Lecture Notes in Computer Science 3631

Commenced Publication in 1973
Founding and Former Series Editors:
Gerhard Goos, Juris Hartmanis, and Jan van Leeuwen

Johann Eder   Hele-Mai Haav
Ahto Kalja   Jaan Penjam (Eds.)

Advances in Databases and Information Systems

9th East European Conference, ADBIS 2005
Tallinn, Estonia, September 12-15, 2005
Proceedings

 Springer

Volume Editors

Johann Eder
University of Klagenfurt, Department of Informatics Systems
Universitätsstrasse 65, 9020 Klagenfurt, Austria
E-mail: eder@isys.uni-klu.ac.at

Hele-Mai Haav
Ahto Kalja
Jaan Penjam
Tallinn University of Technology, Institute of Cybernetics
Akadeemia 21, 12618 Tallinn, Estonia
E-mail: {helemai,ahto,jaan}@cs.ioc.ee

Library of Congress Control Number: 2005932083

CR Subject Classification (1998): H.2, H.3, H.4, H.5, J.1

ISSN   0302-9743
ISBN-10   3-540-28585-7 Springer Berlin Heidelberg New York
ISBN-13   978-3-540-28585-4 Springer Berlin Heidelberg New York

Springer is a part of Springer Science+Business Media

springeronline.com

© Springer-Verlag Berlin Heidelberg 2005
Printed in Germany

Typesetting: Camera-ready by author, data conversion by Scientific Publishing Services, Chennai, India
Printed on acid-free paper   SPIN: 11547686   06/3142   5 4 3 2 1 0

Preface

The 9th East-European Conference on Advances in Databases and Information Systems was held on September 12–15, 2005, in Tallinn, Estonia.

It was organized in a cooperation between the Institute of Cybernetics at Tallinn University of Technology, the Department of Computer Engineering of Tallinn University of Technology, and the Moscow chapter of ACM SIGMOD.

The main objective of the ADBIS series of conferences is to provide a forum for the dissemination of excellent research accomplishments and to promote interaction and collaboration between the Database and Information Systems research communities from Central and East European countries and the rest of the world. The ADBIS conferences provide an international platform for the presentation of research on database theory, the development of advanced DBMS technologies, and their advanced applications in particular in information systems.

The 2005 conference continued the ADBIS conferences held in St. Petersburg (1997), Poznan (1998), Maribor (1999), Prague (2000), Vilnius (2001), Bratislava (2002), Dresden (2003), and Budapest (2004). The conference consisted of regular sessions with technical contributions reviewed and selected by an international Program Committee, as well as of invited talks and tutorials given by leading scientists.

For the first time the ADBIS conferences had a satellite event, a workshop on data mining and knowledge discovery. The ADMKD 2005 workshop, with its own international Program Committee as well as proceedings, served as a forum to encourage researchers and practitioners to discuss and investigate data mining research and implementation issues, and to share experience in developing and deploying data mining systems.

The ADBIS series of conferences continues with growing interest as demonstrated by the large number of 144 submitted papers from 40 countries from all over the world. This volume contains one invited paper and 27 high-quality papers selected in a rigorous reviewing process by the international Program Committee with members from 27 countries. The papers cover a wide range of topics of database and information systems research, in particular, database theory, data modelling and query processing as well as database interoperability and XML databases.

As a tradition, the next 19 papers from the PC ranking were accepted in a be included to separate volume of research communications published by Tallinn University of Technology Press as a local volume of ADBIS 2005 proceedings, and published electronically in the CEUR Workshop Proceedings series: http://SunSITE.Informatik.RWTH-Aachen.DE/Publications/CEUR-WS/.

Many people and organizations contributed to the success of ADBIS 2005. Our thanks go to the authors and invited speakers for their outstanding contribution to the conference and the proceedings. We very much acknowledge the Program Committee members for their reviewing and for accepting a heavy workload. Our thanks go also to the additional referees who carefully reviewed the submissions. Without the willingness and enthusiasm of many scientists sharing their expertise and voluntarily donating their time for thoroughly evaluating the merits of submitted work, this conference would not have been possible.

We wish to thank all the organizing team and our sponsors, who made the conference possible. Our special thanks go to Ms. Kristiina Kindel for maintaining the ADBIS 2005 Web site and Mr. Rein Lõugas for the technical preparation of the manuscript of the conference proceedings.

Last but not least, we are grateful to Springer for supporting the publication of the ADBIS 2005 proceedings in their LNCS series.

September 2005   Johann Eder
                                                           Hele-Mai Haav
                                                           Ahto Kalja
                                                           Jaan Penjam

Conference Organization

General Chair

Jaan Penjam (Institute of Cybernetics at Tallinn University of Technology, Estonia)

General Co-chair

Ahto Kalja (Department of Computer Engineering of Tallinn University of Technology, Estonia)

Program Committee Co-chairs

Johann Eder (University of Klagenfurt, Austria)
Hele-Mai Haav (Institute of Cybernetics at Tallinn University of Technology, Estonia)

Program Committee

Antonia Albani
Luciano Baresi
Janis Barzdins
Andras Benczur
Maria Bielikova
Juris Borzovs
Sjaak Brinkkemper
Bostjan Brumen
Albertas Caplinskas
Wojciech Cellary
Asuman Dogac
Johann Eder
Remigijus Gustas
Hele-Mai Haav
Mirjana Ivanovic
Hannu Jaakkola
Leonid Kalinichenko
Ahto Kalja
Marite Kirikova
Mikhail Kogalovsky

Christoph Koch
Christian Koncilia
John Krogstie
Rein Kuusik
Peri Loucopoulos
Kalle Lyytinen
Yannis Manolopoulos
Rainer Manthey
Saulius Maskeliunas
Mihhail Matskin
Misha Missikoff
Tadeusz Morzy
Pavol Navrat
Nikolay Nikitchenko
Kjetil Norvag
Boris Novikov
Thimios Panagos
Torben Bach Pedersen
Jaan Penjam
Jaroslav Pokorny

Henrikas Pranevichius
Boris Rachev
Jolita Ralyte
Gunter Saake
Klaus-Dieter Schewe
Joachim Schmidt
Vaclav Snasel
Dan Suciu
Eva Söderström
Kuldar Taveter

Jaak Tepandi
Bernhard Thalheim
Olegas Vasilecas
Victor Vianu
Gottfried Vossen
Tatjana Welzer
Viacheslav Wolfengagen
Robert Wrembel
Alexander Zamulin

ADBIS Steering Committee

Chairman: Leonid Kalinichenko (Russian Academy of Science, Russia)

Andras Benczur (Hungary)
Radu Bercaru (Romania)
Albertas Caplinskas (Lithuania)
Johann Eder (Austria)
Janis Eiduks (Latvia)
Hele-Mai Haav (Estonia)
Mirjana Ivanovic (Yugoslavia)
Mikhail Kogalovsky (Russia)
Yannis Manolopoulos (Greece)
Rainer Manthey (Germany)

Tadeusz Morzy (Poland)
Pavol Navrat (Slovakia)
Boris Novikov (Russia)
Jaroslav Pokorny (Czech Republic)
Boris Rachev (Bulgaria)
Anatoly Stogny (Ukraine)
Bernhard Thalheim (Germany)
Tatjana Welzer (Slovenia)
Viacheslav Wolfengagen (Russia)

Organizing Committee

Eve Kann, Kristina Kindel, Sulev Kuiv, Rein Lõugas, Marje Tamm (Institute of
    Cybernetics at Tallinn University of Technology, Estonia)
Marion Lepmets, Tarmo Robal (Department of Computer Engineering, Tallinn
    University of Technology, Estonia)

Additional Referees

B. Akcay
A. Ansper
S. Apel
M. Aziz
G.B. Laleci
G. Barzdins
P. Bertolazzi
V. Bicer
S. Bossung
A. Buldas
R. Butleris
D. Buy
E. Celms
J. Chmielewski
V. Derballa
L. Dmitriy

M. Družovec
D. Eleyan
F.A. Ferrarotti
M. Freudenthal
L. Galambos
M. Garcia
I. Geist
G. Gidofalvi
A. Glazs
S. Hagemann
S. Hartmann
T. Herstel
H. Höpfner
P. Hupe
A. Imada
M. Janssen

Y. Kabak

I. Karydis

A. Kaya

M. Kirchberg

A. Kiss

S. Klöckner

V. Kotkas

J. Laucius

J. Lechtenbörger

T. Leich

N. Leonid

C. Letz

J. Løland

W.M.N. Wan Kadir

W. Martens

N. Mehandjiev

T. Namli

A. Nanopoulos

L. Nemuraite

L. Novak

A. Okcan

M. Olduz

B. Paradauskas

I. Petrounias Karlis Podnieks

P.R.F. Sampaio

M. Rekouts

F. Riaz-ud-Din

A. Riha

F. Rizzolo

P. Rusakovs

J. Rykowski

S. Scherzinger

I. Schmitt

A. Schneidewind

H.-W. Sehring

T. Skopal

F. Taglino

C. Thomsen

I. Timko

L. Tininini

A. Tretiakov

V. Tulit

S. Unal

J. Vain

A. Vakali

M. Vassilakopoulos

P. Vassiliadis

M. Zemlicka

Table of Contents

Query Processing

Heterogeneous Databases and Interoperability

XML and Databases

XML Databases and Beyond-
Plenty of Architectural Challenges Ahead

Theo Härder

University of Kaiserslautern, D-67653 Kaiserslautern, Germany
haerder@informatik.uni-kl.de

Abstract. A key observation is that the invariants in database management determine the mapping steps of the supporting architecture. Referring to the multi-layered architecture of record-oriented database management systems (DBMSs), we sketch the advances made during the past decades. Then, we explore the ways how this proven architecture can be used to implement XML DBMSs (XDBMSs). Major changes and adaptations are needed in most of the layers to support fine-grained XML document processing (XDP). The use of DeweyIDs opens a new paradigm for the management of XML document trees: While preventing node relabeling, even in case arbitrary large subtrees are inserted into an XML document, DeweyIDs offer great benefits for efficient navigation in the document trees, for declarative query processing, and for fine-grained locking thereby avoiding access to external storage as far as possible. The proposed architecture also captures horizontal and vertical distribution of XML processing. Nevertheless, new architectural models are needed beyond record-oriented data types.

1 Introduction

Data independence is accomplished by the data model through set orientation and value-based, declarative requests together with the database management system (DBMS) implementing it. A high degree of logical and physical data independence is urgently needed to provide a flexible view mechanism thereby insulating the users, e.g., application programs, from DB schema evolution and to let the DBMS "survive" the permanent change in computer science in general and in the DB area in particular. Furthermore, DBMSs have a lifetime >20 or even >30 years. Therefore, far-reaching requirements concerning the extensibility and evolution of a DBMS are abundant: growing information demand led to enhanced standards with new object types, constraints, etc.; advances in research and development bred new storage structures and access paths, etc.; rapid changes of the technologies used and especially Moore's law strongly affected storage devices, memory, connectivity (e.g., Web), and so on.

We could already experience that a multi-layered hierarchical DBMS architecture is appropriate to fulfil the design objectives of data independence and to enable long-term system evolution and flexible extensibility as far as relational and object-

J. Eder et al. (Eds.): ADBIS 2005, LNCS 3631, pp. 1–16, 2005.

relational data models and their implementations are concerned [8]. For this reason, we believe that it is a good starting point for architectural considerations of DBMSs beyond them.

Table 1. Description of the DBMS mapping hierarchy

	Level of abstraction	Objects	Auxiliary mapping data
L5	Nonprocedural or algebraic access	Tables, views, tuples	Logical schema description
L4	Record-oriented, navigational access	Records, sets, hierarchies, networks	Logical and physical schema description
L3	Record and access path management	Physical records, access paths	Free space tables, DB-key translation tables
L2	Propagation control	Segments, pages	DB buffer, page tables
L1	File management	Files, blocks	Directories, VTOCs, etc.

1.1 The History of the Layer Model

Mike Senko developed initial architectural concepts named Data Independent Accessing Model [18]. DIAM consists of four hierarchically layered levels called entity set model, string model, encoding model, and physical device level model. Some years later, Härder and Reuter refined these ideas and proposed a mapping model or reference architecture consisting of five hierarchical layers which should cooperate as "abstract machines" and achieve a high degree of information hiding among them to facilitate evolution and extensibility. As depicted in Table 1 [11], the architectural description embodies the major steps of dynamic abstraction from the level of physical storage up to the user interface. At the bottom, the database consists of huge volumes of bits stored on non-volatile storage devices, which are interpreted by the DBMS into meaningful information on which the user can operate. With each level of abstraction (proceeding upwards), the objects become more complex, allowing more powerful operations and being constrained by a growing number of integrity rules. The uppermost interface supports a specific data model, in our case by data access via SQL.

1.2 Major Extensions and Optimizations

While the explanation model concerning the DBMS architecture is still valid, an enormous evolution/progress has been made during the last two decades concerning functionality, performance, and scalability. The fact that all these enhancements and changes could be adopted by the proposed architecture is a strong indication that we refer to a salient DBMS model. We cannot elaborate on all extensions, let alone to discuss them in detail, but we want to sketch some major improvements/changes.

Layer L1 was enhanced by the necessary functionality to attach and operate many new types of storage devices such as SSDs, Worms, DVDs. Furthermore, specialized mapping functions allowed tailored clustering measures or LOB representation on external storage. Disk arrays with various forms of interleaving supported schemes with adjustable degrees of redundancy (e.g., the RAID project) and enabled declustering of objects at various levels to provide for parallel access.

At layer L2, Moore's Law increased the available memory for DB buffers by a factor of 10^4 within the past 20 years thereby achieving an optimization by default. Use of improved replacement algorithms—exploiting reference density combined with LRU (e.g., LRU-K)—, prefetching and pipelined execution in case of scan-based DB processing, etc. greatly improved DB buffer efficiency. Furthermore, configuring a set of buffers (for example, up to 80 in DB2) to separate workloads of different types and optimized to specific data types further boosted performance behavior at level L2.

Of all access path structures, which could potentially fill level L3, the dominant one is still the ubiquitous B-tree. Despite a "firestorm" of research resulting in a few hundred proposals of novel index structures, the B- or B*-tree seem to be sufficient to cover all practical needs. At best, a few other structures such as UB-tree, R-tree, or Grid file are integration candidates for specialized access support. Indeed, the most dramatic performance enhancements at this architectural layer are due to fine-grained locking methods, in particular, applied to index structures, i.e., to B*-trees [16].

To mention a few optimization measures applied at level L4 and referring to the access paths of L3: selection and join algorithms utilizing TIDs of existing indexes thereby avoiding physical I/O as much as possible, hash joins which may also dramatically reduce access to external storage, and adaptive algorithms of various kinds which support load balancing and optimized throughput. Such adaptive techniques include setting or adjusting the degree of parallelism depending on the current workload, reordering and merging ranges to optimize repeated probes into an index, sharing scans among multiple queries, and so on [4].

Compilation and optimization of queries embodies the major functionality of L5. Although the quality of the optimizer—as a kind of landmark concept of a DBMS—has greatly improved in the course of the past two decades, e.g., by using refined statistics and histograms, there still remain open problems and even emerge new challenges. For example, user-defined types have to carry their own cost model to be integrated by cost-based optimizers. Furthermore, effective optimizers for dynamic QEPs (query execution plans) must address the problems of changes in resource availability or at least provide for dynamic plans with alternative algorithms or alternative plan shapes [4].

1.3   The Search for Future DBMS Architectures

The architectural layers sketched so far perfectly match the *invariants of set-oriented, record-like database management*: storage management (L1 and L2), access path and record management (L3), compilation, optimization, and evaluation of queries (L4 and L5). During the recent decade, integration efforts for functionality not fitting into this framework were primarily based on a kind of loose coupling of components—called Extenders, DataBlades, or Cardridges—and a so-called extensibility infrastructure. Because these approaches could neither fulfil the demands for seamless integration nor the overblown performance and scalability expectations, future solutions may face major changes in the architecture.

A hot topic of research is the appropriate integration of XML document management, because messages are data, too. Questions controversially discussed so far are "Will the DBMSs of the future be hybrids, storing both relational and XML?" or "Will everything be stored in XML format?" making myriads of SQL systems "legacy applications". Besides hybrid architectures, which map XML documents and tables by separate storage and access systems and support coexistence/combination of DB requests of both kinds, a futuristic scenario motivated by the questions above was discussed in *ROX: Relational over XML* [15] to support SQL APIs as well as XDP interfaces. While XML operations on native XML structures are the target of optimization in XDBMSs, such future DBMS architectures represent mixed SQL and XQuery systems to run SQL applications on native XML or on hybrid structures concurrently.

A key observation of relational DBMS architectures is that the *invariants in database management determine the mapping steps of the supporting architecture*. Because of the record-oriented nature of fine-grained management of XML documents the invariants of XDP are, at least, similar to the relational ones. Therefore, we explore in Section 2 the ways how the original layer model has to be adjusted to serve for the description and explanation of XDBMS implementations. In Section 3, we consider variants of this model to be applied to data management scenarios where horizontal and vertical distribution of XML database processing is needed. Section 4 sketches a number of new data types which cannot be smoothly integrated into the architectural framework and argues about the need for enhanced adaptivity and dependability properties for future DBMSs. Finally, we conclude with some brief remarks in Section 5.

2 Architectural Requirements for XML Databases

Currently available relational or object-relational (O)RDBMSs only manage structured data well. There is no effective and straightforward way for handling XML data. This is obviously true when simple CLOB types have to be used. In particular, searching of XML documents becomes prohibitively slow. But also more refined mappings do not lead to good solutions per se: An innumerable number of algorithms [19] has been proposed for the mapping of semi-structured XML data to structured relational database tables and columns (the so-called "shredding"). All these approaches have failed to efficiently support the wide spectrum of DB applications and to guarantee satisfactory performance in high-performance transaction environments. Furthermore, as XML documents permeate information systems and databases with increasing pace, they are more and more used in a collaborative way. If you run today an experiment on existing DBMSs with collaborative XML documents, you may experience a "performance catastrophe" meaning that most transactional operations are processed in strict serial order. The challenge for database system development is to provide adequate and fine-grained management for these documents enabling efficient and concurrent read and write operations. Therefore, future XML DBMSs will be judged according to their ability to achieve high transaction parallelism.

2.1 XTC Architecture

First attempts to provide for DB-based XML processing focused on using the lower layer features of relational DBMSs such that roughly the access and storage system layers were *reused and complemented* by the data system functionality tailored to the demands of the XML data model (e.g., DOM, SAX, XQuery); this implied the mapping (called "shredding") of XML document structures onto a set of tables.

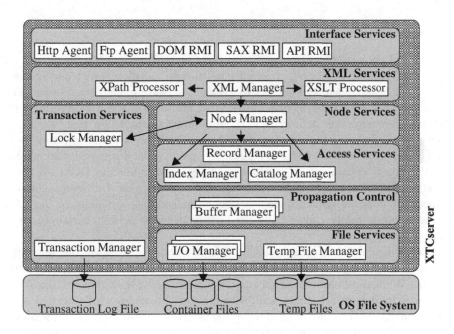

Fig. 1. XTC system – overview

Although viable within our five-layer architecture (by reusing L1 to L4), this idea had serious performance trade-offs, mainly in the areas of query optimization and concurrency control. New concepts and implementation techniques in the reused layers are required to achieve efficient query processing. For these reasons, so-called native XML DBMSs emerged in recent years, an architectural example of which is illustrated in Fig. 1. The current state of the XTC architecture (XML Transaction

Coordinator [12]) perfectly proves that native XDBMSs can be implemented along the lines of our five-layer architecture.

2.2 Storage and Buffer Management

At the layers L1 and L2, reuse of concepts as described in Section 1.2 is obvious. Hence, we can more or less adopt the mechanisms proven in relational DBMS implementations and adjust them to the specific needs of XML document representations. In summary, our storage layer offers an extensible file structure based on the B*-tree mechanism as a container of single XML documents such that updates of an XML document (by IUD operations) can be performed on any of its nodes. We have shown that a very high degree of storage occupancy (> 96%) for XML documents is achieved under a variety of different update workloads.

Although the functionality in the remaining three layers is comparable at an abstract level, the objects and the specific implementation methods exhibit strong distinctions. Due to space restrictions, we can only focus on some new important aspects.

2.3 Access Services

Efficient and effective processing and concurrent operations on XML documents are greatly facilitated, if we use a specialized internal representation, which enables fine-granular management and locking. For this reason, we have implemented in our XTC system the taDOM storage model illustrated in Fig. 3 as a slight extension of the XML tree representation defined in [21]. In contrast to the DOM tree, we do not directly attach attributes to their element node, but introduce separate *attribute roots*, which connect the attribute nodes to the respective elements. String nodes are used to store the actual content of an attribute or a text node. Via the DOM API, this separation enables access of nodes independently of their value. Our representational enhancement does not influence the user operations and their semantics on the XML document, but is solely exploited by the lock manager to achieve certain kinds of optimizations.

Most influential for an access model to the tree nodes of an XML document is a suitable node-labeling scheme for which several candidates have been proposed in the literature. While most of them are adequate to label static XML documents, the design of schemes for dynamic documents allowing arbitrary insertions within the tree—free of reorganization, i.e., no reassignment of labels to existing nodes—remains a challenging research issue. The existing approaches can be classified into range-based and prefix-based labeling schemes. While range-based schemes consisting of independent numbering elements (e.g., DocID, startPos: endPos, level, see [1]) seem to be less amenable to algorithmic use and cannot always avoid relabeling in case of node insertions, prefix-based schemes seem to be more flexible. We believe that they are at least as expressive as range-based schemes, while they guarantee stability of node IDs under arbitrary insertions, in addition. In particular, we favor a scheme supporting efficient insertion and compression while providing the so-called Dewey order (defined by the Dewey Decimal Classification System). Conceptually similar to the ORDPATH scheme [17], our scheme refines the mapping and solves practical problems of the implementation.

Fast access to and identification of all nodes of an XML document is mandatory to enable effective indexing primarily supporting declarative queries and efficient processing of direct-access methods (e. g., *getElementById()*) as well as navigational methods (e. g., *getNextSibling()*). For this reason, we have implemented the node labeling scheme whose advantages should be illuminated by referring to Fig.2. For example, a DeweyID is 1.3.4.3.5 which consists of several so-called *divisions* separated by dots (in the human readable format). The root node of the document is always labeled by DeweyID 1 and consists of only a single division. The children obtain the DeweyID of their parent and attach another division whose value increases from left to right. To allow for later node insertions at a given level, we introduce a parameter *distance* which determines the gap initially left free in the labeling space. In Fig.3, we have chosen the minimum distance value of 2. Furthermore, assigning at a given level a distance to the first child, we always start with *distance + 1*, thereby reserving division value 1 for attribute roots and string nodes (illustrated for the attribute root of 1.3 with DeweyID 1.3.1). Hence, the mechanism of the Dewey order is quite simple when the IDs are initially assigned, e.g., when all nodes of the document are bulk-loaded.

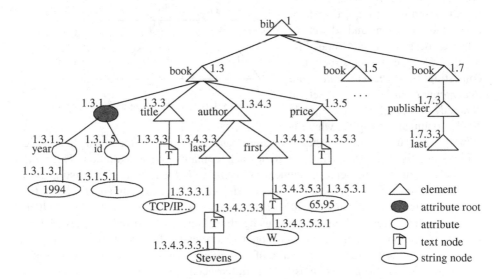

Fig. 2. A sample taDOM tree labeled with DeweyIDs

In the above tree example, the author node is inserted later within the gap 1.3.3 to 1.3.5. Because arbitrary many nodes may be inserted into any gap, we need a kind of overflow mechanism indicating that the labeling scheme remains at the same level when an odd division value is not available anymore for a gap. Thus, we reserve even division values for that purpose; they may occur consecutively (depending on the insertion history) where an uninterrupted sequence of even values just states that the same labeling level is kept [13].

The salient features of a scheme assigning a DeweyID to each tree node include the following properties: Referring to the DeweyID of a node, we can determine the level of the node in the tree and the DeweyID of the parent node. Hence, we can derive its entire ancestor path up to the document root without accessing the document. By comparing the DeweyIDs of two nodes, we can decide which node appears first in the document's node order. If all sibling nodes are known, we can determine the exact position of the node within the document tree. Furthermore, it is possible to insert new nodes at arbitrary locations without relabeling existing nodes. In addition, we can rapidly figure out all nodes accessible via the typical XML navigation steps, if the nodes are stored in document order, i.e., in left-most depth-first order.

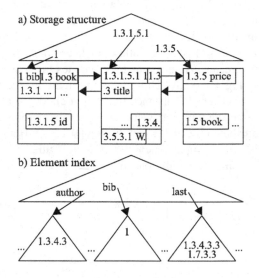

Fast (indexed) access to each node is provided by variants of B*-trees tailored to our requirements of node identification and direct or relative location of any node. Fig. 3a illustrates the storage structure—consisting of *document index* and *document container* as a set of chained pages—for the sample XML document of Fig. 2, which is

Fig. 3. Document storage using B*-trees

stored in document order; the key-value pairs within the document index are referencing the first DeweyID stored in each container page. Additionally to the storage structure of the actual document, an *element index* is created consisting of a *name directory* with all element names occurring in the XML document (Fig. 3b); for each specific element name, in turn, a *node-reference index* is maintained which addresses the corresponding elements using their DeweyIDs. In all cases, variable-length key support is mandatory; additional functionality for prefix compression of DeweyIDs is very effective. Because of reference locality in the B*-trees while processing XML documents, most of the referenced tree pages (at least the ones belonging to the upper tree layers) are expected to reside in DB buffers—thus reducing external accesses to a minimum.

2.4 Node Services—Support of Navigation, Query Evaluation, and Locking

Selection and join algorithms based on index access via TID lists together with the availability of fine-grained index locking boosted the performance of DBMSs [8], because they reduced storage access and minimized blocking situations for concurrent transactions as far as possible. Both factors are even more critical in XDBMS. Hence, when designing such a system, we have to consider them very carefully.

Using the document index sketched in Fig. 3, the five basic navigational axes *parent, previous-sibling, following-sibling, first-child,* and *last-child,* as specified in DOM [21], may be efficiently evaluated—in the best case, they reside in the page of the given context node *cn.* When accessing the previous sibling *ps* of *cn,* e.g., node 1.5 in Fig. 2, an obvious strategy would be to locate the page of 1.5 requiring a traversal of the document index from the root page to the leaf page where 1.5 is stored. This page is often already present in main memory because of reference locality. From the context node, we check all IDs backwards, following the links between the leaf pages of the index, until we find *ps*—the first ID with the same parent as *cn* and the same level. All IDs skipped along this way were descendants of *ps.* Therefore, the number of pages to be accessed depends on the size of the subtree having *ps* as root. An alternative strategy avoids this unwanted dependency: After the page containing 1.5 is loaded, we inspect the ID *d* of the directly preceding node of 1.5, which is 1.3.5.3.1. If *ps* exists, *d* must be a descendant of *ps.* With the level information of *cn,* we can infer the ID of *ps*: 1.3. Now a direct access to 1.3 suffices to locate the result. The second strategy ensures independence from the document structure, i.e., the number of descendants between *ps* and *cn* does not matter anymore. Similar search algorithms for the remaining four axes can be found. The *parent* axis, as well as *first-child* and *next-sibling* can be retrieved directly, requiring only a single document index traversal. The *last-child* axis works similar to the *previous-sibling* axis and, therefore, needs two index traversals in the worst case.

For declarative access via query languages like XQuery, a set-at-a-time processing approach—or more accurately, sequence-at-a-time—and the use of the element index promise in some cases increased performance over a navigational evaluation strategy. Nevertheless, the basic DOM primitives are a fallback solution, if no index support is available. To illuminate the element index use for declarative access, let us consider a simple XQuery predicate that only contains forward and reverse step expressions with name tests: *axis1::name1/.../axisN::nameN.* XQuery contains 13 axes, 8 of which span the four main dimensions in an XML document: *parent–child, ancestor–descendant, preceding-sibling–following-sibling,* and *preceding–following.* For each axis, we provide an algorithm that operates on a duplicate-free input sequence of nodes in document order and

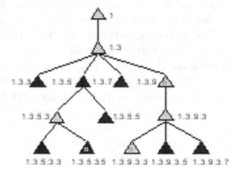

phase 1: creation of a hash table

input	HT
1.3.3	HT(1.3)=1.3.3
1.3.5	
1.3.5.3.3	HT(1.3.5.3)=1.3.5.
1.3.5.3.5	
1.3.5.5	HT(1.3.5)=1.3.5.5
1.3.7	
1.3.9.3.5	HT(1.3.9.3)=1.3.9.
1.3.9.3.7	

Fig. 4. Following-sibling algorithm

produces an output sequence with the same properties and containing for the specified axis all nodes which passed the name test. Therefore, the evaluation of axes is closed in this group of algorithms and we can freely concatenate them to evaluate path expressions having the referenced structure. Our evaluation strategy follows the idea of structural joins [1] adjusted to DeweyIDs, and additionally expanded to support the *preceding-sibling–following-sibling* and *preceding–following* dimensions.

Let us consider the *following-sibling* axis as an example. In Fig. 4, the nodes of the input sequence P, which may be the result of a former path step, are marked in a dark shade. Furthermore, the sequence of nodes F in our document that satisfy the name test for the current evaluation of the *following-sibling* axis carry the letter 'n'. The DeweyIDs of these nodes are retrieved using the element index. A problem of using the *following-sibling* axis is the possible generation of duplicates. For example, node 1.3.9 qualifies as a *following-sibling* for nodes 1.3.3, 1.3.5, and 1.3.7. Because duplicate removal is an expensive operation, our strategy is to avoid duplicates in the first place. The evaluation algorithm works as follows: In a first phase, input P is processed in document order. For each DeweyID d, a pair (key, value) as *(parent(d), d)* is added to a hash table HT. If *parent(d)* is already present in HT, d can be skipped. Because we process P in document order, only the first sibling among a group of siblings is added to HT. In the second phase, we iterate over F and probe each ID f against HT. If *parent(f)* is contained in HT, we simply compare whether or not f is a *following-sibling* of HT*(parent(f))*. This comparison can easily be done by looking at the two DeweyIDs. Assume, the parent of f=1.3.5.3.5 is contained in HT and f is a *following-sibling* of HT(1.3.5.3), then f will be included into the result sequence. For ID f=1.3.9.3.3, this test fails, because f is not a *following-sibling* of 1.3.9.3.5. F is processed in document order, therefore, the output also obtains this order. Similar evaluation algorithms are provided for all other axes.

Fine-grained concurrency control is of outmost importance for collaborative use of XML documents. Although predicate locking of XQuery and XUpdate-like statements [21] would be powerful and elegant, its implementation rapidly leads to severe drawbacks such as the need to acquire large lock granules, e.g., for predicate evaluations as shown in Fig. 4, and undecidability problems—a lesson learned from the (much simpler) relational world. To provide for a multi-lingual solution, we necessarily have to map XQuery operations to a navigational access model to accomplish fine-granular concurrency control. Such an approach implicitly supports other interfaces such as DOM, because their operations correspond more or less directly to a navigational access model. Therefore, we have designed and optimized a group of lock protocols explicitly tailored to the DOM interfaces which are absolutely complex—20 lock modes for nodes and three modes for edges together with the related compatibilities and conversion rules—, but for which we proved their correctness [12] and optimality [1][14].

---

[1] By using so-called meta-synchronization, XTC maps the meta-lock requests to the actual locking algorithm which is achieved by the lock manager's interface. Hence, exchanging the lock manager's interface implementation exchanges the system's complete XML locking mechanism. In this way, we could run XTC in our experiments with 11 different lock protocols. At the same time, all experiments were performed on the taDOM storage model optimized for fine-grained management of XML documents.

2.5 Query Compilation and Optimization

The prime task of layer L5 is to produce QEPs, i.e., to translate, optimize, and bind the multi-lingual requests—declarative as well as navigational—from the language models to the operations available at the logical access model interface (L4). For DOM and SAX requests, this task is straightforward. In contrast, XQuery or XPath requests will be a great challenge for cost-based optimizers for decades. Remember, for complex languages such as SQL:2003 (simpler than the current standard of XQuery), we have experienced a never-ending research and development history—for 30 years to date—and the present optimizers still are far from perfect. For example, selectivity estimation is much more complex, because the cardinality numbers for nodes in variable-depth subtrees have to be determined or estimated. Furthermore, all current or future problems to be solved for relational DBMSs [4] will occur in XDBMSs, too.

3 Architectural Variants

Because the invariants in database management determine the mapping steps of the supporting architecture, we can also use our architectural framework in new data management scenarios where XDBMSs are involved, as long as the basic invariants still hold true: page-oriented mapping to external storage, management of record-oriented data, set-oriented/navigational data processing. Similar to the scenarios evolved in the past for relational database management, equivalent ones may emerge in the future, in case XDBMSs gain the momentum in the market.

3.1 Horizontal Distribution of XDBMS Processing

A variety of DB processing scenarios can be characterized as the horizontal distribution of the entire DB functionality and of partitioned/replicated data to processing nodes connected by a network. As a consequence, the core requirements remain, leading to a simplified architectural model sketched in Fig. 5, which consists of identical layered models for every node together with a *connection layer* responsible for communication, adaptation, or mediation services. In an implementation, this layer could be integrated with one of the existing layers or attached to the node architecture to encapsulate it for the remaining system.

For these reasons, our layer model can serve as a framework for the implementation of XDBMS variants for architectural classes such as *Shared Nothing, Shared Disk, and Parallel DBMSs,* because all of them have to run identical operations in the various layers. Adaptation of processing primarily concerns the handling of partitioning or replication and, as a consequence, issues of invalidation, synchronization, and logging/recovery.

When heterogeneity of the data models or autonomy of database systems comes into play, the primary tasks of the connection layer are concerned with adaptation and mediation. *Federated XDBMSs* could represent the entire spectrum of possible data integration scenarios and would need an adjustment of the DB requests at the level of the data model or a compensation of functionality not generally available. As opposed to distributed homogeneous XDBMSs, some users (transactions) may only refer to a local view thereby abstaining from federated services, while, at the same time, other users exploit the full services of the data federation. The other extreme case among the federation scenarios is represented by *Multi-XDBMSs*, for which the connection layer primarily takes over the role of a global transaction manager passing unmodified DB requests to the participating DB servers.

3.2   Vertical Distribution of XDBMS Processing

Our layer model also fits to client/server database processing. In this category, the major concern is to make XDBMS processing capacity available close (or at least closer) to the application of the client (computer). So far, client/server DBMSs are used in applications relying on long-running transactions with a checkout/checkin mechanism for (versioned) data. Hence, the underlying data management scenarios are primarily tailored to engineering applications. Object-oriented DBMS distinguish between file servers, object servers, and query servers: the most sophisticated ones are the query servers. Their real challenge is declarative, set-oriented query processing thereby using the current content of the query result buffer [3].

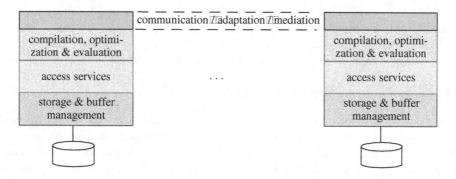

Fig. 5. Horizontal XDBMS distribution

Until recently, query processing in such buffers was typically limited to queries with predicates on single tables (or equivalent object types). Now, a major enhancement is pursued in scenarios called *database caching*. Here, full-fledged DBMSs, used as frontend DBs close to application servers in the Web, take over the role of cache managers for a backend DB. As a special kind of vertical distribution, their performance-enhancing objective is to evaluate more complex queries in the cache which, e.g., span several tables organized as cache groups by equi-joins [10]. The magic concept is *predicate completeness* where the DBMS (i.e., its cache manager) has to guarantee that all objects required for the evaluation of a query predicate are present in the cache and are consistent with the DB state in the backend DB. So far, these concepts are explored for relational models, e.g., SQL. However, we have observed that the idea of predicate completeness can be extended to other types of data models—in particular, XML data models—, too. Thinking about the potential of this idea gives us the vision that we could support the entire user-to-data path in the Internet with a single XML data model [9].

While the locality preservation of the query result buffer in query server architectures can take advantage of application hints [3], *adaptivity* of database caching is a major challenge for future research [2]. Furthermore, precise specification of *relaxed currency and consistency* of data is an important future task to better control the widespread and growing use of distant caches and asynchronous copies 7]. Other interesting research problems occur if transactional updates are directly performed in DB caches. Instead of processing them in the backend DB first, they could be executed in the cache or even jointly in cache and backend DB under a 2PC protocol. Such update models may lead to futuristic considerations where the conventional hierarchic arrangement of frontend cache and backend DB is dissolved: If each of them can play both roles and if together they can provide consistency for DB data, more effective DB support may be gained for new applications such as grid or P2P computing.

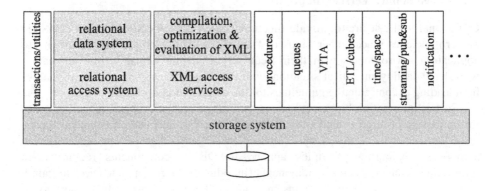

Fig. 6. Desirable extentions for future DBMS architectures

4   New Types of DBMS Architectures

XML data could not be adequately integrated into the original layer model because the processing invariants valid in record-oriented DBMS do not hold true for document trees with other types of DB requests. Therefore, we needed substantial changes and adaptations, especially in layers L3 to L5, while the overall layered framework could be preserved. However, what has to be done when the conceptual differences of the data types such as VITA (video, image, text, audio) or data streams are even larger?

4.1 The Next Database Revolution Ahead

VITA types, for example, are managed in tailored DB buffers and are typically delivered (in variable-length junks) to the application thereby avoiding additional layer crossings. In turn, to avoid data transfers, the application may pass down some operations to the buffer to directly manipulate the buffered object representation. Hence, Fig. 6 illustrates that the OS services or, at best, the storage system represent the least common denominator for the desired DBMS extensions.

If the commonalities in data management invariants for the different types and thus the reuse opportunities for functionality are so marginal, it makes no sense to squeeze all of them into a unified DBMS architecture. As a proposal for future research and development, Jim Gray sketched a framework leading to a diversity of type-specific DBMS architectures [6]. As a consequence, we obtain a collection of heterogeneous DBMSs which have to be made accessible for the applications—as transparently as possible by suitable APIs. Such a collection embodies an "extensible object-relational system where non-procedural relational operators manipulate object sets. Coupled with this, each DBMS is now a Web service" [6]. Furthermore, because they cooperate on behalf of applications, ACID protection has to be assured for all messages and data taking part in a transaction.

4.2 Dependability Versus Adaptivity

Orthogonal to the desire to provide functional extensions, the key role of DBMSs in modern societies places other kinds of "stress" on their architecture. Adaptivity to application environments with their frequently changing demands in combination with dependability in critical situations will become more important design goals—both leading to contradicting guidelines for the architectural design.

So far, information hiding and layers as abstract machines were the cornerstones for the design of large evolutionary DBMSs. Typically, adaptable component (layer) behavior cannot be achieved by exploiting local "self"-observations alone. Hence, autonomic computing principles applied to DBMS components require more information exchange across components (introducing more dependencies) to gain a more accurate view when decisions relevant for behavioral adaptations have to be made. Trouble-free operation of a DBMS primarily comes from adjustment mechanisms automatically applied to problems of administration, tuning, coordination, growth, hardware and software upgrades, etc. Ideally, the human system manager should only set goals, policies, and a budget while the automatic adaptation mechanisms should do the rest [5]. Online feedback control loops are key to achieve such adaptation and "self-*" system properties, which, however, amplify the information channels across system layers.

In contrast, too many information channels increase the inter-component complexity and are directed against salient software engineering principles for highly evolutionary systems. In this respect, they work against the very important dependability objective which is much broader than self-tuning or self-administration. Hence, design challenges are to develop a system which should be always available, i.e., exhibiting an extremely high availability, and which only services authorized uses, i.e., even hackers cannot destroy data or force the system to deny services to authorized users. Jim Gray summarizes the main properties of a dependable and adaptive system as *always-up + secure + trouble-free*. To develop such systems, innovative architectures observing new software engineering principles have to be adopted. However, most of their properties are not easily amenable to mathematical modeling and runtime analysis, because they are non-functional in general. Weikum calls for a highly componentized system architecture with small, well-controlled component interfaces and limited and relatively simple functionality per component which implies the reduction of optional choices [20]. The giant chasm to be closed results from diverging requirements: *growing system complexity* due to new extensions and improved adaptivity as opposed to *urgent simplification needs* mandatory for the development of dependable systems.

5 Conclusions

In this paper, we primarily explored how XDBMSs fit into the framework of a multi-layered hierarchical architecture originally developed for record-oriented data models. We proposed major changes and adaptations for which DeweyIDs embody the fundamentally new concept. Their expressive power and stability enabled new classes of evaluation algorithms for services supporting navigation, declarative queries, and fine-grained locking. Finally, we sketched some ideas for integration data types which cannot be efficiently mapped to the layer architecture and emphasized the need to decidedly improve adaptability and dependability properties in future DBMSs.

References

[1] Al-Khalifa, S. et al.: Structural Joins: A Primitive for Efficient XML Query Pattern Matching. Proc. 18th Int. Conf. on Data Engineering, 141 (2002)

[2] Altinel, M. et al.: Cache Tables: Paving the Way for an Adaptive Database Cache. VLDB 2003: 718-729

[3] Deßloch, S., Härder, T., Mattos, N. M., Mitschang, B., and Thomas, J.: Advanced Data Processing in KRISYS. VLDB J. 7(2): 79-95 (1998)

[4] Graefe, G.: Dynamic Query Evaluation Plans: Some Course Corrections? IEEE Data Eng. Bull. 23(2): 3-6 (2000)

[5] Gray, J.: What next?: A dozen information-technology research goals. J. ACM 50(1): 41-57 (2003) (Journal Version of the 1999 ACM Turing Award Lecture)

[6] Gray, J.: The Next Database Revolution. SIGMOD Conference 2004: 1-4

[7] Guo, H., Larson, P.-A., Ramakrishnan, R., Goldstein, J.: Relaxed Currency and Consistency: How to Say "Good Enough" in SQL. SIGMOD Conference 2004: 815-826

[8] Härder, T.: DBMS Architecture—Still an Open Problem. Proc. Datenbanksysteme in Business, Technologie und Web (BTW 2005), LNI P-65, Springer, 2-28, 2005

[9] Härder, T.: Caching over the Entire User-to-Data Path in the Internet, in: T. Härder, W. Lehner (eds), Data Management in a Connected World, LNCS 3551, 2005, pp. 67–89

[10] Härder, T., Bühmann, A.: Query Processing in Constraint-Based Database Caches. Data Engineering Bulletin 27:2 (2004) 3-10

[11] Härder, T., Reuter, A.: Concepts for Implementing a Centralized Database Management System. Proc. Int. Comp. Symp. on Appl. Systems Development, 1983, Nürnberg, 28-60

[12] Haustein, M., Härder, T.: Optimizing Concurrent XML Processing, submitted (2005)

[13] Haustein, M., Härder, T., Mathis, C., and Wagner, M.: DeweyIDs—The Key to Fine-Grained Management of XML Documents, submitted (2005)

[14] Haustein, M., Härder, T., and Luttenberger, K.: Contest of Lock Protocols—The Winner is taDOM3+, submitted (2005), http://wwwdvs.informatik.uni-kl.de/pubs/p2005.html

[15] Halverson, A., Josifovski, V., Lohman, G., Pirahesh, H., and Mörschel, M. ROX: Relational Over XML. Proc. 30th Int. Conf. on Very Large Data Bases, Toronto (Sept. 2004)

[16] Mohan, C.: ARIES/KVL: A Key-Value Locking Method for Concurrency Control of Multiaction Transactions Operating on B-Tree Indexes. VLDB 1990: 392-405

[17] O'Neil, P. E. et al.: ORDPATHs: Insert-Friendly XML Node Labels. Proc. SIGMOD Conf.: 903-908 (2004)

[18] Senko, M. E., Altman, E. B., Astrahan, M. M., and Fehder, P. L.: Data Structures and Accessing in Data Base Systems. IBM Systems Journal 12(1): 30-93 (1973)

[19] Tatarinov, I. et al.: Storing and Querying Ordered XML Using a Relational Database System. Proc. ACM SIGMOD, Madison, Wisconsin, USA, 204-215 (2002)

[20] Weikum, G., Mönkeberg, A., Hasse, C., and Zabback, P.: Self-tuning Database Technology and Information Services: from Wishful Thinking to Viable Engineering. VLDB 2002: 20-31

[21] W3C Recommendations. http://www.w3c.org (2004)

Usable Recursive Queries

Tomasz Pieciukiewicz[1], Krzysztof Stencel[2], and Kazimierz Subieta[1, 3]

[1] Polish-Japanese Institute of Information Technology, Warsaw, Poland
[2] Institute of Informatics, Warsaw University, Warsaw, Poland
[3] Institute of Computer Science PAS, Warsaw, Poland
`pietia@pjwstk.edu.pl`, `stencel@mimuw.edu.pl`,
`subieta@ipipan.waw.pl`

Abstract. Recursive queries are required for many tasks of database applications. Among them we can mention Bill-Of-Material (BOM), various kinds of networks (transportation, telecommunication, etc.), processing semi-structured data (XML, RDF), and so on. The support for recursive queries in current query languages is limited. In particular, this concerns corresponding extensions of SQL in Oracle and DB2 systems. In this paper we present recursive query processing capabilities for the object-oriented Stack-Based Query Language (SBQL). SBQL offers very powerful and flexible recursive querying capabilities due to the fact that recursive processing operators are fully orthogonal to other capabilities of this language. The presented features aim at the ease of recursive programming in databases and not at building new theoretical foundations. This paper discusses novel SBQL constructs, such as transitive closures, fixed point equations and recursive procedures/views. Their main advantage is that they are seamlessly integrated with object-oriented facilities, computer environment and databases.

1 Introduction

There are many important tasks which require recursive processing. The most widely known is Bill-Of-Material (BOM) which is a part of Materials Requirements Planning (MRP) systems. BOM acts on a recursive data structure representing a hierarchy of parts and subparts of some complex material products. Typical MRP software processes such structures by proprietary routines and applications implemented in a programming language. However, frequently users need to issue *ad hoc* queries addressing such structures. In such cases they need special recursive user-friendly facilities of a query language. Similar problems concern computations on genealogic trees, stock market dependencies, various types of networks (transportation, telecommunication, electricity, gas, water, and so on), etc. The recursion is also necessary for internal purposes of computer systems, such as processing recursive metadata structures (e.g. CORBA Interface Repository), configuration management repositories, hierarchical structures of XML or RDF files, and so on.

In many cases recursion can be substituted by iteration, but this implies much lower abstraction level and less elegant problem specification. The iteration may also cause higher cost of program maintenance, since it implies a clumsy code, more difficult to debug and change.

J. Eder et al. (Eds.): ADBIS 2005, LNCS 3631, pp. 17–28, 2005.

Despite importance, recursion is not supported in SQL standards (SQL-89 and SQL-92). Beyond the standards, it is implemented (differently) in relational DBMSs, in particular, in Oracle and DB2, in the form of transitive closures and linear recursion. Newer SQL standards SQL-99 (aka SQL-3) and SQL 2003 introduce both transitive closure and deductive rules *a la* Datalog. Unfortunately these standards are very huge and eclectic, thus many database professionals doubt if they will ever be fully implemented. The ODMG standard for object-oriented databases and its query language OQL do not mention any corresponding facilities. Recursion is considered a desirable feature of XML-oriented and RDF-oriented query languages, but current proposals and implementations do not introduce corresponding features or introduce them with many limitations.

The possibility of recursive processing has been highlighted in the field of deductive databases, notably Datalog. The paradigm has roots in logic programming and has several variants. Some time ago it was advocated as a true successor of relational databases, as an opposition to the emerging wave of object-oriented databases. Datalog as it has been proposed has sound theoretical foundations (see e.g. [2] and thousands of papers which cannot be cited here). However, it seems that Datalog falls short of the software engineering perspective. It has several recognized disadvantages, in particular: flat structure of programs, limited data structures to be processed, no powerful programming abstraction capabilities, impedance mismatch during conceptual modeling of applications, poor integration with typical software environment (e.g. class/procedure libraries) and poor performance. Thus practical mission-critical Datalog applications are till now unknown. Nevertheless, the idea of Datalog semantics based on fixpoint equations seems to be very attractive to formulate complex recursive tasks. Note however that fixpoint equations can be added not only to languages based on logic programming, but to any query language, including SQL, OQL and XQuery.

Besides transitive closures and fixpoint equations there are classical facilities for recursive processing known from programming languages, namely recursive functions (procedures, methods). In the database domain a similar concept is known as recursive views. Integration of recursive functions or recursive views with a query language requires generalizations beyond the solutions known from typical programming languages or databases. First, functions have to be prepared to return bulk types that a corresponding query language deals with, i.e. a function output should be compatible with the output of queries. Second, both functions and views should possess parameters, which could be bulk types compatible with query output too. Currently very few existing query languages have such possibilities, thus using recursive functions or views in a query language is practically unexplored.

This paper discusses three different approaches to recursive querying:

- transitive closure operators,
- least fixed point equation systems (fixpoint equations, for short),
- recursive procedures and views.

For the first time, we describe all three approaches to recursive processing within a unified framework: the Stack Based Approach (SBA) to object-oriented query/programming languages [5, 6, 7]. SBA treats a query language as a kind of programming languages and therefore, queries are evaluated using mechanisms which are common in programming languages. SBA introduces an own query language Stack-Based Query Language (SBQL) based on abstract, compositional syntax and formal operational semantics. SBQL is equipped with a strong type system.

We have implemented all these three recursive facilities within the framework of SBA and smoothly integrated them with object-oriented ideas, computer environment and databases. The research has been done within the currently developed object-oriented database platform ODRA devoted to Web and grid applications. In this report we compare the approaches on sufficiently complex examples showing their strengths and weakness with respect to problems from database application programming.

The paper is organized as follows. Section 2 presents the Stack-Based Approach and its query language SBQL. Section 3 is devoted to the transitive closure in SBQL. Section 4 describes fixpoint equations in SBQL. Section 5 deals with recursive procedures and views. Section 6 discusses the future work. Section 7 concludes.

2   Stack Based Approach and Stack Based Query Language

2.1   Data Store Models

In the Stack Based Approach four data store models are defined, with increasing functionality and complexity. The M0 model described in [6] is the simplest data store model. In M0 objects can be nested (with no limitations on nesting levels) and can be connected with other objects by links. M0 covers relational and XML-oriented structures. It can be easily extended [7] to comply with more complex models which include classes and static inheritance (M1), dynamic object roles and dynamic inheritance (M2), encapsulation (M3) and other features of object-oriented databases.

In SBA an object has the following properties: *internal object identifier* (OID) which cannot be used in queries nor printed, *external name*, which is used in the application code to access objects, and object content which can be a value, a link, or a set of objects. An SBA store consists of the structure of such objects/subobjects and the set of identifiers of root objects, i.e., starting points for queries.

2.2   Name Binding and Environment Stack

SBA is based on the programming languages' naming-scoping-binding principle. Each name occurring in a query/program is bound to a proper run-time database/program entity according to the name scope. Scopes for names are managed by means of the Environment Stack (ES). ES consists of sections which contain entities called binders. Binders relate names with run-time objects and are used during binding names. A *binder* is a pair (n, v), written as $n(v)$, where n is an external name used in queries and v is a value (most often it is an object identifier).

New sections on ES are built by means of a special function *nested* which returns the content of an object (in case of complex objects) and the pointed object (in case of link objects).

Binding name n occurring in a query is an action of the query interpreter which searches ES for the binder named n that is closest to the top of ES. Binding respects static scoping rules which mean that some sections of ES are invisible during the binding (e.g. sections related to local environments of procedures). The name binding can return multiple binders and this way we handle collections of objects.

2.3 Stack-Based Query Language (SBQL)

Stack-Based Query Language [6, 7] is based on the principle of compositionality, i.e. semantics of a complex query is recursively built from semantics of its components. SBQL queries are defined as follows:

1. A name or a literal is a query; e.g., 2, "Niklaus Wirth", *Book*, *author*.
2. σq, where σ is an unary operator and q is a query, is a query; e.g., *count(Book)*, *sin(x)*.
3. $q_1 \ \tau \ q_2$, where τ is a binary operator, is a query; e.g., 2+2, *Book.title*, *Customer* **where** <condition>.

In SBQL each binary operator is either algebraic or non-algebraic. If Δ is an algebraic operator, then in the query $q_1 \ \Delta \ q_2$ the order of evaluation of queries q_1 and q_2 is inessential. Queries are evaluated independently and their results are combined into the final result depending on Δ. Examples of algebraic operators are numerical and string operators and comparisons, aggregate functions, union, and others.

Non-algebraic operators are the core of the SBA. In a query $q_1 \ \theta \ q_2$ with a non-algebraic operator θ the second subquery is evaluated in context determined by the first subquery. Thus the order of evaluation of queries q_1 and q_2 is significant. Query $q_1 \ \theta \ q_2$ is evaluated as follows. First q_1 is evaluated. Then q_2 is evaluated for each element r of the result returned by q_1. Before each such evaluation ES is augmented with a new scope determined by *nested(r)*. After evaluation the stack is popped to the previous state. A partial result of the evaluation is a combination of r and the result returned by q_2 for this value. The method of the combination depends on θ. Eventually, these partial results are merged into the final result depending on the semantics of operator θ. Examples of non-algebraic operators are selection (**where**), projection/navigation (the dot), join, quantifiers ($\exists$, $\forall$), and transitive closures.

3 Transitive Closures in SBQL

A transitive closure in SBQL is a non-algebraic operator having the following syntax:

   q_1 **close by** q_2

Both q_1 and q_2 are queries. The query is evaluated as follows. Let *final_result* be the final result of the query and $\cup$ the bag union. Below we present the pseudo-code accomplishing abstract implementation of q_1 **close by** q_2:

```
final_result := result_of ( q₁);
for each r ∈ final_result do:
    o    push nested(r) at top of ES.
    o    final_result := final_result ∪ result_of (q₂);
    o    pop ES;
```

Note that each element *r* added to *final_result* by q_2 is subsequently processed by the *for each* command. The above operational semantic can be described in the denotational setting as the least fixed point equation (started from *final_result* = $\varnothing$ and continued till fixpoint):

$final\_result = q_1 \cup final\_result. q_2$

where dot is identical with the dot operator in SBQL. Similarly, the semantics can be expressed by iteration (continued till *result_of* (q_2) = $\varnothing$):

$final\_result = q_1 \cup q_1.q_2 \cup q_1.q_2.q_2 \cup q_1.q_2.q_2.q_2 \cup ....$

Naive implementation of the **close by** operator is as easy as the implementation of the dot operator. Note that if q_2 returns a previously processed element, an infinite loop will occur. Checking for such situations in queries is sometimes troublesome and may introduce unnecessary complexity into the queries. Another operator **close unique by** has been introduced to avoid infinite loops due to duplicates returned by q_2.

As q_1 and q_2 can be any queries, simple or complex, the relation between elements which is used for transitive closure is calculated on the fly during the query evaluation; thus the relation needs not to be explicitly stored in the database.

In Fig.1 we depict a simple data schema used in our examples. It is a description of parts, similar to descriptions used in Bill of Material (BOM) applications. Each *Part* has *name* and *kind*. If *kind* is "detail", the part has also *detailCost* and *detailMass* (the cost and mass of this part) and has no *assemblyCost*, *assemblyMass* attributes. If *kind* is "aggregate", the part has no *detailCost* and *detailMass*, but it has *assemblyCost* and *assemblyMass*. The attributes represent the cost of assembling this part and mass added to the mass of the components as the result of the assembly process. Aggregates have one or more *Component* sub-objects. Each *Component* has the *amount* attribute (number of components of specific type in a part), and a pointer object *leadsTo*, showing the part used to construct this part.

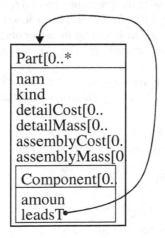

Fig. 1. A sample data schema

The simplest transitive closure SBQL query over this schema finds all components of a part named "engine".

(*Part* **where** *name* = "engine") **close by** (*Component.leadsTo.Part*)

This query first selects parts having *name* attribute equal to "engine". The transitive closure relation is described by the subquery (*Component.leadsTo.Part*). It returns all *Part* objects which are reached by the *leadsTo* pointer from already selected objects.

One of the basic BOM problems, i.e. "find all components of a specific part, along with their amount required to make this part", may be formulated using the transitive closure as follows:

((*Part* **where** *name*="engine"), (1 **as** *howMany*))
close by (*Component.((leadsTo.Part*), (*howMany*amount*) **as** *howMany*))

The query uses a named value in order to calculate the number of components. The number of parts the user wants to assemble (in this case 1) is named *howMany* and paired with the found part. In subsequent iterations the *howMany* value from parent object is used to calculate the required amount of child elements. It is also named *howMany* and paired with the child object.

The above query does not sum up amounts of identical sub-parts from different branches of the BOM lattice. Below we present a modified query which returns aggregated data – sums of distinct components from all branches of the BOM tree:

((((*Part* **where** *name*="engine") **as** *x*, (1 **as** *howMany*))
    close by (*x.Component.((leadsTo.Part*) **as** *x*, (*howMany*amount*) **as**
    howMany))
) **group as** *allEngineParts*
).
((**distinct**(*allEngineParts.x*) **as** *y*).(*y*, **sum**((*allEngineParts* **where** *x=y*).*howMany*)))

This query uses grouping in order to divide the problem into two parts. First, all the components named *x*, along with their amounts named *howMany* are found. The pairs are then grouped and named *allEngineParts*. The grouped pairs are further processed, by finding all distinct elements and summing the amounts for each distinct element.

This query could be further refined, in order to remove all aggregate parts (so only the detail parts will be returned). There are many ways to accomplish this goal. On of them is to use the operator **leaves by** in place of **close by**. The operator **leaves by** returns only leaf objects, i.e. objects which do not result in adding any further objects to the result set:

((((*Part* **where** *name*="engine") **as** *x*, (1 **as** *howMany*))
    leaves by(*x.Component.((leadsTo.Part*) **as** *x*, (*howMany*amount*) **as**
    howMany))
) **group as** *allEngineParts*
).
((**distinct**(*allEngineParts.x*) **as** *y*).(*y*, **sum**((*allEngineParts* **where** *x=y*).*howMany*)))

Such a typical BOM task cannot be formulated in any variant of SQL as a single query. Although the complexity of the SBQL solution is still high, SBQL supports facilities to manage the complexity. In this case the grouping operator allows us to decompose the problem into easier subproblems.

SBQL queries may be used to perform even more complex tasks. The query below calculates the cost and mass of the part named "engine", taking into account cost and mass of each engine part, amount of engine parts and cost and mass increment connected with assembly. This task has been used in [1] as an example of lack of power and flexibility of currently used query languages. In SBQL the task can be formulated with no essential problems:

```
(  (   ((Part where name="engine") as x, (1 as howMany))
       close by x.Component.((leadsTo.Part) as x, (amount*howMany) as
       howMany)
   ) group as allEngineParts
).
(allEngineParts.(
   if x.kind="detail" then
       ((howMany * x.detailCost) as c, (howMany * x.detailMass) as m)
   else
       ((howMany * x.assemblyCost) as c, (howMany* x.assemblyMass) as m)
   )
) group as CostMassIncrease).
(sum(CostMassIncrease.c) as engineCost, sum(CostMassIncrease.m) as engineMass)
```

Due to the full orthogonality (including orthogonal persistence) SBQL can perform calculations without referring to the database; e.g. 2+2 is a regular query. It is impossible in some SQL variants. The query below calculates an approximation the square root of a, using the fixpoint equation $x = (a/x + x)/2$.

```
(  (1 as x, 1 as counter)
   close by (((a/x + x)/2 as x, counter +1 as counter) where counter ≤ 5)
).(x where counter = 5)
```

Cycles in the queried graph can be easily dealt with by means of another variant of the **close by** operator – **close unique by**. This variant removes duplicates after each closure iteration, thus cycles do not imply infinite loops. Another variant of the **close by** operator is the **leaves unique by** operator. It is a combination of the two previous variants. It returns only leaf objects, while preventing problems with graph cycles.

4   Fixpoint Systems in SBQL

SBQL supports many different programming paradigms. Among others, SBQL provides querying capabilities similar to those of Datalog. The currently proposed solution is based on fixpoint systems, i.e. queries of the form $x = q(x)$, where x is a variable, q is an arbitrary SBQL query dependent on x. A system of such equations can have arbitrary number of variables. Such fixpoint systems in comparison to Datalog seem to have essential differences, in particular the following:

- Datalog is used to deduce *facts*, using other *facts* and *rules*. SBQL fixpoint systems are used to find objects or (complex) values which satisfy some conditions.
- Datalog is based on logic, thus some authors expect that it would be possible to *prove mathematically* some properties of a Datalog program and its results. SBQL

theoretical foundations lie elsewhere, and the possibility of proving anything is not among the concerns of the SBQL design.

- The equations in SBQL fixpoint systems (which can be thought of as equivalent to Datalog rules) may use any valid SBQL query;
- SBQL puts no constraints on the negation operator and assumes neither stratification nor CWA. However, negation is not the only operation which may result in a query causing an infinite loop; for instance, another such operator is function *sinus*. SBQL assumes that the programmer takes appropriate care.

In our opinion these differences concern mainly some specific rhetoric, ideological assumptions, terminology, and superficial notions. From the pragmatic point of view SBQL fixpoint systems are syntactically very similar to Datalog programs. Moreover, they can be used in the same situations and can solve the same tasks. For these reasons we consider SBQL fixpoint systems as a direct counterpart of Datalog programs. Taking in account all options, SBQL has the power of universal programming languages thus is incomparably more powerful than Datalog.

The syntax of an SBQL fixpoint system is as follows:

fixpoint$(x_{i1}, x_{i2},..., x_{in})$ $\{x_1 :\text{-} q_1; x_2 :\text{-} q_2;... x_m :\text{-} q_m;\}$

where:

- $x_1, x_2,..., x_m$ are names of variables in this equation system,
- $x_{i1}, x_{i2},..., x_{in}$ are returned variables, $\{x_{i1}, x_{i2},..., x_{in}\} \subseteq \{x_1, x_2,..., x_m\}$,
- $q_1, q_2,..., q_m$ are SBQL queries with free variables $x_1, x_2,..., x_m$;

The semantics of this language construct is the following:

1. Variables $x_1, x_2,..., x_m$ are initialized to empty bags.
2. Queries $q_1, q_2,..., q_m$ are evaluated.
3. If the results of $q_1, q_2,..., q_m$ are equal to the values of $x_1, x_2,..., x_m$, then stop (the fixpoint is reached). Otherwise assign the results of $q_1, q_2,..., q_m$ to the values of $x_1, x_2,..., x_m$ and go to step 2.
4. The values of $x_{i1}, x_{i2},..., x_{in}$ are returned as the result of the fixpoint query.

As queries $q_1, q_2,..., q_m$ can reference variables $x_1, x_2,..., x_m$, the fixpoint system provides recursive capabilities.

The simplest use of a fixpoint system in a query is the calculation of transitive closure. The query below uses a fixpoint system to find all subcomponents of the part named "engine" (the query addresses the schema shown in Fig.1):

fixpoint (*parts*){
    parts :- (*Part* **where** *name*="engine") **union** (*parts.Component.leadsTo.Part*);
}

Fixpoint systems are regular SBQL queries, and as such may be used as parts of other SBQL queries. The query below uses a fixpoint system as a part of a SBQL query, in order to find all unique engine elements:

distinct(**fixpoint** (*parts*){
    parts :- (*Part* **where** *name*="engine") **union** (*parts.Component.leadsTo.Part*);
})

A fixpoint system may use some variables as a way to break down the problem into smaller, more manageable parts. The query below does that in order to calculate the number of different parts in the part named "engine":

fixpoint (*final*) {
   engine **:-** ((*Part* **where** *name*="engine") **as** *x*, 1 **as** *howMany*);
   engineParts **:-** *engine* **union** *engineParts.Component*.
                            ((*leadsTo.Part*) **as** *x*, (*amount*howMany*) **as** *howMany*);
   final **:-** (**distinct**(*engineParts.x*) **as** *y*).(*y*, **sum**(*engineParts* **where** *x=y*).*howMany*);
  }

Only variable *final* is returned as the fixpoint result. The other two variables are used only to perform calculations, as their final values are inessential to the user. Variable *engine* is used to find the top element of the hierarchy (the "engine" part), while *engineParts* is the variable in which the results of recursive calculations are stored. Variables *final* and *engine* do not have to be calculated recursively.

The same principle is used in the next example. The query calculates the total cost and mass of the engine:

fixpoint (*cost*, *mass*){
   engine **:-** ((*Part* **where** *name*="engine") **as** *x*, 1 **as** *howMany*);
   engineParts **:-** *engine* **union** *engineParts.Component*.((*leadsTo.Part*) **as** *x*,
                              (*amount*howMany*) **as** *howMany*);
   detailsMass **:-** **sum**((*engineParts* **where** *x.kind* = "detail").
                              (*howMany*x.detailMass*));
   detailsCost **:-** **sum**((*engineParts* **where** *x.kind* = "detail").
                              (*howMany*x.detailCost*));
   addedMass **:-** **sum**((*engineParts* **where** *x.kind* = "aggregate").
                              (*howMany*x.assemblyMass*));
   *addedCost***:-** **sum**((*engineParts* **where** *x.kind* = "aggregate").
                              (*howMany*x.assemblyCost*));
   cost **:-** *detailsCost* + *addedCost*;
   mass **:-** *detailsMass* + *addedMass*;
  }

Fixpoints, unlike transitive closures, are capable of evaluating more than one recursive problem in each step, in a manner similar to the Datalog. This topic may be an interesting area for further research, although most of the practical recursive problems we are aware of can be solved using only a single recursion.

Similarly to transitive closures, fixpoint systems may be used to perform recursive calculations without referring to the database. The example below shows a fixpoint system version of example calculating the square root of *a*:

fixpoint(*x*){
   y :- (1 **as** *r*, 1 **as** *c*) **union** (*y*.(*a/r* + *r*)/2 **as** *r*, *c*+1 **as** *c*) **where** $c \leq 5$;
   x :- (*y* **where** *c* = 5).*r*;
  }

Fixpoint systems in SBQL fit well with the rest of the language. As they are based on a powerful and flexible approach, they are free from many drawbacks present in Datalog, such as the difficulty with formulating queries based on complex objects.

When compared with transitive closures, fixpoint systems seem to be more readable, as decomposition of the problem is easier.

5   Recursive Procedures and Views in SBQL

SBQL philosophy allows for seamless integration of imperative language constructs, including recursive procedures and functions with query operators. This allows utilizing the most popular recursive processing technique, without sacrificing any of the benefits of query language. In contrast to popular programming languages the new quality of SBQL concerns types of parameters and types of functions output. The basic assumption is that parameters are any SBQL queries and the output from functional procedures is compatible with query output. Thus SBQL procedures and functions are fully and seamlessly integrated with SBQL queries.

Statements in SBQL procedures use SBQL queries. An SBQL query preceded by an imperative operator is a statement. Statements such as *if, while, for each*, etc. can be more complex, see [7]. SBQL includes many such imperative operators (object creation, flow control statements, loops, etc.).

Below we present a recursive procedure which finds all components of a specific part, along with their amount required to make this part. It consists of a single return statement. The returned value is an empty collection or the result from recursive invocation of the same procedure. For simplicity in the examples we skip typing.

```
procedure SubPartsHowMany( myPartsHowMany ){
  return
    if not exists(myPartsHowMany) then bag()
    else bag( myPartsHowMany,
              SubPartsHowMany(myPartsHowMany.c.Component.
                        ((leadsTo.Part) as c, howMany * amount) as howMany))
         )
}
```

The procedure takes a structure or a collection of structures as the parameter (*myPartsHowMany*). Each structure contains *c* (a reference to a part) and *howMany* (the amount of parts). An example procedure call is the following:

SubPartsHowMany(((Part **where** name="engine") **as** c, (1 **as** howMany))

An advantage of recursive procedures is simplicity of the problem decomposition. A recursive task can be easily distributed among several procedures (some of which may be reused in other tasks). A procedure calculating the cost and mass of a part illustrating this possibility is shown below. The procedure utilizes the previously defined *SubPartsHowMany* procedure in order to perform the recursive processing and then performs calculations, on local variables (introduced by *create local*).

```
procedure CostAndMass(myPartsHowMany) {
  if not exists(myPartsHowMany) then return bag();
  create local SubPartsHowMany(myPartsHowMany) as parts;
  create local (parts where c.kind="detail") as details;
```

```
  create local (parts where c.kind="aggregate") as aggregates;
  create local sum(details.(howMany*c.detailMass)) as detailsMass;
  create local sum(details.(howMany*c.detailCost)) as detailsCost;
  create local sum(aggregates.(howMany*c.assemblyMass)) as addedMass;
  create local sum(aggregates.(howMany*c.assemblyCost)) as addedCost;
  return ((addedCost+detailsCost) as cost, (addedMass+detailsMass) as mass);
}
```

Recursive procedures in SBQL offer many advantages when compared to stored procedures in relational DBMSs. Most of them are consequences of the fact that procedures in SBQL are a natural extension of the SBA, working on the same principles and evaluated by the same evaluation engine, while in relational systems stored procedures are an add-on to the system evaluated separately from SQL queries. SBQL queries are valid as expressions, procedure parameters, etc. The type system is the same and there is no impedance mismatch between queries and programs.

SBQL updateable views are based on procedures and as such can be recursive and can utilize any other SBQL option, in particular parameters. Note that recursion without parameters makes little sense, thus if one assumes that views can be recursive then they must have parameters too. Recursive parameterized views are not available in any query language but SBQL. A simple read-only view, returning all subparts of parts which names are passed as a parameter, is shown below.

```
  create view EnginePartsDef {
    virtual objects EngineParts (whichParts){
      if not exists(whichParts) then return bag();
      create local (Part where Name in whichParts) as p;
      return (p union EngineParts(p.Component.leadsTo.Part.name)) as b;
    }
    on retrieve do return b;
  }
```

An example view invocation:

```
  EngineParts("pacer") where kind = "detail"
```

SBQL updateable views are discussed in detail in several publications, e.g. in [4, 7].

6 Future Work

A query language implementation without optimization is hardly accepted by the users due to bad performance. The amount of information stored in current databases would make the evaluation time of most queries unacceptable. The problem is even bigger in the case of recursive queries, as the evaluation cost of such queries is usually higher than in the case of non-recursive ones. It makes query optimization research a high priority task. Clearly defined semantics of SBQL allows for a systematic and disciplined approach to this problem. The adaptation of well-known techniques is possible. Query rewriting optimizations for SBQL are described e.g. in [3] and [7]. The techniques useful for transitive closure queries are also presented there. Other optimization techniques, however, have not been researched in detail yet. This applies to various index-based techniques, fixpoint system optimizations using semi-naïve evaluation and magic set techniques ([8]).

7 Conclusions

We have presented recursive query processing capabilities for the object-oriented Stack-Based Query Language (SBQL). SBQL offers very powerful and flexible recursive querying capabilities.

The transitive closure allow formulating queries more powerful and easily readable than SQL queries when compared with Oracle and DB2 SQL variants of transitive closure operators. Combined with the ease of semi-structured data handling in SBQL this may make XML data processing a much easier task.

Fixpoint systems provide SBQL with recursive capabilities similar to deductive query languages. However SQBL offers much more freedom, as there are no restrictions on operators which may be used within the queries. SBQL is also much better prepared to handle structured and semi-structured data than Datalog and its variants. This freedom, however comes at a cost, because the programmer must make sure that the query does not start an infinite evaluation loop.

Recursive procedures and views provided by SBQL allow to solve complex problems easily through problem decomposition, code reuse and other facilities typical for imperative programming languages. They are seamlessly integrated with the querying capabilities and allow the programmer to fully benefit from all the query language options and DBMS properties, i.e. macroscopic statements, handling of bulk data, persistent storage and optimization for queries used within procedures.

With the recent rise of interest in recursive processing due to the emergence of XML, RDF and other similar standards the SBQL seems to provide an interesting and universal alternative to other query languages.

References

1. Atkinson, M. P., Buneman, P.: Types and Persistence in Database Programming Languages. ACM Computing Surveys 19(2), (1987) 105-190
2. Abiteboul, S., Hull, R., Vianu, V.: Foundations of Databases. Addison-Wesley 1995
3. Płodzień, J., Subieta, K.: Applying Low-Level Query Optimization Techniques by Rewriting, Proc. DEXA Conf., Springer LNCS 2113, (2001) 867-876
4. Kozankiewicz, H., Subieta, K.: SBQL Views –Prototype of Updateable Views. Local Proc. of 8th East-European Conference on Advances in Databases and Information Systems (ADBIS), September 2004, Budapest, Hungary.
5. Subieta, K., Beeri, C., Matthes, F., Schmidt, J. W.: A Stack-Based Approach to Query Languages. Proc. East-West Database Workshop, 1994, Springer Workshops in Computing, (1995) 159-180
6. Subieta, K., Kambayashi, Y., Leszczyłowski, J.: Procedures in Object-Oriented Query Languages. Proc. VLDB Conf., Morgan Kaufmann, (1995) 182-193
7. Subieta, K.: Theory and Construction of Object-Oriented Query Languages. Polish-Japanese Institute of Information Technology Editors, Warsaw (2004)
8. Ullman, J. D.: Principles of Database and Knowledge-Base Systems, volume II, ch. 13, W H Freeman (1990)

Relation-Collapse: An Optimisation Technique for the Similarity Algebra $\mathcal{SA}$

Thomas Herstel and Ingo Schmitt

Fakultät für Informatik, Universität Magdeburg,
PF 4120, D-39016 Magdeburg
{herstel, schmitt}@iti.cs.uni-magdeburg.de

Abstract. Query systems of multimedia database systems should support similarity queries as well as user preferences like query term weighting. The graphical query language WS-QBE integrates these concepts and is a user-friendly query language. For evaluation purposes WS-QBE queries are translated into similarity algebra $\mathcal{SA}$ expressions. Expressions produced by the generation algorithm are very complex and thus need simplification and optimisation. One technique aiming at expression simplification is the relation-collapse technique. This technique, which is focus of this work, drastically reduces the number of basis relation scans and thus promises a more efficient query evaluation. Further, we discuss employing special, efficient implementations for algebra operations.

1 Introduction

The success of classical relational database systems in efficiently managing large amount of data leads to employing such systems to new application scenarios. Most convincing advantages are an integrated and consistent handling of data and declarative query facilities.

New database applications often deal with non-classical media types, such as for images, videos and audio data. These extensions to database systems also demand new query system mechanisms. For example, classical Boolean comparison operators of relational query languages ($<$, $>$, $=$, ...) are insufficient for image retrieval query formulation. Rather, new operators are needed which determine the *similarity* of an object to a given one. E.g., similarity between images can be based on comparing the dominating colours, and songs or music can be compared on containing the same melody. Depending on the media type and application there are diverse different similarity operators imaginable or demanded.

One problem when employing similarity operators in queries concerns the judgement of database objects according to their similarity to a query object. The degree to which every database object is similar w.r.t. a given query object has to be evaluated during query processing and expressed within result presentation. As those comparison operators, rather than deciding in a Boolean true/false manner, determine the degree to which a certain feature is fulfilled, also fuzzy values [24] must be considered. These values stem from the interval $[0, 1]$ and represent the extent of measured similarity. Utilizing fuzzy values also

J. Eder et al. (Eds.): ADBIS 2005, LNCS 3631, pp. 29–42, 2005.

implies a change in the semantics of result sets: sets from relational algebra are replaced by fuzzy sets, where to every set item a membership value is assigned which denotes the degree of membership to this set.

Combining similarity values in the manner of conjunction and disjunction is supported in fuzzy logic by employing so called t-norms and t-conorms respectively. Widely used and thus most prominent functions are 'min' and 'max'.

A query language that supports querying media objects like images, videos and audio data adequately has to provide similarity query facilities as well as query term weighting concepts and features to express user preferences. For example, when querying an image database which contains landscape pictures a user may prioritize the presence of a scenic sunset over the originating artist. Combining weighs with junctors can be done for instance by applying the well-known Fagin's weighting schema [9].

A *graphical* multimedia query language that allows a declarative query formulation including similarity, weighting, and user preferences is WS-QBE [20,19]. However, a graphical and declarative language is not appropriate for efficient query processing. Thus, queries in WS-QBE are translated into an algebra. This similarity algebra $\mathcal{SA}$ [18] like relational algebra is a procedural language and thus prescribes query processing steps. Unfortunately, the translation of WS-QBE queries into similarity algebra expressions following Codd's reduction algorithm results in rather complex expressions.

The problem we focus on here, however, is not specific to relational *similarity* calculus and algebra, but results from the demand of safe expressions. To ensure safety of variable evaluation variables must be bound to evaluable, i.e. finite domains. When conditions on variables are specified in the calculus expression, their values are calculated in the algebra by exploring their actual values in the database relation. These evaluations are connected to the rest of the algebra expression via joins. For example, in a system storing paintings and information about the artists the query

'*Give me all IDs of paintings similar to a given one.*'

is expressed in WS-QBE by simply filling in the similarity condition and indicating the output via the 'P.' symbol:

painting	id	photo	painter	title	technique
	P. $\sim$ ▦				

In a calculus expression the condition on the attribute photo is (implicitly) conjunctively combined with the evaluation of relation variables. Thus, the query corresponds to the expression:

$$\{X_{id} \mid \exists X_{photo}(\exists X_{painter}(\exists X_{title}(\exists X_{technique}($$
$$\text{painting}(X_{id}, X_{photo}, X_{painter}, X_{title}, X_{technique}) \wedge$$
$$(X_{photo} \sim C_{\square}))))) \}.$$

Following Codd's reduction algorithm, to ensure integrity of variable evaluation such conjunctions produce joins in algebra expressions. Reducing the calculus expression to an algebra expression results in[1]:

$$\pi_{\#1}((\text{painting}) \bowtie_{\#2=\#1} \sigma_{\#1 \sim C_{\square}} (\pi_{\#2}(\text{painting}))).$$

In our example, the variable X_{photo} in the similarity condition is evaluated by a projection of the respective attribute in painting. Then, the similarity condition is applied followed by a join with relation painting.

From the optimisation point of view these generated expressions, though correct, are comparatively inefficient to compute. There is no need here to introduce joins. Rather, the selection could have been applied directly to the relation and the join can be neglected, i.e. in our example $\pi_{\#1}(\sigma_{\#2 \sim C_{\square}}(\text{painting}))$ is more efficient. The problem gets even worse with increasing number of attribute conditions, since for *every* attribute condition potentially unnecessary joins are introduced and thus computational complexity rises unjustifiably. Assuming utilising nested loop joins the computational effort for self joining a relation with n tuples is $O(n * n)$ compared to linear effort for selection. With every additional attribute condition the effort increases by factor n. In other words, for m conditions the computational effort is $O(n^{m+1})$ instead of $O(n)$.

Therefore, the generated expressions must be simplified, i.e. optimised for query processing needs. One optimisation problem, which we will further discuss in this work is for example to reduce the number of generated table access operations and applied joins. The technique called **relation-collapse** introduced here reduces the number of access operations by far and thus enables an efficient query processing.

Since the early seventies when Codd proposed his relational calculus and algebra [2,3,4,5] they were aspect of optimisation considerations. Surveys can be found for example in [15,10,14]. The latter two concentrate mainly on physical aspects, particularly [10] contains a comprehensive overview of operator algorithms and behaviour, e.g. for hashing, aggregation, and joins. In our work, we do not concentrate on physical aspects of query optimisation. Rather, we first focus on logical optimisation which must be considered before efficient implementations can be chosen.

Besides, diverse algebra optimisation techniques have been studied. Selections of optimisation rules and heuristics to apply them can be found in almost every database textbook, like [7,6,16]. However, these rules cannot be simply adopted to similarity algebra, mainly for two reasons: They (1) do not cover introduced operators for query term weighting and user preferences, and (2) do not consider integration and treatment of similarity values within operators. While the first is rather obvious, the latter is more subtle. Basically, when evaluating similarity algebra expressions the tuple's membership values are updated subsequently

---

[1] For demonstration purposes distracting projections, e.g. originating from existential quantifiers are neglected here. Hash symbols '#' denote attribute positions and the tilde symbol '$\sim$' in the selection condition stands for the similarity function. For further details of $\mathcal{SA}$, please refer to Section 3.

by every applied operation. An optimisation technique has to guarantee the
same result tuples *and* respective membership values are returned regardless to
a chosen query plan. Yu and Meng discuss optimisation techniques for advanced
databases in [23]. However, the chapter on fuzzy databases which are related to
our work explores adapting techniques to unnest queries, but does not discuss
algebraic equivalences w.r.t. membership values.

The remainder of this work is organised as follows. In the next section we
sketch the graphical multimedia language WS-QBE which is the source language
for the algebra expressions we are optimising. Then, the similarity algebra is
introduced in Section 3. Possible optimisation rules are then discussed in Section 4. Therein, we will especially focus on the relation-collapse technique.
Finally, Section 5 concludes our work and an outlook to future research is given.

2   The WS-QBE Query Language

WS-QBE is a graphical, declarative and user-friendly query language for multimedia queries. It extends the well-known query language QBE by weighting and
similarity query concepts. Here, WS-QBE serves as source language for optimising
generated algebra expressions. As we will focus on these algebra expressions,
WS-QBE is only sketched. For a detailed discussion please refer to [20,19].

The main principle in QBE query formulation is to specify table skeletons,
which are filled with example data. We adopted this concept and added the opportunity to specify a *weighting table* where query term relevance weights are
specified and a *condition tree* that allows to formulate complex query conditions. Additionally to the 'standard' predicates for attribute value conditions
like $<, =, >$ we introduce similarity operators. Of course, similarity predicates
are application and user dependent. Thus, we allow the user to arbitrarily define
operators and their behaviour. Further, in WS-QBE output constraints may be
specified in a *temporal* or *spatial condition* table or frame, respectively. Altogether, WS-QBE supports (1) declarative similarity query formulation, (2) query
term weighting, and (3) output parameterisation.

An exemplary query in a multimedia system managing paintings and some
additional data, might be:

*'Find all IDs of oil paintings that originate from a Dutch painter and are
similar to the picture taken with my digital camera.'*

In WS-QBE this query is specified as follows:

painting	id	photo	painter	title	technique
P.	~ 🖼	_aid		oil	

artist	aid	name	native_country
	_aid		The Netherlands

In the table skeletons, specifying a '**P.**' for an attribute states this particular
attribute belonging to the query output. Matching of attribute values to some
constants is specified by simply simply filling in these constant into the respective attribute column. Operators other than equality, e.g. the image similarity
operator '~', are entered together with the appropriate constant, for example

an image. Joins can be expressed by filling in variables ('_aid' here), which for every occurrence must be equal on evaluation.

When this query is translated into the target language $\mathcal{SA}$, a complex algebra expression is generated. The transformation result is shown in Figure 2.

3   The Similarity Algebra $\mathcal{SA}$

This section informally introduces key operations of the similarity algebra $\mathcal{SA}$. In order to only show the most important operations relevant to this work, it is only briefly introduced here. For a more detailed and formal description we refer to the works [18,20].

The similarity algebra $\mathcal{SA}$ extends every tuple of a relation by a membership value from the interval $[0, 1]$ which expresses its membership to the relation. For example, if the user asks for database objects where the image is similar to a given picture, each tuple within the respective relation is tested against the given image. The result of a tuple's similarity test is a corresponding value from the interval $[0, 1]$. In order to reflect the degree of membership to the result set, the similarity results are integrated into the membership value of a tuple. For this purpose, every tuple reserves the attribute position zero to hold its membership value, i.e. classical relations are extended by an artificial attribute.

Obviously, the boolean junctors conjunction and disjunction cannot be employed. Rather, junctors from fuzzy logic, i.e. t-norms and t-conorms [24] are utilized. Additionally our algebra allows weighting of set operations like intersection and union. For our purpose we employed and adopted the weighting scheme developed by Fagin and Wimmers [9] as described in [21].

In the following we briefly present the most important operations of the similarity algebra $\mathcal{SA}$ together with their formal semantics. The semantics of an algebra expression E is given by its interpretation I^*. Interpretation of expressions utilises a function I, which, e.g. assigns values to constant identifiers and relations to relation names. Further, similarity function names, t-norms and t-conorms are replaced by their actual counterparts.

- Relation R is a 0-ary operation for accessing a classical database relation.
  $I^*(R) = \{(1, v_1, v_2, \ldots, v_n) | (v_1, v_2, \ldots, v_n) \in I(R)\}$ where $A_1, A_2, \ldots, A_n$ are attributes in R.
  All tuples obtain membership value 1, as they are considered true facts. For processing, the original relation is automatically extended by a leading attribute at position 0, which holds the membership value for every tuple.
- R^+ is a 0-ary operation to access an extended relation. This relation already has an attribute at position 0 that holds the membership value. Such relations for example can be the result of an $\mathcal{SA}$ query.
  $I^*(R^+) = I(R^+)$ where $A_1, A_2, \ldots, A_n$ are attributes in R^+ and v_0 is a similarity value from interval $[0, 1]$.
- $\pi_{\#_{p_1}, \#_{p_2}, \ldots, \#_{p_n}}(E)$ performs a projection of an algebra expression E where $\#_{p_1}, \#_{p_2}, \ldots, \#_{p_n}$ are the positions of the projection attributes.

Let $v_{0_1}, \ldots, v_{0_l}$ be all similarity values of a list of attribute values $v_{p_1}, \ldots, v_{p_n}$ of tuples $(v_{0_i}, v_1, \ldots, v_m) \in I^*(E)$ with accordingly identical values $p_i = j \Rightarrow v_{p_i} = v_j$ for $i = 1, \ldots, n$. Then $I^*(\pi_{\#_{p_1}, \#_{p_2}, \ldots, \#_{p_n}}(E)) = \{(u_0, v_{p_1}, v_{p_2}, \ldots, v_{p_n}) | (v_{0_i}, v_1, \ldots, v_m) \in I^*(E)\}$ holds, where u_0 is determined by:

$$u_0 = \begin{cases} I(\vee)(v_{0_1}, \ldots, v_{0_l}) & \text{if } l > 1 \\ v_{0_1} & \text{if } l = 1 \end{cases}.$$

The necessary duplicate removal on projections is performed by employing the t-conorm on the similarity values of those tuples that share the same values in projected attributes.

- $\sigma_{y_i \delta y_j}(E)$ denotes the selection. Note, that the selection predicate can include similarity conditions.
$I^*(\sigma_{y_i \delta y_j}(E)) = \{(u_0, v_1, \ldots, v_n) | (v_0, v_1, \ldots, v_n) \in I^*(E) \wedge u_0 = I(\wedge)(v_0, I(\delta)(\hat{y}_i, \hat{y}_j)) \wedge I(\delta)(\hat{y}_i, \hat{y}_j) > 0\}$. Attributes and constants are replaced by their values:

$$\hat{y}_i = \begin{cases} v_i & \text{if } y_i \text{ denotes an attribute} \\ I(y_i) & \text{if } y_i \text{ denotes a constant.} \end{cases}$$

$$\hat{y}_j = \begin{cases} v_j & \text{if } y_j \text{ denotes an attribute} \\ I(y_j) & \text{if } y_j \text{ denotes a constant.} \end{cases}$$

The utilised function I assigns concrete semantics to each specified similarity function δ, e.g. image similarity calculation or matching character strings. The selection, for each tuple, executes the similarity test on the specified attributes and constants, respectively. The obtained similarity value is then combined with the tuple's prior similarity value employing the t-norm.

- $(E_a \cap E_b)$, $(E_a \overrightarrow{\cap}_\theta E_b)$, $(E_a \overleftarrow{\cap}_\theta E_b)$ are three variants of intersection operators, where the expressions E_a and E_b must be union compatible. Corresponding tuples are combined in a conjunctive (t-norm) manner. The operations $(E_a \overrightarrow{\cap}_\theta E_b)$ and $(E_a \overleftarrow{\cap}_\theta E_b)$ are weighted variants, where the former denotes a stronger weighting to the left and the latter a stronger weighting to the right, respectively. A weighted conjunction according to the weighting schema from [9] is utilized.

  - *Intersection* $(E_a \cap E_b)$:
    $I^*((E_a \cap E_b)) = \{(u_0, v_1, \ldots, v_k) | (v_0, v_1, \ldots, v_k) \in I^*(E_a) \wedge (w_0, v_1, \ldots, v_k) \in I^*(E_b) \wedge u_0 = I(\wedge)(v_0, w_0) > 0\}$.
    Only tuples that originate from both expressions E_a and E_b are retained. Their similarity values are combined by t-norm.

  - *Weighted intersection* $(E_a \overrightarrow{\cap}_\theta E_b)$:
    $I^*((E_a \overrightarrow{\cap}_\theta E_b)) = \{(u_0, v_1, \ldots, v_k) | (v_0, v_1, \ldots, v_k) \in I^*(E_a) \wedge (w_0, v_1, \ldots, v_k) \in I^*(E_b) \wedge u_0 > 0\} \cup \{(u_0, v_1, \ldots, v_k) | (w_0, v_1, \ldots, v_k) \in I^*(E_b) \wedge \forall v_0.(v_0, v_1, \ldots, v_k) \notin I^*(E_a) \wedge u_0 > 0\}$ where u_0 is determined by:

    $$u_0 = \begin{cases} I(\overrightarrow{\wedge}_\theta)(I(\theta), v_0, w_0) & \text{case 1} \\ I(\overrightarrow{\wedge}_\theta)(I(\theta), 0, w_0) & \text{case 2} \end{cases}.$$

The semantics of $(E_a \overleftarrow{\cap}_\theta E_b)$ is given analogously.

Please note, that contrary to 'classic' intersection weighted intersections allow tuples in the result set which originate from only one of the expressions. This behavior is induced by weighted conjunction, which may produce values greater than zero even if one operand is zero.

- The three set union variants $(E_a \cup E_b)$, $(E_a \overrightarrow{\cup}_\theta E_b)$, $(E_a \overleftarrow{\cup}_\theta E_b)$ are analogously defined to their intersection counterparts.
- The Cartesian product $(E_a \times E_b)$ is analogously defined to the respective relational operations. However, the membership values are combined using conjunctions.
- $(E_a \bowtie_{\#_{i_1}=\#_{j_1},\dots,\#_{i_m}=\#_{j_m}} E_b)$ denotes the join operation, where the semantics is given by:

$I^*(E_a \bowtie_{\#_{a_1}=\#_{b_1},\dots,\#_{a_n}=\#_{b_n}} E_b) =$
$\{(u_0, v_1, \dots, v_k, w_1, \dots, w_l | (v_0, v_1, \dots, v_k) \in I^*(E_a) \wedge (w_0, w_1, \dots, w_l)$
$\in I^*(E_b) \wedge \forall i \in \{1, \dots, n\}.v_{a_i} = w_{b_i} \wedge u_0 = I(\wedge)(v_0, w_0)\}.$

Join extends Cartesian product by matching of attribute values. A join without specified equality condition behaves like Cartesian product.

Please note, that operations within our algebra only result in tuples, whose similarity values are greater than zero.

4   Optimisation of $\mathcal{SA}$ Expressions

Algebraic optimisation bases on semantic equivalence of syntactically different algebraic expressions. In addition to relational algebra semantic equivalence in $\mathcal{SA}$ means equality of calculated similarity values. The aim of optimisation is to transform a given algebra expression into an equivalent one, whose evaluation takes minimal computational effort. Often, heuristics are applied to find such expressions.

Due to the special concepts of the $\mathcal{SA}$ language w.r.t. similarity semantics optimisation rules cannot be easily adopted. For example, duplicate removal in $\mathcal{SA}$ projection means to disjunctively combine the corresponding similarity values, which has to be considered. In [13] optimisation limitations regarding commutativity of operators and projection are discussed. They occur, if underlying t-norm and t-conorm lack mutual distributivity. Furthermore, missing associativity of weighted operators [21] result in additional restrictions regarding optimisation.

The $\mathcal{SA}$ expressions are a result of two consecutive steps. First WS-QBE queries are transformed into the similarity domain calculus [20]. The expressions in $\mathcal{SDC}$ are then transformed into $\mathcal{SA}$ expressions, c.f. [18]. Often, this transformation results in rather complex expressions with much optimisation potential.

In the following we present a theorem, that allows a recursive simplification of complex expressions and, thus, promises higher evaluation efficiency.

Theorem 1. *Within similarity algebra $\mathcal{SA}$ the equivalence shown in Figure 1 holds, given that*

- $I(\wedge)(v_0, p) = v_0$ *is true for all similarity values v_0 from S and*
- $\pi_{\#i}(S) \subseteq \pi_{\#j}(R)$ *holds.*

R is a relation and S an arbitrary algebra expression. The projection $\pi_{\#j}(R)$ aggregates membership values of tuples in R sharing a value at attribute position $\#j$. The value p is the aggregated value of a projection tuple, which due to join operation is combined with the corresponding similarity value v_0 from S.

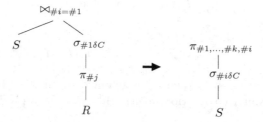

Fig. 1. Optimisation rule `relation-collapse`

Proof. The left side of optimisation rule according to join definition produces the following:

$$\{(u_0, v_1, \ldots, v_k, w_1) | (v_0, \ldots, v_k) \in S \wedge (w_0, w_1) \in \sigma_{\#1\delta C}\left(\pi_{\#j}(R)\right) \wedge v_i = w_1$$
$$\wedge u_0 = I(\wedge)(v_0, w_0)\}.$$

Considering equality $v_i = w_1$ all occurrences of w_1 are set to v_i. Furthermore, the projection can be put outside:

$$\pi_{\#1,\ldots,\#k,\#i}\left(\{(u_0, v_1, \ldots, v_k) | (v_0, \ldots, v_k) \in S \wedge (w_0, v_i) \in \sigma_{\#1\delta C}\left(\pi_{\#j}(R)\right)\right.$$
$$\left.\wedge \; u_0 = I(\wedge)(v_0, w_0)\}\right).$$

The requirement $(w_0, v_i) \in \sigma_{\#1\delta C}\left(\pi_{\#j}(R)\right)$ according to definition of selection can be replaced by $w_0 = I(\wedge)(p, v_i\delta C)^2$ and $v_i\delta C > 0$. The value p is computed in the projection, where the similarity values $p_{i_1}, \ldots, p_{i_l}$ of the v_i-tuples are disjunctively combined, i.e. $p = I(\vee)(p_{i_1}, \ldots, p_{i_l})$. Thus, we get:

$$\pi_{\#1,\ldots,\#k,\#i}\left(\{(u_0, v_1, \ldots, v_k) | (v_0, \ldots, v_k) \in S \wedge v_i\delta C > 0 \wedge\right.$$
$$\left.u_0 = I(\wedge)(v_0, I(\wedge)(p, v_i\delta C))\}\right).$$

Associativity of t-norm leads to:

$$I(\wedge)(v_0, I(\wedge)(p, v_i\delta C)) = I(\wedge)(I(\wedge)(v_0, p), v_i\delta C).$$

---

[2] For sake of simplicity, we use $v_i\delta C$ here instead of $I(\delta)(\hat{y}_i, \hat{y}_j)$.

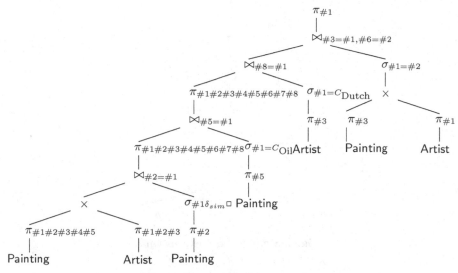

Fig. 2. Generated $\mathcal{SA}$ expression

Together with condition $I(\wedge)(v_0, p) = v_0$ we get:

$$\pi_{\#1,...,\#k,\#i}\left(\{(u_0, v_1, \ldots, v_k) | (v_0, \ldots, v_k) \in S \wedge v_i \delta C > 0 \wedge \right.$$
$$\left. u_0 = I(\wedge)(v_0, v_i \delta C)\}\right).$$

The definition of selection allows to rewrite the whole expression as follows:

$$\pi_{\#1,...,\#k,\#i}\left(\sigma_{\#i\delta C}(S)\right) \qquad\qquad \square$$

Please note, that this optimisation rule is even applicable, when the database relation R is replaced by a similarity relation R^+. Furthermore, this theorem can be adapted easily to selections, where two variables are compared. Theorem 1 induces a question, when the constraint

$$I(\wedge)(v_0, p) = v_0$$

is satisfied. This condition particularly holds, when min and max are used for conjunction and disjunction and additionally constraint $v_0 \leq p$ holds. The value p emerges from projection on similarity values on relation R, i.e. they are combined using disjunction. Thus, the value of p compared to each similarity value in R can only be higher.

Further, if within expression S similarity values originating from R are only combined to values v_0 using conjunction but not disjunction, they can only decrease and condition $v_0 \leq p$ is guaranteed. E.g., such operations with conjunctions in S are selections or Cartesian products. When a projection does not discard any attributes, e.g. they are duplicated or reordered, the tuples' similarity values remain unchanged.

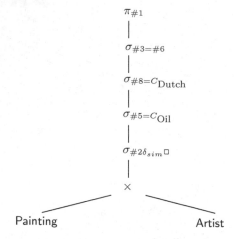

Fig. 3. Simplified $\mathcal{SA}$ expression

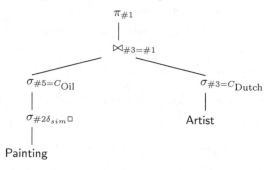

Fig. 4. Optimised algebra expression

The following example demonstrates application of our theorem 1. May the generated expression from Figure 2 be given. Applying the theorem recursively, and additionally removing projections where all attributes are listed, we get the simplified expression shown in Figure 3.

This expression can be further simplified by applying optimisation rules known in database theory:

- The order of subsequent selections may be arbitrarily changed. This directly follows from associativity and commutativity of t-norms.
- The Cartesian product and selection are commutative. Both are defined over t-norm and due to its associativity and commutativity the operations can be swapped.
- A selection with equality condition between two attributes of different relations and a Cartesian product can be substituted by a join. This directly follows from respective definitions.

Applying these rules to our example we finally get the algebra expression shown in Figure 4.

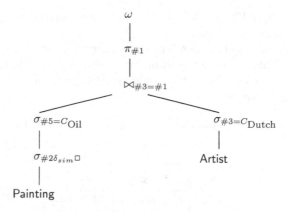

Fig. 5. Initial query evaluation plan

Besides algebraic optimisation in a subsequent step a physical optimisation is needed. Subject of physical optimisation is usually a query evaluation plan. A query evaluation plan discards the set semantics silently implied by algebra. For example, a query evaluation plan considers the tuples' order whereas the concept of order is meaningless in set theory. Further, an algebra operator can have more than one realisation. The query term states chosen implementations and may additionally introduce new operators.

Often, a user expects the result of a similarity query to be sorted according to the similarity values. However, queries, where all database tuples are more or less relevant can easily occur. Obviously, in such a scenario it is quite unhandy to block result presentation until the last result tuple is determined. In order to circumvent delays, results are determined stepwise upon successive requests. Compared with classic databases queries, this characteristic has to be considered particularly. Here, the well-known pipeline technique, where result objects are passed through different operators can be utilised. This is particularly reasonable, if the number of presented object is known in advance and relatively small compared to the number of result objects.

We therefore, for physical optimisation introduce a sort operator, that arranges tuples in decreasing order according to their similarity values. Considering semantics of similarity queries this operator is introduced between result evaluation and presentation, i.e. at the root of the query plan tree. Figure 5. tree. An early sort according to similarity values may have the following advantages:

1. *Ranker:* If a similarity test concerning a relation's media attribute precedes sort operation a so called *ranker* algorithm can be employed. These algorithms realise an index regarding similarity and provide nearest neighbor determination. Rankers present their result in a stream like fashion, i.e. result objects are shown on subsequent requests. For example, rankers can be based on the VA-file [22] approach or the AV-method [1].
2. *Combiner:* If two object streams which are sorted by their similarity values must be merged by a binary operation in $\mathcal{SA}$, special *combiner* al-

gorithms [8,11,17] can be employed. A good survey on different combiner algorithms is given in [12].

3. *Projection:* Projection combines similarity values of duplicates using disjunction. This is very efficient on streams of result object, which are sorted according to their similarity values. In [12] such an algorithm is suggested and named *transferer*.

Applying these three techniques is exemplarily shown in Figure 6.

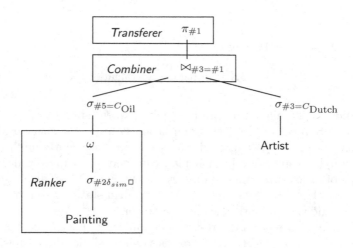

Fig. 6. Query evaluation plan

Our example also demonstrates, that sorting by similarity values as early as possible is not always optimal. For example, in Figure 6 the ranker algorithm must examine all paintings in order to find the most similar one. If however, the succeeding test regarding the painting technique ($\sigma_{\#5=C_{Oil}}$) has high selectivity, e.g. only five of one million paintings show oil technique, this selection should be executed *before* the similarity test ($\sigma_{\#2\delta_{sim}}$). This, on the other hand, precludes employing a ranking algorithm. But in view of the very few number of objects this can be considered negligible.

In order to get satisfactorily and reliable assumptions on how early a selection regarding similarity values fits best, respective statistics on data and knowledge about similarity semantics are vital. A cost model for similarity queries helps to find an optimal query evaluation plan.

5   Conclusion

This work shortly introduces the similarity language $\mathcal{SA}$, which basically extends relational algebra by similarity, weighting and user preferences. The algebra is not considered as a user language but rather is a target language of a graphical, user-friendly, and calculus based language called WS-QBE . For an efficient evaluation in query processing, optimisation of algebra expressions is inevitable. An important principle therein is to reduce the number of relation scans. As shown, this can be achieved by the applying an optimisation rule called relation-collapse. Correctness of this rule was formally shown. Furthermore, some more aspects and limits of optimisation were discussed.

Often optimisation rules without a cost based analysis is not applicable. In the future we will develop an appropriate cost based model for evaluation effort estimation.

As the similarity algebra is an extension of relational algebra, some expressions can be expressed directly in SQL-2003. This benefits from advantages coming with technologically mature SQL databases. We consider this aspect and work on harmonising both, optimisation techniques outside and inside of database systems with each other.

References

1. Balko, S., Schmitt, I., Saake, G.: The Active Vertice Method: A Performant Filtering Approach to High-Dimensional Indexing. Data and Knowledge Engineering (2004) 51(3):369–397
2. Codd, E. F.: A Relational Model of Data for Large Shared Data Banks. Communications of the ACM (1970) 13(6):377–387
3. Codd, E. F.: A Database Sublanguage Founded on the Relational Calculus. In ACM SIGFIDET Workshop on Data Description, Access and Control (1971) 35–61
4. Codd, E. F.: Relational Completeness of Data Base Sublanguages. In R. Rustin, editor, Data Base Systems, volume 6, Prentice Hall, Englewood Cliffs, NJ (1972) 65–98
5. Codd, E. F.: Relational Database: A Practical Foundation for Productivity. Communications of the ACM (1982) 25(2):109–117
6. Date, C., J.: An Introduction to Database Systems. Addison-Wesley, 8th edition (2003)
7. Elmasri, R., Navathe, S. B.: Fundamentals of Database Systems. Benjamin/Cummings, Redwood City, CA, 4th edition (2004)
8. Fagin, R., Lotem, A., Naor, M.: Optimal aggregation algorithms for middleware. Journal of Computer and System Sciences (2003) 66(4):614–656
9. Fagin, R., Wimmers, E. L.: A Formula for Incorporating Weights into Scoring Rules. Special Issue of Theoretical Computer Science (2000)
10. Graefe, G.: Query Evaluation Techniques For Large Databases. ACM Computing Surveys (1993) 25(2):73–170
11. Güntzer, U., Balke, W. T., Kießling, W.: Optimizing Multi-Feature Queries for Image Databases. In A. El Abbadi, M. L. Brodie, S. Chakravarthy, U. Dayal, N. Kamel, G. Schlageter, and K.-Y. Whang, editors, VLDB 2000, Proceedings of 26th International Conference on Very Large Data Bases, September 10-14, 2000, Cairo, Egypt, Morgan Kaufmann (2000) 419–428
12. Henrich, A., Robbert, G.: Ein Ansatz zur Übertragung von Rangordnungen bei der Suche auf strukturierten Daten. In G. Weikum, H. Schöning, and E. Rahm, editors, Datenbanksysteme in Business, Technologie und Web, BTW'03, 10. GI-Fachtagung, Leipzig, Februar 2003, Lecture Notes in Informatics (LNI) Volume P-26, Bonn, Gesellschaft für Informatik. (2003) 167–186

13. Herstel, T., Schmitt, I.: Optimierung von Ausdrücken der Ähnlichkeitsalgebra SA. In Peter Dadam and Manfred Reichert, editors, INFORMATIK 2004 - Informatik verbindet – Beiträge der 34. Jahrestagung der Gesellschaft für Informatik e.V. (GI), Band 2, 20.-24. September 2004, Ulm, Germany, volume P-51 of Lecture Notes in Informatics (LNI), Bonn . Gesellschaft für Informatik, Köllen Druck+Verlag GmbH (2004) 49–53

14. Ioannidis, Y. E.: Query optimization. ACM Computing Surveys (1996) 28(1):121–123

15. Jarke, M., Koch, J.: Query Optimization in Database Systems. ACM Computing Surveys (1984) 16(2):111–152

16. Kifer, M., Bernstein, A., Lewis, P. M.: Database Systems: An Application-Oriented Approach, Introductory Version. Addison-Wesley, 2nd edition (2004)

17. Nepal, S., Ramakrishna, M. V.: Query Processing Issues in Image(multimedia) Databases. In M. Kitsuregawa, editor, Proc. of the 15th IEEE Int. Conf. on Data Engineering, ICDE'99, Sydney, Australia, March, Los Alamitos, CA, 1999. IEEE Computer Society Press (1999) 22–29

18. Schmitt, I., Schulz, N.: Similarity Relational Calculus and its Reduction to a Similarity Algebra. In Dietmar Seipel and J. M. Turull-Torres, editors, Third Intern. Symposium on Foundations of Information and Knowledge Systems (FoIKS'04), Austria, February 17-20, volume 2942 of lncs Springer-Verlag Berlin Heidelberg (2004) 252–272

19. Schmitt, I., Schulz, N., Herstel, T.: WS-QBE: A QBE-like Query Language for Complex Multimedia Queries. In Yi-Ping Phoebe Chen, editor, Proceedings of the 11th International Multimedia Modelling Conference (MMM'05), Melbourne, Australia, January 12-14, 2005, Los Alamitos, CA, jan 2005. IEEE Computer Society Press (2005) 222–229

20. Schulz, N.: Formulierung von Nutzerpräferenzen in Multimedia-Retrieval-Systemen. Dissertation, Otto-von-Guericke-Universität Magdeburg, Fakultät für Informatik (2004)

21. Schulz, N., Schmitt, I.: Relevanzwichtung in komplexen Ähnlichkeitsanfragen. In G. Weikum, H. Schöning, and E. Rahm, editors, Datenbanksysteme in Business, Technologie und Web, BTW'03, 10. GI-Fachtagung, Leipzig, Februar 2003, Lecture Notes in Informatics (LNI) Volume P-26. Gesellschaft für Informatik (2003) 187–196

22. Weber, R., Schek, H. J., Blott, S.: A Quantitative Analysis and Performance Study for Similarity-Search Methods in High-Dimensional Spaces. In A. Gupta, O. Shmueli, and J. Widom, editors, Proc. of the 24th Int. Conf. on Very Large Data Bases (VLDB'98), Ney York City, August 24–27, 1998, San Francisco, CA. Morgan Kaufmann Publishers (1998) 194–205

23. Yu, C. T., Meng, W.: Principles of Database Query Processing for Advanced Applications. Morgan Kaufmann Publishers, San Francisko, CA (1998)

24. Zadeh, L. A.: Fuzzy Logic. IEEE Computer (1988) 21(4):83–93

On Modal Deductive Databases

Linh Anh Nguyen

Institute of Informatics, University of Warsaw,
ul. Banacha 2, 02-097 Warsaw, Poland

Abstract. We present a query language called MDatalog, which is an
extension of Datalog for multimodal deductive databases. We define
modal relational algebras and give the seminaive evaluation algorithm
and the magic-set transformation for MDatalog queries. Results of this
paper are proved for the multimodal logics of belief $KDI4_s5$, $KDI45$,
$KD4_s5_s$, $KD45_{(m)}$, which are extensions of the monomodal logic $KD45$.
We show that MDatalog has PTIME data complexity in these logics.

1 Introduction

Deductive databases are very useful for practical applications. In deductive
databases, intentional relations are defined using extentional relations and logical rules, and users can thus create sophisticated relations from basic ones. The
field of deductive databases is mature and there are well-developed techniques
for computing queries in such databases (see, e.g., [1]). Deductive databases
continuously receive attention from researchers; see, e.g., recent works [2,4].

Modal and temporal logics are used to reason about knowledge, belief, actions, changes, etc. It is desirable to study modal and temporal extensions of
deductive databases. For example, if we treat belief as a kind of uncertainty,
then modal deductive databases using multi-degree belief have potential applications. The field of temporal deductive databases has received a lot of attentions
from researchers (see, e.g., the survey [3]). On the other hand, the term "modal
deductive databases" is hard to find in the literature of computer science.

In [8], we proposed a modal query language MDatalog, which extends Datalog with modal operators. The computational method proposed in that work
is based on building a least L-model for a modal deductive database, where L
is the base modal logic. The technique used in [8] has the good property that it
also works for the logics $KD4$ and $S4$ but has a disadvantage that it does not
fully address advanced techniques of Datalog like the relational algebra or the
magic-set transformation. In [9,10], we developed a modal logic programming
language called MProlog and gave fixpoint semantics and SLD-resolution calculi
for MProlog in basic serial monomodal logics and useful multimodal logics of
belief. (An implementation of MProlog was reported in [11].) We used a special
structure called a *model generator* to represent a Kripke model. A model generator is a set of ground modal atoms, which may contain labelled existential
modal operators. The direct consequence operator of the fixpoint semantics is a
function that maps a model generator to another one. With that feature, we are

J. Eder et al. (Eds.): ADBIS 2005, LNCS 3631, pp. 43–57, 2005.

able to group atoms in a model generator by predicate symbols and this is a key to develop modal relational algebras, which is done in this work.

In this work, we extend the query language MDatalog for multimodal deductive databases. Basing on the existing techniques of Datalog, we define modal relational algebras and give the seminaive evaluation algorithm and the magic-set transformation for MDatalog queries. The language MDatalog is a sublanguage of MProlog and our computational methods for MDatalog are based on the fixpoint semantics of MProlog programs. Results of this paper are proved for the multimodal logics $KDI4_s5$, $KDI45$, $KD4_s5_s$, $KD45_{(m)}$, which are multimodal extensions of the monomodal logic $KD45$. The logics $KDI4_s5$ and $KDI45$ are intended for reasoning about multi-degree belief, while $KD4_s5_s$ can be used for distributed systems of belief, and $KD45_{(m)}$ can be used for reasoning about epistemic states of agents. We show that MDatalog has PTIME data complexity in these logics.

The rest of this work is organized as follows. In Section 2, we give basic definitions for multimodal logics and define the multimodal logic programming language MProlog. In Section 3, we provide fixpoint semantics for MProlog programs in the multimodal logics $KDI4_s5$, $KDI45$, $KD4_s5_s$, $KD45_{(m)}$. In Section 4, we define the MDatalog language and give definitions for multimodal deductive databases. We also show that MDatalog has PTIME data complexity in $KDI4_s5$, $KDI45$, $KD4_s5_s$, $KD45_{(m)}$. In Section 5, we define the L-SPCU algebra, which is an extension of the relational algebra SPCU for a multimodal logic L, and show that nonrecursive MDatalog queries in L can be simulated by L-SPCU queries. In Section 6, we present the seminaive evaluation algorithm and the magic-set transformation for MDatalog queries. Finally, Section 7 contains concluding remarks.

2 Preliminaries

2.1 Syntax and Semantics of Quantified Multimodal Logics

A language for quantified multimodal logics is an extension of a language of classical first-order logic with modal operators $\Box_i$ and $\Diamond_i$, for $1 \leq i \leq m$ (where m is fixed). The modal operators $\Box_i$ and $\Diamond_i$ can take various meanings. For example, $\Box_i$ can stand for "the agent i believes" and $\Diamond_i$ for "it is considered possible by agent i". The operators $\Box_i$ are called universal modal operators, while $\Diamond_i$ are called existential modal operators.

Terms and formulas are defined in the usual way, with the addition that if φ is a formula then $\Box_i\varphi$ and $\Diamond_i\varphi$ are also formulas. The *modal depth* of a formula is the maximal nesting depth of modalities in the formula. The *Herbrand universe* $\mathcal{U}$ and the *Herbrand base* $\mathcal{B}$ (for a fixed language) are defined as usual.

A *Kripke frame* is a tuple $\langle W, \tau, R_1, \ldots, R_m \rangle$, where W is a nonempty set of possible worlds, $\tau \in W$ is the *actual world*, and R_i is a binary relation on W, called the *accessibility relation* for the modal operators $\Box_i$, $\Diamond_i$. If $R_i(w, u)$ holds then we say that the world u is accessible from the world w via R_i.

A *fixed-domain Kripke model with rigid terms*, hereafter simply called a Kripke model or just a model, is a tuple $M = \langle D, W, \tau, R_1, \ldots, R_m, \pi \rangle$, where D is a set called the *domain*, $\langle W, \tau, R_1, \ldots, R_m \rangle$ is a Kripke frame, and π is an interpretation of constant symbols, function symbols and predicate symbols. For a constant symbol a, $\pi(a)$ is an element of D. For an n-ary function symbol f, $\pi(f)$ is a function from D^n to D. For an n-ary predicate symbol p and a world $w \in W$, $\pi(w)(p)$ is an n-ary relation on D.

A *variable assignment* V w.r.t. a Kripke model M is a function that maps each variable to an element of the domain of M. The value of $t^M[V]$ for a term t is defined as usual.

Given a Kripke model $M = \langle D, W, \tau, R_1, \ldots, R_m, \pi \rangle$, a variable assignment V, and a world $w \in W$, the *satisfaction relation* $M, V, w \vDash \varphi$ for a formula φ is defined as follows:

$$
\begin{aligned}
M, V, w \vDash p(t_1, \ldots, t_n) &\quad \text{iff} \quad (t_1^M[V], \ldots, t_n^M[V]) \in \pi(w)(p); \\
M, V, w \vDash \varphi \wedge \psi &\quad \text{iff} \quad M, V, w \vDash \varphi \text{ and } M, V, w \vDash \psi; \\
M, V, w \vDash \Box_i \varphi &\quad \text{iff} \quad \text{for all } v \in W \text{ such that } R_i(w, v), \ M, V, v \vDash \varphi; \\
M, V, w \vDash \forall x\, \varphi &\quad \text{iff} \quad \text{for all } a \in D, \ (M, V', w \vDash \varphi), \\
&\qquad \text{where } V'(x) = a \text{ and } V'(y) = V(y) \text{ for } y \neq x;
\end{aligned}
$$

and as usual for other cases (treating $\Diamond_i \varphi$ as $\neg \Box_i \neg \varphi$, and $\exists x\, \varphi$ as $\neg \forall x\, \neg \varphi$). We write $M, w \vDash \varphi$ to denote that $M, V, w \vDash \varphi$ for every V. We say that M satisfies φ, or φ is true in M, and write $M \vDash \varphi$, if $M, \tau \vDash \varphi$. For a set Γ of formulas, we call M a model of Γ and write $M \vDash \Gamma$ if $M \vDash \alpha$ for every $\alpha \in \Gamma$.

If as the class of admissible interpretations we take the class of all Kripke models (with no restrictions on the accessibility relations) then we obtain a quantified multimodal logic which has a standard Hilbert-style axiomatisation denoted by $K_{(m)}$. Other *normal (multi)modal logics* are obtained by adding certain axioms to $K_{(m)}$.

For a normal modal logic L whose class of admissible interpretations can be characterized by classical first-order formulas using the accessibility relations, we call such formulas *L-frame restrictions*, and call frames with such properties *L-frames*. We call a model M with an L-frame an *L-model*. We say that φ is *L-satisfiable* if there exists an L-model of φ, i.e. an L-model satisfying φ. A formula φ is said to be *L-valid* and called an *L-tautology* if φ is true in every L-model. For a set Γ of formulas, we write $\Gamma \vDash_L \varphi$ and call φ a *logical consequence* of Γ in L if φ is true in every L-model of Γ.

2.2   Multimodal Logics About Belief

To reflect properties of belief, one can extend the system $K_{(m)}$ with some of the following axioms, where axiom (D) states that belief is consistent, axiom (I) states that subscripts indicate degrees of belief, axiom (4) (resp. (4_s)) states that belief satisfies (strong) positive introspection, and axiom (5) (resp. (5_s)) states that belief satisfies (strong) negative introspection.

Name	Schema	Corresponding Condition
(D)	$\Box_i\varphi \to \neg\Box_i\neg\varphi$	$\forall u\,\exists v\,R_i(u,v)$
(I)	$\Box_i\varphi \to \Box_j\varphi$ if $i > j$	$R_j \subseteq R_i$ if $i > j$
(4)	$\Box_i\varphi \to \Box_i\Box_i\varphi$	$\forall u,v,w\ (R_i(u,v) \wedge R_i(v,w) \to R_i(u,w))$
(4_s)	$\Box_i\varphi \to \Box_j\Box_i\varphi$	$\forall u,v,w\ (R_j(u,v) \wedge R_i(v,w) \to R_i(u,w))$
(5)	$\neg\Box_i\varphi \to \Box_i\neg\Box_i\varphi$	$\forall u,v,w\ (R_i(u,v) \wedge R_i(u,w) \to R_i(w,v))$
(5_s)	$\neg\Box_i\varphi \to \Box_j\neg\Box_i\varphi$	$\forall u,v,w\ (R_j(u,v) \wedge R_i(u,w) \to R_i(v,w))$

The following logics are intended for reasoning about multi-degree belief:

$$KDI4_s5 = K_{(m)} + (D) + (I) + (4_s) + (5)$$
$$KDI45 = K_{(m)} + (D) + (I) + (4) + (5)$$

Note that axiom (5_s) is derivable in $KDI4_s5$. Axiom (I) gives $\Box_i\varphi$ the meaning "φ is believed up to degree i", and $\Diamond_i\varphi$ can be read as "it is possible weakly at degree i that φ".

For multi-agent systems, subscripts beside $\Box$ and $\Diamond$ stand for agents. For distributed systems of belief we can use $KD4_s5_s = K_{(m)} + (D) + (4_s) + (5_s)$. In this system, agents have full access to belief bases of each other. They are members of a united system and viewed as "friends". In another kind of multi-agent systems, agents are "opponents" and they play against each other. Each agent tries to simulate epistemic states of the others. To write a program for an agent one may need to use modal operators of other agents. One of suitable logics for this problem is $KD45_{(m)} = K_{(m)} + (D) + (4) + (5)$.

For further reading on modal logics, see, e.g., [6,7].

2.3 Multimodal Logic Programs

We use E and F to denote classical atoms, and $\boxdot$ to denote a sequence of universal modal operators, which may be empty. By $\forall(\varphi)$ we denote the universal closure of φ. Similarly as in classical logic programming, we use the clausal form $\boxdot(\varphi \leftarrow \psi_1, \ldots, \psi_n)$ for $\forall(\boxdot(\varphi \vee \neg\psi_1 \ldots \vee \neg\psi_n))$.

A *program clause* is a formula of the form $\boxdot(A \leftarrow B_1, \ldots, B_n)$, where $n \geq 0$ and $A, B_1, \ldots, B_n$ are formulas of the form E, $\Box_i E$, or $\Diamond_i E$. $\boxdot$ is called the *modal context*, A the *head*, and $B_1, \ldots, B_n$ the *body* of the program clause.

An *MProlog program* is a finite set of program clauses.

When the base logic is intended for reasoning about multi-degree belief, it has little sense to write a program clause in the form $\Box_i\Box_j\varphi$. Besides, in the logics $KDI4_s5$ and $KD4_s5_s$ we have the tautology $\nabla\nabla'\varphi \equiv \nabla'\varphi$, where ∇ and ∇' are modal operators. For these reasons, we introduce a restriction for MProlog programs in these logics: For $L \in \{KDI4_s5, KDI45, KD4_s5_s\}$, an MProlog program is called an *L-MProlog program* if its program clauses have modal context with length bounded by 1.

In the logic $KD45_{(m)}$, we have the tautology $\Box_i\Box_i\varphi \equiv \Box_i\varphi$. So, we introduce a restriction for MProlog programs in $KD45_{(m)}$: An MProlog program is called a $KD45_{(m)}$-*MProlog program* if the modal contexts of its program clauses do not contain subsequences of the form $\Box_i\Box_i$.

It is shown in [10] that the MProlog language (with goals) has the same expressiveness power as the general Horn fragment in normal modal logics. Moreover, the above restrictions do not reduce expressiveness of the language [10].

3   Fixpoint Semantics of MProlog Programs

In this section, we instantiate our framework given in [10] to provide fixpoint semantics for L-MProlog programs, where $L \in \{KDI4_s5, KDI45, KD4_s5_s, KD45_{(m)}\}$. Let L be one of these logics and P be an L-MProlog program.

When applying the "direct consequence operator" $T_{L,P}$, if we obtain an "atom" of the form $\Diamond_i E$, then to simplify the task we label the modal operator $\Diamond_i$. Labelling allows us to address the chosen world(s) in which this particular E must hold. A natural way is to label $\Diamond_i$ by E to obtain $\langle E \rangle_i$.

Throughout this work, we will use the following notations:

- ∇ : $\Box_i$, $\Diamond_i$, or $\langle E \rangle_i$, called a *modal operator*;
- $\triangle$: a (possibly empty) sequence of modal operators, called a *modality*;
- A, B : formulas of the form E or ∇E, called *simple atoms*;
- α, β : formulas of the form $\triangle E$, called *atoms*;
- φ, ψ : *(labelled) formulas*, i.e. formulas that may contain $\langle E \rangle_i$.

A *ground modality* is a modality without variables.

Recall that a simple subscript like i beside $\Box$, $\Diamond$, or $\langle E \rangle$ indicates the *kind* (i.e. degree/agent number) of the modal operator. We use such subscripts beside ∇ for the same aim. To distinguish a number of modal operators we use superscripts of the form (i), e.g. $\Box^{(1)}$, $\Box^{(2)}$, $\nabla^{(i)}$.

Define that a modality $\nabla_{i_1}^{(1)} \ldots \nabla_{i_k}^{(k)}$ is in L-normal form if

- case $L \in \{KDI4_s5, KD4_s5_s\}$: $k \leq 1$,
- case $L = KD45_{(m)}$: $i_j \neq i_{j+1}$ for all $1 \leq j < k$,
- case $L = KDI45$: $i_1 > \ldots > i_k$.

A modality is in *L-normal labelled form* if it is in L-normal form and does not contain[1] $\Diamond_i$. An atom is in *L-normal (labelled) form* if it is of the form $\triangle E$ with $\triangle$ in L-normal (labelled) form. An atom is in *almost L-normal labelled form* if it is of the form $\triangle A$ with $\triangle$ in L-normal labelled form.

We define $\preceq_L$ to be the least reflexive and transitive binary relation between modal operators such that $\Diamond_i \preceq_L \langle E \rangle_i \preceq_L \Box_i$, and if $L \in \{KDI4_s5, KDI45\}$ and $i \leq j$ then $\Box_i \preceq_L \Box_j$ and $\Diamond_j \preceq_L \Diamond_i$. A ground modality $\triangle = \nabla^{(1)} \ldots \nabla^{(n)}$ is called an *L-instance* of a ground modality $\triangle' = \nabla^{(1')} \ldots \nabla^{(n')}$ if $\nabla^{(i)} \preceq_L \nabla^{(i')}$ for every $1 \leq i \leq n$. In that case we say that $\triangle'$ is *equal to* or *more general in L than* $\triangle$ (hereby we define a *pre-order between ground modalities*). If $\triangle$ is an L-instance of $\triangle'$ then we call $\triangle E$ an *L-instance* of the atom $\triangle' E$. For example, $\Box_1 \Diamond_2 E$ is a $KDI4_s5$-instance of $\Box_2 \langle F \rangle_1 E$.

---

[1] In [10], we exclude also $\langle \top \rangle_i$, but $\langle \top \rangle_i$ and $\top$ are not used in this work, as we will omit details of the construction of standard L-models of L-model generators.

A *model generator* is a set of ground atoms not containing $\Diamond_i$. An *L-normal model generator* is a model generator consisting of atoms in *L*-normal labelled form. An *L*-normal model generator I is expected to represent an *L*-model, which is defined in [10] and called the *standard L-model* of I. It is shown in [10] that *"the standard L-model of an L-normal model generator I is a least L-model of I"*.

Given an *L*-normal model generator I, how can $T_{L,P}(I)$ be defined? Basing on the axioms of L, I is first extended to the *L-saturation* of I, denoted by $Sat_L(I)$, which is a set of atoms. Next, *L-instances of program clauses* of P are *applied* to the atoms of $Sat_L(I)$. This is done by the operator $T_{oL,P}$. The set $T_{oL,P}(Sat_L(I))$ is a model generator but not necessary in *L*-normal form. Finally, the *normalization operator* NF_L converts $T_{oL,P}(Sat_L(I))$ to an *L*-normal model generator. $T_{L,P}(I)$ is defined as $NF_L(T_{oL,P}(Sat_L(I)))$.

The *saturation operator* Sat_L is specified by the following rules, in which formulas in both sides are required to be in almost *L*-normal labelled form:

$L = KDI4_s5$: $\quad \Box_i E \to \Box_j E \;$ if $i > j$
$\qquad\qquad\qquad\quad \Box_i E \to \Box_m \Box_i E$
$\qquad\qquad\qquad\quad \langle F \rangle_i E \to \Box_m \Diamond_i E$

$L = KD4_s5_s$: $\quad \Box_i E \to \Box_j \Box_i E$
$\qquad\qquad\qquad\quad \langle F \rangle_i E \to \Box_j \Diamond_i E$

$L = KD45_{(m)}$: $\quad \triangle \Box_i E \to \triangle \Box_i \Box_i E$
$\qquad\qquad\qquad\quad \triangle \langle F \rangle_i E \to \triangle \Box_i \Diamond_i E$

$L = KDI45$: $\quad \triangle \Box_i \alpha \to \triangle \Box_j \alpha \;$ if $i > j$
$\qquad\qquad\qquad\quad \triangle \Box_i \alpha \to \triangle \Box_i \Box_j \alpha \;$ if $i > j$
$\qquad\qquad\qquad\quad \triangle \Box_i \Box_j \alpha \to \triangle \Box_j \alpha \;$ if $i > j$
$\qquad\qquad\qquad\quad \triangle \Box_i E \to \triangle \Box_i \Box_i E$
$\qquad\qquad\qquad\quad \triangle \nabla E \to \triangle \Box_i \Diamond_i E \;$ if $\Diamond_i \preceq_L \nabla$
$\qquad\qquad\qquad\quad \triangle \Box_i \nabla_j E \to \triangle \Diamond_j E \;$ if $i > j$
$\qquad\qquad\qquad\quad \triangle \langle F \rangle_i \nabla_j E \to \triangle \Diamond_i E \;$ if $i > j$

Given an *L*-normal model generator I, $Sat_L(I)$ is the least extension of I that contains all ground atoms in almost *L*-normal labelled form that are derivable from some atom in I using the rules specifying Sat_L. As an example, for $L = KDI4_s5$, we have $Sat_L(\{\Box_2 p(a)\}) = \{\Box_2 p(a), \Box_1 p(a), \Box_m \Box_2 p(a), \Box_m \Box_1 p(a)\}$.

Let $\boxdot$ be a universal modality in *L*-normal form, $\boxdot'$ a modal context of an *L*-MProlog program clause, φ and φ' be program clauses with an empty modal context. We say that $\boxdot$ is an *L-context instance* of $\boxdot'$ if $\boxdot'\psi \to \boxdot\psi$ is *L*-valid (for every ψ), and that $\boxdot\varphi$ is an *L-instance* of (a program clause) $\boxdot'\varphi'$ if $\boxdot$ is an *L*-context instance of $\boxdot'$ and there exists a substitution θ such that $\varphi = \varphi'\theta$.

It is easily seen that $\boxdot$ is an *L*-context instance of $\boxdot'$ iff one of the following condition holds: a) $L \in \{KD45_{(m)}, KD4_s5_s\}$ and $\boxdot = \boxdot'$; b) $L = KDI4_s5$ and $\boxdot$ is an *L*-instance of $\boxdot'$; c) $L = KDI45$, $\boxdot' = \Box_i$, $\boxdot$ is not empty, and every modal operator $\Box_j$ of $\boxdot$ satisfies $j \leq i$.

The *operator* $T_{0L,P}$ is defined as follows: for a set I of ground atoms in almost L-normal labelled form, $T_{0L,P}(I)$ is the least (w.r.t. $\subseteq$) model generator such that if $\boxdot(A \leftarrow B_1, \ldots, B_n)$ is a ground L-instance of some program clause of P and $\triangle$ is a maximally general ground modality in L-normal labelled form such that $\triangle$ is an L-instance of $\boxdot$ and $\triangle B_i$ is an L-instance of some atom of I (for every $1 \leq i \leq n$), then the forward labelled form of $\triangle A$ belongs to $T_{0L,P}(I)$, where the *forward labelled form* of an atom α is the atom α' such that if α is of the form $\triangle'\diamondsuit_i E$ then $\alpha' = \triangle'\langle E\rangle_i E$, else $\alpha' = \alpha$.

For example, if P consists of the only clause $\square_2(\diamondsuit_1 p(x) \leftarrow q(x), r(x), \square_1 s(x), \diamondsuit_2 t(x))$ and $I = \{\langle q(a)\rangle_1 q(a), \langle q(a)\rangle_1 r(a), \square_2\square_2 s(a), \square_2\langle t(a)\rangle_1 t(a)\}$ and $L = KDI4_s5$, then $T_{0L,P}(I) = \{\langle q(a)\rangle_1\langle p(a)\rangle_1 p(a)\}$.

The *normalization operator* NF_L is specified by the following rules, in which formulas in both sides are required to be in almost L-normal labelled form and ∇_i is $\square_i$ or $\langle E\rangle_i$:

$$L \in \{KDI4_s5, KD4_s5_s\} : \quad \nabla'_j \nabla_i E \rightarrow \nabla_i E$$
$$L = KD45_{(m)} : \quad \triangle\nabla'_i\nabla_i E \rightarrow \triangle\nabla_i E$$
$$L = KDI45 : \quad \triangle\nabla'_j\nabla_i E \rightarrow \triangle\nabla_i E \text{ if } j \leq i$$

Given a model generator I, $NF_L(I)$ is the set of all ground atoms in L-normal labelled form that are derivable from some atom of I using the rules specifying NF_L. For example, $NF_{KDI4s5}(\{\langle q(a)\rangle_1\langle p(a)\rangle_1 p(a)\}) = \{\langle p(a)\rangle_1 p(a)\}$.

Define $T_{L,P}(I) = NF_L(T_{0L,P}(Sat_L(I)))$. By definition, the operators Sat_L, $T_{0L,P}$, and NF_L are all increasingly monotonic and compact. Hence the operator $T_{L,P}$ is monotonic and continuous. By the Kleene theorem, it follows that $T_{L,P}$ has the least fixpoint $T_{L,P}\uparrow\omega = \bigcup_{n=0}^{\omega} T_{L,P}\uparrow n$, where $T_{L,P}\uparrow 0 = \emptyset$ and $T_{L,P}\uparrow n = T_{L,P}(T_{L,P}\uparrow(n-1))$ for $n > 0$. Denote the least fixpoint $T_{L,P}\uparrow\omega$ by $I_{L,P}$ and the standard L-model of $I_{L,P}$ by $M_{L,P}$.

It is proved in [10] that "$P \models_L I_{L,P}$ and $M_{L,P}$ is a least L-model of P".

Example 1. Consider the following program P in $L = KDI4_s5$:

$$\diamondsuit_1 s(a) \leftarrow \qquad\qquad \square_1(q(x) \leftarrow r(x), s(x))$$
$$\square_1(\square_1 r(x) \leftarrow s(x)) \qquad \square_2(p(x) \leftarrow \diamondsuit_2 q(x))$$

We have $I_{L,P} = \{\langle s(a)\rangle_1 s(a), \square_1 r(a), \langle s(a)\rangle_1 q(a), \square_2 p(a), \square_1 p(a)\}$.

4   MDatalog and Modal Deductive Databases

In this section, we give definitions for modal deductive databases and define a query language called MDatalog for such databases. We also show that the data complexity of MDatalog in the logics $KDI4_s5$, $KDI45$, $KD4_s5_s$, $KD45_{(m)}$ is in PTIME. Let L be one of these logics.

We first define the L-MDatalog language. An MProlog program clause without function symbols is *allowed* if every variable occurring in the head also occurs in the body. An *L-MDatalog program* is an L-MProlog program free from function symbols and containing only allowed clauses.

An n-ary *L-tuple* is an ordered pair $(\triangle, t)$, where t is a classical n-ary tuple of constant symbols and $\triangle$ is a ground modality in almost *L*-normal labelled form. An n-ary *L-relation* is a set of n-ary *L*-tuples. An *L*-relation is an n-ary *L*-relation for some n. An *L*-relation is said to be in *L-normal form* if each of its tuples is of the form $(\triangle, t)$ with $\triangle$ in *L*-normal labelled form.

A modal deductive database in L consists of an instance I of extentional *L*-relations (*edb*) and an *L*-MDatalog program P for defining intentional relations (*idb*).

If $(\triangle, t)$ is a tuple in an *L*-relation of a predicate p then we also treat it as the atom $\triangle p(t)$. Let $\mathcal{R}$ be a set of predicate symbols. An instance I of *L*-relations of $\mathcal{R}$ will be also treated as a set of atoms of predicates of $\mathcal{R}$. Conversely, a set I of ground atoms of predicates of $\mathcal{R}$ which are in almost *L*-normal labelled form will be also treated as an instance of *L*-relations of $\mathcal{R}$. If I is an instance of *L*-relations of $\mathcal{R}$ and p is a predicate symbol of $\mathcal{R}$, then by $I(p)$ we denote the instance of the *L*-relation p contained in I.

An *L*-MDatalog program P can be treated as the function P_L that maps an instance of *edb* *L*-relations to an instance of *idb* *L*-relations such that $P_L(I)$ is the least (w.r.t. $\subseteq$) *L*-model generator J such that $T_{L,P}(I \cup J) = J$. Let $T_{L,P,I}$ be the operator defined by $T_{L,P,I}(J) = T_{L,P}(I \cup J)$. Then $T_{L,P,I}$ is monotonic and continuous, and $P_L(I)$ is the least fixpoint of $T_{L,P,I}$ specified by $T_{L,P,I} \uparrow \omega = \bigcup_{0 \leq k \leq \omega} T_{L,P,I} \uparrow k$, where $T_{L,P,I} \uparrow k$ is defined in a similar way as $T_{L,P} \uparrow k$.

We define an *L-MDatalog query* to be a pair (P, φ), where P is an *L*-MDatalog program and $\varphi = \boxdot(query(x_1, \ldots, x_k) \leftarrow B_1, \ldots, B_h)$ is an *L*-MDatalog clause (i.e. an allowed program clause not containing function symbols) such that: *query* is a special predicate symbol not occurring in P and the body of φ, the variables $x_1, \ldots, x_k$ are different, and $k \geq 1$. An *L*-MDatalog query (P, φ) takes as input an instance I of *edb* *L*-relations and returns as output the *L*-relation $P'_L(I)(query)$, where $P' = P \cup \{\varphi\}$.

One can show that the (fixpoint) semantics of *L*-MDatalog queries is compatible with the least model semantics of *L*-MProlog programs [10].

Example 2. Let us consider the situation when a company has some branches and a central database. Each of the branches can access and update the database, and suppose that the company wants to distinguish data and knowledge coming from different branches. Also assume that data coming from branches can contain noises and statements expressed by a branch may not be highly recognised by other branches. This means that data and statements expressed by branches are treated as "belief" rather than "knowledge". In this case, we can use the multimodal logic $KD4_s5_s$, where each modal index represent a branch of the company, also called an *agent*. Recall that in this logic each agent has a full access to the belief bases of the other agents. Data put by agent i are of the form $\square_i E$ (agent i believes in E) or $\Diamond_i E$ (agent i considers that E is possible). A statement expressed by agent i is a clause of the form $\square_i(A \leftarrow B_1, \ldots, B_n)$, where A is an atom of the form E, $\square_i E$, or $\Diamond_i E$, and $B_1, \ldots, B_n$ are simple modal atoms that may contain modal operators of the other agents. For communicating with normal users, the central database may contain rules with the empty modal context, i.e. in the form $E \leftarrow B_1, \ldots, B_n$, which hide sources of information. As a concrete example, consider the following program/database in $KD4_s5_s$:

agent 1:

$$\Box_1(\Diamond_1 likes(x, Coca) \leftarrow likes(x, Pepsi)) \tag{1}$$
$$\Box_1(\Diamond_1 likes(x, Pepsi) \leftarrow likes(x, Coca)) \tag{2}$$
$$\Box_1 likes(Tom, Coca) \leftarrow \tag{3}$$
$$\Box_1 likes(Peter, Pepsi) \leftarrow \tag{4}$$

agent 2:

$$\Box_2(likes(x, Coca) \leftarrow likes(x, Pepsi)) \tag{5}$$
$$\Box_2(likes(x, Pepsi) \leftarrow likes(x, Coca)) \tag{6}$$
$$\Box_2 likes(Tom, Pepsi) \leftarrow \tag{7}$$
$$\Box_2 likes(Peter, Coca) \leftarrow \tag{8}$$
$$\Box_2 likes(Peter, beer) \leftarrow \tag{9}$$

agent 3:

$$\Box_3(very\_much\_likes(x, y) \leftarrow likes(x, y), \Box_1 likes(x, y), \Box_2 likes(x, y)) \tag{10}$$
$$\Box_3 likes(Tom, Coca) \leftarrow \tag{11}$$
$$\Diamond_3 likes(Peter, Pepsi) \leftarrow \tag{12}$$
$$\Diamond_3 likes(Peter, beer) \leftarrow \tag{13}$$

for communicating with users:

$$very\_much\_likes(x, y) \leftarrow \Box_3 very\_much\_likes(x, y) \tag{14}$$
$$likes(x, y) \leftarrow \Diamond_3 very\_much\_likes(x, y) \tag{15}$$
$$possibly\_likes(x, y) \leftarrow \Diamond_i likes(x, y) \quad (\text{for } i \in \{1, 2, 3\}) \tag{16}$$

Theorem 1. *For $L \in \{KDI4_s5, KDI45, KD4_s5_s, KD45_{(m)}\}$, the data complexity of L-MDatalog is in PTIME.*

Proof. Let (P_0, φ) be an L-MDatalog query, and I_0 an input to (P_0, φ). Let $P = P_0 \cup \{\varphi\}$, c be the size of P, and n the size of $P \cup I_0$. It is sufficient to show that the complexity of computing $P_L(I_0)$ is bounded by a polynomial of n.

Fix some $k \geq 1$ and let $I = T_{L,P,I_0} \uparrow k$ and $\alpha \in I$. Then the modal depth of α is bounded by 1 for $L \in \{KDI4_s5, KD4_s5_s\}$, by m for $L = KDI45$, and by the modal depth of P for $L = KD45_{(m)}$. Denote this bounce by d.

The key of this proof is that modal depths of atoms appearing in $T_{L,P,I_0} \uparrow \omega$ are bounded by d. Also observe that for any atom β, the sets $Sat_L(\{\beta\})$ and $NF_L(\{\beta\})$ can be computed in a finitely bounded number of steps.

The number of classical atoms that may occur in (the atoms of) I is of rank $O(n^c)$. Hence the size of I is of rank $O(n^{c(d+1)})$. It follows that the size of $Sat_L(I_0 \cup I)$ and the number of steps needed for computing $Sat_L(I_0 \cup I)$ from I_0 and I are also of rank $O(n^{c(d+1)})$. The number of steps needed for computing $T_{0L,P}(Sat_L(I_0 \cup I))$ from $Sat_L(I_0 \cup I)$ is of rank $O(n^{c.c.(d+1)})$. The size of $T_{0L,P}(Sat_L(I_0 \cup I))$ can be estimated in a similar way as the size of I and is of rank $O(n^{c(d+2)})$. The number of steps need for computing $T_{0L,P,I_0} \uparrow (k + 1)$ from $T_{0L,P}(Sat_L(I_0 \cup I))$ is of the same rank as the size of $T_{0L,P}(Sat_L(I_0 \cup I))$. Therefore the number of steps needed to compute $T_{L,P,I_0} \uparrow (k+1)$ from $T_{L,P,I_0} \uparrow k$ is bounded by a polynomial of n. The size of $T_{L,P,I_0} \uparrow \omega$ can be estimated in the same way as the size of I and is of rank $O(n^{c(d+1)})$. Hence the number of steps needed to compute $T_{L,P,I_0} \uparrow \omega$ is bounded by a polynomial of n.

5   Modal Relational Algebras

Let L be one of the multimodal logics $KDI4_s5$, $KDI45$, $KD4_s5_s$, $KD45_{(m)}$. In this section, we first define a modal relational algebra in L, called the L-SPCU algebra. These algebras extend the classical SPCU algebra (see, e.g., [1]) with some operators involving with modalities. We then compare L-SPCU algebra queries with *nonrecursive* L-MDatalog programs (defined later).

The *L-SPCU algebra* is formed by the following operators:

Selection. The two primitive forms are $\sigma_{j=c}$ and $\sigma_{j=k}$, where j, k are positive integers and c is a constant symbol. The operator $\sigma_{j=c}$ takes as input any L-relation I with arity $\geq j$ and returns as output an L-relation of the same arity. In particular, $\sigma_{j=c}(I) = \{(\triangle, \mathfrak{t}) \mid (\triangle, \mathfrak{t}) \in I \text{ and } \mathfrak{t}(j) = c\}$. The operator $\sigma_{j=k}$ is defined analogously for inputs with arity $\geq max\{j, k\}$.

Projection. The general form of this operator is $\pi_{j_1,\ldots,j_n}$, where $j_1, \ldots, j_n$ is a sequence of positive integers, possibly with repeats. This operator takes as input any L-relation with arity $\geq max\{j_1, \ldots, j_n\}$ and returns an L-relation with arity n. In particular, $\pi_{j_1,\ldots,j_n}(I) = \{(\triangle, \langle c_1, \ldots, c_n \rangle) \mid (\triangle, \mathfrak{t}) \in I \text{ for some } \mathfrak{t} \text{ with } \mathfrak{t}(j_i) = c_i \text{ for } 1 \leq i \leq n\}$.

Cross-product. This operator, denoted by $\times$, takes as input a pair of L-relations in L-normal form having arbitrary arities k and h and returns an L-relation with arity $k + h$. In particular, if $arity(I) = k$ and $arity(J) = h$, then $I \times J = \{(\triangle, \langle \mathfrak{t}(1), \ldots, \mathfrak{t}(k), \mathfrak{s}(1), \ldots, \mathfrak{s}(h) \rangle) \mid \text{there exist } \triangle' \text{ and } \triangle'' \text{ such that } (\triangle', \mathfrak{t}) \in I, (\triangle'', \mathfrak{s}) \in J, \text{ and } \triangle \text{ is a maximal } L\text{-instance in } L\text{-normal labelled form of } \triangle' \text{ and } \triangle''\}$.

Union. This operator, denoted by $\cup$, takes as input a pair of L-relations with the same arity and returns an L-relation with the same arity that is the union of the input relations.

Context-shrink. The two primitive forms are $\Box_i$ and $\Diamond_i$, where $1 \leq i \leq m$. These operators take as input any L-relation I and return as output an L-relation of the same arity. In particular, $\Box_i(I) = \{(\triangle, \mathfrak{t}) \mid \text{there exists } (\triangle\nabla, \mathfrak{t}) \in I \text{ such that } \Box_i \preceq_L \nabla\}$. The operator $\Diamond_i$ is defined analogously.

Context-stretch. The two primitive forms are $\Box_i^{\leftarrow}$ and $\Diamond_i^{\leftarrow}$, where $1 \leq i \leq m$. These operators take as input any L-relation I in L-normal form and return as output an L-relation of the same arity. In particular, $\Box_i^{\leftarrow}(I) = \{(\triangle\Box_i, \mathfrak{t}) \mid (\triangle, \mathfrak{t}) \in I\}$ and $\Diamond_i^{\leftarrow}(I) = \{(\triangle\Diamond_i, \mathfrak{t}) \mid (\triangle, \mathfrak{t}) \in I\}$.

Context-selection. The general form of this operator is $\sigma_{\boxdot}$, where $\boxdot$ is the modal context of an L-MDatalog program clause. This operator takes as input any L-relation I in L-normal form and returns as output an L-relation of the same arity. In particular, $\sigma_{\boxdot}(I) = \{(\triangle, \mathfrak{t}) \mid \text{there exist } (\triangle', \mathfrak{t}) \in I \text{ and a universal modality } \boxdot' \text{ being an } L\text{-context instance of } \boxdot \text{ such that } \triangle \text{ is a maximal } L\text{-instance in } L\text{-normal labelled form of } \triangle' \text{ and } \boxdot'\}$.

Saturation. This operator, denoted by Sat_L, takes as input any L-relation I in L-normal form and returns as output an L-relation of the same arity. In particular, $Sat_L(I) = \{(\triangle, \mathfrak{t}) \mid \text{there exists } \triangle' \text{ such that } (\triangle', \mathfrak{t}) \in I \text{ and } \triangle E \in Sat_L(\{\triangle' E\}) \text{ for some } E\}$, where the latter operator Sat_L acts on model generators as defined in Section 3.

Labelling. The general form of this operator is $Label_p$, where p is an n-ary predicate symbol. This operator takes as input any L-relation I with arity n and returns as output an L-relation of the same arity. In particular, $Label_p(I) = \{(\triangle, t) \mid (\triangle, t) \in I$ and $\triangle$ is not of the form $\triangle'\Diamond_i\} \cup \{(\triangle\langle p(c_1, \ldots, c_n)\rangle_i, \langle c_1, \ldots, c_n\rangle) \mid (\triangle\Diamond_i, \langle c_1, \ldots, c_n\rangle) \in I\}$.

Normalization. This operator, denoted by NF_L, takes as input any L-relation I and returns as output an L-relation in L-normal form and of the same arity. In particular, $NF_L(I) = \{(\triangle, t) \mid$ there exists $\triangle'$ such that $(\triangle', t) \in I$ and $\triangle E \in NF_L(\{\triangle'E\})$ for some $E\}$, where the latter operator NF_L acts on model generators as defined in Section 3.

Note that the operators $\times$, $\Box_i$, $\Diamond_i$, and $\sigma_{\boxdot}$ are dependent on the base logic L. However, for simplicity we do not attach the index L to these operators.

Observe that if input consists of finite L-relations, then the above given operations can be effectively computed and they return a finite L-relation (for $L \in \{KDI4_s5, KDI45, KD4_s5_s, KD45_{(m)}\}$).

L-SPCU (algebra) queries are built from input L-relations and unary constant relations $I_L^c = \{(\boxdot, \langle c\rangle) \mid \boxdot$ is a universal modality in L-normal labelled form$\}$, where c is a constant symbol, using the L-SPCU algebra operators.

A predicate p *directly depends* on a predicate q in an L-MDatalog program P if there exists a program clause φ of P containing p in the head and q in the body. Define the relation "*depends*" to be the transitive closure of the relation "directly depends". An L-MDatalog program P is *nonrecursive* if none of its predicates depends on itself.

Theorem 2. *Every L-MDatalog query (P, φ), where $L \in \{KDI4_s5, KDI45, KD4_s5_s, KD45_{(m)}\}$ and P is a nonrecursive L-MDatalog program, is equivalent to an L-SPCU query.*

Proof. We give only a sketch for this proof. Since the L-SPCU algebra contains the union operator, it is sufficient to show that every L-relation *ans* defined by a nonrecursive L-MDatalog program clause is equivalent to an L-SPCU query. For simplicity, we show this using the following representative example

$$\boxdot(\Diamond_i ans(x, x, z, a) \leftarrow \Box_j R(x, b), \Diamond_k S(x, y), T(z))$$

Let $Q = \pi_1(\sigma_{1=3}(\Box_j(Sat_L(\sigma_{2=b}(R))) \times \Diamond_k(Sat_L(S))))$. Then *ans* is equivalent to

$$NF_L(Label_{ans}(\Diamond_i^{\leftarrow}(\sigma_{\boxdot}(\sigma_{1=2}(Q \times Q) \times Sat_L(T) \times I_L^a))))$$

The conversion of the above theorem does not hold because the operators Sat_L, $\Box_i^{\leftarrow}$ and $\Diamond_i^{\leftarrow}$ may return relations which are not in L-normal form.

An additional operator that deserves for consideration is the *redundant elimination* operator $RE_L(I) = \{(\triangle, t) \in I \mid$ there is no $(\triangle', t) \in I$ such that $\triangle' \neq \triangle$ and $\triangle$ is an L-instance of $\triangle'\}$. We believe that this operator has a good behaviour when used in L-SPCU queries.

6   Evaluation of MDatalog

In this section, we extend evaluation techniques of Datalog (see, e.g., [1]) for MDatalog. We concentrate on bottom-up techniques, in particular, the seminaive evaluation and the magic-set transformation. Specific results of this section are formulated for the logics $KDI4_s5$, $KDI45$, $KD4_s5_s$, $KD45_{(m)}$. In this section, let L denote one of these logics.

6.1   The Seminaive Evaluation

Let P be an L-MDatalog program and I an instance of edb L-relations. We first give a *naive* algorithm for computing $P_L(I)$. Since $P_L(I) = T_{L,P,I} \uparrow \omega$, we can obtain $P_L(I)$ by computing $T_{L,P,I} \uparrow k$ for increasing values of k until a fixpoint $T_{L,P,I} \uparrow k = T_{L,P,I} \uparrow (k-1)$ is reached. Suppose that we have already computed $T_{L,P,I} \uparrow k$ and the content of a relation p in $T_{L,P,I} \uparrow k$ is stored in p_k. Let J_k consist of such relations p_k. Then to compute $T_{L,P,I} \uparrow (k+1)$ consider the program P_{k+1} obtained from P by replacing every predicate p in bodies of the clauses of P by p_k. P_{k+1} is a nonrecursive MDatalog program, and hence $P_{k+1}(I \cup J_k)$ can be computed using the L-SPCU algebra operators. The results of $P_{k+1}(I \cup J_k)$ are then assigned to relations p_{k+1} to start the next round (if necessary).

In the naive algorithm, a considerable amount of redundant computation is done, as $T_{L,P,I} \uparrow k \subseteq T_{L,P,I} \uparrow (k+1)$ and each round recomputes all elements of the previous round. To avoid this situation we can apply the *seminaive* evaluation technique in a similar way as for Datalog programs. Let P'_{k+1}, for $k \geq 1$, be the program constructed as follows: for each clause $\boxdot(A \leftarrow B_1, \ldots, B_n)$ of P and each $1 \leq i \leq n$, add to P'_{k+1} the clause $\boxdot(A \leftarrow B'_1, \ldots, B'_{i-1}, B^*_i, B''_{i+1}, \ldots, B''_n)$, where B'_j (resp. B''_j) is obtained from B_j by replacing the predicate of B_j, denoted by p, by p_k (resp. p_{k-1}), and B^*_i is obtained from B_i by replacing the predicate of B_i, denoted by q, by the predicate defined by $(q_k - q_{k-1})$. The key in this evaluation is B^*_i, which contains only new atoms that are derived at round k. Then the seminaive algorithm is the modification of the naive algorithm with P_k replaced by P'_k for $k \geq 2$. It is straightforward to prove that the seminaive algorithm produces $T_{L,P,I} \uparrow k$ at round k. This means that the seminaive algorithm is correct.

6.2   The Magic-Set Transformation Technique

We now consider the *magic-set* transformation technique for MDatalog queries. In logic programming, SLD-resolution is a top-down procedure for computing answers. In SLD-derivations, constant symbols may be push from goals to subgoals through unification, and in this way the search space is restricted. The magic-set technique simulates that kind of search restriction for bottom-up evaluation. It rewrites a given query to another equivalent one that is more effective when used with the seminaive evaluation.

An *adornment* γ for an n-ary predicate p is a sequence of n letters 'b' or 'f', and p *adorned by* γ is denoted by p^γ. For $A = \triangle p(t_1, \ldots, t_n)$, where p is an *idb* predicate, we use A^γ to denote $\triangle p^\gamma(t_1, \ldots, t_n)$ and say that a variable x is *bound* in A^γ if there exists $1 \leq j \leq n$ such that $t_j = x$ and $\gamma(j) = \text{`}b\text{'}$, otherwise x is *free* in A^γ. If $A = \triangle p(t_1, \ldots, t_n)$ and p is an *edb* predicate, then A^γ denotes the atom A itself (this means that we do not use adornments for *edb* predicates). Given a clause $\varphi = \boxdot(A \leftarrow B_1, \ldots, B_k)$ and an adornment γ for the predicate in A, the *adorned version* of φ w.r.t. γ is $\boxdot(A^\gamma \leftarrow B_1^{\gamma_1}, \ldots, B_k^{\gamma_k})$, where γ_i is specified as follows: if B_i is of the form $\triangle p(t_1, \ldots, t_n)$ and t_j is a constant symbol or a variable bound in A^γ or occurring in $B_1, \ldots, B_{j-1}$ then $\gamma_i(j) = \text{`}b\text{'}$, else $\gamma_i(j) = \text{`}f\text{'}$.

Let (P_0, φ) be an L-MDatalog query. Let ψ be the adorned version of φ w.r.t. the adornment containing only ‘f’ with the modification that the head is written without adornment. Let $P = P_0 \cup \{\varphi\}$ and P^{ad} be the program consisting of all adorned versions of all clauses of P_0 plus ψ. We call P^{ad} the *adorned program* corresponding to the query (P_0, φ).

We proceed by giving a further transformation for P^{ad}. We start with auxiliary notations. For an atom A of the form $\triangle p^\gamma(t_1, \ldots, t_n)$, where $|\triangle| \leq 1$ and $i_1, \ldots, i_k$ are all the indexes such that $\gamma(i_j) = \text{`}b\text{'}$ for $1 \leq j \leq k$: by *input_A* we denote the atom $\triangle input\_p^\gamma(t_{i_1}, \ldots, t_{i_k})$; by *input_blf_A* we denote[2] $\Box_i p^\gamma(t_{i_1}, \ldots, t_{i_k})$ if $\triangle = \Diamond_i$, and *input_A* otherwise. Note that we do not write adornment for *query* but it is implicitly the one that contains only ‘f’. For an adorned clause $\varphi_i = \boxdot(A \leftarrow B_1, \ldots, B_k)$ and $1 \leq j \leq k$, let Sup_j^i be the atom of predicate sup_j^i whose arguments are the variables that occur both in *input_A*, $B_1, \ldots, B_{j-1}$ and $B_j, \ldots, B_k, A$.

Let (P_0, φ) be an L-MDatalog query and P^{ad} the corresponding adorned program. We construct P^m as follows: At the beginning let P^m contain only the clause $\boxdot'(input\_query \leftarrow)$, where $\boxdot'$ is the modal context of φ. Then for each clause $\varphi_i = \boxdot(A \leftarrow B_1, \ldots, B_k)$ of P^{ad} with the property that *query* depends on the predicate of A :

- If no *idb* predicate occurs in $B_1, \ldots, B_k$ then add to P^m the clause

$$\boxdot(A \leftarrow input\_A, B_1, \ldots, B_k) \tag{s i.1}$$

- Otherwise, let $i_1, \ldots, i_h$ be all the indexes such that for each $1 \leq j \leq h$, B_{i_j} is an atom of an *idb* predicate. Then add to P^m the following clauses:

$$\boxdot(Sup_{i_1}^i \leftarrow input\_A, B_1, \ldots, B_{i_1-1}) \tag{s i.1}$$
$$\boxdot(Sup_{i_j}^i \leftarrow Sup_{i_{j-1}}^i, B_{i_{j-1}}, \ldots, B_{i_j-1}) \text{ for every } 1 < j \leq h \tag{s i.j}$$
$$\boxdot(A \leftarrow Sup_{i_h}^i, B_{i_h}, \ldots, B_k) \tag{s i.$(h+1)$}$$
$$\boxdot(input\_blf\_B_{i_j} \leftarrow Sup_{i_j}^i) \text{ for every } 1 \leq j \leq h \tag{i i.j}$$

In the last clause given above, we use *input_blf_B_{i_j}* instead of *input_B_{i_j}* because that, in serial modal logics we have that $\boxdot(\Box_i E \rightarrow \Diamond_i E)$, hence we should accept $\boxdot(\Diamond_i input\_E \rightarrow \Box_i input\_E)$.

Among the clauses of P^m there is exactly one clause defining *query*. Denote that clause by φ^m. Then (P^m, φ^m) is the L-MDatalog query obtained from (P_0, φ) by the magic-set transformation.

---

[2] *blf* stands for "□-lifting form"

In order to compare (P^m, φ^m) with (P_0, φ) and obtain an equivalence we need a modification for the operator Sat_L. The problem is that if $\triangle E \rightarrow \triangle' E$ is an instance of a rule specifying Sat_L or NF_L then we should accept also $\triangle' input\_E \rightarrow \triangle input\_E$. We extend the primary set of rules specifying Sat_L with the following rules:

- case $L \in \{KDI4_s5, KDI45\}$: $\triangle input\_E \rightarrow \square_m input\_E$ if $|\triangle| \geq 1$;
- case $L = KD4_s5_s$: $\triangle \nabla_i input\_E \rightarrow \square_i input\_E$;
- case $L = KD45_{(m)}$: $\triangle \nabla_i \triangle' input\_E \rightarrow \triangle \square_i \triangle' input\_E$ and
  $\triangle \nabla_i \nabla'_i input\_E \rightarrow \triangle \square_i input\_E$.

We also need the modification that if α is of the form $\triangle \Diamond_i p^\gamma(t_1, \ldots, t_n)$ then the *forward labelled form* of α is $\triangle \langle p(t_1, \ldots, t_n) \rangle_i p^\gamma(t_1, \ldots, t_n)$ instead of $\triangle \langle p^\gamma(t_1, \ldots, t_n) \rangle_i p^\gamma(t_1, \ldots, t_n)$. The following theorem states that the magic-set transformation for L-MDatalog is correct. See [10] for its proof.

Theorem 3. *Let* $L \in \{KDI4_s5, KDI45, KD4_s5_s, KD45_{(m)}\}$, (P_0, φ) *be an* L-*MDatalog query,* $P = P_0 \cup \{\varphi\}$, (P^m, φ^m) *be the result of the magic-set transformation for* (P_0, φ), *and* I *an edb instance. Then every atom* $\triangle query(c_1, \ldots, c_k) \in P_L^m(I)$ *is an* L-*instance of some atom of* $P_L(I)$, *and every atom* $\triangle query(c_1, \ldots, c_k) \in P_L(I)$ *is an* L-*instance of some atom of* $P_L^m(I)$. *This means that* $REL_L(P_L^m(I)(query)) = REL_L(P_L(I)(query))$.

Given an L-MDatalog query (P_0, φ), to evaluate it we can first transform it into (P^m, φ^m) using the magic-set transformation, and then apply the seminaive evaluation for the new query.

7   Conclusions

In this work, we have presented the modal query language MDatalog and developed modal relational algebras and evaluation methods for MDatalog queries. We have applied our methods for the multimodal logics of belief $KDI4_s5$, $KDI45$, $KD4_s5_s$, $KD45_{(m)}$ and shown that MDatalog has PTIME data complexity in these logics.

Our methods are applicable for other modal logics. In particular, they can be applied for the serial modal logics KD, T, KDB, B, $KD5$, $S5$, and extended for the almost serial modal logics KB, $K5$, $K45$, and $KB5$, as fixpoint semantics for MProlog programs in these logics have been developed in [9].

Looking from the view of modal logic programming, the ability of adopting the fixpoint semantics of MProlog programs for computing MDatalog queries is an evidence for the usefulness of the direct approach used for modal logic programming [9,10]. The translational approaches [5,12] used in modal logic programming are not suitable for modal deductive databases, because they introduce Skolem function symbols and can make clauses not allowed.

In the field of deductive databases, apart from bottom-up methods like the seminaive evaluation or the magic-set transformation, there are also top-down methods. It is known that, for Datalog, the magic-set transformation method is "equivalent" to the top-down QSQ method (see, e.g., [1]). For MDatalog, we did not give any top-down method for evaluation. This remains as an interesting problem for further investigation, at least from the theoretical point of view. There are also other problems deserving for investigation, e.g., behaviours of the redundant elimination operator, efficient representation of *edb* databases, or further optimisations for bottom-up evaluation methods.

This work and our previous work [8] are pioneer works on modal deductive databases. Despite that this work does not cover all problems involving with modal deductive databases, it establishes a fundamental basis for the subject.

Because multimodal logics can be used to reason about multi-degree belief (a kind of uncertainty) and epistemic states of agents, we believe that modal deductive databases will have potential applications.

References

1. Abiteboul, S., Hull, R., Vianu, V.: Foundations of Databases. Addison Wesley (1995)
2. Behrend, A., Manthey, R.: Update propagation in deductive databases using soft stratification. In G. Gottlob, A.A. Benczúr, and J. Demetrovics, editors, Proceedings of ADBIS'04, LNCS 3255, Springer (2004) 22–36
3. Chomicki, J.: Temporal query languages: A survey. In D.M. Gabbay and H.J. Ohlbach, editors, Temporal Logic: ICTL'94, volume 827, Springer-Verlag (1994) 506–534
4. Cumbo, C., Faber, W., Greco, G., Leone, N.: Enhancing the magic-set method for disjunctive datalog programs. In B. Demoen and V. Lifschitz, editors, Proceedings of ICLP'04, LNCS 3132, Springer (2004) 371–385
5. Debart, F., Enjalbert, P., Lescot, M.: Multimodal logic programming using equational and order-sorted logic. Theoretical Computer Science (1992) 105:141–166
6. Fitting, M., Mendelsohn, R. L.: First-Order Modal Logic. Springer (1998)
7. Halpern, J. Y., Moses, Y.: A guide to completeness and complexity for modal logics of knowledge and belief. Artif. Intell. (1992) 54(2):319–379
8. Nguyen, L. A.: The modal query language MDatalog. Fundamenta Informaticae (2001) 46(4):315–342
9. Nguyen, L. A.: A fixpoint semantics and an SLD-resolution calculus for modal logic programs. Fundamenta Informaticae (2003) 55(1):63–100
10. Nguyen, L. A.: Multimodal logic programming and its applications to modal deductive databases. Manuscript (served as a technical report), available on Internet at http://www.mimuw.edu.pl/ nguyen/papers.html (2003)
11. Nguyen, L. A.: The modal logic programming system MProlog. In J.J. Alferes and J.A. Leite, editors, Proceedings of JELIA 2004, LNCS 3229, Springer (2004) 266–278
12. Nonnengart, A.: How to use modalities and sorts in Prolog. In C. MacNish, D. Pearce, and L.M. Pereira, editors, Proceedings of JELIA'94, LNCS 838, Springer (1994) 365–378

Declarative Data Fusion –
Syntax, Semantics, and Implementation

Jens Bleiholder and Felix Naumann

Humboldt-Universität zu Berlin,
Unter den Linden 6, D-10099 Berlin, Germany
{bleiho, naumann}@informatik.hu-berlin.de

Abstract. In today's integrating information systems *data fusion*, i.e., the merging of multiple tuples about the same real-world object into a single tuple, is left to ETL tools and other specialized software. While much attention has been paid to architecture, query languages, and query execution, the final step of actually fusing data from multiple sources into a consistent and homogeneous set is often ignored.

This paper states the formal problem of data fusion in relational databases and discusses which parts of the problem can already be solved with standard SQL. To bridge the final gap, we propose the SQL FUSE BY statement and define its syntax and semantics. A first implementation of the statement in a prototypical database system shows the usefulness and feasibility of the new operator.

1 Data Fusion

Integrated (relational) information systems provide users with only one uniform view to different (relational) data sources. Querying the underlying different data sources, combining the results, and presenting it to the user is done by the integration system.

In this paper we want to present our work on how to do the Data Fusion step in the data integration process. We rely on relational data where conflicts on the schema level already have been solved, but conflicts on the data level remain. Data Fusion is then the process of combining data about the same object from different sources by resolving occurring data conflicts. We assume object identity, that means, it is possible to distinguish between different real-world objects by a globally unique and consistent identifier. In most domains, such an identifier is already present or can easily be created, e.g., by duplicate detection methods.

Figure 1 shows three tables. The first two each represent data of a data source. In the example we talk about real persons (students), identified by their first name. We assume a domain in which these names are unique, consistent and unambiguously identify the students.

The tables overlap intensionally, as well as extensionally. They partially contain the same information about the same objects, but also complement one another: Column CAR is contained in table EE_Students but not in table

J. Eder et al. (Eds.): ADBIS 2005, LNCS 3631, pp. 58–73, 2005.

EE_Students			
NAME	AGE	STUDENT	CAR
Peter	$\perp$	no	Ford
Alice	22	yes	$\perp$
Bob	$\perp$	yes	VW
Charly	25	yes	Pontiac
Paul	26	yes	Chevy
Paul	$\perp$	yes	Chevy

CS_Students			
NAME	AGE	STUDENT	PHONE
Alice	$\perp$	yes	555 1234
Bob	27	$\perp$	555 4321
Charly	24	yes	$\perp$
Alice	21	no	555 9876
Mary	24	yes	$\perp$
Mary	24	yes	$\perp$

Data fusion result of EE_- and CS_Students				
NAME	AGE	STUDENT	CAR	PHONE
Peter	$\perp$	no	Ford	$\perp$
Alice	22	yes	$\perp$	555 9876
Bob	27	yes	VW	555 4321
Charly	25	yes	Pontiac	$\perp$
Paul	26	yes	Chevy	$\perp$
Mary	24	yes	$\perp$	$\perp$

Fig. 1. Two data sources with conflicting data and the result of data fusion; $\perp$ determines NULL values

CS_Students, column PHONE is solely contained in table CS_Students. When integrating data from both tables, inter-group conflicts (e.g., *Bob* and *Charly*) and intra-group conflicts (e.g., *Paul*) on the data level can occur. We distinguish between two kinds of conflicts: a) 'uncertainty' about the value, caused by missing information, aka. NULL values in the table, and b) 'contradictions'. An example for the former would be the age of *Bob*, one for the latter the age of *Charly*.

When fusing data from the two source tables into one single table, one has to decide on how to handle these conflicts. This problem has been first mentioned by Dayal [2]. Since then, a couple of approaches and techniques have emerged, many of them trying to "avoid" the conflicts by resolving only the uncertainty of missing values. Anyhow, there is no system so far and no relational technique that is able to produce a result, such as the one given in Fig. 1 at the bottom. Therefore we propose an extension of SQL, the FUSE BY statement, which not only resolves uncertainties, but also fuses tables by resolving occurring data conflicts.

Contributions. The main contributions of this paper are an extension of the SQL syntax to support data fusion operations. We provide formal semantics of data fusion in the relational model and demonstrate its feasibility in a prototypical implementation.

Structure of this paper. First, we review related work on data fusion, paying attention both to data integration systems and to individual relational operators enabling data fusion (Sec. 2). Combining the advantages of several approaches, we next define syntax and semantics of our FUSE BY statement (Sec. 3). We have implemented the FUSE BY statement in a prototypical RDBMS and provide some initial insights in query processing for data fusion (Sec. 4). Finally, we conclude and point out future directions (Sec. 5).

2   Complete and Concise Data Integration

Data integration has two broad goals: Increasing completeness and increasing conciseness of the data that is available to users and applications. An increase in completeness is achieved by adding more information sources to the system. An increase in conciseness is achieved by fusing duplicate entries and merging common attributes into one. After defining both notions, we analyze conventional and extended relational operators with respect to their ability to achieve complete and concise answers. Thus, the second part of this section covers the related work on data fusion.

2.1   Completeness

Completeness of a data set, such as a query result, measures the amount of data in that set both in terms of the number of tuples (extension) and the number of attributes (intension). *Extensional completeness* is the number of tuples in a data set in relation to the overall number of available tuples in the integrated system. Increase is achieved by adding more tuples using union-type operators.

Intensional completeness is the number of attributes in a data set in relation to the overall number of attributes available in the integrated system. Increase is achieved by integrating sources that supply additional, yet unseen attributes to the relation using join-type operators. This distinction is along the lines of related work [7,9,14].

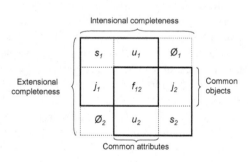

Fig. 2. Extensional and intensional completeness

To illustrate, Fig. 2 labels the different parts of a data set that is integrated from two sources. The generalization to more than two sources is trivial. The data of data source S_1 comprises areas s_1, u_1, j_1, and f_{12}. The data of source S_2 comprises the areas s_2, u_2, j_2, and f_{12}. Areas $\emptyset_1$ and $\emptyset_2$ contain only NULL values. We use the figure to describe what kind of data is produced by different operators.

2.2   Conciseness

Without knowledge of common attributes and common objects, the best that an integrating system can do is produce a result as seen in Fig. 3(a). While this result has a high completeness it is not concise. Knowledge about common attributes, i.e., knowledge about which attribute in one source semantically corresponds to which attribute in the other source, allows results of the shape as seen in Fig. 3(b). Incidentally, this shape is the result of an outer union operation on the two source relations (assuming semantically corresponding attributes are given the same name). We call such results intensionally concise: No real-world property is represented by more than one attribute.

Knowledge about common objects, e.g., using a globally consistent ID, such as the ISBN for books, or using duplicate detection methods, allows results as seen in Fig. 3(c). Here, the only known common attribute is the ID. This result can be formed using the full outer join operation on the IDs of the two source relations. We call such results extensionally concise: No real-world object is represented by more than one tuple.

Finally, Fig. 3(d) shows the result after identifying common attributes *and* common objects. The main feature of this result is that it contains

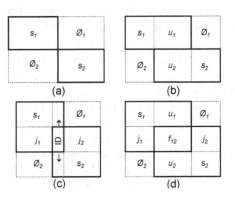

Fig. 3. Four degrees of integration

only one row per represented real-world object *and* each row has only one value per represented attribute. This result is the ultimate goal of data fusion. No common relational operator can express this result in the presence of conflicting data. The motivation of this paper is to find a way to declaratively express this result using the SQL language and some extension.

2.3 Relational Operators

In the following paragraphs we analyze standard and advanced relational operators that somehow perform data integration. In particular we discuss their ability to achieve complete and concise results. Tab. 1 summarizes the discussion.

The **union join** produces results of the shape of Fig. 3(a), the most inconcise result conceivable and merely of theoretical interest. The result of the **union** ($\cup$) operator is more concise, in that it combines tuples from two union-compatible relations and removes exact duplicates. The **outer union** ($\uplus$) operator alleviates the problem of union-compatibility by adding missing attributes to both relations and padding them with NULL values [4]. Outer union increases both extensional and intensional completeness, as represented in Fig. 3(b). Conciseness is as for the union operator. The **minimum union** operator ($\oplus$) is defined by Galindo-Legaria as an outer union followed by a removal of subsumed tuples [4]. Thus, minimum union takes one step towards increased extensional conciseness: Uncertainties caused by subsumed tuples are resolved but tuples representing the same real-world objects with contradictory data remain.

Join operators assume at least one common attribute, the join attribute. The **natural join** ($\bowtie$) and **key join** ($\bowtie_{id=id}$) are not well-suited to fuse tables, because the result contains only objects present in both source tables (low extensional completeness). This disadvantage is removed by the use of the **outer join** operations ($\overset{\circ}{\bowtie}$), which also retains all tuples of either one or both relations (left, right and full outer join). Figure 3(c) shows this result. If the join attribute is a globally consistent ID, the full outer join achieves full extensional conciseness: each real-world object is identified by that ID and appears only once in the result. However, common attributes cannot be combined as long as there are conflicts among the attribute values. Thus, intensional conciseness is low.

Yang and Özsu describe the **match join** operator used in the AURORA system [18]. It can be rewritten as an outer join of all attribute value combinations. The corresponding value of the key attribute is used to perform the join resulting in one large table. Tuples are chosen from this table according to different parameters. Extensional conciseness depends on these parameters and can reach the same level as the full outer join. The operator is able to resolve uncertainties but not conflicts. Based on the match join, Greco et al. define the **merge** ($\boxtimes$) and **prioritized merge** ($\lhd$) operators [6]. They are rewritten as the union of two outer joins and thus increase intensional completeness. The use of the SQL function COALESCE with the join increases intensional conciseness by resolving uncertainties. Contradictions remain and the use of union increases extensional completeness but does not increase extensional conciseness.

The notions of increasing extensional and intensional conciseness are naturally reflected by the concepts of **grouping** and **aggregation**. Even though they are standard features of most DBMS, they cannot be readily used for data fusion: There is seldom a globally consistent ID, so grouping must be based on some form of duplicate detecting similarity function instead of equality. More importantly though, most DBMS restrict aggregation functions to the few numeric functions specified in the SQL standard, i.e., COUNT, MIN, MAX, SUM, AVG, and sometimes STDDEV and VARIANCE which are not sufficient to resolve most arising conflicts.

Several projects have sought to overcome this restriction. For instance, Wang and Zaniolo introduce the AXL system to define aggregate functions in DBMS [17]. While their rewriting is already a step forward, aggregate functions allow only one input parameter, namely the column name. However, there are many cases where conflicts should be resolved by taking other data into account as well. The **FraQL** language and system, developed by Sattler et al., allows user-defined aggregates with more than one parameter [13]. They define four 2-parameter aggregation functions, each of which aggregates one column depending on the values of another column. These functions may be used to implement different conflict resolution strategies, for instance choosing values from a specific source (conflict avoidance), choosing the most recent value, or choosing all possible values (and let the user decide).

Table 1. Summary of operations, compared to the ideal result of data fusion (+ marks satisfactory behaviour, − indicates weaknesses)

Operation	Completeness int.	Completeness ext.	Conciseness int.	Conciseness ext.	Notes
Union-Join	+	+	−	−	
Union	+	+	+	−	assuming union-compatibility
Outer Union	+	+	+	−	
Minimum union	+	+	+	+/−	
Natural join	+	−	+	+	
Key join	+	−	−	+	
Outer natural-join	+	+	+	+	no intra-source duplicates
Outer key-join	+	+	−	+	no intra-source duplicates
Match join	+	+/−	−	+/−	depending on parametrization
Prioritized Merge	+	+	+	−	
User-defined grouping and aggregation	n/a	+	n/a	+	only on single table, thus no effect on intension
Data Fusion	+	+	+	+	all duplicates

We summarize in Tab. 1 how the different data fusion operations behave concerning completeness and conciseness. A "+" marks satisfactory behavior, whereas a "−" indicates weaknesses.

2.4   Data Fusion Systems

There are several integrating information systems that achieve data fusion to certain degrees: **TSIMMIS** integrates semi-structured data from multiple sources [5]. Using a rule-based language, developers of mediators can define how data is fused [10]. Special constructs specify favored data sources in case of conflicts. Values for that attribute are taken only from the favored source. Thus, without looking at other data sources, the system may not even become aware of a data conflict and so *avoids* conflicts. The **Hermes** system also integrates data in the mediator by pre-defined rules [16]. The authors explicitly name five different strategies to resolve conflicts during integration: choosing the newest data, two different strategies to choose a value depending on its source, choosing the value of numerical data, e.g., always the minimum, and choosing the value of the more *reliable* source.

Fusionplex performs data fusion by allowing advanced conflict resolution techniques [8]. Metadata, such as timestamp, cost, accuracy, availability, and clearance, is used to choose the most recent, most accurate, or cheapest data among all available data from different sources. Using this kind of source metadata reduces conflict resolution to favoring a source given some data quality criteria and therefore to conflict *avoidance* as in TSIMMIS. Using the additional metadata is possible only after extending all relational operators. As in grouping and aggregation, the value chosen for an attribute is independent of other attribute values.

Data cleansing systems are less focused on fusing data but on cleansing an existing single table. They provide simple data scrubbing methods, duplicate detection algorithms, and let users specify how duplicates are to be merged. However, typical data cleansing procedures as **Potter's Wheel** [11] or **Ajax** [3] are implemented as separate systems and do not provide declarative data fusion operators.

3   The FUSE BY Statement

The FUSE BY statement represents a simple way of expressing queries that fuse multiple tuples describing the same object into one tuple while resolving uncertainties and contradictions. It is based on the standard SQL syntax and resembles in syntax and semantics the GROUP BY statement.

3.1   Syntax

The syntax diagram of the FUSE BY statement is shown in Fig. 4. Tuples going into the fusion process are from the tables given in the FROM clause. Join conditions may apply and are possible, as are subselects. FUSE FROM indicates combining the given tables by outer union instead of cross product, saving complex subselects in most cases as can be seen further on. Please note that when using FUSE FROM tuples are ordered in the order of the tables specified. (In FUSE FROM t1, t2 all tuples from t1 are considered before the tuples from t2.)

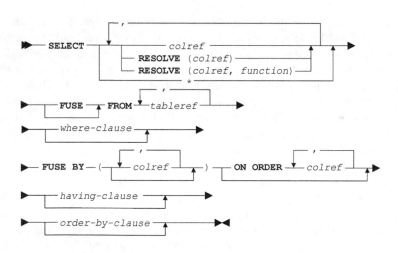

Fig. 4. Syntax diagram of the FUSE BY statement

Similar to the GROUP BY clause, the FUSE BY clause defines which objects are considered as the same real world objects, and are therefore fused into one single tuple. The attributes given here serve as identifier. ON ORDER influences the order in which tuples are considered when resolving conflicts. All attributes that do not appear in the FUSE BY clause may contain data conflicts. The keyword RESOLVE in the SELECT clause marks these columns and also serves to specify a conflict resolution function (*function*) to resolve conflicts in this column. The wildcard '*' or not specifying a conflict resolution function results in a default conflict resolution behavior.

Keep in mind that both the HAVING-clause and ORDER BY clause can be used additionally and keep its original meaning. A small example for a FUSE BY statement is:

```
SELECT Name, RESOLVE(Age, max)
FUSE FROM EE_Student, CS_Students
FUSE BY (Name)
```

This fuses the data on EE- and CS-Students, leaving just one tuple per student. Students are identified by their name and conflicting age values are resolved by taking the higher age (assuming people only get older...).

3.2 Semantics

The overall idea behind FUSE BY is the idea of fusion by grouping and aggregation. Ideally, FUSE FROM and the outer union operator is used. Possible data conflicts are resolved in each group separately.

FUSE BY statements possess an intuitive and beneficiary default behavior: If there is no information of how to group objects, only exact duplicates and subsumed tuples are removed. If there is no information on how to resolve conflicts, known NON-NULL values in the tuples are preferred to NULL values.

Fusion process. The fusion process consists of two phases. First, all the tuples from all the sources involved are combined to form just one single table (Step 1). This increases completeness. In a second phase conciseness is being increased by grouping together tuples representing the same real world object and resolving conflicts (Step 2 through 4).

Step 1: Increasing completeness. To execute a FUSE BY statement, the tuples going into the fusion process are determined first by evaluating the FROM clause as given in the statement and eventually applying an existing WHERE condition to it. If FUSE FROM is used instead of FROM, the given tables are combined by an outer union instead of cross product. Because there is no separate outer union operator in SQL this operation needs to be rewritten (see Sec. 3.2).

Step 2: Identifying tuples to be fused. Second, all the tuples that describe one and the same real world object are grouped together. This is done by doing a grouping on the column(s) given in the FUSE BY clause. We hereby assume that we are able to rely on a globally unique and consistent identifier that we can use to do the grouping. This identifier may be produced by detecting duplicates and assigning equal keys to the same real world objects or using multiple columns as key. For this reason duplicate detection needs to be done in advance to the fusion process. Using the WHERE clause, tuples may be filtered out before the grouping.

Step 3: Increasing conciseness. Then, exact duplicates and subsumed tuples are removed per group. A tuple t_1 subsumes another tuple t_2 if they are defined on the same attributes, t_2 has more $\perp$ values than t_1 and t_1 coincides with t_2 in all NON-NULL attributes [4]. The removal of subsumed tuples is neither a standard operation of the relational algebra, nor does there exist a specific SQL statement. Rao et al. nevertheless show how subsumed tuples can be removed from a single table [12]. However, removing subsumed tuples per group as needed in our case does not yield the same result as removing subsumed tuples from the entire table. Therefore the technique applied by [12] is not feasible in our case. All the remaining tuples of one group are then fused together to just one tuple, at the same time resolving inconsistencies and data conflicts. This is done by applying conflict resolution functions to the columns as indicated in the RESOLVE parts of the SELECT clause. More details on conflict resolution follow in Sec. 3.4.

Step 4: Shaping the result. Finally, only the desired columns as indicated in the SELECT clause are projected to form the final result. Additional HAVING and ORDER BY clauses are applied afterwards on this result.

Figure 5 shows the query that is used to produce the table in Fig. 1 from the introduction. Please note that the order of the tables and the order by Age influences the values chosen, e.g. the phone number of *Alice*.

```
SELECT Name, RESOLVE(Age, max), RESOLVE(Car),
       RESOLVE(Student, vote), RESOLVE(Phone)
FUSE FROM EE_Students, CS_Students
FUSE BY (Name) ON ORDER Age
```

Fig. 5. Example query that produces the Data Fusion result from Fig. 1

Rewriting fusion queries. Parts of FUSE BY can be rewritten by standard SQL and therefore directly executed by any standard DBMS. This rewriting does not include the conflict resolution functions (c.f. Sec. 3.4) and the grouping, as we show in the following paragraphs. Please reconsider the example query from Fig. 5. The rewriting of the query is shown in Fig. 6, the non-standard parts are marked by italic font.

The outer union operation as needed by FUSE FROM, together with the necessary order of the tuples by source table, can be rewritten as shown in lines 4 to 9. For each input table there is a SELECT statement with all the attributes from all tables. Attributes not present in a table are padded with NULL values. The data from the two tables is combined by UNION ALL. Exact intra-source duplicates as well as exact inter-source duplicates are removed by a DISTINCT in the enclosing SELECT. The extension to more than two tables is straightforward, but increases complexity of the rewritten statement.

```
 1: SELECT Name, max(Age), cr_coalesce(Car), cr_vote(Student),
 2:                         cr_coalesce(Phone)
 3: FROM (SELECT DISTINCT Name, Age, Car, Student, Phone
 4:        FROM (SELECT Name, Age, Car, Student, NULL as Phone, 1 as src
 5:              FROM EE_Students
 6:               UNION ALL
 7:              SELECT Name, Age, NULL as Car, Student, Phone, 2 as src
 8:              FROM CS_Students
 9:               ORDER BY src, Age
10:             )
11:      )
12: group by Name
```

Fig. 6. Example query producing the result from Fig. 1, rewritten by means of SQL and using non standard aggregation functions

As Union is not order preserving, the order of the tuples by table (using an additional column src) as required by FUSE BY is guaranteed by the ORDER BY in line 9, as well as the order implied by the ON ORDER clause of FUSE BY.

To do the grouping and prepare for conflict resolution the result is grouped by the attributes given in the FUSE BY clause of the statement (line 12). The attributes with the needed conflict resolution are placed in the SELECT clause (line 1 and 2).

Using GROUP BY in the rewriting requires the use of aggregation functions with all the attributes not present in the GROUP BY clause. As our approach allows the conflict resolution functions to be more general than aggregation functions, this part cannot be further rewritten, simply because such conflict resolution functions are not part of SQL.

As GROUP BY is not order preserving and we cannot influence the order in the resulting groups, only conflict resolution functions that are not order dependant can be used. As soon as order dependant conflict resolution functions are used, an order preserving version of GROUP BY is needed (marked by an italic *group by*). Also, GROUP BY does not allow for removing subsumed tuples in the groups.

Default behavior and wildcards. Wildcards, e.g., *, are replaced by all attributes present as given by the FROM or FUSE FROM clause, if necessary accompanied by RESOLVE. If no explicit conflict resolution function is given, COALESCE is used as default function. COALESCE is an n-ary function and returns its first NON-NULL parameter value. Using COALESCE as default, the order of the tuples is important and directly influences the chosen value. If no attribute is given in the FUSE BY clause, all tuples form one large group, performing removal of exact duplicates and subsumed tuples on all tuples in this large group.

3.3   Examples - Describing Fusion Queries

Query 1 of Fig. 7(a) groups the tuples of one table S1 by the values in column A. All other columns (replacing wildcard *) of table S1 may contain conflicting data that is resolved by the default conflict resolution function COALESCE. This way, the statement behaves like a GROUP BY with a COALESCE aggregation, additionally removing subsumed tuples per group. Fusion by more than one column is possible, replacing A by all desired columns.

```
SELECT *              SELECT *              SELECT *
FROM S1               FROM S1               FUSE FROM S1, S2
FUSE BY (A)           FUSE BY ()            FUSE BY ()
```
(a) Removing data (b) Removing exact (c) Fusing two tables
conflicts   duplicates and sub- by minimum union
                   sumed tuples

Fig. 7. Three simple FUSE BY statements

In Query 2 in Fig. 7(b) there is no column present in the FUSE BY clause. All tuples are treated equally as being in one large group. Exact duplicates and subsumed tuples are removed. Conflicts are not resolved and this corresponds to the result of a DISTINCT operator and the removal of subsumed tuples (indicated as S1 ↓ by [4]).

Query 3 of Fig. 7(c) combines the two tables S1 and S2 by outer union. It completes missing values in columns by NULL values and removes exact duplicates and subsumed tuples. Together with COALESCE as default conflict resolution function this corresponds to the result of a DISTINCT operator and a minimum union operator [4]. Examples with three or more tables look and behave similarly.

3.4 Conflict Resolution

Different conflict resolution functions and strategies are required by different domains, thus encapsulating expert knowledge to fuse data in a domain. Nevertheless, there are some conflict resolution functions that are applicable in a wide variety of domains.

Conflict resolution functions. The concept of conflict resolution is more general than the concept of aggregation, because the functions can be arbitrarily complex and can take more data into account to compute a value. In the most general case, they can use the information given by the query context. This query context consists not only of the conflicting values themselves, but may also consist of the corresponding tuples, all remaining column values or other metadata (e.g. column or table name). This extension of aggregation functions enables the author of a FUSE BY statement to use many different and powerful ways to resolve conflicts.

Table 2 shows a list of useful conflict resolution functions starting with the standard aggregation functions followed by more complex functions. The column containing all conflicting values is passed as a first parameter to all functions. Depending on the function, additional parameters may be used, e.g., the source in function CHOOSE. A FUSE BY query using some of these functions to fuse three movie database tables is presented later in Sec. 4.

Conflict Resolution Strategies. There are several simple strategies to resolve conflicts that are repeatedly mentioned in the literature ([10,16,15]). With FUSE BY all these strategies can be applied in an easy and consistent way.

Preferring one source over others. The FUSE BY statement explicitly orders the tuples by sources as given in the FUSE FROM clause. Therefore, this strategy can be applied by writing the preferred source first and using FIRST as conflict resolution function. COALESCE is used to fall back on values of other sources in case the desired source does not provide a value for the attribute. CHOOSE may also be used.

Choosing the most common value. The intuition behind this strategy is that correct values prevail over incorrect ones, given enough evidence. It is implemented by applying the VOTE function on a column.

Choosing the most recent value. This requires time information about the recentness present in the tables as a separate attribute or by other means. This strategy can then be applied by either ordering on this attribute and using FIRST/COALESCE or using a special function additionally using the time information.

Take all, let the user decide. Using GROUP applies this strategy.

4 Implementation

We are implementing the FUSE BY operator as part of an integrated information system. We base our implementation on the XXL framework — a Java library for building database systems [1]. The library builds on the cursor concept to implement relational database operators. We used the library to implement additional cursors for the outer union operator, the removal of subsumed tuples, and the FUSE BY operator, and to implement a selection of conflict resolution functions. They are used in our experiments, which are currently all performed in main memory.

Computing Fusion Queries. The implementation of the FUSE BY cursor follows the definition of its semantics as described in Sec. 3.2. The implementation of outer union simply concatenates all the input tuples adding NULL values if necessary. Our first naive implementation of the removal of subsumed tuples simply compares every tuple to all other tuples in the same group and tests for subsumption.

Experiments. We conducted several experiments with three data sources of the movie domain, kindly provided to us by the respective organizations: the Internet Movie Database[1] (I), a non-public movie collection (C) and a movie

---

[1] http://www.imdb.com

Table 2. Conflict resolution functions

Function	Description
COUNT	Counts the number of distinct NON-NULL values, i.e., the number of conflicting values. Only indicates conflicts, the actual data values are lost.
MIN / MAX	Returns the minimal/maximal input value with its obvious meaning for numerical data. Lexicographical (or other) order is needed for non numerical data.
SUM / AVG / MEDIAN	Computes sum, average and median of all present NON-NULL data values. Only applicable to numerical data.
VARIANCE / STDDEV	Returns variance and standard deviation of data values. Only applicable to numerical data.
RANDOM	Randomly chooses one data value among all NON-NULL data values.
CHOOSE	Returns the value supplied by a specific source.
COALESCE	Takes the first NON-NULL value appearing.
FIRST / LAST	Takes the first/last value of all values, even if it is a NULL value
VOTE	Returns the value that appears most often among the present values. Ties can be broken by a variety of strategies, e.g., choosing randomly.
GROUP	Returns a set of all conflicting values. Leaves resolution to the user.
SHORTEST / LONGEST	Chooses the value of minimum/maximum length according to a length measure.
(ANNOTATED) CONCAT	Returns the concatenated values. May include annotations, such as source of value.
HIGHEST QUALITY	Evaluates to the value of highest information quality, requiring an underlying quality model.
MOST RECENT	Takes the most recent value. Most recentness is evaluated with the help of another attribute or other data about recentness of tuples/values.
MOST ACTIVE	Returns the most often accessed or used value. Usage statistics of the DBMS can be used in evaluating this function.
CHOOSE CORRESPONDING	Chooses the value that belongs to the value chosen for another column.
MOST COMPLETE	Returns the value from the source that contains the fewest NULL values in the attribute in question.
MOST DISTINGUISHING	Returns the value that is the most distinguishing among all present values in that column.
HIGHEST INFORMATION VALUE	According to an information measure this function returns the value with the highest information value.
MOST GENERAL / SPECIFIC CONCEPT	Using a taxonomy or ontology this function returns the most general or specific value.

collection frequently used in the collaborative filtering community, Movielens[2] (M). We extracted nine different attributes out of all the movie data present in these sources and built an artificial ID. The three sources have significant intensional and small extensional overlap.

Figure 8 shows an example query from this movie domain. It illustrates the application of conflict resolution functions from Table 2. In this query, movie data is fused from the three sources (I, M, and C). Equal movies are identified by the attribute ID and conflicts in all other attributes are resolved as follows: The value for the attribute DIRECTOR is chosen from source I, assuming source I to contain the correct answer. Information about the production company (PROD_COMP) is taken from the source that contains the most information on production companies. Taking the value for the production country (PROD_COUNTRY) from the same source assumes that if a source knows a lot about production companies it also knows a lot about production countries, as these are two related aspects of making a movie. The same applies to RELEASE and DISTRIBUTOR. Worth mentioning is also the conflict resolution for the attribute GENRE. Given a taxonomy of different genre descriptions and given conflicting values, MOSTSPECIFIC returns the most specific of them in the taxonomy.

Conflict resolution for the remaining attributes is straight-forward.

```
SELECT ID,
       RESOLVE (TITLE, Longest),
       RESOLVE (YEAR, Vote),
       RESOLVE (DIRECTOR, Choose(I)),
       RESOLVE (PROD_COMP, MostComplete),
       RESOLVE (PROD_COUNTYR, ChooseCorresponding(PROD_COMP)),
       RESOLVE (GENRE, MostSpecific),
       RESOLVE (RELEASE, Earliest),
       RESOLVE (COLOR, Vote),
       RESOLVE (DISTRIBUTOR, ChooseCorresponding(RELEASE))
FUSE FROM I,M,C FUSE BY (ID)
```

Fig. 8. Complex FUSE BY example query, fusing data from three different movie data sources (I, M and C). Data conflicts are resolved, showing the use of some of the functions from Tab. 2.

Findings/Insights. The FUSE BY operator scales well. In the movie domain it is able to handle simple queries over at least 330,000 tuples using XXL and our implementation. Dominating the runtime is the sort operation. As the extensional overlap in our test tables is not very high (1-3% of the total number of tuples from the sources), the groups consist only of a few (approximately 1-10) tuples (also accounting for fuzzy duplicates in single sources). Therefore the nearly quadratic runtime of the removal of subsumed tuples hardly affects the total runtime.

---

[2] http://www.movielens.org

5 Conclusions

Simple, declarative, and almost automatic data integration is a pressing problem of today's large-scale information systems. This paper deals with the *data fusion* step in the data integration process. In this step, several representations of same real world objects, that may be scattered among several data sources, are fused to a single representation. During this process completeness and conciseness of the integration result are increased, while possible uncertainties and contradictions in the data are resolved.

As no relational technique so far produces such a complete yet concise result, we next propose the FUSE BY extension of SQL, which allows to declaratively specify how to fuse relational tables and thereby resolve data conflicts. Formal syntax and semantics of this new SQL clause are given. A main feature of the operator is the use of conflict resolution functions in the SELECT clause. We give examples and describe how they relate to aggregation functions known from conventional DBMS. Also, FUSE BY has convenient default behavior, such as the elimination of subsumed tuples, allowing sophisticated data fusion already with very simple statements.

The new operator is successfully implemented as part of our research integration system. We are currently enhancing our data fusion DBMS in terms of (i) scalability and optimization techniques, (ii) addition of conflict resolution functions, and (iii) integration with a domain-independent duplicate detection technique. Together with the optimizer already present in the XXL framework, we will be able to support the full life cycle of a query: writing the query, optimizing the query and finally executing it. As more and more efficient functionality is present, interesting optimization issues abound, particularly concerning the execution of conflict resolution functions.

In summary, writing SQL queries using the FUSE BY statement is as simple as writing conventional grouping and aggregation queries, but has the added value of a complete and concise result without contradictory data.

Acknowledgment. This research was supported by the German Research Society (DFG grant no. NA 432).

References

1. v. Bercken, J., Blohsfeld, B., Dittrich, J.-P., Krämer, J., Schäfer, T., Schneider, M., Seeger, B.: XXL - a library approach to supporting efficient implementations of advanced database queries. In Proc. of VLDB (2001) 39–48
2. Dayal, U.: Processing queries over generalization hierarchies in a multidatabase system. In Proc. of VLDB (1983) 342–353
3. Galhardas, H., Florescu, D., Shasha, D., Simon,E.: AJAX: An extensible data cleaning tool. In Proc. of SIGMOD (2000) 590
4. Galindo-Legaria, C.: Outerjoins as disjunctions. In Proc. of SIGMOD (1994) 348–358

5. Garcia-Molina, H., Papakonstantinou, Y., Quass, D., Rajaraman, A., Sagiv, Y., Ullman, J., Vassalos, V., Widom, J.: The TSIMMIS approach to mediation: Data models and languages. J. Intell. Inf. Syst. (1997) 8(2):117–132

6. Greco, S., Pontieri, L., Zumpano, E.: Integrating and managing conflicting data. In Revised Papers from the 4th Int. Andrei Ershov Memorial Conf. on Perspectives of System Informatics (2001) 349–362

7. Motro, A.: Completeness information and its application to query processing. In Proc. of VLDB Kyoto, Aug. (1986) 170–178

8. Motro, A., Anokhin, P.: Fusionplex: resolution of data inconsistencies in the integration of heterogeneous information sources. Information Fusion, (2004) In Press.

9. Naumann, F., Freytag, J.-C., Leser, U.: Completeness of integrated information sources. Information Systems (2004) 29(7):583–615

10. Papakonstantinou, Y., Abiteboul, S., Garcia-Molina, H.: Object fusion in mediator systems. In Proc. of VLDB (1996) 413–424

11. Raman, V., Hellerstein, J.: Potter's Wheel: An interactive data cleaning system. In Proc. of VLDB (2001) 381–390

12. Rao, J., Pirahesh, H., Zuzarte,C.: Canonical abstraction for outerjoin optimization. In Proc. of SIGMOD ACM Press (2004) 671–682

13. Sattler, K., Conrad, S., Saake, G.: Adding Conflict Resolution Features to a Query Language for Database Federations. In Proc. 3rd Int. Workshop on Engineering Federated Information Systems, EFIS (2000) 41–52

14. Scannapieco, M., Batini, C.: Completeness in the relational model: a comprehensive framework. In Proceedings of the International Conference on Information Quality (IQ), Cambridge, MA (2004) 333–345

15. Schallehn, E., Sattler, K.-U., Saake, G.: Efficient similarity-based operations for data integration. Data Knowl. Eng. (2004) 48(3):361–387

16. Subrahmanian, V.S., Adali, S., Brink, A., Emery, R., Lu, J. L., Rajput, A., Rogers, T. J., Ross, R., Ward, C.: Hermes: A heterogeneous reasoning and mediator system. Technical report, University of Maryland, (1995)

17. Wang, H., Zaniolo, C.: Using SQL to build new aggregates and extenders for object- relational systems. In Proc of VLDB (2000) 166–175

18. Yan, L. L., Özsu, M.: Conflict tolerant queries in AURORA. In Proc. of CoopIS (1999) 279

Non-destructive Integration of Form-Based Views

Jan Hidders[1], Jan Paredaens[1], Philippe Thiran[2],
Geert-Jan Houben[2], and Kees van Hee[2]

[1] University of Antwerp, Belgium
[2] Eindhoven University of Technology, The Netherlands

Abstract. Form documents or screen forms bring essential information
on the data manipulated by an organization. They can be considered
as different but often overlapping views of its whole data. This paper
presents a non-destructive approach of their integration. The main idea
of our approach is to keep the original views intact and to specify constraints between overlapping structures. For reasoning over constraints,
we provide a set of inference rules that allows not only to infer implied
constraints but also to detect conflicts. These reasoning rules are proved
to be sound and complete. Although the form-based views are hierarchical structures, our constraints and reasoning rules can also be used in
non-hierarchical data models.

1   Introduction

In the design process for data-intensive applications the design of the global
data model is a crucial step. Often this step involves the integration of different
data models that each describe the information need of different groups of end
users. In the case of workflow and case management systems these data models
or views are usually defined as a form, hence *form-based views* and the tasks that
are managed by the system are typically manipulations of these forms. For large
and complex workflows the task of modeling the forms is often split according
to the different case types. The consequence is often that we obtain a set of
different data models that contain synonyms (different class names that refer to
the same class) and homonyms (the same class name is used in different models
with a different meaning).

A classical solution for resolving this problem is to integrate the different
views into a single global schema [1]. However, in this paper we will integrate
the different views by taking a disjoint union of them and adding constraints that
express semantical relationships between the classes and relations in the different
data models. Since the original views remain part of the global data model we
call this *non-destructive integration*. The fact that the original views remain part
of the global data model is important in the case of workflow systems because the
the views are part of the description of the execution of the workflow. However,
even for other types of data-intensive information systems such a design has

J. Eder et al. (Eds.): ADBIS 2005, LNCS 3631, pp. 74–86, 2005.

benefits. Since the original class and relation names from the views are kept in the global data model this will make communication easier with the end-users for which the views described an information need. Moreover, since the relationships between the different views are made explicit it will be easy to see how changes to the global data model affect the different views and vice versa.

The main contribution of this paper is the presentation of a small but powerful set of semantical relationships between classes and relations in different views, and a sound and complete set of inference rules that allows us to derive implied relationships and in particular whether there is a conflict in the resulting global schema.

The paper is organized as follows. Section 2 develops a small example that allows us to informally present our non-destructive approach of form-based view integration. In Section 3, we formally specify the problem. The schema and their instances are defined as well as the different constraints we consider. Sections 4 and 5 present different sets of inference rules for deriving constraints and detecting conflicts. For each set, we prove their soundness and their completeness. In Section 6, we discuss related works. We give our concluding remarks in Section 7.

2   Informal Problem Definition

We assume that the process of data integration starts with so-called *form-based views* which are essentially hierarchical data structures that describe complex values which can be roughly thought of as tree-shaped graphs. Three examples of such views are given in Figure 1. Each view has the form of a tree which defines all the data that is shown in the view. The nodes of these graphs can be interpreted as classes that contain sets of objects, and the edges can be interpreted as binary relationships between these classes. The root node indicates for which class the view is defined as well as the name of the view. The nodes directly below a node define the attributes of this class. For example, in the Patient view we see that for a patient we have the patient's names, diseases, rooms and treating doctors. At the next level in the view we see that for a disease of a patient we have its types and its names. For the purpose of this paper we will assume that all attributes are set-valued, i.e., they can contain zero, one or more objects.

In the three views in the example we see that there is an overlap in the sense that some objects such as those in the Doctor class in the Patient view and those in the Doctor class in the Doctor view are in fact the same object. In a similar fashion it holds that some of the pairs of the Department-Doctor-Manager relationship in the Doctor view will also be pairs in the Department-Manager relationship. This type of redundancy can be solved by integrating the views into a single new schema, but we propose to leave the original views intact and explicitly specifies such constraint between the different views as illustrated in Figure 2.

There are 8 types of constraints that we will consider:

ISA The ISA constraint between classes is indicated by an edge that is labeled with ⇒. An example is the edge between the Department class in the Doctor

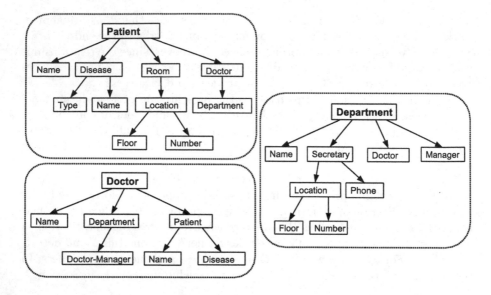

Fig. 1. Three form-based views

view and the Department class in the Department view. The ISA constraint indicates that the objects in one class must also be objects of the other class.

Relational ISA The relational ISA constraint between relationships is indicated by an edge that is labeled with $\Rightarrow^\downarrow$. An example is the edge between the Department-Doctor-Manager relationship in the Doctor view and the Department-Manager relationship in the Department view. This constraint indicates that all pairs of the first relationship are also pairs of the second relationship.

Inverse Relational ISA The inverse relational ISA constraint between relationships is indicated by an edge that is labeled with $\Rightarrow^\uparrow$. An example is the edge between the Patient-Doctor relationship in the Patient view and the Doctor-Patient relationship in the Doctor view. This constraint indicates that all the inverse pairs of the first relationship are also pairs of the second relationship.

Disjointness The disjointness constraint between classes is indicated by an edge that is labeled with $\asymp$. An example is the edge between the Location class in the Patient view and the Location class in the Department view. This constraint indicates that the two classes cannot have common objects.

Relational Disjointness The relational disjointness constraint between relationships is indicated by an edge that is labeled with $\asymp^\downarrow$. This constraint indicates that the two relationships cannot have common pairs.

Inverse Relational Disjointness The inverse relational disjointness constraint between relationships is indicated by an edge that is labeled with $\asymp^\uparrow$. This constraint indicates that there cannot be a pair in one relationship such that the inverse pair is in the other relationship.

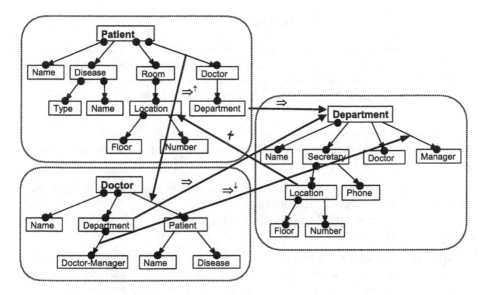

Fig. 2. Three integrated form-based views

Totalness The totalness constraint of a relationship r is indicated by a solid dot at the beginning of the edge of r. It indicates that the relationship r is total, i.e.,. that for every object o in the source class of r there is a pair of r whose first component is o. For example, every patient has a name, a room and a doctor, but probably has no disease.

Surjectivity constraint The surjectivity constraint of a relationship r is indicated by a solid dot at the end of the edge of r. It indicates that the relationship r is surjective, i.e., for every object o in the target class of r there is a pair of r whose second component is o.

The schema of Figure 2 has a straightforward interpretation that is similar to that of FDM [2], binary ORM [3] and the data models that are used in descriptive logics. Note that in all these models the instances of a schema are essentially graphs that somehow match the schema. Since the original views are still present in the schema it is also clear that for each view we can define a projection on the instances of this schema. Although this projection will usually define a graph it can always be transformed into a forest by splitting nodes with two incoming edges. This means that the general approach is here that of the *local as view* (LAV) approach as defined in [4].

When the constraints are added to the views it is possible that conflicts appear. For example, if there is an ISA constraint between the classes A and B and at the same time a disjointness constraint between them then the class A nor B can never be populated.

In the remainder of this paper, we discuss the problem of reasoning over schemas with such constraints in order to infer implied such constraints and to detect conflicts.

3   Formal Problem Definition

For formally specifying the form-based views, we use a graph representation instead of a tree representation as presented in the previous section. We use this simplified data representation since our aim is to provide some constraints that can be used in a context broader than the forms. As such, we are now considering these two types of data models:

- *Frame:* graph structure related to an original form-based view,
- *Schema:* graph structure related to the union of disjoint form-based views, with constraints among them.

In the following paragraphs, we present these types by giving their schema definition and their instance definition.

A *frame* is a multigraph where the nodes represent classes and the edges relationships. More formally:

Definition 1 (Frame). *A* frame *is a tuple* $F = (C, R, s, t)$ *with C a set of classes, R a set of relationships, $s : R \to C$ a function that indicates the source class of a relationship, and $t : R \to C$ a function that indicates the target class of a relationship.*

Definition 2 (Instance). *An* instance *of a frame $F = (C, R, s, t)$ is a tuple $I = (O, [\![\cdot]\!])$ with O a set of objects, and $[\![\cdot]\!]$ the interpretation function that maps classes $c \in C$ to a subset of O, denoted as $[\![c]\!]$, and relationships $r \in R$ to subsets of $O \times O$, denoted as $[\![r]\!]$, such that, for all relationships $r \in R$, it holds that:*

$$[\![r]\!] \subseteq [\![s(r)]\!] \times [\![t(r)]\!] \tag{1}$$

A *schema* is a frame over which some constraints are specified.

Definition 3 (Constraint). *Given a frame $F = (C, R, s, t)$ a constraint is one of the following:*

subclass $c_1 \Rightarrow c_2$, $r_1 \Rightarrow^\downarrow r_2$, $r_1 \Rightarrow^\uparrow r_2$
cardinality $r\cdot$, $\cdot r$
disjointness $c_1 \nsim c_2$, $r_1 \nsim^\downarrow r_2$, $r_1 \nsim^\uparrow r_2$

with $r, r_1, r_2 \in R$ and $c_1, c_2 \in C$. We let $I \vdash k$ denote that constraint k holds for instance $I = (O, [\![\cdot]\!])$. Then we have:

$$I \vdash c_1 \Rightarrow c_2 \text{ iff } [\![c_1]\!] \subseteq [\![c_2]\!] \tag{2}$$

$$I \vdash r_1 \Rightarrow^\downarrow r_2 \text{ iff } [\![r_1]\!] \subseteq [\![r_2]\!] \tag{3}$$

$$I \vdash r_1 \Rightarrow^\uparrow r_2 \text{ iff } [\![r_1]\!]^{-1} \subseteq [\![r_2]\!] \tag{4}$$

$$I \vdash \cdot r \text{ iff } [\![s(r)]\!] = \{o_1 \mid (o_1, o_2) \in [\![r]\!]\} \tag{5}$$

$$I \vdash r\cdot \text{ iff } [\![t(r)]\!] = \{o_2 \mid (o_1, o_2) \in [\![r]\!]\} \tag{6}$$

$$I \vdash c_1 \nsim c_2 \text{ iff } [\![c_1]\!] \cap [\![c_2]\!] = \varnothing \tag{7}$$

$$I \vdash r_1 \nsim^\downarrow r_2 \text{ iff } [\![r_1]\!] \cap [\![r_2]\!] = \varnothing \tag{8}$$

$$I \vdash r_1 \nsim^\uparrow r_2 \text{ iff } [\![r_1]\!]^{-1} \cap [\![r_2]\!] = \varnothing \tag{9}$$

Definition 4 (Schema). *A schema is a tuple $S = (F, K)$ with F a frame and K a finite set of constraints over F.*

Definition 5 (Instance). *An instance of schema S is an instance I of frame F such that $I \vdash k$ for all constraints $k \in K$.*

4 Inference Rules for Subclass and Cardinality Constraints

In this section, we present the sets of inference rules M_1 and M_2 that only derive constraints of the forms $c_1 \Rightarrow c_2$, $r_1 \Rightarrow^\downarrow r_2$, $r_1 \Rightarrow^\uparrow r_2$ and of the forms $\cdot r$ and $r \cdot$, respectively. In Figure 3, we give the set of rules $M1$ and in Figure 4, we give the set of rules M_2. We assume that the inference rules are defined given a frame $F = (C, R, s, t)$ and variables $c, c_1, c_2, \ldots$ range over C and $r, r_1, r_2, \ldots$ range over R. If for a relationship $r \in R$, it holds that $s(r) = c_1$ and $t(r) = c_2$ then this is denoted as $c_1 \xrightarrow{r} c_2$. We will also assume that K^* is the closure of K under the rules in $M_1 \cup M_2$.

$$\text{Refl} \frac{}{c \Rightarrow c} \qquad \text{Trans} \frac{c_1 \Rightarrow c_2 \quad c_2 \Rightarrow c_3}{c_1 \Rightarrow c_3} \qquad \text{RelRefl} \frac{}{r \Rightarrow^\downarrow r}$$

$$\text{RelTr1} \frac{r_1 \Rightarrow^\downarrow r_2 \quad r_2 \Rightarrow^\downarrow r_3}{r_1 \Rightarrow^\downarrow r_3} \qquad\qquad \text{RelTr2} \frac{r_1 \Rightarrow^\downarrow r_2 \quad r_2 \Rightarrow^\uparrow r_3}{r_1 \Rightarrow^\uparrow r_3}$$

$$\text{RelTr3} \frac{r_1 \Rightarrow^\uparrow r_2 \quad r_2 \Rightarrow^\downarrow r_3}{r_1 \Rightarrow^\uparrow r_3} \qquad\qquad \text{RelTr4} \frac{r_1 \Rightarrow^\uparrow r_2 \quad r_2 \Rightarrow^\uparrow r_3}{r_1 \Rightarrow^\downarrow r_3}$$

$$\text{IsaPr1} \frac{c_1 \xrightarrow{r_1} c_2 \quad c_3 \xrightarrow{r_2} c_4 \quad r_1 \cdot \quad r_1 \Rightarrow^\downarrow r_2}{c_2 \Rightarrow c_4} \qquad \text{IsaPr2} \frac{c_1 \xrightarrow{r_1} c_2 \quad c_3 \xrightarrow{r_2} c_4 \quad r_1 \cdot \quad r_1 \Rightarrow^\uparrow r_2}{c_2 \Rightarrow c_3}$$

$$\text{IsaPr3} \frac{c_1 \xrightarrow{r_1} c_2 \quad c_3 \xrightarrow{r_2} c_4 \quad \cdot r_1 \quad r_1 \Rightarrow^\downarrow r_2}{c_1 \Rightarrow c_3} \qquad \text{IsaPr4} \frac{c_1 \xrightarrow{r_1} c_2 \quad c_3 \xrightarrow{r_2} c_4 \quad \cdot r_1 \quad r_1 \Rightarrow^\uparrow r_2}{c_1 \Rightarrow c_4}$$

Fig. 3. Set of inference rules M_1

4.1 Instance Construction

For proving the completeness of inference rules in $M_1 \cup M_2$, we construct the instances I^{tot}, I^{surj} given a schema $S = (F, K)$ with $\cdot r \notin K^*$ and $r \cdot \notin K^*$, respectively. Informally, the instance I^{tot} is constructed as follows. It is assumed that $\cdot r \notin K^*$. We introduce two objects, o_1 and o_2 where o_1 is in only the super-classes of $s(r)$ and o_2 is simply in all classes of the schema. Then we fill

$$c_1 \xrightarrow{r_1} c_2 \quad c_3 \xrightarrow{r_2} c_4$$
$$c_3 \Rightarrow c_1 \quad \cdot r_1$$
RELPR1 $$\dfrac{r_1 \Rightarrow^{\downarrow} r_2}{\cdot r_2}$$

$$c_1 \xrightarrow{r_1} c_2 \quad c_3 \xrightarrow{r_2} c_4$$
$$c_4 \Rightarrow c_1 \quad \cdot r_1$$
RELPR2 $$\dfrac{r_1 \Rightarrow^{\uparrow} r_2}{r_2 \cdot}$$

$$c_1 \xrightarrow{r_1} c_2 \quad c_3 \xrightarrow{r_2} c_4$$
$$c_4 \Rightarrow c_2 \quad r_1 \cdot$$
RELPR3 $$\dfrac{r_1 \Rightarrow^{\downarrow} r_2}{r_2 \cdot}$$

$$c_1 \xrightarrow{r_1} c_2 \quad c_3 \xrightarrow{r_2} c_4$$
$$c_3 \Rightarrow c_2 \quad r_1 \cdot$$
RELPR4 $$\dfrac{r_1 \Rightarrow^{\uparrow} r_2}{\cdot r_2}$$

Fig. 4. Set of inference rules M_2

the relations with pairs that contain o_1 to satisfy the surjectivity and totalness constraints. The construction of I^{surj} is similar except we assume that $r \cdot \notin K^*$ and replace $s(r)$ with $t(r)$. This leads to the following formal definition.

Definition 6 (Instances I^{tot} and I^{surj}). *Given a schema S with $\cdot r \notin K^*$, we define $I^{tot} = (O^{tot}, [\![\cdot]\!]^{tot})$ such that $O^{tot} = \{o_1, o_2\}$ and $[\![\cdot]\!]^{tot}$ the smallest function[3] that satisfies the following rules for all classes c:*

$$o_1 \in [\![c]\!] \; if \, s(r) \Rightarrow c \in K^* \tag{10}$$
$$o_2 \in [\![c]\!] \tag{11}$$

and the following rules for all relationships r:

$$(o_1, o_2) \in [\![r]\!] \; if \, \cdot r_1 \in K^* \wedge s(r) \Rightarrow s(r_1) \in K^* \wedge r_1 \Rightarrow^{\downarrow} r \in K^* \tag{12}$$
$$(o_1, o_2) \in [\![r]\!] \; if \, r_1 \cdot \in K^* \wedge s(r) \Rightarrow t(r_1) \in K^* \wedge r_1 \Rightarrow^{\uparrow} r \in K^* \tag{13}$$
$$(o_2, o_1) \in [\![r]\!] \; if \, \cdot r_1 \in K^* \wedge s(r) \Rightarrow s(r_1) \in K^* \wedge r_1 \Rightarrow^{\uparrow} r \in K^* \tag{14}$$
$$(o_2, o_1) \in [\![r]\!] \; if \, r_1 \cdot \in K^* \wedge s(r) \Rightarrow t(r_1) \in K^* \wedge r_1 \Rightarrow^{\downarrow} r \in K^* \tag{15}$$
$$(o_2, o_2) \in [\![r]\!] \tag{16}$$

The construction of I^{surj} is identical except that $s(r)$ is replaced with $t(r)$.

4.2   Soundness and Completeness of Rules

Theorem 1. *Given a schema $S = (F, K)$ with K containing only subclass constraints and cardinality constraints and K^* the closure of K under the rules in $M_1 \cup M_2$ then*

1. *$c_1 \Rightarrow c_2 \in K^*$ iff $I \vdash c_1 \Rightarrow c_2$ for all instances I of S,*
2. *$r_1 \Rightarrow^{\downarrow} r_2 \in K^*$ iff $I \vdash r_1 \Rightarrow^{\downarrow} r_2$ for all instances I of S,*
3. *$r_1 \Rightarrow^{\uparrow} r_2 \in K^*$ iff $I \vdash r_1 \Rightarrow^{\uparrow} r_2$ for all instances I of S,*

---

[3] The ordering over set-valued functions over the same domain is defined such that f is smaller than g iff $f(x) \subseteq g(x)$ for all x in the domain.

4. $\cdot r \in K^*$ *iff* $I \vdash \cdot r$ *for all instances* I *of* S*, and*
5. $r \cdot \in K^*$ *iff* $I \vdash r \cdot$ *for all instances* I *of* S.

Proof. (Sketch) The *only-if* part of all the propositions is easily proved by verifying that all the inference rules in $M_1 \cup M_2$ are sound which follows from the semantics of the constraints as defined in Definition 3.

The *if* part proceeds by showing that for all constraints it holds that if it is not in K^*, then it does not hold in at least one of I^{tot} and I^{surj}. It can also be shown that I^{tot} and I^{surj} are instances of S. Finally, it can be shown that if $\cdot r \notin K^*$ ($r \cdot \notin K^*$) then this constraint is not satisfied by I^{tot} (I^{surj}). $\square$

5   Inference Rules for Deriving Disjointness Constraints

In this section we will also consider constraints of the forms $c_1 \nsim c_2$, $r_1 \nsim^{\downarrow} r_2$ and $r_1 \nsim^{\uparrow} r_3$. We give three sets of these rules, namely M_3 (Figure 5) and M_4 (Figure 6). We will assume from now on that K^* is the closure of K under the rules in $M_1, \ldots, M_4$.

With disjointness constraints it is possible to define schemas in which certain classes and relations cannot be populated. To find such conflicts we introduce the following syntactical notion of conflict.

Definition 7 (conflict). *A conflict is a constraint of the form* $c \nsim c$ *or* $r \nsim^{\downarrow} r$. *If a set of constraints* K *does not contain such a conflict then it is said to be* conflict-free.

Note that $r \nsim^{\uparrow} r$ is not a conflict since there are non-empty relations for which it holds.

5.1   Instance Construction

For proving the completeness of the inference rules in $M_1, \ldots, M_4$, we construct the instances I^{base}, $I^{\nsim}$, $I^{\nsim^{\uparrow}}$ and $I^{\nsim^{\downarrow}}$ given a schema $S = (F, K)$ with $F = (C, R, s, t)$.

Informally we can describe the construction of I^{base} as follows. For each class c we introduce a distinct object o_c that is in c and all its super-classes. For each relation r we introduce the objects o_r^1 (and o_r^2) that are in the source (target) class of r and all its (implied) super-classes. Next we add the pair (o_r^1, o_r^2) to relation r and all its super-relations, and the inverse to all its inverse super-relations. Finally, to satisfy the totalness and surjectivity constraints we add for relations q with such a constraint and each object o in a class c a pair with o and either o_q^1 or o_q^2 to q and its inverse and normal sub-relations. This leads to the following formal definition:

Definition 8 (Instance I^{base}). *Given a schema* $S = (F, K)$ *with* $F = (C, R, s, t)$ *we define* $I^{base} = (O^{base}, \llbracket \cdot \rrbracket^{base})$ *such that* $O^{base} = \{o_c \mid c \in C\} \cup \{o_r^1, o_r^2 \mid r \in R\}$

82   J. Hidders et al.

$$\text{DsjSym } \frac{c_1 \nsim c_2}{c_2 \nsim c_1} \qquad\qquad \text{DsjDnSym } \frac{r_1 \nsim^\downarrow r_2}{r_2 \nsim^\downarrow r_1}$$

$$\text{DsjUpSym } \frac{r_1 \nsim^\uparrow r_2}{r_2 \nsim^\uparrow r_1} \qquad\qquad \text{DsjInh } \frac{c_1 \nsim c_2 \quad c_3 \Rightarrow c_2}{c_1 \nsim c_3}$$

$$\text{DsjInh1 } \frac{r_1 \nsim^\downarrow r_2 \quad r_3 \Rightarrow^\downarrow r_2}{r_1 \nsim^\downarrow r_3} \qquad\qquad \text{DsjInh2 } \frac{r_1 \nsim^\downarrow r_2 \quad r_3 \Rightarrow^\uparrow r_2}{r_1 \nsim^\uparrow r_3}$$

$$\text{DsjInh3 } \frac{r_1 \nsim^\uparrow r_2 \quad r_3 \Rightarrow^\downarrow r_2}{r_1 \nsim^\uparrow r_3} \qquad\qquad \text{DsjInh4 } \frac{r_1 \nsim^\uparrow r_2 \quad r_3 \Rightarrow^\uparrow r_2}{r_1 \nsim^\downarrow r_3}$$

$$\text{DsjPr1 } \frac{c_1 \xrightarrow{r_1} c_2 \quad c_3 \xrightarrow{r_2} c_4 \quad c_2 \nsim c_4}{r_1 \nsim^\downarrow r_2} \qquad\qquad \text{DsjPr2 } \frac{c_1 \xrightarrow{r_1} c_2 \quad c_3 \xrightarrow{r_2} c_4 \quad c_2 \nsim c_3}{r_1 \nsim^\uparrow r_2}$$

$$\text{DsjPr3 } \frac{c_1 \xrightarrow{r_1} c_2 \quad c_3 \xrightarrow{r_2} c_4 \quad c_1 \nsim c_3}{r_1 \nsim^\downarrow r_2} \qquad\qquad \text{DsjPr4 } \frac{c_1 \xrightarrow{r_1} c_2 \quad c_3 \xrightarrow{r_2} c_4 \quad c_1 \nsim c_4}{r_1 \nsim^\uparrow r_2}$$

Fig. 5. Set of inference rules M_3

and the interpretation function is defined as the smallest interpretation function that satisfies the following rules for all classes c:

$$o_d \in [c] \text{ if } d \Rightarrow c \in K^* \tag{17}$$
$$o_r^1 \in [c] \text{ if } r \Rightarrow^\downarrow q \in K^* \wedge s(q) \Rightarrow c \in K^* \tag{18}$$
$$o_r^1 \in [c] \text{ if } r \Rightarrow^\uparrow q \in K^* \wedge t(q) \Rightarrow c \in K^* \tag{19}$$
$$o_r^2 \in [c] \text{ if } r \Rightarrow^\downarrow q \in K^* \wedge t(q) \Rightarrow c \in K^* \tag{20}$$
$$o_r^2 \in [c] \text{ if } r \Rightarrow^\uparrow q \in K^* \wedge s(q) \Rightarrow c \in K^* \tag{21}$$

and the following rules for all relationships r:

$$(o_q^1, o_q^2) \in [r] \text{ if } q \Rightarrow^\downarrow r \in K^* \tag{22}$$
$$(o_q^2, o_q^1) \in [r] \text{ if } q \Rightarrow^\uparrow r \in K^* \tag{23}$$
$$(o, o_q^2) \in [r] \text{ if } o \in [s(q)] \wedge q \Rightarrow^\downarrow r \in K^* \wedge \cdot q \in K^* \tag{24}$$
$$(o_q^1, o) \in [r] \text{ if } o \in [t(q)] \wedge q \Rightarrow^\downarrow r \in K^* \wedge q \cdot \in K^* \tag{25}$$
$$(o, o_q^1) \in [r] \text{ if } o \in [t(q)] \wedge q \Rightarrow^\uparrow r \in K^* \wedge q \cdot \in K^* \tag{26}$$
$$(o_q^2, o) \in [r] \text{ if } o \in [s(q)] \wedge q \Rightarrow^\uparrow r \in K^* \wedge \cdot q \in K^* \tag{27}$$

Lemma 1. *Given a schema $S = (F, K)$ such that K^* is conflict-free, then the corresponding I^{base} is an instance of S.*

$$\text{CnflPr1} \quad \frac{c_1 \xrightarrow{r} c_2 \qquad r \approx^\downarrow r \qquad \cdot r}{c_1 \approx c_1} \qquad\qquad \text{CnflPr2} \quad \frac{c_1 \xrightarrow{r} c_2 \qquad r \approx^\downarrow r \qquad r \cdot}{c_2 \approx c_2}$$

$$\text{IsaCnfl} \quad \frac{c_1 \approx c_1}{c_1 \Rightarrow c_2} \qquad\qquad\qquad \text{IsaDnCnfl} \quad \frac{r_1 \approx^\downarrow r_1}{r_1 \Rightarrow^\downarrow r_2}$$

$$\text{IsaUpCnfl} \quad \frac{r_1 \approx^\downarrow r_1}{r_1 \Rightarrow^\uparrow r_2} \qquad\qquad \text{TotCnfl} \quad \frac{c_1 \xrightarrow{r} c_2 \qquad c_1 \approx c_1}{\cdot r}$$

$$\text{SurjCnfl} \quad \frac{c_1 \xrightarrow{r} c_2 \qquad c_2 \approx c_2}{r \cdot} \qquad\qquad \text{DisjCnfl} \quad \frac{c_1 \approx c_1}{c_1 \approx c_2}$$

$$\text{DisjDnCnfl} \quad \frac{r_1 \approx^\downarrow r_1}{r_1 \approx^\downarrow r_2} \qquad\qquad \text{DisjUpCnfl} \quad \frac{r_1 \approx^\downarrow r_1}{r_1 \approx^\uparrow r_2}$$

Fig. 6. Set of inference rules M_4

Proof. (Sketch) We first show that I^{base} is an instance of F (i.e., the proposition (1) holds). We then can show that all constraints in K will also hold for I^{base}. Finally we verify that the constraints from (2) to (9)) are satisfied. □

Informally we can describe the construction of $I^{\approx}$ as follows. We assume that $a \approx b \notin K^*$. Then we construct the instance as for I^{base} except that we introduce a special object o_{ab} that is placed both in class a and in class b and in all their super-classes. This leads to the following formal definition:

Definition 9 (Instance $I^{\approx}$). *Given a schema $S = (F, K)$ with $F = (C, R, s, t)$ and $a \approx b \notin K^*$ we define $I^{\approx} = (O^{\approx}, [\![\cdot]\!]^{\approx})$ such that $O^{\approx} = O^{base} \cup \{o_{ab}\}$ and the interpretation as for I^{base} but with the following additional rule:*

$$o_{ab} \in [\![c]\!] \; if \, a \Rightarrow c \in K^* \vee b \Rightarrow c \in K^* \tag{28}$$

Lemma 2. *Given a schema $S = (F, K)$ such that K^* is conflict-free and $a \approx b \notin K^*$, then the corresponding $I^{\approx}$ is an instance of S.*

Proof. (Sketch) The proof proceeds similar to that of Lemma 1 except that for some propositions we need to consider extra cases. □

Informally we can describe the construction of $I^{\approx^\downarrow}$ as follows. We assume that $p \approx^\downarrow q \notin K^*$. Then we construct the instance as for I^{base} except that we introduce a special pair (o^1_{pq}, o^2_{pq}) that is placed both in the relation p and in the relation q and in all their super-relations, and the inverse is placed in all the inverse super-relations. This leads to the following formal definition:

Definition 10 (Instance $I^{\approx^\downarrow}$). *Given a schema $S = (F, K)$ with $F = (C, R, s, t)$ and $p \approx^\downarrow q \notin K^*$ we define $I^{\approx^\downarrow} = (O^{\approx^\downarrow}, [\![\cdot]\!]^{\approx^\downarrow})$ such that $O^{\approx^\downarrow} = O^{base} \cup \{o^1_{pq}, o^2_{pq}\}$*

and the interpretation function as for I^{base} but with the following additional rules for all classes c:

$$o_{pq}^1 \in [\![c]\!] \; if \, (p \Rightarrow^{\downarrow} r \in K^* \vee q \Rightarrow^{\downarrow} r \in K^*) \wedge s(r) \Rightarrow c \in K^* \qquad (29)$$

$$o_{pq}^1 \in [\![c]\!] \; if \, (p \Rightarrow^{\uparrow} r \in K^* \vee q \Rightarrow^{\uparrow} r \in K^*) \wedge t(r) \Rightarrow c \in K^* \qquad (30)$$

$$o_{pq}^2 \in [\![c]\!] \; if \, (p \Rightarrow^{\downarrow} r \in K^* \vee q \Rightarrow^{\downarrow} r \in K^*) \wedge t(r) \Rightarrow c \in K^* \qquad (31)$$

$$o_{pq}^2 \in [\![c]\!] \; if \, (p \Rightarrow^{\uparrow} r \in K^* \vee q \Rightarrow^{\uparrow} r \in K^*) \wedge s(r) \Rightarrow c \in K^* \qquad (32)$$

and for all relationships r:

$$(o_{pq}^1, o_{pq}^2) \in [\![r]\!] \; if \, p \Rightarrow^{\downarrow} r \in K^* \vee q \Rightarrow^{\downarrow} r \in K^* \qquad (33)$$

$$(o_{pq}^2, o_{pq}^1) \in [\![r]\!] \; if \, p \Rightarrow^{\uparrow} r \in K^* \vee q \Rightarrow^{\uparrow} r \in K^* \qquad (34)$$

Informally we can describe (o_{pq}^1, o_{pq}^2) as the typical pair that is both in the relationship p and q.

Lemma 3. *Given a schema $S = (F, K)$ such that K^* is conflict-free and $p \wr^{\downarrow} q \notin K^*$, then the corresponding $I^{\wr^{\downarrow}}$ is an instance of S.*

Proof. The proof proceeds similar to that of Lemma 2 and considers the extra cases for Prop. (1), Constr. (7), Constr. (8) and Constr. (9) using the assumption that $p \wr^{\downarrow} q \notin K^*$.   □

Definition 11 (Instance $I^{\wr^{\uparrow}}$). *Given a schema $S = (F, K)$ with $F = (C, R, s, t)$ and $p \wr^{\uparrow} q \notin K^*$ we define $I^{\wr^{\uparrow}}$ similar to $I^{\wr^{\downarrow}}$ but here we add a pair $(o_{pq}^{12}, o_{pq}^{21})$ such that it is in $[\![p]\!]^{\wr^{\uparrow}}$ and its inverse, $(o_{pq}^{21}, o_{pq}^{12})$, is in $[\![q]\!]^{\wr^{\uparrow}}$.*

Lemma 4. *Given a schema $S = (F, K)$ such that K^* is conflict-free and $p \wr^{\uparrow} q \notin K^*$, then the corresponding $I^{\wr^{\uparrow}}$ is an instance of S.*

Proof. The proof proceeds similar to that of Lemma 3.   □

5.2   Soundness and Completeness of Rules

Theorem 2. *Given a schema $S = (F, K)$ with K^* the closure of K under the rules in $M_1, \ldots, M_4$ then*

1. $c_1 \Rightarrow c_2 \in K^*$ iff $I \vdash c_1 \Rightarrow c_2$ for all instances I of S,
2. $r_1 \Rightarrow^{\downarrow} r_2 \in K^*$ iff $I \vdash r_1 \Rightarrow^{\downarrow} r_2$ for all instances I of S,
3. $r_1 \Rightarrow^{\uparrow} r_2 \in K^*$ iff $I \vdash r_1 \Rightarrow^{\uparrow} r_2$ for all instances I of S,
4. $\cdot r \in K^*$ iff $I \vdash \cdot r$ for all instances I of S,
5. $r \cdot \in K^*$ iff $I \vdash r \cdot$ for all instances I of S,
6. $c_1 \wr c_2 \in K^*$ iff $I \vdash r_1 \wr r_2$ for all instances I of S,
7. $r_1 \wr^{\downarrow} r_2 \in K^*$ iff $I \vdash r_1 \wr^{\downarrow} r_2$ for all instances I of S, and
8. $r_1 \wr^{\uparrow} r_2 \in K^*$ iff $I \vdash r_1 \wr^{\uparrow} r_2$ for all instances I of S.

Proof. (Sketch) The *only-if* part of all the propositions is easily proved by verifying that all the inference rules in $M_1, \ldots, M_4$ are sound, which follows straightforwardly from the semantics of the constraints as defined in Definition 3.

The *if* part is proven in two steps. We first show that for each type of constraint that if K^* is conflict-free then it holds, and then we show that from this it follows that it holds for any K.   □

Corollary 1. *The rules in $M_1, \ldots, M_3$ are sufficient to detect if K^* is conflict-free.*

Proof. From the preceding corollary it follows that if the closure of K under $M_1, \ldots, M_3$ does not contain a conflict then the closure under $M_1, \ldots, M_4$ will also not contain a conflict. It is also clear that if the first closure contains a conflict then so does the second closure. Therefore the first closure contains a conflict iff the second closure does.   □

6 Related Work

There has already been a large amount of research on the topic of data integration [4] and reasoning about taxonomies in general [5] and database schemas in particular [6]. As is argued in [7] the two subjects are closely linked together since the ability to reason over the views can be used to check the representation for inconsistencies and redundancies, and to maintain the system in response to changes in the data needs. In particular, [8] presents a reasoning approach for automating a significant part of the schema integration process and [9] relies on a reasoning support to improve the quality of data.

Description Logics (DL) are a well-known family of knowledge representation formalisms that descend from KL-ONE [10]. Long since, they have been applied to data management [11] and information integration [12]. The basic idea is to express database schemas as DL knowledge bases so that DL reasoning techniques can be used to reason about the schema. Although this approach can be restricted to useful fragments where reasoning is still tractable, e.g. [13] and [14], it often already becomes intractable for relatively small fragments [15] and even more so when the concept of *inverse role* is added [16]. It was to the best of our knowledge not yet known that the fragment that is proposed in this paper, which can express such inverse roles, has a relatively simple set of inference rules that is sound and complete and allows tractable reasoning.

7 Conclusion

In this paper we have proposed a view integration method that leaves the original views intact and allows their relationships to be defined by constraints that explicitly express semantical relationships between the components of the different views. Although the motivation of this approach comes from workflow and case management systems where the original views are important for the description of the workflow, this approach can also be beneficial for data integration in more general settings. To support the integration process we have proposed a set of inference rules that allows us to derive implied semantical relationships and especially whether there are conflicts in the integrated schema. We have shown that these sets of rules are sound and complete for all proposed types of constraints, and that subsets of these rules can be already complete for certain subsets of the constraints. Finally it was shown that the inference rules provide in all cases a tractable inference mechanism.

References

1. Batini, C., Lenzerini, M., Navathe, S.B.: A comparative analysis of methodologies for database schema integration. ACM Comput. Surv. 18 (1986) 323–364
2. Shipman, D.W.: The functional data model and the data language DAPLEX. ACM Trans. Database Syst. 6 (1981) 140–173
3. Halpin, T.: Information modeling and relational databases: from conceptual analysis to logical design. Morgan Kaufmann Publishers (2001)
4. Lenzerini, M.: Data integration: A theoretical perspective. In: PODS. (2002) 233–246
5. Bergamaschi, S., Sartori, C.: On taxonomic reasoning in conceptual design. ACM Trans. Database Syst. 17 (1992) 385–422
6. Formica, A., Missikoff, M.: Inheritance processing and conflicts in structural generalization hierarchies. ACM Comput. Surv. 36 (2004) 263–290
7. Calvanese, D., De Giacomo, G., Lenzerini, M., Nardi, D., Rosati, R.: Information integration: Conceptual modeling and reasoning support. In: Proc. of the 6th Int. Conf. on Cooperative Information Systems (CoopIS'98). (1998) 280–291
8. Kashyap, V., Sheth, A.P.: Semantic and schematic similarities between database objects: A context-based approach. VLDB J. 5 (1996) 276–304
9. Calvanese, D., De Giacomo, G., Lenzerini, M., Nardi, D., Rosati, R.: Source integration in data warehousing. In: Proc. of the 9th Int. Workshop on Database and Expert Systems Applications (DEXA'98), IEEE Computer Society Press (1998) 192–197
10. Brachman, R., Schmolze, J.: An overview of the KL-ONE knowledge representation system. Cognitive Science (1985) 171–216
11. Kirk, T., Levy, A.Y., Sagiv, Y., Srivastava, D.: The Information Manifold. In Knoblock, C., Levy, A., eds.: Information Gathering from Heterogeneous, Distributed Environments, Stanford University, Stanford, California (1995)
12. Calvanese, D., Giacomo, G.D., Lenzerini, M., Nardi, D., Rosati, R.: Description logic framework for information integration. In: KR. (1998) 2–13
13. Brachman, R., Levesque, H.: The tractability of subsumption in frame-based description languages. In: AAAI-84, Austin, Texas (1984) 34–37
14. Borgida, A., Brachman, R.J., McGuinness, D.L., Resnick, L.A.: CLASSIC: a structural data model for objects. In: Proc. of the ACM SIGMOD International Conference on Management of Data, Portland, Oregon (1989) 58–67
15. Nutt, W., Donini, F.M., Lenzerini, M., Nardi, D.: The complexity of concept languages. Inf. Comput. 134 (1997) 1–58
16. Horrocks, I., Sattler, U.: A description logic with transitive and inverse roles and role hierarchies. Journal of Logic and Computation 9 (1999) 385–410

A Multi-version Data Model and Semantic-Based Transaction Processing Protocol

Alexander Yakovlev

Department of Computer Science, Saint-Petersburg State University,
Universitetsky prospekt, 28, Peterhof, St. Petersburg, Russia, 198504
yakki@mail.ru

Abstract. Data processing delays are becoming one of the most serious problems in a mobile environment. A not-the-latest version of data item cannot be inserted because of data fluctuation in subsequent versions. In this paper there is presented a multi-version data model capable of preserving full version history. Such a model allows updates not ordered chronologically. It is obtained by using semantics received from applications. The version of data item is defined by operation with a set of attributes and acceptance timestamp. Consistency requirements "by demand" allow non-conflict commutative versions defined by commutative operations. Transaction protocol to be used with data model presented is also described.

1 Introduction

Advances in mobile services are increasing now very high. We can meet mobile applications in GIS, navigation and others. One can see problem of unstable channels in distributed mobile systems. Other problem is low passing ability of wireless channels.

Some of mobile applications need to process data modification operations initiated by mobile hosts. If some mobile hosts are in disconnected mode - hasn't connection with remaining part of system- the problem of transaction delays appears. Transaction restrictions, like consistency and others and non-commutative data modification operations order that there are no processed transactions without connection to other hosts. So they will not be committed or aborted until reinstatement of connection, if using distributed database with multiple replicas of data.

The objective of this paper is to introduce a multi-version data model that store semantic operations on data items and version vitality time bounds. This model may allow committing of outdated transactions and decrease network traffic. Introduced transaction model doesn't fully satisfy the consistency property of ACID properties [15] –it has relaxed.

The main advantage of such data model is the possibility of data history modification. This can be achieved by using semantic of modification operations. In this paper data domains with supported operation list are used for mining semantic information. In experimental part of this research there are counts of committed transactions with different conflict rates done by discussed model.

J. Eder et al. (Eds.): ADBIS 2005, LNCS 3631, pp. 87–96, 2005.

2 Related Works

Classical approach on the transaction management is not applicable for a mobile environment [16]. Pessimistic concurrency control systems leads to blocking transactions, since mobile host can't update any cached objects while it is disconnected. There are a lot of approaches that includes specifics of mobile environment. One part of the works on mobile transactions cover the design of efficient concurrency control protocols [2, 11]. Other aims in enable working with replicated database fragment in disconnected mode [5, 6, 9, 13].

Pessimistic approaches don't support replication and disconnected operations and cannot serve successfully in mobile environment [6]. Optimistic approach where the commitment is processed on local replica is proposed in [4].

Different notions of consistency can be maintained by systems with architecture like GLOMAR [11] – middleware layer for distributed systems that allows development specific consistency models in scope of environmental constraints.

A multi-version data broadcasting method is introduced at first to resolve the problem of reading inconsistent data values for read-only transactions [13]. In this method all the previous versions within the time frame need to be broadcast as well further to the most updated version. Mobile transactions can use stale data versions since they are allowed to read this version by the relative consistency. Transaction defined in [13] by quintuple of values: transaction type; the set of operations of transaction; the transaction deadline; the partial order of operations. Every version of data item has validity time bounds, the lower one is defined by timestamp of inserting/updating this item, when the upper one by committing new version of item.

Various techniques, such as absolute and relative consistency, have been proposed to define correctness of temporal data items [9]. Some of them use external consistency based on the definition of absolute validity interval (AVI). This interval is defined for each temporal data item related to maximum rate of changes. If the difference exceeds predefined tolerance limit or AVI is exceeded, then the system becomes externally inconsistent. Relative consistency defines the consistency for data items that are accessed by the same transaction. Due to this requirement data items have to be valid at the same time point.

Other type of algorithms aims in early detecting conflicts on mobile host site with decreasing communication between mobile host and stationary network. Data dependencies are used in [18] for this aims –the clients receive from the server dependency information, from which they build partial serialization graph. Dependency information there can be fully calculated on server side and then broadcasts to clients. Using dynamic adjustment of timestamp ordering and partial validation on mobile clients is presented in [22]. This transaction processing algorithm aims in early detecting conflicts within update transactions on mobile clients and resolving them based on timestamps.

TCOT one phase protocol is based on timeouts calculation and tries to make transaction decision - commit or abort – with help of calculated value of timeout. It reduces communication between sites [19].

Semantic based transaction processing models used to increase concurrency by using commutative operations [2]. In optimistic concurrency control systems cached objects stored on mobile hosts can be updated without any coordination. But all the updates need to be validated for the commitment of transaction. If checking updates validity is failed then transaction that corresponds to this update rollbacks by this scheme.

Weak and strict operations on data items have been proposed for mobile computing in [3]. Strict operations have semantics same with the normal read and write operations. The weak ones are local operations, processed only on mobile host without any exchanging with external environment within a process.

3 System Model

Distributed mobile database system consists of mobile hosts (MH), fixed hosts (FH) and mobile support stations (MSS) [16]. Every mobile host has wireless connection to the network. A high-speed fixed network connects fixed hosts to each other. Wireless connection speed is much smaller then in a fixed network. Mobile hosts can communicate with fixed hosts only through the mobile support stations. The database is distributed on MH and FH. MH or FH may maintain primary copy of fragment and there are cashed secondary copies on MH and FH. We always have backup copy of data items that have primary copies situated on MH, if it is possible.

4 Data Model

Database consists of simple data items, unbound between them. For storing semantic information data domains with sets of acceptable operations are used – updates are available via data domain operations only. Attributes of operation are kept with operation ids to make possible recalculation process. In lifetime information part version vitality bounds and version real create timestamp are kept. This model suggests each data item to be associated with the following structure (Fig. 1):

Definition 1. anchor timestamp is time-stamp that indicates moment from that one can make new versions. It is defined by last fixed version upper life-bound timestamp or another timestamp if it is required.

The application defines the fixing history strategy(for example tax need to be calculated at the end of year and we need to fix all accounts, on that tax applies).

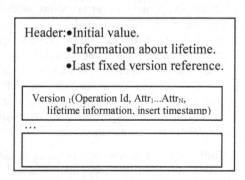

Fig. 1. Multi-version data item structure

Each data item as multi-version one has its change history stored. It is starting from the initialization timestamp. On the data item initialization the starting value is always specified, there are default values for each data domain. That value is used for computations of all the later data item version's values.

The database is updated with new operations applied to the data item as the newer versions appear. If there is a data item fixation necessary for the time moment <t>, the versions of the data item becomes to be fixed until <t>. Because of fixing, values of the versions can be computed by applying operations taking place until <t>.

Data domains that are considered in this paper can be not-numerical, have complex structure and contain information about non-conflict operations in special commutative table of a special format that contains information about all requirements to avoid conflicts. Some of these tables pointed in [17, 21] are useful for improving concurrency.

5   Accumulators and External Functions

In [21] concept of accumulators is introduced. Accumulators store operations applied to some initial value of simple type like described below data model.

Definition 2. External function is used to get additional information about the accumulator. External function may depend not only on one accumulator, its base value and operations history, but possibly on other accumulators and other different parameters.

Definition 3. An external function depends on the period of time if it depends on operations that have been applied during this period.

External functions can be used on application layer for wide area of aims. Value of version stored in accumulator can be returned by external function. A lot of mobile service provider billing system functions can be wrapped into external function, for example balance request by mobile station. Another application is in different kinds of aggregate functions – average or maximum value in case of numeric domain etc.

There are two concepts of accumulators – list-accumulator and set-accumulator types. List-accumulator stores versions in strong order of timestamps instead of Set-accumulator, which stores versions without any order. In this work only List accumulator type is considered.

Because of strictly defined order, each operation stored in the list-accumulator has a context of other operations. (By the way, the list-accumulator may be applied as a set, because each operation has its unique identifier, and the context may be ignored in the application.) There are two kinds of list-accumulators: insert-only and insert-and-remove list-accumulators. Inserting or removing the new operations in such accumulator occurs as inserting or removing the element in the set. The replaying strategies for the list-accumulator follow.

Definition 4. An insert-only list-accumulator supports only one way for replaying: insertion of a compensational operation and insertion of the new operation.

There are following cases related to time-dependency of the external functions and the commutativity of the defined operations:

Case 1. There are some time-dependent external functions in the accumulator

- If all operations in the accumulator commutate with each other, inserting of the compensational and new operations occurs according to the rules of detection of the ETS.

- Else, if some operations in accumulator do not commutate with each other, inserting of the compensational and new operations occurs according to the rules of detection of the ETS. Because the operations do not commutate, the application should warrant the semantic correctness of the replaying.

Case 2. All external functions are time-independent

- If some operations in accumulator do not commutate with each other, inserting of the new element in any place of the list does not damage the rules of detection of the ETS because all external functions are time independent. Thus, there are several cases to replay the operations:
  - o Insertion of the compensational operation and the new operation just after the old operation
  - o Insertion of the compensational operation just after the old operation and inserting the new operation according to its ETS
  - o Insertion of the compensational and the new operations according to their ETS

The compensational operation and the method of replaying are defined by the application. Purging of out-of-date operations is hardly needed to improve performance, because number of operations stored in accumulator have tendency to grow up. We will purge out-of-date version if there will be no external functions that depends on lifetime of this version.

6 Timestamp Consistency

Absolute consistency constraints are defined on base items, when the relative consistency ones on the set of base items and the set of items, derived from the set of base items. A Transaction observes absolute consistency if all its accessed data items truly reflect the status of the corresponding objects in the external environment. Absolute consistency constraints can be applied to this kind of multi-version data model as well, as relative consistency constraints.

Absolute consistency can be easily described by this definition: the value of data item is outdated since a new update for this item is generated [15]. Relative consistency guarantees that base and derived items in the transaction represents status of data at the same point [13]. Because of restrictions of a mobile environment we need to solve problems, caused by disconnection and network delays. We illustrate this problem by the following scenario: transaction needs two data items, one of them to be accessed by it, when another one may be transmitted only after a long delay. During such a long transaction, an update of the previously accessed items may be created. To maintain absolute consistency following the unapplied update, described above, the transaction must to be restarted.

Absolute consistency requirements can be relaxed in order to reduce the number of transaction restarts. The timestamps seem to be useful. Transaction may consider accessed data items valid if all data items are valid by the time of a transaction initialization. It can be useful because the timestamps that are stored with operations –

their values can be restricted for all operations from this transaction by the value of timestamp that indicates the transaction initialization.

Definition 5. Transaction fully satisfies timestamp consistency requirements if all items, read by transaction, are relatively consistent at timestamp of transaction initialization.

By this we don't need to require any data item to be valid after initialization of transaction and return all the requested data items.

7   Transaction Protocol

Transactions are presented in terms of operation sets, according to given data model. Every reading operation has a time restrictions as a parameter, within the requirements for versions that needed. Every writing operation creates a record that contains operation identifier, attributes required for given operation, and timestamp of version vitality lower bound.

For application specific tasks we need to support stronger requirements on consistency. It can be aimed by using "strict" operations.

Definition 6. Operation is "strict" if it needs for fixing computed value for version of data item that reads or creates.

Operations with this requirement will be prefixed by "Strict" ("StrictRead", "StrictWrite") in this paper. "Strict" operation in transaction causes this transaction to be strict. Every derived value is written by transaction as an operation. It must have timestamp, which is equal to the moment of live connection to server. By this durability of values that must be fixed is guaranteed – all derived new versions are computed with fixed values if it needed by using "StrictRead".

In our model we will maintain local copy by algorithm, described in [18], using data dependency to decrease network using. Transaction coordinator will serve information about versions that become to be stale, received by broadcasting channels Processing of strict transactions is already described in a lot of works and uses pessimistic approach. We will discuss just processing of non-strict transactions.

Definition 7. *read_set* - It is list of data items that are read by a transaction.

Definition 8. *write_set* - It is list of data items which are written by a transaction.
  1.   We check *read_set:*

- If we have all *read_set* values, then calculate all values from *write_set* locally on mobile host, mark them by timestamp of last successful connection to fixed network (successful means that we received all information from coordinator and it is confirmed by coordinator).
- If we haven't some values from *read_set*, then request values through coordinator and after receiving all needed information calculate *write_set* and so on.
  2.   Send results of work to coordinator, including (*read_set, write_set*)
- If coordinator finds in read set some stale versions, then restart transaction because MH was in disconnected mode more time then it is possible.

- If *write_set* checking inside database management system is fault because of some conflicts with Strict-transactions, then restart transaction.

3. If we have no conflicts then make decision about commit of this transaction and include versions from *write_set* into accumulator. Then send *write_set* through all coordinators for excluding stale versions.

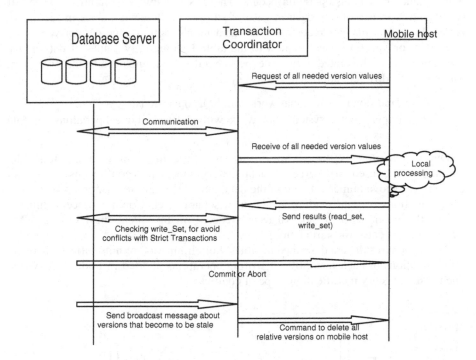

Fig. 2. Processing of non-strict transaction

This protocol relaxes the consistency property among ACID properties as the fixing of values of data items can be required by the transaction, but it is unnecessary.

Also other properties are guaranteed in terms of operations: durability is reached because of the absence to allow deleting any version of data item, atomicity can be guaranteed checking procedure transaction processing and by fixed network services, isolation is reached by using transaction management systems. The lasts are not aimed in this paper.

8 Experiments and Optimization

In experimental part of this research count of committed transactions with different conflict rates is obtained. Model of transaction flow with available merging for data item versions is build. Aims of this work cause to check successful processing of outdated transactions. For experimental needs we use numeric domain and arithmetic operations on it. Actually there are two binary operations in numeric domain: adding and multiplying.

For experimental realization of given algorithm Microsoft SQL Server 2000 SDK chosen to be used.

Multi-version data model described above assumes necessity of calculation of data item's values if reading operation occurs. There is possibility to minimize speed of reading. It is in use of approach in case of storage of elements values in secondary tables. In such a manner request for the data item's value of the certain version is equivalent on speed to usual request to the table keeping only values of data items. This approach is illustrated with the experimental system enclosed to the given job. There are two different approaches in test system:

- Traditional system that work with SQL operations.
- Experimental system that work with defined above operations on data items.

During experiments the set of operations above the data with the following parameters are used: a degree of data history modifying conflicts is 50 %, all operations - above numerical type of the data, binary. Fixing of a history is switched - off. Operations of data reading are born in separate set. Commit process initiated every 50 operations in thread. All tests executed on Intel Pentium 4-1700(256 Mb RAM, one test database started only).

Experiment results are described in tables. For elimination of noise effects there are 1000 iterations of each test. 50% of writing operations aborted in traditional system due to "data history modification" type of conflict.

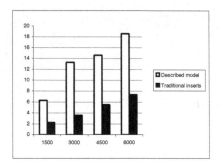
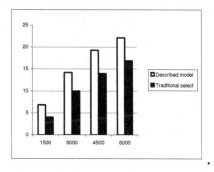

Fig. 2. Time results for insert (create version) Operations (horizontal-count of operations, vertical-time elapsed in seconds)

Fig. 3. Time results for select (get value) operations (horizontal-count of operations, vertical-time elapsed in seconds)

According to the executed experiments cost of operation of record increases on the average in 2,28 times, cost of operation of reading in 1,44 times. The tendency is kept at increase in amount of shorthanded operations.

9 Performance Analyses

In this paper a multi-version data model is presented. It requires the values of data items to be recalculated during each reading operation. In experiments cost of ability of data history modification is shown properly. Reading operation speed increases in 1,3-1,5 times, writing operation speed – in 2,1-2,5 times. But a set of operations includes half of aborted in traditional system parts. Then we have some other results for writing operations – 4,2-5 times increasing of cost in speed.

In the following way using of suggested model enables data history modification, but always it has cost – speed decreased.

10 Conclusions

In this paper, a data model and a transaction model for working with timestamp consistency is proposed. Semantic information about operations on data items is used to allow working with fragment of database in disconnected mode. Ability of including work that done on disconnected host realized.

Transaction protocol presented in this paper allows for the commitment of data item versions to be made not only in chronological order. Contrary to the traditional transaction protocols data item version's values can be recalculated upon the commitment of older version of data.

Durability property from ACID transaction properties is achieved in sense of durability of the operations performed on data items instead of data item version values. Consistency property is relaxed to timestamp consistency that can restrict history modification by timestamp, which is the lowest possible bound of updateable version history.

References

1. Weikum, G., Vossen, G.: Transactional Information Systems – Theory, Algorithms and the Practice of Concurrency Control and Recovery. Morgan Kaufmann Publishers (2002)
2. Walborn, G. D., Chrysanthis, P. K.: Transaction Processing in Pro-Motion. In Proceedings of ACM Symposium on Applied Computing (1999)
3. Pitoura, E., Bhargava, B.: Building Information Systems for Mobile Environments. In Proceedings of 3rd International Conference on Information and Knowledge Managment (1994) 371-378
4. Pitoura, E., Bhargava, B.: Data Consistency in Intermittently Connected Distributed Systems. In Transactions on Knowledge and Data Engineering, (1999)
5. Madria, S. K., Bhargava, B.: System Defined Prewrites to Increase Concurrency in Databases. In Proceedings of First East Europian Symposium on Advances in Databases and Information Systems. St.-Petersburg (1997)
6. Madria, S. K., Bhargava, B.: A Transaction Model for Improving Data Availability in Mobile Computing. In Distributed and Parallel Databases, 10(2) (2001)
7. Lu, Q., Satyanaraynan, M.: Improving Data Consistency in Mobile Computing Using Isolation-Only Transactions. In Proceedings of The 5th Workshop on Hot Topics in Operating Systems, Orcas Island, Washington (1995)

8. Pitoura, E., Chrisanthis, P.: Scalable Processing of Read-Only Transactions in Broadcast Push, IEEE International Conference on Distributed Computing Systems, Austin (1999)

9. Kao, B., Kam-Yiu, L., Adelberg, B., Cheng, R., Lee T.: Updates and View Maintenance in Soft Real-Time Databases. In Proceedings of Conference on Information and Knowledge Management, Kansas City (1999)

10. Eich, M. H., Helal, A.: A Mobile Transaction Model That Captures Both Data and Movement Behaviour. ACM/Baltzer Journal on Special Topics on Mobile Networks and Applications (1997)

11. Cuce, S., Zaslavsky, A.: Adaptable Consistency Control Mechanism for a Mobility Enabled File System, Third International Conference on Mobile Data Management, MDM 2002, Singapore, IEEE CS Press (2002) 27-34

12. Dunham, M., Helal, A., Balakrishnan, S.: A mobile transaction model that captures both the data and movement behavior. Mobile Networks and Applications, 2 (1997)

13. Kam-Yiu, L., GuoHui, L., Tei-Wei, K.: A Multi-Version Data Model for Executing Real-time Transactions in a Mobile Environment. In Proceedings of MobiDe'2001 (2001)

14. Barbara, D.: Mobile Computing and Databases – A Survey. IEEE Transactions on Knowledge and Data Engineering, Vol. 11, No.1 (1999)

15. Date, C.: An Introduction to Database Systems, 7th ed., Addison-Wesley (1999)

16. Mascolo, C., Capra, L., Zachariadis, S., Emmerich, W.: XMIDDLE: A Data-Sharing Middleware for Mobile Computing. Int. Journal on Personal and Wireless Communications (2002)

17. Novikov, B., Proskurnin, O.: Towards collaborate video authoring. In Proc. of the ADBIS'2003, Dresden, Germany (2003) 370-384

18. Chung, I. Y., Bhagava, B., Mahoui, M., Lilien, L.: Autonomous Transaction Processing Using Data Dependency in Mobile Environments. In Proc. of the 9th IEEE Workshop on Future Trends of Distributed Computing Systems.(FTDCS'03), San Juan, Puerto Rico (2003) 138

19. Kumar, V., Prabhu, N., Dunham, M., Saydim, Y. A.: TCOT – a timeout-based mobile transaction commitment protocol, IEEE Transaction on Computers, vol. 51 (2002)

20. Demers, A. J., Petersen, K., Spreitzer, M. J., Terry, D. B., Theimer, M. M., Welch, B. B.: The Bayou architecture: Support for data sharing among mobile users. In IEEE Workshop of Mobile Computing Systems and Applications (WMCSA), Santa Cruz, California, USA (1994)

21. Kozlova, A., Kochnev, D., Novikov, B.: The Middleware Support for Consistency in Distributed Mobile Applications, In Proc. of BalticDBIS'2004 (2004)

22. Victor, C. S., Lee, Lam, S., K. W., Son, S. H., Chan E. Y. M.: On Transaction Processing with Partial Validation and Timestamp Ordering in Mobile Broadcast Environments, IEEE Transaction on Computers, vol. 51, No.10 (2002) 1196-1211

Managing Schema Versions in Object-Oriented Databases

Xian Liu, David Nelson, Simon Stobart, and Sue Stirk

School of Computing and Technology, The Sir Tom Cowie Campus at St. Peter's,
University of Sunderland, Sunderland, SR6 0DD UK
{xian.liu, david.nelson, simon.stobart,
sue.stirk}@sunderland.ac.uk

Abstract. The schemas of object-oriented databases are frequently changed in advanced applications such as Computer-Aided Design. This generates many schema versions that are used to model the evolving structure of a real world entity. Thus, there exists a need for an adequate method of managing the schema versions effectively, so that the user can trace the history of the changing schema with ease. In this paper, we propose a nested matrix model for the management of schema versions in object-oriented databases. The model maintains a semantic set of relationships between the schema versions. The advantages of our work include the provision of a logical representation for schema versions that are not addressed sufficiently in exiting models and the development of a graphic querying interface.

1 Introduction

Advanced applications such as Computer-Aided Design rely on object-oriented databases to facilitate the design process of artifacts that have a complex data structure [1, 2]. As a result of incremental design, the structure of the objects modeled is frequently modified. This gives rise to schema changes. There are two general approaches to schema changes: schema evolution and schema versioning. The former allows the database to be updated to the new schema without any loss of data [3], while the latter retains all versions (both current and past) of the schema and the data associated with them [4]. This forms a complete history of the evolution of the database.

The schema versioning approach is often preferred, in that it enables the user to go back to previous versions of the schema. This is essentially important in advanced applications like engineering design. However, existing models of schema versioning have limited capabilities. For example, most of them can only handle situations where a schema version is derived from another one; merging schema versions is not considered. The logical representation of schema versions is not addressed sufficiently. Some models are not implemented to validate its correctness.

In this paper, we propose a nested matrix model of schema versioning, which supports a richer set of relationships between schema versions by introducing the merging type. We present a logical representation of schema versions designed to increase the modeling power of the model. We discuss our prototype implementation of the model including a graphic querying interface which enables a casual user to access schema versions with ease.

J. Eder et al. (Eds.): ADBIS 2005, LNCS 3631, pp. 97 – 108, 2005.

The remainder of the paper is organized as follows. Section 2 introduces the model formally. Section 3 describes the prototype implementation of the model and its graphic querying interface features. Section 4 is an overview of related work. Section 5 concludes the paper.

2 Nested Matrix Model

In this section, we first introduce the basic concepts of the model using a simplified example of the structural evolution of a design object. The formal definitions of the model are given later.

2.1 Basic Concepts

The schema of an object-oriented database is a set of classes. A class consists of attributes and methods that represent the state and behavior of the objects modeled. Each attribute has a unique name in the scope of the class and a type (either a system-defined type such as character and number or a user defined type). Each method also has a name. It may receive a set of parameters and does or does not return a value. The combination of the name and parameters, called the signature of the method, must be unique within the class. In addition to defining its own attributes and methods, a class may inherit those of another class. Thus, the schema can be seen as a set of class inheritance hierarchies as shown in Figure 1.

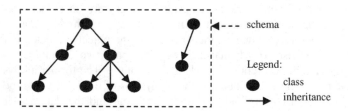

Fig. 1. Schema Graph – Showing Class Inheritance

The schema evolves when one or more of its classes are changed. The changes are the results of adding, deleting and/or updating the classes in terms of their superclass, attributes and methods. We have defined a set of primitive change types as listed below. They describe all possible changes to the schema based on the definition in the preceding paragraph.

Changes to the structure of the tree graph:

- add a class to the schema,
- delete a class from the schema,
- assign a class as the superclass of another class if it does not have one,
- remove its superclass from a class (but not from the schema),
- replace the superclass of a class.

Changes to a node of the tree graph:

- rename a class,
- add an attribute to a class,
- delete an attribute from a class,
- rename an attribute of a class,
- add a method to a class,
- delete a method from a class,
- rename a method of a class.

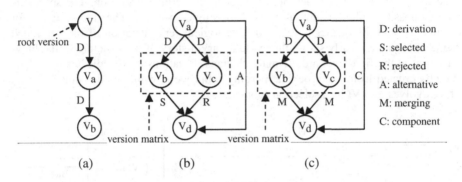

Fig. 2. Types of Relationship of Schema Versions

A versioned schema is a collection of snapshots (called versions) of the schema over time that describe the history of changes in the structure of the objects modeled. A new version is always created from one or more existing versions. There are six types of relationship between versions as shown in Figure 2. Firstly, the derivation type means that the new version is derived from a single existing version (Figure 2(a)). Secondly, a version may derive more than one version as alternatives, and out of them, one is selected and the rest, rejected. That is, the rejected versions stop being involved in the evolutionary process of the schema and are not allowed to create other versions (Figure 2(b)). To represent these semantics, we create a new version Vd and a set of selected/rejected relationships. Physically, Vd has an identical set of class definitions with Vb. However, logically, they are not the same, in that different semantics are represented: Vb is an alternative to Vc in parallel, while Vd is the result of a selection from Vb and Vc. Vd can continue to evolve by creating new versions, but Vb and Vc can not, since they have been replaced by Vd. Selecting the best one from multiple alternatives is an important step forward, for example, in engineering design applications, and therefore is considered in the model using a logical version Vd. Thirdly, versions originating from the same version can be merged as components to form a new version (Figure 2(c)).

To provide a logical representation for a versioned schema, a root version is automatically created as the start of its evolution as shown in Figure 2(a). The alternative and component versions that always originate from one version Va and end at another one Vd are enclosed in a logical container called version matrix. We add between Va and Vd an alternative (A) / component (C) relationship to represent the semantics that Va evolves into Vd indirectly through an alternative / component version matrix. A version matrix may host other lower level version matrices. Thus, we have a multiple level organization of version matrices. The first level is the main evolutionary path of a linear feature. The version matrices that are associated with it form the second level, and those nested in the second level in turn form the third level, and so on. We use a simplified example below to illustrate these concepts.

Figure 3 illustrates the structural evolution/development of a bicycle design. The design undergoes 3 main stages: frame V_a, wheels V_g, and crank V_h, the order of which must be preserved, in that each stage serves a base for the next one. In the second stage, the front wheel V_b and the back wheel V_c plus the associated sprockets V_f are designed separately and then put together by a merging operation. The sprockets have two possible solutions: multi-speed V_d or single-speed V_e. They are designed for experiments, and the former is selected. The logical representation of the versioned schema in Figure 3 clearly shows the evolutionary history of the structure of the bicycle design: at the first level are the main changes. Relationship C indicates that V_g is indirectly created from V_a through a merging subprocess, while relationship A shows that V_c evolves into V_f by a selection subprocess.

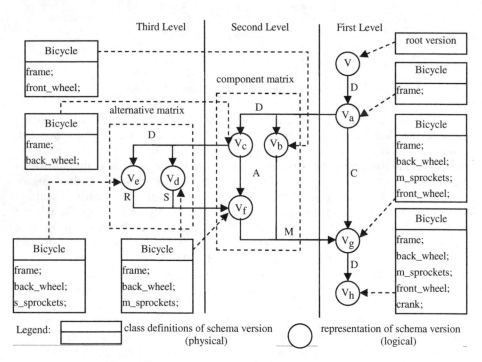

Fig. 3. Bicycle Design Modeled as Versioned Schema

As shown in Figure 3, a schema version is always associated with a set of class definitions except for the root version. The same set of class definitions may be shared by two or more schema versions. This is consistent with real world situations. For example, in engineering design, parts of the same type/structure are often used in more than one place of a product. This feature gives rise to the concept that there are two facets of a schema version: a physical one and a logical one. The user works with the logical facet, and the system is responsible for transparently providing the physical facet, i.e., the associated class definitions.

2.2 Definitions of the Model

A versioned schema is represented by a DAG graph extended to accommodate version matrices. We define the DAG graph and the version matrix, respectively.

The DAG is defined as $G = (V, E, l)$, where $V = \{ v_a, v_b, ..., v_n \}$ is a set of nodes representing the versions of the schema; E is a set of edges of the nodes labeled D, S, R, A, M, or C indicating the relationship types between the versions; and l is a function for retrieving the label of an edge, that is, the relationship type of the two versions concerned: $l (v_i, v_j) \rightarrow t \in \{D, S, R, A, M, C, N\}$, where N means that there does not exist an edge from v_i to v_j.

To define version matrices, we must first introduce the concept of matrix paths. A matrix path is a sequence of all adjacent edges, (v_{i+1}, v_{i+2}), (v_{i+2}, v_{i+3}), ..., (v_{i+n-1}, v_{i+n}), such that the number of outgoing edges of v_e is equal to the number of incoming edges of v_{e+1}, where $e = i+1, i+2, ..., i+n-1$. If $\exists$ edges (v_i, v_{i+1}) and (v_{i+n}, v_j) such that the number of outgoing edges of v_i is not equal to the number of incoming edges of v_{i+1} and that the number of outgoing edges of v_{i+n} is not equal to the number of incoming edges of v_j, then v_i and v_j are called the starting version and the ending version of the matrix path, respectively. A version matrix is/contains a set of matrix paths that share the same starting and ending versions.

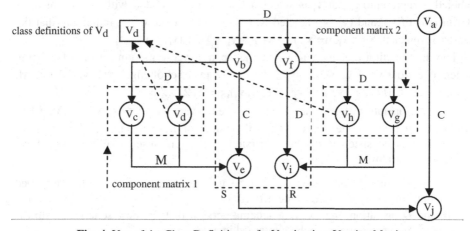

Fig. 4. Use of the Class Definitions of a Version in a Version Matrix

A version matrix is used to describe the way that a version evolves into another one through a set of alternative or component versions. Thus, there should be only two versions associated with it: its starting and ending versions. To be in compliance with this, we specify that the existing versions for a selection or merging operation must be leaf versions and that when the version matrix is formed upon completion of the operation, it is closed, that is, no version may logically be created from the versions inside it. However, the user can still take advantage of the class definitions associated with them using the sharing mechanism. Consider Figure 4. Suppose that V_i needs to merge the class definitions of V_d and V_g after component matrix 1 is formed and closed. Since V_d can not create new versions, V_h is created which shares the set of class definitions of V_d. The directed edge from V_f to V_h represents the logical relationship between them, that is, V_f has outdated and been replaced with V_h. The set of class definitions of V_h is not necessarily obtained by modifying those of V_f. It may be created from scratch or use those of an existing version. This is similar to the case of object versioning [5].

To manipulate the versioned schema in the graph, we have defined four operations as explained below.

The D operation creates from an existing version v_i a new version v_j and an edge (v_i, v_j) labeled D by applying a set of primitive changes $c = \{ c_a, c_b, ..., c_n \}$ to v_i, or by using the class definitions of another existing version v_e, or by defining a set of class definitions d from scratch. Thus, it has three forms:

1. $D (v_i, c, n='v_j') \rightarrow v_j + D(v_i, v_j)$, n is the name given to the new version, $D(v_i, v_j)$ represents an edge (v_i, v_j) labeled D;
2. $D (v_i, v_e, n='v_j') \rightarrow v_j + D(v_i, v_j)$;
3. $D (v_i, d, n='v_j') \rightarrow v_j + D(v_i, v_j)$, d is a set of class definitions.

The S operation creates a new schema version v_j by selecting one v_i from a set of existing schema versions $v = \{ v_a, v_b, ..., v_n \}$. It also creates a set of edges: (v_i, v_j) labeled S representing that v_i is selected (i.e., v_j is associated with the set of class definitions of v_i), and (v_e, v_j) labeled R, e = a, b, ..., n and $e \neq i$, indicating that the rest v_e is rejected. $S (v, v_i, n='v_j') \rightarrow v_j + S(v_i, v_j) + R(v_e, v_j)$.

The M operation creates a new schema version v_j by merging a set of existing schema versions $v = \{ v_a, v_b, ..., v_n \}$. It also creates a set of edges: (v_e, v_j) labeled M, e = a, b, ..., n. $M (v, n='v_j') \rightarrow v_j + M(v_e, v_j)$, e = 1, 2, ..., n.

The Del operation deletes an existing schema version v_i: $Del (v_i) \rightarrow V, v_i \notin V$, where V is the set of nodes representing all versions of the schema.

To maintain consistency of schema versions, we specify a set of rules for the above operations as follows:

- The names of schema versions must be unique in the scope of the versioned schema, since they are used as identifiers.
- For the D operation, the existing schema version that the new schema version is created from can not already be contained in a version matrix.
- For the M and S operations, the existing schema versions to be merged or selected from must be leaf versions, that is, no versions are already created from them, and the matrix paths associated with them have the same starting version.
- If attributes/methods with the same name/signature are encountered in a class when merging schema versions, the user must delete or rename some of them to guaran-

tee that the merged class does not have any attributes/methods with the same name/signature.

- For the *Del* operation, the existing schema version to be deleted must be a leaf version.

3 Implementation

In this section, we present a prototype implementation of the model. We first discuss its architecture in Subsection 3.1. Its schema version management unit is described in Subsection 3.2, followed by discussions on the graphic querying interface in Subsection 3.3. Finally, in Subsection 3.4, we address the physical organization issue.

3.1 Architecture

The implementation adopts a two-layer architecture (Figure 5). The first layer is a schema version management unit. It implements the concepts and rules defined in the model by creating a set of objects that represent schema versions and their relationships. The second layer is to make the objects persistent using an ODMG compliant object-oriented database system, so that the user can retrieve and manipulate the schema versions beyond the program sessions that create them. The main advantage of the architecture is that the implementation is portable, that is, it can be transferred to any object-oriented database system that meets the ODMD standards.

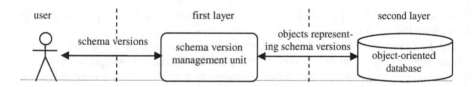

Fig. 5. Architecture of the Implementation

3.2 Schema Version Management Unit

As shown in Figure 6, the schema version management unit consists of a number of modules for performing various tasks of managing schema versions and a graphic user interface (GUI) that provides a convenient means of communications with the user.

The top part of the GUI, titled Schema, is used to manipulate versioned schemas as a whole. When the New button is selected, the Schema module is called that creates a new versioned schema with the name given in the Name field by the user. It also creates a Root version for the schema automatically as specified in the model. The Open button is to retrieve an existing versioned schema and display its logical representation, that is, a DAG graph with version matrices, in the Display area in the middle part of the GUI. We explain how to use the graph to access schema versions in the next subsection. The last button, DelSch, removes from the system the versioned schema named in the Name field. If errors occur during the above operations, for

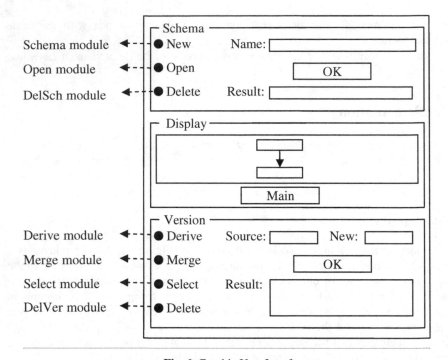

Fig. 6. Graphic User Interface

example, trying to delete a nonexistent schema, message windows pop up to give the reasons for the failure.

The bottom part of the GUI is for manipulating schema versions of the versioned schema opened. The four buttons on the left perform derivation, merge, selection and deletion operations, respectively. When interactions with the user are needed, various windows pop up for confirmation or input purposes. For example, in merging schema versions, if two attributes with the same name are encountered in a class, a window is opened to show these attributes, and the user must delete or rename one of them before the merging operation continues. The Result area on the right bottom corner of the GUI reports the results of each step of the performed operation, so that problems that may arise can easily be identified.

3.3 Graphic Querying Interface of Schema Versions

We have designed a graphic querying interface for easy access to schema versions. When a versioned schema is opened, its logical representation is shown in the Display part of the GUI (Figure 7). Initially, only the schema versions at the main (first) level are displayed. If there is an edge labeled C or A, this means that a version matrix is nested between the two associated schema versions. Thus, the user can click on the edge to have the nested matrix at the second level displayed. If it also hosts other version matrices, he or she can access them by clicking on the corresponding C or A edges. The Main button brings back the schema versions at the main level, that is,

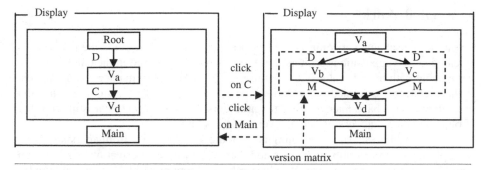

Fig. 7. Graphic Querying Interface

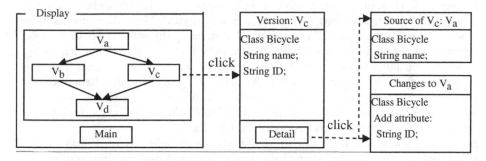

Fig. 8. Access to Schema Versions

returning to the starting point of the graphic navigation. In this way, schema versions at any level can be reached by simply clicking on edges.

To access a particular schema version, the user clicks on the node labeled its name in the graph (Figure 8). This pops up a window that shows all class definitions of the schema version. The Detail button on the window is used to trace the historical information on how it was created, such as its source schema version and the class changes made.

3.4 Physical Organization

A versioned schema consists of a number of schema versions, and each schema version is always associated with a set of class definitions. Thus, there arises a need to maintain these class definition sets physically. We use the file management facilities provided by the underlying operating system to do this.

When a versioned schema is initialized, a home directory is created for it. This directory is used to hold a database for storing the logical representations of its schema versions and some subdirectories. Each subdirectory in turn holds a set of class definitions that is associated with one or more schema versions (in a sharing case, see Section 2) and a database to store the objects created under the schema versions. Thus, when the user (or a program) needs to access objects of a schema version, the system transparently opens the database in the subdirectory associated with it.

4 Related Work

Research into schema versioning in object-oriented databases began in the mid 1980's when advanced applications such as CAD required objects stored in the database to be changeable both in their value and structure [6, 7, 8]. Most schema versioning models in the literature are defined by extending the concepts of object versioning, since the two related fields have many similar requirements. However, in comparison with that of object versioning, work on schema versioning is limited.

One approach to schema versioning is to create a new version from an existing one by applying a set of primitive changes and then establishing a derivation link between them. This forms a version derivation hierarchy, or more precisely, a tree structure [9, 10, 11, 12, 13]. However, the user may want to take advantage of two or more existing versions. Thus, the system needs to have the ability to merge versions.

Another approach is based around the concept of view. Most view models allow modifications of the structure of objects by generating different views of a global schema [14, 15]; [16] can also derive a new view from an existing one and merge views by renaming classes with the same names from different sources. The main drawback of the view approach is that the derivation and merging relationships between views that describe the way of evolution of the schema are not maintained. In other words, all views are derived from the global schema. Thus, the user has no means to trace the evolutionary history of the schema.

Some models use class versioning to handle schema changes [17, 18, 19], in which a new class version is created when changes are made to an existing version of a class. All versions of the class form a version hierarchy, that is, a tree structure. In general, the database schema consists of more than one class in the form of a set of class inheritance hierarchies. Thus, a configuration mechanism of existing class versions is needed. One proposed configuration method is to use a logical container such as that in [20]. However, at the schema level, the containers of class versions that represent schema versions are related only with derivation links. The merging of schema versions is not supported.

More recently, progress on temporal object-oriented databases has brought a new approach to schema versioning in which each schema version is assigned a timestamp corresponding to its valid and/or transaction time [21, 22, 23]. However, due to the linear nature of time, temporal models allow only one version at one point of time in a given dimension, while multiple current versions as alternatives are required in applications such as CAD.

5 Conclusions and Future Work

We have proposed a nested matrix model for schema versioning in object-oriented databases and develop a prototype implementation. The model consists of a structure of schema versions and a set of rules. The structure, defined in a formal way, is a DAG extended to accommodate version matrices: the nodes represent schema versions; the labeled edges indicate the relationship types between schema versions; and the matrices organize related schema versions in a meaningful way. The rules are used to guarantee consistency of schema versions. The advantages of the model include its increased modeling capabilities that provide a richer set of relationships (i.e., derivation, component, merging, alternative, selection, rejection) between schema versions than existing models and a logical representation of the versioned schema that can be decomposed into different levels. Unlike many models in the literature, this model is validated with a prototype implementation. A distinct feature of the implementation is the development of a graphic querying facility, which enables a casual user to access schema versions with ease.

The concepts of the model may be extended to accommodate object versioning. Thus, the system is able to provide both schema versioning and object versioning capabilities in a unified way. Another direction of the future work is to design a set of handlers like those in [17] to enable programs that are written for a schema version to access objects created under other schema versions.

References

1. Ketabchi, M.: Object-oriented data models and management of CAD databases. In: Proceedings of the 1986 international workshop on object-oriented database systems. Pacific Grove, California, United States (1986) 223-224
2. Hong, B., Lee, S.: CAD Data management using object-oriented paradigms. In: Proceedings of the first international conference on industrial and engineering applications of artificial intelligence and expert systems. Volume 2. Tullahoma, Tennessee, United States (1988) 1044-048
3. Peters, R., et al.: An axiomatic model of dynamic schema evolution in objectbase systems. In: ACM Transactions on Database Systems. 22(1) (1997) 75–114
4. Roddick, J.: A survey of schema versioning issues for database systems. Information and Software Technology, Volume 37, Issue 7 (1995) 383-393.
5. Katz, R.: Toward a unified framework for version modeling in engineering databases. In: ACM Computing Surveys. Volume 22 , Issue 4 (1990) 375-409
6. Dittrich, K., R. Lorie, R.: Version support for engineering database system. IBM Research Report: RJ4769. California, USA (1985)
7. Katz, R., et al.: Version modeling concepts for computer-aided design databases. In: Proceedings of the 1986 ACM SIGMOD international conference on management of data. Washington, D.C., USA (1986) 379-386
8. Banerjee, J., et al.: Semantics and implementation of schema evolution in object-oriented databases. In: ACM SIGMOD Record, Vol. 16, Issue 3 (1987) 311-322.
9. Kim, W., Chou, T.: Versions of schema for object-oriented databases. In: Proceedings of the 14th VLDB Conference. Los Angeles, USA (1988)
10. Biliris, A.: Database support for evolving design objects. In: Proceedings of the 26th ACM conference on design automation. Las Vegas, USA (1989) 258-263
11. Cheval, J.: A version model for object-oriented databases. In: Proceedings of the 8th British national conference on databases. York, UK (1990)
12. Oussalah, C., Urtado, C.: Complex object versioning. In: Proceedings of the 9th conference on advanced information systems engineering. Barcelona, Spain (1997) 259-272
13. Lautemann, S.: Schema versions in object-oriented systems. In: Proceedings of the 5th international conference on database systems for advanced applications. Melbourne, Australia (1997)
14. Santos, C., et al.: Virtual Schemas and Bases. In: Proceedings of the 4th international conference on extending database technology. Cambridge (1994) 81-94

15. Bertino, E., Guerrini, G.: Viewpoints in object database systems. In: Proceedings of the second international software architecture workshop. San Francisco, USA (1996) 289-293
16. Jones, M., Rundensteiner, E.: View materialization techniques for complex hierarchical objects. in: Proceedings of the sixth international conference on Information and knowledge management. Las Vegas, USA (1997) 222-229
17. Monk, S., Sommerville, I.: A model for versioning of classes in object-oriented databases. In: Proceedings of the 10th British national conference on databases. Aberdeen, UK (1992) 42-58
18. Li, X., Tari, Z.: Class versioning for the schema evolution. Internet: http://citeseer. ist.psu.edu/360381.html (1998)
19. Nacer, M., Estublier, J.: Schema evolution in software engineering databases: a new approach in Adele environment. In: Computers and Artificial Intelligence, Volume 19 (2000)
20. Gancarski, S., Jomier, G.: A framework for programming multiversion databases. In: Data & Knowledge Engineering, Volume 36 (2001) 29-53.
21. Iqbal, A., et al.: A temporal approach to managing schema evolution in object database systems. In: Data & Knowledge Engineering, 28(1) (1998) 73-105
22. Rodríguez, L., et al.: TVOO: A temporal versioned object-oriented data model. In: Information Science, Volume 114, No. 1-4 (1999) 281-300
23. Grandi, F., et al.: A formal model for temporal schema versioning in object-oriented databases. In: Data & Knowledge Engineering, 46(2) (2003) 123-167

Efficient Integrity Checking
for Databases with Recursive Views

Davide Martinenghi and Henning Christiansen

Roskilde University, Computer Science Dept.,
P.O.Box 260, DK-4000 Roskilde, Denmark
{dm, henning}@ruc.dk

Abstract. Efficient and incremental maintenance of integrity constraints involving recursive views is a difficult issue that has received some attention in the past years, but for which no widely accepted solution exists yet. In this paper a technique is proposed for compiling such integrity constraints into incremental and optimized tests specialized for given update patterns. These tests may involve the introduction of new views, but for relevant cases of recursion, simplified integrity constraints are obtained that can be checked more efficiently than the original ones and without auxiliary views. Notably, these simplified tests are derived at design time and can be executed before the particular database update is made and without simulating the updated state. In this way all overhead due to optimization or execution of compensative actions at run time is avoided. It is argued that, in the recursive case, earlier approaches have not achieved comparable optimization with the same level of generality.

1 Introduction

Recursive views are generally regarded as a welcome extension to relational databases, as they allow a large class of query problems to be formulated within a declarative query language. To this end, we can mention flexible query answering based on taxonomies stored in the database, and various kinds of path-finding problems, such as network routing and travel planning. The introduction of recursion (since 1999 in the SQL standard [13] as *stratified linear* recursion based on fixpoint semantics) naturally raises a need for a satisfactory treatment of recursion in integrity constraints (ICs) which, in real-world applications, usually include complex data dependencies and "business logic". In this respect, database management systems should provide means to automatically verify, in an efficient way, that database updates do not introduce any violation of integrity. Maintaining compliance of data with respect to ICs is a crucial database issue, as, if data consistency is not guaranteed, then query answers cannot be trusted.

ICs are properties that must hold throughout the existence of a database for it to represent a meaningful set of data. While a complete check of integrity is prohibitive in any realistic case, it gives good sense to search for incremental

J. Eder et al. (Eds.): ADBIS 2005, LNCS 3631, pp. 109–124, 2005.

strategies checking only the consequences of a database update, based on the hypothesis that the database was consistent before the update itself. This principle, called simplification, has been studied at least since [24], both for relational and deductive databases. The majority of existing methods either disregard recursion completely or disallow recursively defined relations to occur in ICs. Earlier approaches to simplification produce constraints that need to be checked in the updated database. We emphasize, however, that it is possible to decide, in the current state, whether a proposed update will introduce inconsistency (i.e., if it were executed). The framework we propose can handle a very general class of updates specified with a rule-based language that allows one to express parametric update patterns. Such patterns are used on the ICs at design time, when only the schema exists and not yet any database state, in order to generate simplified parametric constraints. Later, at runtime, the parametric constraints are instantiated with the specific update values and tested in the actual state.

The main contributions of this paper are as follows. *(i)* We formalize the general problem of finding simplified, incremental integrity checks for databases with recursive views, based on our previous contribution for the non-recursive case [6]. *(ii)* We develop a terminating procedure, based on the identification of specific recursive patterns, that generates efficient simplified tests that are necessary and sufficient conditions for integrity of the updated database. The method allows more general updates and provides finer results than previous approaches. The procedure takes in input a parametric update pattern and a set of ICs and produces, as output, a set of optimized ICs.

The paper is organized as follows. The simplification framework is shown in section 2 and refined for recursion in section 3; its ability to handle recursive cases is demonstrated through a series of examples in section 4. A detailed comparison of methods that handle recursion is given in section 5, followed by experimental evaluation in section 6. Concluding remarks are provided in section 7.

2   A Framework for Simplification of Integrity Constraints

2.1   Basic Notions

For simplicity, we apply notation and concepts from deductive databases, more specifically Datalog programs with stratified negation [10], but we stress that our results are also applicable in a relational setting, since translation techniques from Datalog to SQL are available [7]. In particular, we assume familiarity with the notions of *predicates* $(p, q, \ldots)$, *constants* $(a, b, \ldots)$, *variables* $(x, y, \ldots)$, function-free *terms*, *atoms*, *literals*, *logical formulas*, *substitutions*, *renaming*, *instances* of formulas and *subsumption*. Sequences of terms are indicated by vector notation, e.g., $\vec{t}$. Substitutions are written as $\{\vec{x}/\vec{t}\}$ in order to indicate which variables are mapped to which terms. A *clause* is a formula $A \leftarrow L_1 \wedge \cdots \wedge L_n$ where A is an atom and $L_1, \ldots, L_n$ are literals and with the usual understanding of variables being implicitly universally quantified; A is called the *head* and $L_1 \wedge \cdots \wedge L_n$ the *body* of the clause. If the head is missing (understood as *false*) the clause is called a *denial*; if the body is missing (understood as *true*) it is a *fact*; all other clauses are called *rules*. Clauses are assumed to be *range restricted*, i.e., all clause variables must occur in a positive database literal in the body.

As stressed in the introduction, ICs need to be specialized for update patterns rather than for specific updates. In order to integrate this in our framework, a special category of symbols called *parameters* is introduced. Parameters are written in boldface ($\mathbf{a}, \mathbf{b}, \ldots$) and can appear anywhere in a formula where a constant is expected. Parameters behave like variables that are universally quantified at a metalevel; they are not expected to be part of any actual database nor of any query or update actually given to a database, but we may have parametric expressions of these categories.

Unique name axioms are assumed for (non-parametric) constants, i.e., distinct constants denote distinct values. A *parameter substitution* is a mapping from parameters to constants. Whenever E is an expression containing parameters $\vec{\mathbf{a}}$, and π is a parameter substitution of the form $\{\vec{\mathbf{a}}/\vec{c}\}$, $E\pi$ denotes the expression that arises from E when each occurrence of a parameter is replaced by its value specified by π; $E\pi$ is called a *parametric instance* of E.

Definition 1 (Database). *A (database) schema consists of disjoint sets of* extensional *and* intensional *predicates (collectively called* database predicates*) and a pair* $\langle IDB, IC \rangle$*, where IDB is a finite set of range restricted rules defining intensional predicates and IC a finite set of denials called a* constraint theory*. A database with schema* $\langle IDB, IC \rangle$ *is a triple* $\langle IDB, IC, EDB \rangle$*, where EDB is a finite set of facts of extensional predicates.*

When the schema is understood, the database may be identified with *EDB*. By virtue of the one-to-one correspondence between these logical notions and relational databases, we will use interchangeably the notions of intensional predicate and *view*, extensional predicate and *relation*, fact and *tuple*.

Definition 2 (Recursion). *For two predicates p and q, p derives q (written $p \hookrightarrow q$) if p occurs in the body of a rule whose head predicate is q. Let $\hookrightarrow^+$ be the transitive closure of $\hookrightarrow$. A predicate p is recursive iff $p \hookrightarrow^+ p$.*

As in [4], we can limit our attention to bilinear systems (those whose rules have at most two predicates mutually recursive with the head predicate), as any stratified program can be rewritten as an equivalent bilinear program. We only focus on *stratified* databases [1], that do not allow mixing negation and recursion. We refer to the semantics of the *standard model*, and write $D \models \phi$, where D is a (stratified) database and ϕ is a closed formula, to indicate that ϕ holds in D's standard model. The notation $A \models B$ is extended to parametric expressions with the meaning that it holds for all its parametric instances; similarly for $\equiv$ and "iff". We view satisfaction of ICs *by entailment* [10].

Definition 3. *A database $D = \langle IDB, IC, EDB \rangle$ is consistent whenever $D \models IC$.*

Definition 4 (Defining formula). *Given an IDB and an intensional predicate p defined in it by the rules $\{p(\vec{t}_1) \leftarrow F_1, \ldots, p(\vec{t}_n) \leftarrow F_n\}$, where the $\vec{t}_i$'s are sequences of terms and the F_i's are conjunctions of literals, the* defining formula of p is $(F_1 \wedge \vec{x} = \vec{t}_1)\rho_1 \vee \ldots \vee (F_n \wedge \vec{x} = \vec{t}_n)\rho_n$, where $\vec{x}$ is a sequence of new distinct variables and each ρ_i is a renaming giving fresh new names to the variables of F_i not in $\vec{x}$. The variables in $\vec{x}$ are the distinguished variables of the defining formula; all other variables in it are the non-distinguished variables.

Example 1. Let D be a database representing an acyclic directed graph and let S be its schema $\langle IDB, \Gamma \rangle$, where

$$IDB = \{\, p(x, y) \leftarrow e(x, y),$$
$$p(x, y) \leftarrow e(x, z) \wedge p(z, y)\}.$$

and $\Gamma = \{\leftarrow p(x, x)\}$. Direct connection of nodes is stored in relation $e/2$. Directed paths are expressed by $p/2$. Acyclicity of the graph is imposed by Γ. The defining formula of p is $e(x, y) \vee (e(x, z) \wedge p(z, y))$, where x, y are distinguished variables and z is a non-distinguished variable.

For convenience, we include *queries* in intensional predicates; when no ambiguity arises, a given query may be indicated by means of its defining formula.

Definition 5 (Update). *A* predicate update *for an extensional predicate p is an expression of the form $p(\vec{x}) \Leftarrow p'(\vec{x})$ where $\Leftarrow p'(\vec{x})$ is a query; p is said to be* affected *by the update. A (database)* update *is a set of predicate updates for distinct predicates. For a given database D and an update U, the updated database D^U is as D, but for every extensional predicate p affected by a predicate update $p(\vec{x}) \Leftarrow p'(\vec{x})$ in U, the subset $\{p(\vec{t}) \mid D \models p(\vec{t})\}$ of EDB is replaced by the set $\{p(\vec{t}) \mid D \models p'(\vec{t})\}$.*

This definition subsumes others that separately specify the added and deleted parts of a predicate. As mentioned, updates can be parametric as input to the transformations to follow.

Example 2. Update $U_1 = \{p(x) \Leftarrow p(x) \vee x = a\}$ describes the addition of fact $p(a)$, whereas $U_2 = \{r(x, y) \Leftarrow (r(x, y) \wedge x \neq \mathbf{a}) \vee (r(\mathbf{a}, y) \wedge x = \mathbf{b})\}$ is parametric and means "change any $r(\mathbf{a}, x)$ into $r(\mathbf{b}, x)$". If $\mathbf{a}$ and $\mathbf{b}$ are instantiated to the same constant, U_2 is immaterial.

In order to simplify the notation for tuple additions and deletions, we write in the following $p(\vec{\mathbf{a}})$ as a shorthand for $p(\vec{x}) \Leftarrow p(\vec{x}) \vee \vec{x} = \vec{\mathbf{a}}$ and $\neg p(\vec{\mathbf{a}})$ for $p(\vec{x}) \Leftarrow p(\vec{x}) \wedge \vec{x} \neq \vec{\mathbf{a}}$.

2.2   Weakest Preconditions

In order to capture the effect of an update U on a constraint theory Γ we introduce the After operator below, which returns a formula that evaluates, in the present state, in the same way as Γ would evaluate in the updated state. In order to make the definition precise, we need to make use of *unfolding* to repeatedly replace every non-recursive intensional predicate by its defining formula until only extensional or recursive predicates appear in the constraint theory.

Definition 6 (Unfolding). *Let Γ be a formula and IDB a set of rules defining predicates $p_1, \ldots, p_n$. Let $F_i(\vec{x}_i, \vec{y}_i)$ be the defining formula of p_i in IDB, where $\vec{x}_i$ are the distinguished and $\vec{y}_i$ the non-distinguished variables. Unfold$_{IDB}(\Gamma)$ is the formula obtained by replacing as long as possible, in Γ, each occurrence of an atom of the form $p_i(\vec{t})$ by $(\exists \vec{y}_i F_i(\vec{t}, \vec{y}_i))$, for each non-recursive predicate p_i defined in IDB.*

Definition 7. *Let U be an update, IDB a set of rules of a schema S and Γ a constraint theory.*

- *Let us indicate with Γ^U a copy of Γ in which any atom $p(\vec{t})$ whose predicate is affected by a predicate update $p(\vec{x}) \Leftarrow p^U(\vec{x})$ in U is simultaneously replaced by the expression $p^U(\vec{t})$ and every intensional predicate q is replaced by a new predicate q^U.*
- *Similarly, let us indicate with IDB^U a copy of IDB in which the same replacements are simultaneously made.*

We define After$_S^U(\Gamma) = $ Unfold$_{IDB \cup IDB^U}(\Gamma^U)$.

Without including details, it may be assumed that After performs standard rewriting in order to have the resulting formula in denial form. The subscript S is always omitted when clear from the context[1].

Example 3. Consider the updates of example 2. Let Γ_1 be $\{\leftarrow p(x) \wedge q(x)\}$ (p and q are mutually exclusive). We have, then:

$$\text{After}^{U_1}(\Gamma_1) = \{ \leftarrow p(x) \wedge q(x),$$
$$\leftarrow q(a) \quad\quad \}.$$

For $\Gamma_2 = \{\leftarrow r(c, x) \wedge q(x)\}$, we have:

$$\text{After}^{U_2}(\Gamma_2) = \{ \leftarrow r(c, x) \wedge c \neq \mathbf{a} \wedge q(x),$$
$$\leftarrow r(\mathbf{a}, x) \wedge c = \mathbf{b} \wedge q(x) \}.$$

Note that these (non)equalities cannot be evaluated; if both parameters are instantiated to the same constant, the result collapses to Γ_2 (the update is neutral).

The characteristic property of the After transformation is captured by the notion of weakest precondition, i.e., a test that can be checked in the present state but indicating properties of the new state.

Definition 8 (Weakest precondition). *Let Γ and Γ' be constraint theories referring to the same schema S, and U an update. Then Γ' is a weakest precondition (WP) of Γ wrt U whenever $D \models \Gamma'$ iff $D^U \models \Gamma$ for any database state D with schema S.*

---

[1] Note, however, that, in the body of the resulting formula, some of the conjuncts might be expressions of the form $\neg \exists \vec{x}[\ldots]$, with nested levels of existentially quantified variables. Although the framework can be adapted to these cases, for reasons of space we will focus on standard denials.

Proposition 1. *For any constraint theory Γ and update U, $\text{After}^U(\Gamma)$ is a WP of Γ wrt U; for any other Ψ which is a WP of Γ wrt U, we have $\Psi \equiv \text{After}^U(\Gamma)$.*

To simplify means then to optimize a WP based on the invariant that the constraint theory holds in the present state.

Definition 9 (Conditional WP). *Let Γ and Γ' be constraint theories referring to the same schema S, and U an update. Then Γ' is a conditional weakest precondition (CWP) of Γ wrt U whenever $D \models \Gamma'$ iff $D^U \models \Gamma$ for any database state D consistent with Γ.*

A WP is also a CWP but not necessarily the other way round. For instance, $\{\leftarrow q(a)\}$ is a CWP (but not a WP) of Γ_1 wrt U_1 of example 3.

2.3   Optimizing Transformations on Integrity Constraints

An essential step in the simplification process is the achievement of constraints that are easier to evaluate than the original ICs. Several measures of the evaluation cost exist: the checking space [26] (the tuples to be accessed in order to evaluate the constraint), the "weakness" of the constraint theory [26], the number of literals in it [5], its level of instantiation [7]. However, all these criteria are only estimates of the effort that is needed to evaluate an IC, as the actual execution time will also depend on the database state as well as on the physical data structure. Furthermore, due to theoretical limitations, no procedure can produce an optimal constraint theory in all cases (for any of the above measures).

In order to remove as many unnecessary checks as possible from After's output, such as redundant denials and sub-formulas, we define a transformation Optimize that simplifies a given constraint theory using a set of trusted hypotheses. Typically, the input to Optimize is After's output theory and the hypotheses are After's input theory. Optimize applies sound and terminating rewrite rules to remove from the input theory all denials and literals that can be proved redundant. *Reduction* [11] is used to eliminate redundancies within a single denial.

Definition 10 (Reduction). *For a denial ϕ, the reduction ϕ^- of ϕ is the result of applying on ϕ the following rules as long as possible, where c_1, c_2 are distinct constants, $\mathbf{a}$ is a parameter, t a term, A an atom, C, D (possibly empty) conjunctions of literals, vars indicates the set of variables occurring in its argument and dom the set of variables in a substitution domain.*

$$
\begin{aligned}
&\leftarrow c_1 = c_2 \wedge C &&\Rightarrow & &true \\
&\leftarrow c_1 \neq c_2 \wedge C &&\Rightarrow & &\leftarrow C \\
&\leftarrow t \neq t \wedge C &&\Rightarrow & &true \\
&\leftarrow t = t \wedge C &&\Rightarrow & &\leftarrow C \\
&\leftarrow x = t \wedge C &&\Rightarrow & &\leftarrow C\{x/t\} \\
&\leftarrow x \neq t \wedge C &&\Rightarrow & &\leftarrow C \ \textit{if } \{x,t\} \cap \text{vars}(C) = \emptyset \textit{ and } t \textit{ is not } x \\
&\leftarrow \mathbf{a} = c_2 \wedge C &&\Rightarrow & &\leftarrow \mathbf{a} = c_2 \wedge C\{\mathbf{a}/c_2\}^2 \\
&\leftarrow A \wedge \neg A \wedge C &&\Rightarrow & &true \\
&\leftarrow C \wedge D &&\Rightarrow & &\leftarrow D \ \textit{if } \exists \sigma \textit{ s.t. } C\sigma \textit{ subclause of } D \textit{ and } \text{dom}(\sigma) \cap \text{vars}(D) = \emptyset
\end{aligned}
$$

---

[2] We assume that each equality is only processed once.

Obviously, for any denial ϕ we have $\phi^- \equiv \phi$. The last rule (*subsumption factoring* [9]) includes the elimination of duplicate literals. The *expansion* [10] of a clause, indicated with a "+" superscript, replaces every constant in a database predicate (or variable already occurring elsewhere in database predicates) by a new variable, and equals it to the replacing item.

Example 4. Let $\phi = \leftarrow p(x, a, x)$. Then $\phi^+ = \leftarrow p(x, y, z) \wedge y = a \wedge z = x$.

For some classes of constraints, such as sets of Horn clauses[3], a resolution-based procedure limiting the size of resolvents to the size of the biggest denial is known to be refutation-complete[4], i.e., it derives *false* iff the set is unsatisfiable. We refer to [27] for the resolution principle and other related notions.

Definition 11. *For a constraint theory Γ, the notation $\Gamma \vdash_R \phi$ indicates that there is a resolution derivation of a denial ψ from Γ^+ such that in each resolution step the resolvent has at most n literals and ψ^- subsumes ϕ, where n is the number of literals of the largest denial in Γ^+.*

The boundedness we have imposed guarantees termination, as Γ is function-free.

Proposition 2. $\vdash_R$ *is sound and terminates on any input.*

Definition 12. *Given two constraint theories Δ and Γ, $\mathsf{Optimize}_\Delta(\Gamma)$ is the result of applying the following rewrite rules on Γ as long as possible; ϕ, ψ are denials, Γ' is a constraint theory, $\sqcup$ is disjoint union.*

$$
\begin{aligned}
\{\phi\} \sqcup \Gamma' &\Rightarrow \Gamma' \text{ if } \phi^- = true \\
\{\phi\} \sqcup \Gamma' &\Rightarrow \Gamma' \text{ if } (\Gamma' \cup \Delta) \vdash_R \phi \\
\{\phi\} \sqcup \Gamma' &\Rightarrow \{\phi^-\} \cup \Gamma' \text{ if } \phi \neq \phi^- \\
\{\phi\} \sqcup \Gamma' &\Rightarrow \{\psi^-\} \cup \Gamma' \text{ if } (\{\phi\} \sqcup \Gamma' \cup \Delta) \vdash_R \psi \text{ and } \psi^- \text{ strictly subsumes } \phi
\end{aligned}
$$

The last rewrite rule allows the removal of literals from a denial; the other rules are self-explanatory.

Proposition 3 (Correctness of $\mathsf{Optimize}$). $\mathsf{Optimize}_\Delta(\Gamma)$ *terminates for any Γ, Δ and $D \models \Gamma$ iff $D \models \mathsf{Optimize}_\Delta(\Gamma)$ in any database D consistent with Δ.*

Definition 13. *For a schema $S = \langle IDB, \Gamma \rangle$ and an update U, let $\Delta = \mathsf{Unfold}_{IDB}(\Gamma)$. We define $\mathsf{Simp}_S^U(\Gamma) = \mathsf{Optimize}_\Delta(\mathsf{After}_S^U(\Gamma))$.*

¿From the previous results we get immediately the following.

Proposition 4. *Let $S = \langle IDB, \Gamma \rangle$ be a schema and U an update. Then $\mathsf{Simp}_S^U(\Gamma)$ is a CWP of Γ wrt U.*

Example 5. With Γ_1 and U_1 from example 2, we have $\mathsf{Simp}^{U_1}(\Gamma_1) = \{\leftarrow q(a)\}$.

---

[3] Here denials with at most one negative literal.
[4] With *factoring, paramodulation* for inequalities and the *reflexivity* axiom [16].

Each step in Optimize reduces the number of literals or instantiates them. Simp is indeed guaranteed to reach a minimal result (by the *subsumption theorem* [25]) for all constraint classes for which $\vdash_R$ is refutation complete[5]. The high complexity of Simp (subsumption alone is in general NP-complete [15]) does not affect the quality of the approach, as simplification takes place at design time (runtime simplification could indeed outweigh the optimization gained), which is justified by the following property.

Proposition 5. *Let Γ be a constraint theory, U an update, and π a parametric substitution. Then* $(\mathsf{Simp}^U(\Gamma))\pi \equiv \mathsf{Simp}^{U\pi}(\Gamma\pi)$.

The present technique is based on an a priori knowledge of the update patterns allowed by a database designer. However, if such patterns are not given in advance, the method is still applicable. We may, e.g., generate all simplifications corresponding to single additions or deletions of any database relation and, thus, obtain optimized behavior for these cases.

3   Refinements for Ordered Linear Recursion

In Simp, recursive predicates in ICs are replaced by new recursive predicates. For an important class of linear recursion that embraces some of the most commonly used recursive patterns (such as left- and right-linear recursion [23]), known as *ordered linear recursion* (OLR) [29], the simplification process can be refined, by possibly eliminating the introduction of new recursive views.

Definition 14. *A predicate r is an OLR predicate if it is defined as follows*

$$\{ \; r(\vec{x}, \vec{y}) \leftarrow q(\vec{x}, \vec{y}) \\ r(\vec{x}, \vec{y}) \leftarrow p(\vec{x}, \vec{z}) \wedge r(\vec{z}, \vec{y}) \; \}, \tag{1}$$

where p and q are predicates on which r does not depend and $\vec{x}, \vec{y}, \vec{z}$ are disjoint sequences of distinct variables. The first rule is the exit rule, *while the other is the* recursive rule.

There may in principle be several exit rules and recursive rules for the same OLR predicate r; however, these can always be reduced to one single exit rule and recursive rule by introducing suitable new views. Note thus that p and q need not be base predicates.

We first transform the definition of r as to decompose it in two parts: a nonrecursive definition and a transitive closure definition (r_p below). If p and q are the same predicate, then no transformation is needed, as the definition of r is already the transitive closure of p. Otherwise we replace r's definition with the following, equivalent set of rules:

$$\{ \; r(\vec{x}, \vec{y}) \leftarrow q(\vec{x}, \vec{y}) \\ r(\vec{x}, \vec{y}) \leftarrow r_p(\vec{x}, \vec{z}) \wedge q(\vec{z}, \vec{y}) \\ r_p(\vec{x}, \vec{y}) \leftarrow p(\vec{x}, \vec{y}) \\ r_p(\vec{x}, \vec{y}) \leftarrow p(\vec{x}, \vec{z}) \wedge r_p(\vec{z}, \vec{y}) \; \}. \tag{2}$$

---

[5] Outside these classes, there are (practically unlikely) cases where the simplification may contain some redundancies.

Note that the argument is perfectly symmetric when r's recursive rule is of the form $r(\vec{x}, \vec{y}) \leftarrow r(\vec{x}, \vec{z}) \wedge p(\vec{z}, \vec{y})$. In this case the second rule in (2) becomes $r(\vec{x}, \vec{y}) \leftarrow q(\vec{x}, \vec{z}) \wedge r_p(\vec{z}, \vec{y})$ and r_p is defined as before.

All occurrences of r in a constraint theory can now be unfolded wrt the first two rules in (2), which introduce q and r_p, the latter being the transitive closure of p. Intuitively, it is easy to characterize the set of tuples that are added to r_p upon addition of a p-tuple, as r_p can be thought of as a representation of paths of a directed graph of p-edges. Suppose that update U is the addition of tuple $\langle \vec{a}, \vec{b} \rangle$ to p, then all added r_p paths are those that pass by the new p-arc and that were not there before the update. If $\delta_U^+ r_p(\vec{x}, \vec{y})$ indicates that there is a new path from $\vec{x}$ to $\vec{y}$ after update U, this can be expressed as:

$$\delta_U^+ r_p(\vec{x}, \vec{y}) \leftarrow (r_p(\vec{x}, \vec{a}) \vee \vec{x} = \vec{a})) \wedge (r_p(\vec{b}, \vec{y}) \vee \vec{y} = \vec{b})) \wedge \neg r_p(\vec{x}, \vec{y}),$$

However, U is not necessarily a single tuple update, so $\delta_U^+ r_p$ needs, in general, to be characterized in terms of r_p in the updated state.

Definition 15. *Let U be an update and r_p the transitive closure of non-recursive predicate p in schema $S = \langle IDB, \Gamma \rangle$; let r_p^U, p^U, IDB^U be defined as to obtain* $\text{After}_S^U(\Gamma)$ *in definition 7. Let $OLR(r_p, S)$ be the following set of rules:*

$$\{r_p^U(\vec{x}, \vec{y}) \leftarrow (r_p(\vec{x}, \vec{y}) \wedge \neg \delta_U^- r_p^U(\vec{x}, \vec{y})) \vee \delta_U^+ r_p^U(\vec{x}, \vec{y}),$$
$$\delta_U^+ r_p(\vec{x}, \vec{y}) \leftarrow (r_p^U(\vec{x}, \vec{w}_1) \vee \vec{x} = \vec{w}_1) \wedge (r_p^U(\vec{w}_2, \vec{y}) \vee \vec{y} = \vec{w}_2) \wedge$$
$$\delta_U^+ p(\vec{w}_1, \vec{w}_2) \wedge \neg r_p(\vec{x}, \vec{y}),$$
$$\delta_U^- r_p(\vec{x}, \vec{y}) \leftarrow (r_p(\vec{x}, \vec{w}_1) \vee \vec{x} = \vec{w}_1) \wedge (r_p(\vec{w}_2, \vec{y}) \vee \vec{y} = \vec{w}_2) \wedge$$
$$\delta_U^- p(\vec{w}_1, \vec{w}_2) \wedge \neg r_p^U(\vec{x}, \vec{y}),$$
$$\delta_U^+ p(\vec{x}) \leftarrow p^U(\vec{x}) \wedge \neg p(\vec{x}),$$
$$\delta_U^- p(\vec{x}) \leftarrow \neg p^U(\vec{x}) \wedge p(\vec{x})\}$$

If, in $OLR(r_p, S)$, $\delta_U^+ p(\vec{w}_1, \vec{w}_2) \equiv \vec{w}_1 = \vec{c}_1 \wedge \vec{w}_2 = \vec{c}_2 \wedge A$, where A is a conjunction of literals and c_1, c_2 are constants, then the second rule is replaced by

$$\delta_U^+ r_p(\vec{x}, \vec{y}) \leftarrow (r_p(\vec{x}, \vec{c}_1) \vee \vec{x} = \vec{c}_1) \wedge (r_p(\vec{c}_2, \vec{y}) \vee \vec{y} = \vec{c}_2) \wedge \tag{3}$$
$$\vec{w}_1 = \vec{c}_1 \wedge \vec{w}_2 = \vec{c}_2 \wedge A \wedge \neg r_p(\vec{x}, \vec{y}).$$

The notation $OLR(S)$ indicates the rules obtained from $IDB \cup IDB^U$ by replacing the clauses defining each transitive closure predicate r_p^U with $OLR(r_p^U, S)$.

Definition 16. *Let U be an update, $S = \langle IDB, \Gamma \rangle$ a schema and Γ^U be defined as in definition 7. Let S^* be the same as S but in which, for all OLR predicate r, its definition (1) is replaced as in (2). Then $\text{AfterRec}_S^U(\Gamma)$ is defined as $\text{Unfold}_{OLR(S^*)}(\Gamma^U)$.*

Proposition 6. *For any constraint theory Γ and update U, $\text{AfterRec}_S^U(\Gamma)$ is a WP of Γ wrt U.*

OptimizeRec is as Optimize, but for any transitive closure predicate r_p, it also considers that $r_p(\vec{t_1}, \vec{t_2})$ subsumes $r_p(\vec{t_1}, \vec{x}) \wedge r_p(\vec{x}, \vec{t_2})$ if $\vec{x}$ does not occur elsewhere[6]. $\mathsf{SimpRec}_S^U(\Gamma)$ is defined as $\mathsf{OptimizeRec}_\Delta(\mathsf{AfterRec}_S^U(\Gamma))$, where Δ contains $\mathsf{Unfold}_S(\Gamma)$ plus the set of all transitive closure rules in S rewritten as denials, e.g., for a predicate r_p defined as in (2) the constraints are $\leftarrow \neg r_p(\vec{x}, \vec{y}) \wedge p(\vec{x}, \vec{y})$ and $\leftarrow \neg r_p(\vec{x}, \vec{y}) \wedge p(\vec{x}, \vec{z}) \wedge r_p(\vec{z}, \vec{y})$. Proposition 4 extends to $\mathsf{SimpRec}$.

The characterization of $\delta_U^- r_p$ given in proposition 6 requires the evaluation of $\neg r_p^U$. However, in many interesting cases $\delta_U^- r_p$ is going to be simplified away. The new views introduced by $\mathsf{AfterRec}$ can be completely disregarded if r_p^U does not occur in the simplified constraints. If both the new and the old state are available, as in some trigger implementations, r_p^U can be evaluated as "r_p in the new state". However, these are precisely the cases where the simplification was, to some extent, unsuccessful, as accessing or simulating the new state clearly requires extra work.

4   Examples

We first observe that many important problems can be reduced to OLR.

Example 6. In [22] the following recursive predicate b is described:

$$\{\, b(x,y) \leftarrow k(x,z) \wedge b(z,y) \wedge c(y),$$
$$b(x,y) \leftarrow d(x,y) \qquad\qquad \},$$

where b stands for "buys", k for "knows", c for "cheap" and d for "definitely buys". These definitions can be rewritten [14] as:

$$\{\, b'(x,y) \leftarrow k(x,z) \wedge b'(z,y),$$
$$b'(x,y) \leftarrow k(x,z) \wedge d(z,y) \wedge c(y),$$
$$b(x,y) \leftarrow b'(x,y),$$
$$b(x,y) \leftarrow d(x,y) \qquad\qquad\qquad \}.$$

Replacing the body of b''s exit rule with a new view e, makes b' OLR:

$$\{\, b'(x,y) \leftarrow k(x,z) \wedge b'(z,y),$$
$$b'(x,y) \leftarrow e(x,y),$$
$$e(x,y) \leftarrow k(x,z) \wedge d(z,y) \wedge c(y),$$
$$b(x,y) \leftarrow b'(x,y),$$
$$b(x,y) \leftarrow d(x,y) \qquad\qquad\qquad \}.$$

The next example will be used in section 5 to compare the present work with previous methods.

Example 7. Consider the database from example 1. Let $U = \{e(\mathbf{a}, \mathbf{b})\}$ be an update pattern that adds an arc. We have

$$\mathsf{AfterRec}_S^U(\Gamma) \equiv \{\, \leftarrow (p(x,x) \wedge \neg \delta_U^- p(x,x)) \vee \delta_U^+ p(x,x)\}$$
$$\equiv \{\, \leftarrow p(x,x) \wedge \neg \delta_U^- p(x,x),$$
$$\leftarrow \delta_U^+ p(x,x)\}.$$

---

[6] It also subsumes $p(\vec{t_1}, \vec{x}) \wedge r_p(\vec{x}, \vec{t_2})$ and $r_p(\vec{t_1}, \vec{x}) \wedge p(\vec{x}, \vec{t_2})$.

When OptimizeRec is applied to $\mathsf{AfterRec}_S^U(\Gamma)$, every unfolding of the first constraint is removed (it is subsumed by the original constraint in Γ). Furthermore, $\delta_U^+ e(x, y)$ bounds both x and y, as $\delta_U^+ e(x, y) \equiv \neg e(\mathbf{a}, \mathbf{b}) \wedge x = \mathbf{a} \wedge y = \mathbf{b}$. Therefore we can replace $\delta_U^+ p$ as in (3)

$$\delta_U^+ p(x, y) \equiv (p(x, \mathbf{a}) \vee x = \mathbf{a}) \wedge (p(\mathbf{b}, y) \vee y = \mathbf{b}) \wedge \neg e(\mathbf{a}, \mathbf{b}) \wedge \neg p(x, y),$$

which unfolds in the remaining $\leftarrow \delta_U^+ p(x, x)$ expression as follows:

$$\{ \leftarrow p(x, \mathbf{a}) \wedge p(\mathbf{b}, x) \wedge \neg e(\mathbf{a}, \mathbf{b}) \wedge \neg p(x, x),$$
$$\leftarrow p(\mathbf{b}, \mathbf{a}) \wedge \neg e(\mathbf{a}, \mathbf{b}) \wedge \neg p(\mathbf{b}, \mathbf{b}),$$
$$\leftarrow p(\mathbf{b}, \mathbf{a}) \wedge \neg e(\mathbf{a}, \mathbf{b}) \wedge \neg p(\mathbf{b}, \mathbf{b}),$$
$$\leftarrow \mathbf{a} = \mathbf{b} \wedge \neg e(\mathbf{a}, \mathbf{b}) \wedge \neg p(\mathbf{a}, \mathbf{a}) \qquad \}.$$

The second and third constraints are identical, and therefore either can be removed. The $\neg p(-, -)$ literals are removed in OptimizeRec via resolution with the constraint in Γ. Similarly, the $\neg e(\mathbf{a}, \mathbf{b})$ literals, in all constraints but the first one, can be removed by reduction and resolution via the intermediate $\vdash_R$-derivations of $\leftarrow e(x, x)$ and $\leftarrow e(x, z) \wedge p(z, x)$. Finally, the first IC is removed as $p(\mathbf{b}, \mathbf{a})$ subsumes $p(\mathbf{b}, x) \wedge p(x, \mathbf{a})$.

$$\mathsf{SimpRec}_S^U(\Gamma) = \{ \leftarrow p(\mathbf{b}, \mathbf{a}),$$
$$\leftarrow \mathbf{a} = \mathbf{b} \quad \}.$$

Note that $\mathsf{SimpRec}_S^U(\Gamma)$ is a much simpler test than Γ as it basically requires to check whether there exists a path between two given nodes, whereas Γ implies testing the existence of a cyclic path for all the nodes in the graph.

A straightforward SQL translation of this simplified result (with p defined as a WITH view with columns c1 and c2) is, e.g., the following query

```
SELECT "ko" FROM p WHERE (p.c1=$B AND p.c2=$A) OR $A=$B
```

in which $A and $B are replaced by the corresponding parameter values and an empty answer indicates consistency, whereas ko indicates inconsistency.

Example 8. [6 continued] Consider a schema S defining the *IDB* of example 6 and a scenario in which a given person p does not want to buy cheap products, expressed by $\Gamma = \{\leftarrow b(p, x) \wedge c(x)\}$. Suppose that a person meets another person who is definitely going to buy something. This event can be represented by the update $U = \{k(\mathbf{a}, \mathbf{b}), d(\mathbf{b}, \mathbf{c})\}$. We have [7]:

$$\mathsf{SimpRec}_S^U(\Gamma) = \{ \leftarrow c(\mathbf{c}) \wedge [p = \mathbf{a} \vee p = \mathbf{b} \vee k'(p, \mathbf{a}) \vee k'(p, \mathbf{b})],$$
$$\leftarrow c(x) \wedge [p = \mathbf{a} \vee k'(p, \mathbf{a})] \wedge \{d(\mathbf{b}, x) \vee [k'(\mathbf{b}, z) \wedge d(z, x)]\}\},$$

where k' is the transitive closure of k. The result indicates that U introduces an inconsistency whenever:

- $\mathbf{c}$ is cheap, and p is or (in)directly knows $\mathbf{a}$ or $\mathbf{b}$, or
- p is or (in)directly knows $\mathbf{a}$, and $\mathbf{b}$ definitely buys (or (in)directly knows someone who does) something cheap.

---

[7] For readability, the resulting formula is presented with disjunctions and rearranged via other trivial, cosmetic steps. Calculations are not shown due to space constraints.

5   Related Works

Several authors have provided results directly related to integrity checking. Most methods have been explicitly designed for relational databases with no views or disallow recursion in ICs; we refer to the survey [21] for references falling under these categories. We also point out that integrity checking is often regarded as an instance of materialized view maintenance: ICs are defined as views that must always remain empty for the database to be consistent. The database literature is rich in methods that deal with relational view/integrity maintenance; the book [12] and the survey [8] provide insightful discussion on the subject.

We now compare our approach with the methods that apply to recursive databases and show that our results have wider applicability and are at least as good. We discuss example 7 and use constants a, b instead of parameters $\mathbf{a}$, $\mathbf{b}$ for compatibility with these methods.

The technique described in [19] requires the calculation of two sets, P and N, that represent the positive and, respectively, negative potential updates generated by a given update. A set Θ is then computed, which contains all the mgus of the atoms in P and N with the atoms of corresponding sign in the IC. For example 7, we have $P = \{e(a,b), p(x,y)\}$, $N = \emptyset$ and $\Theta = \{y/x\}$. The updated database is consistent iff every condition $\Gamma\theta$ holds in it, for all $\theta \in \Theta$, Γ being the original constraint theory. Unlike our method, in this case the obtained condition is identical to Γ and therefore there is no simplification.

In [17], the authors determine low-cost pre-tests which are sufficient conditions that guarantee the integrity of the database. If the pre-tests fail, then integrity needs to be checked with an exact method, such as ours. A set of literal/condition pairs, called *relevant set*, is calculated. If the update in question unifies with any of the literals in the relevant set and the attached condition succeeds, then the pre-test fails; otherwise we are sure that the update cannot falsify the ICs. For example 7 the relevant set is $\{p(x,x)/true, e(x,x)/true, e(x,z)/true, p(z,x)/e_N(x,z)\}$ (e_N refers to e in the updated state). The update $e(a,b)$ unifies with $e(x,z)$, whose associated condition trivially succeeds, therefore the pre-test fails and an exact test needs to be executed.

In [18] partial evaluation of a meta-interpreter is used to produce logic programs that correspond to simplified constraints. The partial evaluator is given a meta-interpreter that constitutes a general integrity checker and produces as output a version of the meta-interpreter specialized to specific update patterns to be checked in the updated state (and employing the hypothesis that integrity holds before the update). The method *could* work for recursive databases, if a perfect partial evaluator were at disposal, but a loop check needs to be included in the program to ensure termination. This does not partially evaluate satisfactorily, resulting in an explosion of (possibly unreachable) alternatives.

With the method described in [5], which is based on the notion of *partial subsumption*, database rules are annotated with *residues* to capture the relevant parts that are concerned by the ICs. When doing semantic query optimization, such parts can often allow faster query evaluation times. However, when it comes to integrity checking, the method typically leaves things unchanged in the presence of recursive rules. In example 7 we need to calculate the residue of the constraint in Γ associated with the extensional relation e. The partial subsumption algorithm stops immediately, as no resolution step is possible, thus resulting in no simplification at all.

Seljée's *inconsistency indicators* (IIs) [29] are based on incremental expressions for OLR. We have improved on his method as follows. Firstly, our update language is more general, allowing compound updates and any kind of bulk operation expressible with rules (IIs cannot handle example 8). Secondly, the simplified constraints produced by SimpRec only need to consult the present database state, whereas IIs require, in general, the availability of both the old and the new state, even in the non-recursive case. For the treatment of recursion IIs impose a number of restrictions on the language (no negation, no existentially quantified variables) that we do not need. For example 7 the II, to be checked *after* the update, is $\leftarrow (p(b, x) \vee b = x) \wedge (p(x, a) \vee a = x)$. We evaluate the performance of this result in section 6.

In [3], integrity checking is regarded as an instance of *update propagation*, i.e., the problem of determining the effect of an update on a set of rules. The method extends the database with rules that express the incremental evaluation of the new state and the ICs themselves are defined by rules. A *soft consequence* operator [2] is then used to compute the model of this augmented database. Instead of a symbolic simplification of the original constraints, this method rather provides an efficient way for evaluating the new state. In this respect, it can be seen as orthogonal to ours, at least when our method does not eliminate references to the new state.

6   Experiments

In order to demonstrate the effectiveness of the simplification procedure, we have tested it on random update sets for example 7. Our tests were run on a machine with a 2 GHz processor, 1 GB of RAM and 80 GB of hard disk, using DES 1.1 [28], which is a Datalog system featuring full recursive evaluation and stratified negation. DES is implemented on top of Prolog; we could therefore program our tests in Prolog and simulate insertions by means of `assert` and deletions by `retract`. The DES query engine is optimized with memoization techniques for answering queries based on previous answers. In this context we always pose the same query $\leftarrow p(x, x)$ to check whether the graph is acyclic, and therefore answers can be reused for subsequent queries. Our method greatly improves performance even in the presence of an already optimized system.

Average execution times are indicated in milliseconds (within a time frame of 50 seconds) and the number of attempted insertions of edge facts is indicated on the x-axis. Each figure reports the execution times needed to update the database and check its consistency according to:

- The un-optimized IC (diamonds).
- The II produced by Seljée's method [29] (squares).
- The formula $\leftarrow p(b, a)$ (II*), produced by improving the II manually (crosses).

– The simplification obtained with Simp (triangles). Note that in this case consistency is checked before the update.

The third curve (a "perfect" post-test), although not generated by any known method, was included for comparison with the test-before-update strategy. In particular, in figure 1 we randomly generated 1500 arcs between 1000 different nodes, whereas in figure 2 we only used 50 different nodes. In the former case the formation of cycles is less likely and the times are generally better. In the latter, however, updates are much more likely to be rejected (44% of the updates were rejected in total, while only 12% in the former case); Simp in this case performs significantly better, with improvements around 20% even wrt the manually produced formula. The interpretation of these results is in accordance with the following observations:

– The comparison between the performance of the optimized and un-optimized checks shows that the optimized version is always more efficient than the original one.
– In both the un-optimized and II methods many more paths need to be computed, which is an expensive operation.
– The gain of early detection of inconsistency, which is a distinctive feature of our approach, is unquestionable in the case of illegal updates. In such a case, with our optimized strategy, the simplified constraint immediately reports an integrity violation wrt the proposed update, which is therefore *not* executed. On the other hand, the other methods require to execute the update, perform a consistency test and then roll back the update.

Note that the extra burden due to the execution and subsequent rollback of an illegal update is even more evident for compound updates, such as those of example 8; in these cases the benefits of a pretest wrt a post-test are even greater. We observe that the above comparisons did not take into account the time spent to produce the optimized constraints[8], as these can be generated at schema design time and thus do not interfere with run time performance.

7   Conclusion and Future Work

We have described a simplification framework for integrity checking in databases with recursive views. A general methodology based on the introduction of new recursive views has been described. This allows checking in the state before the update whether the database will be consistent in the updated state. While for recursive problems we cannot guarantee, in general, that the resulting test will be more efficient than the original one, this is indeed the case for the important class of OLR problems, for which differential expressions can be easily derived that indicate the incremental variations of the recursive predicate.

---

[8] All symbolic simplifications in this paper were obtained with an experimental implementation of the simplification procedure [20].

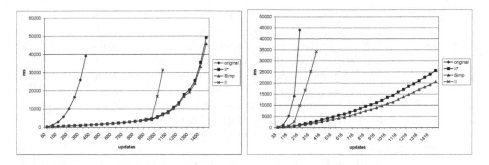

Fig. 1. Sparse data   **Fig. 2.** Dense data

The simplified ICs can be regarded as queries and can therefore make use of all known traditional query optimization methods, including specific techniques for recursive queries evaluation, such as, e.g., magic sets.

There are numerous ways to extend this work. First of all, more cases for which useful differential expressions exist could be identified; regular-chain programs are a likely candidate. The literature is rich in decidable rewriting techniques that reduce recursive problems to easier ones; these could be integrated in the framework.

References

1. Apt, K. R., Blair, H. A., Walker, A.: Towards a theory of declarative knowledge. In Foundations of Deductive Databases and Logic Programming. Morgan Kaufmann (1988) 89–148
2. Behrend, A.: Soft stratification for magic set based query evaluation in deductive databases. In Proceedings of the twenty-second ACM SIGMOD-SIGACT-SIGART symposium on Principles of database systems. ACM Press (2003) 102–110
3. Behrend, A.: Soft Stratification for Transformation-Based Approaches to Deductive Databases. PhD thesis, University of Bonn (2004)
4. Catarci, T., Cruz, I. F.: On expressing stratified datalog. In 2nd ICLP Workshop on Deductive Databases and Logic Programming (1994) 85–100
5. Chakravarthy, U. S., Grant, J., J. Minker, J.: Logic-based approach to semantic query optimization. ACM Transactions on Database Systems (TODS) (1990) 15(2):162–207
6. Christiansen, H., Martinenghi, D.: Simplification of database integrity constraints revisited: A transformational approach. In LOPSTR'03, volume 3018 of LNCS Springer (2004) 178–197
7. Decker, H.: Translating advanced integrity checking technology to sql. In Database integrity: challenges and solutions. Idea Group Publishing (2002) 203–249
8. Dong, G., Su, J.: Incremental Maintenance of Recursive Views Using Relational Calculus/SQL. SIGMOD Record (2000) 29(1):44–51
9. Eisinger, N., Ohlbach, H. J.: Deduction systems based on resolution. In Handbook of Logic in Artificial Intelligence and Logic Programming - Vol 1: Logical Foundations., Clarendon Press, Oxford (1993) 183–271

10. Godfrey, P., Grant, J., Gryz, J., Minker, J.: Integrity constraints: Semantics and applications. In Logics for Databases and Information Systems (1998) 265–306
11. Grant, J., Minker, J.: Integrity constraints in knowledge based systems. In Knowledge Engineering Vol II, Applications. McGraw-Hill (1990) 1–25
12. Gupta, A., and I. S. Mumick, I. S. editors.: Materialized views: techniques, implementations, and applications. MIT Press (1999)
13. INCITS. Information technology - Database languages - SQL - Part 2: Foundation (SQL/Foundation) - INCITS/ISO/IEC 9075-2-1999 (1999)
14. Ioannidis, Y. E., Wong, E.: Towards an algebraic theory of recursion. J. ACM (1991) 38(2):329–381
15. Kapur, D., Narendran, P.: Np-completeness of the set unification and matching problems. In CADE (1986) 489–495
16. Knuth, D., Bendix, P.: Simple word problems in universal algebras. Computational Problems in Abstract Algebras (1970) 263–297
17. Lee, S. Y., Ling, T. W.: Further improvements on integrity constraint checking for stratifiable deductive databases. In VLDB'96, Proceedings of 22th International Conference on Very Large Data Bases, Morgan Kaufmann (1996) 495–505
18. Leuschel, M., de Schreye, D.: Creating specialised integrity checks through partial evaluation of meta-interpreters. JLP (1998) 36(2):149–193
19. Lloyd, J. W., Sonenberg, L., Topor, R. W.: Integrity constraint checking in stratified databases. JLP (1987) 4(4):331–343
20. Martinenghi, D.:   A simplification procedure for integrity constraints. http://www.dat.ruc.dk/ dm/spic/index.html (2004)
21. Mayol, E., Teniente, E.: A survey of current methods for integrity constraint maintenance and view updating. In Advances in Conceptual Modeling: ER '99 Workshops, volume 1727 of LNCS, Springer (1999) 62–73
22. Naughton, J. F.: Minimizing function-free recursive inference rules. J. ACM (1989) 36(1):69–91
23. Naughton, J. F., Ramakrishnan, R., Sagiv, Y., Ullman, J. D.: Efficient evaluation of right-, left-, and mult-lineare rules. In J. Clifford, B. G. Lindsay, and D. Maier, editors, Proceedings of the 1989 ACM SIGMOD International Conference on Management of Data, Portland, Oregon, May 31 - June 2, 1989. ACM Press (1989) 235–242
24. Nicolas, J. M.: Logic for improving integrity checking in relational data bases. Acta Informatica (1982) 18:227–253
25. Nienhuys-Cheng, S. H., de Wolf, R.: The equivalence of the subsumption theorem and the refutation-completeness for unconstrained resolution. In ASIAN (1995) 269–285
26. Qian, X.: An effective method for integrity constraint simplification. In Proceedings of the Fourth International Conference on Data Engineering, IEEE Computer Society (1988) 338–345
27. Robinson, J. A.: A machine-oriented logic based on the resolution principle. J. ACM (1965) 12(1):23–41
28. Sáenz-Pérez, F.:   Datalog educational system v1.1. user's manual. Technical Report 139-04, Faculty of Computer Science, UCM (2004) Available from http://www.fdi.ucm.es/profesor/fernan/DES/.
29. Seljée, R.: A Fact Integrity Constraint Checking System for the Validation of Semantic Integrity Constraints after Updating Consistent Deductive Databases. PhD thesis, Tilburg University (1997)

A Formal Model for the Problem
of View Selection for Aggregate Queries

Jingni Li[1], Zohreh Asgharzadeh Talebi[1],
Rada Chirkova[2,*], and Yahya Fathi[1,**]

[1] Operations Research Program, NC State University, Raleigh, NC 27695
{jli, zasghar, fathi}@ncsu.edu
[2] Computer Science Department, NC State University, Raleigh, NC 27695
chirkova@csc.ncsu.edu

Abstract. We present a formal analysis of the following view-selection
problem: Given a set of queries and a database, return definitions of views
that, when materialized in the database, would reduce the evaluation
costs of the queries. Optimizing the layout of stored data using view
selection has a direct impact on the performance of the entire database
system. At the same time, the optimization problem is intractable, even
under natural restrictions on the types of queries of interest. In this paper
we use an integer-programming model to obtain optimal solutions to the
problem of view selection for aggregate queries on data warehouses. We
also report the results of the post-optimality analysis that we performed
to determine/observe the impact of changing certain input characteristics
on the optimal solution.

1 Introduction

As relational databases and data warehouses keep growing in size, evaluating
many common queries — such as aggregate queries — by database-management
systems (DBMS) may require significant transformations of large volumes of
stored data. As a result, the requirement of good overall performance of frequent
and important user queries necessitates optimal DBMS choices in choosing and
executing query plans. A significant aspect of query performance is the choice
of auxiliary data used in query answering, such as which indexes are used in
a query plan to access a given stored relation. In modern commercial database
systems, another common type of auxiliary data is *materialized views* — relations that were computed by answering certain queries on the (original) stored
data in the database and that can be used to provide, without time-consuming
runtime transformations, "precompiled" information relevant to the user query
in question. We give an example of using materialized views to answer select-
project-join queries with aggregation in a star-schema [21] data warehouse.

---

* This author's work is partially supported by the National Science Foundation under
Grant No. 0321635.
** This author's work on this material has been supported by the National Science
Foundation under Grant No. 0307072.

J. Eder et al. (Eds.): ADBIS 2005, LNCS 3631, pp. 125–138, 2005.

Example 1. Consider a data warehouse with three stored relations:

```
Sales(CID,DateID,QtySold,Discount)
Customer(CID,CustName,Address,City,State)
Time(DateID,Day,Week,Month,Year)
```

Sales is the fact table, and Customer and Time are dimension tables.

Let the query workload of interest have two aggregate queries, Q1 and Q2, expressed here in SQL. Query Q1 asks for the total quantity of products sold per customer in the last quarter of the year 2004. Q2 asks for the total product quantity sold per year for all years after 1999 to customers in North Carolina.

```
Q1: SELECT c.CID, SUM(QtySold)        Q2: SELECT t.Year, SUM(QtySold)
    FROM Sales s, Time t, Customer c       FROM Sales s, Time t, Customer c
    WHERE s.DateID=t.DateID                WHERE s.DateID=t.DateID
    AND s.CID=c.CID AND Year=2004          AND s.CID=c.CID
    AND Month >= 10 AND Month <= 12        AND Year > 1999 AND State = 'NC'
    GROUP BY c.CID;                        GROUP BY t.Year;
```

We can use techniques from [19] to show that the following view V can be used to give exact answers to each of Q1 and Q2.

```
V: SELECT s.CID, Year, Month, State, SUM(QtySold) AS SumQS
   FROM Sales s, Time t, Customer c
   WHERE s.DateID = t.DateID AND s.CID = c.CID
   GROUP BY s.CID, Year, Month, State;
```

That is, suppose the view V is materialized in the data warehouse, which means that the answer to the query V on the database is precomputed and stored as a new relation V[1] alongside Sales, Customer, and Time. Then the answer to each of Q1 and Q2 can be computed by accessing just the data in the materialized view V. For instance, the query Q1 can be evaluated as

```
Q1: SELECT CID, SUM(SumQS) FROM V
    WHERE Year=2004 AND Month >= 10 AND Month <= 12 GROUP BY CID;
```

Note that evaluating Q1 using the view V is likely to be more efficient than evaluating Q1 using its original definition, as using V allows the DBMS to avoid taking an expensive join of Sales, Customer, and Time and also — because V is an aggregate view — may save some time in the grouping/aggregation step.

In this paper we consider the following view-selection problem: Given a set of queries, a database, and a set of constraints on derived data (e.g., a storage limit on the amount of disk space that can be used to store materialized views), return definitions of views that, when materialized in the database, would satisfy the constraints and reduce the evaluation costs of the queries. As automated design of materialized views to answer queries is an important component of query processing in data warehouses [5,19,32] and of automated query-performance

---

[1] We follow the tradition of using the same name for a view query and its answer.

tuning [20,26,28], the problems of selecting views and of answering queries using materialized views have been studied thoroughly in the literature.

Generally, spending more time on designing materialized views for a given query workload tends to pay off, as greater improvement can thereby be achieved in the performance of the queries using the resulting stored derived data. As the number of potentially beneficial views or indexes tends to be prohibitive even for simple query workloads [3,11,19], in many cases it is not practical to use exhaustive enumeration to obtain derived data that would *globally minimize* query-evaluation costs. Several approaches (see, e.g., [3,17,19,29]) have been proposed to design good-quality sets of derived data for evaluating SQL queries, without spending an inordinate amount of time on the design. We continue the work of [17,19] of studying view-selection algorithms that are competitive, that is, algorithms that provide optimality guarantees on their outputs without necessarily exploring the entire search space of views. In this paper we present a formal model of the view-selection problem for queries on star-schema data warehouses and explore competitive techniques for designing and using materialized views in this context. Our techniques and results are applicable to a practically important class of range-aggregate queries on star-schema data warehouses.

Our contributions are as follows:

- we model view selection as an integer-programming (IP) problem and give references to similar IP structures in the literature,
- we use standard IP-solver software to solve optimally several realistic-size instances of the problem on the popular TPC-H benchmark [33], and
- we perform a post-optimality analysis to determine/observe the impact of changing certain input characteristics on the optimal solution.

After outlining related work, in Section 3 we provide the background and formal definitions. Section 4 introduces our IP model of the view-selection problem. Section 5 describes our framework for analysis and experimentation. We report our experimental results in Section 6 and conclude in Section 7.

2   Related Work

Designing and using derived data to improve query performance has long been a direction of research and practical efforts in data-intensive systems. Over time, a wealth of theoretical results (see [18] for a survey) and some practical solutions [4,8,10] have been accumulated on using views and indexes in query answering. The problem of answering aggregate queries using views has been considered in relation to data warehouses and data cubes [2,7,15,34]; results on answering each query using a single view are presented in [16,31]. Recent work [1,12] has considered the problem of rewriting aggregate queries using multiple views.

Considerable work has been done on efficiently selecting views and indexes for general SQL queries [3,9] and in particular for aggregate queries (e.g., [1,17,19,29]). [35] proposes algorithms, including an IP approach, for selecting materialized views to minimize the sum cost of processing the given queries and of maintaining all the views. [3,4] have introduced an end-to-end approach and a system architecture for designing and using materialized views and indexes to answer queries. In this paper we study the problem of selecting views for aggregate queries on star-schema data warehouses. The setting and assumptions we use are similar to those in [17,19] (rather than to those in [35]) — that is, we seek to minimize the total execution costs of the given queries under a storage-limit constraint. At the same time, the novelty of our work is in obtaining efficiently optimal solutions for problem instances of realistic sizes, or competitive heuristics using lower-bound relaxation for larger problem instances.

3   Preliminaries and Problem Specification

The setting and assumptions we use are similar to those in [17,19]. We consider select-project-join queries with equality-based joins and with aggregation sum, count, max, or min. Our approach is applicable to queries with inequality comparisons, including the important class of range-aggregate queries. (We consider comparisons of the form $A \; \theta \; c$, where A is an attribute in a relation, c is a constant, and θ is one of $>, \geq, <, \leq, =, \neq$.) We study workloads of *parameterized* queries: The parameterized version of a query with constants has placeholders instead of all the constants. In this paper we concentrate on the special case of *star-schema queries*: We assume that the database schema is a star schema [21], with a fact table and dimension tables. Further, in each star-schema query, each join is a natural join of the fact table with a dimension table.

To measure query-evaluation performance in presence of views, our cost model is as follows. We consider the costs of answering queries using unindexed materialized views, such that each query can be evaluated by processing just one view relation and no other data, as in Example 1. (This setting is the same as in [19].) Thus, the cost of evaluating each query is proportional to the *size* of the view chosen for the evaluation. We use two metrics for view sizes: (1) the number of rows in the view relations (this is a common assumption in the literature on view selection), and (2) the number of bytes in the view relation. In Section 6 we will see that these metrics give us different experimental results. Finally, given a query workload Q and a set of views V that have been precomputed on a database D, the *total cost* of evaluating Q using V is the sum of the costs of evaluating all the queries in Q, such that each query is evaluated using a view in V. The sum can be weighted to reflect the relative frequency or importance of individual workload queries. Similarly to [19], we assume that a view resulting from joining all the base relations in the star schema — we call this view the *raw data* — is always part of the available set V of materialized views.

We consider the following view-selection problem: Our goal is to minimize the evaluation costs of a given workload of parameterized aggregate queries defined on a star schema, by selecting and precomputing materialized views that can be used in answering the queries. (We consider only *equivalent* rewritings of the queries in Q using the set V, i.e., we require that exact answers to all the queries in Q can be computed using V.) We consider this minimization problem under a storage-space limit, which is an upper bound on the amount of disk space that can be allocated for the materialized views. Thus, our *problem inputs* are of the form $\mathcal{I} = (\mathcal{D}, \mathcal{Q}, b)$, where $\mathcal{D}$ is a database, $\mathcal{Q}$ is a workload of parameterized queries, and b is the (positive integer) value of the storage limit.

For any parameterized query in the given workload, our goal is to design views that can be used in evaluating *any instance* of the query. Thus, similarly to [17,19] we consider only views without comparisons with constants. We use the following definitions of solutions and of the optimal viewset problem (OVP):

Definition 1. *(Admissible viewset/solution) Let $\mathcal{I} = (\mathcal{D}, \mathcal{Q}, b)$ be a problem input. A set of views $\mathcal{V}$ is an* admissible viewset *for $\mathcal{I}$ if (1) each query in $\mathcal{Q}$ can be rewritten equivalently using $\mathcal{V}$, and (2) $\mathcal{V}$ satisfies the storage limit b.*

Definition 2. *(Optimal viewset/solution) For a problem input $\mathcal{I} = (\mathcal{D}, \mathcal{Q}, b)$, an* optimal viewset *is a set of views $\mathcal{V}$ defined on $\mathcal{D}$, such that (1) $\mathcal{V}$ is an admissible viewset for $\mathcal{I}$, and (2) $\mathcal{V}$ minimizes the cost of evaluating $\mathcal{Q}$ on the database $\mathcal{D}_{\mathcal{V}}$, among all admissible viewsets for $\mathcal{I}$. Here, $\mathcal{D}_{\mathcal{V}}$ is the database that results from adding to $\mathcal{D}$ the relations for all the views in $\mathcal{V}$ computed on $\mathcal{D}$.*

Definition 3. *(Optimal viewset problem, OVP) For a given problem input $\mathcal{I} = (\mathcal{D}, \mathcal{Q}, b)$, find an optimal viewset. A solution for a given instance of OVP consists of a collection of materialized views $\mathcal{V}$ (which includes the raw data on $\mathcal{D}$ [19] and all additional views that we choose to materialize) and an association between each element of $\mathcal{Q}$ and its corresponding element of $\mathcal{V}$.*

4   The Formal Model

In this section we propose an integer programming (IP) model for the optimal viewset problem (OVP) and discuss methodologies for solving this IP model. We use the following notation to represent the input $\mathcal{I} = (\mathcal{D}, \mathcal{Q}, b)$ in this model:

a_i :   Size of the view i, for all $i \in IV$,
               where IV is the index set for all possible views;
b :   storage limit;
c_{ij} :   evaluation cost of answering query j by using view i,
               for all $i \in IV$ and $j \in \mathcal{Q}$.

We let $c_{ij} = +\infty$ if view i cannot be used to answer query j. We further define the following decision variables for the IP model.

$$x_i = \begin{cases} 1 & \text{if view i is materialized} \\ 0 & \text{otherwise} \end{cases} \quad \text{for all } i \in IV$$

and

$$y_{ij} = \begin{cases} 1 & \text{if we use view i to answer query j} \\ 0 & \text{otherwise} \end{cases} \quad \text{for all } i \in IV \text{ and } j \in \mathcal{Q}$$

The optimal viewset problem can now be stated as the following IP model.

Minimize $\sum_{i \in IV} \sum_{j \in Q} c_{ij} y_{ij}$ (OVIP) subject to $\quad\quad \sum_{i \in IV} a_i x_i \leq b$ $\hfill$ (1)

$\quad\quad\quad\quad\quad \sum_{i \in IV} y_{ij} = 1$ $\quad\quad$ for all j $\hfill$ (2)

$\quad\quad\quad\quad\quad y_{ij} \leq x_i$ $\quad\quad$ for all i, j such that $c_{ij} \neq +\infty$ $\hfill$ (3)

$\quad\quad\quad\quad\quad x_1 = 1$ $\hfill$ (4)

$\quad\quad\quad\quad\quad x_i, y_{ij} \in \{0, 1\}$ $\quad\quad$ for all i, j

Constraint (1) limits the size of the materialized views to be no more than the available storage space b. Constraint (2) states that each query is answered by exactly one view in the set of materialized views. Constraint (3) guarantees that query j can be answered by view i only if view i is already materialized. Constraint (4) states that the raw data table is always materialized, and the remaining constraints are simply the binary requirements for x_i and y_{ij}. It is noteworthy that the binary requirement for y_{ij} can be replaced by a simple non-negativity restriction without affecting the corresponding optimal solution for this model. This modification, however, has a significant impact in reducing the overall computational effort required to solve this IP model.

The structure of this IP model is similar to those for the uncapacitated facility location problem (UFL) and the k-median problem. These two problems are well studied in the open literature, and it is reported that relatively large instances of the corresponding IP models can be solved within reasonable time. Several heuristic approaches for solving these problems have also been reported. See [13] and [22] for the facility location problem and [24] for the k-median problem.

We can also employ the linear programing (LP) relaxation or the Lagrangean relaxation of this IP model to develop lower bounds for the optimum value of the objective function. In [30] it is observed that the LP relaxation of the IP model for the facility location problem can provide strong lower bounds for it, and in [25] it is shown that the Lagrangean relaxation of this IP model can provide even stronger lower bounds. Due to the similarity of the structure of OVIP with these models we expect that similarly strong lower bounds for OVIP can also be obtained. These lower bounds are typically obtained with modest amount of computational effort, hence they can be used to devise exact algorithms (such as a branch and bound algorithm) for solving this problem. We can also employ the lower bound for each instance to evaluate the solution obtained via an inexact algorithm (i.e., a heuristic procedure) for that instance, hence providing an upper bound on the performance ratio of the algorithm in that instance.

5   Our Framework

In the experimental results reported in this paper we consider view design for star-schema queries. To design aggregate views for a workload of star-schema queries, we use a data structure — view lattice — that was introduced in [19]. A view lattice is a representation of the search space of views for the workload, where nodes represent views and directed edges between the views denote which view can be evaluated using another view. For any view we choose to materialize from the view lattice, if the view is usable in evaluating some query in the given query workload, then the answer to the view is the only relation needed in the evaluation. That is, our view-selection procedures determine joinless rewritings of queries. In addition to joinless rewritings, we plan to consider rewritings that are computed via joins of aggregate views with other relations [1,12].

To define an instance of the problem and to construct input data for our IP formalism, we start out by selecting a query workload, that is, frequent and important queries whose evaluation costs we want to reduce by materializing views. We then construct for the query workload a view lattice using the approach of [19]. In constructing the view lattice, we associate each query in our query workload with a node in the lattice. More specifically, we construct from the query workload a set of grouping and aggregated attributes of interest — these are all the attributes mentioned in the queries, except the attributes in the join conditions. We then use these attributes to construct a view lattice as described in [19]. For instance, suppose we select queries Q1 and Q2 in Example 1 to be our workload queries. We then use attributes mentioned in the two queries to construct two sets of attributes of interest for us — grouping and aggregated attributes. Attributes CID, Year, Month, and State are our grouping attributes in Example 1, and attribute QtySold is the aggregated attribute.

Once we have constructed a view lattice, we calculate the sizes of the answers to all the views in the lattice. We can estimate the sizes by using methods mentioned in [19], for instance by using sampling. Finally, to complete the input data, we specify a storage limit.

To illustrate, we present the following numerical example adopted from [19]. Figure 1 shows a part of the view lattice for this example that consists of the raw data (source node a) and a collection of views $\{b, c, d, e, f, g, h\}$ as indicated. The space requirement for each node in the lattice is given next to that node, and the edges represent the relationship between views as discussed above. In this example we assume that the query workload consists of all nodes in the lattice, and the

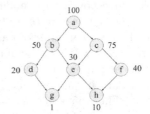

Fig. 1. Lattice example with space costs [19]

problem is to determine a collection of at most three additional views to materialize (in addition to the raw data a) so that the total cost of answering all the workload queries is minimized. Note that in this example, in order to be consistent with the example given in [19] we restrict the *number of views*, rather than their corresponding storage space requirement as we stated earlier.

The IP model (OVIP1) for this example can be written as follows.

Minimize $\quad \sum_{i=1}^{8} \sum_{j=1}^{8} c_{ij} y_{ij}$ $\hfill (OVIP1)$

subject to $\quad \sum_{i=1}^{8} x_i \leq 4$

$\sum_{i=1}^{8} y_{ij} = 1 \qquad$ for all $j = 1$ to 8

$y_{ij} \leq x_i \qquad$ for all i, j such that $c_{ij} \neq +\infty$

$x_1 = 1$

$x_i, y_{ij} \in \{0, 1\} \qquad$ for all $i, j = 1$ to 8

The matrix of objective-function coefficients c_{ij} for the model OVIP1 is the following matrix, where nodes a, b, c, d, e, f, g, and h correspond to the rows (and columns) 1 through 8, respectively.

$$
\begin{bmatrix}
100 & 100 & 100 & 100 & 100 & 100 & 100 & 100 \\
\infty & 50 & \infty & 50 & 50 & \infty & 50 & 50 \\
\infty & \infty & 75 & \infty & 75 & 75 & 75 & 75 \\
\infty & \infty & \infty & 20 & \infty & \infty & 20 & \infty \\
\infty & \infty & \infty & \infty & 30 & \infty & 30 & 30 \\
\infty & \infty & \infty & \infty & \infty & 40 & \infty & 40 \\
\infty & \infty & \infty & \infty & \infty & \infty & 1 & \infty \\
\infty & \infty & \infty & \infty & \infty & \infty & \infty & 10
\end{bmatrix}
$$

The model OVIP1 has 8 binary variables and 64 continuous variables. We solved this problem using the IP solver CPLEX [27] with an AMPL interface [14] and obtained the following optimal solution: $x_1 = x_2 = x_4 = x_6 = 1$ (corresponding to nodes a, b, d, and f in the lattice), $y_{11} = y_{22} = y_{13} = y_{44} = y_{25} = y_{66} = y_{47} = y_{68} = 1$, with all remaining variables equal to zero. The total cost associated with this solution is 420. Incidentally, this solution is identical to the solution obtained using the heuristic procedure reported in [19].

In order to represent the lattice associated with a large data set (for a realistic instance of the view-selection problem), we use a table format. Each row in this table corresponds to a node in the lattice; in each row, we have two entries representing the *view ID* and the *view size* for that node, respectively. Thus, this table has two columns and as many rows as the number of nodes in the lattice.

In each row (i.e., node of the lattice) the view size is represented in units that we choose for our analysis (e.g., number of rows in the view, number of bytes of stored data in the view, etc.), and the view ID is a binary (0 and 1) vector of size K. The ith element in this vector corresponds to the ith grouping attribute in the database, and K represents the total number of grouping attributes. For each view, an entry of 1 in the ith position of its view ID implies that the corresponding attribute is used to group the associated rows in the database (to form this view), and an entry of 0 means otherwise. In other words, a 1 entry in the ith position of the view ID for a node (view) implies that this node (view) can be used to answer a query that requires the ith attribute, and a 0 entry in the ith position implies otherwise. We give SQL examples in Section 6.

It follows that the dependency relationship among views (nodes) can be derived expressively from their corresponding view IDs. A query e in the lattice can be computed directly from a view f (i.e., f is an ancestor of e in the lattice) if the set of positions with entry 1 in the view ID for e is a subset of the set of positions with similar entry in the view ID for f (e.g., $f = \{1, 1, 0, 0, 1\}$ is an ancestor for $e = \{0, 1, 0, 0, 1\}$, but it is not an ancestor for $e' = \{0, 1, 0, 1, 0\}$). Note that the number of nodes in the lattice is 2^K and increases exponentially as the number of attributes K increases. For this reason, in order to keep the size of the IP model as small as possible, it is important that in each instance we only maintain those rows of the table (nodes of the lattice) that are potential ancestors to at least one of the queries in our query workload for that instance.

The evaluation cost of a query e using a view f is taken to be the storage cost of the view f if e can be answered by f, and is set equal to infinity otherwise. Following the above criteria, the cost matrix to answer a query workload can be easily computed and transformed to the input of the IP model.

6 Implementation and Experimental Evaluation

We have conducted experiments to evaluate the IP model and framework presented in Sections 4 and 5. All experiments were run on a machine with a 3GHz Intel P4 processor, 1GB RAM, and a 80GB hard drive running Windows XP SP2 and CPLEX/AMPL 9.0. The experimental results show the following:

- relatively large instances of the view-selection problem, including instances of practically important sizes, can be solved optimally;
- our LP relaxation of the IP model provides very strong lower bounds for each optimal value;
- we can get different *optimal* solutions depending on whether we measure query costs and view sizes in rows or bytes.

We give here just a brief summary of the experiments; a detailed account of the experimental setup and results can be found in [23]. The goal of the experiments was to obtain optimal solutions and lower bounds on problem instances of realistic sizes. We did the experiments on a TPC-H database benchmark [33]; the sizes of the stored tables are shown in Figure 2. The size estimates for the nodes in the view lattices were obtained by running the queries for all possible lattice views on the TPC-H stored data with scale factor of 0.1 and

TPC-H Tables

Name	Size (bytes)
Lineitem	2,147,483,647
Part	1,193,906
Supplier	14,188,544
PartSupp	5,830,541
Customer	244,883,456
Orders	482,877,440
Nation1	2,103
Nation2	2,103
Region	396

Fig. 2. Sizes of TPC-H tables (in bytes)

by extrapolating the sizes of the answers to the queries to the sizes of the stored data used to evaluate the workload queries and their rewritings.

For the experiments we used three datasets — raw data with 7, 13, and 15 attributes. (To obtain some raw tables for the experiments, we used joins of TPC-H tables.) The numbers of nodes in the view lattices for these datasets are 128, 8192, and 32768, respectively.

For each raw table we constructed the IP model for several instances of the problem, each instance with a different query workload and different storage limit b. For each instance, given the corresponding lattice, query workload, and storage limit, we constructed the input files for the IP model, as described in Section 5. We solved each instance using the software package CPLEX/AMPL as described earlier, and in each instance we were able to find an optimal solution. For illustrative purposes, in Table 1 we give detailed characteristics of three different instances in our experiment. (We have solved many more instances of the problem for each view lattice, but due to space constraints we cannot give here the details; these three instances are typical). Each row of this table

Table 1. Description of three problem instances in the experiments

Ins. ID	View lattice	Maximum no. nodes	Query workload	Capacity no. rows	No. of nodes	No. of x_j's	No. of y_{ij}'s
1	7	128	{ 5, 7, 17, 69, 81, 88, 112 }	702,709	60	60	60×7
2	13	8,192	{ 88, 112, 593, 912, 2050, 2368, 6656, 7936 }	1,264,194	4,104	4,104	$4,104 \times 8$
3	15	32,768	{ 152, 224, 2848, 3201, 8194, 8832, 26624, 31232 }	1,522,810	17,464	17,464	$17,464 \times 8$

corresponds to one instance and gives the view lattice (raw data) and query workload corresponding to that instance. The maximum number of nodes in each instance is 2^K, where K is the number of attributes in the view lattice. Note that in our IP model we only include those nodes that could be used as potential ancestors for one or more queries in the query workload for that instance. Thus, the number of nodes we included in the IP model is in fact smaller than 2^K, as stated in the table. For each instance we also give the number of variables in the corresponding IP model.

The execution time for CPLEX /AMPL to solve the three instances in Table 1 was 0.05 seconds, 3.04 seconds, and 18.64 seconds, respectively. The execution time is expected to grow at an exponential rate with the size of the instance; hence we do not expect it to be practical to solve much larger instances of this IP model using CPLEX/AMPL. At the same time, the instances that we are able to solve are of realistic sizes in practice, as exemplified in the three instances described in

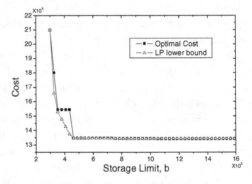

Fig. 3. Sensitivity analysis and LP lower bound for the view-7 instance

Table 1. This demonstrates that we can use a standard IP solver to solve practical instances of our proposed IP model.

We have performed a post-optimality analysis to observe the impact of changing the storage limit b on the optimal value of the objective cost function. In realistic view-selection scenarios, the total space available to store the materialized views is usually smaller than the total size of the input query workload; otherwise we can precompute all the queries in advance and store them on disk, which would be a globally optimal solution to the view-selection problem. At the same time, the storage limit has to be at least as large as the size of the raw data table [19]. Hence, to explore the tradeoff between the amount of available storage space and the resulting total query costs, in our experiments we varied the value of storage space b between one and five times the size of the raw data.

Figures 3 and 4 show the results for two instances of Table 1, with 7 and 13 attributes respectively. In each instance and for each value of b we also solved the corresponding LP problem to obtain the associated lower bound; the lower bounds are also shown on the graphs. (The step curves in Figures 3 and 4 give the optimal cost value, whereas the smooth curves show the lower bounds.) Intuitively, in optimal solutions, the only possible change as the value of b increases is to add another materialized view to the solution. Note that if we have limited space that can only store the raw data, then each query would be computed directly from the raw data; as the number of materialized views increases with the increase in the value of b, the optimal query costs decrease. Finally, our experiments show that the LP lower bound is very close to the optimal value of the IP problem most of the time: Linear-programming relaxation provided a good lower bound in all the instances, and the ratio of the lower bound to the optimum varied between 0.92 and 0.99.

In another set of experiments we used bytes, rather than rows, to measure view sizes. In the literature, view sizes and query costs are typically measured in units of rows (see, e.g., [17,19,29]). At the same time, the units of bytes are the actual measure of storage requirements and query costs in query processing in database-management systems, because the cost of answering a given query using a given view is proportional to the number of disk blocks occupied by the view. Thus, in some

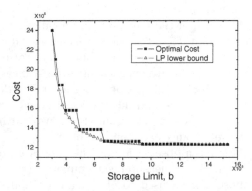

Fig. 4. Sensitivity analysis and LP lower bound for the view-13 instance

of our experiments we expressed in bytes both the storage requirements for the views and the costs of answering queries using those views. Note that if we state the problem this way for units of bytes, we do not need to change the formulation (equalities and constraints) of our IP model in Section 4.

In our experiments, for some problem instances we obtain identical optimal solutions when view sizes and query costs are measured in rows *and* bytes; for other instances, we obtained different results. In Table 2 we report some results where we obtained different optimal solutions for units of rows and for units of bytes. The table shows experimental results for two problem instances on the view lattice for seven grouping attributes (instance IDs 1 and 2), and for two problem instances on the view lattice for thirteen grouping attributes (instance IDs 3 and 4); the raw data for both lattices come from the TPC-H dataset [33]. For each instance we report the index of the root node of the lattice; the root node is the raw data, which is (similarly to [19]) always required to be part of the viewsets we output as solutions for the problem instances.

Table 2. Solving the problem for units of rows and bytes

Inst-ance ID	No. of grouping attrib.	Root node index	Query workload (query indexes)	Units of rows		Units of bytes	
				storage limit	optimal viewset	storage limit	optimal viewset
1	7	127	{ 55, 59, 125, 126 }	899,418	{ 55, 126, 127 }	4,487,825	{ 55, 127 }
2	7	127	{ 1, 7, 53, 76, 111, 115 }	1,084,770	{ 1, 53, 76, 127 }	5,412,766	{ 1, 7, 76, 127 }
3	13	8,191	{ 1792, 3013, 5392, 6096, 7063 }	900,541	{ 1792, 5392, 8191 }	6,889,391	{ 5392, 6096, 8191 }
4	13	8,191	{ 1185, 5224, 6401, 6672 }	836,835	{ 6401, 6672, 8191 }	6,402,022	{ 6929, 8191 }

For each of the four problem instances we did two experiments — one for a storage limit, b, and all view sizes measured in rows, and the other for a storage limit and view sizes measured in bytes. For example, the second row of Table 2 gives results for two experiments for instance ID 2 — that is, for query workload $\{1, 7, 53, 76, 111, 115\}$. One experiment was done for the value of storage limit b = 1,084,770 rows, and the other was done for a storage limit b = 5,412,766 bytes. (We set the value of b in units of rows and in units of bytes in such a manner that the instances are comparable.)

Our main observation on the results reported in Table 2 is that regardless of the units of measurement employed (rows or bytes), the IP model that we propose can be used to obtain an optimal solution for the problem within a reasonable amount of execution time (less than 20 seconds for the instances reported earlier), and using the units of bytes in this context does not impose any additional computational burden for solving the IP model. Further, the two optimal solutions obtained when we use these units of measurement are not necessarily identical. As units of bytes (instead of rows) is a more realistic measure in the context of view selection, we posit that bytes should be employed as the primary units of measurement in problem inputs.

7   Conclusions and Future Work

In this paper we considered the following view-selection problem: Given a set of queries, a database, and a storage limit on the amount of disk space that can be used to store materialized views, return definitions of views that, when materialized in the database, would satisfy the constraints and reduce the evaluation costs of the queries. We focused on practically important range-aggregate queries on star-schema data warehouses. We described our approach to obtaining *globally optimal* sets of views. The approach is an IP model that allows us to obtain optimal solutions without having to exhaustively enumerate all possible candidate solutions. We presented the formulation of the IP model and introduced an

LP relaxation. We reported our experimental results that show the practicality of our approach for problem instances of realistic sizes.

Our experiments show that the computational requirements of solving the OVIP problem (see Section 4) become prohibitive once the size of the problem exceeds certain limits. Hence, to solve larger instances of OVIP, we are investigating techniques for designing and developing an algorithm (and the corresponding software) that takes advantage of the special structure of the problem. Further, solving even larger instances of the problem using exact methods might prove to be altogether too time consuming; thus, we may have to employ an appropriate heuristic procedure that exploits the structure of OVIP, such as a Lagrangean heuristic. Such heuristic procedures have been developed for the facility location problem [6] and for the k-median problem [24], and the computational results show that these procedures obtain good solutions with a modest amount of computational effort. We expect that similar heuristic procedures can be developed for solving the view-selection problem OVP as well.

In addition to designing competitive heuristics for selecting views, we are extending our approach to selecting indexes alongside views (see, e.g., the setting of [17]). We plan to apply and extend our results to generalizations of range-aggregate queries, where queries can be answered using *joins* of views [1,12]. We are also interested in studying the view-and index-selection problems under the maintenance-cost constraint on materialized views and indexes.

References

1. Afrati, F., Chirkova, R.: Selecting and using views to compute aggregate queries. In Proceedings of the International Conference on Database Theory (ICDT) (2005)
2. Agarwal, S., Agrawal, R., Deshpande, P., Gupta, A., Naughton, J. F., Ramakrishnan, R., S. Sarawagi, S.: On the computation of multidimensional aggregates. In Proceedings of VLDB (1996) 506–521
3. Agrawal, S., Chaudhuri, S., Narasayya, V. R.: Automated selection of materialized views and indexes in SQL databases. In Proc. VLDB (2000) 496–505
4. Agrawal, S., Chaudhuri, S., Narasayya, V. R.: Materialized view and index selection tool for Microsoft SQL Server 2000. In Proc. ACM SIGMOD (2001)
5. Baralis, E., Paraboschi, S., Teniente, E.: Materialized view selection in a multidimensional database. In Proc. VLDB (1997) 156–165
6. Barcelo, J., Casanovas, J.: A heuristic lagrangean algorithm for the capacitated plant location problem. European J. Operations Research (1984) 15:212–226
7. Chaudhuri, S., Dayal, U.: An overview of data warehousing and OLAP technology. SIGMOD Record (1997) 26(1):65–74
8. Chaudhuri, S., Krishnamurthy, R., Potamianos, S., Shim, K.: Optimizing queries with materialized views. In Proceedings of ICDE (1995) 190–200
9. Chaudhuri, S., Narasayya, V. R.: An efficient cost-driven index selection tool for Microsoft SQL server. In Proceedings of VLDB (1997) 146–155
10. Chaudhuri, S., Narasayya, V. R.: AutoAdmin 'What-if' index analysis utility. In Proceedings of ACM SIGMOD (1998) 367–378
11. Chirkova, R., Halevy, A. Y., Suciu, D.: A formal perspective on the view selection problem. VLDB Journal (2002) 11(3):216–237

12. Cohen, S., Nutt, W., Serebrenik, A.: Rewriting aggregate queries using views. In Proceedings of PODS (1999) 155–166
13. Cornuejols, G., Nemhauser, G. L., Wolsey, L.A.: The uncapacitated facility location problem. Technical Report 605, Operations Research and Industrial Engineering, Cornell University (1984)
14. Fourer, R., Gay, D. M., Kernighan, B. W.: AMPL: A Modeling Language for Mathematical Programming. Boyd and Fraser, Danvers, Mass. (2002)
15. Gray, J., Chaudhuri, S., Bosworth, A., Layman, A., Reichart, D., Venkatrao, M.: Data cube: A relational aggregation operator generalizing Group-by, Cross-Tab, and Sub Totals. Data Mining and Knowledge Discovery (1997) 1(1):29–53
16. Gupta, A., Harinarayan, V., Quass, D.: Aggregate-query processing in data warehousing environments. In Proceedings of VLDB (1995) 358–369
17. Gupta, H.,, Harinarayan, V., Rajaraman, A., Ullman, J. D.: Index selection for OLAP. In Proceedings of ICDE (1997) 208–219
18. Halevy, A. Y.: Answering queries using views: A survey. VLDB Journal (2001) 10(4):270–294
19. Harinarayan, V., Rajaraman, A., Ullman, J. D.: Implementing data cubes efficiently. In Proceedings of ACM SIGMOD (1996) 205–216
20. IBM. Autonomic Computing. http://www.research.ibm.com/autonomic/
21. Kimball, R., Ross, M.: The Data Warehouse Toolkit (second edition). Wiley Computer Publishing (2002)
22. Krarup, J., Pruzan, P. M.: The simple plant location problem: Survey and synthesis. European Journal of Operations Research (1983) 12:36–81
23. Li, J., Chirkova, R., and Fathi, V.: An IP Model for the View Selection Problem. Technical report, NC State University (2005)
24. Mulvey, J. M., Crowder, H. P.: Cluster analysis: An application of lagrangian relaxation. Management Science (1979) 25:329–340
25. Parker, R. G., Rardin, R. L.: Discrete Optimization. Academic Press (1988)
26. Microsoft Research AutoAdmin Project. Self-Tuning and Self-Administering Databases. http://research.microsoft.com/dmx/autoadmin/default.asp
27. ILOG S.A. CPLEX 7.0 software package. http://www.ilog.com (2000)
28. Shasha, D., Bonnet, P.: Database Tuning: Principles, Experiments, and Troubleshooting Techniques. Morgan Kaufmann (2002)
29. Shukla, A., Deshpande, P., Naughton, J. F.: Materialized view selection for multidimensional datasets. In Proceedings of VLDB (1998) 488–499
30. Spielberg, K.: Algorithms for the simple plant location problem with some side constraints. Operations Research (1969) 17:85–111
31. Srivastava, D., Dar, S., H.V. Jagadish, H. V., Levy, A. Y.: Answering queries with aggregation using views. In Proceedings of VLDB (1996) 318–329
32. Theodoratos, D., Sellis, T.: Data warehouse configuration. In Proceedings of VLDB (1997) 126–135
33. TPC-H:. TPC Benchmark H (Decision Support). Available from http://www.tpc.org/tpch/spec/tpch2.1.0.pdf
34. Widom, J.: Research problems in data warehousing. In Proc. CIKM (1995)
35. Yang, J., Karlapalem, K., Li, Q.: Algorithms for materialized view design in data warehousing environment. In Proceedings of VLDB (1997) 136–145

Efficient Main-Memory Algorithms for Set Containment Join Using Inverted Lists

Dmitry Shaporenkov

University of Saint-Petersburg, Russia
dsha@acm.org

Abstract. We present two algorithms for set containment joins based on inverted lists. The first algorithm scans the left relation and determines for each tuple all the qualifying tuples by querying the inverted file for the right relation. The second algorithm employs the common inverted file for both relations. We focus on improving performance of algorithms in main memory by reducing number of L2 cache misses which is achieved by applying such techniques as partitioning and compression. We study algorithms analytically and experimentally and determine which one is better depending on parameters of the input relations. We also demonstrate that both algorithms are superior to some other known methods for set containment joins.

1 Introduction

Set-valued attributes have become more important in recent years with growing distribution of object-relational database systems (ORDBMS) and rapid development of such application areas as information retrieval and data mining. In practice it is often required to evaluate join queries on set-valued attributes. In such cases the join predicate is a set predicate, such as set containment or intersection. Many real-world queries can be naturally expressed as set containment and intersection joins. For example, a query that finds appropriate candidates among job seekers includes a condition that the set of candidate's skills contains the set of skills required for the job as a subset. If we are interested in retrieving all documents containing the specified set of terms from the collection, this again can be considered a set containment query. A relation *People* that includes a set-valued attribute *Hobbies* poses the problem of finding all pairs of people sharing common hobbies that can be formulated as a set intersection self-join.

Set-valued attributes are not directly supported in a traditional relational DMBS, since already the first normal form explicitly requires an attribute be atomic, i.e. forbids the value of an attribute to be a set. However, set-valued attributes in a relational DBMS can be simulated using unnested external representation ([3]) that creates an auxiliary relation connected to the original relation by a foreign key, thus representing one-to-many relationship between record of the original relation and the elements of the value of its set-valued attribute. It can be easily noticed ([7]) that many complex joins on atomic attributes that arise in relational DMBS in fact hide set predicates behind sophisticated expressions involving aggregation. However, as study [3] shows, relational query optimizers are generally unable to deal with such queries in an efficient manner,

J. Eder et al. (Eds.): ADBIS 2005, LNCS 3631, pp. 139–152, 2005.

since set predicates are unknown for them. Nested-loops algorithm is the most common way to handle joins with complex predicates. In case of joins with set predicates, however, nested loops algorithm falls short because of its poor performance ([2]), so better methods are required.

Main-memory DBMS (MMDBMS) have attracted much attention during recent decade. A MMDBMS stores all the data and support structures (such as indexes) in RAM of the database server. Constantly growing amount of memory in modern database servers already enables to store small and medium-size databases directly in main memory. It has been shown that MMDMBS provide huge performance gain over traditional, disk-based DBMS, since retrieving the necessary data in MMDBMS usually does not involve disk access at all. Slow disk device is used only for logging and recovery. Many researchers ([12,1,15,9]) have recognized that the crucial factor for performance of a MMDBMS is CPU cache utilization, that is, how many cache misses database operations incur. If the number of cache misses is high, CPU will spend most of time waiting the data to be fetched from RAM (so-called CPU *stall*).

In this paper we present two efficient algorithms based on inverted files for set-containment joins in main memory. Inverted files are well-known and widely used tool for indexing text documents. The first algorithm employs the inverted file S_{IF}^A built for the right relation S to find all qualifying tuples for each tuple of the left relation R. The second algorithm scans the common inverted file RS_{IF}^A built on the set-valued attribute A for R and S and processes the inverted lists in such a way that the resulting structure is exactly a set of $(t_R, t_{S_1}, ..., t_{S_k})$ lists where $t_R.A \subseteq t_{S_i}.A, i = 1, .., k$. Both algorithms are based on simple ideas, and we focus our study on tailoring the algorithms for MMDBMS by improving CPU cache utilization. We try to achieve this by applying such optimizations as partitioning algorithms into stages and compressing intermediate results. We present experimental study showing that our optimizations give significant effect as compared with straightforward implementations. We also demonstrate that both algorithms are superior to some other algorithms for set-containment joins.

The structure of the paper is as follows. The section 2 presents a survey of related work in the area of algorithms for joins with set predicates. In the section 3 we first describe the basic versions of both algorithms, and then discuss various performance optimizations. The section 4 shows the results of experimental evaluation of the algorithms. The section 5 concludes the paper and outlines directions for future work.

2   Related Work

Helmer and Moerkotte ([2]) seem to be the first researchers who addressed specifically set containment joins. They evaluated several algorithms for set containment join in main memory. The first group of algorithms includes variations of nested-loops join which differ in how the set comparison is implemented. Several implementations of set comparison were considered, and a method that uses signatures turned out to be the best one. The second algorithm employs signature-based approach by hashing all the signatures of the relation R (assuming that the join condition is $t_R.A \subseteq t_S.A, t_R \in R, t_S \in S$), enumerating subsets of each set of the relation S, and matching each subset with hashed signatures of R.

Melnik and Garcia-Molina ([7]) describe two algorithms for set containment joins. Both algorithms, Adaptive Pick-and-Sweep Join (that extends Pick-and-Sweep Join proposed in [8]) and Adaptive Divide-and-Conquer Join exploit essentially the same idea, namely, partitioning the relations being joined in such a way that the join result can be computed by joining only sets from each pair of corresponding partitions and then merging results. Algorithms use sophisticated methods for constructing the set of partitions (details can be found in [7]).

Mamoulis ([4]) considers several algorithms for set containment, intersection and overlap join (two sets $s1$ and $s2$ are said to k-overlap if they have at least k elements in common). He proposes Block Nested-Loops algorithm (BNL) that uses inverted file S_{IF} built on the relation S. The S_{IF} is partitioned into blocks each of which can fit into the main memory. The BNL algorithm proceeds by reading each block of S_{IF} and scanning the relation R to find qualifing tuples. Mamoulis also discusses the algorithm that joins two inverted files R_{IF} and S_{IF} (IFJ), but rejects this algorithm as inefficient. Mamoulis' BNL and IFJ algorithms are based on the same principles as our algorithms. However, we consider our algorithms in a context of MMDBMS, and estimate their performance from the viewpoint of L2 cache efficiency, not I/O. This allows us to apply hashing to intermediate results where Mamoulis had to use the sort/merge approach. Moreover, we discuss a technique for improving locality of hashing with the aim to better utilize the L2 CPU cache.

During the last decade, many algorithms commonly used in DBMS in the course of many years were reconsidered from the viewpoint of their optimality for main-memory DBMS ([12,9,15,6]). [12] was one of the first works concerning this problem. It suggests cache-conscious versions of several well-known database algorithms such as hash-join, and also demonstrates some fundamental techniques that can be used for improving performance of main-memory algorithms. This and other works have made great contribution by increasing researchers' and developers' awareness of cache performance issues.

3 Algorithms

Both our algorithms employ so-called *inverted files*. Inverted files are well-known tool for document indexing that is widely used in the information retrieval area. We apply inverted files in a slightly different environment, but the general idea remains unchanged. We drop the requirement of the relational first normal form that an attribute should be atomic and allow set-valued attributes. We consider two relations R and S with the common set-valued attribute A. $Domain(A)$ stands for the domain from which elements of values of A in tuples of R and S are drawn. We assume that tuples of relations are identified by record ID (RID), and we denote the value of an attribute P in the tuple t $t.P$. An inverted file R_{IF} maps an element v of the $Domain(A)$ into the list of RIDs $t_1.rid, ..., t_k.rid$ where $t_1, ..., t_k$ are the tuples of R such that (for the sake of brevity we will speak that a tuple t_j contains an element v if the condition (1) is satisfied)

$$v \in t_j.A, 1 \le j \le k. \tag{1}$$

One of our algorithms exploits the idea of *join indexes* ([13,10]) that has been long known in the database research community. Join indexes essentially precompute the join result thereby allowing very fast join processing. Our join index has the form of a *common inverted file*. Instead of building two separate inverted files R_{IF} and S_{IF} we construct one inverted file RS_{IF} that maps an element v of the $Domain(A)$ into two lists of the RIDs, l_R^v and l_S^v, where l_R^v and l_S^v consist of all RIDs of tuples from R and S, respectively, each of which meets the condition (1). This enables us to find all tuples from R and S containing the given element using only single lookup in the inverted file. As noticed in [10], this property comes at the cost of some loss in efficiency in case if RS_{IF} is used in role of either R_{IF} or S_{IF} (that is, if RS_{IF} is used for finding all tuples from either R or S containing an element). How big is the loss depends on the implementation of the inverted file. In the implementation we used it is quite affordable. On the positive side, combining two inverted files into one gives us a very efficient way for traversing all elements of the $Domain(A)$ and their corresponding inverted lists in both relations without using index lookup.

We have to make a note about handling the case when $t.A = \emptyset$, t is a tuple of R. For any such t all the tuples of S match, but the inverted files R_{IF} and RS_{IF} originally do not contain information about t. Therefore any join algorithm based solely on inverted files will miss all pairs (t, t'), where t' is a tuple of S. One approach to this problem is to produce all such pairs in an additional pass over the left relation. Another approach would be to incorporate information about t into the inverted file, for instance, by introducing a special fake value v_{fake} and mapping it into a list of all tuples. Thus we virtually increase each set by adding the fake element v_{fake} and eliminating empty sets, so they no longer need special care. Either of methods has its own advantages and disadvantages. In the following we will tacitly assume that one of these techniques is used, and the case of empty sets does not require special handling.

To analyse performance of the algorithms analytically, we introduce the following definitions. We need to estimate the average length of lists in inverted file. Let $|V|$ be the number of different values in the inverted file R_{IF}, $|R|$ - cardinality of the relation R, and $|r|$ - average cardinality of $t.A$, where t is a tuple of R. Assuming that the values are uniformly distributed accross tuples, the probability for a tuple t to have a value v among the elements of the set $t.A$ is equal to $P_{v \in t.A} = 1 - (1 - \frac{1}{|V|})^{|r|}$. Hence for the average length of the inverted list in the inverted file R_{IF} we get $|l_R| = |R|P_{v \in t.A}$. If the inverted lists are implemented as arrays of integers, their average length in bytes equals to $|l_R|sizeof(int)$. As we dicuss below, techniques for compressing an increasing sequence of integers enable to significantly reduce this value. Let also $CacheSize$ be the size of the L2 cache in bytes, $CacheLine$ be the size of the $L2$ cache line in bytes, and $size(o)$ - the size of an object o in bytes, where the object o is any object occupying a contiguous region of memory. For cost estimation, we will also need the join selectivity $\phi(R, S)$, and the average number of qualifying tuples of S for a tuple t of R in the result $L(R, S) = \phi(R, S)|S|$.

It has been recognized ([9,6]) that number of L2 cache misses is an important performance metrics for main-memory database algorithms like number of I/O for traditional databases. Therefore, our cost model should take into account not only computational cost (which is proportional to the number of primitive operations) but also number of L2 cache misses. When describing algorithms we use prefix ↑ for distinguishing pointers from objects; our intention is to clarify all points in an algorithm where memory accesses (and thus cache misses) happen.

Our cost model includes several basic operations, so the cost of an algorithm can be obtained by properly combining the cost of these operations. For each operation its cumulative cost ($TotalCost$) consists of the computational cost ($CompCost$) plus the L2 cache misses cost ($CacheCost$), all costs are in abstract time units. The operations include:

1. *Inverted file lookup:* $IFLookup(ifile, v) \rightarrow\uparrow l$. This operation retrieves a pointer to the inverted list l corresponding to the given element $v \in Domain(A)$ in the inverted file $ifile$. We will assume that the inverted file $ifile$ is implemented in the form of hash table. Hence if the hash function is good enough, the computational cost of the lookup can treated as a constant. Since for large relations inverted files cannot fit into the $L2$ cache, an arbitrary lookup involves a L2 cache miss, unless the required data have already been loaded into the L2 cache and still can be found there (they might have been evicted from the cache and replaced with some other data). So in the worst case the cost of the lookup can be estimated as follows: $TotalCost(IFLookup(ifile, v)) = C_1 + C_{miss}$, where C_1 is a fixed computational cost of hash table lookup and C_{miss} is the time wasted because of the cache miss.

2. *Intersecton of inverted lists:* $Intersect(\uparrow l_1, \uparrow l_2) \rightarrow\uparrow l$. This operation computes an inverted list l that contains common elements from two inverted lists l_1 and l_2 and returns a pointer to the resulting list. Since inverted lists are kept in ascending order, this operation can be efficiently implemented as synchronous traversal of both inverted lists. Its computational cost is $C_{comp}(|l_1| + |l_2|)$, where C_{comp} is a constant accounting for integer comparison. The operation generally incurs number of cache misses that is equal to $\frac{size(l_1) + size(l_2)}{CacheLine}$.

3. *Workmap lookup:* $WorkmapLookup(workmap, rid) \rightarrow\uparrow o$. This operation returns a pointer to an object o associated with the given RID rid using the map $workmap$ (which we call *working map*). A natural way to implement such a working map is a hash table, because we are not interested in preserving the order of keys. An array would be even better, but since the set of keys is not guaranteed to fit into a limited integer range, array may waste large amount of space. We can apply the same reasoning as for the inverted file lookup, moreover, in this case a good hash function definitely exists. Hence we have $TotalCost(WorkmapLookup(workmap, rid)) = C_2 + C_{miss}$, where C_2 is the cost of lookup into the working map.

3.1   Algorithm Using Inverted File for the Right Relation

This algorithm is similar to the traditional index join on atomic attributes. We traverse the left relation, and for each tuple issue a set-containment query that finds all qualifying tuples of the right relation. The algorithm which we call *IndexJoin* is depicted in the Figure 1

The cost of the algorithm can be estimated as follows. Obviously, the computation cost is

$$CompCost = |R|\Big(|r|CompCost(IFLookup) + (|r| - 1)CompCost(Intersect)\Big).$$

```
foreach (RID t.rid in R)
{
    let t.A = {v}∪(t.A)_rest; // separate one element of the set t.A
    l : ↑ list of RID;
    l = IFLookup(S_IF, v);
    foreach (v ∈ (t.A)_rest)
    {
        l' : ↑ list of RID;
        l' = IFLookup(S_IF, v);
        l = Intersect(l, l');
    }
    foreach (RID s.rid in l) add (t.rid, s.rid) to the result;
}
```

Fig. 1. Algorithm using inverted file for the right relation

For simplicity we ignore the fact that l shrinks in the inner loop, and assume that $|l| = L(R,S) = \phi(R,S)|S|$. The cache misses estimation is more difficult, since both $IFLookup$ and $Intersect$ may benefit from the data previously loaded into the cache. This happens if an inverted list l_R^v has been loaded into the cache during a previous iteration of the outer loop and has not been evicted yet. The inverted list l_R^v was loaded at the time the $IFLookup(v)$ was previously performed. Under the assumption that values of the $Domain(A)$ are distributed uniformly across tuples, $IFLookup$ has been performed $|V|$ times since that moment, and each $IFLookup$ transferred $size(l)$ bytes into the cache. Let us assume that the L2 cache is fully-associative, i.e. a block of memory can be loaded into any cache line. Then the probablity for l_R^v to reside entirely in the cache between two subsequent calls to $IFLookup(v)$ is $P_{hit} = (1 - \frac{size(l)}{CacheSize})^{|V|}$, since the probability of replacing a cache line holding data from l_R^v is $size(l)/CacheSize$.

It is therefore evident that with grow of $|V|$ P_{hit} is decreasing fast, and the number of cache misses caused by $Intersect$ grows. However, if $|S|$ is fixed, $|l|$ and hence $size(l)$ grow with decrease of $|V|$, and P_{hit} is also decreasing. So the algorithm exhibits poor temporal (because the probability of reusing cache lines is low due to relatively large interval between subsequent access to the same data) and spatial (because any part of S_{IF} can be accessed on each iteration) locality and is suboptimal in main memory.

The locality of the algorithm can be improved by breaking the algorithm into stages so that only a part of S_{IF} is accessed on each stage. A simple way to do this is to order all values in the S_{IF} and split the resulting sequence of values into the given number of intervals $[v_1, v_2)...[v_{n-1}, v_n]$ so that each interval contains approximately the same number of values from S_{IF}. On the stage k of the modified algorithm (we call it *Staged index join*, or *IndexJoin(s)*, where s is the number of stages), only values that fit in the interval $[v_k, v_{k+1})$ are considered. The modified algorithm maintains a list of $WorkEntry$ structures (eash is associated with a tuple t of R) which to the beginning of the stage k contain a $t.rid$, the ordered values of $t.A$ and the list of RIDs of tuples $t'_1, ..., t'_{l_t}$ such that $v \in t.A \Rightarrow v \in t'_m(A), m = 1, ..., l_t$, where $v \in [v_1, v_2)...[v_{k-1}, v_k)$. This way $WorkEntry$ contains a list of RIDs of tuples of

S which are currently considered qualifying the containment predicate for the tuple t. This list shrinks as the algorithm proceeds.

The modified algorithm should exhibit better cache behavior than the original one, since the likelyhood of reusing the l_R^v in cache is increased due to better locality. There is, however, extra overhead in the modified version caused by necessity to find the values of $t(A)$ to be processed on the current stage. To speed up this search, values of $t(A)$ in the $WorkEntry$ are kept ordered.

3.2   Algorithm Using Common Inverted File

Using common inverted file enables us to avoid $IFLookup$ altogether. Indeed, simultaneous traversal of inverted lists l_R^v and l_S^v gives us an information about tuples from R and S which have intersecting values of A. Repeating this procedure for all values of $v \in t(A)$ (t - tuple of R) and intersecting the resulting sets of tuples of S produces all tuples of S matching the containment predicate for t. The basic algorithm (called *Inverted File Join* or IFJ) is presented in the Figure 2:

```
Workmap : map : RID -> ↑ list of RID;
foreach (Value v in RS_IF)
{
    let l_R^v, l_S^v - inverted lists corresponding to v in RS_IF;
    foreach (t_R.rid in l_R^v)
    {
        L_t : ↑ list of RID;
        L_t = WorkmapLookup(Workmap, t_R.rid);
        if (L_t = NULL)
            L_t = l_S^v;
        else
            L_t = Intersect(L_t, l_S^v);
        Put L_t into the Workmap with the key t_R.rid;
    }
}
```

Fig. 2. Basic algorithm using common inverted file

The computational cost of this algorithm is similar to that of the algorithm based on inverted file for the right relation:

$$CompCost = |R|\Big(|r|CompCost(WorkmapLookup) + (|r|-1)CompCost(Intersect)\Big).$$

There is a difference in cache behavior of algorithms, since $IndexJoin$ repeatedly loads into the cache inverted lists of S_{IF}, and the size of these inverted lists does not change as the algorithm proceeds. In the IFJ, on the contrary, most heavy processing is concentrated on the lists L_t, which shrink in size as more RIDs are discarded as a result of intersection. To estimate number of cache misses, we nevertheless treat $|L_t|$ as a constant. Applying the same reasoning as for the $IndexJoin$, for the probability of reusing cache lines previously loaded by data from L_t we get: $P_{hit} = (1 - \frac{size(L')}{CacheSize})^{|R|}$.

Here $size(L')$ is normally much smaller than $size(l)$ in the corresponding formula for the $IndexJoin$, however, $|R|$ is expected to be much greater than $|V|$. So the cache behavior of the IFJ is again suboptimal. To improve it, we apply the same technique as in the case of $IndexJoin$. This time we split the algorithm into stages so that only a part of $Workmap$ is accessed on each stage. All RIDs of tuples of RID are ordered and split into a number of intervals each of which contains approximately the same number of RIDs. On each stage only the RIDs that fit into the corresponding interval are considered, other RIDs are discarded. Since l_R^v is already kept ordered in the inverted file, the relevant RIDs can be selected quite efficiently.

The modified version of the IFJ (called $IFJ(s)$, where s is again the number of stages) suffers much fewer cache misses, since only a small part of $Workmap$ is accessed on each stage. As in the case of $IndexJoin(s)$ there exists an additional overhead for selecting the relevant RIDs for processing.

The number of stages can be estimated as follows. Since it is desirable that all L_t fit into the cache, the number of tuples to be processed on each stage should not exceed $\frac{|CacheSize|}{size(L_t)}$, and hence the number of stages should be the minimal number that is greater than $\frac{|R|size(L_t)}{CacheSize}$. $|L_t|$ decreases as the algorithm proceeds, but its average value remains in the bounds $[L(R, S), l_S]$, where $L(R, S)$ and l_S are the average number of qualifying tuples of S for a tuple of R, and average length of inverted lists l_S^v in RS_{IF}, respectively. This observation enables to get an upper and a lower bounds for the number of stages, but the interval between them can be quite large. So in practice, the number of stages needs to be carefully tuned.

Note that both algorithms have much in common, since the values of $Domain(A)$ in the IFJ play the role of RIDs in the $IndexJoin$ and vice versa. Another important note concerns the staged versions of the algorithms. Though we use the term 'stage' to denote the effect of the partitioned processing, there is no real data dependency between subsequent stages in both cases. This means that both algorithms can be easily parallelized by putting each stage on a separate processor or server. Examination of parallel versions of the algorithms is beyond the scope of the paper.

4   Experimental Study

We have implemented both algorithms in Memphis. Memphis (a brief description can be found in [11]) is a framework for experiments on main-memory algorithms and index structures. Implementations are written in the C# programming language ([16]) and run under the .NET framework. For inverted files we used a custom hash table implementation. However, for hash function we reused the standard .NET $GetHashCode$ method that for integers simply returns the value of the integer. Hash table implementation is based on linear hashing.

All experiments were conducted on a laptop with Intel P4 2.8 GHz CPU and 1 Gb RAM running under Windows XP. This machine features Intel Pentium 4 Mobile processor with 2-level on-chip cache. The size of the L2 cache is 512 Kb, and the size of the L2 cache line is 128 bytes (these parameters were measured using Stefan Manegold's Calibrator tool [5]). For measuring the number of L2 cache misses we used the Intel VTune Performance Analyser ([17]) that provides a graphical user interface to various

CPU counters. All reported times were estimated using *QueryPerformanceCounter / QueryPerformanceFrequency* Windows API that give a programmatic access to the high-resolution hardware performance counter. To reduce level of noise in measurements, we present average times based on results of several runs.

For our experiments we used synthetic datasets. These datasets were generated by a program that takes desired characteristics of the dataset (relations cardinalities, average set cardinality, distributions of set cardinalities and set elements, size of the element domain etc.) as input and produces the resulting dataset in the form of a text file. Unless mentioned explicitly we do not include the time necessary for constructing the inverted files into the response time of a join algorithm. The reason is that in a practical situation it is expected that inverted files have already been built prior to computing the join.

4.1   Case Study 1: Tuning Number of Stages for $IFJ(n)$

In this case study, we use a dataset containing two relations, each of which consists of two attributes - the first is used as a primary key, and the second is a set-valued attribute. The characteristics of relations are: $|r| = |s| = 5, |V| = 5000, |R| = 150000, |S| = 300000$, the join selectivity is $\frac{5007}{|R||S|} = 1.2 * 10^{-7}$. The results are presented in the Table 1 and on the Figure 3. It is evident that the best performance is achieved with 2-staged processing, 2 stages provide a balance between reduced number of cache misses and extra overhead of the multi-staged algorithm.

Table 1. Dependency of join time and number of L2 cache misses on n for *IFJ(n)*

Stages	Time, sec	Cache Misses ($*10^6$)
1	9.3	60
2	8.4	55
3	8.6	54
5	8.7	53
9	8.9	52

At the same time we observed that $IndexJoin(n)$ does not benefit from partitioning - the execution time grows steadily with increasing number of stages. We attribute this effect to the large cost of selecting relevant values in case of $IndexJoin(n)$. In the $IndexJoin(n)$ this operation is performed for each tuple of R on each stage, or, in other words, $n * |R|$ times. In the $IFJ(n)$ this selection of relevant tuples is necessary for each value, so its cost is proportional to $n * |V|$. Given that normally $|V| \ll |R|$, this seems to be a plausible explanation for inefficiency of staging for $IndexJoin$. In the further discussion we will assume that $n = 1$ for $IndexJoin(n)$.

4.2   Case Study 2: Comparing Performance of $IndexJoin$ and IFJ

It might seem from the previous experiment that IFJ is dominated by $IndexJoin$, but this is not indeed the case. To demonstrate this, we take relations with the following parameters: $|r| = 17, |s| = 25, |R| = 250000$ and vary $|S|$. The results of $IndexJoin(1)$

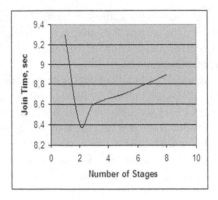

Fig. 3. Dependency of join time on number of stages for IFJ

Table 2. Comparing performance of $IndexJoin$ and IFJ

$|S|(*10^5)$	Time, sec		Cache misses	
	IndexJoin(1)	IFJ(3)	IndexJoin(1)	IFJ (3)
1	1.2	2.3	$42 * 10^6$	$60 * 10^6$
3	6	9	$1,3 * 10^7$	$1 * 10^7$
5	10	11	-	-
7	19	18	-	-

and $IFJ(3)$ (it has been observed that 3 stages provide the best result in the case) are presented in the Table 2 and on the Figure 4.3.

The explanation for the fact that $IFJ(3)$ eventually outperforms $IndexJoin(1)$ is that with approximately equal computational cost IFJ exhibits better locality than $IndexJoin(1)$, and importance of this factor increases with $|S|$. This is also confirmed by our measurements of number of cache misses in the Table 2 (some cells are omitted because the program ran out of memory and crashed when VTune profiling was enabled).

4.3   Case Study 3: Effect of Compression

Compression of increasing sequence of integers is a compelling technique that enables to reduce the size of inverted lists and increase both cache utilization and cardinality of relations that can be joined in memory without trashing. In our implementation we used well-known Gamma-encoding ([14]). In this experiment the cardinalities of relations are kept fixed: $|R| = 100000, |S| = 250000$. The dependency among running time, total memory used by the program (to retrieve this value, the code was instrumented by a call to the $GC.GetTotalMemory$ function from the .NET standard library. This function performs garbage collection before calculating the size of the heap), the average lengths of inverted lists and the cardinality of the result $|Result|$ are illustrated in the Table 3. The table shows results for both versions of the IFJ, with and without com-

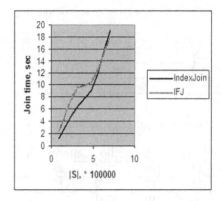

Fig. 4. Dependency of join time on $|S|$ for $IndexJoin$ and IFJ

Table 3. Effect of compression on IFJ

$|l_R|$	$|l_S|$	$|Result|$	Uncompressed		Compressed	
			Time, sec	Mem. Usage, Mb	Time, sec	Mem. Usage, Mb
20	50	137	1.5	110	3.2	113
75	188	1759	1.8	113	3.9	90
3000	7500	0	73	144	115	146
500	2250	$50 * 10^6$	-	300	151	91

pression. One cell is missed because the algorithm was not able to finish due to exhaustion of all the available memory. This experiment was not performed for $IndexJoin$ but we suspect that it would show similar results.

From the presented results it becomes clear that more compact inverted lists in the 'compressed' version, though reducing the number of compulsory L2 cache misses, do not pay off the increase in the cost of intersection operation. So the most important effect of using compression is smaller memory footprint. As the third and the fourth rows of the table demonstrate this effect is achieved only when all l_R, l_S and $|Result|$ are large enough. This fact quite matches the intuitive expectations, since the less the cardinality of the result (in the extreme case of the third row the result is empty), the shorter inverted lists in the intermediate results, and the less benefits we obtain compressing them.

4.4 Case Study 4: Comparison with Other Algorithms

To demonstrate the efficiency of the proposed methods in comparison with other known algorithms for set-containment joins, we have also implemented signature nested-loops join (SNL, [2]) and partitioned set join (PSJ, [8]). We consider the single relation with fixed parameters $|r| = 5, |V| = 10000$. The relation is joined with itself. For the PSJ and SNL we tuned such parameters as signature size and number of partitions according to recommendations in respective papers and our own experiments. The results are depicted in the Table 4 (for the $IndexJoin$ and IFJ we include the time spent in

Table 4. Comparison with other algorithms, large $|V|$

$|R|$	$|Result|$	SNL, sec	PSJ, sec	IFJ, sec	IndexJoin, sec
20000	20019	53	45	0.23	0.3
75000	75000	-	70	1.11	1.17
150000	150000	-	140	2.43	2.37

Table 5. Comparison with other algorithms, decreasing $|V|$

$|V|$	$|Result|$	PSJ, sec	IFJ, sec	IndexJoin, sec
1000	15727	10	0.21	0.23
500	15727	10.8	0.22	0.26
250	26537	10.9	0.31	0.34
100	26537	15	0.7	0.78
50	339421	32	1.6	1.45
25	1544713	71	4.7	4.2
10	-	282	49	45

constructing the inverted files in the reported time). SNL has been quickly recognized as a dominated algorithm, so we gave up experiments with it.

Since the performance of $IndexJoin$ and IFJ heavily depends on the average length of inverted lists in S_{IF} and RS_{IF}, one might expect that it deteriorates fast with decrease of $|V|$. To verify this hypothesis, we performed another experiment under the same conditions as the previous one except for the $|R| = 15000$ is fixed, and $|V|$ is decreasing. The results are given in the Table 5 and illustrated by the chart on the Figure 5 (one cell is missing because in all cases the program ran out of memory). As these measurements and the curves on the Figure 5 show, $IndexJoin$ and IFJ are indeed more sensitive to decreasing $|V|$ than PSJ (decreasing $|V|$ from 1000 to 10 resulted in ≈ 28 times slowdown of PSJ and ≈ 200 times slowdown of IFJ and $IndexJoin$). However, in all cases inverted files-based algorithms still demonstrated much better performance than PSJ.

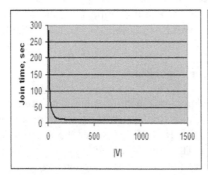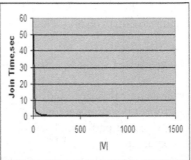

Fig. 5. Dependency of join time on $|V|$ for PSJ (left) and IFJ (right)

5   Conclusion

We presented two algorithms for set-containment join based on inverted files. We examined a technique for improving cache behavior of algorithms that splits an algorithm into stages so that only a small part of data is accessed on each stage. It turned out that this technique is quite efficient for the second algorithm, IFJ, but does not benefit the first algorithm, $IndexJoin$, because in the case of $IndexJoin$ it does not pay off the extra overhead caused by selecting relevant values for processing on each stage.

Both algorithms provide competitive performance. Our experiments reveal that generally speaking $IndexJoin$ is more effective for relations of small and medium cardinalities and if the average cardinality of the set-valued attribute is not large. IFJ is better suited for relations of large cardinalities, since it better scales with grow of $|S|$. We also discovered that compression of the inverted lists may provide large savings of memory space if the length of inverted lists and result cardinality are large enough. At the same time compression achieves better cache utilization at too expensive cost of extra computations required to unpack the compressed data.

Future research may focus on improving cache behavior of $IndexJoin$, since our current approach has turned out ineffective. Both algorithms discussed in this paper can be easily parallelized, and studying the paralled and distributed versions of algorithms is an interesting unexplored problem. Another research direction is development of main-memory variants of algorithms for other set predicates like intersection or overlap.

References

1. Boncz, P. A., Manegold, S., Kersten, M. L.: Database Architecture Optimized for the New Bottleneck: Memory Access. In Proceedings of the 25th VLDB Conference (1999) 54–65
2. Helmer, S., Moerkotte, G.: Evaluation of main memory join algorithms for joins with set comparison join predicates. In Proceedings of the 23rd VLDB Conference (1997) 386–395
3. Helmer, S., Moerkotte, G.: Compiling away set containment and intersection joins (technical report) (2002)
4. Mamoulis, N.: Efficient processing of joins on set-valued attributes. In Proceedings of the SIGMOD 2003 Conference (2003) 157–168
5. Manegold, S.: The Calibrator, a Cache-Memory and TLB Calibration Tool. http://homepages.cwi.nl/~manegold/Calibrator/
6. Manegold, S., Boncz, P., Nes, N., Kersten, M.: Cache-conscious radix-decluster projections. In Proceeding of the SIGMOD 2004 Conference (2004)
7. Melnik, S., Garcia-Molina, H.: Adaptive Algorithms for Set Containment Joins. ACM Transactions on Database Systems (2003) 28:56–99
8. Ramasamy, K. et al.: Set containment joins: The good, the bad and the ugly. In Proceedings of the 26th VLDB Conference (2000) 351–362
9. Rao, J., Ross, K. A.: Making B+-Trees Cache-Conscious in Main Memory. In Proceedings of the 2000 ACM SIGMOD International Conference on Management of Data (2000) 475–486
10. Shaporenkov, D.: Multi-indices - a tool for optimizing join processing in main memory. In Proceedings of the Baltic DBIS 2004 Conference (2004)
11. Shaporenkov, D.: Performance comparison of main-memory algorithms for set containment joins. In Proceedings of the SYRCoDIS'04 (2004)
12. Shatdal, A., Kant, C., Naughton, J. F.: Cache Conscious Algorithms for Relational Query Processing. In Proceedings of the 20th VLDB Conference (1994) 510–521

13. Valduriez, P.: Join Indices. ACM Transactions on Database Systems (1987) 12:218–246
14. Witten, I., Moffat, A., Bell, T.: Managing Gigabytes : Compressing and Indexing Documents and Images. Morgan Kaufmann publishers, second edition (1999)
15. Zhou, J., Ross, K. A.: Buffering Accesses to Memory-Resident Index Structures. In Proceedings of the 29th VLDB Conference (2003)
16. C# Language Specification. ECMA-334 International Standard (2001)
17. Intel VTune Performance Analyzer. http://www.intel.com/software/products/vtune

VA-Files vs. R*-Trees in Distance Join Queries[*]

Antonio Corral[1], Alejandro D'Ermiliis[1], Yannis Manolopoulos[2],
and Michael Vassilakopoulos[3]

[1] Department of Languages and Computing, University of Almeria, 04120 Almeria, Spain
{acorral, sandro}@ual.es
[2] Department of Informatics, Aristotle University, GR-54124 Thessaloniki, Greece
manolopo@csd.auth.gr
[3] Department of Informatics, Technological Educational Institute of Thessaloniki,
P.O. BOX 141, GR-57400, Thessaloniki, Greece
vasilako@it.teithe.gr

Abstract. In modern database applications the similarity of complex objects is examined by performing distance-based queries (e.g. nearest neighbour search) on data of high dimensionality. Most multidimensional indexing methods have failed to efficiently support these queries in arbitrary high-dimensional datasets (due to the dimensionality curse). Similarity join queries and K closest pairs queries are the most representative distance join queries, where two high-dimensional datasets are combined. These queries are very expensive in terms of response time and I/O activity in case of high-dimensional spaces. On the other hand, the filtering-based approach, as applied by the VA-file, has turned out to be a very promising alternative for nearest neighbour search. In general, the filtering-based approach represents vectors as compact approximations, whereas by first scanning these approximations, only a small fraction of the real vectors is visited. Here, we elaborate on VA-files and develop VA-file based algorithms for answering similarity join and K closest pairs queries on high-dimensional data. Also, performance-wise we compare the use of VA-files and R*-trees (a structure that has been proven to be of robust nature) for answering these queries. The results of the comparison do not lead to a clear winner.

1 Introduction

Large sets of complex objects are used in modern applications (e.g. multimedia databases [11], medical images databases [15], etc.). To examine the similarity of these objects, high-dimensional feature vectors (i.e. points in the high-dimensional spaces) are extracted from them and organized in multidimensional indexes. Then, distance-based queries (e.g. nearest neighbour, similarity join, K closest pairs, etc.) are applied on the high-dimensional points. The most representative high-dimensional *distance join queries* (DJQ), where two datasets are involved, are the *similarity join*

[*] Supported by the ARCHIMEDES project 2.2.14, «Management of Moving Objects and the WWW», of the Technological Educational Institute of Thessaloniki (EPEAEK II), co-funded by the Greek Ministry of Education and Religious Affairs and the European Union, INDALOG TIC2002-03968 project «A Database Language Based on Functional Logic Programming» of the Spanish Ministry of Science and Technology under FEDER funds, and the framework of the Greek-Serbian bilateral protocol.

J. Eder et al. (Eds.): ADBIS 2005, LNCS 3631, pp. 153–166, 2005.
© Springer-Verlag Berlin Heidelberg 2005

query (SJ) and the *K closest pairs query* (*K*-CPQ). The SJ query discovers all pairs of points from two different point datasets, where the distance does not exceed a distance threshold δ. The *K*-CPQ discovers *K*>0 distinct pairs of points formed from two different point datasets that have the *K* smallest distances between them. The former does not take into account the cardinality and order of the final result (but only the user-defined distance threshold δ), whereas the latter does not consider any distance bound (but only the user-defined final result cardinality *K*). Note that these queries have been successfully applied in data mining algorithms (e.g. clustering algorithms based on similarity join [3] and closest pairs [16]).

Here, we focus on performing DJQ using a *filtering-based approach* that has proven to outperform a sequential scan for high dimensionalities, when a tree index fails to process a *K* nearest neighbour query (*K*-NNQ) efficiently (dimensionality curse). The VA-file (vector-approximation file) is the most representative access method of this category [20]. Instead of partitioning, the VA-file constructs the *index file* by compressing each feature vector. With respect to query processing, the compact vector approximations are sequentially scanned and filtered in the first stage so that a small fraction of them remains to be visited in the second stage. The improvement for *K*-NNQ arises due to the reduced I/O accesses (as the index file size is small) and due to the smaller response time (because of the fewer distance computations).

The main goal of this paper is to develop VA-file based algorithms for DJQ involving two sets of high-dimensional data. More specifically, we develop algorithms for SJs and *K*-CPQs in high-dimensional spaces, where both point datasets are indexed by VA-files. To achieve this goal, we propose new bounds on the distance between pairs of points and new pruning conditions. Moreover, we present experimental results comparing the performance of these algorithms with analogous algorithms that make use of R*-trees [1], in terms of the I/O activity and the response time. Based on these results, we draw conclusions about the behaviour of the algorithms that use VA-files for DJQ in high-dimensional spaces.

The paper is organized as follows. In Section 2, we review the related literature and motivate the research reported here. In Section 3, a brief description of the VA-file structure, definitions of the most representative DJQ, approximation-based distance functions and pruning conditions are presented. In Section 4, algorithms based on distance bounds and pruning conditions over VA-files for *K*-CPQ and SJ are examined. In Section 5, a comparative performance study of these algorithms is reported. Finally, in Section 6, conclusions on the contribution of this paper and future work are summarized.

2   Related Work and Motivation

Numerous algorithms have been proposed for satisfying DJQ in high-dimensional environments. For similarity joins on high-dimensional point datasets, the most representative papers are [18, 14, 10, 4]. In [18] an index structure (ε-kdB tree) and an algorithm for similarity self-join on high-dimensional points was presented. The basic idea is to partition the dataset perpendicularly to a selected dimension into stripes of the width ε to restrict the join algorithm to pairs of subsequent stripes. In [14] the problem of computing high-dimensional similarity joins between two high-dimensional point datasets, where neither input is indexed (Multidimensional Spatial Join, MSJ), was investigated. The basic idea of this access method is to partition the dataset into level-files, each of which contains the points of a level in the order of their Hilbert values. In [10] a new algorithm (Generic External Space Sweep, GESS), which introduces a rate of data replication to reduce the number of distance computations as an enhancement of MSJ, was proposed. In [4], a complex and interesting index architecture (Multipage Index, MuX) and join algorithm (MuX-join), which allows a separate optimization CPU time and I/O time, were presented. On the other hand, the K-CPQ has not been studied in-depth for high-dimensionality data. In [8], DFS-based approximate algorithms for the K-CPQ using R-trees [13] have been proposed (in order to get suboptimal results in reasonable time). One of the main objectives of this work was to examine the influence of the approximate parameters on the trade-off between accuracy and efficiency of such algorithms.

Many approaches have been proposed to overcome the *curse of dimensionality* in the context of K-NNQ. They are usually classified into five major categories: (1) tree index structures by partitioning the data space or data-partitioning; (2) space-filling curves, (3) dimensionality reduction approaches; (4) approximate algorithms and (5) filtering-based (i.e. approximation) approaches. In this paper, we are going to focus on the last category. The filtering-based approach overcomes the dimensionality curse by filtering the points so that only a small fraction of them must be visited during a search. In this respect, the most representative access method is the VA-file [20], which divides the data space into 2^b rectangular cells, where b denotes a user-specified number of bits. The VA-file allocates a unique bit-string of length b to each cell and approximates data points that fall into a cell by that bit-string. In general, the VA-file itself is simply an array on disk of these compact approximations of points.

Following the ideas of the VA-file, many variants have proposed to improve the performance of K-NNQ. The VA$^+$-file [12] combines a linear decorrelation using KLT (Karhunen-Loève Transformation) along with a variance specific quantization scheme using the VA-file principles. The LPC-file [6] enhances the VA-file by adding polar coordinate information of the point (vector) to approximation, increasing the discriminatory power. The GC-tree [5] pursues a hybrid strategy which incorporates a quad-tree-like hierarchical space partitioning with bit-encoded clusters and a point approximation based on local polar coordinates on the leaf nodes. In the IQ-tree [2], all points are globally approximated according to one fixed grid (like the VA-file) and it also maintains a flat directory containing the minimum bounding rectangles (MBRs) of the approximate data representations. The A-tree [17] combines hierarchical indexing and local approximation by quantization. The MBRs of point clusters are approximated by quantization in so-called virtual bounding rectangles (VBRs). And recently, the SA-tree [9] was proposed, which combines data clustering and compression (i.e. it employs the characteristics of each cluster to adaptively compress points to bit-string) to speed up processing of high-dimensional K-NNQ.

All the previous efforts have been mainly focused on enhancing the VA-file to improve the performance during the K-NNQ (a query applied on a single set of high-dimensional data). The main objective of this paper is to investigate the behaviour of VA-files on DJQ involving pairs of high-dimensional data sets (SJs and K-CPQs). For this reason, we propose new bounds of the distance between pairs of points, new pruning conditions and lead to algorithms for these DJQ using VA-files.

3   Distance Join Queries for VA-Files

3.1   Distance Join Queries

Let us consider points in the *dim*-dimensional data space ($D^{dim} = \Re^{dim}$) and a distance function for a pair of these points. A general distance function is the L_t-distance (d_t) or Minkowski distance between two points p_i and q_j from two different datasets ($P = \{p_i: 0 \leq i \leq |P|-1\}$ and $Q = \{q_j: 0 \leq j \leq |Q|-1\}$, respectively) in D^{dim} ($p_i = (p_i[0], p_i[1],\ldots, p_i[\text{dim}-1])$ and $q_j = (q_j[0], q_j[1],\ldots, q_j[\text{dim}-1])$), where $p_i[d]$ ($q_j[d]$) is the coordinate value of p_i (q_j) in dimension d, that is defined by:

$$d_t(p_i,q_j) = \left(\sum_{d=0}^{dim-1} |p_i[d]-q_j[d]|\right)^{\frac{1}{t}}, \text{ if } 1 \leq t < \infty, \text{ and } d_\infty(p_i,q_j) = \max_{0 \leq d \leq dim-1} |p_i[d]-q_j[d]|$$

For $t = 2$ and $t = 1$ we have the Euclidean and the Manhattan distances. They are the most known L_t-distances. Often, the Euclidean distance is used as a distance function, but, depending on the application, other distance functions may be more appropriate. The *dim*-dimensional Euclidean space (metric space), E^{dim}, is the pair (D^{dim}, d_2). In the following, we will use *dist* instead of d_2. The most representative DJQ in E^{dim} are the following:

Definition. Similarity Join (SJ). Let P and Q be two point datasets ($P \neq \varnothing$ and $Q \neq \varnothing$) in E^{dim} and δ a real number $\delta \geq 0$. Then, the result of the Similarity Join is the set $SJ(P,Q,\delta) \subseteq P \times Q$ containing all possible pairs of points of $P \times Q$ that can be formed by choosing one point of P and one point of Q, having a distance smaller than or equal to δ: **SJ(P, Q, δ)** = $\{(p_i,q_j) \in P \times Q: \text{dist}(p_i,q_j) \leq \delta\}$.

Definition. K closest pairs query (K-CPQ). Let P and Q be two point datasets ($P \neq \varnothing$ and $Q \neq \varnothing$) in E^{dim} and K an integer number in the range $1 \leq K \leq |P| \cdot |Q|$. Then, the result of the K closest pairs query is the set K-CPQ(P,Q,K) $\subseteq P \times Q$ containing all the ordered sequences of K different pairs of points of $P \times Q$ with the K smallest distances between all possible pairs of points that can be formed by choosing one point of P and one point of Q: **K-CPQ(P,Q,K)** = $\{((p_1,q_1), (p_2,q_2), \ldots, (p_K,q_K)) \in (P \times Q)^K: p_1, p_2, \ldots, p_K \in P, q_1, q_2, \ldots, q_K \in Q, (p_i,q_i) \neq (p_j,q_j)\ i \neq j\ 1 \leq i,j \leq K, \forall (p_i,q_i) \in P \times Q - \{(p_1,q_1), (p_2,q_2), \ldots, (p_K,q_K)\}$ and $\text{dist}(p_1,q_1) \leq \text{dist}(p_2,q_2) \leq \ldots \leq \text{dist}(p_K,q_K) \leq \text{dist}(p_i,q_j)\}$.

For SJ, if the sets *P* and *Q* coincide, then the DJQ is called *similarity self-join* (widely studied in [18, 14, 10, 4]). Fig. 1 illustrates these DJQs, where the points of *P* and *Q* are represented by starts (*) and crosses (+), respectively. In the left part of Fig. 1, we can observe that $SJ(P,Q,\delta) = \{(p_3,q_1), (p_4,q_6), (p_6,q_6), (p_8,q_8), (p_8,q_9), (p_8,q_{10}), (p_{11},q_9), (p_{11},q_{10})\}$ where $\delta = 0.8$. If we want to obtain the four closest pairs ($K = 4$) of the two data-sets depicted in the right part of Fig. 1, the result is $K\text{-}CPQ(P,Q,K) = \{(p_8,q_8), (p_{11},q_{10}), (p_4,q_6), (p_8,q_9)\}$.

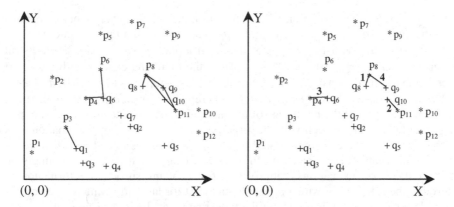

Fig. 1. Examples of SJ and K-CPQ using 2-dimensional points

3.2 The VA-File (Vector-Approximation File)

The VA-file [20] does not partition the data, but the data space is partitioned into rectangular cells which are used to generate bit-encoded approximations of the points. Therefore, the VA-file consists of two files: one contains an approximation of the feature representation of each point *(approximation file)*, whereas the other one the exact representation of each point *(vector file)*. They are connected by indexes, since they are simple arrays on disk. The quantization is obtained by laying a grid over the data space and approximating the points by their surrounding cells (see left part of Fig. 2). The grid has 2^{b_d} intervals along dimension d ($0 \leq d \leq dim-1$), where $b = \sum_d b_d$ is the number of bits per approximation, b_d is the number of bits for dimension d and *dim* the dimensionality of the data space. In Fig. 2, $b_d = 2$ and $dim = 2$ (a realistic b_d value for nearest neighbour search would be between 6 and 8 according to [20]). The *intervals* of this grid are numbered from 0 to $2^{b_d} - 1$ (see left part of Fig. 2), and the *partition points* $m[d, 0]$, $m[d, 1]$, ..., $m[d, 2^{b_d}]$ bound them. That is, $m[d, k]$ represents the k-th partition point in dimension d; and in total, there are $2^{b_d} + 1$ partition points

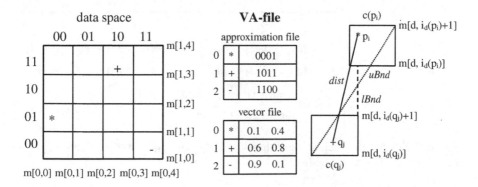

Fig. 2. Structure of the VA-file and, distances between points and cells

and 2^{b_d} intervals. These partition points are determined so that each interval contains the same number of vectors. Given a point p_i, $i_d(p_i)$ denotes the *interval* in dimension d that p_i falls into, i.e. it is the approximation of a point p_i ($P = \{p_i: 0 \leq i \leq |P|-1\}$) in dimension d and $i_d(p_i) \in \{0,1,\ldots, 2^{b_d} - 1\}$. Thus, the following expression holds ($p_i[d]$ is the value of p_i in dimension d): $m[d, i_d(p_i)] \leq p_i[d] < m[d, i_d(p_i)+1]$, $\forall d: 0 \leq d \leq dim-1$.

A *bit-string* of length $b = \sum_d b_d$ ($0 \leq d \leq dim-1$) represents each *cell*. Such a bit-string is the concatenation of the bit-strings of the interval numbers of the cell (for example, the point (+) falls into the cell with the bit-string 1011). Thus, the approximation of p_i is the bit-string of the cell (represented by $c(p_i)$) that contains p_i and it is denoted by $a(p_i)$ (i.e. elements of approximation file). Thus, the approximation file is simply an array of these approximations. Intuitively, $a(p_i)$ contains sufficient information to determine the cell $c(p_i)$ in which p_i lies. Notice that for large *dim* values, the volume of a cell is so small that it is highly unlikely the two points lie in the same cell.

3.3 Distance Bounds Between Cells and Pruning Conditions

Next, we are going to show how pairs of cells can be used to derive (lower and upper) bounds between pairs of points. Given two points from two different points datasets $p_i \in P$ and $q_j \in Q$, the minimum (maximum) distance between their cells ($c(p_i)$ and $c(q_j)$, respectively) is a lower (upper) bound of its distance. Thus, given the cells of two points from two different datasets, we can bound from below and above their distance ($dist(p_i,q_j)$) as follows (according to the terminology of [20]): $lBnd(c(p_i), c(q_j)) \leq dist(p_i, q_j) \leq uBnd(c(p_i), c(q_j))$.

The lower bound, $lBnd(c(p_i), c(q_j))$, is the smallest distance between the cells of p_i and q_j. Obviously, $lBnd(c(p_i),c(q_j),d) \leq lBnd(c(p_i),c(q_j))$, $\forall d: 0 \leq d \leq dim-1$ [7]. Analogously, we can obtain the upper bound, $uBnd(c(p_i), c(q_j))$. The right part of the Fig. 2 shows these distance bounds and its relation with $dist(p_i, q_j)$.

$$lBnd\big(c(p_i),c(q_j)\big) = \sqrt{\sum_{d=0}^{dim-1} \begin{cases} \left(m[d,i_d(p_i)]-m[d,i_d(q_j)+1]\right)^2, & m[d,i_d(p_i)] > m[d,i_d(q_j)+1] \\ \left(m[d,i_d(q_j)]-m[d,i_d(p_i)+1]\right)^2, & m[d,i_d(q_j)] > m[d,i_d(p_i)+1] \\ 0, & otherwise \end{cases}}$$

$$uBnd\big(c(p_i),c(q_j)\big) = \sqrt{\sum_{d=0}^{dim-1} \begin{cases} \left(m[d,i_d(p_i)+1]-m[d,i_d(q_j)]\right)^2, & m[d,i_d(p_i)] > m[d,i_d(q_j)+1] \\ \left(m[d,i_d(q_j)+1]-m[d,i_d(p_i)]\right)^2, & m[d,i_d(q_j)] > m[d,i_d(p_i)+1] \\ \max \begin{cases} \left(m[d,i_d(p_i)+1]-m[d,i_d(q_j)]\right)^2, \\ \left(m[d,i_d(q_j)+1]-m[d,i_d(p_i)]\right)^2 \end{cases}, & otherwise \end{cases}}$$

In order to design efficient algorithms for DJQ using the VA-file structure, pruning conditions need to be defined.

Pruning Condition 1. If $lBnd(c(p_i),c(q_j)) > z$, then the pair of points (p_i,q_j) will be discarded from the final result, where z is the δ distance threshold for SJ, or the distance value of the K-th closest pair that has been found so far ($K\text{-}cp^{dist}(p,q)$) for K-CPQ. $lBnd(c(p_i), c(q_j)) \leq \delta \Rightarrow (p_i, q_j) \in SJ(P, Q, \delta)$ and $lBnd(c(p_i), c(q_j)) \leq K\text{-}cp^{dist}(p, q)) \Rightarrow (p_i, q_j) \in KCPQ(P, Q, K)$

Pruning Condition 2. If $lBnd(c(p_i),c(q_j)) > y$, then the pair of points (p_i, q_j) will be discarded from the final result, where y is the δ distance threshold for SJ, or the distance value of the K-th largest upper bound encountered so far ($K\text{-}cp^{uBnd}(c(p), c(q))$) for K-CPQ. $lBnd(c(p_i), c(q_j)) > \delta \Rightarrow (p_i, q_j) \notin SJ(P, Q, \delta)$ and $lBnd(c(p_i), c(q_j)) > K\text{-}cp^{uBnd}(c(p), c(q)) \Rightarrow (p_i, q_j) \notin KCPQ(P, Q, K)$. Note that in the case of SJ the two pruning conditions are the same.

4 Algorithms for Distance Join Queries Using VA-Files

The previous distance bounds between cells and pruning conditions can be embedded into search algorithms for VA-files and obtain the result of DJQ. In this section we describe additional data structures needed for DJQ, a distance-based sweeping technique for fast pruning, and two search algorithms using VA-files as in [20].

4.1 Data Structures for the Result and Distance-Based Sweep Technique

In order to design algorithms for processing K-CPQ in a non-incremental way (K must be fixed in advance) [7], an extra data structure that holds the K closest pairs (result of K-CPQ) is needed. This data structure is organized as a maximum binary heap, called *Kheap* [8]. The closest pair with the largest distance ($K\text{-}cp^{dist}(p,q)$) resides on top of the Kheap (the root), and it will be used in *pruning condition 1*. Notice that this data structure will also be used to calculate $K\text{-}cp^{uBnd}(c(p),c(q))$, used in *pruning condition 2*. On the other hand, the result of the SJ must not be ordered, and the Kheap is not needed. Therefore, the data structure that holds the result set is (instead of Kheap) a file of records (*resultFile*) of three fields, where the first field will be the distance, whereas the second and the third ones will be the pair of points (p_i,q_j). To accelerate the performance of SJs, a page buffer is used in main memory to hold the records as they are computed and as soon as it gets full, we add a new page to the result file.

Since the approximation file itself is simply a *flat array on disk* of all the approximations of points (approximation file), we can adapt the *distance-based plane-sweep technique* [7] for the high-dimensional space to avoid processing all possible combinations of pairs from two approximations files. In general, this technique consists of choosing a sweeping dimension and sorting the approximations on this dimension in increasing order (if both files are sorted already on a common dimension, no sorting is necessary). First, the sweeping dimension ($0 \leq sd \leq dim-1$) is established (e.g. $sd = 0$ or X-axis). After that, two pointers are maintained initially pointing to the first entry of each sorted approximation file. Let *pivot* be the entry of the smallest value of the approximation over the sweeping dimension pointed by one of these two pointers, e.g. $pivot = a(p_0)$ {$a(p_i)$: $0 \leq i \leq |P|-1$}. The cell of the pivot must be paired up with the cells determined by the approximations stored in the other approximation file {$a(q_j)$: $0 \leq j \leq |Q|-1$} from left to right that satisfy $lBnd(c(pivot),$

$c(q_j),sd) \leq z$ (where z is a pruning distance, e.g. $z = \delta$ for SJs), obtaining a set of candidate pairs of approximations where the element *pivot* is fixed. After all possible pairs of approximations that contain *pivot* have been found, the pointer of the pivot is increased to the next entry, *pivot* is updated with the approximation of the next smallest value of the approximation over the sweeping dimension pointed by one of the two pointers and the process is repeated until one of the approximation file is completely scanned.

Notice that we apply $lBnd(c(p_i),c(q_j),sd)$ because in this technique, the sweeping takes place only over one dimension. Moreover, the search is only restricted to the closest cells (obtained from approximations of points) with respect to the cell of the *pivot* entry according to the current z value. No duplicated pairs are obtained, since the cells are always scanned over sorted approximation files.

4.2 Distance-Based Sweep Algorithm (VA-DBSA)

The general schema for search algorithms using the VA-file structure has two phases. In the first phase *(filtering step)*, the approximations of points (approximation file) are scanned to determine lower bounds on the distance of cells pairs, and pairs of points are pruned according to the distance-based sweep technique and the pruning conditions. In the second phase *(refinement step)*, the filtered points (vector file) are visited and the pairs of points that satisfy the distance condition (SJ or K-CPQ) are chosen for the final result. Notice that the performance of this algorithm depends upon the ordering of the approximations and points. The algorithm for processing the K-CPQ is described by the following steps ($z = K\text{-}cp^{dist}(p,q)$; at the beginning $z = \infty$):

- *Filtering step*: Apply the *distance-based sweep technique* over the two approximation files, according to $lBnd(c(p_i),c(q_j),sd)$. Then, from these filtered pairs of approximations $(a(p_i),a(q_j))$ select only those that satisfy the *pruning condition 1*, i.e. $lBnd(c(p_i),c(q_j)) \leq z$.
- *Refinement step*: From the final candidates of the filtering step, select only those pairs of points from vector files having $dist(p_i,q_j) \leq z$. Insert all of them into Kheap until it gets full. Then remove the root of the Kheap and insert the new pair of points (p_i,q_j), updating this data structure and $z = K\text{-}cp^{dist}(p,q)$.

The adaptation of this algorithm (VA-DBSA) from K-CPQ to the SJ is very simple. In the filtering and refinement steps, replace z with δ. Notice that Kheap is now unnecessary and the final result is stored in *resultFile*.

4.3 Near Optimal Distance-Based Sweep Algorithm (VA-NODBSA)

In [20] a near optimal algorithm for K-NNQ which minimizes the number of vectors visited was proposed. Here, we present a version of near optimal algorithm for DJQ, although it is *more complex, time-consuming* and has *memory-overhead*. It has also two phases. (1) During the *filtering step* the approximations are scanned, the distance-based sweep technique is applied and, the $lBnd$ and $uBnd$ are computed for each pair of approximations. Assuming that $K\text{-}cp^{uBnd}(c(p),c(q))$ is also calculated using a Kheap, if a pair of approximations is encountered such that $lBnd(c(p_i),c(q_j)) > K\text{-}cp^{uBnd}(c(p),c(q))$, then the pair of points (p_i,q_j) can be discarded. The selected pairs of approximations and their *lBnd* are organized as a minimum binary heap, called *Nheap* [7]. The size of Nheap could be very large with the increase of *dim* and the cardinality of the datasets, and a hybrid memory/disk scheme and techniques based on range partitioning could be needed [8]. (2) During the *refinement step* the pairs stored in Nheap are visited in increasing order of *lBnd* to determine the final answer set. Not all these candidate pairs of points are visited, but this phase ends when $lBnd(c(p_i),c(q_j)) > K\text{-}cp^{dist}(p,q)$, (recall that $K\text{-}cp^{dist}(p,q)$ is also calculated using a *Kheap*). The algorithm for *K*-CPQ is described by the following steps ($z = K\text{-}cp^{dist}(p,q)$ and $y = K\text{-}cp^{uBnd}(c(p),c(q))$, at the beginning $z = \infty$ and $y = -\infty$):

- *Filtering step*: Create Nheap, and a Kheap structure based on *uBnd*, called *KheapU*. Apply the *distance-based sweep technique* over the two approximation files, according to $lBnd(c(p_i),c(q_j),sd)$. Then, from these pairs of approximations $(a(p_i),\ a(q_j))$ select only those that satisfy the *pruning condition 2*, i.e. $lBnd(c(p_i),c(q_j)) \le y$, and store them in Nheap. $y = K\text{-}cp^{uBnd}(c(p),\ c(q))$ is computed using KheapU.
- *Refinement step*: Process Nheap from these pairs of approximations $(a(p_i),\ a(q_j))$ while $lBnd(c(p_i),c(q_j)) \le z$, i.e. using the *pruning condition 1*. $z = K\text{-}cp^{dist}(p,q)$ is computed using a Kheap structure based on *dist*, called *KheapD*. Moreover, select only those pairs of points from vector files having $dist(p_i,\ q_j) \le z$, and insert all of them into KheapD until it gets full. Then remove the root of the KheapD and insert the new pair of points $(p_i,\ q_j)$, updating this data structure and $z = K\text{-}cp^{dist}(p,q)$.

The adaptation of this algorithm (VA-NODBSA) from *K*-CPQ to the SJ is analogous to the adaptation of VA-DBSA for both phases (filtering and refinement).

5   Experimental Results

In this section, we have evaluated the performance of our algorithms over real high-dimensional datasets of image features (unlike [20] where uniform data have been used) extracted from a Corel image collection (http://corel.digitalriver.com/), available from [21]. We have chosen two datasets of features based on the colour histogram (CH) and colour histogram layout (HL). Each real dataset contains 68,040 feature vectors of *dim* = 32. From each 32-dimensional vector, we have chosen the first 4, 8, 12, 16 and 32 dimensions, giving rise to pairs of points datasets with different dimensionalities and the same cardinality (68,040). These pairs of datasets are used in *K*-CPQ and SJ.

All experiments were performed on an Intel/Linux workstation with a Pentium IV 2.5 GHz processor, 1 GByte of main memory, and several GBytes of secondary storage, using the gcc compiler. The index page size was 8 Kb, and the number of items sharing the same disk page decreased as the dimensionality increased. All the elements were fetched directly from the disk without caching. The performance measurements are mainly: (a) the elapsed time (wall-clock time) reported in seconds and (b) the number of page accesses. For comparison purposes, we have also implemented distance join algorithms using nested loops over the vector files and R-tree-based distance join algorithms [8], applying in both cases the *distance-based sweep technique* described previously. Besides, the index construction was not taken into account for the total elapsed time.

Our first experiment seeks the most appropriate number of bits per dimension (b_d) for VA-files that will be used in the next experiments. The suggested value in [20] for b_d was 8, although here we have obtained (after many experiments) that $b_d = 10$ reports better results for DJQ. For higher values of b_d the size of the approximation file can be larger than the size of the vector file, and the filtering power is seriously affected, since the vectors themselves are used without being approximated. We have also observed that VA-NODBSA minimizes the number of vectors visited, although it is time-consuming (slower than VA-DBSA), because in the filtering step it is necessary to maintain two auxiliary structures Nheap and KheapU (variable sizes).

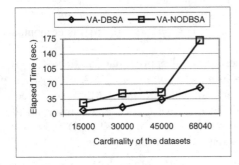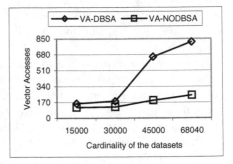

Fig. 3. Performance of VA-files algorithms for *K*-CPQ with respect to the dataset sizes

In the second experiment, we have studied the behaviour of the VA-file-based algorithms for *K*-CPQ when the cardinality of the datasets varies. We have the following configuration: *dim* = 16, |*P*| = |*Q*| = 15,000, 30,000, 45,000 and 68,040, *K* = 100 and b_d = 10. Fig. 3 shows that VA-DBSA is faster than VA-NODBSA, although it requires a smaller number of vector accesses (in the refinement step). In addition, we can also observe the effect of the increase of the size of the datasets for VA-NODBSA. This results to the increase of the consumed time and the increase of the memory-overhead, since more items have to be combined in the filtering step.

In the third experiment, we compare the performance of the VA-file-based algorithms (VA-DBSA = DB and VA-NODBSA = NO) with a nested loops algorithm only using vector files (NL) and with an R*-tree distance join algorithm (Rtree), varying the dimensionality (*dim* = 4, 8, 12, 16 and 32). Fig. 4 shows the performance measurements for the following configuration: |*P*| = |*Q*| = 68,040, *K*=100, b_d = 10 and, the maximum branching factors for R*-trees were 227, 120, 81, 62 and 31 for each *dim* value, using a node size of 8 Kb. When comparing the results of the *K*-CPQ algorithms with respect to the I/O activity and the elapsed time, we observe that this query becomes more expensive as the dimensionality grows, in particular for values larger than 16. Notice, also, that the huge number of pages accesses (the sum of the number of approximation and vector accesses in the VA-file structure) in all algorithms is due to the absence of global buffering. The R-tree version was the fastest in all cases (e.g. 5 times faster than NL for *dim* = 2), although for low and medium dimensions it needed many page accesses. NL is also an interesting alternative with respect to the total elapsed time because the expensive filtering step is avoided, but for *dim* = 32 it obtained the largest value of page accesses. DB is better than NO for these two performance metrics, but the latter gets the minimum number of vector accesses after an expensive filtering phase over the two approximation files. For example, for *dim* = 32 the total number of vector accesses was 277 for NO and 2,811 for DB, whereas the number of approximation accesses was 17,227,051 and 8,255,818, respectively.

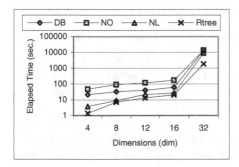 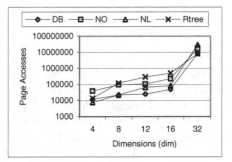

Fig. 4. Performance of distance-join algorithms where the dimensionality is increased

The forth experiment compares the performance of the VA-file-based algorithms (DB and NO) with NL and Rtree, varying K from 1 to 100,000. Fig. 5 illustrates the performance measurements for the configuration: $dim = 16$, $|P| = |Q| = 68,040$, $b_d = 10$ and the maximum branching factor for R*-trees was 62. In the left chart, we see that the slowest was NO, due to its time and memory consumption, although it needs the minimum number of vector accesses (e.g. $K = 100,000$, it was 83,033). The DB obtains interesting results for the total number of page accesses, when we have large K values. NL reports very good results since it avoids the filtering step and only works over the vector files using the distance-based sweep technique. For example, it was the fastest and the cheapest in terms of I/O activity for small K values (1 and 10). Finally, the results of the K-CPQ algorithm over R*-trees are very interesting as well, since it is the fastest for large K values and it obtains a small number of page accesses, mainly due to the high pruning in the internal nodes on the R*-trees, the use of distance-based sweep technique and the use of large fan-outs of the R-tree nodes.

The last experiment studies the performance of the best VA-file-based algorithm (VA-DBSA), NL and the Rtree variant, for similarity join (SJ) using different δ values (0.001, 0.003, 0.005, 0.008, 0.01, 0.03 and 0.05). Fig. 6 illustrates the performance measurements for the configuration: $dim = 16$, $|P| = |Q| = 68,040$, $b_d = 10$ and the maximum branching factor for R*-trees was 62. We can deduce that the R-tree distance join algorithm using distance-based sweep technique is the best alternative. For example, it was 10.7 times faster than NL for $\delta = 0.001$ (in the result, each point has an average of 7.1 join mates) and 8.1 times for $\delta = 0.05$ (141.8 join mates per point). NL (the filtering step is not performed) is slightly faster than

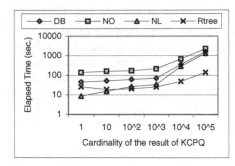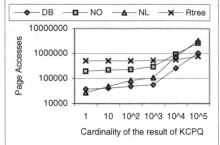

Fig. 5. Performance of *K*-CPQ when *K* is varied from 1 to 100,000

VA-DBSA, but it needs more page accesses. An interesting behaviour of the R-tree variant is that from $\delta = 0.01$ to $\delta = 0.05$, it needed 3.3 times more page accesses than for $\delta = 0.001$, whereas for VA-DBSA this was of 17.5 times.

From the previous performance comparison for real high-dimensional datasets, the most important conclusions are the following: (1) the filtering power of VA-file-based algorithms for DJQ is reduced when the dimensionality, cardinality of the datasets, *K* and δ are increased. (2) VA-NODBSA minimizes the number of vector accesses at the expense of time consumption and memory-overhead. (3) Including the distance-based sweep technique in the R-tree distance join algorithm improves notably its performance mainly with respect to the CPU cost. (4) And finally, the most important conclusion is that for DJQ where two real high-dimensional datasets are involved, the use of hierarchical multidimensional access methods (as R*-trees) with optimization techniques (like distance-based sweep) to the processing of index nodes (controlling the trade-off between I/O and CPU cost with respect to the page size [KoS01]) is the best alternative since its filtering power is increased, when *K* and δ are not very large (in this case the nested loops is the best alternative because it has no additional index overhead).

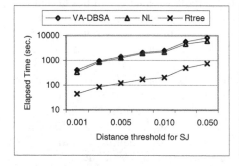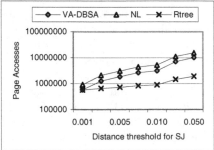

Fig. 6. Performance of SJ when δ is varied

6 Conclusions and Future Work

The contribution of this paper is twofold. (1) It reports the first development of algorithms for DJQ on pairs of high-dimensional data sets using VA-files. For this purpose, special bounds and pruning conditions have been proposed and employed. (2) It reports a detailed performance comparison of VA-files vs. R*-trees with respect to DJQ using real data. More specifically, for K-NNQs and distance range queries, where one real high-dimensional dataset and one query point are involved, one of the best alternatives to overcome the *dimensionality curse* is the use of VA-files (a filtering-based approach). For K-CPQs and SJs, where two real high-dimensional datasets are combined, this is not the best alternative with respect to the CPU cost, because the filtering step is overloaded, while it is competitive with respect to the I/O cost. The use of efficient hierarchical multi-dimensional access methods with optimization techniques in the processing of index nodes is a very interesting choice (since the filtering power can be improved notably). Future research may include the use of approximation techniques on VA-files [19, 8], the cost estimation of VA-file-based DJQ [19] and the study of the buffering impact over these DJQs, as in [4].

References

1. Beckmann, N., Kriegel, H. P., Schneider, R., Seeger, B.: "The R*-tree: an Efficient and Robust Access Method for Points and Rectangles", Proc. SIGMOD Conf. (1990) 322-331
2. Berchtold, S., Böhm, C., Jagadish, H., Kriegel, H. P., Sander, J.: "Independent Quantization: an Index Compression Technique for High-Dimensional Data Spaces", Proc. ICDE Conf. (2000) 577-588
3. Böhm, C., Braunmuller, B., Breuning, M. M., Kriegel, H. P.: "High Performance Clustering based on Similarity Join", Proc. CIKM Conf. (2000) 298-305
4. Böhm, C., Kriegel, H. P.: "A Cost Model and Index Architecture for the Similarity Join", Proc. ICDE Conf. (2001) 411-420
5. Cha, G. H., Chung, C. W.: "The GC-tree: a High-Dimensional Index Structure for Similarity Search in Image Databases", Transactions on Multimedia, Vol. 4, No. 2 (2002) 235-247
6. Cha, G. H., Zhu, X., Petkovic, D, Chung, C.W.: "An Efficient Indexing Method for Nearest Neighbor Searches in High-Dimensional Image Databases", Transactions on Multimedia, Vol. 4, No. 1 (2002) 76-87
7. Corral, A., Manolopoulos, Y., Theodoridis, Y., Vassilakopoulos, M.: "Algorithms for Processing K-Closest-Pair Queries in Spatial Databases", Data and Knowledge Engineering Journal, Vol. 49, No. 1 (2004) 67-104
8. Corral, A., Vassilakopoulos, M.: "On Approximate Algorithms for Distance-Based Queries using R-trees", The Computer Journal, Vol. 48, No. 2 (2005) 220-238
9. Cui, B., Hu, J., Shen, H., Yu, C.: "Adaptive Quantization of the High-Dimensional Data for Efficient KNN Processing", Proc. DASFAA Conf. (2004) 302-313
10. Dittrich, J. P., Seeger, B.: "GESS: a Scalable Similarity-Join Algorithm for Mining Large Data Sets in High Dimensional Spaces", Proc. SIGKDD Conf. (2001) 47-56
11. Faloutsos, C., Barber, R., Flickner, M., Hafner, J., Niblack, W., Petkovic, D., Equitz, W.: "Efficient and Effective Querying by Image Content", Journal of Intelligent Information System, Vol.3, No.3-4 (1994) 231-262

12. Ferhatosmanoglu, H., Tuncel, E., Agrawal, D., Abbadi, A. E.: "Vector Approximation Based Indexing for Non-Uniform High Dimensional Data Sets", Proc. CIKM Conf. (2000) 202-209
13. Guttman, A.: "R-trees: a Dynamic Index Structure for Spatial Searching", Proc. SIGMOD Conf. (1984) 47-57
14. Koudas, N., Sevcik, K. C.: "High Dimensional Similarity Joins: Algorithms and Performance Evaluation", Transactions on Knowledge and Data Engineering, Vol. 12, No. 1 (2000) 3-18
15. Korn, F., Sidiropoulos, N., Faloutsos, C., Siegel, C., Protopapas, Z.: "Fast Nearest Neighbor Search in Medical Images Databases", Proc. VLDB Conf. (1996) 215-226
16. Nanopoulos, A., Theodoridis, Y., Manolopoulos, Y.: "C^2P: Clustering based on Closest Pairs", Proc. VLDB Conf. (2001) 331-340
17. Sakurai, Y., Yoshikawa, M., Uemura, S., Kojima, H.: "The A-tree: an Index Structure for High-Dimensional Spaces using Relative Approximation", Proc. VLDB Conf. (2000) 516-526
18. Shim, K., Srikant, R., Agrawal, R.: "High-Dimensional Similarity Joins", Proc. of ICDE Conf. (1997) 301-311
19. Weber, R., Böhm, K.: "Trading Quality for Time with Nearest Neighbor Search", Proc. EDBT Conf. (2000) 21-35
20. Weber, R., Schek, H. J., Blott, S.: "A Quantitative Analysis and Performance Study for Similarity-Search Methods in High-Dimensional Spaces", Proc. VLDB Conf. (1998) 194-205
21. Web site: http://kdd.ics.uci.edu/databases/CorelFeatures/CorelFeatures.html

The Expressivity of Constraint Query Languages with Boolean Algebra Linear Cardinality Constraints*

Peter Revesz

Department of Computer Science and Engineering,
University of Nebraska-Lincoln, Lincoln, NE 68588, USA
revesz@cse.unl.edu

Abstract. Constraint query languages with Boolean algebra linear cardinality constraints were introduced recently and shown to be evaluable using a quantifier elimination method in [22]. However, the expressive power of constraint query languages with linear cardinality constraints is still poorly understood in comparison with other cases of constraint query languages. This paper makes several contributions to the analysis of their expressive power. Several problems that were previously provably impossible to express even in $FO + POLY$ are shown to be expressible using first-order query languages with linear cardinality constraints $FO + BALC$. We also show that all monadic Datalog queries are expressible in $FO + BALC$. Finally, we also show a new results for $FO + LINEAR$ by expressing in it the problem of finding the time when two linearly moving point objects are closest to each other.

1 Introduction

An important question for *constraint databases* [13] is their expressive power, that is, to know what problems they can or cannot express [17,20]. Since constraint databases generalize relational databases with the extension of a tuple to *constraint tuples*, which are conjunctions of constraints, it seems intuitive that constraint databases can express more types of problems. However, the fact is that most results regarding the expressive power of constraint query languages are negative. Consider the following problems:

Definition 1. [MAJORITY] *The input has two unary relations R_1 and R_2. The output is true if and only if $R_1 \subseteq R_2$ and $|R_2| \leq 2|R_1|$.*

Definition 2. [TRANSITIVE CLOSURE] *The input is a binary relation R. The output is a binary relation that is the transitive closure of R, that is, all pairs (a_0, a_n) such that there are elements $(a_0, a_1), \ldots, (a_{n-1}, a_n)$ in R.*

---

* This work was supported in part by USA National Science Foundation grant EIA-0091530 and a NASA Space and EPSCoR grant.

J. Eder et al. (Eds.): ADBIS 2005, LNCS 3631, pp. 167–182, 2005.

One very powerful-looking first-order query language is Relational Calculus with polynomial constraints over the real numbers. We call this language $FO + POLY$. The following is a surprising theorem:

Theorem 1 (Benedikt et al. [3]). MAJORITY *and* TRANSITIVE CLOSURE *are not expressible in* $FO + POLY$.

Recently, Revesz [22] presented a first-order language with Boolean algebras and linear cardinality constraints. We call this language $FO + BALC$. In this paper we show the following:

Theorem 2. MAJORITY *and* TRANSITIVE CLOSURE *are expressible in* $FO+BALC$.

There are some known expressibility results also for first-order queries with linear constraints over the rational numbers, which we denote as $FO+LINEAR$. Afrati et al. [1] show that $FO+LINEAR$ can express a query that returns *true* if and only if the database consists of exactly c parallel lines where c is a constant. Similarly, they show that $FO+LINEAR$ can also express the query that returns *true* if and only if the database consists of two lines intersecting at a point.

In this paper we move beyond just static spatial objects and consider moving point objects. There is a growing interest in representing moving objects. For example, Cai et al. [4,23], Chomicki et al. [6,7,8], Güting et al. [11], Kollios et al. [14], Saltenis et al. [24], and Wolfson et al. [26] describe moving object data models and techniques to query moving objects. Constraint databases are a natural representation of moving objects. A natural query on moving objects is the following.

Definition 3. [TIME CLOSEST] *Given two moving points that move along two different lines with uniform speed, find the time when they are closest to each other.*

In this paper we show the following:

Theorem 3. TIME CLOSEST *is expressible in* $FO + LINEAR$.

While in this paper we focus on first-order query languages, there are also some interesting expressibility results for recursive query languages. For example, Kuijpers and Smits [15] show that if the constraint database input is a binary relation $R(x, y)$ that describes a polynomial spatial relation, i.e., relations expressible using quantifier-free real polynomial constraints, then there is no Datalog query with linear constraints that returns *true* if and only if R is topologically connected.

We only consider in this paper the class of *monadic Datalog* queries, i.e., those queries in which each defined relation (in the head of the rules) is a unary relation. We show the following theorem for monadic Datalog queries:

Theorem 4. *Any monadic Datalog query is expressible in $FO + BALC$.*

The rest of the paper is organized as follows. Section 2 is a brief review of basic concepts. Section 3 proves Theorem 2. This section also shows that several other graph problems, such as SAME COLOR and MAXIMAL CLIQUE as well as the N-QUEENS problem are also expressible in $FO + BALC$. Section 4 proves Theorem 4. Section 5 proves Theorem 3. Section 6 discusses related work. Finally, Section 7 gives some conclusions.

2   Constraint Databases

Constraint databases [13] and constraint logic programming [12] both represent input information as a set of constraint tuples. For example, to describe a graph with vertices $V = \{1, 2, 3, 4\}$ and edges $E = \{(1, 2), (2, 3), (1, 4)\}$, a constraint database over the Boolean algebras of sets of subsets of the integers could be the following, where comma means "and":

Edge

X Y		
X Y	$X = \{1\}$,	$Y = \{2\}$
X Y	$X = \{2\}$,	$Y = \{3\}$
X Y	$X = \{1\}$,	$Y = \{4\}$

We will use this type of representation for several graph problems in Section 3. The intended meaning of a constraint tuple is that any instantiation of the variables that satisfies the constraint belongs to the relation. In the above example the satisfying instantiations are obvious, but they are less obvious when the constraints are more complex. In particular, we allow besides the equality constraints above any *linear cardinality constraint* [22] of the form:

$$c_1|t_1| + \ldots + c_k|t_k| \ \theta \ b$$

where each t_i for $1 \le i \le k$ is a Boolean term –composed of set constants or variables, and the intersection, union, and set complement with respect to the whole set of integers–, each c_i for $1 \le i \le k$ and b are integer constants and θ is:

$=$ for the equality relation,
$\ge$ for the greater than or equal comparison operator,
$\le$ for the less than or equal comparison operator, or
$\equiv_n$ for the congruence relation modulus some positive integer constant n.

Note: Boolean cardinality constraints can express other common constraints over sets. For example, the constraint that t_1 is a subset of t_2, denoted

$$t_1 \subseteq t_2 \quad \text{is equivalent to} \quad |t_1 \wedge \overline{t_2}| = 0$$

where t_1 and t_2 are Boolean terms and $\overline{t_2}$ is the complement of t_2. For the sake of greater readability, in the following we will use $\subseteq$ constraints, because readers are more familiar with it.

In this paper we consider first-order languages FO with existential $\exists$ and universal $\forall$ quantifiers, and the connectives logical *and* $\wedge$, *or* $\vee$, and *not* $\neg$, and variables and constants with the usual composition.

We also consider Datalog, which is a rule-based language that is related to Prolog. Each Datalog query contains a Datalog program and an input database. We divide the set of relation names $\mathcal{R}$ into defined relation names and input relation names. Each Datalog query consists of a finite set of rules of the form:

$$R_0(x_1, \ldots, x_k) :\!- R_1(x_{1,1}, \ldots, x_{1,k_1}), \ldots R_n(x_{n,1}, \ldots, x_{n,k_n}), C_1, \ldots, C_m.$$

where each R_i is either an input relation name or a defined relation name, and the xs are either variables or constants, and each C_i is a constraint. The relation names $R_0, \ldots, R_n$ are not necessarily distinct. For a good introduction of Datalog queries and examples see [17,20].

3   Problems Expressible in $FO + BALC$

In this section, we study the expressive power of $FO + BALC$. This language seems to be a natural language to express a variety of problems, including MAJORITY, several graph problems, and the N-QUEENS problem, which is a familiar search problem in AI.

3.1   The MAJORITY Problem

To express the MAJORITY query in $FO + BALC$ we assume that the two input relations $R_1(X)$ and $R_2(Y)$ each contain one equality constraint that sets the value of X and Y equal to a set of numbers. Then the $FO + BALC$ query:

$$\exists X, Y \;\; R_1(X) \;\wedge\; R_2(Y) \;\wedge\; X \subseteq Y \;\wedge\; 2|X| - |Y| \geq 0.$$

correctly expresses MAJORITY. The simplicity of the above formula suggests that $FO + BALC$ is a natural language to express this and similar queries.

3.2   The TRANSITIVE CLOSURE Problem

To express transitive closure, we at first introduce the following definition.

Definition 4. *Let S and X be any two set variables. Then,*

$$S[X] \;=_{def}\; |X| = 1 \;\wedge\; X \subseteq S.$$

The above definition says that $S[X]$ is true if and only if X is a singleton set, which is a subset of S. Using this definition, it becomes easier to express transitive closure. We express it as follows:

$$\phi_{TC}(Z_1, Z_2) = \forall S \; (S[Z_1] \wedge \forall X, Y \; S[X] \wedge R(X, Y) \rightarrow S[Y]) \rightarrow S[Z_2].$$

The $\phi_{TC}(Z_1, Z_2)$ is a formula with two free variables, namely Z_1 and Z_2. Let us consider any substitution for these two variables. Suppose that Z_1 is substituted by a_0 and Z_2 is substituted by a_n, such that, there are elements $(a_0, a_1), \ldots, (a_{n-1}, a_n)$ in R.

The substituted formula $\phi_{TC}(a_0, a_n)$ says that for all S if ($a_0 \in S$, and if every time the first argument of R is in S, then the second argument of R is also in S), then $a_n \in S$. Since we assumed that there is a sequence of elements $(a_0, a_1), \ldots, (a_{n-1}, a_n)$ in R, the condition of the main implication within ϕ is true if and only if $a_0, \ldots, a_n \in S$. Then clearly $a_n \in S$, hence the then clause is also true. Therefore, the main implication of ϕ is true, and (a_0, a_n) is a substitution into ϕ_{TC} that makes it true.

Conversely, if there is no sequence of elements of the form (a_0, a_1), $\ldots$, (a_{n-1}, a_n) in R, then there must exist an S which has in it a_0 and only those which are "reachable" by a sequence of elements from a_0. Then the condition of the main implication in ϕ_{TC} is true, but since a_n is not "reachable" from a_0 the then clause is false. That makes the main implication false, showing that (a_0, a_n) is not a satisfying substitution in this case. This shows that Theorem 2 holds.

3.3   The SAME COLOR Problem

Given an undirected graph that is 2-colorable, we would like to know which pairs of vertices can be colored the same color. Suppose that the colors we consider are *blue* and *red*. The following expresses that Z_1 and Z_2 can be both colored blue.

$$\phi_B \;=\; \exists B \; B[Z_1] \;\wedge\; B[Z_2]$$

where each vertex which is in set B is assumed to be colored blue, and each vertex not in B is assumed to be colored red. The following formula expresses that the vertices that are connected to a blue vertex are red.

$$\phi_{B-Neighbor} \;=\; \forall X, Y \; B[X] \;\wedge\; Edge(X,Y) \;\rightarrow\; \neg B[Y].$$

Similarly, the following asserts that the vertices connected to a red vertex are blue.

$$\phi_{R-Neighbor} \;=\; \forall X, Y \; \neg B[X] \;\wedge\; Edge(X,Y) \;\rightarrow\; B[Y].$$

Then the formula:

$$\phi_{SC} \;=\; \phi_B \;\wedge\; \phi_{B-Neighbor} \;\wedge\; \phi_{R-Neighbor}$$

expresses the SAME COLOR problem.

3.4   The MAXIMAL CLIQUE Problem

In an undirected graph, a clique is a subgraph in which every vertex is connected with every other vertex. The size of a clique is the number of vertices it contains.

We represent an undirected graph by a binary relation $Edge$ where $Edge$ is symmetric, that is, it represents an undirected edge between X and Y by containing both (X, Y) and (Y, X) as two elements.

Given an undirected graph and an integer constant k, the MAXIMAL CLIQUE problem asks whether the size of the maximum clique in the graph is k. To express MAXIMAL CLIQUE, at first we express that a graph has a clique with k vertices as follows:

$$\phi_k = \exists S \ |S| = k \wedge \forall X, Y \ (S[X] \wedge S[Y] \wedge X \neq Y) \rightarrow Edge(X, Y).$$

In the above, S contains the vertices that belong to a clique. Clearly, if the maximal clique has size k, then the graph has a clique of size k but does not have a clique of size $k + 1$. That is,

$$\phi_{MC} = \phi_k \wedge \neg\phi_{k+1}.$$

3.5 The N-QUEENS Problem

Given a chess-board of size $n \times n$ for some integer n, the N-QUEENS problem asks to place n queens on the chess-board so that no two queens are in the same row, column, or diagonal. The N-QUEENS problem is a quite challenging search problem that is not easy to implement in a procedural language like C++. We give a high-level declarative solution to this problem.

While the following solution can be generalized to any n, let us assume for the sake of simplicity that $n = 5$. Then let's count the squares on the chess-board in the usual way, that is, from left to right in each row, and from the top row to the bottom row, as shown below.

1	2	3	4	5
6	7	8	9	10
11	12	13	14	15
16	17	18	19	20
21	22	23	24	25

Then let variables R_i for $1 \leq i \leq 5$ be those locations in the ith row that contain a queen. We know the following:

$$\phi_R = R_1 \subseteq \{1, 2, 3, 4, 5\} \wedge \ldots \wedge R_5 \subseteq \{21, 22, 23, 24, 25\}.$$

Similarly, let variables C_i for $1 \leq i \leq 5$ be those locations in the ith column that contain a queen. We know that:

$$\phi_C = C_1 \subseteq \{1, 6, 11, 16, 21\} \wedge \ldots \wedge C_5 \subseteq \{5, 10, 15, 20, 25\}.$$

Further, let variables D_i for $1 \leq i \leq 7$ be the set of locations of queens on the diagonals that run downwards from left to right and have at least two squares. We know that:

$$\phi_D = D_1 \subseteq \{4, 10\} \wedge \ldots \wedge D_7 \subseteq \{16, 22\}.$$

The symmetric case is the variables L_i for $1 \leq i \leq 7$ that contain the set of locations of queens on the diagonals that run downwards from right to left and have at least two squares. For those we have:

$$\phi_L = L_1 \subseteq \{2, 6\} \wedge \ldots \wedge L_7 \subseteq \{20, 24\}.$$

Since no row or column can have more than one queen, there must be exactly one queen in each row and in each column. Further, on each diagonal there may be at most one queen. Therefore, the formula:

$$\phi_R \wedge \phi_C \wedge \phi_D \wedge \phi_L \wedge (\bigwedge_i |R_i| = 1) \wedge (\bigwedge_i |C_i| = 1) \wedge (\bigwedge_i |D_i| \leq 1) \wedge (\bigwedge_i |L_i| \leq 1)$$

correctly expresses the N-QUEENS problem.

4 Monadic Datalog is Expressible in $FO + BALC$

The problems expressed in Section 3 give interesting examples that can be expressed in $FO + BALC$. In this section, instead of giving just examples, we show that an entire class of Datalog programs, namely the class of *monadic Datalog programs*, is expressible in $FO + BALC$.

In a monadic Datalog program P the defined relations are monadic, that is, have arity one. Without loss of generality we assume that the variables range over the integers and the defined (or intensional) relations are $S_1, \ldots, S_m$ and the input (or extensional) relations are $R_1, \ldots, R_n$.

For each rule r_j of P with the form:

$$A_0 :— A_1, \ldots, A_k.$$

where each A_i for $1 \leq i \leq k$ is an atom (i.e., a relation name with variables from the set $X_1, \ldots, X_l$), we write the following expression:

$$\phi_j = \forall X_1, \ldots, X_l \ \ B_1 \wedge \ldots \wedge B_k \rightarrow B_0.$$

where B_i is A_i if A_i contains an input relation name, and B_i is $S_j[X]$ if A_i is $S_j(X)$ for some defined relation name S_j and X is either one of the variables $X_1, \ldots, X_l$ or a concrete set of integer constants. Note that ϕ_j may contain only $S_1, \ldots, S_m$ as free variables ranging over the subsets of the integers. Clearly, the essential difference between the monadic Datalog program and the conjunction:

$$\bigwedge_j \phi_j$$

is that for the monadic Datalog program the least model is returned while the conjunction can have many models. The intersection of all the models of the conjunction is the least model of the monadic Datalog program. To select the least model, we have to add an assertion that the model returned must be the minimal model. We can do that by writing the following expression:

$$\phi_{MoD} = \left(\bigwedge_j \phi_j\right) \wedge \left(\forall S_1^+ \ldots, S_k^+ \left(\bigwedge_j \phi_j^+\right) \rightarrow \left(\bigwedge_i S_i \subseteq S_i^+\right)\right)$$

where ϕ_j^+ is like ϕ_j with S_i replaced by S_i^+. Then ϕ_{MoD} expresses what we need. Each monadic Datalog program has a least model $S_1, \ldots, S_k$, which is the output database, i.e., the assignment to $S_1, \ldots, S_k$ returned by an evaluation of the program on an input database. Clearly, ϕ_{MoD} enforces that $S_1, \ldots, S_k$ is a minimal model by constraining all other models $S_1^+ \ldots, S_k^+$ to be bigger or equal to it. Let us see a concrete example.

Example 1. Consider the following monadic Datalog program P.

$$S(X) :\!- Start(X).$$
$$S(Y) :\!- S(X), \ Edge(X,Y).$$

Here program P finds the vertices that are reachable from the start vertices contained in the input relation *Start*. The first rule can be expressed by:

$$\phi_1 \ = \ \forall X \quad Start(X) \rightarrow S[X].$$

The second rule can be expressed by:

$$\phi_2 \ = \ \forall X, Y \quad S[X] \wedge Edge(X,Y) \rightarrow S[Y].$$

Then P can be expressed in $FO + BALC$ as:

$$\phi_P \ = \ (\phi_1 \wedge \phi_2) \wedge \left(\forall S^+ (\phi_1^+ \wedge \phi_2^+) \rightarrow S \subseteq S^+\right).$$

Since S is a model of the rules of P, and for any other model S^+ of the rules of P we have $S \subseteq S^+$, it follows that S must be the least model.

5   The TIME CLOSEST Problem in $FO + LINEAR$

Suppose that two cars, which both move linearly in the plane, want to radio-communicate with each other. What is the best time to attempt the radio communication? Intuitively, the best time would be when the two cars are closest to each other, hence that time instance needs to be found. We show that it can be found using only linear constraints, which is surprising, because at first glance the problem seems to require the Euclidean distance function, which is a quadratic polynomial constraint.

The two cars can be represented by two constraint database relations $P_1(x, y, t)$ and $P_2(x, y, t)$. For example, an input database instance could be the following (see also Figure 1):

$$P_1(x, y, t) :\!- x = t, \ y = 2t + 4.$$
$$P_2(x, y, t) :\!- x = 3t, \ y = 4t.$$

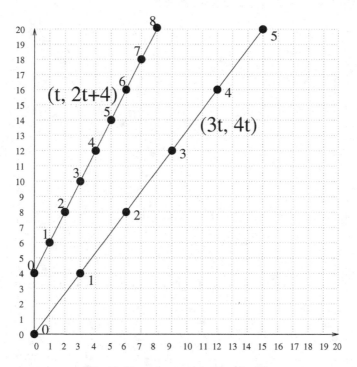

Fig. 1. Two cars moving in the plane

Suppose that we would like to find the time instance t when the two cars are closest to each other. We can define first the difference between the two cars at any time t as follows:

$$\Delta P(x, y, t) = \exists x_1, x_2, y_1, y_2 \ P_1(x_1, y_1, t) \wedge P_2(x_2, y_2, t) \wedge x = x_2 - x_1 \wedge$$
$$y = y_2 - y_1.$$

ΔP is also a moving point in the plane as shown in Figure 2. The difference between the two cars is exactly the difference between ΔP and the origin at any time t. Therefore, the two cars are closest to each other when ΔP is closest to the origin. Now the projection of ΔP onto the plane is a line, which is the path along which ΔP travels. We can find this by:

$$\Delta Pline(x, y) = \exists t \ \Delta P(x, y, t).$$

Let us now take the line which goes through the origin and is perpendicular to $\Delta Pline$. If (x_1, y_1) and (x_2, y_2) are two points on $\Delta Pline$, then the slope of $\Delta Pline$ is:

$$\frac{y_2 - y_1}{x_2 - x_1}.$$

The perpendicular line will have a negative reciprocal slope and will go through the origin. Hence its line equation is:

$$y = -\frac{x_2 - x_1}{y_2 - y_1} x \tag{1}$$

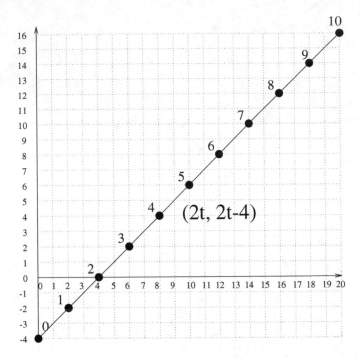

Fig. 2. The ΔP moving point

Now we can chose any two distinct points on the line $\Delta Pline$ for expressing the line equation. Let us choose (x_1, y_1) to be the intersection point of $\Delta Pline$ and the line perpendicular to it and going through the origin. Further, let us chose the second point (x_2, y_2) such that

$$y_2 = x_1 + y_1. \tag{2}$$

Clearly, this is always possible to do when the line is not vertical. Now what is the intersection point? It will satisfy Equations (1) and (2), that is:

$$y_1 = -\frac{x_2 - x_1}{y_2 - y_1} x_1$$
$$x_1 = y_2 - y_1. \tag{3}$$

The above can be simplified to:

$$y_1 = x_1 - x_2$$
$$x_1 = y_2 - y_1. \tag{4}$$

Therefore, if $\Delta Pline$ is not vertical, that is, $x_1 \neq x_2$, then the point of $\Delta Pline$ that is closest to the origin is exactly the intersection point, hence:

$$Closest\_Point(x_1, y_1) = \exists x_2, y_2 \ \Delta Pline(x_1, y_1) \ \wedge \ \Delta Pline(x_2, y_2) \ \wedge$$
$$y_1 = x_1 - x_2 \ \wedge \ x_1 = y_2 - y_1 \ \wedge \ x_1 \neq x_2.$$

Otherwise, if $\Delta Pline$ is vertical, that is, for any two different points $x_1 = x_2$, then the closest point is:

$$Closest\_Point(x_1, y_1) = \exists x_2, y_2 \; \Delta Pline(x_1, y_1) \; \wedge \; \Delta Pline(x_2, y_2) \; \wedge$$
$$y_1 = 0 \; \wedge \; x_1 = x_2 \; \wedge \; y_2 \neq 0.$$

Hence putting the above two cases together, we have:

$$Closest\_Point(x_1, y_1) = \exists x_2, y_2 \; \Delta Pline(x_1, y_1) \; \wedge \; \Delta Pline(x_2, y_2) \; \wedge$$
$$((y_1 = x_1 - x_2 \; \wedge \; x_1 = y_2 - y_1 \; \wedge \; x_1 \neq x_2) \; \vee$$
$$(y_1 = 0 \; \wedge \; x_1 = x_2 \; \wedge \; y_2 \neq 0)).$$

The time when the two cars are closest to each other is:

$$Closest\_Time(t) = \exists x, y \; \Delta P(x, y, t) \; \wedge \; Closest\_Point(x, y).$$

Clearly, the above formula is in $FO + LINEAR$, which shows Theorem 3.

Example 2. Let us look at what will happen when we have the input database instance P_1 and P_2 as given above. In that case, we obtain:

$$\Delta P(x, y, t) \quad :- x = 2t, \; y = 2t - 4.$$

$$\Delta Pline(x, y) :- x = y + 4.$$

For *Closest_Point*, we get after simplifications:

$$Closest\_Point(x_1, y_1) \; = \; \exists x_2, y_2 \; x_1 = y_1 + 4 \; \wedge x_2 = y_2 + 4 \; \wedge$$
$$y_1 = x_1 - x_2 \; \wedge \; x_1 = y_2 - y_1 \; \wedge \; x_1 \neq x_2.$$

Eliminating x_2 and y_2 we get:

$$Closest\_Point(x_1, y_1) \; = \; x_1 = 2 \; \wedge \; y_1 = -2.$$

Finally, the closest time is calculated as:

$$Closest\_Time(t) \; = \; \exists x, y \; x = 2t \; \wedge \; y = 2t - 4 \; \wedge \; x = 2 \; \wedge \; y = -2.$$

Eliminating x and y we get:

$$Closest\_Time(1).$$

Therefore, the two cars are closest at time 1. It is at that time that the two cars should attempt to radio-communicate with each other.

6 Related Work

The present work extends the author's earlier work that presented a quantifier elimination for the first-order theory of atomic Boolean algebras of sets with linear cardinality constraints [21,22] but did not examine its expressive power.

Feferman and Vaught (see Theorem 8.1 in [10]) proved the decidability of the first-order theory of atomic Boolean algebras of sets with *set-theoretical equivalence* which are also commonly called today *equicardinality* constraints. Let us denote this logic by $FO + EC$. An equicardinality constraint between sets A and B, denoted $A \sim B$, simply means that sets A and B have the same cardinality and can be easily expressed by the linear cardinality constraint $|A| - |B| = 0$. Hence obviously $FO + BALC$ includes $FO + EC$. Interestingly, however, the two logics have the same expressive power, because $FO + EC$ can express any linear cardinality constraint. For example, the $FO + BALC$ formula:

$$\exists X \quad 2|X| - |Y| = 0$$

can be expressed by the $FO + EC$ formula:

$$\exists X, Z \quad X \cap Z \sim \emptyset \quad \wedge \quad X \sim Z \quad \wedge \quad X \cup Z \sim Y$$

where $\emptyset$ is the symbol for the empty set. The formula says that there exist sets X and Z that do not intersect, have an equal cardinality, and whose union has an equal cardinality with Y.

Although equal in expressive power, $FO + EC$ has some limitations, because while we can eliminate the variable from the first formula and obtain:

$$|Y| \equiv_2 0$$

we cannot eliminate the variables from the second formula and get a quantifier-free formula with only equicardinality constraints. This shows that:

Theorem 5. $FO + EC$ *does not admit quantifier elimination.*

Now let's try to consider a multi-sorted logic, that is, one where each of the variables and quantifiers ranges either over the integers (this is not allowed in $FO + BALC$) or the subsets of the integers. This kind of multi-sorted logic was first considered by Zarba [27], who gave a quantifier elimination method for the fragment that contains only quantifiers ranging over the integers and conjectured the whole logic to be undecidable. Kuncak et al. [16] showed this logic, which they called Boolean algebra with Presburger arithmetic and can be denoted by $FO + BAPA$, to be decidable and admitting quantifier elimination.

Obviously $FO + BAPA$ includes $FO + BALC$. However, in this case too, it can be shown that $FO + BAPA$ and $FO + BALC$ have the same expressive power. The proof reduces any $FO + BAPA$ formula to a logically equivalent $FO + BALC$ formula as follows.

An integer variable can occur in a $FO + BAPA$ formula only within the Presburger arithmetic constraints of addition of the form $x + y = z$, comparison of the form $x \geq y$, and congruence of the form $x \equiv_n b$, where x, y and z are integer variables and b is an integer constant. For every integer variable x introduce a new set variable X. Then translate every addition constraint of the above form into:

$$|X| + |Y| - |Z| = 0 \tag{5}$$

every comparison constraint of the above form into:

$$|X| - |Y| \geq 0 \tag{6}$$

and every congruence constraint of the above form into:

$$|X| \equiv_n b. \tag{7}$$

Clearly, the Presburger addition (comparison and congruence) constraint is true for some assignment of integer constants c_1, c_2, and c_3 to x, y, and z if and only if Equation (5) (respectively, Equation (6) and Equation (7)) is true for any arbitrary assignment of set constants C_1, C_2, and C_3 for X, Y, and Z with the only restriction that $|C_1| = c_1$, $|C_2| = c_2$, and $|C_3| = c_3$.

The above gives a reduction of $FO + BAPA$ formulas to $FO + BALC$ formulas. Further, it is obvious that from any solution of the $FO + BALC$ formula, it is easy to generate a solution of the $FO + BAPA$ formula by simply taking the cardinalities of those set variables that were introduced in the reduction from $FO + BAPA$ to $FO + BALC$. (Remember that the set variables introduced in the conversion into $FO + BALC$ are simply integer variables in $FO + BAPA$.) Hence we have:

Theorem 6. *$FO + BALC$ and $FO + BAPA$ and $FO + EC$ have the same expressive power.*

Besides expressive power another important consideration for the above related logics is their computational complexities which turns out to be reducible to cases of Presburger arithmetic. Recall that any formula can be easily put into a prenex normal form where all the quantifiers precede the rest of the formula.

When read left to right, the quantifiers at the beginning of the prenex formula show a certain pattern of alternations between sequences of existential and sequences of universal quantifiers. The number of alternations turns out to be complexity-wise important as shown by the following theorem.

Theorem 7 (Reddy and Loveland [18]). *The validity of a Presburger arithmetic sentence with n quantifiers, length $O(n)$, and m quantifier alternations can be decided in $2^{n^{O(m)}}$ space.*

Revesz [21,22] noted the following.

Theorem 8 (Revesz [21,22]). *Quantifier elimination of any $FO + BALC$ formula with n quantifiers and length $O(n)$ and m quantifier alternations reduces to a quantifier elimination of a Presburger arithmetic formula with 2^n quantifiers and length $2^{O(n)}$ and m or $m + 1$ quantifier alternations.*

The reason for the above is that the quantifier-elimination in [21,22] is based on a reduction of a $FO + BALC$ formula into a Presburger arithmetic formula by introducing into the prenex part of the formula a single sequence of 2^n existentially quantified integer variables. Kuncak et al. [16] use a similar reduction together with Theorem 7, which allows them to show that:

Theorem 9 (Kuncak et al [16]). *The validity of a $FO + BAPA$ sentence with n quantifiers, length $O(n)$ and m quantifier alternations can be decided in $2^{n^{O(mn)}}$ space.*

Similarly, Theorems 7 and 8 can be combined to show that:

Theorem 10. *The validity of a $FO+BALC$ sentence with n quantifiers, length $O(n)$ and m quantifier alternations can be decided in $2^{n^{O(mn)}}$ space.*

In summary, $FO+BALC$, $FO+BAPA$ and $FO+EC$ are closely related logics that have the same expressive power and computational complexity. Therefore, the choice among these three logics is only a stylistic preference as far as decision problems are concerned. However, when considering constraint query languages, where the constraint query evaluation requires quantifier elimination, then only $FO + BALC$ and $FO + BAPA$ can be considered.

Although all three logics assume the domain of variables to be atomic Boolean algebras (which are isomorphic to Boolean algebras of subsets of the integers), some mention must be made of the case when the domain is an *atomless* Boolean algebra. For example, consider the atomless Boolean algebra where the variables denote areas in the real plane, and the operators are interpreted as intersection and union of areas, and area complement with respect to the real plane. In this logic it is possible to introduce polynomial constraints such as $|A|^2 > |B \cap C|^3$, which expresses that the square of the area A is greater than the cube of the area that is the intersection of B and C. Note that here $|A|$ is the measure of the area of an element of the atomless Boolean algebra and not the cardinality of an element of an atomic Boolean algebra. Formulas with polynomial constraints over areas, abbreviated $FO+POLYA$, can be reduced to $FO+POLY$ similarly to the reduction of $FO+BALC$ to Presburger arithmetic. In particular, a $FO+POLYA$ formula with n area variables will be reduced to a $FO+POLY$ formula with 2^n real number variables. Each real number variable will represent one of the 2^n areas that are obtained by considering the intersections of the n area variables or their complements.

For example, if we have only the three area variables A, B, and C, then we need to consider eight areas $A \cap B \cap C, \ldots, \overline{A} \cap \overline{B} \cap \overline{C}$. Note that any polynomial constraint over the measures of Boolean terms over A, B, and C is expressible as a polynomial constraint over the measures of the eight areas. For instance, $|A|^2 > |B \cap C|^3$ can be expressed by:

$$(|A \cap B \cap C| + |A \cap B \cap \overline{C}| + |A \cap \overline{B} \cap C| + |A \cap \overline{B} \cap \overline{C}|)^2 > (|A \cap B \cap C| + |\overline{A} \cap B \cap C|)^3.$$

The measures of the eight areas are independent of each other. Hence the validity of a $FO + POLYA$ formula can be tested by considering a $FO + POLY$ formula where each of the eight measures are replaced by a unique real number variable and the three Boolean variables A, B, and C are replaced by real number variables that are constrained to be equal to a linear combination of the eight independent variables. Therefore, we have that:

Theorem 11. *The validity of a $FO + POLYA$ sentence with n quantifiers, length $O(n)$, and m quantifier alternations can be reduced to deciding the validity of a $FO + POLY$ sentence of length $2^{O(n)}$ with m or $m+1$ quantifier alternations.*

Since $FO + POLY$ formulas admit quantifier elimination, we also can show:

Theorem 12. $FO + POLYA$ *admits quantifier elimination.*

Tarski [25] gave the first decision procedure and quantifier elimination algorithm for the real closed fields, but more efficient algorithms include [2,5,9,19].

7 Conclusions

We gave several positive results about the expressivity of constraint queries. There are many interesting open questions regarding expressivity. For example, can we express some more graph problems using constraint queries, such as, the chromatic number of a graph? Some earlier negative results gave the impression that constraint queries are not too useful. However, it is still currently being discovered what are the best application areas for various constraint queries. For the problems that we considered, the solutions found are simpler than the procedural language solutions. This suggests that by providing high-level declarative query languages, constraint database systems could be beneficial for users in practice on problems related to the ones presented in this paper.

References

1. Afrati, F., Andronikos, T., Kavalieros, T.: On the expressiveness of query languages with linear constraints: Capturing desirable spatial properties. In *Proc. Workshop on Constraint Databases and Their Applications*, volume 1191 of *Lecture Notes in Computer Science*. Springer-Verlag (1997) 105–115
2. Basu, S.: New results on quantifier elimination over real closed fields and applications to constraint databases. Journal of the ACM (1999) 46(4):537–55
3. Benedikt, M., Dong, G., Libkin, L., Wong, L.: Relational expressive power of constraint query languages. Journal of the ACM (1998) 45(1):1–34
4. Cai, M., Keshwani, D., Revesz, P.: Parametric rectangles: A model for querying and animating spatiotemporal databases. In Proc. 7th International Conference on Extending Database Technology, volume 1777 of Lecture Notes in Computer Science. Springer-Verlag (2000) 430–440
5. Caviness, B. F., J. R. Johnson, J. R.: editors. Quantifier Elimination and Cylindrical Algebraic Decomposition. Springer-Verlag (1998)
6. Chomicki, J., Haesevoets, S., Kuijpers, B., Revesz, P.: Classes of spatiotemporal objects and their closure properties. Annals of Mathematics and Artificial Intelligence (2003) 39(4):431–461
7. Chomicki, J., Revesz, P.: Constraint-based interoperability of spatiotemporal databases. Geoinformatica (1999) 3(3):211–43
8. Chomicki, J., Revesz, P.: A geometric framework for specifying spatiotemporal objects. In Proc. International Workshop on Time Representation and Reasoning (1999) 41–6

9. Collins, G. E.: Quantifier elimination for real closed fields by cylindrical algebraic decomposition. In H. Brakhage, editor, Automata Theory and Formal Languages, volume 33 of Lecture Notes in Computer Science, Springer (1975) 134–83

10. Feferman, S., Vaught, R. L.: The first-order properties of products of algebraic systems. Fundamenta Mathematicae (1959) 47:57–103

11. Güting, R. H., Böhlen, M. H., Erwig, M., Jenssen, C. C., Lorentzos, N. A., Schneider, M., Vazirgiannis, M.: A foundation for representing and querying moving objects. ACM Transactions on Database Systems, 25 (2000)

12. Jaffar, J., Lassez, J. L.: Constraint logic programming. In Proc. 14th ACM Symposium on Principles of Programming Languages (1987) 111–9

13. Kanellakis, P. C., Kuper, G. M., Revesz, P.: Constraint query languages. Journal of Computer and System Sciences (1995) 51(1):26–52

14. Kollios, G., Gunopulos, D., Tsotras, V. J.: On indexing mobile objects. In Proc. ACM Symposium on Principles of Database Systems (1999) 261–72

15. Kuijpers, B., Smits, M.: On expressing topological connectivity in spatial Datalog. In Proc. Workshop on Constraint Databases and Their Applications, volume 1191 of Lecture Notes in Computer Science, Springer-Verlag (1997) 116–33

16. Kuncak, V., Nguyen, H. H., Rinard, M.: An algorithm for deciding BAPA: Boolean algebra with Presburger arithmetic. In Proc. 20th International Conference on Automated Deduction, Lecture Notes in Computer Science. Springer-Verlag (2005)

17. Kuper, G. M., Libkin, L., Paredaens, J.: editors. Constraint Databases. Springer-Verlag (2000)

18. Reddy, C. R., Loveland, D. W.: Presburger arithmetic with bounded quantifier alternation. In Proc. ACM Symp. on Theory of Comp. (1978) 320–325

19. Renegar, J.: On the computational complexity and geometry of the first-order theory of the reals. Journal of Symbolic Computation (1992) 13(3):255–352

20. Revesz, P.: Introduction to Constraint Databases. Springer-Verlag, New York (2002)

21. Revesz, P.: Cardinality constraint databases. In Manuscript submitted to 23rd ACM Symposium on Principles of Database Systems (2003)

22. Revesz, P.: Quantifier-elimination for the first-order theory of Boolean algebras with linear cardinality constraints. In Proc. 8th East European Conference on Advances in Databases and Information Systems, volume 3255 of Lecture Notes in Computer Science, Springer-Verlag (2004) 1–21

23. Revesz, P., Cai, M.: Efficient querying of periodic spatio-temporal databases. Annals of Mathematics and Artificial Intelligence (2002) 36(4):437–457

24. Saltenis, S., Jensen, C. S., Leutenegger, S. T., Lopez, M. A.: Indexing the positions of continuously moving objects. In Proc. ACM SIGMOD International Conference on Management of Data (2000) 331–42

25. Tarski, A.: A Decision Method for Elementary Algebra and Geometry. University of California Press, Berkeley (1951)

26. Wolfson, O., Sistla, A., Xu, B., Zhou, J., Chamberlain, S.: DOMINO: Databases for moving objects tracking. In Proc. ACM SIGMOD International Conference on Management of Data (1999) 547–9

27. Zarba, C. G.: A quantifier elimination algorithm for a fragment of set theory involving the cardinality operator. In 18th Int. Workshop on Unification (2004)

Extensible Canonical Process Model Synthesis Applying Formal Interpretation

Leonid Kalinichenko, Sergey Stupnikov, and Nikolay Zemtsov

Institute of Informatics Problems, Russian Academy of Science
{leonidk, ssa, nazem}@ipi.ac.ru

Abstract. The current period of IT development is characterized by an explosive growth of diverse information representation languages. Applying integration and composition of heterogeneous information components it is required to develop the canonical information model serving for adequate expression of semantics of various information models used in the environment encompassing required heterogeneous components. Basic principles of the canonical model synthesis include fixing of its kernel, constructing the kernel extensions for each specific information model of the environment so that this extension together with the kernel could be *refined* by this information model, and forming the canonical model as a union of all such extensions. Previously these principles have been successfully applied to the synthesis of structural and object canonical models. This paper[1] applies this technique to synthesis of the process canonical model. The method proposed is based on interpretation of process model semantics in logics, and specifically, in the Abstract Machine Notation that made possible to construct provable refinements of process specifications. This method has been applied to the environment of process models defined by workflow patterns classified by W.M.P. van der Aalst. Thus the canonical process model synthesized possesses a property of completeness with respect to broad class of process models used in various Workflow Management Systems as well as the languages used for process composition of Web services.

1 Introduction

The present period of IT development is characterized by the process of explosive growth of various information representation models. This development takes place in frame of specific distributed infrastructures (such as OMG architectures (in particular, the model driven architecture (MDA)), semantic Web and Web services architectures, digital library architectures as collective memories of information in various subject domains, architectures of the information grid), as well as in the standards of languages and data models (such as, for example, ODMG, SQL, UML, XML and RDF stacks of data models), process models and

---

[1] This research has been partially supported by the grant N 05-07-90413 of the Russian Foundation for Basic Research as well as by the Program of Basic Research of the Department of Information Technologies and Computing Systems of RAS.

J. Eder et al. (Eds.): ADBIS 2005, LNCS 3631, pp. 183–198, 2005.

workflow models, semantic models (including ontological models and models of metadata), models of digital repositories of data and knowledge in particular scientific domains (e.g., virtual observatories in astronomy).

This process is accompanied by another trend — the accumulation of based on such models information components and services, the number of which grows exponentially. This growth causes the accelerating need for integration of components and services represented in heterogeneous models in various applications, as well as their reuse and composition implementing new information systems. The indicated trends are contradictory: the more variety of used models we meet in various components and services, the more complex become problems of their integration and composition. These trends are not new, but with time, the diversity of various models and their complexity grow together with the increasing need for integration and composition of components and tools represented in different models. Scale of these phenomena, determining possibilities of designing of distributed information systems in various domains, reusing, trading and compositions of components, reaching their semantic interoperability, integration of heterogeneous information sources, is sufficient motivation for research and development of adequate methods for manipulation of various information representation models.

The basis of these methods is constituted by the concept of the canonical information model serving as the common language, "Esperanto", for adequate expression of semantics of various information models, surrounding us. To prove that a definition in a language can be substituted with a definition in another one, formal specification facilities and commutative model mappings are provided.

Initially ideas of mapping structured data models and canonical model construction for them were developed. The basic definitions of equivalence of database states, database schemas and data models were introduced to preserve operations and information while constructing of mappings of various structured data models into the canonical one [11,12]. According to this approach, each data model was defined by syntax and semantics of two languages – data definition language (DDL) and data manipulation language (DML). The main principle of mapping of an arbitrary source data model into the target one (the canonical model) constituted *the principle of commutative data model mapping* . According to it preserving of operations and information of a source data model while mapping it into the canonical one could be reached under the condition, that the diagram of DDL (schemas) mapping and diagram of DML (operators) mapping are commutative [12]. At that time in the process of data model mappings construction the denotational semantics was used as a formalism (metamodel), allowing to prove a commutativity of the diagrams mentioned [12]. Such a proof had to be carried out manually.

Later, for the object data models, the method of data model mapping and canonical models constructions was modified as follows. As a formalism (metamodel) of the method the Abstract Machine Notation (AMN) was used instead of the denotational semantics. It allowed to define the model-theoretic specifications in the first order logics and to prove the fact of specification *refinement*

[3,4]. The theory of refinement provided for developing of fundamental definitions of relationships between data types, data schemas, data models so that
instead of equivalence of respective specifications, it could be possible to reason
on their refinement [14]. It is said that specification A *refines* specification D,
if it is possible to use A instead of D so that the user of D does not notice
this substitution. Existence of special tools for AMN (B-technology)provides for
conducting proofs of commutativity of mappings semi-automatically: theorems
required for the proof of refinement are generated by B automatically, and their
proof is (generally) conducted with the human assistance.

The main principle of canonical model synthesis is that its *extensibility* is
required for semantic integration and information interoperability in heterogeneous environment, including various models. A kernel of the canonical model
is fixed. For each specific information model M of the environment an extension
of the kernel is defined so that this extension together with the kernel *is refined*
by M. Such refining transformation of models should be *provably correct*. The
canonical model for the environment is synthesized as *the union of extensions*,
constructed for models M of the environment.

Applying similar principles, this paper deals with process models, required
for describing activities of various organizations for solving of their tasks. For
example, virtual organization models are based on composition of processes of
real organizations involved in sphere of activity of the virtual organization. Another example is trading of processes and composition of processes implementing
a required process (this is one of well-known tasks in semantic Web or in mobile
systems). The processes are implemented in workflows in various Workflow Management Systems (WfMS). For the process languages they apply various concepts
and paradigms incompatible for various WfMS. Irrespective of the model used,
workflow specification is a complex construction, integrated with specifications
of other types (usually, object-oriented).

While mapping processes at synthesis of their canonical model, it is required
to preserve the semantics of concurrency. The main problem of such synthesis is that there is no general theory of concurrency. The early research has
shown [15], that process algebras do not possess sufficient expressive power to
serve as a kernel of the canonical process model. At the same time combining
of two requirements – completeness of the canonical process model ability of
interpretation of various workflow models with an ability to prove of correctness of arbitrary process model interpretation in the canonical process model –
remained hard-reachable for quite a long time period . The possibility of interpretation of concurrent events, typical for process models, in logics, and specifically,
in the Abstract Machine Notation has been discovered recently [8,19,17]. Algorithms of process specifications mappings into AMN were constructed [7,18].
This approach allows to construct provable refinements of process specifications,
applying the B-technology. This achievement is the necessary prerequisite for
commutative mapping of process models. Simultaneously it was succeeded to
classify and describe the diversity of workflow models by means of *workflow patterns* [1]. Due to these two events, the possibility of choice of a canonical process

model kernel and construction of its extensions, refined by various workflow patterns, became possible. Thus, the way to the canonical process model synthesis has been opened, and such synthesis has been developed [16] in the context of the work reported here.

The text of the paper is organized as follows. In section 2 an approach to the synthesis of extensible canonical process model is described. In section 3 the technique of construction of refining extensions for process model is considered. In conclusion the results are summarized, and perspectives of application of the methods described are discussed.

2   Construction of Canonical Process Model

The analysis of large number of WfMS process models [1] resulted in 20 workflow patterns – process constructions being typical in practice.

The set of the patterns mentioned is complete; it has appeared to be enough for representation of process models of various WfMS. This result allows to select the workflow patterns as the source process models for synthesis of the canonical process model. Thus it is possible to combine process completeness of the selected set of constructions with a possibility to interpret with this set an arbitrary process, expressed in process models of various WfMS's.

2.1   Definition of the Kernel of Canonical Process Model

According to the principles of the canonical model synthesis, the canonical process model is developed as a kernel, including basic primitives of process specifications, and extensions of the kernel.

A subset of scripts of the SYNTHESIS language [13,15] was selected as the canonical process model kernel. Its capabilities are close to the colored Petri nets [10]. The kernel has the following properties.

1. It is based on the well-known model of Petri nets.
2. It embeds Petri nets in the object environment. As a result the control flow and the data flow are combined by means of tokens – objects of certain types having unique identifiers.
3. It provides for binding of Petri net transitions with functions, which should be called at firing of these transitions. The rules of binding input and output tokens of a transition with input and output parameters of the respective function can be defined. Such bindings are necessary for modeling of information system as a whole, what is not taken into account in more abstract models [10,2].

The declaration of any entity in the SYNTHESIS language (for example, types, classes, functions) syntactically is given by means of a *frame*. Generally frame may be considered as a structured symbolic model of some entity or concept, used to represent their instances. Syntactically a frame is separated with braces. The slot names and their values are separated by a colon. The values of a slot are separated by commas. Atomic .value, frame, collection of formulae of object calculus, set of values may be used as slot values. Different slots in a frame are separated by semicolons.

Scripts are defined applying a generic script type in the SYNTHESIS language. They form a subtyping hierarchy. Each instance of a script type corresponds to an execution of the process, defined by the script. An example of script specification is given in the following section.

2.2 Generic Types as Extensions of the Canonical Model Kernel

Extensions of the canonical process model kernel were constructed [16] for workflow patterns defined in [1]. Here we consider the extension technique of the canonical model kernel for the *discriminator* pattern as an example.

This pattern describes a situation when a completion of one of (concurrent) branches is expected. After that the subsequent transition is activated, and all remaining branches are cancelled.

In canonical model each pattern corresponds to a generic script type, treated as an extension of the kernel. This type defines rules, according to which process control flow is organized. Various script elements (such as functions and data types) can be used as parameters of the type.

Graphically scripts are represented by a bipartite graph with two sorts of nodes – places (represented by circles) and transitions (represented by squares). Nodes of different sorts are connected by the incidence relation (arrows). Places can accumulate tokens of various types. Transitions may fire when a certain conditions are met, consuming tokens from input places of a transition and producing tokens in its output places.

The *discriminator* pattern is represented in the canonical model with the generic script type `discriminator` (fig. 1). Without loss of generality we consider the pattern to be a junction of two branches. In the figure the `Trunk` transition is connected with a dashed line to a dashed rectangle with rounded corners. This graphically denotes that at firing of the transition `Trunk` all tokens are to be removed from the marked area. In this way the cancellation of the remaining (concurrent) branches is realized.

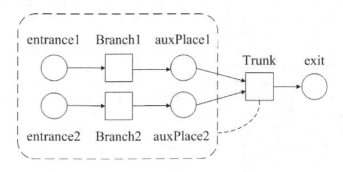

Fig. 1. The discriminator pattern

```
{ discriminator; in: script;
  params: {branch1/function, branch2/function, trunk/function,
           entrance1TokenType/type, entrance2TokenType/type,
           auxPlaceTokenType/type, exitTokenType/type };
```

Here `discriminator` – is a name of the script type. The formal parameters of a type are set in the optional `params` slot. So, each transition (for example, `Trunk`) is parameterized with the function type (in this case – `trunk`), which is called at transition firing. Each place (for example, `entrance1`) is parameterized with the token type, admissible for the given place (here – `entrance1TokenType`).

```
states:
  {entrance1; token: entrance1TokenType},
  {entrance2; token: entrance2TokenType},
  {auxPlace1; token: auxPlaceTokenType},
  {auxPlace2; token: auxPlaceTokenType},
  {exit; token: exitTokenType};
```

The `states` slot defines the set of places of a specific net. Each place is characterized by a name and an admissible token type.

```
transitions:
{ Branch1;
  from: entrance1;  bind_from: {entrance1, in};
  to: auxPlace1;      bind_to: {auxPlace1, out};
  activity: {in: function;
    params: {+ in/entrance1TokenType, -out/auxPlaceTokenType};
     {{branch1(in,out)}};
  }
}
```

In the `transitions` slot a set of transitions of a specific net is defined. Each transition is characterized by name (for example, `Branch1`), list of input places (`from`), list of output places (`to`), optional list of conditions (`conditions`), function, which is called at firing of the transition (`activity`), and also binding lists of input and output parameters of this function (`bind_from`, `bind_to`). The body of the function for transition `Branch1` consists of respective function call with a correct set of parameters (`branch1(in,out)`). The given script fragment works as follows. A token of type `entrance1TokenType` is selected in place `entrance1`. If a token is found, the transition fires – the token is passed into the input parameter `in` of the `branch1` function (according to the slot `bind_from`). A token at the output of the function (`out` parameter) is passed into `auxPlace1` place by virtue of the binding, defined in `bind_to` slot.

The specification for `Branch2` transition looks similarly. Transition `Trunk` concludes specification of the generic script type.

```
{ Trunk;
  from: auxPlace1, auxPlace2;
  bind_from: {auxPlace1, in}, {auxPlace2, in};
  to: exit;
  bind_to: {exit, out};
  activity: {in: function;
   params: {+ in/auxPlaceTokenType, -out/exitTokenType};
   {{
      trunk (in, out) &
      isempty (entrance1') & isempty (entrance2') &
      isempty (auxPlace1') & isempty (auxPlace2')
   }};
  }
}
```

A function, substituted as a script parameter (for example, trunk), should have, besides other, certain number of input and output parameters of definite types (in our case these are two input parameters of types auxPlace1TokenType and auxPlace2TokenType, and one output parameter of a type exitTokenType). Primed state names denote post-states of operations. The body of the function also contains formula, according to which certain places are cleared of tokens.

In this work we use the following notation. Input and output places of a pattern are named as entrance and exit, respectively (with addition of index if required). Additional places are named auxPlace1, auxPlace2, etc. Transitions are named either Trans, or, if the pattern deals with branching, "trunk" transition is named Trunk, and transitions in branches as Branch. If required, an additional indexing can be added. Such notational agreement is not impose any limitations on the way patterns are used or implemented. They are introduced for readability.

2.3   Semantics of the Canonical Process Model in AMN

The synthesis of the extensible canonical process model is realized on the basis of the formal system (Abstract Machine Notation (AMN)) [3,4]. In this section we consider a part of the semantics of the kernel and semantics of the extension, required for understanding of the example below.

AMN, as a model-theoretic notation, allows to consider specifications of state space and behavior (defined by operations on states) in an integrated way . The specification of a machine state is introduced by state variables together with invariants – constraints, which should always be satisfied. Operations are defined on the basis of the extended formalism of the Dijkstra's guarded commands [9].

The *refinement* as a key concept of AMN, provides for correlation of system specifications of various levels of abstraction. A refining specification can be significantly more detailed, than a refined one. The refining specification is constructed on the basis of the algorithmic and data refinement [3]. The refinement is formalized in AMN by formulation of a number of theorems of special sort, so-called *proof obligations*. Such theorems are formulated automatically by tools supporting B-technology (e.g., B-Toolkit, AntelierB) on the basis of *gluing invariants* – the invariants, correlating states of refined and refining systems.

The theorems can be proved with the help of tools supporting automatic and (or) interactive proof.

Due to [7,18,19,8,17,5], common understanding of how one should interpret process models in AMN has been formed. This understanding, in its turn, has allowed to develop a method of script model mapping into AMN.

The main idea of mapping scripts into AMN consists in modeling of system state (i.e. places of a script) as variables of AMN, and modeling of transitions through AMN operations bodies of which are expressed in guarded substitutions. Such idea is characteristic for all approaches of representation of process models in AMN.

The **discriminator** script described above is represented in AMN as RE-FINEMENT with a name *DiscriminatorScript*.

REFINEMENT *DiscriminatorScript*
SETS *Obj*
CONSTANTS *ext_entrance1 TokenType*, *ext_auxState1 TokenType*, . . .
PROPERTIES
   $ext\_entrance1\,TokenType \in \mathbb{P}(Obj) \wedge$
   $ext\_auxState1\,TokenType \in \mathbb{P}(Obj) \wedge \ldots$
VARIABLES *entrance1, auxState1*, . . .
INVARIANT
   $entrance1 \in \mathbb{P}(ext\_entrance1\,TokenType) \wedge$
   $auxState1 \in \mathbb{P}(ext\_auxState1\,TokenType) \wedge \ldots$
INITIALISATION *entrance1* := $\varnothing$ || *auxState1* := $\varnothing$ || . . .
OPERATIONS . . .

REFINEMENT is the most universal AMN construction, since it can be used both as refined and as refining construction. Therefore this construction is most preferable for homogeneous representation of scripts in AMN.

In AMN specifications we shall represent types as extents, which are defined in the section of constants. For example, an extent *ext _entrance1 TokenType* is introduced for place *entrance1*. Then in the section of properties the types are represented as subsets of the deferred set *Obj* , which is interpreted as the union of extents of all object types. Each place of the script, defined in **states** slot, is represented in AMN as an individual variable which is typed in the INVARIANT section appropriately. In the INITIALISATION section variables are initialised with empty sets, corresponding to initial absence of tokens in the script places.

Each transition of the script, defined in **transitions** slot, is represented in AMN by an operation of the machine *DiscriminatorScript* .

The operations of abstract machines are based on the generalized substitutions. We shall use operations of sort

$$op = S$$

Here *op* is an operation name, S – substitution, defining the effect of the operation on the state space.

The Generalized Substitution Language (GSL) provides for description of transitions between system states. Each generalized substitution S defines a Predicate transformer, linking some postcondition R with its *weakest* precondition $[S]R$. This guarantees preservation of R after the operation execution. In such case we say that S *establishes* R. We shall use substitutions given in the table 1. Here S, T, S_1, S_2 stand for substitutions, x, y, t are variables, E, F denote expressions, G, G_1, G_2, P are predicates, $P\{x \to E\}$ denotes predicate P having all free occurrences of variable x replaced by E.

Table 1. The Generalized substitutions and their semantics

The generalized substitution S	$[S]P$
$X := E$	$P\{x \to E\}$
$X := E \parallel y := F$	$[x, y := E, F]P$
SELECT G_1 THEN T_1 WHEN G_2 THEN T_2 END	$(G_1 \Rightarrow [T_1]P) \wedge (G_2 \Rightarrow [T_2]P)$
ANY t WHERE G THEN T END	$\forall t \bullet (G \Rightarrow [T]P)$
$S\,;\ T$	$[S][T]P$

Now we proceed to the OPERATIONS section of the machine.

The SELECT substitution, with guarding predicate representing a condition of the transition firing, taken from bindings of the slot `bind_from`, constitutes the body of the script operation. For example, for operation *Branch1* such condition requires an occurrence of some token t in place *entrance1*. For operation *Trunk* the condition requires an occurrence of a token in one of the input places *auxState1*, *auxState2*, and absence of tokens in the others.

$Branch1 =$
SELECT
   $\exists t \bullet (t \in entrance1)$
THEN
   ANY t WHERE $t \in entrance1$
   THEN
     $entrance1 := entrance1 - \{t\} \parallel$
     ANY r WHERE $r \in ext\_auxState1\,TokenType$
     THEN
       SELECT $TRUE = TRUE$
       THEN $auxState1 := auxState1 \cup \{r\}$
       END
     END
   END
END

If the conditions of transition firing are met, appropriate tokens are taken from places defined by bindings of the slot `bind_from`. These tokens are passed as input parameters to the transition function. Selected tokens are removed from the input places. For operation *branch1* a token t from place *entrance1* is removed: $entrance1 := entrance1 - \{t\}$. For operation *trunk* a token t, satisfying the guarding predicate of substitution SELECT, is removed from the place it occupied. Simultaneously (that is specified by simultaneous substitution $\|$) another substitution is executed, consisting of sequential composition of two substitutions. The first of them represents the transition function, the second represents correct allocation of an output token of the transition. In our example the transition functions are absent, since we consider the generic type, so the sequential composition is degenerated. In case of operation *branch1* only token allocation is interpreted: with the help of ANY substitution a token r is selected from the extension of a type *auxState1TokenType*. This token is passed into place *auxState1*, an output place for the transition. In case of operation *trunk* an allocation of a token r of admissible type *exitTokenType* in an *exit* place of the transition is interpreted. After that with the help of sequential substitution $\langle\,;\,\rangle$ a cancellation of concurrent branches is realized so that tokens are removed from the respective script places.

Trunk =
SELECT
$\quad\quad \exists\, t_1 \bullet (t_1 \in auxState1 \wedge auxState2 = \varnothing) \vee$
$\quad\quad \exists\, t_2 \bullet (t_2 \in auxState2 \wedge auxState1 = \varnothing)$
THEN
$\quad$ ANY t WHERE $t \in Obj \wedge$
$\quad\quad (t \in auxState1 \wedge auxState2 = \varnothing \vee$
$\quad\quad t \in auxState2 \wedge auxState1 = \varnothing)$
$\quad$ THEN
$\quad\quad auxState1 := auxState1 - \{t\} \parallel auxState2 := auxState2 - \{t\} \parallel$
$\quad\quad$ ANY r WHERE $r \in ext\_exitTokenType$
$\quad\quad$ THEN
$\quad\quad\quad$ SELECT $TRUE = TRUE$ THEN $exit := exit \cup \{r\}$ END
$\quad\quad$ END ;
$\quad\quad (entrance1 := \varnothing \parallel entrance2 := \varnothing \parallel$
$\quad\quad\quad auxState1 := \varnothing \parallel auxState2 := \varnothing)$
$\quad$ END
END

3   Construction of Refining Extensions of the Canonical Process Model Kernel

Two process models, source and target, are required for the refining extensions construction technique. The canonical model stands for the target model. In section 2 it was shown how extensions of the canonical model kernel are specified by means of generic types for workflow patterns (for the discriminator example). Constructing an extension, it is necessary to show, that the extension of the kernel is refined by the source workflow pattern model. Here it is convenient to use the source models of workflow patterns given in YAWL (Yet Another Workflow Language) [2]. This language has constructions sufficient for expression of all workflow patterns [1]. At construction of the extension of the process model kernel it is necessary to prove that the source model refines the target one. In this section we show this for the discriminator pattern.

The workflow process specification in YAWL is a set of the Extended Workflow Nets (EWF-nets) [2], forming a tree-like structure. In this paper for simplicity we shall not go beyond YAWL facilities sufficient for description of the the discriminator pattern example. The specification will be given as a single EWF-net.

In general a data model mapping requires to construct 1) mapping of a source model M_j into an extension of a target model M_i; 2) AMN semantics for M_j; 3) AMN semantics for extended M_i. After that the B technology is applied to prove a) state-based properties of the mapping (commutativity of the data type state mapping diagrams); b) behavioral properties of the mapping for all types, defined for the source data model. This leads to a proof that M_j is a refinement of the extension of M_i.

Thus, for our example nothing else left but to construct AMN semantics of the discriminator pattern defined in YAWL.

The discriminator as the EWF-net is defined as the following 8-tuple:

$Discriminator = \langle C, i, o, T, F, join, split, rem \rangle$

$C = \{ enter1, enter2, auxState1, auxState2, exit \}$
$T = \{ branch1, branch2, trunk \}$
$F = \{ enter1 \mapsto branch1, enter2 \mapsto branch2,$
$\qquad branch1 \mapsto auxSatate1, branch2 \mapsto auxSatate2,$
$\qquad auxSatate1 \mapsto trunk, auxSatate2 \mapsto trunk,$
$\qquad trunk \mapsto exit \}$
$join = \{ trunk \mapsto XOR \}$
$split = \varnothing$
$rem = \{ trunk \mapsto \{ enter1, enter2, auxState1, auxState2, branch1, branch2 \} \}$

Here C is a set of places (in Petri nets terminology). T is a set of tasks. For the purpose of this paper it is sufficient to consider a *task* as a subnet showed in the Fig. 2.

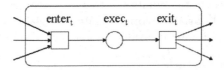

Fig. 2. EWF-net task structure

If the place $exec_t$ contains a token then t is said to be *executed*.

F is an incidence relation, i.e. a set of the ordered pairs of nodes. Such pairs define a possibility of moving tokens through the net. *join* is a function describing a mode of consuming tokens by a transition. There are three possible modes: *XOR* (only one token is consumed from all input places), *AND* (one token is consumed from each of the input places) and *OR* (one token is consumed from each of the several input places). If a transition has more than one input place (for example, incidence relation has two pairs related to *trunk* transition: $auxSatate1 \mapsto trunk$, $AuxSatate2 \mapsto trunk$), we should define join-behavior (in ur case as $trunk \mapsto XOR$). *split* is a function describing split-behaviour of transitions, i.e. a mode of token appearance in output places of the transitions at their firing. This function is reciprocal to the function *join* and is described similarly. *rem* is the function associating transitions with places, which should additionally be removed of tokens at firing of these transitions (thus cancellation is realized). In our case firing of the *trunk* transition leads to removing tokens from *enter1*, *enter2*, *auxState1*, *auxState2*, *branch1*, *branch2* places.

Such net is represented in AMN by a construction

REFINEMENT *Discriminator*
SETS *States* = {*state_enter*1, *state_enter*2,
        *state_auxState*1, *state_auxState*2, *state_exit*}
VARIABLES *States*, *Exec_branch*1, *exec_branch*2, *exec_trunk*
INVARIANT *states* ∈ *States* → *NAT* ∧ *exec_branch*1 ∈ *NAT* ∧
    *exec_branch*2 ∈ *NAT* ∧ *exec_trunk* ∈ *NAT*
INITIALISATION
    ANY *states*1 WHERE
        *states*1 ∈ *States* → *NAT* ∧ ∀ *st* • (*st* ∈ dom (*states*1) ⇒ *states*1(*st*) = 0)
    THEN
        States := *states*1
    END ||
    *exec_branch*1 := 0 || *exec_branch*2 := 0 || *exec_trunk* := 0
OPERATIONS ...

In the SETS section the *States* set is defined, which represents the set of a string constants conforming to names of places. In general, each task $t_i \in T$ is represented in AMN with the two operations $enter\_t_i$, $exit\_t_i$, and with a variable $exec\_t_i$ of the respective machine. Variable $exec\_t_i$ is typed in the *INVARIANT* section by the type of natural numbers. A natural number stored in $states(state\_c_i)$ reflects the number of tokens contained in the c_i place. The variable *states* and all variables corresponding to places are initialised in the INITIALISATION section as zero values, so that in the initial moment the net had no tokens.

In the OPERATIONS section an arbitrary operation $enter\_t_i$ is defined as follows, where a kind of predicate P_{enter} and a kind of substitution S_{enter} depend on join-behavior of task t_i (value of $join(t_i)$):

$enter\_t_i =$
SELECT $exec\_t_i = 0 \land P_{enter}$
THEN $S_{enter} \parallel exec\_t_i = exec\_t_i + 1$
END

For example, for operation $enter\_trunk$ of task $trunk$, P_{enter} looks as follows (what is characteristic for the XOR-join behavior):

$(states(state\_auxState1) > 0 \land states(state\_auxState2) = 0 \lor$
$(states(state\_auxState1) = 0 \land states(state\_auxState2) > 0)$

For the same operation a substitution S_{enter} realizes consumption of a single token from one input place.

IF $states(state\_auxState1) > 0$
THEN
   $states(state\_auxState1) := states(state\_auxState1) - 1$
ELSIF $states(state\_auxState2) > 0$
THEN
   $states(state\_auxState2) := states(state\_auxState2) - 1$
END

An arbitrary operation $exit\_t_i$ is defined so that a kind of substitution S_{exit} depends on split-behavior of task t_i (of the value of $split(t_i)$).

$exit\_t_i =$
SELECT $exec\_t_i > 0$
THEN $(S_{exit} \parallel exec\_t_i = exec\_t_i - 1); R_{exit}$
END

For example, for the operation $exit\_trunk$ the S_{exit} is defined as $State\_exit :=$ $state\_exit + 1$. R_{exit} for the same operation looks as follows.

$states :=$
   $States \lhdplus \{st \mapsto num \mid num = 0 \land$
      $st \in \{state\_enter1, state\_enter2,$
            $state\_auxState1, state\_auxState2\}\} \parallel$
   $exec\_branch1 := 0 \parallel exec\_branch2 := 0$

Here tokens are removed from places $enter1$, $enter2$, $auxState1$, $auxState2$ (respective variables are set to zero) and execution of tasks $branch1$, $branch2$ is cancelled. $r_1 \lhdplus r_2$ denotes a relation r_1 overridden by a relation r_2.

The extension of the canonical process model for the *Discriminator* pattern has been defined by means of the generic script type described in the previous section.

The last stage of the proof, that the extension of the canonical model by the generic script type is correct, consists in applying of the automation facilities of B-Technology to prove that machine *DiscriminatorScript* is refined by machine *Discriminator*. For this purpose it is necessary to *conform* machines *DiscriminatorScript* and *Discriminator*. The conformance process consists of the following steps:

- point the refinement direction adding the REFINES section in the *Discriminator* machine.

  REFINES *DiscriminatorScript*

- conform operation names in refined and refining machines: for each transition t of the script rename the respective operation t of *DiscriminatorScript* machine into the operation *exit_t*; add the empty operation *enter_t* to *DiscriminatorScript* machine.

  $enter\_t = skip;$

- add of a *refinement invariant* in section INVARIANT of *Discriminator* machine. The invariant should describe a relationship between states of refined and refining machines.

  $card\,(entrance1) = states(state\_entrance1) + exec\_branch1 \wedge$
  $card\,(entrance2) = states(state\_entrance2) + exec\_branch2 \wedge$
  $(\,card\,(auxState1) = states(state\_auxState1) + exec\_trunk \wedge$
  $card\,(auxState2) = states(state\_auxState2) \vee$
  $card\,(auxState2) = states(state\_auxState2) + exec\_trunk \wedge$
  $card\,(auxState1) = states(state\_auxState1)) \wedge$
  $card\,(exit) = states(state\_exit)$

  $card\,(s)$ denotes a cardinality of a state s as a set.

At the end of the conformance process the tool for the automated AMN refinement proof has been applied (B-Toolkit 5.1.4). It had automatically formulated 65 theorems, expressing the fact that machine *DiscriminatorScript* is refined by machine *Discriminator*. Large number of theorems is explained by automatically subdividing complex theorems by the tool into simpler ones to prove them independently. For example, the theorem of initialisation refinement was subdivided into 6 theorems. 38 theorems were proved automatically by the tool, the others were proved interactively. In the table 2 total number of theorems formulated and number of theorems automatically proved are shown.

Table 2. The number of theorems

	Number of theorems	Number of automatically proved theorems
The theorem of the unified state non-emptines	1	0
Theorems of the initialisation refinement	6	6
Theorems of refinement for operation *enter_branch*1	7	5
Theorems of refinement for operation *exit_branch*1	7	4
Theorems of refinement for operation *enter_branch*2	7	5
Theorems of refinement for operation *exit_branch*2	8	5
Theorems of refinement for operation *enter_trunk*	16	11
Theorems of refinement for operation *exit_trunk*	13	2
Total number of theorems	65	38

4 Conclusion

The provable synthesis of the canonical process model shown here appeared to be feasible due to: 1) the recently discovered possibility of interpretation of concurrent events, characteristic for process models, in logics and 2) the reduction of the workflow models diversity to a relatively small number of workflow patterns. These premises have served as necessary precondition for the canonical process model synthesis, following the principles proclaimed earlier. The methods developed constitute necessary basis for reaching semantic interoperability, reuse and composition of heterogeneous process components in distributed information systems.

At the same time, due to the exploding growth of number and variety of information representation models, it is difficult to cope with such variety of information models manually preserving the basic principles of mapping and synthesis of canonical models applying the refinement techniques. Therefore the methods developed should be supplemented with a compositional approach to the canonical models synthesis. This approach in general consists in registering of data types of each source data model in the canonical model so that they could serve as refinements of types or compositions of types already included into the canonical model. If there are no appropriate types in the current canonical model, we should construct its extension. Specifications of components (data types) of the canonical and source models are stored in a repository. Special tools are needed to discover necessary components, to match them, to eliminate structural and behavioral discrepancies of components, to form their compositions, and to prove commutativity of the resulting mappings. This idea is planned to be developed on the basis of the existing approach for compositional development of information systems [6].

References

1. van der Aalst, W. M. P. et al.: Workflow Patterns. – Distributed and Parallel Databases (2003) 14(3):5-51
2. van der Aalst, W. M. P., ter Hofstede, A. H. M.: YAWL: Yet Another Workflow Language (Revised version). – QUT Technical report, FIT-TR-2003-04. Brisbane (2003)
3. Abrial J.-R.: B-Technology. Technical overview. – BP International Ltd. (1992)
4. Abrial, J. R.: The B-Book. – Cambridge University Press (1996)
5. Abrial, J. R.: B# : Toward a synthesis between Z and B. – In Proc. of the International Conference of Z and B Users ZB'2003. Springer (2003)
6. Briukhov, D., Kalinichenko, L.: Component-based information systems development tool supporting the SYNTHESIS design method. – In Proc. of the Second East European Conference ADBIS'1998. Springer (1998)
7. Butler, M.: csp2B: A Practical Approach to Combining CSP and B. – Formal Aspects of Computing, Vol. 12 (2000)
8. Butler, M., Snook, C.: Verifying Dynamic Properties of UML Models by Translation to the B Language and Toolkit. – In Proc. of the UML 2000 Workshop Dynamic Behaviour in UML Models: Semantic Questions.
9. Edsger, W., Dijkstra, E.W.: A discipline of programming. – Prentice Hall (1976)
10. Jensen, K.: Coloured Petri Nets: a High Level Language for System Design and Analysis. – Springer (1991)
11. Kalinichenko, L. A.: Data model transformation method based on axiomatic data model extension. – Proc. of the 4th International Conference on Very Large Data Bases (1978)
12. Kalinichenko, L. A.: Methods and tools for equivalent data model mapping construction. – Proc. of the International Conference on Extending Database Technology EDBT'90. Springer (1990)
13. Kalinichenko, L. A.: SYNTHESIS: the language for desription, design and programming of the heterogeneous interoperable information resource environment. – Moscow (1995)
14. Kalinichenko, L. A.: Method for Data Models Integration in the Common Paradigm. – In Proc. of the First East-European Conference, ADBIS'97. St.Petersburg (1997)
15. Kalinichenko, L. A.: Workflow Reuse and Semantic Interoperation Issues. – Advances in workflow management systems and interoperability; A.Dogac, L.Kalinichenko, M.T. Ozsu, A.Sheth (Eds.). NATO Advanced Study Institute (1997)
16. Kalinichenko, L. A., Stupnikov, S. A., Zemtsov, N. A.: Canonical models synthesis for heterogeneous information sources integration. – Moscow (2005)
17. Ledang, H., Souquieres, J.: Contributions for Modeling UML State-Charts In B. – In Proc. of the Third International Conference on Integrated Formal Methods IFM 2002. Springer (2002)
18. Stupnikov, S. A., Kalinichenko, L. A., Dong, J. S.: Applying CSP-like Workflow Process Specifications for their Refinement in AMN by Pre- existing Workflows. – In Proc. of the Sixth East-European Conference on Advances in Databases and Information Systems ADBIS'2002. Slovak University of Technology (2000)
19. Treharne, H., Schneider, S.: How to Drive a B machine. – In Proc. of the First International Conference of Z and B Users ZB'2000. Springer (2000)

Location Awareness of Information Agents

Merik Meriste, Jüri Helekivi, Tõnis Kelder, Andres Marandi[1],
Leo Mõtus, and Jürgo Preden[2]

[1] Tartu University Institute of Technology, Estonia
merik.meriste@ut.ee
[2] Tallinn Technical University, Estonia
leo.motus@dcc.ttu.ee

Abstract. This paper discusses the use of generic geospatial agents (provided by agent development environment KRATT) for collecting and processing location aware information. The approach is essentially based on agent-based digital map processing software that is capable of handling raster or vector maps, and maps with different colour schemes, with different packing methods, with different systems of signs, etc. Each application can be configured and reconfigured dynamically. Agents, and the applications that use services provided by agents, are not in one-to-one relationship; one agent can simultaneously work with many applications. Also, an agent may use services from different agents in different situations. The approach is illustrated by pilot applications, such as participatory GIS, tracking of active objects, information collection and navigation in a sensor network with beacons.

1 Introduction

Steadily increasing number of computer applications exhibit location aware behaviour. Location- and time-awareness is often a crucial non-functional requirement for new applications. As the need for spatial and real-time data increases, and access to that data improves, the need for appropriate software tools becomes urgent. A prevailing trend in developing such systems is the wide use of autonomous, interactive software entities [1] – supported by component-based development, agent-based technologies, innovations in software modelling and analysis methods, and respective tools. The architecture of those systems should be dynamically modifiable (or, preferably, able to evolve by itself due to proactive behaviour of components).

Two concepts are today considered reasonable for addressing the development of such systems – web services and autonomous agents. Geospatial technology developers are embracing web services as a mechanism for providing spatial and time-aware capabilities in enterprise applications. The Open Geospatial Consortium [4, 5] tackles the challenge of developing tools to support the integration of spatial capabilities into applications that do not depend on a full-featured Geographic Information Systems (GIS). The major problem is that of embedding location- and time-aware autonomous components into information systems and other applications.

This paper discusses the use of generic geospatial agents (provided by agent development environment KRATT) for collecting and processing location- and time-

J. Eder et al. (Eds.): ADBIS 2005, LNCS 3631, pp. 199–208, 2005.

aware information. The approach relies essentially on agent-based digital map processing software that is capable of handling raster or vector maps, and maps with different colour schemes, with different packing methods, with different systems of signs, etc. Each application can be configured and reconfigured dynamically, i.e. forms a community of location- and time-aware agents. Agents, and the applications that use services provided by agents, are not necessarily in one-to-one relationship; one agent can simultaneously work with many applications. Also, an agent may use services from different agents in different situations. A community of agents has a distinctive property that is not common in artificial systems – the complete list of interacting components and the structure of their interactions cannot be fixed completely at the specification and design stage.

The more sophisticated computations and the more context-sensitive (i.e. depending on location and time of processed information) interactions are, the larger will be the share of emergent behaviour in the overall behaviour of systems. Consequently, the more difficult its is to satisfy the requirements imposed on quality of service of the future systems during the operation of implemented systems. The issues of engineering agents and, especially multi-agents, have received rather scanty attention - current interests of agent-based systems are mostly focused on agents' intelligence related issues.

This paper illustrates the use of a prototype for an agent development environment KRATT [6], for building generic geospatial agents. The conceptual line of development as well as some typical geospatial tasks with appropriate pilot applications is superficially described, and the obtained experience discussed in section 2. Basic collection of geospatial agents is introduced in section 3. A short overview of further developments, work-in-progress and open problems will conclude the presentation.

2 Spatial Agents

Agents exist and interact in a multi-agent system that is distributed across a set of, not necessarily homogeneous, networks. Some agents can exist completely in a virtual world – interacting only with the other agents, or also interacting with non-agent components of the system, some other agents may be essentially related to their physical body. A multi-agent system, as an application, consists of administrative agents, and application agents. All the agents are generated from pre-specified classes and form together a community of agents. The class of an agent determines its capabilities and lists related components that are to be applied when generating an instance of this agent. Majority of agents, i.e. application agents carry out their autonomous (and maybe proactive) tasks. Administrative agents are specific in a sense that they store and execute the rules for the community of agents, and provide common services, as required for dependable operation of application agents. Agents, and the applications that use services provided by agents are not in one-to-one relation; one agent can simultaneously work with many applications. Also, an application may use services from different agents in different situations. An application is configured dynamically, depending on which agents are active and accessible at this particular moment.

A spatial multi-agent system acquires the information from different GIS, IS and DB, as well as represents and manages the information supplied by agents involved. The acquired information is processed and used to update the required databases, or to satisfy other requests from a particular client. A multi-agent system comprises following types of autonomous agents:

- configurable *information agent* implements queries and management of databases interacting with particular DB agents;
- *map agents* search, pre-process, and deliver fragments of the base map;
- *spatial agents* manage the vector information for images or situations activated on the user's view of the map;

related information agents manage the map objects related information, e.g. record of a lot related information, historic or environmental information, etc. ;

location agents, that periodically transmit position of active objects (GPS devices, radio beacons, motes etc.).

This set of types for agent classes forms the basis of any multi-agent system applied to digital map processing. The set of types is easily extendable and depends on tasks required by the customer, types of digital base-maps, additional databases to be used, and on other factors. Each agent is to be programmed as required by the specific application. However, many agents have generic features that facilitate their usage in a variety of applications with minimal modifications. The first experience shows that dynamic compilation of agents' intermediated map frames offers a reasonable processing speed, better than that of typical fixed menu of web services of a traditional GIS.

3 Agent-Based Solutions to Geospatial Tasks

Agent based digital map software can display different areas from a variety of digital maps (raster or vector based maps, maps with different colour schemes, maps with different packing methods, maps with different systems of conventional signs, etc). Reasonably short response time of the agent-based map system is achieved due to carefully designed network usage, combined with caching and parallel processing of source maps and databases in the servers.

The prototype software development is carried out in C# and .NET since this platform appears to be the most suitable for controlling multiple simultaneous threads needed in agents. The customer's computer must have a web browser, and sufficient memory space for automatically downloaded *active map object* together with some other active objects, necessary to solve the particular task stated by the customer.

The map-specific part of the web browser's page in a customer's computer is *map_object* (presented as ActiveX component). The other parts of the page depend on the specific requirements of the application and are usually based on JavaScript, cater for dynamic support of the page, and for interactions between the *map_object*, the customer, and web-servers. The whole page or parts of it are typically generated by a web-server based application (see Figure 1). The main operational response and support to the queries from the *map_object* and the web-server application comes from a dedicated multi-agent system.

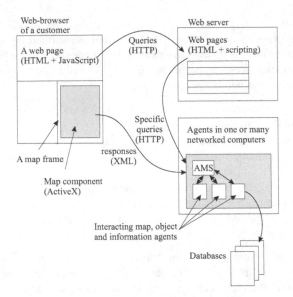

Fig. 1. A multi-agent digital map application cooperates with web-server

3.1 Participatory GIS

Participatory GIS for regional planning and management was tested as one of the pilot applications. The aim of this application is to view and update the information distributed in a variety of proprietary databases — e.g. technological communications (water, sewerage, electricity, etc.) built for Tartu City. The proprietary information is presented as a dynamic collection of spatial and information frames integrated into one application. The task comes from the city government, who needs the information of different infrastructures (gas-, water-, sewerage-, heating pipelines, power lines and phone lines) for planning and coordinating daily maintenance and construction activities. In reality, the infrastructure is maintained by different organizations and the information, therefore, is also kept in different GIS and databases.

The prototype of the participatory GIS for the tasks described above is implemented as a community of agents (see also Figure 2). This multi-agent system provides the updated information from different information sources as well as represents and manages the information supplied by agents involved. The collection consists of following types of agents:

- configurable information agent implements queries and management of databases that interact with particular DB agents;
- map agents that search, pre-process, and send fragments of a digital base-map, requested by the *map_object*
- spatial agents for searching, processing, and sending the vector information for the image or situation that has been activated in the *map_object*
- information agents that manage, search, and forward the map objects related information, f.e. records of lot related information, pipeline data etc. Map related information is known to map and spatial agents, it is requested by the web-server or the *map_object* depending on user's or agents' activities.

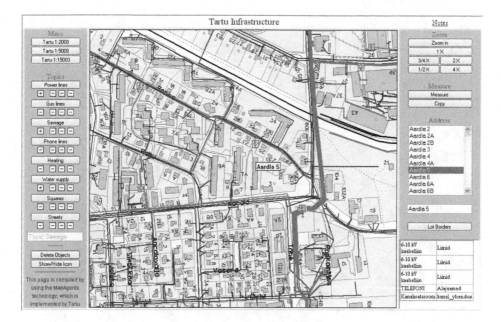

Fig. 2. Participatory GIS

The user can select one main theme and compare it with different sub-themes. Borders of a lot and map positioning by address can additionally be applied.

The number of base maps and different data categories used in an application depends on maps and data which are available to users. As a result, the users can have overview of the existing infrastructure in the area they are interested of, e.g. the location of pipelines, availability of gas line, or central heating system etc.

3.2 Using GPS for Tracking Active Objects

To include active or mobile objects in the framework of geospatial agents, a prototype for tracking vehicles was developed. As usually, a GPS module, which is attached to the moving object, receives the signal from satellites and transmits the coordinates with the unique ID of object to operator agent. The agents provide the map application with coordinates of the particular mobile object. The map application (Figure 3) displays moving objects as icons on the map, each icon is labelled with additional information (precise coordinates, time value, speed and azimuth, etc).

The tracking multi-agent is a community of agents comprising following types of agents:

- agents processing fragments of the map;
- agents searching, processing, and sending the vector information for the image or situation that has been activated in the *map object*.
- GPS agents, that periodically transmit to other agents the position of active objects equipped with standard GPS device.
- agents to manage, search, and forward information related to active objects.

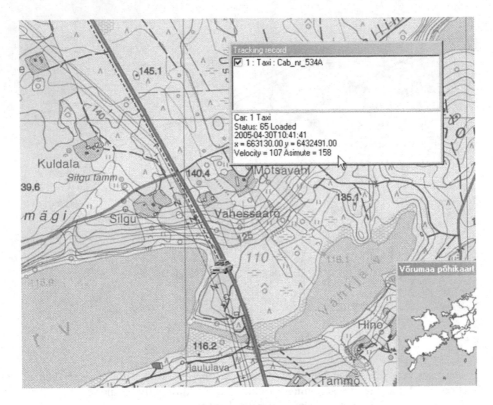

Fig. 3. Tracking active objects

3.3 Tracking Active Objects Without GPS

In many applications the GPS services are not available – for instance in buildings, caves, or for many other reasons. Such applications are typically related to monitoring and surveillance of the environment, remote monitoring and maintenance of technical devices, operational situations in rescue, police and security services. In such cases the navigation, tracking, and displaying functions are based on information collected from ad hoc sensor networks, extended with beacons, or in some cases with identifiable landmarks with known position. It is highly recommendable that applications could be built from basically the same set of components as described above in this paper, independently of the availability of GPS.

Ad hoc sensor networks form a subclass of multi-hop ad hoc networks (MANET) – that usually are with dynamically changing topology and highly irregular traffic load, and are built on heterogeneous hard- and software platforms [3]. Ideologically they are quite close to agent technology – like interacting autonomous agents, the nodes in a multi-hop sensor network exhibit proactive behaviour and may behave differently in different communication acts [7].

The recently started, and ongoing pilot project (*Hopadhoc*) for experimenting with map agents without GPS support starts by building an artificial environment with a number of fixed beacons with known coordinates, installing a number of stationary sensors (with unknown coordinates), introducing a number of mobile platforms equipped with necessary sensors, signal processors, plus other devices and software necessary for autonomous proactive behaviour.

The digitized schema of this artificial environment is used as a conventional digital map, processed by the above described community of (may be slightly modified) map agents. The mobile platforms compute their coordinates in the environment (relying on signals from the beacons), based on their computed location coordinates the mobile platforms reason about their next destination and tasks to be performed. The reasoning is supported by regularly improved digital schema of the environment – available for mobile platforms from an agent that is responsible for collecting information sent from the mobile platforms and fitting the incoming information with the already existing information.

A heterogeneous computer network (combined from the regular internet, WiFi and radio-frequency sensor network) serves as a communication infrastructure for the artificial environment. The sensor network is based on "Berkeley motes". Motes are small computing devices that have three key capabilities: computing, sensing, and (radio)communication capabilities. Sufficient memory to store and in some cases pre-process collected data locally is a feature that increases the number of possible applications. Motes are battery powered to enable their autonomous operation. Each mote can have a diverse set of sensors, for example the sensor boards used in Hopadhoc project have light, temperature, microphone, sounder, tone detection, 2-axis accelerometer and 2-axis magnetometer sensors. Each mote is able to communicate with any other mote in the ad hoc sensor network. The network can also be connected to a PC, or to a wired or WiFi network.

The use of motes is increasing rapidly in military, as well as civilian applications: monitoring wildlife, monitoring applications in agriculture, monitoring and maintaining huge civil constructions (the Golden Gate Bridge, and the new Hong Kong bridges are equipped with tens of thousand sensors and actuators).

However the data provided by motes has little value without time and location identifiers. One option for solving the location problem is to hand-place the motes at known locations, providing each mote with some ID and location identifiers (as it was done for the Hong Kong Bridge). This is essentially using the motes in a way very similar to how we are using conventional (wired) sensors – each sensor is in a fixed position and the output of that sensor serves as a predefined input to our control or monitoring system. It cannot be expected in every application that each mote will be carefully hand-placed and that there is an opportunity, will or means to identify the mote's locations during the placement of the mote.

The second solution for solving the sensor localization task is to determine the mote's location after the mote has been deployed. Again there are several options: to equip each mote with some localization hardware or to determine the mote's location after its deployment and then either store the coordinates in the mote or in some central database. Adding some localization hardware to each mote is quite costly.

Naturally the approach where each mote's position is not predetermined is more attractive for most applications. As an indoor solution we suggest to use Cricket motes that provide means for solving the indoor localization task. For instance, Cricket beacons are fixed in the ceiling of the room and each Cricket beacon sends out radio and ultrasonic pulses. The radio packet contains data on the beacon's coordinates (predefined) and the beacon's identifier. The Cricket receivers listen to the radio pulses and after receiving the first bits of the radio pulse the receiver starts to listen to the ultrasonic pulse. Based on the time difference of the arrival of these two pulses the distance to the specific beacon can be determined. Obviously one beacon is not enough to determine the receiver's location. But with three beacons it is possible to calculate the receiver's location based on the coordinates of the beacons (provided by the beacons) and the distance to each beacon.

The above-described map agent solution (KRATT) provides the basic ideology that can be extended for application on mobile & thin platforms. The first step in developing a location-aware computing platform is recursive updating of the map by positioning the mobile node on a map in a master map server for this environment.

Sensor motes are placed randomly in an area for which there is a map in the KRATT system. A mobile robot navigates in the area and communicates with sensor motes. Once communication with a mote is initiated the mobile robot makes a rough estimation on the mote's location (using the sounder and the tone detection circuit on the mote). The mobile robot can communicate the mote's location estimation to the mote (which will then be stored locally at the mote) and all further sensor data originated from the mote will have a location identifier associated with it. Such an approach assumes stationary motes. If there are several mobile agents then the mote's location can be gradually improved, until the reasonable precision is achieved.

Once a mobile node is aware of its location with respect to the beacons, the context awareness issues can be addressed directly. This includes, for instance, context awareness in terms of positioning the mobile platform on the map in relation to the other static objects on the map (walls, doors, etc) and in relation to the other mobile platforms. The location data can be used for better analysis and processing of sensor data (if advanced algorithms are used then for example sound waves reflecting from a nearby wall can be filtered out if necessary, etc). Also a mobile node can query nearby stationary motes and or mobile nodes for additional sensor data to improve its own perception of the environment.

Based on the additional information collected, a mobile robot can improve its reasoning processes -- such as, to better assess its performance, to better plan future activities, to improve its understanding of the environment and about the intentions of other actors in the environment. This leads to step-by-step improvement of independent navigational capabilities of any mobile node using a collectively updated map. This includes route planning, sub-goal selection, considering the potential intentions of other mobile and non-mobile nodes (if the node is aware of those intentions), and of course executing the plan by following the selected route. In a long run, a whole range of new topics can be stated, researched, and hopefully resolved – cooperation, competition, self-organization, and others.

4   Conclusions

A clear increase of interest can be observed on applying agents, and multi-agent systems in situations that require location-awareness, and time-awareness. This could be caused by the successful practice of component-based systems, combined with the fact that autonomous and proactive components are being used increasingly. An obvious demand for appropriate active components is initiated by the high level GIS community needs. The theory of modelling of a family of agents with complex time sensitive and location sensitive interactions among its members remains today a fundamental problem in artificial intelligence and computer science. On the other hand, the evolution of computer science is gradually reaching the understanding that interactive systems represent a new paradigm in computation that cannot be modelled using traditional tools [2, 8]. The basis for this *empirical* computer science research relies on two contradictive concepts – inside-view in order to prescribe the behaviour of an agent (i.e. programming), and outside-view in order to design and analyse (i.e. modelling).

To develop applications in this context requires an approach to software architecture that helps developers evolve their solutions in flexible ways. A prevailing trend in developing such systems is the wide use of autonomous, interactive software entities – supported by component-based development, agent-based technologies, innovations in software modelling and analysis methods, and respective tools. The architecture of those systems should be dynamically modifiable (or, preferably, able to evolve by itself due to proactive behaviour of components). Two concepts are considered reasonable today – web services and agents. The major problem is also that of embedding location- and time-aware autonomous components (i.e. proactive context-aware agents) into information systems and other applications.

Some aspects of implementation of generic geospatial agents in a prototype agent development environment KRATT were presented in this paper. A collection of geospatial agents as well as conceptual line of development, and the first experience were superficially described. Agents can display different areas from a variety of digital maps (raster or vector based maps, maps with different colour schemes, maps with different packing methods, maps with different systems of conventional signs, etc). Reasonably short response time of the agent-based map system is achieved due to carefully designed network usage, combined with caching and parallel processing of source maps and databases in the servers.

The developed collection of agent classes forms the basis of any multi-agent system applied to digital map processing. The collection is easily extendable and depends on tasks required by the customer, types of digital base-maps, additional databases to be used, and on other factors. Each agent is to be programmed as required by the specific application. However, many agents have generic features that facilitate their usage in a variety of applications with minimal modifications. The first experience shows that dynamic compilation of agents' intermediated map frames offers a reasonable processing speed, better than that of typical fixed menu of web services of a traditional GIS.

The above-described map agent solution (KRATT) provides the basic ideology that can be extended for application on mobile & thin platforms. The first step in developing a location-aware computing platform is recursive updating of the map by positioning the mobile node on a map in a master map server for this environment. Further experiments and developments of the instrumental software and particular types of geospatial agents are needed, certainly in pair with carefully selected application areas.

This paper is based on interim results of an ongoing larger project on time-aware and location aware agents, carried out in the Estonian Centre for Dependable Computing (CDC) – a joint venture of Tallinn Technical University and Tartu University.

Acknowledgment

The partial financial support provided by ETF grant 4860 and grants nr 0140237s98, 0250556s98 from Estonian Ministry of Education is acknowledged.

References

1. Bigus, J. P., Schlosnagle, D. A., Pilgrim, J. R., Mills, W. N., Diao, Y.: ABLE: A toolkit for building multi-agent autonomic systems. IBM Systems Journal, vol. 41, no. 3 (2002) 350–371
2. Blass, A., Gurevich, Y.: Algorithms: A quest for absolute definitions. Bulletin of European Association for Theoretical Computer Science. no. 81 (2003)
3. Chlamtac, I., Conti, M., Liu, J. J.-N.: Mobile ad hoc networking: imperatives and challenges, Ad Hoc Networks, Volume 1, Issue 1 (2003) 13–64
4. McKee, L.: The Importance of Going "Open". Open Geospatial Consortium. (2003) www.opengis.org
5. McKee, L.: The Spatial Web. Open Geospatial Consortium. (2003) www.opengis.org
6. Motus, L., Meriste, M., Kelder, T., Helekivi, J.: An Architecture for a Multi-agent System Test-bed. Proc. of the 15th IFAC World Congress, vol. L (2002)
7. Tschudin, C., Gunningberg, P., Lundgren,. H., Nordström, E.: Lessons from experimental MANET research, Ad Hoc Networks, Volume 3, Issue 2 (2005) 221–233
8. Wegner, P.: Interactive foundations of computing. Theor. Computer Science, vol. 192 (1998) 315–351

Algebraic Semantics of XML Schema

Leonid Novak[1] and Alexandre Zamulin[2],[*]

[1] Institute of System Programming, Russian Academy of Sciences,
25, B. Kommunisticheskaia str., Moscow 109104, Russia
novak@ispras.ru
[2] A.P. Ershov Institute of Informatics Systems,
Siberian Branch of Russian Academy of Sciences,Novosibirsk 630090, Russia
zam@iis.nsk.su

Abstract. The semantics of the core features of XML Schema in terms of the XQuery 1.0 and XPath 2.0 data model algebraically defined is given. The database state is represented as a many-sorted algebra whose sorts are sets of data type values and different kinds of nodes and whose operations are data type operations and node accessors. It is shown that a document can be easily mapped to its implementation in terms of nodes and accessors defined on them.

1 Introduction

In this paper, we present a formalization of some core ideas of XML Schema [11,12] (which is nowadays a widely used standard of XML databases) by means of algebraic techniques. The benefits of a formal description are well known: it is both concise and precise [1]. This paper is not the first attempt to formalize an XML language. A detailed review of related work is given in Section 9. It is sufficient to mention at the moment that in all previous work an XML document rather than an XML database is practically formalized. For this reason, one cannot easily map a document to its implementation in terms of nodes and accessors defined on them. Moreover, any operation of an XML algebra should be defined as a function on the underlining sets. Therefore an algebraic model of the XML database is needed for definition of such operations.

A data model [13] is designed to support the query language XQuery [14] and any other specification that references it. Since XML Schema is designed for defining databases that may be searched by XQuery (in fact, the type system of XQuery is based on XML Schema), it is natural to use this model as semantics of XML Schema. For this purpose, we need to define formally the model and map syntactic constructs of XML Schema to the components of the model. As a result, we can get an abstract implementation of XML Schema, which may be helpful both in the concise description of XML Schema and the understanding of its implementation.

To save space, we define only the semantics of a representative part of XML Schema, simplifying many of its constructions. In this way, we consider only the most important document components: elements and attributes, other compo-

---

[*] The work of this author is supported in part by Russian Foundation for Basic Research under Grant 04-01-00272.

J. Eder et al. (Eds.): ADBIS 2005, LNCS 3631, pp. 209–222, 2005.

nents such as comments, namespaces, and processing instructions can be easily
added to the presented model without its redefinition.

It is assumed that the reader is familiar with XML [10] and some document type definition language like DTD. The familiarity with XML Schema is
desirable, but not mandatory.

The rest of the paper is organized as follows. The abstract syntax of element
declarations and type definitions in XML Schema is presented in Section 2, and
the abstract syntax of the document schema is given in Section 3. Basic types of
XML Schema are listed in Section 4. Base classes of the data model are described
in Section 5. The database itself is defined in Section 6, and the document order
is defined in Section 7. It is shown in Section 8 that an XML document can
be converted into a database tree and vice versa. A review of related work is
presented in Section 9, and concluding remarks are given in Section 10.

2   Element Declarations and Type Definitions

In this section we present an abstract syntax of element declarations and type
definitions in XML Schema. The syntax is given in terms of syntactic types representing syntactic domains and the following type constructors:

$Seq(T)$ — type of ordered sets of values of type T (empty set included).
$FM(T_1, T_2)$ — type of ordered sets (empty set included) of pairs of values of
    types T_1 and T_2 defining final mappings from T_1 to T_2.
$Union(T_1, ..., T_n)$ — type of the disjoint union of values of types $T_1, ..., T_n$.
$Enumeration$ — enumeration type constructor.
$Pair(T_1, T_2)$ — type of pairs of values of types T_1 and T_2.
$Interleave(T_1, T_2)$ — type of two-item sets of values of types T_1 and T_2 (if a and
    b are values of respective types T_1 and T_2, then both $a\&b$ and $b\&a$ are
    instances of this type).
$Tuple(T_1, ..., T_n)$ — type of tuples of values of types T_1, ..., T_n.

The presentation is supplied with examples written in the XML Schema language. The correspondence between abstract syntax constructions and their
XML representations is straightforward.

There is a predefined syntactic type, $Name$, whose elements are used for
denoting different document entities. Depending on the context where this type
is used, we denote it either by $ElemName$ or $AttrName$ or $SimpleTypeName$
or $ComplexTypeName$.

$ElementDeclaration =$
    $Tuple(ElemName, Type, RepetitionFactor, NillOption)$
$RepetitionFactor = Pair(Minimum, Maximum)$
$Minimum = NaturalNumber$
$Maximum = Union(NaturalNumber, \{\texttt{unbounded}\})$
$NillOption = Boolean$

The $RepetitionFactor$ indicates here how many element information items with
this $ElemName$ a document may have. The $NillOption$ indicates whether the

element may have the nil value. $NaturalNumber$ and $Boolean$ are conventional natural number and Boolean values.

Example 1:
```
<xsd:element name="annotation" type="xsd:string" nillable="true"/>
<xsd:element name="Book" type="Book-type" minOccurs="1"
                                        maxOccurs="unbounded"/>
<xsd:element name="A">
  <xsd:complexType>
       ...
  </xsd:complexType>
</xsd:element>
```

Three element declarations are presented in the example. The $RepetitionFactor$ is indicated by the pair (`minOccurs, maxOccurs`); in the first and third element declarations the default value (1, 1) is used, in the second declaration the value is set explicitly. An anonymous complex type is used in the third declaration. $NillOption$ is set to $false$ by default in the second and third declarations. Thus only the first element may have the nil value.

$$GroupDefinition = Tuple(Seq(LocalGroupDefinition),$$
$$CombinationFactor, RepetitionFactor)$$
$$LocalGroupDefinition = Union(ElementDeclaration, GroupDefinition)$$
$$CombinationFactor = Enumeration(\texttt{sequence}, \texttt{choice})$$

A group definition consists of a sequence of local group definitions, which are either element declarations or group definitions. The $CombinationFactor$ indicates whether the group defines a sequence or choice. The definition has the *empty content* if the sequence of local group definitions is empty. A nested group definition is presented in Example 2.

Example 2:
```
<xsd:sequence minOccurs="0" maxOccurs="unbounded">
  <xsd:sequence minOccurs="0" maxOccurs="unbounded">
    <xsd:element name="work" type="xsd:string"/>
    <xsd:element name="eat" type="xsd:string"/>
  </xsd: sequence>
  <xsd:choice>
    <xsd:element name="work" type="xsd:string"/>
    <xsd:element name="play" type="xsd:string"/>
  </xsd:choice>
  <xsd:element name="sleep" type="xsd:string"/>
</xsd:sequence>
```

$$Type = Union(TypeName, AnonymousTypeDefinition)$$

A type may be defined inline in an element declaration (third declaration in Example 1) or supplied with a name in a type definition (Example 7). Some type names are predefined, they denote primitive simple types (for instance, the type `xsd:string` in the above examples).

$$TypeName = Union(SimpleTypeName, ComplexTypeName)$$

A simple type in an element declaration means the definition of zero or more tree leaves. A complex type in an element declaration means, as a rule, the definition of zero or more intermediate nodes of a tree. We consider in the sequel that all simple types are predefined and have a name.

$$AllOptionDefinition =$$
$$\qquad FM(ElemName, Tuple(Type, OptionFactor, NillOption))$$
$$OptionFactor = \{0, 1\}$$

This is the declaration of a special group containing the declared elements in any order. This group may not consist of nested groups. An element of the group is optional in a document if the value of the *OptionFactor* is 0, and it must be present if the value is 1. The declaration has the *empty* content if the final mapping is empty.

Example 3:
```
<xsd:all>
    <xsd:element name="Title" type="xsd:string"/>
    <xsd:element name="Author" type="xsd:string"/>
    <xsd:element name="Date" type="xsd:string"/>
    <xsd:element name="ISBN" type="xsd:string"/>
    <xsd:element name="Publisher" type="xsd:string"/>
</xsd:all>
```

In the above example the *OptionFactor* has the default value 1 (each element must be present in a document).

$$AttributeDeclarations = FM(AttrName, SimpleTypeName)$$

AttributeDeclarations introduce a number of attributes with different names. The type of an attribute is always a simple type. For simplicity, we do not indicate properties (REQUIRED, PROHIBITED, OPTIONAL) and default values.

Example 4:
```
<xsd:attribute name="InStock" type="xsd:boolean"/>
<xsd:attribute name="Reviewer" type="xsd:string"/>
```

$$AnonymousTypeDefinition =$$
$$\qquad Union(SimpleContentDefinition, ComplexContentDefinition)$$
$$SimpleContentDefinition = Pair(SimpleTypeName, AttributeDeclarations)$$
$$ComplexContentDefinition = Pair(MixedOption, ComplexTypeContent)$$
$$ComplexTypeContent =$$
$$\qquad Union(LocalElementDeclarations, AttributeDeclarations,$$
$$\qquad\qquad Pair(LocalElementDeclarations, AttributeDeclarations))$$
$$MixedOption = Boolean$$
$$LocalElementDeclarations = Union(AllOptionDefinition, GroupDefinition)$$

A complex type may have either a simple content or a complex content. In the first case, a simple type is extended by attribute definitions. In the second case, the definition of a complex type typically consists of (local) element declarations or attribute declarations or both. If the *MixedOption* in the *ComplexContentDefinition* is set to *true*, then a document may contain text nodes in between element nodes of the corresponding group.

Example 5:
```
<xsd:complexType>
  <xsd:simpleContent>
    <xsd:extension base="xsd:decimal">
      <xsd:attribute name="currency" type="xsd:string"/>
    </xsd:extension>
  </xsd:simpleContent>
</xsd:complexType>
```

A complex type with a simple content is defined. An element of this type may have a decimal value and an attribute.

Example 6:
```
<xsd:complexType mixed="true">
  <xsd:sequence>
    <xsd:element name="Book" minOccurs=0 maxOccurs="1000">
      <xsd:complexType>
        <xsd:all>
          <xsd:element name="Title" type="xsd:string"/>
          <xsd:element name="Author" type="xsd:string"/>
          <xsd:element name="Date" type="xsd:string"/>
          <xsd:element name="ISBN" type="xsd:string"/>
          <xsd:element name="Publisher" type="xsd:string"/>
        </xsd:all>
      </xsd:complexType>
    </xsd:element>
  </xsd:sequence>
  <xsd:attribute name="InStock" type="xsd:boolean"/>
  <xsd:attribute name="Reviewer" type="xsd:string"/>
</xsd:complexType>
```

A complex type with complex content is defined. The *MixedOption* of the outer type indicates that Book elements can be interleaved by texts.

3   Document Schema

In this model we permit only one element information item as a child of the document information item. This model is more restrictive than the one specified in [13] (where several element information items may be children of the document information item), but it strictly follows the model specified in [11].

$DocumentSchema =$
    $Interleave(ComplexTypeDefinitionSet, GlobElementDeclaration)$
$ComplexTypeDefinitionSet =$
    $FM(ComplexTypeName, AnonymousTypeDefinition)$
$GlobElementDeclaration = Tuple(ElemName, Type, NillOption)$

Thus, a document schema defines a set of documents each having a root element with the same name. The schema may contain a number of complex type definitions preceding or following $GlobElementDeclaration$ and introducing type names used within $GlobElementDeclaration$ and $ComplexTypeDefinitionSet$[3]. For any type T used in a document schema with the complex type definition set ctd, the following requirement on type usage must be satisfied: $T \in SimpleTypeName$ or $T \in AnonymousTypeDefinition$ or $T \in dom(ctd)$[4]

Example 7:
```
<?xml version="1.0"?>
<xsd:schema xmlns:xsd="http://www.w3.org/2001/XMLSchema"
     targetNamespace="http://www.books.org"
     xmlns="http://www.books.org"
     elementFormDefault="qualified">
  <xsd:complexType name="BookPublication">
     <xsd:sequence>
        <xsd:element name="Title" type="xsd:string"/>
        <xsd:element name="Author" type="xsd:string"/>
        <xsd:element name="Date" type="xsd:string"/>
        <xsd:element name="ISBN" type="xsd:string"/>
        <xsd:element name="Publisher" type="xsd:string"/>
     </xsd:sequence>
  </xsd:complexType>
  <xsd:element name="BookStore">
     <xsd:complexType>
        <xsd:sequence>
           <xsd:element name="Book" type="BookPublication"
                                    maxOccurs="unbounded"/>
        </xsd:sequence>
     </xsd:complexType>
  </xsd:element>
</xsd:schema>
```
A named and an anonymous data type are defined in the example.

---

[3] In fact, the document schema may also contain a number of other element declarations and attribute declarations. However, attributes are always part of complex types and may be declared inline. Multiple global element declarations may also be considered as a kind of syntactic sugar permitting one either to combine several document schemas in one schema or save space by referencing an element declaration from within several complex types.

[4] Here and in the sequel, $dom(f)$ denotes the domain of a finite mapping f.

4   Basic Types

We consider that the data model contains all primitive types listed in [12]. These are *string, boolean, decimal, float, double, duration, dateTime, time, date, gYear, gYearMonth, gYearDay, gDay, gMonth, hexBinary, base64Binary, anyURI,* and *QName.* An *atomic type* is a primitive type or a type derived by restriction from another atomic type [12]. A *simple type* is an atomic type or list type or union type or a type derived by restriction from another simple type.

Simple types create a type hierarchy resembling that of object-oriented languages. The type `xs:anyType` is at the top of the hierarchy (i.e., it is the base type of all types). The type `xs:anySimpleType` is a subtype of `xs:anyType` and is the base type of all simple types. The type `xdt:anyAtomicType` is a subtype of `xs:anySimpleType` and is the base type for all the primitive atomic types, and `xdt:untypedAtomic` is its subtype not including some specific atomic types such as `xs:integer`, `xs:string`, and `xdt:dayTimeDuration` [14].

In this paper, we additionally use the type constructor $Seq(T)$ defining the set of all sequences (ordered sets) of elements of type T. Any sequence type possesses the following operations among the others: $|s|$ returns the length of the sequence s, $s_1 + s_2$ attaches the sequence s_2 to the sequence s_1, and $s[i]$ returns the i-th element of the sequence s.

5   Base Classes

The data model defined in [13] has a flavor of an object-oriented model [5] in the sense that its main building entities are unique *nodes* possessing the state that can be viewed by a number of *accessor* functions. There are several disjoint classes of nodes (elements, attributes, etc.) representing different document information items. All of these classes may be considered as subclasses of the base class *Node*. Therefore, the following class hierarchy may be designed:

Node: base class with the following accessors:
  base-uri: Seq(anyURI) (empty or one-element sequence),
  node-kind: string,
  node-name: Seq(QName) (empty or one-element sequence),
  parent: Seq(Node) (empty or one-element sequence),
  string-value: string,
  typed-value: Seq(anyAtomicType) (sequence of zero or more atomic values)[5],
  type: Seq(QName) (empty or one-element sequence),
  children: Seq(Node) (sequence of zero or more nodes),
  attributes: Seq(Node) (sequence of zero or more nodes),
  nilled: Seq(boolean) (empty or one-element sequence).

Document: a subclass of the class *Node* with three extra accessors not considered in this paper.

---

[5] Because of complex rules of computing this value for different kinds of nodes, we do not consider this accessor in the sequel.

Element: a subclass of the class *Node* without extra accessors.

Attribute: a subclass of the class *Node* without extra accessors.

Text: a subclass of the class *Node* without extra accessors.

Instances of these classes serve for representing document information items, element information items, attributes and texts, respectively.

6   Database

6.1   State Algebra

Because of frequent insertion of new documents, updating existing documents and deleting obsolete documents, a database evolves through different database states. Each state can be formally represented as a many-sorted algebra called a *state algebra* in the sequel (algebra components are written in the true type font). Each class C is supplied in a state algebra A with a set of node identifiers A_C in such a way that the sets of identifiers $A_{Document}$, $A_{Element}$, $A_{Attribute}$, A_{Text}, etc. are disjoint and the set A_{Node} is the union of the above sets. In the sequel, the node identifier is meant each time a node is mentioned (in the same way as an object identifier, or reference, represents an object in object-oriented languages and databases, see [5] for a formal definition of an object-oriented model).

Each simple data type T is supplied in A with a set of values A_T and a set of meaningful operations. One of these operations, denoted by the type name and called *constructor*, converts a string value into an atomic value of this type.

The following node accessor values are set in any state algebra A:

- for each nd $\in A_{Document}$: node-kind(nd) = ''document'', node-name(nd), parent(nd), type(nd), attributes(nd), and nilled(nd) are set to empty sequences;
- for each nd $\in A_{Element}$: node-kind(nd) = ''element'';
- for each nd $\in A_{Attribute}$: node-kind(nd) = ''attribute'', children(nd), attributes(nd), and nilled(nd) are set to empty sequences;
- for each nd $\in A_{Text}$: node-kind(nd) = ''text'', node-name(nd), children(nd), attributes(nd), and nilled(nd) are set to empty sequences.

A state algebra A sets values of the other accessors. The following variables are used in the definition of the state algebra:

$el, el_1, el_2, ...$ — element names,
eld — element declaration,
$leds$ — local element declarations,
ctd — set of complex type definitions,
$atds$ — attribute declarations,
$gd, gd_1, gd_2, ...$ — group definitions,
gds — sequence of group definitions,
$T, T_1, T_2, ...$ — data types,
cf — combination factor,

$min_1, min_2, \ldots$ — minimum number of occurrences of an element or group,
$max_1, max_2, \ldots$ — maximum number of occurrences of an element or group,
mix — mixed content option,
nid — nil option.

The state algebra extensively uses trees of nodes. A parent node in such a tree is either a document node or an element node. The children of a particular parent node are those nodes that are indicated by the accessors *children* and/or *attributes*. Formally:

- a node nd is a tree with the root nd;
- if s is a tree with root nd and $s_1, \ldots, s_n$ are trees with roots $nd_1, \ldots, nd_n$ such that `children(nd)` $= (nd_1, \ldots, nd_n)$, then $\langle s, (s_1, \ldots, s_n) \rangle$ is a tree with the root nd;
- if s is a tree with root nd and $nd_1, \ldots, nd_n$ are nodes such that `attributes(nd)` $= (nd_1, \ldots, nd_n)$, then $\langle s, (nd_1, \ldots, nd_n) \rangle$ is a tree with the root nd.

The set of these trees constitute the set of values of the data type *Tree*. The function *root* : *Tree* → *Node* applied to a tree yields its root node and the function *roots* : *Seq(Tree)* → *Seq(Node)* applied to a sequence of trees yields the sequence of their root nodes.

6.2   Document Tree

A document schema $S = (eld, ctd)$ or $S = (ctd, eld)$, where $eld = (el, T, nid)$ is an element declaration and ctd a set of complex type definitions, is mapped in a state algebra **A** to zero or more trees of nodes. Denote such a tree by s. It must satisfy the following requirements:

1. nd = `root(s)` $\in A_{\text{Document}}$, `base-uri(nd)` $\in A_{\text{anyUri}}$, and `string-value(nd)` = `string-value((children(nd))`. Thus, the string value of the document node is the string value of its single child.

2. A node end $\in$ s is associated with the element declaration $eld = (el, T, nid)$ so that:

3. end $\in A_{\text{Element}}$, `parent(end)` = nd, `children(nd)` = (end) (i.e., a document node has only one child, an element node, it is the node with name "BookStore" in a tree associated with the Example 9 schema); and

4. `node-name(end)` = el, `base-uri (end)` = `base-uri(parent(end))`, `type(end)` = T if T is a type name, `type(end)` = "xs:anyType" if T is an anonymous type definition, and `string-value(end)` and `typed-value(end)` are computed according to the algorithms described in [13], Section 6.2.2.

5. If nid = $false$ (i.e., the element may not have the nil value), then `nilled(end)` = $false$, and

5.1. If T is a simple type, then:

5.1.1. There is in s a node tnd $\in A_{\text{Text}}$ such that `parent(tnd)` = end, `type(tnd)` = "xdt:untypedAtomic", `string-value(tnd)` $\in A_{\text{String}}$, `base-uri(tnd)` = `base-uri(end)`, and `children(end)` = (tnd).

For instance, a text node is associated with each of the element nodes with names Title, Author, Date, ISBN, and Publisher in a tree associated with the Example 7 schema.

5.2. If T is a complex type with simple content $(T', atds)$, where $atds = \{at_1 \mapsto T_1, ..., at_u \mapsto T_u\}$ (attributes are declared), then items 5.1.1 and 5.3.1 hold. For instance, a text node and attribute node will be associated with an element declared with the type presented in Example 5.

5.3. If T is a complex type with complex content $(mix, leds, atds)$ or $(mix, atds)$, where $atds = \{at_1 \mapsto T_1, ..., at_u \mapsto T_u\}$ (attributes are declared), then

5.3.1. s contains a sequence of leaf nodes $\mathtt{as} = (\mathtt{and}_1, ..., \mathtt{and}_u)$ such that $\mathtt{attributes(end)} = \mathtt{as}$ (the sequence consists of two nodes for the attribute declarations of Example 4) and, having an automorphism σ on $\{1, ..., u\}$ (we need it because the sequence of nodes may be different from the sequence of the corresponding attribute declarations), it holds for each $\mathtt{and}_j \in \mathtt{as}$:

$\mathtt{and}_j \in \mathtt{A_{Attribute}}$, $\mathtt{parent(and}_j) = \mathtt{end}$, $\mathtt{base\text{-}uri(and}_j) = \mathtt{base\text{-}uri(end)}$, $\mathtt{node\text{-}name(and}_j) = at_{\sigma(j)}$, $\mathtt{type(and}_j) = T_{\sigma(j)}$, $\mathtt{string\text{-}value(and}_j) \in \mathtt{A_{String}}$, $\mathtt{typed\text{-}value(and}_j) = T_{\sigma(j)}(\mathtt{string\text{-}value(and}_j))$.

5.4. If T is a complex type with complex content $(mix, leds, atds)$ or $(mix, leds)$ (subelements are declared), then:

5.4.1. If $leds$ is empty (i.e., the type has the empty content), then

5.4.1.1. If $mix = true$ (mixed type definition), then

- $\mathtt{children(end)} = ()$ or
- $\mathtt{children(end)} = (\mathtt{tnd})$ where $\mathtt{tnd}$ is a text node ($\mathtt{tnd} \in \mathtt{A_{Text}}$) with the following accessor values: $\mathtt{parent(tnd)} = \mathtt{end}$, $\mathtt{base\text{-}uri(tnd)} = \mathtt{base\text{-}uri(end)}$, $\mathtt{type(tnd)} = \text{``xdt:untypedAtomic''}$, and $\mathtt{string\text{-}value(tnd)} \in \mathtt{A_{String}}$.

Thus, only a text node may be attached to an element node if it has no element child. For instance, an element node corresponding to the element declared with the type presented in Example 6 may have only one text node as child if there are no subordinated "Book" elements.

5.4.1.2. If $mix = false$ (no text node is allowed), then $\mathtt{children(end)} = ()$.

5.4.2. If $leds$ is not empty, then there is in s a sequence of trees ss such that, for each $\mathtt{rnd} \in \mathtt{roots(ss)}$, it holds: $\mathtt{parent(rnd)} = \mathtt{end}$ and $\mathtt{rnd} \in \mathtt{A_{Element}}$. For instance, a sequence of trees may be associated with a $\mathtt{BookStore}$ element node (roots of these trees are children of the $\mathtt{BookStore}$ node) and a sequence of trees may be associated with a $\mathtt{Book}$ element node (roots of these trees are children of the $\mathtt{Book}$ node) in a tree associated with the Example 7 schema.

5.4.2.1. If $mix = false$ (intermediate text nodes are not allowed), then $\mathtt{children(end)} = \mathtt{roots(ss)}$.

5.4.2.2 If $mix = true$ (mixed type definition), then

- there is in s a sequence of text nodes ts, such that, for each $\mathtt{tnd} \in \mathtt{ts}$, it holds: $\mathtt{tnd} \in \mathtt{A_{Text}}$, $\mathtt{parent(tnd)} = \mathtt{end}$, $\mathtt{base\text{-}uri(tnd)} = \mathtt{base\text{-}uri(end)}$, $\mathtt{type(tnd)} = \text{``}xdt : untypedAtomic\text{''}$, $\mathtt{string\text{-}value(tnd)} \in \mathtt{A_{String}}$, and $\mathtt{typed\text{-}value(tnd)} = xdt : untypedAtomic(\mathtt{string\text{-}value(tnd)})$,
- $\mathtt{children(end)} = \mathtt{sss}$, where the sequence of nodes sss involves all the nodes of the sequences $\mathtt{roots(ss)}$ and ts in such a way that $\forall i \in \{1, ..., |sss| - 1\}$

there do not exist nodes $\mathtt{sss[i]}$ and $\mathtt{sss[i+1]}$ such that $\mathtt{sss[i]} \in \mathtt{A_{Text}}$ and $\mathtt{sss[i+1]} \in \mathtt{A_{Text}}$ (there are no adjacent text nodes). Thus, $\mathtt{Book}$ nodes of Example 6 may be interleaved with text nodes (note that the children nodes of a $\mathtt{Book}$ node may not).

5.4.2.3. If $leds$ is an AllOptionDefinition $\{el_1 \mapsto (T_1, min_1, nid_1), ..., el_u \mapsto (T_u, min_u, nid_u)\}$, then $\mathtt{ss}$ is a sequence of q trees $(1 \leq q \leq u)$ so that zero or one tree is associated with the element declaration $el_j \mapsto (T_j, min_j, nid_j)$, $j = 1, ..., u$, if $min_j = 0$ and exactly one tree if $min_j = 1$, and each $\mathtt{end_i} \in \mathtt{roots(ss)}$ satisfies the requirements starting from item 4, assuming that $\mathtt{end} = \mathtt{end_i}$, $el = el_{\sigma(i)}$, $T = T_{\sigma(i)}$, and $nid = nid_{\sigma(i)}$, where $\sigma : \{1, ..., q\} \rightarrow \{1, ..., u\}$ and $i = 1, ..., q$. For instance, an $\mathtt{ss}$ associated with the group definition of Example 3 is a sequence of five trees whose root nodes are element nodes with the declared names sequenced in any order.

5.4.2.4. If $leds$ is a GroupDefinition $(gds, cf, (m, n))$, then $\mathtt{ss}$ consists of k $(m \leq k \leq n)$ subsequences of trees $\mathtt{ss_1}, ..., \mathtt{ss_k}$ (multiple occurrences of complex type values)[6] and it holds for a subsequence $\mathtt{ss_j}$, $j = 1, ..., k$:

- if $gds = (gds_1, ..., gds_u)$ and $cf = \mathtt{sequence}$, then $\mathtt{ss_j}$ consists of u subsequences (one for each group definition)[7] of trees $\mathtt{ss_q^j}$, $q = 1, ..., u$, and
  - if gds_q is an element declaration $(el_q, T_q, (min_q, max_q), nid_q)$, then $\mathtt{ss_q^j}$ is a sequence of v $(min_q \leq v \leq max_q)$ trees such that (if $\mathtt{ss_q^j}$ is not empty) each $\mathtt{end} \in \mathtt{roots(ss_q^j)}$ satisfies the requirements starting from item 4, assuming that $el = el_q$, $T = T_q$, and $nid = nid_q$ (for instance, $\mathtt{ss_q^j}$ is a sequence consisting of one tree for the declaration of the element with the name $\mathtt{sleep}$ in the group definition presented in Example 2);
  - if gds_q is a group definition (for instance, the first or second inner group definition in Example 2), then $\mathtt{ss_q^j}$ satisfies the requirements starting from item 5.4.2.4, assuming that $leds = gds_q$ and $\mathtt{ss} = \mathtt{ss_q^j}$.
- if $gds = (gds_1, ..., gds_u)$ and $cf = \mathtt{union}$, then $\mathtt{ss_j}$ is associated with a gds_q, $q \in \{1, ..., u\}$ (for instance, $\mathtt{ss_j}$ is associated either with the declaration of the element $\mathtt{work}$ or with the declaration of the element $\mathtt{play}$ in the second inner group definition in Example 2), and
  - if gds_q is an element declaration $(el_q, T_q, (min_q, max_q), nid_q)$, then $\mathtt{ss_j}$ is a sequence of v $(min_q \leq vmax_q)$ trees (exactly one tree for any element declaration in the second inner group definition in Example 2) such that (if $\mathtt{ss_j}$ is not empty) each $\mathtt{end} \in \mathtt{roots(ss_j)}$ satisfies the requirements starting from item 4, assuming that $el = el_q$, $T = T_q$, and $nid = nid_q$;
  - if gds_q is a group definition, then $\mathtt{ss_j}$ satisfies the requirements starting from item 5.4.2.4, assuming that $leds = gds_q$ and $\mathtt{ss} = \mathtt{ss_j}$.

---

[6] For instance, an $\mathtt{ss}$ associated with the group definition presented in Example 2 may be empty or consist of any number of such subsequences. The same refers to the first inner group definition of this example. The second inner group definition may result only in an $\mathtt{ss}$ consisting of one tree.

[7] For instance, each $\mathtt{ss_j}$ that is part of an $\mathtt{ss}$ associated with the group definition presented in Example 2 consists of three such subsequences.

6. If $nid = true$ (i.e., the element may have the nil value), then:

6.1. If T is a simple type, then either $\mathtt{children(end)} = ()$ and $\mathtt{nilled(end)} = true$ or $\mathtt{nilled(end)} = false$ and item 5.1.1 holds.

6.2. If T is a complex type with simple content $(T_1, atds)$, where $atds = \{at_1 \mapsto T_1, ..., at_u \mapsto T_u\}$, then either $\mathtt{children(end)} = ()$ and $\mathtt{nilled(end)} = true$ and item 5.3.1 holds or $\mathtt{nilled(end)} = false$ and items 5.1.1 and 5.3.1 hold.

6.3. If T is a complex type with complex content, then either $\mathtt{children(end)} = ()$ and $\mathtt{nilled(end)} = true$ and item 5.3 holds or $\mathtt{nilled(end)} = false$ and items 5.3 and 5.4 hold.

7. There are no other nodes in s.

7   Document Order

The ordering of nodes in the tree s defines the document order, which is used in some operations of XQuery [14] and other XML query languages. As in XQuery, the notation $\mathtt{nd_1} << \mathtt{nd_2}$ means in this paper that the node $\mathtt{nd_1}$ occurs in s before the node $\mathtt{nd_2}$ and the notation $\mathtt{tree(nd_1)} << \mathtt{tree(nd_2)}$ means that any node in the tree with the root node $\mathtt{nd_1}$ occurs in s before any node in the tree with the root node $\mathtt{nd_2}$. The relation $<<$ is a total order. Recall that the root node in s is the document node nd. The tree s is ordered as follows:

- let $\mathtt{children(nd)} = \mathtt{(end)}$, then $\mathtt{nd} << \mathtt{end}$;
- for any element node $\mathtt{end} \in$ s, let $\mathtt{attributes(end)} = (\mathtt{and_1}, ..., \mathtt{and_k})$ and $\mathtt{children(end)} = (\mathtt{end_1}, ..., \mathtt{end_m})$, then $\mathtt{end} << \mathtt{and_1}$, $\mathtt{and_i} << \mathtt{and_{i+1}}$, $i = 1, ..., k\text{-}1$, $\mathtt{and_k} << \mathtt{end_1}$, and $\mathtt{tree(end_j)} << \mathtt{tree(end_{j+1})}$, $j = 1, ..., m\text{-}1$.

8   XML-Document vs. Document Tree

In this section, we address the issue of expressive power and correctness of the data model presented in the paper. In order to do this, we formulate the proposition of the existence of a mapping between XML-documents and document trees that preserves the document validity and content. We respectively write *S-document* and *S-tree* for an XML-document and document tree valid with respect to the document schema S.

First, we introduce an equivalence relation on the set of XML-documents that is based on the document content - *content equality* denoted by $=_c$. The relation is an important basis for formalization of one of the basic notions of the paper, the XML-document. Second we state and prove the following theorem:

Theorem. For any document schema S, there is a function f that maps a set of S-documents to a set of S-trees and a function g that serializes an S-tree to an S-document such that $g(f(X)) =_c X$.

The proof of the theorem can be found in [8].

9   Related Work

There are very few papers devoted to formal foundation of XML Schema or another document definition language. More popular subjects are, to our knowledge, validation of a document against a schema [6,7] and development of an algebra for an XML query language [3,4].

The paper [1] is a work that directly concerns the problem of formal semantics of XML Schema. Like our paper, it formalizes some core ideas of XML Schema. Model Schema Language (MSL) is designed for this purpose. It is described with an inference rule notation originally developed by logicians. These inference rules show in what cases a document validates against a document schema. Thus, the main difference between this paper and our paper is in the fact that this paper does not suggest any internal model of the document schema. As a result, such important aspects as node identity constraints and mappings from XML Schema syntax into internal model components are not touched in the paper. The authors have mentioned that they had begun to work on these topics, but we have not managed to find a paper presenting such a work.

Inference rules are also used in defining the semantics of another popular XML schema language, RELAX NG [2]. The way of defining the semantics in this work resembles that of [1] in the sense that the semantics of a schema consists of the specification of what XML documents are valid with respect to that schema. Like the work [1], this work has the same shortcomings and the same differences with our work.

Formal semantics of values, types, and named typing in XML Schema are defined in [9]. We have not touched these problems, considering that they are successfully solved in that paper.

The representation of an XML document as a data tree is also described in [4]. However, the work is not related with both XML Schema and XQuery 1.0 Data Model. For this reason, the tree consists only of element nodes, the node does not possess an identifier, the majority of node accessors are not defined, etc. In contrast to this work, our document tree is much closer to the tree informally specified in [13].

10   Conclusion

We have presented the semantics of the core features of XML Schema in terms of the XQuery 1.0 and XPath 2.0 data model algebraically defined. The database state is represented as a many-sorted algebra whose sorts are sets of data type values and different kinds of nodes and whose operations are data type operations and node accessors. The values of some node accessors, such as `parent`, `children` and `attributes`, define a document tree with a definite order of nodes. The values of other node accessors help to make difference between kinds of nodes, learn the names, types and values associated with the corresponding document entities, etc., i.e., provide primitive facilities for a query language. As a result, a document can be easily mapped to its implementation in terms of nodes and accessors defined on them. The main theorem of the paper proves this.

It is worth to note that, with this kind of semantics, the XQuery 1.0 and XPath 2.0 data model may be considered as an abstract implementation of XML Schema. Hence, XML Schema and the XQuery 1.0 and XPath 2.0 data model become tightly related, which may serve as a significant help for the XML Schema implementor.

Finally, the presented semantics may serve as a base of an XML algebra supporting a query language such as XQuery. We are proceeding with this work.

References

1. Brown, A., Fuchs, M., Robie, J., Wadler, P.: MSL: A model for W3C XML Schema. Proc. 10th Int'l World Wide Web Conf., Hong Kong (2001) 191–200
2. Clarke, C., Makoto, M.: RELAX NG specification. Oasis (2001) http://www.relaxng.org/spec-20011203.html
3. Fernandez, M., Siméon, J., Wadler, P.: An Algebra for XML Query. FST TCS, Delhi (2000) 11–45
4. Jagodish, H. V., Lakshmanan, V. S., Srivastatva, D., Thompson, K.: Tax: A Tree Algebra for XML. Proc. Intl. Workshop on databases and Programming Languages, Marino, Italy (2001)
5. Lellahi, K., Zamulin, A.: An object-oriented database as a dynamic system with implicit state. A. Caplinskas and J. Eder (eds.). Advances in Databases and Information Systems (Proceedings of the 5th East European Conference, ADBIS 2001, Vilnus, Lithuania, September 2001), LNCS, vol. 2151, (2001) 239–252
6. Murata, M., Lee, D., Mani. M.: Taxonomy of XML Schema Languages using Formal Language Theory. Extreme Markup Languages, Montreal, Canada (2001)
7. Novak, L., Kuznetsov, S.: Canonical Forms of XML Schemas. Programming and Computer Software, No. 5 (2003) 65–80
8. Novak, L., Zamulin, A.: Algebraic Semantics of XML Schema. Preprint No. 117, Institute of Informatics Systems of the Siberian Branch of the Russian Academy of Sciences (2004) http://www.iis.nsk.su/persons/zamulin/zam-preprint117.ps.
9. Siméon, J., Wadler, P.: The Essence of XML. POPL'03, January 15-17, New Orlean, Loisiana, USA (2003)
10. Extensible Markup Language (XML) 1.0 (Third Edition). W3C Working Draft (2004) http://www.w3.org/TR/2004/REC-xml-20040204
11. XML Schema Part 1: Structures Second Edition, W3C Working Draft (2004) http://www.w3.org/TR/xmlschema-1
12. XML Schema Part 2: Datatypes Second Edition. W3C Working Draft (2004) http://www.w3.org/TR/xmlschema-2
13. XQuery 1.0 and XPath 2.0 Data Model, W3C Working Draft (2005) http://www.w3.org/TR/xpath-datamodel
14. XQuery 1.0: An XML Query Language. W3C Working Draft (2005) http://www.w3.org/TR/xquery
15. XML Information Set, W3C Working Draft (2004) http://www.w3.org/TR/xml-infoset

Efficient XPath Evaluation

Bing Wang[1], Ling Feng[2], and Yun Shen[1]

[1] Department of Computer Science, University of Hull,
Hull, HU6 7RX, United Kingdom
{B.Wang, Y.Shen}@dcs.hull.ac.uk
[2] Department of Computer Science, University of Twente,
PO Box 217, 7500 Enschede The Netherlands
ling@cs.utwente.nl

Abstract. Inspired by the best querying performance of ViST among the rest of the approaches in the literature, and meanwhile to overcome its shortcomings, in this paper, we present another efficient and novel geometric sequence mechanism, which transforms XML documents and XPath queries into the corresponding geometric data/query sequences. XML querying is thus converted to finding non-contiguous geometric sub-sequence matches. Our approach ensures correct (i.e., without semantic false) and fast (i.e., without the costly post-processing phase) evaluation of XPath queries, while at the same time guaranteeing the linear space complexity. We demonstrate the significant performance improvement of our approach through a set of experiments on both synthetic and real-life data.

1 Introduction

With the advent of XML as a standard for data representation and exchange on the Web, indexing and querying XML documents becomes increasingly important for current and future data-centric applications. Substantial research efforts [4,7,5,11] have been conducted to structurally index and retrieve data from XML documents.

The first problem of retrieving data from XML documents is how to deal with specific queries containing constraints related to the content of the documents. Providing a uniform index structure [15] for both the structure and content information of an XML document is thereupon desirable. More importantly, the mechanism should be preferably implemented using some well-supported DBMS data structures like B+Tree.

The second problem is that a query compatible to XPath is modeled as a tree, referred to as a *twig*, and can be complicated [6] when wildcards "*" and self-or-descendent axis("//") are presented (for example, Q5 in Table 3). To match such a complex query against a document tree without corresponding preprocessing mechanism is equivalent to the tree inclusion problem and has been proved to be NP-complete [1].

Previous research efforts have been devoted to twig pattern matching for several years. XISS [10] is the first to break twig pattern query into binary twigs,

J. Eder et al. (Eds.): ADBIS 2005, LNCS 3631, pp. 223–237, 2005.

and "stitch" the binary twigs (i.e. two nodes with parent-child relationship) together to obtain the final results. State-of-the-art mechanisms, i.e. structural join [3], holistic twig join [12], have been proposed to stitch root-to-node paths together by using specially designed stacks. Additionally, some index structures, such as XR-Tree [8] and XB-Tree [12], have been proposed to optimize the above twig join operations. However, the performance of all the above mechanisms is suffered from the time-consuming join operations.

Wang et al. proposed a novel ViST mechanism [15], which transforms both XML documents and XPath queries into structure-encoded sequences so that the twig pattern matching problem is converted to subsequence matching problem. The advantage of this approach is that it does not need to break down a twig pattern into root-to-leaf paths and process them individually, thus avoiding the heavy join operations to join intermediate results. This method improves all the previous searching mechanisms significantly. However, ViST has three major shortcomings. First, its structure-encoded sequence model can cause the semantic false problem. That is, an XML fragment which semantically matches a query may not be returned. Second, ViST may lead to false answers (false alarms) because its encoding method can not fully sustain the structures of XML data trees. Time-consuming refinement phase or post-processing phase has to be called to eliminate the false answers. Although Wang et al. [14] further proposed a way to eliminate the post-processing phase with $O(n^2)$ total size complexity (where n is the total node number in a data tree), it depends on specialized *trie + path link* structure to find sibling-cover in the trie and remove the false answers, in which the semantic false still exists. Third, ViST can not guarantee the linear size complexity of structure-encoded sequence. In the worst case, the total size of structure-encoded sequence is $O(n^2)$ when a document is a unary tree.

To overcome the above three problems, in this paper, we present another encoding mechanism to transform XML documents and XML queries into geometric sequences. Our objective is to ensure correct (i.e. without semantic false) and fast (i.e. without the post-processing phase) evaluation of XPath queries, while at the same time guaranteeing the linear size complexity of the sequence. This approach enables us to achieve better storage and query performance than ViST.

2   The Problems with ViST

As proposed in [15], a structure-encoded sequence is derived from a prefix traversal of an XML document, in format of a sequence of (*symbol, prefix*) pairs, $(a_1, p_1), (a_2, p_2), ..., (a_n, p_n)$, where a_i represents a node in the XML document tree ($a_1 a_2 ... a_n$ is the pre-order sequence) and p_i is the encoded path from root to a_i. In the same spirit, XML queries are converted into structure-encoded query sequences in which "*" and "//" are explicitly encoded. Querying XML is equivalent to finding non-continuous subsequence matches in ViST. The corresponding structure-encoded sequence of the XML document example in Figure 1 is illustrated in Figure 2. Let T_{Str} denote the structure encode sequence.

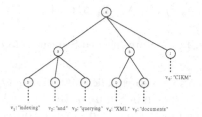

Fig. 1. An Example of XML Document in Tree Structure

T_{Str} = **(A, ε) (B, A) (D, AB) (v₁, ABD) (E, AB) (v₂, ABE) (F, AB) (v₃, ABF) (B, A) (D, AB) (v₄, ABD) (K, AB) (v₅, ABK) (J, A) (v₆, AJ)**

Fig. 2. Structure-Encoded Sequence of the XML Document in ViST Approach

The problem of false answers (a.k.a false alarms) arises immediately in ViST in which an XML document is represented by a structure-encoded sequence. For example, given a query Q2: $/A/B[./E][./K]$, its tree structure is shown in Figure 8(b), and its corresponding structure-encoded query sequence is shown in Figure 3. The underlined non-continuous subsequence in T_{Str} marks a result (matching). However, it is a false answer since the structure expressed in Q2 does not exist in the XML document example. We call this kind of queries *non-existence false*.

$$Q2_{Str} = \textbf{(A, } \varepsilon\textbf{) (B, A) (E, AB) (K, AB)}$$

Fig. 3. Structure-Encoded Sequence of Q2

Consider, for another example, Q3 shown in Figure 8(c), its structure-encoded sequence is shown in Figure 4. In ViST, Q2 and Q3 may return the same results because Q2 is a subsequence of Q3. We call this kind of query pairs *non-equivalence false*. It implies that refinement phase or post-processing phase has to be called to eliminate the false answers in these two cases. However, the process may not be always trivial.

Moreover, ViST has a serious semantic flaw in transforming XPath queries into structure-encoded sequences. Suppose we have an XML fragment:

$$< A >< B >< K >< C >< /C >< /K >< /B >< /A >$$

and its corresponding structure-encoded sequence:

$$Frag_{Str} =< A, \varepsilon >< B, A >< K, AB >< C, ABK >$$

If Q: $/A[./B//C][//K]$ is transformed into a structure-encoded query sequence and evaluated against this fragment:

$$Q_{Str} =< A, \varepsilon >< B, A >< C, AB// >< K, A// >$$

$$Q3_{Str} = \mathbf{(A, \, \varepsilon) \, (B, \, A) \, (E, \, AB) \, (B, \, A) \, (K, \, AB)}$$

Fig. 4. structure-encoded Sequence of Q3

we can see that there is no such subsequence matching of Q_{Str} in $Frag_{str}$ since K appear after C in ViST, as shown in Figure 5. However, Q semantically matches the fragment. This flaw can hardly be fixed since the order among the items in a structure-encoded sequence is indispensable in ViST. We call this semantic flaw of ViST *semantic false*.

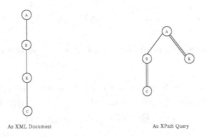

An XML Document   An XPath Query

Fig. 5. A Semantic False Query Evaluation in ViST

3   Proposed Method

To overcome the shortcomings of ViST, in this section, we present a geometric-encoding mechanism, which transforms XML documents/queries into geometric data/query sequences. Further enhancement to our geometric encoding approach is also described.

3.1   Mapping XML Documents into Geometric Data Sequences

We firstly model XML as an ordered, node labeled, rooted tree. More formally, consider a graph $\mathbf{T} = (\mathbf{V_G}, \mathbf{V_T}, \mathbf{v_r}, \mathbf{E_G}, \mathbf{label_{node}}, \mathbf{nid}, \sum_{\mathbf{T}})$. V_G is the set of element nodes and V_T is the set of text nodes. $\forall v \in V_T$, v has no outgoing edge. v_r is the root of the XML data tree, where there exists a path from v_r to v, $\forall v \in V_G \cup V_T$. Moreover, it implies that v_r has no incoming edge. Each node $v \in V_G \cup V_T$ is labeled through the function $label_{node}$ over the set of terms, $\sum_T$. The label of a node $v \in V_G$ is referred to as the tag name. The label of $v \in V_T$ is referred to as a distinct keyword contained in the corresponding text. We use quotation mark in future figures to distinguish the label in V_T.

Each edge e, $e \in E_G$, is a parent-child edge, denoting the parent-child relationship. The parent node is denoted as v_{e_p}, and the child node is denoted as v_{e_c}. A path is a sequence of edges starting from the node v_i to the node v_j, denoted as $e_i, e_{i+1}, ..., e_j$. A node v_i is ancestor of v_j *iff* a path to v_j goes through v_i. The order among the sibling nodes is distinguished. Each node is assigned a unique nid number for indexing and querying purpose. We refer T_{v_i} as the subtree induced by node v_i. Figure 1 shows an example of our data model. The solid edges represent E_G. The dashed edge denotes a edge e, $v_{e_p} \in V_G$, and $v_{e_c} \in V_T$. The quoted string represents a label of a node $v \in V_T$.

We secondly transform an XML document into a sequence by pre-order traversing the above XML data tree, recording a node's parent when backtracking. For the example in Figure 1, its sequence representation is shown in Figure 6.

$$\textbf{ABDv}_1\textbf{DBEv}_2\textbf{EBFv}_3\textbf{FBABDv}_4\textbf{DBKv}_5\textbf{KBAJv}_6\textbf{JA}$$

Fig. 6. A Sequence Representation of the Example XML Document

To clearly represent a sequence, we slightly modify the above sequence to indicate the start (s), intermediate(i), end (e) positions of a specific node which appears multiple times in the sequence. The modified sequence representation is shown in Figure 7. Let T_{Geo} denote the modified sequence, and $\mathbf{f}$: T $\rightarrow T_{Geo}$. Easily we can see $\mathbf{f}$ is a bijection between T_{Geo} and T. In the rest of the paper, we call the modified sequence *geometric sequence*. We later show in Section 4 that those extra *symbol*$_i$ and *symbol*$_e$ require trivial processing in both indexing and querying process.

$$T_{Geo}=\underline{\mathbf{A}_s}\mathbf{B}_s\underline{\mathbf{D}_s}\mathbf{v}_1\underline{\mathbf{D}_e}\mathbf{B}_i\mathbf{E}_s\mathbf{v}_2\mathbf{E}_e\mathbf{B}_i\mathbf{F}_s\mathbf{v}_3\mathbf{F}_e\underline{\mathbf{B}_e}\mathbf{A}_i\mathbf{B}_s\mathbf{D}_s\mathbf{v}_4\mathbf{D}_e\mathbf{B}_i\underline{\mathbf{K}_s}\mathbf{v}_5\underline{\mathbf{K}_e}\mathbf{B}_e\mathbf{A}_i\ \mathbf{J}_s\mathbf{v}_6\mathbf{J}_e\underline{\mathbf{A}_e}$$

Fig. 7. A Geometric Sequence Representation of the Example XML Document

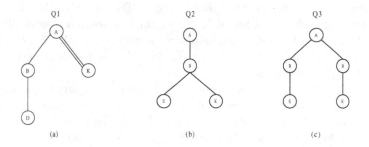

Fig. 8. Example of Query Sequences in Tree Form

3.2   Transforming XPath Query into Geometric Query Sequence

A query compatible to XPath is modeled as a tree, as shown in Figure 8. The core of evaluating an XPath query at an XML document is finding all the answers of such a twig pattern matching the constraints (axes, nested structure, terms etc.) of the query. Moreover, a query can be complicated when wildcards "*" and self-or-descendent axis("//") are presented. When we transform an XPath query

Table 1. List of Q1, Q2, and Q3 in Geometric Query Sequences

Path Expression	Geometric Query Sequence
Q1: /A[B/D][//K]	$Q1_{Geo}$: A_s B_s D_s $D_e{}^p$ $B_e{}^p$ $A_i{}^u$ K_s K_e A_e
Q2: /A/B[./E][./K]	$Q2_{Geo}$: A_s B_s E_s $E_e{}^p$ B_i K_s $K_e{}^p$ $B_e{}^p$ A_e
Q3: /A/B[E]/following-sibling::B/K	$Q3_{Geo}$: A_s B_s E_s $E_e{}^p$ $B_e{}^p$ A_i B_s K_s $K_e{}^p$ $B_e{}^p$ A_e

into a geometric query sequence in a similar way of mapping XML documents into geometric sequences, we ensure that all the information in the XPath query is preserved. We show this by using example queries Q1, Q2, and Q3 in Table 1. Their tree structures are shown in Figure 8.

Consider the example query Q2: /A/B[./E][./K], its tree structure is shown in Figure 8(b). When we transform it into a geometric query sequence, we must preserve: (1) A is parent of B, and (2) B is parent of both E and K. In this paper, Q2 is transformed into a geometric query sequence: A_s B_s E_s $E_e{}^p$ B_i K_s $K_e{}^p$ $B_e{}^p$ A_e, where p implies that the upcoming item is *parent* of the current item. As we can observe, any internal node is followed by its $parent_e$ or $parent_i$ in the geometric sequence. However, a E_e may be followed by B_i in real data sequence not B_e. This issue can be easily solve by defining B_i *equals to* B_e when determining the parent relationship. If p is not explicitly stated, the relationship is ancestor-descendant ("//") by default.

Similarly, for query Q1: /A[B/D][//K], its tree structure is shown in Figure 8(a). When we transform it into geometric sequence, we must preserve: (1) D is a child node of B which, in turn, a child node of A and (2) K is a descendant of A. As we state in previous section, ViST may incur semantic false when transforming Q1 into structure-encoded query sequence since there is no explicit information of the relationship between K and B (D) stated. In this case, we add "u" to a specific node which has at least two child nodes and meanwhile "//" is involved. Q1 is transformed into a geometric sequence: A_s B_s D_s $D_e{}^p$ $B_e{}^p$ $A_i{}^u$ K_s K_e A_e as shown in Table 1, where u signifies that semantic uncertainty may occur in the upcoming item.

After an XPath Query is transformed into a geometric query sequence, querying XML documents is equivalent to finding (under the guidance of flag 'p' and/or 'u') non-contiguous subsequence matches in the corresponding geometric data sequences. For query Q1, the underlined non-contiguous subsequence matching in Figure 7 marks a correct matching (i.e. the example document satisfies the query).

Revert to the semantic false problem presented in ViST, as illustrated in Section 2. Let's see how our geometric encoding mechanism avoids the problem. The geometric data/query sequence of the XML fragment and the query (Figure 5)is as follows:

$$Frag_{Geo} = A_s B_s K_s C_s C_e K_e B_e A_e$$

$$Q_{Geo} = A_s B_s C_s C_e^p B_e^p A_i^u K_s K_e A_e$$

To match Q_{Geo} against $Frag_{Geo}$, when we evaluate A_i^u, we resume the range information of A_s. It implies that we will search for K_e in $Frag_{Geo}$ within the range of A_s instead of B_e, starting with which, we can find K_s, K_e and A_e. Section 4 will introduce an elegant stack mechanism to implement the method.

3.3   Numbered Geometric Sequence

Furthermore, consider the fact that in an XML document, the same element names may appear several times. Given the data tree in Figure 1 and query Q2 in Figure 8(b), Q2 should return no result. However, in Table 1, $Q2_{Geo}$ does not provide enough information to eliminate the second B_e, which implies that a result would be returned if the second B_e is included.

$$T_{Geonum} \quad = \quad \mathbf{A_{1s}B_{1s}D_{1s}v_1D_{1e}B_{1i}E_{1s}v_2E_{1e}B_{1i}F_{1s}v_3F_{1e}B_{1e}A_{1i}}$$
$$\mathbf{B_{2s}D_{2s}v_4D_{2e}B_{2i}K_{1s}\ v_5K_{1e}B_{2e}A_{1i}J_{1s}v_6J_{1e}A_{1e}}$$

Fig. 9. Numbered Geometric Sequence Representation of XML Document

To tackle this problem, we enhance the basic geometric-encoding data sequence by numbering each (repeated) item, so that a geometric sequence is sequence of $symbol_{number_{(s|i|e)}}$. Figure 9 gives a numbered geometric data sequence. Note that we do not number the geometric query sequence. We can see that there is no such subsequence matching in $T_{Geo_{num}}$. Additionally, for each query sequence having $symbol_i$, we only choose the first one in T_{Geo} on the basis of the fact that the rest $symbol_i$ is redundant in querying process. Moreover, for queries having the same child nodes in branches, it is equal to find all the non-decreasing subsequence matching in geometric sequence for all the nodes with the same names. "*" is handled as a range query as the same to ViST. If p is not explicitly stated in geometric sequence model, "//" is then default and not instanced on the basis of the fact that "//" only represents ancestor-descendant relationship. By contrasting to ViST's instance step, resource-consuming prefix checking and range query steps connected with "//" are eliminated in our geometric sequence model. Due to lack of space, the correctness of querying XML through numbered geometric data/query sequence matching is not provided.

4   Holistic Sequence Matching

To acclerate XPath evaluation, the challenge of our geometric model is to (i) avoid the semantic false problem, (ii) eliminate the false answers without refinement or post-processing phases, and (iii) provide a linear storage complexity mechanism to reduce the size of index. In section 3, we show that the total size of numbered geometric sequence is O(n). In this section, we demonstrate our subsequence matching can find all the correct answers without refinement or post-processing phase which is inevitable in ViST.

Table 2. List of Q1, Q2, and Q3 in Optimized Geometric Query Sequences

Path Expression	Geometric Sequence
Q1: /A[B/D][//K]	$Q1_{OptGeo}$: $A_s\ D_e^{\ p}\ B_e^{\ p}\ A_i^{\ u}\ K_e\ A_e$
Q2: /A/B[./E][./K]	$Q2_{OptGeo}$: $E_e^{\ p}\ B_i\ K_e^{\ p}\ B_e^{\ p}\ A_e$
Q3: /A/B[E]/following-sibling::B/K	$Q3_{OptGeo}$: $E_e^{\ p}\ B_e^{\ p}\ A_i\ B_s\ K_e^{\ p}\ B_e^{\ p}\ A_e$

4.1   Index Structure

We adopt a hierarchical indexing structure similar to ViST with some modifications. Each item in a geometric data sequence is in form of $(symbol_{number_{(s|i|e)}})$. Items in a geometric sequence are first put into a trie-like structure. Then each node in the trie is assigned two extra elements "preorder" and "size", where "preoder" is the pre-order traversal position of the node in the data tree, and "size" is used for dynamic scope allocation purpose, whose detail study can be found in the [13]. To build the index structure, each node in the trie, in format of $(symbol_{number_{(s|i|e)}}$, preorder, size), is firstly inserted into a sequence B+Tree index (i.e. SB-Index) using its $symbol_{(s|i|e)}$ as the key. For all the nodes with the same $symbol_{(s|i|e)}$, they are inserted into a position B+Tree (i.e. PB-Index) using its preorder as the key. Figure 10 illustrates the index structure used.

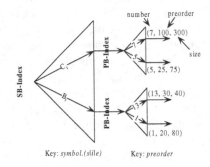

Fig. 10. Index Structure: SB-Index and PB-Index

4.2   Bottom-Up XPath Evaluation

Observing that the performance of evaluating XPath queries over XML documents is significantly affected by the lengths of geometric query sequences, we improve our subsequence matching algorithm on the basis of optimized geometric query sequence transformation. The rational behind is that instead of keeping pairs of nodes like B_s and B_e in a query sequence, we can actually remove one of them without loss of semantics while performing subsequence matching.

Here, we propose a geometric query sequence transformation rule, with an aim to minimize the length of the query sequence. That is: *removing all the*

$symbol_s$ *unless it connects with a* $symbol_i^u$. [3] Examples of the optimized XPath query sequences after transformation are listed in Table 2.

Interestingly, the transformed query subsequences enable us to perform query evaluation in a bottom-up manner, since we start our subsequence matching from a $symbol_e$. For example, given the query $Q_2 : /A/B/[./E][./K]$ in Figure 8 and its optimized geometric query sequence: $E_e^p \ B_i \ K_e^p \ B_e^p \ A_e$, we start the evaluation process from E_e instead of A_s. In comparison, the matching algorithm described in ViST exhibits the top-down flavor.

To facilitate the optimized geometric subsequence matching, we improve our stack mechanism accordingly, where only one set of stacks called **symbol** stacks are involved. We use $Stack_{symbol}$ to denote the stack which accommodates items having *symbol*.

Given an optimized geometric query sequence $q_{1_{v_1}}^{l_1} \ q_{2_{v_2}}^{l_2} \ \dots \ q_{m_{v_m}}^{l_m}$ and a geometric data sequence $d_{1_{num_1, V_1}} d_{2_{num_2, V_2}} \dots d_{n_{num_n, V_n}}$, where $(m \leq n)$, $\forall x (1 \leq x \leq m) \ (v_x = s|i|e) \wedge (l_x = u|p)$), and $\forall y (1 \leq y \leq n) \ (V_y = s|i|e)$. Starting with the empty stacks, we scan across the two sequences from left to right. When two equal symbols encounter (i.e., $q_x = d_y$ and $v_x = V_y$) in $q_{x_{v_x}}^{l_x}$ and $d_{y_{num_y}, V_y}$, we consider the following situations.

[Case 1] $\underline{(v_x = V_y = s)}$
    We push $d_{y_{num_y}, s}$ into the symbol stack $Stack_{d_y}$.
[Case 2] $\underline{(v_x = V_y = e)}$
    There exist two possibilities. 1) When the top item of $Stack_{d_y}$ has a subscript *intermediate* flag i, we check whether $d_{y_{num_y}, i}$ has the same num_y as this top item. If they are the same, we push $d_{y_{num_y}, i}$ into $Stack_{d_y}$; otherwise a mismatch happens and we start our backtracking process. That is, we pop all those candidate items, which lie between $d_{y_{num_y}, e}$ and the top item in $Stack_{d_y}$, out of the corresponding symbol stacks including this top item, and continue to re-search these candidate items in the data sequence.
    2) When the top item of $Stack_{d_y}$ has a subscript *end* flag e, we check whether $d_{y_{num_y}, i}$ has the same num_y as this top item. If they are not the same, we push $d_{y_{num_y}, i}$ into $Stack_{d_y}$; otherwise a mismatch happens and we start the above backtracking process.
[Case 3] $\underline{(v_x = V_y = i)}$
    We check whether $d_{y_{num_y}, i}$ has the same num_y as the top item in $Stack_{d_y}$. If they are the same, we push it into $Stack_{d_y}$; otherwise, a mismatch happens, and we start our backtracking process.
    Note that when we encounter $q_{x_i}^u$ in the query sequence, we need to shift the search pointer in the data sequence backward to $d_{y_{num_y}, s}$ to avoid the semantic false problem (as specified in Section 3).

To illustrate our optimized geometric subsequence matching procedure, let's take query Q_2 as the example. A snapshot of the symbol stacks is given in Figure 11. Detailed algorithmic description can be found in the Algorithm 1(*pc*

---

[3] Recall in Section 4, $symbol_s^u$ signifies that we need to *resume* the range information of $symbol_s$ so as to cope with the semantic false problem.

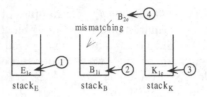

Fig. 11. Stack Status Avoiding Non-existence Query in OptGeoMatching

denotes parent-child relationship and *ad* denotes ancestor-descendant relationship). Firstly, E_{1e} is pushed into $Stack_E$ (Step 1). Since p is in E_e^p in the query sequence, the only item in Figure 9 that satisfies the parent-child constraint is B_{1i}, and is thus pushed into $Stack_B$ (Step 2). K_{1e} is further pushed into $Stack_K$ (Step 3). As p is in K_e^p, B_{2e} is the only possible parent item. However, its number 2 does not conform to the number 1 of the top item B_{1i} in $Stack_B$ (Step 4). Thus B_{2e} cannot be pushed into $Stack_B$, and a mismatch happens. We need to backtrack to B_i and re-start the searching in the data sequence from B_{2i}, returning no satisfactory query answer in the end.

5   Experimental Results

We implement our proposed sequence matching mechanism, *OptGeoMatching*, in C++. We also implemented ViST, and a classical indexing and querying mechanism, XISS [10], for comparison purpose. XISS breaks down the queries into binary twigs and "stitches" them together to obtain the final results. ViST treats both XML documents and XML queries as sequences and obtains the final results by using subsequence matching phase to get preliminary results and post-processing phase to eliminate false answers. We encode the string as they are in ViST and use substring matching algorithm to detect the prefix matching.

We use the B+Tree library in Berkeley DB provided by Sleepycat software. All the experiments are carried out on a Pentium III 750MHZ machine with 512MB main memory. We use disk pages of 8k for Berkeley B+Tree index. To evaluate both the efficiency and scalability of the proposed method, we perform the experiments on both real-world datasets and synthetic datasets.

Experiments on Real-World Datasets
Data Sets

For our experiments, we use public XML databases DBLP [9] and the public XML benchmark XMARK [2].

- DBLP is popularly used in benchmarking XML indexing methods. In the version we used in this study, it has 3,332,130 elements and 404,276 attributes, totally 130,726KB data. The maximum depth of DBLP is 6. The average length of geometric sequence is 39.
- XMARK is widely used in benchmarking XML indexing mechanism with complex nesting structure. In this version we used in this study, it has 1,666,315 elements and 381,878 attributes, totally 115,775KB. The maximum depth of XMARK is 12.

input: SB-Index: index of symbol names; **PB-Index**: index of (preorder, size) labels; $\mathbf{Q_{Geo}} = Q_{Geo_1}, ..., Q_{Geo_{len}}$: XML query in geometric sequence format; **j**: the jth point in Q_{Geo}; **range**: in format of (preorder, size); **len**: length of XPath query sequence.
output: all the matchings of Q_{Geo} in the XML data
if $j \leq len$ **then**

    if u *is in* Q_{Geo_j} **then**

        resume range of corresponding $symbol_s$, say (n', size');
        $OptGeoMatching(n', size', j + 1)$;

    else

        $T \leftarrow$ All the matchings of Q_{Geo_j} in SB-Index;
        $R \leftarrow$ All the matchings of T in PB-Index satisfying *range*;
        for *each* $r_k \in R$ **do**

            if $stack_{symbol}.isempty()$ *or* s *is in* Q_{Geo_j} **then**
                $stack_{symbol}.push(r_k)$;

            else

                if $r_k.number = stack_{symbol}.top().number$ *and* i *is in* Q_{Geo_j} **then**
                    $stack_{symbol}.push(r_k)$;

                if $r_k.number = stack_{symbol}.top().number$ *and* e *is in* Q_{Geo_j} *and* i *is in* $stack_{symbol}.top()$ **then**
                    $stack_{symbol}.push(r_k)$;

                if $r_k.number \;!= stack_{symbol}.top().number$ *and* e *is in* Q_{Geo_j} *and* e *is in* $stack_{symbol}.top()$ **then**
                    $stack_{symbol}.push(r_k)$;

            if $r_k = stack_{symbol}.top()$ **then**
                Assume range of r_k *is* (n', size');
                if $size' \geq len - j$ **then**

                    if p *is in* Q_{Geo_j} *and parent constraint is satisfied* **then**

                        if i *is in* $Q_{Geo_{j+1}}$ **then**
                            $OptGeoMatching(n', size', j + 1)$ //pc;

                        else
                            $OptGeoMatching(n', size', j + 1)$ //ad;

                  else
                      $OptGeoMatching(n', size', j + 1)$;
                    if i *or* e *is in* Q_{Geo_j} **then**
                      skip to r_h, where $r_h.n \geq (r_k.n + r_k.size)$

            $stack_{symbol}.pop()$;

else
  output a matching of Q_{Geo};

Algorithm 1: OptGeoMatching

Table 3. List of XPath Queries

T: title; A: article; AU: author; I: inproceedings; N: namerica; P: payment; PE: person-ref; PER: person; O: open_auction; C: closed_auctions; CA: closed_auction; B: bidder; BU: buyer;

XPath Queries	Data Sets
Q1: //T[text()="On views and XML"]	DBLP
Q2: //A[./AU[text()="Dan Suciu"]][./AU[text()="Tan"]]	DBLP
Q3: /*//I/AU[text()="Peter Buneman"]/following-sibling::AU	DBLP
Q4: //N/*/P[text()="Cash"]	XMARK
Q5: //*/O[./B/PE[@PER="person0"]][./B/PE[@PER="person23"]]	XMARK
Q6: //C/CA/BU[@PER="person11"]/following-silbing::BU	XMARK

Performance of Query Processing
We used 6 queries on the DBLP and XMARK, and compared the proposed method with ViST and XISS. Table 3 lists 6 different queries for DBLP and XMARK, respectively. The experimental results of using the proposed method, ViST and XISS are shown in Table 4.

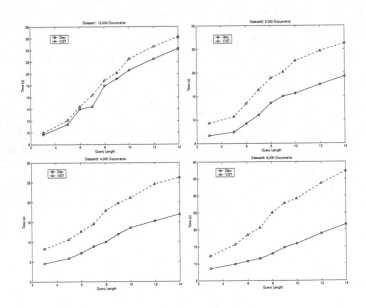

Fig. 12. Queries over Synthetic Data

Q1 is a simple query, "find all the titles with 'On views and XML'". We find out our geometric sequence model performs slightly better that ViST cause there is no instantiation step in geometric sequence model which is inevitable in ViST. Q2 and Q3 are relatively complex queries, respectively, "find all the articles written by 'Dan Suciu' and 'Tan'" and "find the authors co-writting inproceeding papers with 'Peter Buneman'". This time, our geometric sequence model outperforms ViST because (1) we do not need to perform substring matching in validating and instancing structure-encoded query sequences. The substring matching increases the disk I/O since enormous data is retrieved from the index; (2) there exists no post-processing phase in our proposed method; (3) most importantly, we performs bottom-up query evaluation strategy. Since the number of the nodes with specific authors' names are comparatively small and their ranges are narrow, we can thereupon achieve significant evaluation performance. Q6 is a query which should return no result since there exists only one buyer in one closed auction. The structure expressed by Q6 is a kind of *false alarm*. Again, without exception, our geometric sequence model is significantly faster than ViST because there is no answer during the subsequence matching in our proposed method. We can confidently say that there is no such structure existing in XMARK file, while time-consuming refinement phase has to be called by ViST to eliminate enormous false answers.

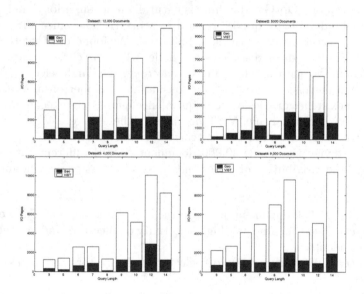

Fig. 13. I/O Performance: Geo vs. ViST

Experiments on Synthetic Data
Datasets

To evaluate the extensibility of the proposed method, we generate our own synthetic datasets. In our experimental environment, there are totally 30,000 documents with 20 different symbols. The maximum depth of our datasets is 16, and maximum fan-out of a node is set to 4. We still use 8KB disk page for B+Tree index and 8-byte integer for pre-order number. We generate geometric sequences directly instead of generating documents.

Table 4. Proposed Method vs. ViST and XISS

Query	Our Method (s)	ViST (s)	XISS (s)
$Q1$	2.81	2.94	7.22
$Q2$	7.14	13.33	319.28
$Q3$	17.49	69.82	612.13
$Q4$	7.86	9.12	467.26
$Q5$	12.27	18.13	392.85
$Q6$	9.73	39.20	729.21

Performance of Query Processing

We set the length of queries to 3, 5, 6, 7, 8, 9, 10, 12, and 14 respectively. All the queries are non-existence queries. To focus on the impact of refinement or post-processing phase in ViST, we do not use queries with content constraints since our bottom-up OptGeoMatching is naturally more superior than top-down ViST. We also do not use queries related to semantic false since ViST can not handle these queries at all. In the scalability test, We found out that the performance of ViST depends on distribution of nodes which are chosen as ancestors or descendants in the queries, referred to as *selectivity*. The high selectivity of both ancestors and descendants generates a considerable number of false answers in ViST if non-existence queries or non-equivalence queries are executed, implying that the query performance of ViST degrades in these cases.

In order to demonstrate the extensibility and stability of our proposed method, we divide the above 30,000 documents into 4 different categories on the basis of the distribution of nodes chosen as ancestors or descendants in the queries.

- $Dataset_1$ (12,000 documents): low selectivity of ancestors and descendants
- $Dataset_2$ (5,000 documents): high selectivity of ancestors and low selectivity of descendants
- $Dataset_3$ (4,000 documents): low selectivity of ancestors and high selectivity of descendants
- $Dataset_4$ (9,000 documents): high selectivity of ancestors and descendants

The results are shown in Figure 12 and Figure 13. We find out that our proposed method performs better than ViST in $Dataset_1$ because the post-processing phase is trivial in dataset1. However, for the rest of the three datasets, our proposed method performs significantly better than ViST since refinement phase requires enormous efforts to eliminate the false answer. Contrasting to ViST, our proposed method performs stably in these three datasets. We notice that even content constraint is not involved in our synthetic data experiments, we can see that OptGeoMatching demonstrates significant disk I/O performance comparing with ViST since top-down ViST is uncertain of its descendants and has to search its full *range* for correct answers. In contrasting to top-down ViST, OptGeoMatching performs a bottom-up subsequence matching and only needs to search a more specific *range* where an ancestor node may exist.

6   Conclusion

In this paper, we report an efficient mechanism for accelerating XPath evaluation steps based on the proposed geometric sequence. A bottom-up holistic subsequence matching algorithm is proposed on the basis of a novel geometric sequence model for XML documents. We demonstrate that our proposed mechanism can significantly improve the current best approach ViST, finding all the correct answers without refinement or post-processing phase with linear size complexity of geometric sequence and guaranteeing the completeness of XPath evaluation without semantic false.

References

1. Aho, A. V., Hopcroft, J. E., Ullman, J. D.: The Design and Analysis of Computer Algorithms. Addison-Wesley (1974)
2. Busse, R., Carey, M., Florescu, D., Kersten, M., Manolescu, I., Schmidt, A., Florian Waas, F.: Xmark an xml benchmark project (2001) http://monetdb.cwi.nl/xml/index.html
3. Chien, S. Y., Tsotras, V. J., Zaniolo, C., Zhang, D.: Efficient complex query support for multiversion XML documents. In EDBT (2002) 161–178
4. Cooper, B., Sample, N., Franklin, M. J., Hjaltason, G. R., Shadmon, M.: A fast index for semistructured data. In The VLDB Conference (2001) 341–350
5. Goldman, R., Widom, J.: Dataguides: Enabling query formulation and optimization in semistructured databases. In VLDB, Springer-Verlag (1997) 436 – 445
6. Gottlob, G., Koch, C., Pichler, R.: The complexity of xpath query evaluation. In PODS, ACM (2003) 179–190
7. Grust, T.: Accelerating xpath location steps. In SIGMOD, ACM Press (2002) 109–120
8. Jiang, H., Lu, H., Wang, W.: Xr-tree: Indexing xml data for efficient structural joins. In 19th International Conference on Data Engineering (2003) 253–264
9. Ley, M.: Dblp bibliography (2004) http://www.informatik.uni-trier.de/ ley/db
10. Li, Q., Moon, B.: Indexing and querying XML data for regular path expressions. In The VLDB Journal (2001) 361–370
11. Milo, T., Suciu, D.: Index structures for path expressions. In Proceedings of the 8th International Conference on Database Theory (1999) 277–295
12. Bruno, N., Koudas, N., Srivastava, D.: Holistic twig joins: Optimal xml pattern matching. In ACM SIGMOD (2002)
13. Shen, Y., Feng, L., Shen, T., Wang, B.: A self-adaptive scope allocation scheme for labeling dynamic xml documents. In DEXA (2004) 811–821
14. Wang, H.: On the sequencing of tree structures for xml indexing (technical report) (2004) http://magna.cs.ucla.edu/ hxwang/publications/xmlrpt.pdf
15. Wang, H., Park, S., Fan, W., Yu, P. S.: Vist: a dynamic index method for querying xml data by tree structures. In SIGMOD, ACM Press (2003) 110–121

A Prototype for Translating XQuery Expressions into XSLT Stylesheets

Niklas Klein[1], Sven Groppe[1], Stefan Böttcher[1], and Le Gruenwald[2]

[1] University of Paderborn, Faculty 5,
Fürstenallee 11,
D-33102 Paderborn, Germany
{niklask, sg, stb}@uni-paderborn.de
[2] University of Oklahoma,
School of Computer Science,
Norman, Oklahoma 73019, U.S.A
ggruenwald@ou.edu

Abstract. The need for a user-friendly query language becomes increasingly important since the introduction of XML. The W3C developed XQuery for the purpose of querying XML data, but XQuery is not available in every tool. Because of historical reasons, many tools only support processing XSLT stylesheets. It is desirable to use tools with XQuery, the design goals of which are, among other goals, to be more human readable and to be less error-prone than XSLT. Instead of implementing XQuery support for every tool, we propose to use an XQuery to XSLT translator. Following this idea, XQuery will be available for all tools, which currently support XSLT stylesheets. In this paper, we propose a translator which transforms XQuery expressions into XSLT stylesheets and we analyze the performance of the translation and XSLT processing in comparison to native XQuery processing.

1 Introduction

1.1 Problem Definition and Motivation

With the wide-spread use of the Extensible Markup Language (XML) accompanied with increasing document sizes, there is an increasing need for user-friendly XML query languages. While the Extensible Stylesheet Language Transformations (XSLT) [11], which also can be used as a query language, is established in the market for years, XQuery [12] is relatively new.

Whereas XSLT is conceived as a transformation language, XQuery was aimed to be an easy human readable query language. Furthermore, both languages are used to grab, filter and associate data from XML-documents. There exists already a large repository of tools, especially commercial products, for supporting XSLT, but not the XQuery language. Examples of such products are BizTalk [8], Cocoon [1] and Xalan [2]. Whenever an application based on these tools is required to use XQuery as the XML query language, it is a big advantage to

J. Eder et al. (Eds.): ADBIS 2005, LNCS 3631, pp. 238–253, 2005.

have a translation from XQuery expressions to XSLT stylesheets such that the XQuery language can be used.

Although both languages were developed with different aims, their application possibilities and expressive power are similar. Both languages use XPath as the path-language for retrieving XML node sets, and both languages have corresponding language constructs for the iteration on an XML node set, the definition of variables, XML node constructors and the definition and call of user-defined functions. However there are some differences between the two languages which we will discuss in Section 2.3.

In this paper, we propose a translation tool from XQuery expressions into XSLT stylesheets that covers the XQuery language except for a few exceptions.

The rest of this paper is organized as follows. Section 2 provides a comparison of XQuery and XSLT. Section 3 describes how we would translate XQuery expressions into XSLT stylesheets. Section 4 presents experimental results comparing the execution times of XSLT stylesheets translated by our approach with the execution times of direct executed XQuery expressions. Finally, Section 5 concludes the paper.

1.2   Related Work

There exists works that compare the languages XSLT and XQuery. [7] shows that many XQuery constructs are easily mappable to XSLT, but presents only examples of mappings and does not provide an algorithm for translating XQuery expressions into XSLT stylesheets. [6] introduces an algorithmic approach of translating XQuery expressions into XSLT stylesheets, but includes neither a detailed algorithm for a subset of XQuery nor a report on experimental results.

Saxon [5] is a processor for both, XQuery expressions and XSLT stylesheets. First, Saxon translates an XQuery expression or an XSLT stylesheet into an object model, where most but not all components are common for XQuery and XSLT. After that, Saxon executes the objects of the object model in order to retrieve the results, but does not provide a source to source translation so that XQuery can be used in XSLT tools.

In this paper we describe a detailed algorithm for translating a subset of XQuery expressions into XSLT stylesheets. Furthermore, we give a detailed performance analysis of the execution of the original XQuery expession compared to the execution of the translated XSLT stylesheet.

2   Comparison of XQuery and XSLT Features

2.1   XQuery Essentials

XQuery is a *functional language*,which means that expressions can be nested with full generality. XQuery is also a *strongly-typed language* in which the operands of various expressions, operators, and functions must conform to the expected types.

XQuery embeds XPath as the path language to locate XML nodes in XML structures. An XPath expression itself is a simple XQuery expression. Furthermore, the XQuery language extends the XPath language by constructors for XML structures like elements and attributes, by FLWOR expressions, which can combine and restructure information from XML documents, by user-defined functions and many more language elements.

FLWOR is an acronym, standing for the first letters of the clauses that may occur in an FLWOR expression:

- `for` clauses associate one or more variables to expressions, creating a tuple stream in which each tuple binds a given variable to one of the items to which its associated expression evaluates. There can be an arbitrary amount of `for` clauses.
- `let` clauses bind variables to the entire result of an expression. There can be an arbitrary number of `let` clauses, but there must be at least one `let` or `for` clause.
- `where` clauses filter tuples, retaining only those tuples that satisfy a condition. The `where` clause is optional.
- `order by` clauses sort the tuples in a tuple stream. The `order by` clause is optional.
- `return` clauses build the result of the FLWOR expression for a given tuple. The `return` clause is required in every FLWOR expression.

2.2 XSLT Essentials

The W3C developed the declarative language XSLT, which describes the transformation of XML documents into a document formulated in XML, HTML, PDF or text by template rules. An XSLT stylesheet itself is an XML document with the root element `<xsl:stylesheet>`. The `xsl` namespace is used to distinguish XSLT elements from other elements. Template rules are expressed by an `<xsl:template>` element. Its `match` attribute contains a pattern in form of an XPath expression. Whenever a current input XML node fulfills the pattern of the `match` attribute, the template is executed. An XSLT processor starts the transformation of an input XML document with the current input XML node assigned to the document root. Using a short form, the output of the executed template is the XML nodes, which are not XSLT instructions, and the text inside the executed template. This output can also be described by a long form with the XSLT instructions `<xsl:element>` for generating XML elements, `<xsl:attribute>` for generating attributes of an XML element and `<xsl:text>` for generating text. Output is also described by the XSLT instruction `<xsl:value-of>`, which converts the result of an XPath expression to a string. The XSLT instruction `<xsl:apply-templates>` recursively applies the templates to all XML nodes in the result node set of the XPath expression given by its `select` attribute. We refer to [11] for a complete list of XSLT instructions.

2.3   Comparison of the XQuery and the XSLT Data Model and Language Constructs

XSLT 2.0 and XQuery 1.0 are both based on the XPath data model [3] and both embed XPath as the path language for determining XML node sets. Therefore, a majority of the XQuery language constructs can be translated into XSLT language constructs and vice versa. For example, `xsl:for each` has similar functionality as `for`, `xsl:if` has similar functionality as `where`, and `xsl:sort` has similar functionality as `order by`. However there are some differences between the two languages which we will discuss here.

Differences in handling intermediate results: XQuery and XSLT handle intermediate results differently.

– Whereas XQuery expressions can be nested with full generality, most XSLT expressions cannot be nested. Therefore, nested XQuery expressions must be translated into a construct, where the intermediate results of the nested XQuery expression are first stored in an intermediate variable using the `xsl:variable` XSLT instruction. After that the intermediate variable is referred for the results of the nested XQuery expression. XSLT variables, which are defined by `xsl:variable`, can only store element nodes. In particular, XSLT variables cannot store attribute nodes, comment nodes and text nodes. Whenever the translated XSLT stylesheets have to store other XML nodes besides element nodes, the translation process can use the work-around presented in Section 2.4.
– Both XQuery and XSLT embed XPath 2.0, which contains the `is` operator. This operator compares the two nodes identities. In the underlying data model of XQuery and XSLT, each node has its own identity. XQuery expressions never copy XML nodes, but always refer to the original XML nodes. Contrary to XQuery expressions, XSLT expressions can only refer in variables to original XML nodes, which can be described by an XPath expression XP and when using the `<xsl:variable select="XP">` instruction. While computing the result of more complex XSLT expressions, which contain functionality outside the possibilities of XPath like iterating in a sorted node set XP by `<xsl:for-each select="XP"><xsl:sort/>...</xsl:for-each>`, XSLT expressions have to copy XML nodes by using `xsl:copy` or `xsl:copy-of`, where the copied XML nodes get new identities different from those of the original XML nodes or other copied XML nodes. Therefore, whenever an XQuery expression uses the `is` operator and variables store a node set that cannot be expressed by an XPath expression, the translation process must offer a work-around, which ensures that the identities of XML nodes in the translated XSLT stylesheet to be considered in the same way as the identities of XML nodes in the original XQuery expression. Section 2.5 describes such a work-around.

Differences in language constructs: The translation process must consider the following differences in the language constructs of XQuery and XSLT:

- Whereas XQuery binds parameters in function calls by order of appearance, XSLT binds parameters of calls of functions and of named templates by parameter names.
- The `order by` construct of XQuery corresponds to `xsl:sort`. XQuery supports four order modifiers: `ascending`, `descending`, `empty greatest` and `empty least`. XSLT supports only `ascending` and `descending`. Therefore, `empty greatest` and `empty least` can not be translated yet. Furthermore `xsl:sort` has to be the first child of the surrounding `xsl:for-each` XSLT instruction. The `order by` clause can contain a variable $v, which is defined after the `for` expression. Therefore, the translated variable definition of $v occurs after the `xsl:sort` instruction, which must be the first child of `xsl:for-each`, but translation of $v is defined later in the translated XSLT stylesheet and cannot be used in the `xsl:sort` instruction. In the special case where the variable $v is defined by an XPath expression XP, we can replace the reference to the translation of $v in the `xsl:sort` XSLT instruction by XP. Furthermore, nested variables in XP must be already defined before the `xsl:for-each` XSLT instruction or, again, must be defined by an XPath expression such that the nested variables can be replaced in XP. In all other cases, the `order by` clause cannot be translated into equivalent XSLT instructions.

2.4 The Transforming XML Nodes to Element Nodes Approach

Whenever XML nodes, which are not element nodes, must be stored as intermediate results, a preprocessing step of the original XML document is needed to transform these XML nodes into element nodes as only element nodes can be stored in XSLT variables of the translated XSLT stylesheet. We use a namespace t in order to identify element nodes, which are transformed from not element nodes. Tests on XML nodes, which are not element nodes, are translated into tests on the corresponding element nodes (see Figure 1). As the result of the translated XSLT stylesheet contains copied element nodes, which are not element nodes of the original document, a postprocessing step must be applied to the result of the XSLT stylesheet, which then transforms these element nodes back to the corresponding XML nodes.

```
site/people/person/@name
```

is translated into

```
site/people/person/t:name
```

Fig. 1. Translating tests on attribute nodes

2.5 The Node Identifier Insertion Approach

In the following, we summarize the work-around presented in [6], which ensures that the identities of XML nodes in the translated XSLT stylesheet are considered in the same way as the identities of XML nodes in the original XQuery expression.

Whenever the `is` operator occurs in the XQuery expression, it is necessary to preprocess the source-document in order to add a new attribute `t:id` containing an unambiguous identifier to every XML element and postprocess the result of the XSLT stylesheet in order to remove the attribute `t:id`. Then the `is` operator can be translated into the `=` operator evaluated on the attribute `t:id`.

When elements are created as intermediate results, the translated XSLT stylesheet does not provide a mechism to set the `t:id` attributes of these elements. Using the `is` operator would work in these cases (see Figure 2). In order to consider both, the case that we have to consider the identity of XML nodes of the input XML document and of intermediate results, we will translate the `is` operator into two operations concatenated with the `or` operator (see Figure 3). One operation compares the `t:id` attributes the result of which is false in the case that there are no `t:id` attributes. The other operation uses the `t:is` operator the result of which is false if two copied XML nodes are compared.

The result of

```
let $a:= <z/>
return $a is $a
```

is "true", but the result of the wrong translation

```
<?xml version="1.0"?>
<xsl:stylesheet xmlns:xsl='http://www.w3.org/1999/XSL/Transform' version="2.0">
<xsl:template match="/">
        <xsl:variable name='let0a'>
                <xsl:element name='z'/>
        </xsl:variable>
        <xsl:copy-of select="$let0a/@t:id = $let0a/@t:id"/>
</xsl:template>
</xsl:stylesheet>
```

is "false".

Fig. 2. Problems when translating the `is` operator in the case that elements are created as intermediate results

```
. is /site[last()]
```

is translated into

```
(./@t:id = /site[last()]/@t:id) or (. is /site[last()])
```

Fig. 3. Translating the `is` operator

2.6   Optimization

Our proposed translation algorithm checks

- whether non-element nodes must be stored as intermediate results and, only then, applies the transforming XML nodes to element nodes approach discussed in Section 2.4, and, otherwise, optimizes by avoiding the processing of this approach.

- whether the is operator is used and, only then, applies the node identifier insertion approach discussed in Section 2.5, and, otherwise, optimizes by avoiding the processing of this approach.

Furthermore, if necessary, both the preprocessing steps and postprocessing steps presented in the transforming XML nodes to element nodes approach and in the node identifier insertion approach can be applied in one step.

2.7   Handling Intermediate Results and Function Calls

XQuery supports closure by allowing nesting XQuery expressions with full generality. Due to the lack of closure in XSLT, query results must be stored in XSLT variables. The results can then be referenced by the names of the variables (see Figure 4).

```
for $i in doc("auction.xml")/site/closed_auctions/closed_auction
        where   $i/price/text() >= 40
        return $i/price
```

is translated into

```
<?xml version="1.0"?>
<xsl:stylesheet version="2.0"
xmlns:xsl='http://www.w3.org/1999/XSL/Transform'>
    <xsl:variable name='rootVar1'>
        <xsl:copy-of select='document("auction.xml")'/>
    </xsl:variable>
    <xsl:template match="/">
        <xsl:variable name="for0_aux">
            <xsl:copy-of select='$rootVar1/site/closed_auctions/closed_auction'/>
        </xsl:variable>
        <xsl:for-each select="$for0_aux/*">
            <xsl:variable name="for0i" select="."/>
            <xsl:if test='$for0i/price/text()>=40'>
                <xsl:copy-of select="$for0i/price"/>
            </xsl:if>
        </xsl:for-each>
    </xsl:template>
</xsl:stylesheet>
```

Fig. 4. Translating a query with intermediate results

While translating a function, we store the function name, the names of its parameters and their order in a global data structure. Whenever we translate a function call, we access this global data structure in order to retrieve the necessary information of the names and the order of the parameters. Then the problem of parameter binding can be solved by mapping the names in the order of their appearance in the function call to the corresponding xsl:param tags (see Figure 5).

```
declare function local:mult($y, $x){ $y * $x };
local:mult(10, 10)
```

is translated into

```
<xsl:template name='mult'>
    <xsl:param name='y'/>
    <xsl:param name='x'/>
    <xsl:copy-of select='$y*$x'/>
</xsl:template>
<xsl:template match="/">
    <xsl:call-template name='mult'>
        <xsl:with-param name='y' select='10'/>
        <xsl:with-param name='x' select='10'/>
    </xsl:call-template>
</xsl:template>
```

Fig. 5. Translating a function

3 Translating XQuery Expressions into XSLT Stylesheets

In this section, we describe the algorithm to translate XQuery expressions into XSLT stylesheets.

3.1 Translation of an XQuery Expression

The translation from an XQuery expression into an XSLT stylesheet is done in two phases. In phase one, we parse the XQuery expression in order to generate the abstract syntax tree of the XQuery expression. For an example, see the XQuery expression in Figure 4 and its abstract syntax tree in Figure 6. In phase two, we evaluate the attribute grammar, which we do not present here due to space limitations. After evaluating the attribute grammar, a DOM [4] representation of the translated XSLT stylesheet is stored in the attribute MainModul.docFrag (see Figure 6). Figure 6 presents the evaluation of attributes for every node in the abstract syntax tree of the XQuery expression in Figure 4. Figure 4 presents also the final results of the translation process.

3.2 Processing of the Translated XSLT Stylesheet

See Figure 7 for an example of the entire translation process (step 1) and transformation process, which consists of the preprocessing step of the input XML document (step 2), the execution of the translated XSLT stylesheet (step 3) and the postprocessing step (step 4) of the results of the XSLT stylesheet.

If we can optimize according to what we have discussed in Section 2.6, then we will avoid the preprocessing step (step 2) and the postprocessing step (step 4).

4 Performance Analysis

This section describes the experiments that we have conducted to compare the execution time of translated XQuery expressions (i.e. XSLT stylesheets) in-

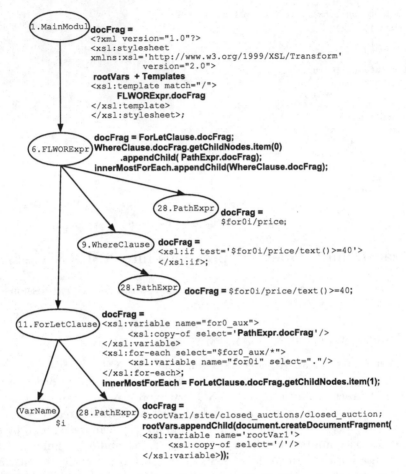

Fig. 6. The abstract syntax tree including computed attributes showing the translation of the XQuery expression in Figure 4

cluding the translation time with the time for executing the original XQuery expression.

4.1   Experimental Environment

We have used the XMark benchmark [10] for all our experiments. This benchmark consists of 20 XQuery queries and an XML data generator. This generator generates XML documents, the size of which can be scaled, containing auction data. The XMark developers chose the 20 XQuery queries that cover many aspects of XQuery. Furthermore, XMark is one of the most used benchmarks for XQuery in research. We have used documents of size 0.317 MB, 0.558 MB, 1.2 MB, 1.7 MB, 2.3 MB, 2.8 MB, 5.5 MB and 12 MB for the experiments.

We have used three different query evaluators: Saxon [5], Xalan [2] and Qexo [9]. Saxon has the capability to evaluate both XQuery expressions and XSLT

XQuery

```
for $b in /site
where $b is /site[last()]
return $b
```

XSLT

1

```
<?xml version="1.0"?>
<xsl:stylesheet xmlns:xsl='http://www.w3.org/1999/XSL/Transform'
version="2.0">
<xsl:template match="/">
    <xsl:variable name="for0_aux">
        <xsl:copy-of select='/site'/>
    </xsl:variable>
    <xsl:for-each select="$for0_aux/*">
        <xsl:variable name="for0b" select="."/>
        <xsl:if test='$for0b/@t:id = /site[last()]/@t:id'>
            <xsl:copy-of select="$for0b"/>
        </xsl:if>
    </xsl:for-each>
</xsl:template>
</xsl:stylesheet>
```

Source-XML

```
<site editor='Miller'>
    one
<site>
<site editor='Fisher'>
    two
</site>
```

2

```
<site t:id='1'>
    <t:editor Attribute=''  t:id='1.1'>
        Miller
    </t:editor>
    one
</site>
<site t:id='2'>
    <t:editor Attribute='' t:id='2.1'>
        Fisher
    </t:editor>
    two
</site>
```

Result-XML

3

```
<site t:id='2'>
    <t:editor Attribute='' t:id='2.1'>
        Fisher
    </t:editor>
    two
</site>
```

4

```
<site editor='Fisher'>
    two
</site>
```

Fig. 7. The transformation process

stylesheets. Whereas Xalan is an XSLT evaluator, which is integrated in the Sun Java Development Kit, Qexo is an XQuery evaluator. Qexo is one of the few XQuery evaluators developed in Java, which implements most language constructs of the current XQuery specifications.

We present the average execution times of 20 executions for every XMark query in combination with every query evaluator.

We have run the experiments on an AMD Athlon 2 Gigahertz with 1 Gigabytes main memory, where 800 Megabytes are assigned to the Java virtual machine. The system runs a Linux kernel 2.6.4 and Java version 1.4.2.

4.2   Analysis of Experimental Results

We present the average execution times of twenty experiments of all 20 XMark queries and their translated XSLT stylesheets for a fixed document file size of 5.5 Megabytes in Figure 14. For the XSLT stylesheets in Figure 14 we have used optimized evaluation (i.e. without the pre- and postprocessing step) except for the unoptimized XSLT stylesheet of query 10, which cannot be optimized because query 10 uses the *is* operator. Saxon processes the XQuery queries 22 % faster on average compared to evaluateing the translated XSLT stylesheets. When we only consider queries without joins, i.e. all queries except the queries 8, 9 and 10, Saxon evaluates the XQuery queries 12 % faster on average. Figure 14 shows that Saxon evaluates the translated XSLT stylesheets of the queries 8, 9 and 10 up to 132 times slower compared to evaluating the original XQuery queries, which shows that Saxon does not optimize the execution of the translated XSLT stylesheets of the queries 8, 9 and 10 with joins. The execution of the translated XSLT stylesheets of the Xalan XSLT processor is 0.8 % faster on average compared to the execution of the Qexo XQuery evaluator of the XMark queries. Note that Xalan and Qexo can not evaluate all queries because they do not implement all used XPath functions. Furthermore, the evaluation time of the Qexo XQuery evaluator is large when evaluating queries containing joins. In fact, Qexo evaluates query 9 (containing two joins) over 7000 times slower than query 1 (no join). The translation needs linear time in the size of the input XQuery query, which is under 7 msec in all cases and can be neglected.

Optimized processing is on average 13 % faster than processing with the preprocessing step and postprocessing step. Only the XMark query 10 cannot be optimized (because it uses the *is* operator), such that the preprocessing step and the postprocessing step must be performed.

Furthermore, we present the average results of twenty experiments of six queries (XMark query 1, 2, 3, 8, 9 and 18) where we vary the document file sizes: Figure 8 shows the execution times of query 1, where the Saxon XQuery evaluator is 18 % faster on average compared to the Saxon XSLT processor with optimization (about 6 sec in the slowest case) and 33 % faster than Saxon XSLT without optimization. Using Xalan XSLT (optimized) is faster than Saxon XQuery for document sizes less than 10 MB, the Xalan XSLT processor is 32 % faster on average compared to Saxon XQuery. The Qexo XQuery evaluator is again 58 % faster than Xalan.

We have retrieved similar results for query 2 (see Figure 9), query 3 (see Figure 10) and query 18 (see Figure 13) compared to query 1. Note that Qexo cannot evaluate query 3 and query 18.

XMark Query 8 contains one join and XMark query 9 contains two joins. The execution times of query 8 (see Figure 11) and the execution times of query 9 (see Figure 12) show that XSLT processors evaluate the translated XSLT stylesheets

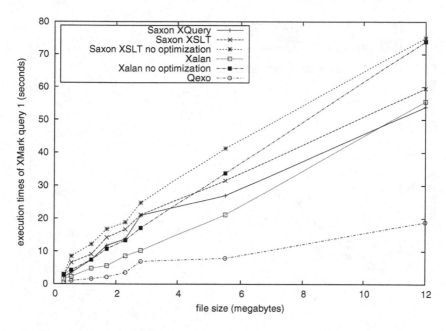

Fig. 8. Execution times (y-axis) of XMark Query 1 and of its translated XSLT stylesheet depending on the file size (x-axis)

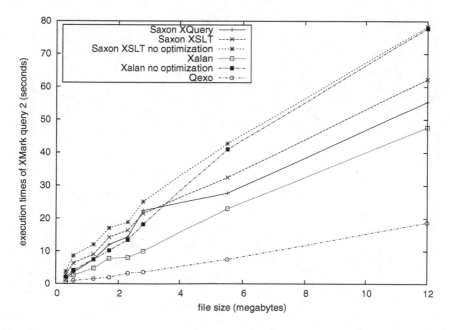

Fig. 9. Execution times (y-axis) of XMark Query 2 and of its translated XSLT stylesheet depending on the file size (x-axis)

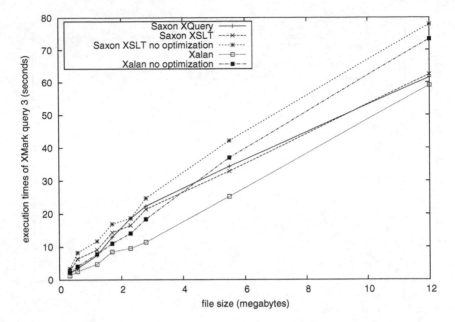

Fig. 10. Execution times (y-axis) of XMark Query 3 and of its translated XSLT stylesheet depending on the file size (x-axis)

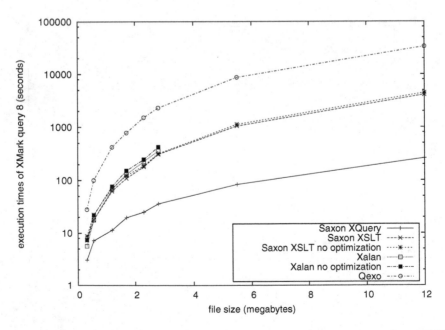

Fig. 11. Execution times (y-axis) of XMark Query 8 and of its translated XSLT stylesheet depending on the file size (x-axis)

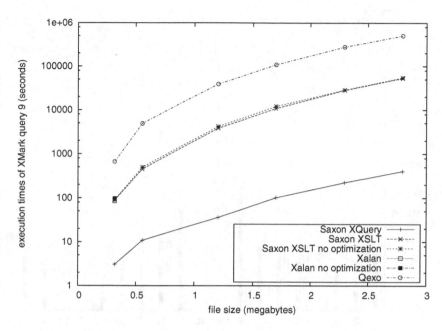

Fig. 12. Execution times (y-axis) of XMark Query 9 and of its translated XSLT stylesheet depending on the file size (x-axis)

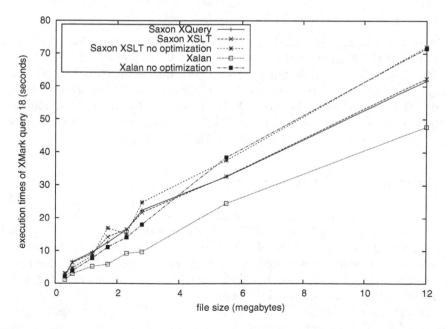

Fig. 13. Execution times (y-axis) of XMark Query 18 and of its translated XSLT stylesheet depending on the file size (x-axis)

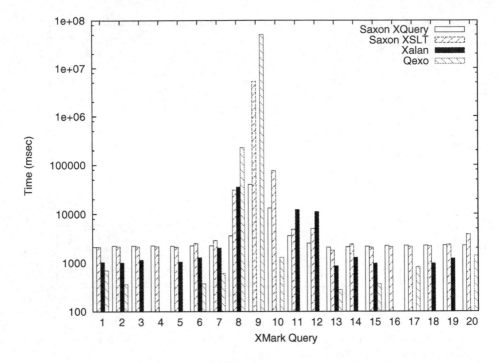

Fig. 14. The execution time of all XMark queries for a file size of 5.5 Megabytes

of queries containing joins much slower compared to the execution of XQuery evaluators of the XQuery queries.

The Saxon XQuery evaluator processes both queries much faster, 80 % for query 8 and 98 % for query 9, compared to the execution of the optimized translated XSLT stylesheets of the Saxon XSLT processor. Contrary, the evaluation of the translated queries of the Saxon XSLT processor is 85 % faster for query 8 and 90 % faster for query 9 compared to the Qexo XQuery evaluator.

5   Summary and Conclusions

We have presented an approach for translating XQuery expressions into XSLT stylesheets. We described the algorithm for the translation process in terms of an attribute grammar, which we do not present here due to space limitations. In general, there must be a preprocessing step for the original XML document before executing the translated XSLT stylesheet and a postprocessing step for the result of the translated XSLT stylesheet.

The experiments considering the XMark queries showed that executing the translated XSLT stylesheet is 12 % slower than native XQuery processing (except queries containing joins). We show that in most cases, but at least for all XMark queries except one XMark query, we can optimize and avoid the preprocessing step and the postprocessing step. Optimized processing is on average 13 % faster than processing with the preprocessing step and postprocessing step. Therefore, we have achieved the goal to make XQuery practically useable for the broad field of XSLT tools.

References

1. apache.org. Cocoon (2004) http://cocoon.apache.org
2. apache.org. Xalan (2004) http://xml.apache.org/xalan-j
3. Fernandez, M., Robie, J. (Eds): "XQuery 1.0 and XPath 2.0 Data Model". W3C Working Draft, June (2001) http://www.w3.org/TR/2001/WD-query-datamodel/
4. Hors, A. L., Hegaret, P. L., Nicol, G., Robie, J., Champion, M., Byrne, S. (Eds): "Document Object Model (DOM) Level 2 Core Specification Version 1.0". W3C Recommendation, Nov. (2000) http://www.w3.org/TR/DOM-Level-2-Core/
5. Kay, M. H.: Saxon (2004) http://saxon.sourceforge.net
6. Lechner, S., Preuner, G., Schrefl, M.: Translating XQueryinto XSLT. In Revised Papers from the HUMACS, DASWIS, ECOMO, and DAMA on ER 2001 Workshops, Springer-Verlag (2002) 239–252
7. Lenz, E.: XQuery: Reinventing the Wheel? (2004) http://www.xmlportfolio.com/xquery.html
8. Microsoft. Biztalk (2004) http://www.biztalk.org/
9. qexo.org. Qexo (2004) http://www.gnu.org/software/qexo
10. Schmidt, A., Waas, F., Manolescu, I., Kersten, M., Carey, M. J., Busse, B.: XMark: A benchmark for XML data management. In Proc. of the 28th International Conference on Very Large Data Bases (VLDB 2002), Hong Kong, China, July 02 (2002)
11. W3C. XSL Transformations (XSLT) (2003) http://www.w3.org/TR/xslt
12. W3C. XML Query (2004) http://www.w3.org/XML/Query

Combining Tree Structure Indexes with Structural Indexes in Query Evaluation on XML Data

Attila Kiss and Vu Le Anh

Department of Information systems, ELTE University
kiss@ullman.inf.elte.hu, leanhvu@inf.elte.hu

Abstract. There are a variety of structural indexes which have been proposed to speed up path expression queries over XML data. They usually work by partitioning nodes in the data graph into equivalence classes and storing equivalence classes as index nodes. The size of a structural index is never larger than the size of the data graph. In the literature it is not always mentioned that the basic structure of XML document is tree-structure. In prior work [1], we introduce and describe a new improved approach for query evaluation on XML data. We consider the data graph of an XML data as the union of the basic tree and the link graph. The basic tree is indexed, that improves the query evaluation more efficiently. In this paper, we introduce and describe a new approach combining two technics: structural- and tree structure indexes. The data graph is simulated by a strong 1-index, in which the basic tree structure remains. Moreover, tree structure index can be built on the new structural index in linear complexity with efficient algorithms. Our experiments show that the new combinational approach is more efficient than we just apply tree structure or structural indexes separately.

1 Introduction

In recent years, the XML has become the dominant standard for exchanging and querying documents over the Internet. The basic structure of an XML document, which comprises hierarchically nested collection of *tagged elements*, can be represented by an ordered labelled tree, in which each element can be only atomic or contains subelements. In general, when a reference can be made from one element to another using ID/IDREF pair, an XML document can be represented by a rooted directed labelled graph. There is a variety of query languages proposed to query XML: *UnQL* [2,3], *Lorel* [4,5], *XML-QL* [6], *XPath* [15], *XQuery* [16], etc. *Path expressions* are the basic building blocks of XML queries. To summarize the structure of XML data and speed up path expression evaluation, structural indexes have been proposed [7,8,9,10]. One of the most popular ones is the 1-index [7], based on the notion of graph bisimilarity. Evaluating regular queries on the 1-index graph, which is never larger than the data graph, is precise and often cheaper than on the naive data graph. However, in most of structural indexes, the data graph model is the general model used for any semi structured data. The basic tree structure of XML data is not mentioned.

J. Eder et al. (Eds.): ADBIS 2005, LNCS 3631, pp. 254–267, 2005.
© Springer-Verlag Berlin Heidelberg 2005

In the prior work [1] we introduce a new approach for regular query evaluation on XML data. The data graph is considered as the union of two components: the basic tree and the link graph. The result of a regular query on the data graph can be considered as the union and concatenation of two sub-results of this query on the link graph and the basic tree. The sizes of the link graph, the number of nodes and edges, are linear functions of the number of reference edges, which is smaller compare to the number of the data graph edges. With the index on the basic tree and the the size of the link graph is small, our algorithm is more efficient than the naive algorithm.

In our work, we use the bulk semantic evaluation with input-, output node sets concepts [3]. It brings us several following advantages: easy implementation in traditional database systems; the evaluation can be parallel executed; adaptive and efficient query decomposition, so that we can support complex queries: tree structured queries, value based select queries, etc. The complexity of this evaluation can be reduced by using graph simulation with structural indexes.

Our Contribution. In this paper, we introduce and describe the new approach, in which the data graph is simulated by the strong 1-index graph and the efficiency of the query evaluation is improved by using tree structure index on the strong 1-index. We also introduce and describe algorithms for constructing the tree structure indexes in linear complexity. Our experiments show that the new approach is more efficient than the old approaches, when we apply tree structure index or structural structure index separately.

Organization. The remainder of the paper is organized as follows. Section 2 is the preliminary and the prior work. We introduce basic concepts and definitions, we also talk about the naive algorithm by using bulk sematic evaluation, and the improved algorithm in our prior work. In section 3, we talk about structural indexes. We introduce and describe the naive algorithm using naive 1-index and our new algorithm which is based on the strong 1-index and tree structure index. In section 4, we introduce and describe algorithms using for our indexes construction. In section 5, we represent our experiments. We discuss the related works in section 6. Section 7 concludes the paper.

2   Preliminary and Prior Work

2.1   Data- and Query Graphs

Data model. In this paper, we model XML as a rooted directed labelled graph $\mathcal{G} = (V, E, \Sigma, r)$. V is the set of nodes, representing XML nodes. $E = E_b \cup E_f$ is the set of edges, representing relationships between nodes. E_b is the set of basic tree edges, representing element-subelement relationship; E_f is the set of reference edges, representing $IDREF$ relationship. Each edge is labelled by a value in the finite set of label values Σ. r is the single root of the graph, with no incoming edges. An example of XML document under this model is shown in Figure 1, where basic tree edges are solid lines, and reference edges are dotted lines.

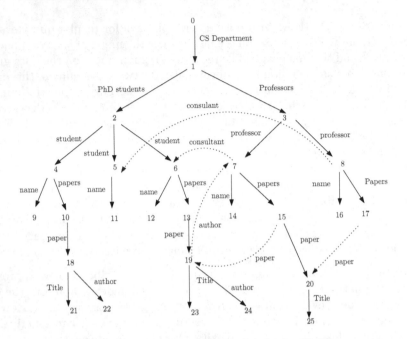

Fig. 1. An Example of data model for XML

Let $a \in \Sigma$, and $@a$ be a new label value. We denote $u \xrightarrow{a} v$, iff there exists an edge from u to v labelled by a; in the case this edge is a basic edge, we denote $u \xrightarrow{a} v$; and in the case this edge is a reference edge, we denote $u \xrightarrow{@a} v$. $\Sigma' = \Sigma \cup \{@a | a \in \Sigma\}$ is denoted as the extension set of label values of $\mathcal{G}$.

Data graph, union of basic tree and link graph. We consider the data graph $\mathcal{G}$ as the union of the basic tree $\mathcal{T}$ and the link graph $\mathcal{L}$. The basic tree is the remainder when we delete all reference edges. The link graph $\mathcal{L} = (V_L, E_L)$ is a labelled directed graph, in which between two nodes there may exist more than one edge, and each edge is labelled by a sequence of label values. $V_L = S_L \cup D_L$, the set of the nodes in $\mathcal{L}$, is the union of the set of the source nodes of the reference edges, S_L, and the set of the destination nodes of the reference edges, D_L. $E_L = E_f \cup E_{sym}$, the set of the edges in $\mathcal{L}$, is the union of the set of the reference edges, E_f, and the set of symbol edges, E_{sym}. We add a symbol edge e from u to v $(u, v \in V_L)$, if there exists a basic path (contains only basic tree edges) from u to v, which does not contain another node in V_L except u and v. The symbol edge e is labelled by the label path of the basic path. The link graph of the data graph in Figure 1 is shown in Figure 2.

The size of a link graph is linear function of the number of the reference edges [1]. More precisely, if k denotes the number reference edges, then $|V_L| \leq 2k$ and $|E_L| \leq 3k - 1$. In practice, the number of the reference edges is often small compared with the number of the edges of the data graph, so the size of the link graph is often small compared with the size of the data graph.

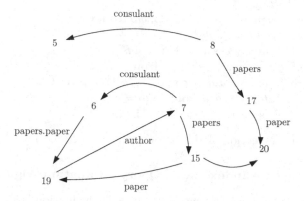

Fig. 2. Link graph of the data graph in Figure 1

Regular queries. A regular expression over Σ alphabet is defined as follows:

$$R = \varepsilon \mid a \mid R_1.R_2 \mid R_1|R_2 \mid R_1^*$$

where ε is the empty word; $a \in \Sigma$ is a letter; R_1, R_2, R are regular expressions; (.), (|), (*) are the concatenation-, the alternation-, and the iteration opera-
tions respectively. Each regular query is defined by a regular expression, and each regular expression also defines a regular language over Σ, which contains all words over Σ marching the regular expression. We call the rooted labelled directed graph of the finite deterministic automata, which computes the regular language defined by the regular expression, the query graph of the query.

2.2   Naive Query Evaluation Algorithm

The result of the regular query $\mathcal{Q}$ given by the regular expression R on the data graph $\mathcal{G}$ with the input node set I, and the output node set O is defined as follows: $\mathcal{R}_O^I(\mathcal{G},\mathcal{Q}) = \{(x,y) \in I \times O | x \xrightarrow{R} y\}$, where $x \xrightarrow{R} y$, iff there exists a path from x to y which matches the regular expression R. For example, let $\mathcal{G}$ be the data graph shown in Figure 1. If $\mathcal{Q}$ is given by $R = professor.name$, and $I = \{2,3\}$, $O = V(\mathcal{G})$, then $\mathcal{R}_O^I(\mathcal{G},\mathcal{Q}) = \{(3,14),(3,16)\}$.

Naive regular query evaluation. We use $G(dfrom, label, dto)$ and $Q(qfrom, label, qto)$ relations to represent all edges of the data graph $\mathcal{G}$ and the query graph $\mathcal{Q}$ respectively; $I(dnode)$, $O(dnode)$ relations to represent the input- and the output node set; q_0, $F(qnode)$ to represent the start state and the set of the final states of $\mathcal{Q}$; $S(dfrom, qfrom, label, dto, qto) = G \underset{label}{\bowtie} Q$ to represent all edges of the state-data graph of the data graph $\mathcal{G}$ and the query graph $\mathcal{Q}$ [1]; $T(dfrom, qfrom, dto, qto)$ to represent the transitive closure relation of S. The naive regular query evaluation algorithm is shown as follows:

Naive-Algorithm
Input: G, Q, I, O, q_0, F
Output: R

1 $S \leftarrow$ **select** *dfrom, qfrom, label, dto, qto* **from** G, Q
    where $G.label = Q.label$
2 Compute T, transitive closure relation of S
3 $T \leftarrow$ **select** *dfrom, qfrom, dto, qto* **from** T, I, O, F
    where $T.dfrom = I.dnode$ **and** $T.qfrom = q_0$ **and**
        $T.dto = O.dnode$ **and** $T.qto = F.qnode$
4 **return** $R \leftarrow$ **select**   *dfrom, dto*   **from** T

The proof for the correction of this algorithm can be found in [1].

2.3   Tree Structure Index Based Query Evaluation Algorithm

Query decomposition. In our scenario, the process evaluation is shown in Figure
3. The input query Q is given by a regular path expression and the input-, output
node sets. The input node set I contains only the root of the data graph. The
output node set O is a subset of the set nodes[1].

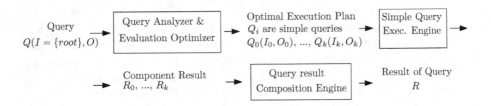

Fig. 3. Query Evaluation Process

We define the concatenation, the union-, and the iteration operations between regular queries [1], based on the operations between regular expressions.
The composed regular query can be evaluated based on its components [1].
In practice, simple queries are the most important regular queries: one-letter
query $\mathcal{Q}_1$ matching an arbitrary letter, universal query $\mathcal{Q}_\infty$ matching an arbitrary word; and primary query $\mathcal{Q}_\alpha$ matching a given word α. We rewrite the
input query Q as an equivalent system of simple queries $Q_i(I_i, O_i)$, where I_i,
O_i are the input-, the output node set of Q_i. The system $\{Q_i(I_i, O_i)\}$ satisfies
following conditions: (1) if Q_i is concatenated by Q_j then $O_i = I_j$; (2) if Q_i and
Q_j is unified then $I_i = I_j$ and $O_i = O_j$; (3) if we want to evaluate Q_i^* then I_i,
O_i should be the set of data nodes. The execution plan as ordered sequence to
evaluate Q_i strongly decide the cost of the query evaluation. The execution plan
can be top-down, bottom-up or hybrid (combining top-down and bottom-up)
approaches. However, in this paper, we mention on the question that evaluating
the primary queries with the input-, the output node set efficiently.

    Tree structure index. Each node is indexed by three parameter $(f, g, address)$,
where $address \in \Sigma^*$ is the label path of the unique basic path from the root

---

[1] The output node set is the set of nodes, whose data satisfies the given selective
conditions

to the node; the pair $(f,g) \in \mathbb{N} \times \mathbb{N}$ system, called *AD system*, helps us to check quickly the ancestor-descendant relationship on the basic tree $\mathcal{T}$. (f,g) is an AD system, iff it satisfies following properties: i. $\forall u \in V : f(u) \leq g(u)$; ii. $\forall v, u \in V : u$ is an ancestor of v, iff $f(u) < f(v) \leq g(u)$. A simple AD system can be constructed by choosing f as the position of the data node and g as the position of the last descendent node of the data node in the pre-order sequence of the basic tree.

Corollary 1. *Let* $\alpha \in \Sigma^*$. *In the basic tree* $\mathcal{T}$:

$$u \xrightarrow{\alpha} v \Leftrightarrow f(u) \leq f(v) \leq g(u) \ \wedge \ address(u).\alpha = address(v)$$

Improved algorithm. We divide all paths matching the word α into two classes: basic paths (contain only basic tree edges) and complex paths (contain at least one reference edge). The set of basic paths can be quickly determined by using tree structure index (Corollary 1). With a complex path p from u to v, we cut it into three sections as follows: the first section is from u to $w \in S_L$, which is the source node of the first reference edge of p; the second section from w to $t \in D_L$, which is the destination node of the last reference reference edge of p; the third section is from t to v. Because the first and third sections are basic paths, and their label path is the prefix (in the case of the first section) or suffix (in the case of the third section) of α, so we can determine them by the tree structure index. The second section can be determined by using the transitive closure relation of the state data of the link graph $\mathcal{L}$ and *the complex representation of query graph* $\mathcal{Q}_\alpha{}^2$ [1].

We represent the nodes of the data graph by relation $N(dnode, f, g, address)$; the link source nodes and the link destination nodes by relations $SL(dnode, f, g, address)$ and $DL(dnode, f, g, address)$ respectively; the edges of the link graph by relation $L(dfrom, slabel, dto)$; the complex representation of the query Q_α by relation $Q_c(qfrom, slabel, qto)$; the edges of the state data graph of the link graph and the query graph by relation $S_c(qfrom, dfrom, slabel, qto, dto)$; the transitive closure relation of S_c by relation $T_c(qfrom, dfrom, qto, dto)$; the basic and complex paths from the input node set to the output nodes by relations $R_1(from, to)$, $R_2(from, to)$; the first, second, and third sections of complex paths from the input node set to the output nodes by relations $R_1'(dfrom, dto, qto)$, $R_2'(dfrom, dto, qfrom, qto)$ and $R_3'(dfrom, dto, qfrom)$ respectively. We denote 0 as the start state and m as the final state of the automata of the primary query. The $Concat(st_1, st_2)$ function returns the concatenation string of two strings st_1, st_2. The improved algorithm for primary queries is shown as follows:

Improved-Algorithm
Input: N, L, SL, DL, $\alpha = a_1.a_2....a_m$, I, O
Output: R
1 $I' \leftarrow$ **select * from** N

---

[2] The complex representation of primary query Q_α is the graph, whose has the same nodes as Q_α and there is an edge from u to v, iff there exists a path on Q_α from u to v; the edge is labelled by the label path of the associated path.

where exists (select * from I **where** $I.dnode = N.dnode$**)**
1 $O' \leftarrow$ **select * from** N
    where exists (select * from I **where** $O.dnode = N.dnode$**)**
2 $R_1 \leftarrow$ **select** $I'.dnode, O'.dnode$ **from** I', O'
    where $I'.f \leq O'.f \leq I'.g \wedge Concat(I'.address, \alpha) = O'.address$
3 Compute Q_c as the complex representation of Q_α
4 $S_c \leftarrow$ **select** $qfrom, dfrom, slabel, qto, dto$ **from** L, Q_c
    where $L.slabel = Q_c.slabel$
5 Compute T_c as the transitive relation of S_c
6 $R_1' \leftarrow$ **select** $I'.dnode, \quad SL.dnode, \quad Q_c.qto$
    from $\quad I', \quad SL, \quad Q_c$
    where $Q_c.qfrom = 0 \ \wedge \ (I'.f \leq SL.f \leq I'.g) \ \wedge$
    $\qquad SL.address = Concat(I'.address, Q_c.slabel)$
7 $R_2' \leftarrow T_c$
8 $R_3' \leftarrow$ **select** $DL.dnode, \quad O'.dnode, \quad Q_c.qfrom$
    from $\quad O', \quad DL, \quad Q_c$
    where $Q_c.qto = m \ \wedge \ (DL.f \leq O'.f \leq DL.g) \ \wedge$
    $\qquad O'.address = Concat(DL.address, Q_c.slabel)$
9 $R_2 \leftarrow$ **select** $R_1'.dfrom, R_3'.dto$ **from** R_1', R_2', R_3'
    where $R_1'.(dto, qto) = R_2'.(dfrom, qfrom) \ \wedge$
    $\qquad R_2'.(dto, qto) = R_3'.(dfrom, qfrom)$
10 **return** $\quad R \leftarrow$ (**select * from** R_1) **union** (**select * from** R_2)

In both two algorithms, the most complicated step is that when we compute the transitive closure relations (step 2 in the naive algorithm, and step 5 in the improved algorithm). In the improved algorithm we only have to compute the state-data graph of the query graph and the link graph, which is smaller compare to the data graph. There are several different modified algorithms proposed in [1] to reduce the complexity in different scenarios.

3   Structural Indexes Based Query Evaluation Algorithms

Structural indexes. A structural index of the data graph $\mathcal{G}$ is a labelled directed graph $I(\mathcal{G}) = (V_I, E_I, \Sigma)$, which is built by the following general procedure: (1) partition the data nodes into classes according to some equivalence relation, (2) make an index node for each equivalence class, with all data nodes in this class being its extent, and (3) add an index edge from index node I to index node J and labelled with $a \in \Sigma$ if there is a data edge from some data node in the extent of I to some data node in the extent of J, whose label is a. Two data edges are equivalent with each other, if they have the same label value and their source- and destination nodes are equivalent respectively. Two equivalent edges are symbolized by the same index edge. We denote the symbol index node of data node u by $I(u)$, and the symbol index edge of data edge e by $I(e)$. Certainly, the size of a structural index is smaller than the size of the associated data graph. Moreover, structural indexes are *safe*. It means if in the data graph $u \xrightarrow{R} v$ then in each structural index of the data graph we have $I(u) \xrightarrow{R} I(v)$, where R is a path regular expression.

1-index. The 1-index is introduced and described by [7]. We denote $A_\infty(\mathcal{G})$ for the 1-index of the data graph $\mathcal{G}$. In the 1-index, the equivalent relation between nodes is *bisimilarity* relation.

Definition 1. *The bisimilarity ($\approx$) relation is a symmetric binary relation, which satisfies following two conditions:*

1. The root node is only equivalent with itself.

2. If $u \approx v$ then for any edge $u' \xrightarrow{a} u$ there exists an edge $v' \xrightarrow{a} v$, such that $u' \approx v'$

Paige and Tarjan [11] describe an $O(m \log n)$ time algorithm for computing $\approx$ on a unlabelled graph with n nodes and m edges, which can be easily adapted to a $O(m \log m)$ algorithm for labelled graphs [12].

The 1-index graph is not only *safe* but also *backward precise*. It means for all $R \in \Sigma^*$, if $I \xrightarrow{R} J$ in $A_\infty(\mathcal{G})$ then for all $v \in J$ there exists $u \in I$, such that $u \xrightarrow{R} v$. Hence, if the input node set is contained only *root*, and the output node set is the set of all data nodes, the result of a regular query on 1-index coincides with the result of this query on the data graph.

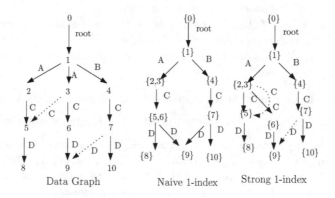

Fig. 4. An example for structural indexes

Strong 1-index. The 1-indexes are structural indexes based on *strong bisimilarity* relations. The difference between the definition of strong bisimilarity relations and bisimilarity relations is that we replace $\rightarrow$ relation by $\rightharpoonup$ relation in second condition of Definition 1, and the set of label values is extended, Σ'. As a result, the basic tree-structure remains in strong 1-indexes. Precisely, the definition of strong bisimilarity relations is below:

Definition 2. *The strong bisimilarity ($\simeq$) relation is a symmetric binary relation, which satisfies following two conditions:*

1. The root node is only equivalent with itself.

2. *If* $u \simeq v$ *and* $u' \xrightarrow{a'} u$ *then there exists* v', *such that* $v' \xrightarrow{a'} v$ *and* $u' \simeq v'$ $(a' \in \Sigma')$.

From definitions, we have:

Corollary 2. *A strong bisimilarity relation is also a bisimilarity relation.*

Corollary 2. shows that we can compute $\simeq$ by Paige and Tarjan algorithm with the complexity $O(m \ log \ m)$ [11]. Moreover, if we already have the 1-index, we can use it as the initial node partition to improve the constructor algorithm.

In the strong 1-indexes, we add a *(basic/reference)* index edge from index node I to index node J and labelled with a if there is a (basic/reference) data edge from some data node in the extent of I to some data node in the extent of J, whose label is a. We can build strong 1-indexes similarly to 1-indexes, as replacing Σ by Σ'.

Similar to the data graph, in the strong 1-indexes there are two kinds of edges: basic edges and reference edges, and the basic edges also create a tree. The strong 1-indexes are *strong backward precise*, that if $I_0 \xrightarrow{a_1'} I_1 \xrightarrow{a_2'} ... \xrightarrow{a_k'} I_k$ $(a_i' \in \Sigma')$ then for all $v_k \in I_k$ there exists $v_0 \in I_0, ..., v_{n-1} \in I_{k-1}$ that $v_0 \xrightarrow{a_1'} v_1 \xrightarrow{a_2'} ... \xrightarrow{a_k'} v_k$.

Proposition 1. *Let* $A_\infty'(\mathcal{G})$ *be a strong 1-index of the data graph G. We have:*

1. $A_\infty'(\mathcal{G})$ *is strong backward precise and safe.*

2. The basic edges of $A_\infty'(\mathcal{G})$ *create a basic tree, denoted by* T_I, *and the root of this tree is the index node contains only the root of* $\mathcal{G}$.

3. All data nodes in an index node have the same address and equal to the address of the index node.

Proof. $A_\infty'(\mathcal{G})$ is safe as it is a structural index. Induction by k, we have if $I_0 \xrightarrow{a_1'} I_1 \xrightarrow{a_2'} ... \xrightarrow{a_k'} I_k$ $(a_i' \in \Sigma')$ then for all $v_k \in I_k$ there exists $v_0 \in I_0, ...,$ $v_{n-1} \in I_{k-1}$ that $v_0 \xrightarrow{a_1'} v_1 \xrightarrow{a_2'} ... \xrightarrow{a_k'} v_k$. Hence, $A_\infty'(\mathcal{G})$ is strong backward precise.

Let I be an index node, u be a data node, such that $u \in I$. The basic path from the root to u is $u_0.u_1. \ ... \ .u_k$, such that u_i are data nodes, u_0 is the *root* of $\mathcal{G}$, $u_k = u$, and there exists a basic edge from u_i to u_{i+1}. Hence, there exists a basic edge from $extent(u_i)$ to $extent(u_{i+1})$, and $extent(u_0).extent(u_1). \ ... \ .extent(u_k)$ is a basic path from the root to I. If there exist two different basic paths from the root of $A_\infty'(\mathcal{G})$ to index node I then because $A_\infty'(\mathcal{G})$ is strong backward precise, so for all $u \in I$ there exist two different basic paths from the root to u, which is impossible. Hence, there is one and only one basic path from the root to every index node. It follows that the basic edges of $A_\infty'(\mathcal{G})$ create a basic tree. Finally, two basic paths $u_0.u_1. \ ... \ .u_k$ and $extent(u_0).extent(u_1). \ ... \ .extent(u_k)$ have the same label path, so all data nodes in an index node have the same address and equal to the address of the index node.

Query Evaluation. In our scenario, after rewriting the input regular query Q we evaluate the component primary queries Q_i on a (strong) 1-index of the data graph and combine them at the end of the execution. The result of the query Q is the data nodes in the union of the extent of index nodes, matching the expression path of the query on the (strong) 1-index. Because the (strong) 1-indexes are backward precise, so the result is precise.

The structure of the strong 1-indexes is similar to the structure of the data graph, so we suggest to build the tree structure index on the basic tree. The query evaluation algorithm on the strong indexes is quite similar to the improved algorithm. In the 1-indexes with no difference between reference edges and basic edges, the query evaluation algorithm is similar to the naive algorithm.

4 Indexes Construction

4.1 Tree Structure Index Construction

We can choose the first parameter f as the position of the data node in the pre-order sequence of the basic tree; the second parameter g as the position of the last descendent node in the pre-order sequence; the third parameter $address$ can be computed from the $address$ of the parent. The algorithm is shown below:

> **Tree Structure Index Constructor Algorithm**
> **Input:** $\mathcal{T}$ is a labelled tree
> **Output:** A tree structure index on $\mathcal{T}$
> **begin**
> 1 $curF \leftarrow 1$
> 2 $ADD(Root, \varepsilon)$
> **end**
>
> **ADD**(I: $IndexNode$, $curAdd : \Sigma^*$)
> **begin**
> 1 Let u be a data node in the extent of I
> 2 $I.address \leftarrow curAdd$
> 3 $I.f \leftarrow curF$
> 4 $curF \leftarrow curF + 1$
> 5 **for all** $J \in Children(I)$ **do** $ADD(J, Concat(curAdd, label(I, J)))$
>   /* $label(I, J)$ is the label of edge from I to J*/
> 6 $I.g \leftarrow curF - 1$
> **end**

In practice, if we parse XML documents by the SAX (Simple API for XML), where the the order sequence of parsing nodes is also the pre-order sequence of the basic tree, then we can build the tree structure index on data graph while parsing XML document. The complexity of the algorithm is $O(n)$, where n is the number of nodes.

4.2 Link Graph Construction

After building the tree structure, we can build the link graph in linear time of the number of reference edges. Let $V_L = \{n_1, n_2, ..., n_t\}$, where n_i are the destination nodes or the source nodes of the link edges. We assume that $n_1.f < n_2.f < ... < n_t.f$. We remark our reader that in the tree structure index constructor algorithm the nodes are automatically sorted by f parameter. The reference edges of the link graph can be easily determined. We use following corollary to determine the symbol paths:

Corollary 3. *There exists a symbol path from n_i to n_j, iff:*
1. $n_i.f < n_j.f \leq n_j.g \leq n_i.g$
2. $\nexists\, n_s : n_i.f < n_s.f < n_j.f \leq n_j.g \leq n_s.g \leq n_i.g$

The link graph constructor algorithm is shown as below:

> **Link Graph Constructor Algorithm**
> **Input:** $\mathcal{G}$ with tree structure index, $V_L = \{n_1, ..., n_t\}$ sorted by f parameter
> **Output:** The link graph $\mathcal{L} = (V_L, E_L)$
> **begin**
> 1 **insert into** E_L all reference edges of $\mathcal{G}$
> 2 *EmptyStack*(S)
> 3 **for** $i = t$ **down to** 1 **do**
> 4   **begin**
> 5   **while** $NotEmpty(S) \wedge (n_{top(S)}.f < n_i.g)$ **do**
> 6   **begin**
> 7   **insert into** E_L symbol edge from n_i to $n_{top(S)}$
> 8 $Pop(S)$
> 9   **end**
> 10 $Push(S, i)$
> 11   **end**
> **end**

Proposition 2. *The link graph constructor algorithm is correct and the complexity is $O(k)$, where k is the number of reference edges.*

Proof. We parse the v_i from the right to the left and bottom-up direction. Hence, if $n_{top(S)}.f < n_i.g$ then n_i is the nearest ancestor of $n_{top(S)}$, so there exists an symbol path from n_i to $n_{top(S)}$. With a given node n_i there may exist only one symbol edges, in which n_i is the destination node. Moreover, if there exists the symbol edge from n_i to n_j then $i < j$. Hence the algorithm find all symbol edges, that follows the correction of the algorithm.

The complexity of step in line 1 is $O(k)$. For each node, we push exactly one time into stack S, and get out maximum one time. So totaly we t times push in and get out maximum t times nodes. Because $t \leq 2k$ so the complexity of the algorithm is $O(k)$.

5   Experiments

We compare the performance between 4 algorithms: the naive algorithm (NA algorithm), the naive algorithm on the 1-index (NI algorithm), the tree structure based improved algorithm (NT algorithm), and the tree structure based improved algorithm on the strong 1-index (TI algorithm) on the same large data sets. The experiments are performed on Celeron R (2.4 G.hz), platform with MS-Windows XP and 512 MBytes of main memory. The Xerces Java SAX parser 1 [14] and the xmlgen the The Benchmark Data Generator [13] are used to parse and to generate XML data. We have implemented the 4 algorithms in PL/SQL language and represented the data sets in ORACLE 9.i. The data sets and the query workload are chosen as follows.

Data sets. Using the Benchmark Data Generator, we generated three data sets D_0, D_1 and D_2 with the sizes 17MB, 30MB and 47 MB respectively. The properties of 3 data sets are as below:

Data set	No. of Nodes	No. of Edges	No. of ref. edges	No. of Labels
D_0	250732	296101	45370	76
D_1	421006	497491	76486	76
D_2	673241	796329	123089	76

For each data set we also built the 1-index and strong 1-index. The properties of the index graphes are as below:

Data set	1-index		strong 1-index	
	No. of Nodes	No. of Edges	No. of b. edges	No. of r. edges
D_0	113004	150353	123003	37350
D_1	189461	252451	189460	62991
D_2	302663	404432	302662	101770

Query Workload. We generated 144 primary queries above 3 data sets. The lengths of queries are between 8 and 12. For the simplicity, we assume that the input set contains only the root, $I = \{root\}$, and the output set is the whole set of nodes, $O = V$. We used the top down approach for the query evaluation.

5.1   Performance Result

Cost model. Because there no standard storage scheme and query cost model exists for graph structured data we adopt the same main-memory cost metric similar to those used in [8,9]. The cost of the NI and NA algorithm is the number of visited edges in step 2, when we compute the transitive closure relation of the state data graph. The cost of the NT and TI algorithms with top-down approach is the sum of following numbers: (1) The number of the records in relation R_1 in step 2; (2) The number of the records in relation R_1' (3) The number of the visited edges of the link graph in relation R_2' using R_1' as the first rule [1] (4) The number of the records in relation R_3' as we use R_2' as semi join precondition [1]. Note that we do not count the data nodes in the extents of index nodes in the TI and NI algorithms, and the complexity in join operations are ignored.

With the above cost metric the average of the cost of the queries evaluation with 4 algorithms is shown below.

Data set	Algorithms			
	N	NI	NT	TI
D_0	4780	2030	932	634
D_1	8146	3401	1592	1077
D_2	13088	5446	2544	1722

The average cost of the TI algorithm is about 13% of the N algorithm's, about 36% of the NI algorithm's and about 68% of the NT algorithm's. The results demonstrate the performance of the TI algorithm over other algorithms.

6   Related Work

Several more recent query languages and DBMS's [2,3,4,5,6] have been considered for semi-structured data. Two of the most famous DBMS's for semi-structured data are: *UnQL* [2,3] and *Lore* [4,5]. Structural recursion is the basis of the syntax and semantics of query languages for semi-structured data and XML in *UnQL*. Queries are translated into structural recursion. The queries evaluation optimization is based on the properties of structural recursion. Bulk semantics of structural recursion is the spirit of our naive query evaluation algorithm. *Lore* decomposes queries into simple path expressions. With two main operators, *Scan* and *Join*, the problem of optimizing a path expression is similar to the join ordering in relational databases. The basic tree structure of XML data is not mentioned in both of *Lore* and *UnQL* since they are designed for semi-structured data.

The most popular structural indexes are the 1-index [7], the $A(k)$-index [8], the $D(k)$-index [9], the $M(k)$-index and the $M^*(k)$-index [10]. The 1-index is based on the notion of bisimulation. All nodes in the same partition have the same set of incoming label paths. We can evaluate accurately any path expression on the 1-index. The $A(k)$-index is based on the notion of k-bisimilarity, which can be considered as weakening of the bisimulation. All nodes in the same partition have the same set of incoming label paths not longer than k. Thus, with the $A(k)$-index all path expressions not longer than k can be evaluated accurately. The $D(k)-$, the $M(k)-$ and the $M^*(k)$-indexes are based on the notion of the dynamic local similarity, which means different index nodes have different local similarity requirements that can be tailored to support a given set of frequently used path expressions. The values of k depend on the length of the path expressions and they can be adjusted dynamically to adapt changing query load. All of these structural indexes do not distinguishe between the tree structure of a document and its link structure.

7   Conclusion

We have introduced and described a new approach for query evaluation on XML data by combining tree structure- and structural indexes. We propose the strong

1-indexes to simulate data graph, which are safe and backward precise and the basic tree is preserved in the strong 1-indexes. Building tree structure index on the basic trees of the strong indexes improves the efficiency of the query bulk-semantic evaluation. We also described and introduced efficient algorithms to construct these indexes. Our experiments show that our new approach yields the query evaluation higher effectiveness than just applying tree-structure or structural indexes separately. By implementing all algorithms in PL/SQL (using ORACLE 9i), we believe that our algorithms can be implemented for trade.

References

1. Kiss, A., Anh, V. L.: A solution for regular queries on XML Data. In 5th Joint Conference on Mathematics and Computer Science. Full paper at http://people.inf.elte.hu/leanhvu/papers/macs-abs.pdf (2004)
2. Buneman, P., Davidson, S., Hillebrand, G., Suciu, D.: A query language and optimization techniques for unstructured data. In Proceedings of ACM-SIGMOD International Conference on Management of Data (1996) 505-516
3. Buneman, P., Fernandez, M., Suciu, D.: UNQL: A query language and algebra for semi-structured data based on structural recursion. In VLDB J.9, 1 (2000) 76-110
4. McHugh, J., Abiteboul, S., Goldman, R., Quass, D., Widom, J.: The Lorel query language for semi-structured data. In International Journal on Digital Libraries (1997) 68-88
5. McHugh, J., Widom, J.: Query optimization for xml. In In Proceedings of VLDB, Edinburgh, UK, September (1999)
6. Deutsch, A., Fernandez, M., Florescu, D., Levy, A., Suciu, D. M.: A query language for xml. In Proceedings of the Eights International World Wide Web Conference (WWW8), Toronto (1999)
7. Milo, T., Suciu, D.: Index Structures for Path Expressions. In ICDT (1999)
8. Kaushik, R., Shenoy, P., Bohannon, P., Gudes, E.: Exploiting Local Similarity for Efficient Indexing of Paths in Graph Structured Data. In ICDE (2002)
9. Chen, Q., Lim, A., Ong, K. W.: D(K)-Index: An Adaptive structural Summary for Graph-Structured Data. In ACM SIGMOD (2003)
10. He, H., Yang, J.: Multiresolution Indexing of XML for Frequent Queries. In Proceedings of the 20th International Conference on Data Engineering (2004)
11. R.Paige, R., Tarjan, R.: Three Partition Refinement Algorithms. In SIAM Journal of Computing (1987) 16:973-988
12. Buneman, P., Davidson, S. B., Fernandez, M. F., Suciu, D.: 1997. Adding Structure to Unstructured Data. In Proceedings of the 6th International Conference on Database Theory (1997) 336-350
13. XMark: The xml benmark project. http://monetdb.cwi.nl/xml/index.html
14. The apache xml project - Xerces Java Parsers. http://xml.apache.org/xerces-j/
15. XML Path Language (XPath) 2.0. http://www.w3.org/TR/xpath20/, 04 April (2005)
16. XQuery 1.0: An XML Query Language. http://www.w3.org/TR/xquery/, 04 April (2005)

A DataGuide-Based Concurrency Control Protocol for Cooperation on XML Data[*]

Peter Pleshachkov[1], Petr Chardin[2], and Sergey Kuznetsov[3]

[1] Institute for System Programming RAS, Russia
peter@ispras.ru
[2] Moscow State University, Russia
pchardin@acm.org
[3] Institute for System Programming RAS, Russia
kuzloc@ispras.ru

Abstract. Concurrency control has been a hot area for quite some time. Today, when XML gains more and more attention, new concurrency control methods for accessing XML data are developed. There was proposed a number of protocols suited for XML. Grabs et al. presented DGLOCK locking protocol based on the DataGuide. This approach resulted in a major concurrency increase for XML data.

In this paper, we propose a new XPath-based DataGuide locking protocol, which extends and generalizes on the hierarchical data locking protocol. Our protocol (1) may be implemented on top of any existing system, (2) provides a high degree of concurrency and (3) produces serializable schedules. The protocol suites for XPath operations very well, as it captures XPath navigational behaviour. Our method also takes into account the semantics of update operations to increase concurrency. The paper presents formal proof of correctness for the protocol.

1 Introduction

Whenever a user deals with a Database Management System (DBMS) he expects it to behave as if he were the only person working with the system. Concurrent operations executed by other users should not interfere with his work. Without proper protection one may experience all kinds of problems, starting with reading dirty or inconsistent data and ending with loosing up large data pieces. DBMS should provide such protection for the users.

For this purpose, a number of concurrecy control protocols has been proposed. Basically, concurrency control protocols use two ways to resolve a conflict. They can either block or rollback one of the conflicting transactions. And since in the case of rollback we loose a lot of resources, already spent to process a transaction, locking techniques are more popular.

Locking-based methods require a transaction to lock objects it is going to work with. Transaction is allowed to proceed if the locks it requested on desired objects are compatible with locks held by other transactions.

---

[*] This work was partially supported by the grant of the Russian Basic Research Foundation (RBRF) N 05-07-90204.

J. Eder et al. (Eds.): ADBIS 2005, LNCS 3631, pp. 268–282, 2005.

Today, when networking changes the face of computer systems, applications require easy and well-structured way to exchange and describe data. eXtensible Markup Language [1] was proposed to answer these needs.

Widespread usage of XML in digital libraries, scientific repositories and across the web resulted in huge XML document collections, which are hard to manage. The need of effective XML processing prompted the development of concurrency control techniques suited specifically for XML.

Most of such methods provide node-level locking [2,3,5]. On the one hand, these methods provide a high degree of concurrency. On the other hand, the lock manager should manage a large number of locks to process large documents. It leads to significant increase of the lock manager's table, which results in the system performance loss. To alleviate this problem, lock escalation procedure should be employed. The procedure handles the conversion of many fine-granularity locks into fewer carse-granularity locks. Unfortunately, this method usually leads to a major concurrency decrease.

Experimental evaluation made by Grabs et al. [4] showed that utilizing of the DataGuide structure allows to improve performance of concurrent queries and updates of XML data. Besides, DataGuide approach significantly reduces the lock manager's memory requirements.

A DataGuide is a data structure that is essentially a compact representation of the document tree. It is concise and accurate because DataGuide describes every unique label path of a document exactly once, regardless of the number of times it appears in that document, and encodes no label path that does not appear in the document [6,7]. It serves as a dynamic schema and plays an important role in query formulation, query optimization and indexing XML documents.

Grabs et al. [4] proposed to extend the usage of this structure. In the DGLOCK protocol, DataGuide also serves for locking. An important benefit of this scheme is an ability to perform fine-grained locking without giving the locking algorithm access to the XML documents themselves. This is quite useful as the tree representation of the documents in some cases is not available to the lock manager.

As it has been already mentioned, the main task of concurrency control system is to protect concurrently executing transactions from each other. Usually, we would like to check that transactions are serialized properly. Serializability [8] requires that concurrent transactions produce the same result that we would get if they were executed in a certain sequential order. This simple condition guarantees that we won't get any problems because of concurrent execution.

In a short paper [9], we presented a research snapshot of XPath-based DataGuide Locking protocol (XDGL). In this paper we give more formal description of the protocol and present a formal proof of correctness.

Our protocol ensures serializability and provides high degree of concurrency within the same XML document. In the proposed method, we use a subset of well-known XPath [10] language to access the document nodes and insert/delete operators to modify document. In our locking method, we employ the DataGuide structure for locking purposes rather than document itself. We use combination of tree and node locks on DataGuide. We also take into account the semantics of update operations to increase concurrency. Our locking method enforces strict serializability and prevents appearance of phantoms [11]. We also present the proof of correctness for XDGL.

The rest of the paper is organized as follows. The next section gives an overview of related work, section 3 introduces some definitions, the XML query and update languages, we refer through the paper. Section 4 presents the proposed locking protocol. It is followed by a section devoted to the proof of correctness for XDGL. We make conclusions in the section 6.

2   Related Work

Various scheduling mechanisms have been developed to deal with XML data effectively. In this section, we will discuss these techniques, their pitfalls and benefits.

The first category of scheduling methods is based on existing technologies originally developed for relational, hierarchical and object-oriented DBMSs. Some of these methods use RDBMS's internal locking mechanisms to provide concurrency control. Unfortunately, for all representations of XML data, these methods usually tend to cause locks that are too restrictive. This is due to the fact that RDBMS lock manager does not take into account the tree-like structure of the document, stored in the tables. This results in a quite low concurrency level for read and update operations. For a bit more detailed overview of these problems see [5].

Another group of well-known methods adopted in order to deal with XML consists of hierarchical and tree locking methods. One might think that these methods should handle XML data rather well because of the hierarchical nature of XML documents. However, these methods do not provide sufficient level of concurrency at first, and do not suite well for XPath queries at second. Detailed studies of these problems may be found in [5]. The problem with XPath queries stems from the locking rules of these protocols. According to these protocols, lock must be acquired top-down. That is, if one has locked a certain node, he cannot lock a parent or sibling node. This retricts the usage of the parent, following sibling and preceding sibling axes in XPath expressions. The third problem, which is a common one for the majority proposed locking methods, is the growth of the locking structures size. The size could be really huge for large documents.

Now we will give an overview of concurrency control methods, specifically tailored for XML data.

Several protocols [2,3] based on the DOM operations were proposed. The protocols use different kinds of locks to latch nodes on different levels. Besides Helmer et al.'s [3] method utilizes Document Type Definition (DTD) to reduce the number of conflicts. These seem to work fine for DOM operations, but there is no research done to see whether they could suite well the evaluation of path expressions.

The protocols developed in [5,12,13] rely on the fact that XML is usually accessed by means of XPath query language. They propose to use "path locks" to increase concurrency and provide the best results for XPath queries. But unfortunately, these methods have a number of shortcomings. In [5], the authors deal with too restrictive subset of XPath. The other works deal with more complex XPath queries, but the conflict determination for them becomes too expensive. Besides these methods are also quite "memory-hungry". If we have to deal with huge documents, it becomes a major problem.

As it has been already mentioned, all previously considered methods tend to request too many locks while working with large documents. Besides, many of them require direct access to the XML document, which is not possible in many cases. The solution to these problems was proposed by Grabs et al. in [4]. They developed a DGLOCK protocol, which utilizes a DataGuide for locking purposes.

We consider this approach to be the most promising. However, the original protocol has a number of serious drawbacks. At first, DGLOCK does not prevent phantoms and does not guarantee for serializability of produced schedules. These problems are the most serious. Another important disadvantage of Grabs's method is the fact that it does not support the use of the descendant axis, which is very important for XPath query processing. The method presented in this paper solves these problems.

3   Preliminaries

This section introduces the notions, which are of interest in this paper, and gives an overview of query and update languages. Moreover, in the Fig. 1 we present an example of XML document *Gtree*, its DTD and DataGuide. We will use *Gtree* document in all examples throughout the paper.

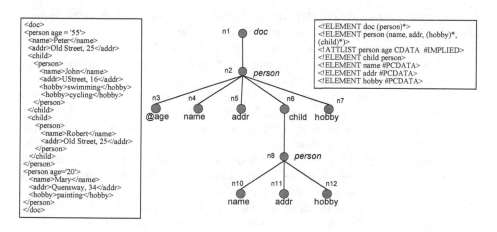

Fig. 1. An XML document *GTree*, its DataGuide and DTD

Definition 1. *An action is a pair a(op, t); where op is one of the operations defined in Sections 3.1, 3.2; t is a transaction identifier.*

Definition 2. *A transaction T is a finite list of actions that have the same transaction identifier t and the last T's operation is commit.*

Definition 3. *Commit (C for short) operation is one that terminates the execution of transaction. It releases all locks acquired by transaction and removes DataGuide's label paths which are not actually present in the document (see the delete operation semantics for details).*

3.1   XPath

The user can access the documents through XPath [10] queries. XPath provides a restricted variation of regular path expressions. XPath is widely recognized in the industry and used within XQuery [14] and XSLT [15]. In this paper, we focus on XPath although our framework is applicable to any regular path expression. We are based on a restricted version of XPath language. Its syntax is defined by the following grammar:

```
locpath := '/' relpath | '//' relpath
relpath := locstep ('/' | '//') locstep | locstep
locstep := axis '::' ntest ('[' spred ']')?
axis    := 'self' | 'child' | 'attribute' | 'descendant' |
           'descendant-or-self'
ntest   := NCName | '@' NCName | '*' | '@' '*'
spred   := ntest relop const
relop   := '=' | '!=' | '<' | '<=' | '>' | '>='
const   := number | string
```

The main syntactical construction in XPath is location path. A location path consists of several location steps syntactically separated by '/' or '//'. A location step may optionally include a simple predicate enclosed in square brackets. At last, 'ntest' denotes names labeling document nodes (elements or attributes) or the wildcard '*' that matches all nodes.

A location path evaluates from left to right. A sequence of context nodes provides the initial point from which each location step starts with. For each context node a step generates a sequence of items and then filters the sequence by predicate. A step returns a sequence of nodes in turn that are reachable from the context node via specified axis. An axis defines the 'direction of movement' for the step. A node test selects nodes based on their name. The resulting sequences are unioned together to form the sequence of context nodes for a subsequent step, if there are any. The final result of the location path is the result of the last location step. Thus, the last location step defines the *target nodes* of location path.

Location path imposes two kinds of constraints on the desired nodes: (1) *structural constraints* expressed via axes and node test, (2) *value-based constraints* expressed via predicates.

The *main branch* of location path is the one that matches the target nodes of location path. We will call other branches of location path, which impose value-based predicate, *additional branches*.

Our grammar describes the unabbreviated and abbreviated syntax of location paths, but in our examples we will follow an abbreviated syntax where it is possible. An abbreviation Q denotes any query expressed in XPath.

Here we should note that though we restrict XPath for the ease of presentation, there are no principal constraints which deny XDGL from dealing with full set of XPath operations.

3.2   Update Language

Now we describe a set of update operations on XML documents. We define only two kinds of primitive updates: insert and delete operators. It is obvious, that any complex update operation may be expressed as a combination of inserts and deletes.

```
update  := 'InsertInto' '(' constr1 ',' locpath ')' |
           'InsertBefore' '(' constr2 ',' locpath ')' |
           'InsertAfter' '(' constr2 ',' locpath ')' |
           'Delete' '(' locpath ')'
constr1:= 'element' '{' NCName '}'  content |
           'attribute' '{' NCName '}' content
constr2 := 'element' '{' NCName '}'  content
content    := '{' PCDATA '}' | '{' '}'
```

The update operations take a set of parameters (*constr1*, *constr2*, and *locpath*). The *constr1* or *constr2* defines a new node to be inserted. It is possibly an empty element (or attribute). The *locpath* matches *target nodes* to be updated.

- *InsertInto(constr1, locpath)*: inserts new node (element or attribute) as the last child for each target node. An attempt to insert an attribute with the same name as an existing attribute fails.
- *InsertBefore(constr2, locpath)*: inserts new node (only element, not attribute) as the preceding sibling for each target node. *InsertAfter(constr2, locpath)* is defined analogously.
- *Delete(locpath)*: removes subtrees specified by *target* nodes. That is, our delete operator uses the deep deletion semantics. There is an important feature of the delete operator: if it removes *all* nodes in the document which correspond to the label path in the DataGuide then this label path is not deleted until the end of transaction.

Our update language is the subset of Tatarinov et al. proposal. For more details see [16].

Below in this paper, we use I_I, I_A, I_B and D to denote *InsertInto*, *InsertAfter*, *InsertBefore* and *Delete* operations (respectively). Besides, we use I_* to denote arbitrary insert operation.

4   Proposed Locking Method

In this section, we introduce granular locking protocol on DataGuide called *XDGL*. It is based on the Grabs et al.'s work [4], which propose DataGuide-based locking (DGLOCK) protocol.

XDGL requires transaction to follow the strict two-phase locking protocol (S2PL)[11]. According to S2PL, a transaction acquired a lock keeps it until the end.

As well as Grabs's method, XDGL requires transaction to obtain intention locks on ancestors of x before accessing a data item x. It ensures that there are no locks in the conflicting mode on the coarser granules (containing x).

According to DGLOCK, a lock on a coarser granule x explicitly locks x and implicitly locks all of x's proper descendants, which are finer granules contained in x. But this requirement is too restrictive for concurrent Q and I_* XML operations. For details see example 1. However, due to the semantics of D operation transaction must lock the entire subtree to remove it. For these reasons in XDGL we use both (1) locks on the DataGuide's nodes and (2) locks on the DataGuide's subtrees. The locks of the first and second type we will call *node locks* and *tree locks* respectively.

Example 1. Let us suppose that transaction T_1 has issued the query /doc/person/name. It should be possible for transaction T_2 to perform the *InsertInto(element {person} {}, /doc)* operation concurrently. However, according to DGLOCK locking rules, transactions T_1 and T_2 are in conflict since the intention shared lock on n_2 required by T_1 is not compatible with the exclusive lock on n_2 required by T_2 (see Fig. 1). Thus, T_1 and T_2 cannot be executed concurrently.

Like DGLOCK, XDGL takes into account both structural and value-based constraints. In XDGL the node and tree locks have to cope with structural constraints. To deal with value-based constraints, each lock has an annotated value-based predicate (VBP).

Another issue, which should be carefully handled, is the phantoms problem [11] that is not solved by DGLOCK. For example, the queries with descendant axes may suffer from phantoms. The straightforward solution of this problem is to lock coarser granules (usually the entire document). Obviously, in some cases this solution is too restrictive. In XDGL, we employ special logical locks to prevent phantoms.

Finally, we introduce some special node locks that prevent the *document order conflicts* during the execution of concurrent I_* operations. For example, the document order conflict arises if one transaction inserts new node as the last child into a node and at the same time another transaction also inserts new node as the last child into the same node.

4.1   Node and Tree Locks

Below we describe a set of all node and tree locks used in XDGL.

– *SI* (shared into) lock. This *node lock* is used by I_I operation. It is set on the DataGuide's nodes which matches the target nodes of I_I. This lock prevents the deletion of I_I's target nodes and insertion of another nodes *into* the target nodes by concurrent transactions. The *SA* (shared after) and *SB* (shared before) locks are defined in a similar way.

- *X* (exclusive) lock. This *node lock* is used by I_* operations. It is set on the DataGuide's node which matches the newly created node in the document. This lock serves for preventing the reading and deletion of new node by concurrent Q, I_* and D operations of another transaction.
- *ST* (shared tree) lock. This *tree lock* is used by Q, I_* and D operations. It is set on the DataGuide's node and implicitly locks all its descendants. That is, *ST* lock prevents any updates inside the entire subtree.
- *XT* (exclusive tree) lock. This *tree lock* is used by D operations. It is set on the DataGuide's node which matches the target nodes of D operation. The *XT* lock prevents any readings and updates inside the entire subtree defined by target nodes. Note that D operation does not affect the DataGuide. This is the responsibility of C operation to remove the DataGuide's nodes, if all nodes in the document related to them were deleted.
- *IS* (intention shared) lock. This *node lock* must be obtained on each ancestor of the node, which is to be locked in one of the shared modes. It ensures for lack of any locks on the coarser granules containing the node in the conflicting mode. *IX* (intention exclusive) lock is defined in a similar way.

Each of these locks is annotated with VBPs which impose additional constraints on the node's value in the *document*. *IX* and *IS* locks are always annotated with $\#t$ (true) predicate. The XDGL's compatibility matrix for node and tree locks is shown in Fig. 2.

There are no strict incompatibilities in matrix. Symbol 'P' in matrix means that the requested lock is compatible with granted locks only if $\cup_i P_i^{granted} \cap P^{requested} = \emptyset$; where $P_i^{granted}$ ($P^{requested}$) are the VBPs of granted (requested) lock.

requested	granted							
	SI	SA	SB	X	ST	XT	IS	IX
SI	P	+	+	P	+	P	+	+
SA	+	P	+	P	+	P	+	+
SB	+	+	P	P	+	P	+	+
X	P	P	P	P	P	P	+	+
ST	+	+	+	P	+	P	+	P
XT	P	P	P	P	P	P	P	P
IS	+	+	+	+	+	P	+	+
IX	+	+	+	+	P	P	+	+

Fig. 2. Lock Compatibility Matrix

Note, that IX and X locks are strictly compatible since IX lock on a node only implies the intention to update the descendants of the node. But it does not imply any updates on the node itself. For the same reasons, S and IX locks are also compatible. SI (SA, SB) lock is not compatible with SI (SA, SB) lock, which prevents concurrent I_I (I_A, I_B) operations upon the same node. Thus, SI, SA and SB locks serve for preventing document order conflicts.

4.2   Logical Locks

Now we turn to the discussion of the logical locks, which are used to prevent phantoms. Let us show how a phantom could appear. Suppose that transaction T_1 reads all of *age* attributes in *GTree*(i.e. T_1 issued //@age query). In the meantime transaction T_2 inserts new *age* attribute into *person* element with *name* 'John' (see Fig. 1). The new *age* attribute is the phantom for transaction T_1. Generally speaking, phantoms can appear when (a) the I_* operation extends the DataGuide (adds new path to DataGuide) and (b) the insertion of new node results in the changing of target nodes of previously executed operations.

Thus, we introduce two locks. The first lock is L (logical) lock, which must be set on DataGuide's node to protect the node's subtrees in the document from a phantom appearance. A logical lock specifies a set of *properties*. Essentially, a property is a logical condition on nodes. This lock prohibits the insertion of new nodes, which possess these properties. The second lock is IN (insert new node) lock, which specifies the properties of new node. The I_* operation, which extends the DataGuide, should obtain the IN lock on each ancestor of the new node.

Here we list all possible combinations of properties for L lock: (1) node-name='name1' (e.g. //person), (2) node-name='name1', node-value *relop* 'val1' (e.g. //name[.≠'John']), (3) node-name='name1', child-name='name2', child-value *relop* 'val1' (e.g. //person[name ≠ 'John']). Here *relop* is a comparison operation (see XPath grammar in the section 3.1).

To check that the new node's properties do not interfere with the L lock properties, the IN lock should specify three properties of a new node: new-node-parent-name, new-node-name, new-node-value.

Thus, L and IN locks are incompatible if one of the following conditions holds:

- If IN's new-node-name equals to a node-name of L lock and L does not contain any other properties (case (1) from the above).
- If IN's new-node-name and new-node-value both match appropriate values of L lock consisting of two properties. That is, node-name=new-node-name and new-node-value relop 'val1' ≠ #f (case (2) from the above).
- If all IN's properties match three properties of L lock. That is node-name=new-node-parent-name, child-name=new-node-name and new-node-value relop 'val1' ≠ #f (case (3)).

If node's name is a wildcard '*' then it equals to any node-name.

4.3   XDGL Scheduler

Now we describe the XDGL scheduler steps for a new action $a(op_i, t_j)$.

1. Extract the *data-path-set* DP of all label paths in DataGuide that lead to data queried or updated by $a(op_i, t_j)$.
2. Compute the *node-predicate-set* $NP = \{(n_j, p_j)\}$; where n_j is the node of DataGuide that matches any label path from DP and p_j is the VBP on n_j extracted from op_i.
3. Compute the *phantom-set* $PH = \{(n_j, properties_j)\}$; where n_j defines the DataGuide's node where a phantom could appear, $properties_j$ specify the properties of nodes to be logically locked.
4. If op_i is an I_* operation and it extends the DataGuide then compute the $properties_i$ of new node.
5. Obtain the node and tree locks needed for op_i
   - Let op_i be a Q operation. For each $n_j \in NP$ performs: (1) obtain (ST, p_j) lock on n_j, (2) obtain $(IS, \#t)$ lock on n_j's ancestors.
   - Let op_i be an I_I operation. For each $n_j \in NP$ performs: (1) if n_j matches the target nodes of I_I then obtain (SI, p_j) lock on n_j and $(IS, \#t)$ lock on its ancestors, (2) if n_j matches the additional branches of I_I's location path then obtain (ST, p_j) lock on n_j and $(IS, \#t)$ lock on its ancestors, (3) if n_j matches the new node inserted by I_I then obtain (X, p_j) lock on n_j and $(IX, \#t)$ lock on its ancestors.
   - Let op_i be an I_A or I_B operation. Perform the steps similar to the previous point's steps.
   - Let op_i be a D operation. For each $n_j \in NP$ performs: (1) if n_j matches the target nodes of D then obtain (XT, p_j) lock on n_j and $(IX, \#t)$ lock on its ancestors, (2) if n_j matches the additional branches of D's location path then obtain (ST, p_j) lock on n_j and $(IS, \#t)$ lock on its ancestors
6. For each $n_j \in PH$ set $(L, properties_j)$ lock on n_j.
7. If op_i is an I_* operation and it extends the DataGuide then obtain *(IN, properties_i)* lock on ancestors of DataGuide's node which matches the new node inserted by I_*.
8. If two locks are not compatible then XDGL scheduler delays $a(op_i, t_j)$.

Next we consider a couple of examples to illustrate the above points.

Example 2. Consider transactions $T_1 = \{/doc/person[@age=`55`]/name\}$ and $T_2 = \{InsertInto(/doc, element\{person\}\{\})\}$ (see Fig. 1). We will show that XDGL scheduler allows to run T_1 and T_2 concurrently.

   Let us apply XDGL rules to T_1: $DP = \{/doc/person/@age, /doc/person/name\}$, $NP = \{(n_3, @age=`55`), (n_4, \#t)\}$, $PH = \{\}$, $n_3:(ST, @age=`55`)$, $n_1, n_2:(IS, \#t)$, $n_4: (ST, \#t)$.

   For T_2 XDGL rules produce the following results: $DP = \{/doc, /doc/person\}$, $NP = \{(n_1, \#t), (n_2, \#t)\}$, $PH = \{\}$, $n_1:(SI, \#t)$, $n_2:(X, \#t)$, $n_1: (IX, \#t)$

   Since locks on n_1 and n_2, required by T_1 and T_2 are compatible, we conclude that T_1 and T_2 can be executed concurrently.

Example 3. Now we will study XDGL behavior in processing transactions $T_1 = \{/doc/person[name='Peter']//@age[. \neq 10]\}$ and $T_2 = \{InsertInto(/doc/person/child/person, attribute\{age\}\{9\})\}$. Let us show that XDGL scheduler prevents the insertion of the phantom (*age* attribute). In other words if T_1 starts before T_2 then T_2 could only proceed when T_1 has ended.

Here are results of XDGL rules, applied to T_1: $DP=\{/doc/person/name, doc/person/@age\}$, $NP=\{(n_4, name = 'Peter'), (n_3, @age \neq 10)\}$, $PH=\{(n_2, (node-name='age', node-value \neq 10))\}$, $n_4:(ST, name='Peter')$, n_1, $n_2:(IS, \#t)$, $n_3:(ST, @age \neq 10)$, $n_2:(L, (node-name='age', node-value \neq 10))$.

Now, let us apply XDGL rules to T_2: $DP=\{/doc/person/child/person, /doc/person/child/person/@age\}$, $NP=\{(n_8, \#t), (n_9, @age=9)\}$; where n_9 is the identifier of the DataGuide's new node; $PH=\{\}$, $n_8:(SI, \#t)$, n_1, n_2, $n_6:(IS, \#t)$, $n_9:(X, @age=9)$, n_1, n_2, n_6, $n_8:(IX, \#t)$. Since n_9 is a new node in DataGuide XDGL also requires the following locks: $n_8,n_6,n_2,n_1:(IN, (new-node-parent-name ='person', new-node-name='@age', new-node-value=9))$.

As the properties of L lock on n_2 (obtained by T_1) match the properties of IN lock on the same node (requested by T_2), XDGL delays the execution of T_2.

5   Correctness of XDGL Scheduler

This section contains the proof of correctness for XDGL locking method. Here we introduce required definitions and notions.

Definition 4. *A schedule S is an interleaving of a set of transactions.*

Definition 5. *We say that a schedule S is a legal schedule if and only if at any step i, a set of all obtained locks L_i^S contains only compatible locks.*

Definition 6. *Schedules S and S' are called equivalent, if (1) the first is a permutation (preserving the order of actions within a transaction) of the second, (2) the resulting document is in both cases the same, and (3) all the queries in the first schedule return the same result as the corresponding queries in the second schedule.*

Definition 7. *Schedule S is serializable, if it is equivalent to some serial schedule.*

To prove that XDGL scheduler is correct, we have to prove that all schedules it could produce are serializable. Our proof consists of two steps. First, we prove some properties of XDGL's schedules in lemmas 1, 2 and 3. Then, we prove that any schedule with these properties is serializable.

We presume some ordering on the transaction identifiers used in S such that $t_i < t_j$ if the commit of t_j follows commit of t_i in S or there is a commit of t_i but there are no commit of t_j in S. According to this order we will serialize the schedule S generated by XDGL.

Let schedule S' be a schedule resulted in swapping two consecutive actions $a(op_i, t_i)$ and $a(op_{i+1}, t_j)$ in S ($t_j < t_i$). We use L_i^S to denote the set of all locks obtained by transactions after processing the i-th step of S. The $l_i^S(op_i)$ denotes a set of all locks acquired (or released) by op_i in schedule S. D_i^S denotes the resulting document after the i-th step.

Lemma 1. *If S is a legal schedule then S' is also a legal schedule.*

Proof. It is clear that S' is a legal schedule if the following conditions hold: (1) all locks in $L_i^{S'}$ are compatible, (2) $L_{i+1}^{S'} \subseteq L_{i+1}^S$

- $op_i, op_{i+1} \in \{Q, I_*, D\}$. Since Q, I_* and D operations do not remove locks, we have $L_{i+1}^S = L_{i-1}^S \cup l_i^S(op_i) \cup l_{i+1}^S(op_{i+1})$ and $L_i^{S'} = L_{i-1}^{S'} \cup l_i^{S'}(op_{i+1}) \cup l_{i+1}^{S'}(op_i)$.
  Suppose $op_i, op_{i+1} \in \{Q, D\}$. Since Q and D does not change the DataGuide, it follows that $l_{i+1}^{S'}(op_i) = l_i^S(op_i)$ and $l_i^{S'}(op_{i+1}) = l_{i+1}^S(op_{i+1})$.
  If $op_i, op_{i+1} \in \{Q, I_*, D\}$. The only case $l_{i+1}^{S'}(op_i) \neq l_i^S(op_i)$ ($l_i^{S'}(op_{i+1}) \neq l_{i+1}^S(op_i)$) when the *target nodes* of op_i (op_{i+1}) contains the nodes inserted by op_{i+1} (op_i) i.e. $op_{i+1} \in I_*$ ($op_{i+1} \in I_*$). Since each of locks ST, SI, SA, SB and XT are not compatible with X lock (taking into account VBPs), we have got a contradiction.
  We have $L_i^{S'} = L_i^S$ and $L_{i+1}^{S'} = L_{i+1}^S$. Thus, we proved (1) and (2).
- $op_{i+1} \in C$ (if $op_i \in C$ then the swapping is not needed). Since C removes locks from the DataGuide it follows $L_{i+1}^S = L_{i-1}^S \cup l_i^S(op_i) \setminus l_{i+1}^S(op_{i+1})$ and $L_i^{S'} = L_{i-1}^{S'} \setminus l_i^{S'}(op_{i+1})$. Since $l_{i+1}^S(op_{i+1}) = l_i^{S'}(op_{i+1})$, we obtain $L_i^{S'} \subseteq L_{i+1}^S$. Therefore (1) is correct.
  If $L_{i+1}^{S'} \neq L_{i+1}^S$, then the commit removes the nodes that are the *target nodes* of op_i. It is impossible as ST, SI, SA, SB and XT locks are not compatible with XT lock (taking VBPs into account). □

Lemma 2. *If S is a legal schedule and at least one of the operations op_i or op_{i+1} in S is a query then results of op_i and op_{i+1} in S' are the same.*

Proof. Since query does not change the document, we only have to consider all combinations of a query and update (non-query) operations.

- $(I_*, Q) \rightarrow (Q, I_*)$. If I_* changes the result of Q then ST lock and X (or IX) lock (taking VBPs into account) are obtained by different transactions on the same node. We have got a contradiction. Thus, in this case the lemma's statement is correct.
- $(Q, I_*) \rightarrow (I_*, Q)$. If I_* inserts new node, which matches the existing label path in DataGuide, then the outcome of Q does not change with the same reasons as in the previous point. So, we need to consider a situation, when I_* extends the DataGuide. In other words, the I_* inserts the phantom. But because of XDGL locking rules the Q is protected against phantoms by means of L lock.
- $(D, Q) \rightarrow (Q, D)$. If D changes the outcome of the query then the query needs ST lock which conflicts with XT (or IX) lock that D requires.

- $(Q, D) \rightarrow (D, Q)$. See previous point
- $(Q, C) \rightarrow (C, Q)$. Since C does not change the document (it only releases locks and removes edges from DataGuide, if any) it cannot change the result of the Q.
- $(C, Q) \rightarrow (Q, C)$. This permutation is not needed for reduction S to the serial schedule. ☐

Lemma 3. *If S is a legal schedule, then $D_{i+1}^S = D_{i+1}^{S'}$*

Proof. Since a query does not change the document, the documents are equal when at least one op_i (or op_j) is a query.

- $(I_I, I_I) \rightarrow (I_I, I_I)$. There are two cases when two I_I operations do not commute. (1) op_i and op_{i+1} insert into the same node. Then swapping of two operations resulted in the document order violation. (2) op_{i+1} inserts into the node created by op_i. Then, after swapping the *target nodes* of op_{i+1} will be empty and op_{i+1} does not insert any nodes.
  The first case is not possible since SI locks are not compatible with SI locks (taking VBPs into account), and S is a legal schedule. The second one is not possible because op_{i+1} requires SI locks on *target nodes*, but SI lock is not compatible with X lock (taking VBPs into account) required by op_i on newly created node.
  This way, we see that the swapping of (I_A, I_A) or (I_B, I_B) do not change resulting document, when the first $i + 1$ actions of the schedules S and S' are undertaken.
- $(I_I, I_A) \rightarrow (I_A, I_I)$. The only questionable situation about the document order preservation arises when I_A inserts the node n_x as the last right sibling of node n_y and I_I inserts a new node n_z into the parent of n_y. But it is obvious that such situation does not result to a problem.
  Similarly, any other combinations of I_I, I_A and I_B also leaves the document the same.
- $(I_*, D) \rightarrow (D, I_*)$ The only case when I_* and D do not commute arises when D deletes nodes inserted by I_*. But I_* acquires X lock on the created node (and IX on its ancestors); D must acquire XT on the same node (or its ancestors). As locks required by I_* and D are not compatible (taking VBPs into account), such situation is not possible.
- $(D, I_*) \rightarrow (I_*, D)$. This case is similar to the previous one.
- $(D, D) \rightarrow (D, D)$. By definition, these operations commute.
- The permutations $(C, I_*) \rightarrow (I_*, C)$ and $(C, D) \rightarrow (D, C)$ are not needed for reduction S to the serial schedule.
- $(D, C) \rightarrow (C, D)$, $(I_*, C) \rightarrow (C, I_*)$. There could be no problem with permutation of these operations.

We have considered all possible combinations of two adjacent operations and proved that the swapping of these operations does not change the document after $i + 1$ step or in other words $D_{i+1}^S = D_{i+1}^{S'}$. ☐

Theorem 1. *All schedules S generated by XDGL scheduler are serializable.*

Proof. We will consequently reduce a legal schedule S to a serial schedule S^{serial} by means of swapping two adjacent actions $a(op_i, t_i)$ and $a(op_{i+1}, t_j)$ where $(t_j < t_i)$. It is obvious, that the schedule is serial if there are no more such pairs.

Taking into account lemmas 2 and 3, we obtain that schedules S and S' are equivalent. Here S' was produced from S by swapping of two consecutive operations. In lemma 1 we proved that S' is a legal schedule. Thus, swapping of two consecutive operations in S' also resultes in equivalent schedule S''. Since a schedule is a finite list of actions and two actions should be swapped at the utmost only once, we conclude, that S can be reduced to S^{serial} by a finite number of swaps.   □

6   Conclusions

XML data is stored in many different ways today. Some methods rely on existing relational or object-oriented technologies to store and process XML. Other proposals prefer a Native XML approach. But any XML-processing system should provide a good means of concurrency control.

In this paper, we have presented a new XPath-based concurrency control protocol (XDGL), which might be implemented on top of any existing database management system. The usage of the DataGuide structure for locking allows to decrease memory requirements for the locking structures. Unlike previously proposed solutions, our protocol ensures strict serilizability and combines predicate and logical locks to provide protection from phantom appearance. It also provides higher degree of concurrency then existing DataGuide-based solutions. Finally, we have presented a formal proof of correctness for the XDGL.

References

1. Yergeau, F., Bray, T., Paoli, J., Sperberg-McQueen, C. M., Maler,E.: Extensible Markup Language, W3C Recommendation, http://w3.org/TR/2004/REC-xml-20040204, 4th February (2004)
2. Haustein, M., Harder, T.: taDOM: A Tailored Synchronization Concept with Tunable Lock Granularity for the DOM API. Proc. ADBIS , Dresden, Germany (2003)
3. Helmer, S., Kanne, C., Moerkotte, G.: Lock-based protocols for cooperation on XML documents. Proc. of the 14th Int. Workshop on Database and Expert Systems Applications (DEXA), Prague, Czech Republic.
4. Grabs, T., Bohm, K., Schek, H.–J.: XMLTM: efficient transaction management for XML documents, Proc. ACM CIKM, McLean, Virginia, USA (2002)
5. Dekeyser, S., Hidders, J.: Conflict Scheduling of Transactions on XML Documents. Proc. ADC, Dunedin, New Zealand (2004)
6. Goldman, R., Widom, J.: DataGuides: Enabling Query Formulation and Optimization in Semistructured DataBases. Proc. VLDB, Athens, Greece (1997)
7. McHugh, J., Abiteboul, S., Goldman, R., Quass, D., Widom, J.: Lore: A DataBase Management System for Semistructured Data. SIGMOD Record Vol. 26(3) (1997)

8. Weikum, G., Vossen, G.: Transactional Information Systems, Morgan Kaufmann (2002)
9. Pleshachkov, P., Chardin, P., Kuznetsov, S.: XDGL: XPath-Based Concurrency Control Protocol for XML Data. Proc. BNCOD Sunderland, UK (2005)
10. Berglund, A., Boag, S., Chamberlin, D., Fernandez, M. F., Kay, M., Robie, J., Simeon, J.: XML Path Language (XPath) 2.0. W3C Working Draft, http://www.w3.org/TR/2005/WD-xpath20-20050211/, 11 February (2005)
11. Eswaran, K. P., Gray, J., Lorie, R., Traiger, I.: The notions of consistency and predicate locks in a database systems. Comm of ACM, Vol. 19, No 11, November (1976) 624-633
12. Hye Choi, E., Kanai, T.: XPath-based Concurrency Control for XML Data. Proc. DEWS, Kaga city, Ishikawa, Japan (2003)
13. Jea, K., Chen, S., Wang, S.: Concurrency Control in XML Document DataBases: XPath Locking Protocol. Proc. ICPADS 2002, Taiwan, ROC, IEEE (2002)
14. Boag, S., Chamberlin, D., Fernandez, M., Florescu, D., Robie, J., Simeon, J.: XQuery 1.0: An XML Query Language. W3C Working Draft, http://www.w3.org/TR/xquery/, 11 February (2005)
15. Kay, M.: XSL Transformations (XSLT) Version 2.0. W3C Working Draft, http://www.w3.org/TR/2005/WD-xslt20-20050211/, 11 February (2005)
16. Tatarinov, I., Ives, Z., Halevy, A., Weld, D.: Updating XML. Proc. ACM SIGMOD, Santa Barbara, California, USA (2001)

Mining Fuzzy Classification Rules Using an Artificial Immune System with Boosting

Bilal Alatas and Erhan Akin

Department of Computer Engineering, Faculty of Engineering, Firat University, 23119, Elazig, Turkey
{balatas, eakin}@firat.edu.tr

Abstract. In this study, a classification model including fuzzy system, artificial immune system (AIS), and boosting is proposed. The model is mainly focused on the clonal selection principle of biological immune system and evolves a population of antibodies, where each antibody represents the antecedent of a fuzzy classification rule while each antigen represents an instance. The fuzzy classification rules are mined in an incremental fashion, in that the AIS optimizes one rule at a time. The boosting mechanism that is used to increase the accuracy rates of the rules reduces the weight of training instances that are correctly classified by the new rule. Whenever AIS mines a rule, this rule is added to the mined rule list and mining of next rule focuses on rules that account for the currently uncovered or misclassified instances. The results obtained by proposed approach are analyzed with respect to predictive accuracy and simplicity and compared with C4.5Rules.

1 Introduction

Data mining is the extraction of implicit, valid, potentially useful, and comprehensible knowledge from large volumes of raw data. The most common use of data mining is in the area of classification that is the task of inducing a model that assigns instances to their respective categories from an input data. The two most important evaluation criteria used in classification techniques are predictive accuracy, i.e. generalization, and comprehensibility, i.e. understandability by a human user. This classification model is useful for serving as an explanatory tool to distinguish between objects of different classes and determining the class label of unknown instances [1].

The vast majority of the classification models work within classic logic framework. However, to cope with continuous attributes, fuzzy logic is a natural way. Furthermore, fuzzy logic is a powerful, flexible method to cope with uncertainty and improves the rule comprehensibility.

This work proposes an algorithm for mining fuzzy classification rules of the form "IF (fuzzy conditions) THEN (class)" based on an AIS and boosting mechanism. AIS is a relatively new computational system based on metaphors of the natural immune system and designed to solve real-world problems [2]. Numerous immune algorithms now exist, based on theoretical immunology and observed immune functions, principles and models. The AIS used in this work is based on clonal selection principle [3] that is a form of natural selection. Boosting is a general method of

J. Eder et al. (Eds.): ADBIS 2005, LNCS 3631, pp. 283–293, 2005.

generating many simple classification rules and combining them into a single, highly accurate rule [4]. In this proposed approach, the boosting mechanism adapts the distribution of training instances in iterations, namely AIS pays more attention to the previously misclassified or uncovered instances. Thereby, cooperation among fuzzy rules is implicitly promoted.

One AIS for mining IF-THEN rules is proposed that is based on extending the negative selection algorithm with a genetic algorithm [5]. However, this method has some conceptual problems in the context of classification task, as discussed in [6]. The first AIS, called IFRAIS, is proposed for mining fuzzy classification rules in [7]. It starts with a full training set, creates a 'best' rule that covers a subset of the training data, adds the best rule to its discovered rule list, removes the instances covered by said rule from the training data, and starts again with a reduced training set. Namely, IFRAIS uses a 'separate-and-conquer' approach. Rules mined in later stages are unaware of the previously removed instances and therefore might be in conflict with rules mined earlier. Unexpected interactions between rules can appear when an instance is covered by several rules of different classes.

Let T rules of a class have been mined and we wish to mine the $T+1$ rule for the same class. The information that the system has about the T rules, are the instances from the training set that were not covered by them, but for the system is not known as the T rules affect on the instances from other classes. Furthermore, when working with fuzzy rules and instances, this problem increases since the instances are covered by a rule in a degree. This can cause unexpected interaction between rules during the inference process. That is why, in this study 'separate-and-conquer' approach is not followed and a boosting mechanism is used instead.

This paper is organized as follows. Section 2 explains the details of the algorithm. Section 3 briefly describes the used data set and discusses the experimental results. Finally section 4 concludes the paper with future works.

2   The Proposed Method

The AIS used in this work is based on clonal selection principle that is a form of natural selection. The antigen imposes a selective pressure on the antibody population by allowing only those cells that specifically recognize the antigen to be selected for proliferation and differentiation. The computational model of the clonal selection principle, like many other artificial immune system models, borrows heavily from immunological theory but is not an exact copy of the immune system's behavior [2].

Attributes are fuzzified by user-specified membership functions as a pre-process. Then AIS follows an iterative rule learning approach [8]. The overall architecture of the proposed approach is shown in Fig. 1. The rules are mined in an incremental fashion by repeatedly invoking AIS that identifies the fuzzy rule that best match and correctly classify the instances of selected class in the set of training instances. The boosting mechanism that will be repeated until no more rules are needed adapts the distribution of training instances in a way that AIS pays more attention to the previously misclassified or uncovered instances. Thereby, the boosting implicitly promotes cooperation among fuzzy rules. When all rules for a class have been mined the same process is repeated for the other classes.

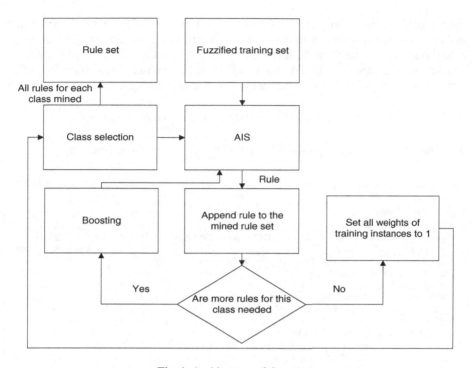

Fig. 1. Architecture of the system

2.1 Mining of Rules

In the proposed algorithm, each antibody that is encoded by a string with n genes, where n is the number of attributes represents the antecedent of a fuzzy classification rule while each antigen represents an instance. Each gene of an antibody consists of two elements; a value V_i that specifies the value or linguistic term of the i-th attribute in the i-th rule condition, and a Boolean flag B_i indicating whether or not the i-th condition occurs in the antecedent decoded from the antibody. The rule consequent is not evolved and all the antibodies of a given AIS are run with the same rule consequent [7]. That is why; the algorithm is run multiple times to mine rules predicting different classes. The main steps of the proposed algorithm are described in Fig. 2.

The proposed algorithm starts by initializing the *MinedRuleSet* to the empty set, and then it performs a loop over the classes to be predicted. For each class, the algorithm initializes weights of all instances with 1; then iteratively finds the best evolved rule, which is then stored in *BestRule*. Next the algorithm adds the *BestRule* to the *MinedRuleSet* and weights the instances that have been correctly covered by the *BestRule* with Boosting mechanism that will be explained later. An instance is correctly covered by a rule if and only if the instance satisfies the rule antecedent and the instance has the same class as predicted by the rule. In order to compute how much an instance satisfies a rule antecedent, the affinity between the rule and the instance is computed as follows.

Assume a training set of K instances $D=\{(x^1, c^1), ..., (x^K, c^K)\}$ where $x^k=\{x^k_1, ..., x^k_N\}$ is an instance taken from some attribute space $\{X_1, ..., X_n\}$, and $c^k \in \{C_1, ..., C_m\}$ is the class label associated with x^k. Upper indices k is used to denote the k-th training instance, and lower indices n to denote the n-th attribute x^k_n of a training instance x^k. Fuzzy rules are of the form R_i: if X_1 is A_{1i} and . . . X_N is A_{Ni} then $Y=c_i$ in which X_n denotes the n-th input variable, A_{ni} the fuzzy set associated to X_n and $c_i \in \{C_1, ..., C_M\}$ represents the class label of rule R_i. For a particular instance x_k,

$$Affinity(Ab, Ag) = \mu_{Ri}(x^k) = \mu_{Ri}(\{x^k_1, ..., x^k_n\}) = \min_{n=1}^{N} \mu_{A_{ni}}\left(x^k_n\right) \tag{1}$$

describes the affinity between the rule (antibody) and the instance (antigen).

```
MinedRuleSet=∅
For Each class c
  Weights of all training instances=1
  While (Number of unweighted instances>MaxUnweigthInstances OR yielding
                                             a positive fitness)
   Generate initial antibody population uniformly
   Prune each rule antecedent
   Compute fitness of each antibody
   For i=1 to NumberOfGenerations
        Perform tournament selection T times, getting T winners to be
cloned
     For Each antibody to be cloned
           Generate C clones of the antibody
           For Each just-generated clone
               Mutate clone
               Prune each clone
               Compute fitness of the clone
           End For Each clone
     End For Each antibody
           Replace T worst antibodies in the population by the T
best clones
   End For i
   BestRule=The rule whose antecedent consists of the antibody with the
           best fitness among all antibodies produced in all generations
   MinedRuleSet=MinedRuleSet ∪ BestRule
   Weight the instances that are correctly covered by the BestRule
  End While
End For Each class
```

Fig. 2. Main steps of the proposed algorithm

The While loop is iteratively performed until the number of unweighted instances is smaller than a user-specified threshold *MaxUnweightInstances* or fitness becomes zero to mine as many rules as necessary to cover the vast majority of the training instances.

Forming of best rules is started by generating an initial antibody population uniformly. Initial population is distributed over antibody space using uniform population (UP) method used for genetic algorithms in [9]. Random initial population method has some drawbacks because it may be created in the infeasible region, or all the antibodies in population may be in the nearest neighborhood and far away to solution, thus search of solution may get a local solution that can not be get rid of.

UP is a method to generate a population of high quality in order to overcome the random method. For simplicity, let $x = (x_1, x_2, ..., x_s)$ be a row vector (antibody) and $x_i \in \{0,1\}$, $1 \le i \le s$. There is a dividing factor r for this method. If $r=1$, then initially, an antibody is randomly created and then, inversion of this antibody is also selected as another antibody. If $r=2$, then randomly created antibody is divided into two equal parts: First, the inversion of the first part is taken and this yields another antibody. Taking inversion of the second part will yield another antibody, and inversion of all genes of randomly generated antibody is also another antibody. Therefore, three extra antibodies are obtained from randomly created antibody. All these antibodies are related to each other. For example, a population of size $4m$ is created from m randomly created antibody (m is a positive integer) in case of $r=2$. Let a be a randomly created antibody; and b, c, and d derived antibodies from a for $r=2$. Then,

$$a = (x_1, x_2, ..., x_n) \qquad\qquad\qquad b = (\bar{x}_1, \bar{x}_2, ..., \bar{x}_n) \qquad (2)$$

$$c = (\bar{x}_1, \bar{x}_2, ... \bar{x}_{\left\lfloor \frac{n}{2} \right\rfloor}, x_{\left\lfloor \frac{n}{2} \right\rfloor + 1}, ..., x_n) \qquad d = (x_1, x_2, ..., x_{\left\lfloor \frac{n}{2} \right\rfloor}, \bar{x}_{\left\lfloor \frac{n}{2} \right\rfloor + 1}, ..., \bar{x}_n)$$

If there are r-dividing points selected in each randomly generated antibody, then the number of derived antibodies from randomly generated antibody is $2^r - 1$. Thus, the number of antibodies in the initial population will be (the number of randomly generated antibodies is m)

$$(2^r - 1) \times m + m = m \times 2^r \qquad (3)$$

Taking inversion of parts for other encoding techniques can easily be formed. In this study, inversion of flags is performed in this way while inversion of values is performed by uniformly transforming one linguistic term to another in a cyclic order.

In the experiments, r was selected as 3, and 6 antibodies were randomly generated. That is why $6 \times 2^3 = 48$ antibodies were used as initial population.

Each rule is pruned to reduce the overfitting of rules to the data and improve comprehensibility of the rules and then fitness is computed. The basic idea of this rule pruning is that the more information gain of a condition [10], the more likely the condition will be removed from this rule. After rule pruning the second For loop over a fixed number of generations is performed.

This For loop starts by performing T tournament selection [11] with tournament size of 10 procedures, in order to select T winner antibodies that will be cloned in the next step. Once T antibodies have been selected, the algorithm performs its core step, which is inspired by the clonal selection principle. This step consists of several sub-steps, as follows. First, for each of the T antibodies to be cloned, the algorithm produces C clones. The value of C is proportional to the fitness of the antibody and is computed as shown in Equation (4) [7], where $fit(Ab)$ denotes the fitness of a given antibody Ab that will be described later and $MaxNumberOfClones$ denotes the maximum number of clones for an antibody. The number of clones increases linearly with the fitness when $0 < fit(Ab) < 0.5$, and any antibody with a fitness greater than or equal to 0.5 will have $MaxNumberOfClones$ clones. $MaxNumberOfClones$ was set to 10 to prevent the clone population from being very large, which would not only be inefficient but also possibly lead to overfitting of the rules to the data.

$$C = \begin{cases} 1 & if \ fit(Ab) \leq 0 \\ MaxNumberOfClones & if \ fit(Ab) \geq 5 \\ \left\lceil \dfrac{MaxNumberOfClones \times fit(Ab)}{5} \right\rceil & otherwise \end{cases} \tag{4}$$

Next, a hypermutation process is applied to each of the just-generated clones. The lower the fitness of a clone (parent antibody), the higher its mutation rate. More precisely, the mutation rate for a given clone cl, denoted $mutrate(cl)$, is given by

$$mutrate(cl) = (1 - fit(cl)) \times (mutrate_{max} - mutrate_{min}) + mutrate_{min} \tag{5}$$

where $mutrate_{min}$ and $mutrate_{max}$ are the smallest and greatest possible mutation rates that have been set to 20% and 50% in the experiments respectively, and $fit(cl)$ is the fitness of clone cl. Once a clone has undergone hypermutation, its corresponding rule antecedent is pruned and finally, the fitness of the clone is recomputed.

In the next step, the population is updated. More precisely, the T worst-fitness antibodies in the current population (not including the clones created by the clonal selection procedure) are replaced by the T best-fitness clones out of all clones generated by the clonal selection procedure. The parameter T and the number of generations were set to 10 and 50 respectively in the experiments.

Next, the best evolved rule consists of the rule antecedent represented by the antibody with the best fitness, across all antibodies produced in all generations, and of the rule consequent containing the class c, which was the class associated with all the generated antibodies is added to the set of mined rules. Finally the boosting mechanism that will be explained later is performed for weighting the training instances.

2.2 Fitness Function

The fitness function, fitness of an antibody ($fit(Ab)$) used in the algorithm shows the quality of a rule and consists of three parts. The first part considers sensitivity, specificity, and accuracy criteria and can be defined as

$$Q_1 = \frac{Sensitivity \times Specificity + aw \times Accuracy'}{1 + aw} \tag{6}$$

$$Sensitivity = \frac{TP}{TP + FN} \tag{7}$$

$$Specificity = \frac{TN}{TN + FP} \tag{8}$$

$$Accuracy = \frac{TP + TN}{TP + TN + FP + FN} \tag{9}$$

Accuracy'=Accuracy when *Accuracy>*0.7 and *Accuracy'*=0 otherwise. *aw* is the weight of the accuracy and is set to 0.01. This term of this part of fitness slightly reinforces the fitness of high-accuracy rules.

In case of categorical attributes, sensitivity is the accuracy among positive instances, and specificity is the accuracy among negative instances. *TP* is true positives, the number of instances covered by the rule that have the same class label as the rule; *FP* is false positives, the number of instances covered by the rule that have a different class label from the rule; *FN* is false negatives, the number of instances that are not covered by the rule but have the same class label as the rule, and *TN* is true negatives, the number of instances that are not covered by the rule and do not have the same class label as the rule. However, in this study fuzzy classification rules are mined, and an instance can be covered by a rule antecedent to a certain degree in the range [0...1], which corresponds to the membership degree of that instance in that rule antecedent. Therefore, the system computes fuzzy values for *TP*, *FP*, *FN*, and *TN*. Let p is the number of instances in the training data set and w^k weight of the instance specified by boosting mechanism. Then

$$TP = \sum_{k|c^k=c_i}^{p} w^k \mu R_i(x^k) \tag{10}$$

$$TN = \sum_{k|c^k \neq c_i}^{p} \left(1 - w^k \mu R_i(x^k)\right) \tag{11}$$

$$FP = \sum_{k|c^k \neq c_i}^{p} w^k \mu R_i(x^k) \tag{12}$$

$$FN = \sum_{k|c^k=c_i}^{p} \left(1 - w^k \mu R_i(x^k)\right) \tag{13}$$

The number of correctly and incorrectly classified instances irrespective of their weight is a consistency criterion and is included in the fitness function as second part. The rationale is to avoid that rules mined in later iterations make inaccurate generalizations based on the few remaining instances with high weights, while ignoring previously down-weighted instances. Part of the fitness for rule consistency of unweighted instances is accordingly computed by considering the number of correctly and incorrectly classified instances covered by the rule R_i and can be defined as

$$Q_2 = \begin{cases} 0 & \sum_{k|c_k=c_i} \mu R_i(x^k) < \sum_{k|c_k \neq c_i} \mu R_i(x^k) \\ \dfrac{\sum_{k|c_k=c_i} \mu R_i(x^k) - \sum_{k|c_k \neq c_i} \mu R_i(x^k)}{\sum_{k|c_k=c_i} \mu R_i(x^k)} & \text{otherwise} \end{cases} \tag{14}$$

Another criterion considered for fitness function, third part, is length of the rule. This part of fitness rewards a concise rule and is computed as

$$Q_3 = 1 - \frac{NumberOfTerms}{20} \tag{15}$$

where *NumberOfTerms* is the number of terms in the antibody, namely the number of flags having value of 1 in the genes of the antibody.

The final fitness function is weighted sum of these described criteria:

$$fit(Ab) = \sum_{i=1}^{3} weight_i Q_i \tag{16}$$

weight₁, *weight₂*, and *weight₃* were set to 1, 1, and 0.0005 respectively.

2.3 Boosting Mechanism

The boosting mechanism is performed as follows. Initially, all training instances are weighted uniformly with the $w^k(t=0)=1$. Each time a best rule for the selected class is included in the list, weights of the instances covered by this rule, $w^k(t+1)$, are changed according to the following formula [12]:

$$w^k(t+1) = \begin{cases} w^k(t) & ,c_i = c_k \\ w^k(t) \times \chi^k & ,c_i \neq c_k \end{cases} \tag{17}$$

$$\chi^k = \left(\frac{E(R_t)}{1 - E(R_t)} \right)^{\mu_{R_t}(x^k)} \tag{18}$$

Here $E(R_t)$ is the error of the fuzzy rule R_t mined at iteration t. $E(R_t)$ of a fuzzy rule R_t is weighted by the degree of matching $\mu R_t(x^k)$ between the k-th training instance (x^k, c^k) and the rule antecedent as well as its weight w^k and can be defined as

$$E(R_t) = \frac{\sum_{k|c_k \neq c_i} w^k \mu R_t(x^k)}{\sum_k w^k \mu R_t(x^k)} \tag{19}$$

2.4 Classifying Test Instances

The rules mined from the training set are used to classify new instances in the test set. Each possible classification C_m accumulates the affinity of fuzzy rules R_i with a matching consequent $c_i=C_m$. The instance x^k is classified according to the class label

$$C_{max}(x^k) = \text{argmax}_{Cm} \left(\left(\sum_{R_i|c_i=C_m} \log(1/\chi_t) \mu_{R_i}(x^k) \right) \right) \tag{20}$$

that consists of the greatest value of the product of the affinity between the rule and the instance by the fitness of the rule and the rule-weighting factor. Rule-weighting factor allows the rules with small classification error, $E(R_t)$, obtain a larger weight. χ_t value used in rule weighting factor $\log(1/\chi_t)$ is computed as

$$\chi_t = \frac{E(R_t)}{1 - E(R_t)} \tag{21}$$

3 Experimental Results

Six data sets described in Table 1 available from the UCI ML repository were used for the experiments. The first column gives the name of the data set, the second the number attributes (excluding the conclusion attribute), the third the total number of instances in the data set, and the last column gives the number of class labels. Three of the data sets have binary class labels while the other three represent multi-class domains. Continuous attributes are fuzzified using a set of linguistic terms that are represented by triangular membership functions. Note that some of the number of instances includes the missing valued instances. In this study, instances that had any attribute with missing value were removed from the data sets.

Table 1. The used data sets

Data sets	# Attributes	# Instances	# Classes
Breast W	9	699	2
Bupa	6	345	2
Diabetes	8	768	2
Glass	9	214	6
Iris	4	150	3
Wine	13	178	3

In the simulations, ten iterations of the whole ten-fold cross-validation (10-CV) procedure were used for estimating predictive accuracy. Since the algorithm is based on a stochastic process and the results produced therefore vary from one 10-CV to the next, the same folds were used for each of the ten 10-CV tests. That is, the data set was not re-shuffled and split into different subsets before each of the ten 10-CV runs. This was done in order to test the deviation in the performance statistics arising from the algorithm, and not due to any changes in the folds used.

Table 2 shows the average accuracy rates on test data and standard deviations for this implementation and C4.5Rules [13]. In this table, this implementation has better performance than C4.5Rules in terms of accuracy rates; the rules obtained by this implementation have higher accuracy than the rules obtained by C4.5Rules in four out of six data sets. However, the differences in accuracy rates are not so significant. C4.5Rules found rules that have higher accuracy than this implementation in Bupa and Glass data sets and the difference is not significant. Too simple rules mined by this implementation that are underfitted to the data seem the reason of this situation.

Table 2. Comparison of accuracy rates

Data sets	This work	C4.5Rules
Breast W	95.36 ± 0.89	94.0 ± 1.22
Bupa	65.3 ± 2.28	66.3 ± 1.50
Diabetes	75.8 ± 1.29	73.0 ± 0.89
Glass	78.8 ± 0.78	78.9 ± 1.2
Iris	94.9 ± 1.15	93.33 ± 5.92
Wine	96.82 ± 1.72	93.3 ± 1.03

Table 3. Comparison of simplicity

Datasets	# Rules		#Terms	
	This work	C4.5Rules	This work	C4.5Rules
Breast W	7.2 ± 0.21	8.1 ± 0.59	11.8 ± 0.12	19.8 ± 2.81
Bupa	8.3 ± 0.46	14.0 ± 0.96	17.1 ± 0.24	36.8 ± 4.04
Diabetes	11.8 ± 0.23	13.1 ± 1.29	24.5 ± 1.05	29.7 ± 1.71
Glass	13.9 ± 1.1	14.0 ± 2.19	28.0 ± 1.02	29.1 ± 2.01
Iris	4.9 ± 1.12	5.5 ± 0.4	8.6 ± 0.5	10.6 ± 0.9
Wine	5.3 ± 0.28	4.6 ± 0.52	12.5 ± 0.8	14.5 ± 1.45

The results of the simplicity of the mined rule set measured by the number of mined rules and the average total number of terms in all mined rules of both this implementation and C4.5Rules are shown in Table 3. This implementation mines fewer rules with fewer numbers of terms than C4.5Rules in five out of all data sets. This is mainly due to the fact that C4.5Rules starts with the unpruned C4.5 decision tree that contains a large amount of superfluous rules and terms. This implementation mined a slight more number of rules in Wine data set, however it mined simpler rules.

4   Conclusion

An AIS-based fuzzy classification rule mining that used a boosting mechanism was presented and compared with C4.5Rules algorithm in six real-world data sets. AIS was proposed as a search strategy to mine accurate and comprehensible knowledge within databases which might be considered as search spaces. The mined rules were presented in such a way that user could easily understand the concise set of comprehensible rules. The appeal of AIS approach is that it provides an effective mechanism for conducting a global search and can cope better with attribute interaction than greedy rule induction algorithms. These results are promising since C4.5Rules has been evolving from the research of decades in decision tree and rule induction algorithms.

The strategy used in this study is different from 'divide-and-conquer' and 'separate-and-conquer' approaches used by decision trees and lists respectively. It used a boosting mechanism to adapt the distribution of training instances in iterations, namely AIS paid more attention to the previously misclassified or uncovered instances. Thereby, cooperation among fuzzy rules was implicitly promoted.

Automatically determining the membership function for each continuous attribute is a future research that can improve the predictive accuracy. Another research direction consists of simultaneously searching for intervals of continuous attributes and mining of classification rules that these intervals conform to avoid from conveying a loss of information. Further testing with more elaborated experiments by using optimized parameters on various databases is also in progress to test the robustness of the proposed method.

References

1. Han, J., Kamber, M.: Data Mining: Concepts and Techniques. Morgan Kaufmann Publishers Academic Press (2001)
2. Castro, L.N., Timmis, J.: Artificial Immune Systems: A New Computation Intelligence Approach. Springer-Verlag, Berlin (2002)
3. de Castro, L.N., Von Zuben, F.J.: Learning and Optimization Using the Clonal Selection Principle, IEEE Transaction on Evolutionary Computation, 6:3 (2002) 239-251.
4. Freund, Y., Schapire R. E.: Experiments with a New Boosting Algorithm. Proc. of the 13th Int. Conf. on Machine Learning ML-96 (1996) 148-156
5. Gonzales, F.A., Dasgupta, D.: An Immunogenetic Technique to Detect Anomalies in Network Traffic. Proceedings of Genetic and Evolutionary Computation. Morgan Kaufmann, San Mateo (2002) 1081-1088
6. Freitas, A.A., Timmis, J.: Revisiting the Foundations of Artificial Immune Systems: a Problem Oriented Perspective. ICARIS 2003. LNCS, Vol. 2787. Springer-Verlag, Berlin (2003) 229-241
7. Alves, R.T., Degado M. R., Lopes H.S., Freitas, A.A.: An Artificial Immune System for Fuzzy-Rule Induction in Data Mining. In: Yao, X. et al. (eds) Parallel Problem Solving from Nature - PPSN VIII, LNCS Vol. 3242 Springer-Verlag, Berlin (2004) 1011-1020
8. Gonzáles, A., Herrera, F.: Multi-Stage Genetic Fuzzy Systems based on the Iterative Rule Learning Approach. Mathware & Soft Computing (1997) 233-249
9. Karcı, A.: Novelty in the Generation of Initial Population for Genetic Algorithms. Knowledge-Based Intelligent Information and Engineering Systems. 8th International Conference KES 2004 LNAI, Vol. 3214. Part II, Springer-Verlag, Berlin (2004) 268-276
10. Alataş, B., Arslan, A.: Mining of Interesting Prediction Rules with Uniform Two-Level Genetic Algorithm. International Journal of Computational Intelligence, 1:1 (2004) 65-70
11. Back, T., Fogel, D.B., and Michalewicz, T. (Eds.): Evolutionary Computation. Vol. 1. IoP Publishing, Oxford, UK (2000)
12. del Jesus, M.J., Hoffman, F., Navacués, L.J., Sánches, L.: Induction of Fuzzy-Rule-Based Classifiers with Evolutionary Boosting Algorithms. IEEE Transactions on Fuzzy Systems, 12:3 (2004) 296-308
13. Quinlan, J.R.: C4.5: Programs For Machine Learning. Morgan Kaufmann, San Mateo (1993)

Continuous Trend-Based Classification of Streaming Time Series

Maria Kontaki*, Apostolos N. Papadopoulos, and Yannis Manolopoulos

Department of Informatics, Aristotle University,
GR-54124 Thessaloniki, Greece
{kontaki, apostol, manolopo}@delab.csd.auth.gr

Abstract. Trend analysis of time series data is an important research direction. In streaming time series the problem is more challenging, taking into account the fact that new values arrive for the series, probably in very high rates. Therefore, effective and efficient methods are required in order to classify a streaming time series based on its trend. Since new values are continuously arrive for each stream, the classification is performed by means of a sliding window which focuses on the last values of each stream. Each streaming time series is transformed to a vector by means of a Piecewise Linear Approximation (PLA) technique. The PLA vector is a sequence of symbols denoting the trend of the series (either UP or DOWN), and it is constructed incrementally. Efficient in-memory methods are used in order to: 1) determine the class of each streaming time series and 2) determine the streaming time series that comprise a specific trend class. Performance evaluation based on real-life datasets is performed, which shows the efficiency of the proposed approach both with respect to classification time and storage requirements. The proposed method can be used in order to continuously classify a set of streaming time series according to their trends, to monitor the behavior of a set of streams and to monitor the contents of a set of trend classes.

Keywords: data streams, time series, trend detection, classification, data mining.

1 Introduction

The study of query processing and data mining techniques for data stream processing has recently attracted the interest of the research community [2], due to the fact that many applications deal with data that change very frequently with respect to time. Examples of such application domains are network monitoring, financial data analysis, sensor networks to name a few. The most important property of data streams is that new values are continuously arrive, and therefore efficient storage and processing techniques are required to cope with the high update rate.

* This research is supported by the *State Scholarships Foundation (I.K.Y.)*.

J. Eder et al. (Eds.): ADBIS 2005, LNCS 3631, pp. 294–308, 2005.

A streaming time series S is a sequence of real values s_1, s_2, ..., where new values are continuously appended as time progresses. For example, a temperature sensor which monitors the environmental temperature every five minutes, produces a streaming time series of temperature values. As another example, consider a car equipped with a GPS device and a communication module, which transmits its position to a server every ten minutes. A streaming time series of two-dimensional points (the x and y coordinates of its position) is produced. Note that, in a streaming time series data values are ordered with respect to the arrival time. New values are appended at the end of the series.

A class of algorithms for stream processing focuses on the recent past of data streams by applying a *sliding window* on the data stream [2,3]. In this way, only the last W values of each streaming time series is considered for query processing, whereas older values are considered obsolete and they are not taken into account. As it is illustrated in Figure 1, streams that are non-similar for a window of length W (left), may be similar if the window is shifted in the time axis (right).

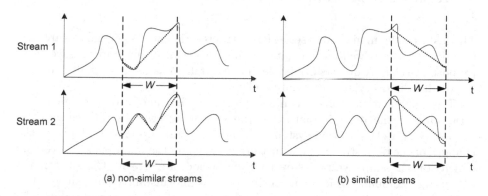

Fig. 1. Similarity using a sliding window of length W

We use trends as a base to classify streaming time series for two reasons. First, *trend* is an important characteristic of a streaming time series. In several applications the way that stream values are modified is considered important, since useful conclusions can be drawn. For example, in a stock data monitoring system it is important to know which stocks have an increasing trend and which ones have a decreasing trend. Second, trend-based representation of time series is more close to the human intuition. In the literature, many papers [6,7] use the values of the data streams and a distance function like Euclidean distance to cluster streams. Although a distance can be large for a pair of streams, these two streams can be intuitively considered similar, if their plots are examined. Thus, distance functions aren't always good metrics to cluster or to classify objects.

In this paper, we focus on the problem of continuous time series classification based on the trends of the series as time progresses. Evidently, we expect that the same series will show different trend for different time intervals. The classification is performed by considering the last W values of each stream (in a sliding window manner). Again, two streaming time series that show similar trends for a specific time interval may be totally dissimilar for another time interval. This effect is illustrated in Figure 1, where the trends of the time series are represented by dotted lines. We note also that two series which show similar trends may be completely different with respect to the values they assume.

The rest of the article is organized as follows. In Section 2 we give significant related work on the issue of trend analysis in streams. Section 3 discusses in detail the proposed approach which is based on two important issues: 1) an effective in-memory representation of the streams by means of an approximation and 2) an efficient in-memory organization in order to quickly categorize a stream when new values for that stream are available. Experimental results based on real-life datasets are offered in Section 4, whereas Section 5 concludes the work and raises some issues for further research in the area.

2   Related Work and Contribution

The last decade, mining time series has attracted the interest of the researchers. Classification is a well-known data mining problem. Many papers have been proposed to classify objects from different research domains as machine learning, knowledge discovery and artificial intelligence.

The classification problem is more challenging in the case of streaming time series due to the dynamic nature of the streaming case. In the recent past, [1] proposed a classification system in which the training model adapts to the changes of the data streams. The method is based on the micro-clusters, vectors which contain simple statistics over a time period of a stream. Classification is achieved by combining micro-clusters in different time instances (snapshots). The method uses a periodically scheme to update the micro-clusters and reports the classification on demand. Our method incrementally computes and continuously reports the classification. Moreover the scheme, that was used, needs a training set in opposition to our scheme that has a restricted number of classifiers and the classifiers are a priori known. In [12] used info-fuzzy networks to address the problem. Other approaches include one-pass mining algorithms [4,8], in which the classification model is constructed in the beginning, and therefore do not recognize possible changes in the underlying concept.

Piecewise linear approximation has been used to represent efficiently time series in many topics as clustering, classification and indexing [16,17]. Many variations have been proposed, among them are the piecewise aggregate approximation (PAA) [11] that stores the mean value of equal-length segments and the adaptive piecewise constant approximation (APCA) [10] that stores the mean value and the right end-point of variable-length segments.

Trend analysis has been used to cluster time series in many domains such as time series [18,13], bioinformatics [14] and ubiquitous computing [15]. Yoon et al proposed six trend indicators. A time series is represented as a partial order of the indicators. A bitmap index is used to encode indicators into bit strings in order to compute the distance between two time series with the XOR operator. In [13,14] modifications of PLA are used to detect trends and three types of them are used (up, down and steady) to cluster time series. These methods study the clustering problem in time series. They do not use an incremental way to compute the trend representation. Additionally the clustering algorithms were proposed are not one-pass algorithms. So the methods are not appropriate in a streaming case. In comparison with our method the trend representation is incrementally computed and the classification is continuously reported using an efficient in-memory access method. Recently, [16] proposed trend analysis to address the problem of subsequence matching in financial data streams. The Bollinger Band indicator (%b) is used to smooth time series and then the PLA is applied. The %b indicator uses simple moving average and thus the whole sliding window is required to compute next values of %b. So the pla representation is not computed incrementally and in case of thousand of streams the memory requisites are enormous.

The contribution of the work is summarized as follows:

- An incremental computation of the PLA approximation is presented, which enables the continuous representation of the time series trends under the sliding window paradigm.
- An efficient in-memory access method is proposed which facilitates fundamental operations such as: determine the class of a stream, insert a stream into another class, delete a stream from an existing class.
- Continuous trend-based classification is supported, which enables the monitoring trend classes or the monitoring of data stream.
- The proposed technique can be applied even in the case where only a subset of the data streams change their values at some time instance. Therefore, it is not required to have stream values at every time instance for all streams.

3   Trend Representation and Classification

In data stream processing there are two important requirements posed by the nature of the data. The first requirement states that processing must be very efficient in order to allow continuous processing due to the large number of updates. This suggests the use of the main memory in order to avoid costly I/O operations. The second requirement states that random access to past stream data is not supported. Therefore, any computations that must be performed on the stream should be incremental, in order to avoid reading past stream values. In order to be consistent with the previous requirements, we propose a continuous classification scheme which requires small storage overhead and performs the classification in an incremental manner, taking into consideration the synopsis of each stream. Each stream synopsis requires significantly less storage than the raw stream data, and therefore, better memory utilization is

Table 1. Basic notations used throughout the study

Symbol	Description
S	a streaming time series
$S(t)$	the value of stream S at time t
N	number of streaming time series
n	length of a streaming time series
W	sliding window length
p	period of moving average ($p \leq W$)
$EMAi_p(t)$	the i-th exponential moving average of period p ($t \geq p$)
$TRIX(t)$	percentage differences of $EMA3_p(t)$ signal
PLA	piecewise linear approximation
$PLA(i)$	the i-th segment of the PLA
k	the number of segments of the PLA
tl_{min}	the minimum time instance of a bucket list
tl_{max}	the maximum time instance of a bucket list
tb_{min}	the minimum time instance of a bucket
tb_{max}	the maximum time instance of a bucket

achieved. Before we describe the proposed method in detail we give the basic symbols used throughout the study in Table 1.

3.1 Time Series Synopsis

In this section we study the problem of the incremental determination of each stream synopsis, in order to reduce the required storage requirements and enable stream classification based on trend. Trend detection has been extensively studied in statistics and related disciplines [5,9]. In fact, there are several indices that can be used in order to determine trend in a time series. Among the various approaches we choose to use the TRIX indicator [9] which is computed by means of a triple moving average on the raw stream data. We note that before trend analysis is performed, a smoothing process should be applied towards removing noise and producing a smoother curve, revealing the time series trend for a specific time interval. This smoothing is facilitated by means of the TRIX indicator, which is based on a triple exponential moving average calculation of the logarithm of the time series values. In the sequel, we first explain the use of the exponential moving average and then we introduce the TRIX indicator.

Definition 1.
The exponential moving average of period p over a streaming time series S is calculated by means of the following formula:

$$EMA_p(t) = EMA_p(t-1) + \frac{2}{1+p} \cdot (S(t) - EMA_p(t-1)) \qquad (1)$$

Definition 2.
The TRIX indicator of period p over a streaming time series S is calculated by means of the following formula:

$$TRIX(t) = 100 \cdot \frac{EMA3_p(t) - EMA3_p(t-1)}{EMA3_p(t-1)} \qquad (2)$$

where $EMA3_p$ is a signal generated by the application of a triple exponential moving average of the input time series.

The signal $TRIX(t)$ oscillates around the zero line. Whenever $TRIX(t)$ crosses the zero line, it is an indication of trend change. This is exactly what we need in order to perform a trend representation of an input time series. Figure 2 illustrates an example. Note that the zero line is crossed by the $TRIX(t)$ signal, whenever there is a trend change in the input signal. Figure 2 also depicts the smoothing achieved by the application of the exponential moving average.

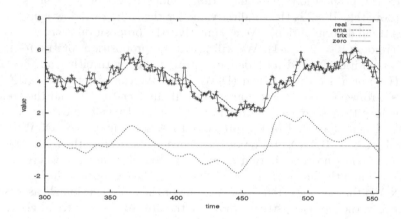

Fig. 2. Example of a time series and the corresponding $TRIX(t)$ signal

Definition 3.

The PLA representation of a streaming time series S for a time interval of W values is a sequence of at most W-1 pairs of the form $(t, trend)$, where t defines the left-point time of the segment and $trend$ denotes the trend of the stream (UP or DOWN) in the specified segment.

Each time a new value arrives, the PLA is updated. Three operations (ADD, UPDATE, EXPIRE) are implemented to support incremental computation of the PLA. The ADD operation is applied when a trend change detected and adds a new PLA-point. The UPDATE operation is applied when the trend is stable and updates the timestamp of the last PLA-point. The EXPIRE operation is applied when the first segment of the PLA is expired and deletes the first PLA-point. Notice that when the UPDATE operation is applied the class of the stream does not change.

3.2   Continuous Classification

In this section we study the way continuous classification is performed. Taking into account that each PLA segment has an UP or DOWN direction, the number of possible trend classes for a sliding window of length W is given by $C_W = 2 \cdot (W - 1)$ as it is illustrated by the following proposition.

Proposition.
The number of different classes C_W of streaming time series is given by:

$$C_W = 2 \cdot (W - 1) \tag{3}$$

where W is the sliding window length.

Proof.
To prove this proposition we use induction. Evidently, the proposition is true for $W=2$ (note that $W=2$ is the smallest value for the sliding window length which enables trend determination). We assume that the proposition is true for $W=n$, and therefore $C_n = 2 \cdot (n-1)$. We will prove the proposition for $W=n+1$. The values at positions n and $n+1$ define a straight line with either an increasing trend (UP) or a decreasing trend (DOWN) (in the case where the TRIX indicator is zero, we retain the previous trend). If the trend is UP and the trend of the previous PLA segment is also UP, then the final result is UP. If the trend is DOWN and the trend of the previous PLA segment is also DOWN, then the final result is DOWN. If one of the above cases is true, then the $(n+1)$-th stream value has no contribution at all. Now consider the case where the last trend is UP and the previous trend is DOWN, or the case where the last trend is DOWN and the previous trend is UP. If one of the aforementioned cases is true then clearly, the $(n+1)$-th stream value contributes to another trend class. This means that the $(n+1)$-th stream value can give two more trend classes. This means that $C_{n+1} = C_n + 2$. By the induction hypothesis we know that $C_n = 2 \cdot (n-1)$. Therefore, $C_{n+1} = 2 \cdot (n-1) + 2 = 2 \cdot n$, and this completes the proof. □

Every time a new value for a streaming time series arrives, the corresponding stream may change from a trend class to another. We illustrate the way continuous classification can be achieved efficiently, by means of an in-memory access method which organizes the streams according to the trend class they belong and by taking into account time information to facilitate efficient search. During continuous classification the following operations must be supported:

- We must quickly locate the class that the corresponding stream belongs to,
- We must delete (if necessary) the corresponding stream from the old class and assign it to a new one, and
- We must report efficiently the stream identifiers that belong to a specific trend class.

Each trend class is supported by several lists of buckets. The first bucket of each list is the *primary bucket* whereas the other buckets are *overflow buckets*. The *overflow buckets* are used only in the case where the stream must be inserted in an existing list (step 2 of Algorithm Insert) and the *primary bucket* of the list is full (bucket size exceeded). Each bucket list is characterized by two time instances tl_{min} and tl_{max}, denoting the minimum and the maximum time instances which corresponds to the $k-1$-th PLA point, where k is the number of points contained in the PLA representation. We use the one before the last PLA point as base to insert streams in bucket lists because is the last stable point (the last point maybe changed if an update happens) and thus we have to update the classification structure only when the stream changes class. Each bucket is composed of a set of stream identifiers and two time instances tb_{min} and tb_{max}. These time instances denote the time interval that each stream in the bucket has been inserted.

In Figure 3 an example of the structure is depicted. The class DUD consists of two bucket lists. The first list contains additionally an *overflow bucket*. For the first list the tl_{min} is 10 and the tl_{max} is 15. This means that the streams 1,2,5,8 have the one before the last PLA point between time 10 and 15. For the *primary bucket* of the first list the tb_{min} is 12 and the tb_{max} is 17 and contains the streams 2,5 and 8. Therefore streams 2,5 and 8 were inserted in this class between time 12 and 17. For the *overflow bucket* of the first list the tb_{min} is 18 and the tb_{max} is 18 and contains the stream 1. Stream 1 was inserted at time instance 18. The description of the second list is the same.

We will explain how we use the bucket lists structure to continuous classify streams with an example. Assume the two bucket lists of the classes DUD and DUDU of the Figure 3. The bucket size is 3 and the window size is 16. At time instance 21 a new value for the stream 1 is arrived. The following operations take place: a) we search the stream 1 in the bucket lists of class DUD, b) we delete it, c) we update PLA and d) we insert it in the bucket lists of class DUDU. The stream 1 has the one before last PLA point at time 14. We search for the bucket list in which tl_{min} and tl_{max} enclose time 14 (step 1 of search algorithm). This is the first list. The first list contains an *overflow bucket* so we must find the insertion time of the stream 1 (insertion time algorithm). The stream 1 was inserted in this class either when a new PLA-point was added ($PLA(k-1)$-point + 1) or when the first segment expired ($W + PLA(0)$-point - 1). The maximum of these two times is the time that the stream was inserted. Therefore the insertion time is 18. We search in the list, a bucket in which tb_{min} and tb_{max} enclose time 18 (step 3 of search algorithm). This is the *overflow bucket* (figure 8). We delete stream 1 and then we delete the bucket because is empty (delete algorithm). Then we update the PLA of the stream. The new class is the DUDU class. Now the one before the last PLA point is at time 20. Since the bucket lists of this class is not empty (step 1 of the insert algorithm) and since the tl_{max} of the one before the last bucket list is smaller than 20 (step 2), we check if the last bucket list is full (step 3). In the Figure 9 we can see that the *primary bucket* of this list is not full. So we update the tl_{max} (step 3) and the tb_{max} and we insert the stream in the *primary bucket* of this list (step 5). The algorithms for insert, search and delete are given in Figure 4, Figure 5 and Figure 7 respectively.

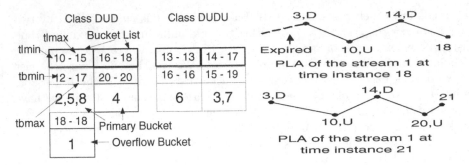

Fig. 3. Example of search algorithm with bucket size 3

Algorithm. Insert

/* Determine the list to insert the stream */
1. If the corresponding class is empty, then a new list is created and the values tl_{min} and tl_{max} are set to the time instance t_{n-1} of the $(n-1)$-th PLA point.
2. Otherwise, check if t_{n-1} is less than the tl_{max} value of the last list. If yes, then the stream identifier is inserted into one of the existing bucket lists. The appropriate bucket list is the list in which the tl_{min} and tl_{max} enclose the t_{n-1}.
3. Otherwise, check if the primary bucket of the last list is full. If the primary bucket is not full then the stream is inserted into that list by updating the corresponding value tl_{max}. If the primary bucket is full, a new bucket list is generated and the values tl_{min} and tl_{max} are set to the time instance t_{n-1} of the $(n-1)$-th PLA point.
/* Determine the bucket to insert the stream */
4. If the primary bucket of the current list does not exist, then a primary bucket is created and the stream is inserted. The tb_{min} and tb_{max} values are updated with the current time.
5. If the primary bucket of the current list is not full, then the stream is inserted into that bucket and the tb_{max} value is updated with the current time.
6. Otherwise the stream is inserted into the last overflow bucket of the list, by updating accordingly the tb_{max} value. If the last overflow bucket is full, a new overflow bucket is generated.

Fig. 4. Insertion algorithm

Algorithm. Search

1. Determine the bucket list by checking for the values of tl_{min} and tl_{max} that enclose the time instance t_{n-1} of the stream.
2. If the list contains only a primary bucket, then the stream identifier is found into that bucket.
3. If the list contains a number of overflow buckets, then by using the time instance that the stream has been inserted (Fig. 6), the corresponding overflow bucket which contains the stream is easily detected.

Fig. 5. Search algorithm

4   Performance Study

The proposed trend-based classification scheme has been implemented in C++, and the experimental evaluation has been performed on a Pentium IV machine

---
Algorithm. Insertion Time
---

1. Compute the time that the last expiration has occurred. The time is given by $lastEXP = W + PLA(0)$-point - 1.
2. Compute the time that the last ADD operation has occurred. The time is given by $lastADD = PLA(k-1)$-point + 1.
3. The time that the stream has been inserted is given by $max(lastEXP, lastADD)$.

Fig. 6. Insertion Time algorithm

Algorithm. Delete
---

1. Call algorithm Search in order to determine the position of the stream.
2. Remove the stream identifier from the bucket.
3. If the bucket is empty it is removed.
4. If the bucket list is empty it is removed.

Fig. 7. Deletion algorithm

with 1GByte RAM running Windows 2000. Two real-life datasets with different characteristics have been used:

- **STOCKS**: is the daily stock prices obtained from http://finance.yahoo.com. The data set consists of 93 time sequences, and the maximum length of each one is set to 3,000.
- **TAO**: this dataset (Tropical Atmosphere Ocean) contains the wind speed of 65 sites on Pacific and Atlantic Ocean since 1974, obtained from the Pacific Marine Environmental Laboratory (http://www.pmal.noaa.gov/tao). We have used the highest data resolution (e.g. the sampling time interval) that was available. About 12,000 streams form the data set, and the maximum length of each one is set to 1,000.

In the sequel we give the performance results for different parameter values for the sliding window length (W), the exponential moving average period (p), the number of the streaming time series (N), the bucket size (B). The experiments are divided into two categories. The first category studies the quality of the clustering and the second studies the performance. We focus on two performance measures: the computational cost required to perform continuous classification and the memory requirements of the proposed approach because they are the most important metrics in determining the effectiveness and the robustness of a stream processing system. The CPU cost was measured in seconds. Finally, the proposed method works both in cases where all the streams or part of them are updated. For the experiments below, the first case was used.

4.1 Quality of PLA

The underlying idea of the approach is to cluster streams using an abstractive representation of the streams that is closer to the "human sense" despite using the values of the streams and the Euclidean distance or others distance metrics. In this section we examined the conforming between the piecewise linear approximation of a stream and the general shape of a stream without micro changes.

Next, we give some classification examples. Figure 8 shows classification patterns and a sample of streams that are associated with each one. For each stream, both the raw data and the PLA are illustrated. The classification instances are peaked after a random number of updates. Notice that if we are not contented with the representation, we can choose a greater p for a more abstractive description of the stream, or a smaller p for a more comprehensive description.

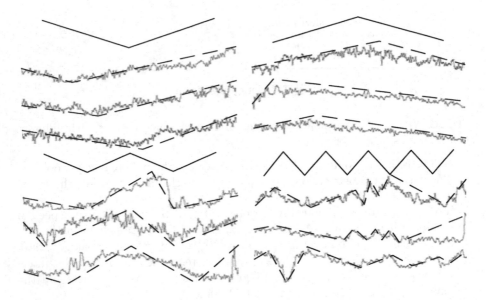

Fig. 8. Classification examples

Additionally, Figure 9 shows the number of clusters for different values of p with respect to W for the TAO and STOCKS data sets. The term CL_raw is used for the possible number of clusters that is entirely depended on the window size W. It was expected the number of clusters, that is actually used, is reduced as the p is increased because less details are represented by the PLA. Therefore some streams are moved in classes with smaller number of segments.

4.2   Performance Evaluation

We first examine the performance of the method with respect to window length. Figure 10 illustrates the total CPU cost (10a) and the CPU cost to compute the PLA of all streams for all the updates (10b) for the TAO data set. Different values for p are used. From Figure 10, the total CPU cost is determined from

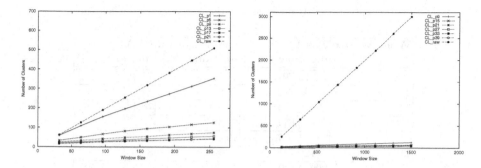

Fig. 9. Number of clusters vs window length for a) TAO and b) STOCKS data sets

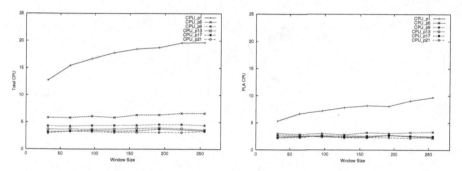

Fig. 10. a) Total CPU cost and b) PLA CPU cost vs window length

the PLA CPU cost. The latter is independent from the window size due to the use of the TRIX indicator.

Table 2 illustrates the total memory for the STOCKS data set and partial memory prerequisites for the PLA representation and the classification structure. Total memory is essentially affected by the PLA memory. The PLA memory is increased as the window size increases.

Next we examine the performance of our method with respect to the number of streams. Figure 11a depicts the CPU cost for all the streams (12145) and for all the updates (about 700) for the TAO data set. The term TOTAL_CPU is used for the sum of the PLA and the classification CPU cost. The CPU cost increases linearly with respect to the number of streams.

The memory prerequisites of the PLA per update for the TAO data set are illustrated in Figure 11b. The term MEM_raw is used for the memory prerequisites of the raw data. Notice that the y-axis scales logarithmically. The PLA memory increases steadily with respect to the number of streams but it is less than the 10% of raw data memory.

To better understand the influence of the bucket size in the classification method, Figure 3 shows the CPU cost and the memory prerequisites of the classification method. Large bucket size reduces the memory prerequisites but increases CPU cost, whereas a small bucket size has the opposite results. The bucket size is a trade-off between memory resources and computation time.

Table 2. Total CPU and classification memory vs bucket size

Window Size	Total memory (KB)	Classification memory (%)	PLA memory (%)
128	13013.797	28.6%	71.4%
324	16065.762	25.9%	74.1%
520	19059.859	23.9%	76.1%
716	21772.871	21.4%	78.6%
912	24441.957	19.6%	80.4%
1108	27129.715	18.1%	81.9%
1304	29934.621	17.2%	82.8%
1500	32726.527	16.5%	83.5%

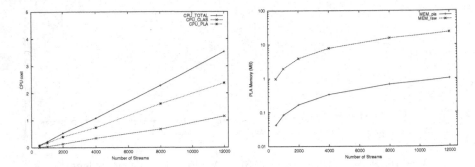

Fig. 11. a) CPU cost and b) memory prerequisites of PLA vs number of streams for TAO

Table 3. Total CPU and classification memory vs bucket size

Bucket Size	Total CPU	Classification memory (MB)
50	3.745	25.061
100	3.7842	14.803
200	3.6836	8.573
300	3.73	6.082
400	3.801	4.764
500	3.9377	3.876
600	4.0029	3.286

5   Conclusions and Future Work

Trend analysis of time evolving data streams is a challenging problem due to the fact that the trend of a time series changes with respect to time. In this paper we studied the problem of continuous trend-based classification of streaming time series, by using a compact representation for each stream and an in-memory access method to facilitate efficient search, insert and delete operations. A piecewise linear approximation (PLA) has been used in order to determine the trend curve of each stream. The PLA representation has been applied on a smoothed version of each stream. We have used the TRIX indicator for smoothing. Moreover, a continuous classification method has been presented which reassigns a stream to new trend class if necessary. Performance evaluation results based on real-life datasets have shown the feasibility and the efficiency of the proposed approach.

In the near future we plan to extend the current work towards continuous clustering of streaming time series, by taking into account the similarity between trend classes.

References

1. Aggarwal, C. C., Han, J., Yu, P. S.: On Demand Classification of Data Streams, Proceedings of the International Conference of Knowledge Discovery and Data Mining(KDD), WA, USA (2004)
2. Babcock, B. Babu, S., Datar, M., Motwani, R., Widom, J.: Models and Issues in Data Stream Systems, Proceedings ACM PODS, Madison, Wisconsin (2002) 1–16
3. Datar, M., Gionis, A., Indyk, P., Motwani, R.: Maintaining stream statistics over sliding windows, Proceedings of the 2002 Annual ACM-SIAM Symp. on Discrete Algorithms (2002) 635–644
4. Domingos, P., Hulten, G.: Mining High-Speed Data Streams, Proceedings of ACM SIGKDD Conference (2000)
5. Fung, G. P. C., Yu, J. X., Lam, W.: News Sensitive Stock Trend Prediction, In PAKDD (2002) 481-493
6. Guha, S., Meyerson, A., Mishra, N., Motwani, R., OCallaghan, L.: Clustering Data Streams: Theory and Practic, IEEE TKDE, Vol. 15, No. 3 (2003) 515-528
7. Guha, S., Mishra, N., Motwani, R.., OÆCallaghan, L.: Clustering data streams, In Proc. of the 2000 Annual IEEE Symp. on Foundations of Computer Science (2000) 359–366
8. Hulten, G., Spencer, L., Domingos. P.: Mining Time Changing Data Streams, Proceedings of ACM KDD Conference (2001)
9. Hutson, J. K.: TRIX - Triple Exponential Smoothing Oscillator, Technical Analysis of Stocks and Commodities (1983) 105–108
10. Keogh, E., Chakrabarti, K., Mehrotra, S., Pazzani, M.: Locally Dimensionality Reduction for Indexing Large Time Series Databases, Proceedings of ACM SIGMOD Conference, California, USA (2001)
11. Keogh, E., Pazzani, M.: A simple dimensionality reduction technique for fast similarity search in large time series databases, Proceedings of Pacific- Asia Conf. on Knowledge Discovery and Data Mining (2000) 122-133
12. Last, M.: Online Classification of Nonstationary Data Streams, Intelligent Data Analysis, Vol. 6, No. 2 (2002) 129-147
13. Ljubic, P., Todorovski, L., Lavrac, N., Bullas, J. C.: Time-series analysis of UK traffic accident data, Proceedings of the Conference on Data Mining and WareHouses (SiKDD), Ljubljana, Slovenia (2002)

14. Sacchi, L., Bellazzi, R., Larizza, C., Magni, P., Curk, T., U. Petrovic, U., Zupan, B.: Clustering and Classifying Gene Expressions Data through Temporal Abstractions, Proceedings of 8th Intelligence Data Analysis in Medicine and Pharmacology Workshop(IDAMAP 2003), Protaras, Cyprus (2003)
15. Takada, T., Kurihara, S., Hirotsu, T., Sugawara, T.: Proximity Mining: Finding Proximity using sensor Data History, Proceedings of 5th IEEE Workshop on Mobile Computing Systems and Applications (WMCSA), CA, USA (2003)
16. Wu, H., Salzberg, B., Zhang, D.: Online Event-driven Subsequence Matching over Financial Data Streams, Proceedings of ACM SIGMOD Conference, Paris, France (2004)
17. Yi, B.-K., Faloutsos, C.: Fast Time Sequence Indexing for Arbitrary Lp Norms, Proceedings of 26th International Conference on Very Large Databases (VLDB), Cairo, Egypt (2000)
18. Yoon, J. P., Luo, Y., Nam, J.: A Bitmap Approach to Trend Clustering for Prediction in Time-Series Databases, Proceedings of Data Mining and Knowledge Discovery: Theory, Tools, and Technology II, Florida, USA (2001)

Conceptual Content Management for Software Engineering Processes

Sebastian Bossung, Hans-Werner Sehring, Michael Skusa,
and Joachim W. Schmidt

Software Technology and Systems Institute (STS),
Hamburg University of Science and Technology (TUHH)
{sebastian.bossung, hw.sehring,
skusa,j.w.schmidt}@tu-harburg.de

Abstract. A major application area of information systems technology and multimedia content management is that of support systems for engineering processes. This includes the particularly important area of software engineering. Effective support of software engineering processes requires large amounts of content (texts, diagrams, code, data, executables etc.) from different conceptual domains. The term "software crisis" disappeared gradually when content modelling and management addressed domains from application analysis and system design in addition to the sheer computational code domain.

In this paper we introduce an innovative conceptual content model and apply it in support of software engineering processes and their artefacts. We base our approach on the core model, of the computational domain which abstracts computational content (bodies of function code) by the computational concept of signatures (lists of typed function parameters). We generalise this *functional abstraction* model beyond the computational domain by introducing the notion of *asset abstraction* which models entities domain-independently by general content-concept pairs. We introduce an asset language and discuss the essentials of an asset system implementation.

In the application part of the paper we argue that software engineering can be substantially simplified by modelling SE entities from all the domains involved in an SE process homogeneously in an asset-oriented approach—entities ranging from application domains over intermediate architectural and design domains down to the computational domain. Furthermore, we discuss how the mappings between such domains can be substantially supported by services based on asset-oriented information systems.

1 Introduction: Content Management for Software Engineering

Heavy demands for data modelling and content management support dominate all kinds of engineering processes and are the major reasons for the ongoing commercial and scientific success of database technology. A wide variety of domain-specific data and content models has been developed and applied to computer-aided engineering environments.

J. Eder et al. (Eds.): ADBIS 2005, LNCS 3631, pp. 309–323, 2005.

An engineering area of specific interest and challenge to computer scientists is their home ground of software engineering (SE) (e.g., [26]). SE processes are particularly demanding since they span a wide variety of domains ranging from application entities in the analysis phase via intermediate entities required for system design and architecture down to computational entities for software implementation and execution.

The content models involved in SE processes usually include separate models for texts, diagrams, code, data, executables etc. This heterogeneity of the models causes much of the complexity of SE processes. SE environments, instead of providing homogeneous working support, are often subdivided into disparate tool contexts for diverse domains and their preferred representations: texts for analysis, diagrams for designs, code for executables, etc. This subdivision puts severe limitations particularly on those process steps which have to span several SE phases over various domains such as mapping steps, coherence tests or simple search and navigation tasks. This situation is only partially improved by approaches like those presented, e.g., in [4,27].

Consequently, we see a demand for a conceptual content model which can be homogeneously applied to all the domains involved in SE processes: to entities from application domains, to those in the intermediate architectural and design area as well as to entities from the computational domain.

In this paper we introduce an innovative conceptual content model applicable to a wide variety of domains and we apply that model to SE processes and their artefacts.

In section 2 we base our content model on the core model of the computational domain which abstracts computational content by the computational concept of signatures. This *functional abstraction* model is then generalised beyond the computational domain (section 3) by introducing the notion of *asset abstraction* which models entities domain-independently. We introduce an asset language and discuss the essentials of asset-based information system implementation. In the application part of the paper (section 4) we discuss how SE can be substantially simplified by modelling all SE entities homogeneously in an asset-oriented model. Furthermore, we argue that the mappings between such domains and other domain-spanning tasks can be supported by services based on asset-oriented information systems. The paper concludes with a short summary and a task outlook in section 5.

2   Conceptual Modelling of Computational Entities

It is historically interesting to observe, how means of abstraction available in programming languages evolved over time. In the assembly language of the early days, the main abstraction was providing human-understandable names (mnemonics) for operation codes. Later more and more abstraction mechanisms were introduced, amongst them functional abstraction and typing (see, e.g., [14] on the history of programming languages).

2.1   Functional Abstraction and Types

Most of even the smallest programs will exhibit near duplicate code if written in a sequential fashion. Introducing the concept of functions to parameterise and factor out this code has several benefits: (1) It makes understanding the program easier as it is broken down into semantically self-contained pieces, (2) it facilitates maintenance, as bugs only have to be fixed in a single place, and (3) it reduces the program's size. Functions usually consist of two important parts: the signature (its formal parameters and its return type) and the function body (the implementing code) [5].

The main power of functions thus lies in the introduction of an abstraction layer that associates conceptual information (the signature) with the code body of the function and hides implementational details. Right from the early days functions had a strong formal foundation to build on: the λ-calculus [16], which provides the theoretical basis for general function semantics: function definition (abstraction) and function invocation (application) form central parts.

Essentially any program deals with data, which the computer handles in the form of a particular internal representation. Generally speaking, any computer-representable data can be see as a string of bits. Depending on its proper interpretation, different operations are possible, for example addition, concatenation, or execution. To support the programmer in making the appropriate assumptions on the interpretation of data, programming languages introduced the concept of types. Types have become a central part of most computer languages by allowing the definition of appropriate computational entities and by formally checking the correctness of their use.

2.2   On Function Signatures over Function Code

Conceptual information on a function is captured in the function's signature to provide enough information to anybody who wants to use the function. The evolution of programming languages brought along new features that take the mechanism of signatures to higher levels of abstraction. Signatures can be found on function, class, and even component level, though the latter is still subject to research [3].

Computational entities are usually modelled in a dualistic way as pairs of code and signature, or, more generally speaking, of value and type. In section 3 we generalise this model to non-computational domains by means of content-concept pairs.

2.3   Operational Support for Computational Model Coherence

Based on functional abstraction, coherence of collections of computational entities can be supported by various technologies including compilers, linkers, runtime bindings, and remote invocations across system boundaries. Compilers make use of type abstractions as well as function signatures in, e.g., decorated abstract syntax trees or symbol tables [1]. This enables important features of compiler technology such as type checking, late binding or type coercion. In addition, by means of function signatures, functions themselves become first class citizens. This allows the introduction of higher-order functions [10].

Function signatures and typing enable runtime systems to select and bind computational entities. A common application is polymorphism.

A third field of application is that of cross system communication. Here signatures are of primary importance, as the full implementation is usually not available to a remote caller. Instead, calling programs are written against signatures, which serve as a language of mutual understanding to both systems. In the same context, named types allow the (un)marshalling of data to be communicated between the systems.

3   Conceptual Modelling of General Domain Entities

The concept of signatures (section 3.1) can be generalised to represent entities of any domain (section 3.2). We introduce a conceptual content modelling language (section 3.3) which drives the automatic generation of *conceptual content management system* (*CCMS*) (section 3.4).

3.1   Functional Abstraction as Special Case of Entity Description

Insights into type systems and their achievements influenced the definition, implementation and utilisation of a series of languages [18,19,10]. Starting from Pascal/R and DBPL this led to the orthogonally persistent object systems Tycoon-1 and 2 (Typed Communicating Objects in Open Environments 2) [7].

Viewing functional abstraction from a content management perspective, the code of a function body can be seen as well-formed content which is abstracted by a signature for management purposes such as type checking, late binding, information hiding etc. (see section 2.3).

In a series of application projects we applied the general idea—viewing code as computational content and describing it by a signature as its computational concept—to entity descriptions for arbitrary domains.

Often content is used to describe real-world entities—concrete or abstract ones. Just like a piece of code can be used properly only if its signature is known to the caller, content descriptions of the actual entities have to be paired with a conceptual understanding of the entities' nature. E.g., (John, Smith, 5000) represents the customer John Smith whose balance is $5000 only if the conceptual model [2] of a customer is clear to the viewer.

Therefore, entity descriptions in general consist of content coupled with a conceptual model of the kind of entity it refers to. For such *[content, concept]* pairs we use the notion of an *asset* as an indivisible union of perceivable content and a set of expressions describing it abstractly. This notion is detailed in the subsequent sections.

Managing entities from the computational domain can be understood as a special case of general entity descriptions. Returning to the example of function code, one can view source code as a specific kind of text which follows the constraints of a certain programming language. Therefore, the existence of a pair *[text, Java program]* augments a text to Java source code.

3.2 Assets: On Concept-Content-Oriented Modelling

The notion of an asset as introduced in the previous section has been developed in projects carried out in cooperation with project partners from the humanities. One main source of insights is the project *Warburg Electronic Library* (*WEL*) [21]. In this project we support art historians from the domain of political iconography.

For general domain models much can be reclaimed from computational models: the pairing of content and concept, the subsumption of content of specific concepts under more general concepts, the substitutability of content from sub concepts of a given concept etc.

Nevertheless, in some respects the entity models we looked at are fundamentally different from computational models. There is a duality of structure and domain semantics of assets. In the above example records with a structure (first name, family name, balance) can describe domain entities of both the kinds "debtor" as well as "creditor", e.g., depending on the balance.

The most severe distinction between descriptions of computational entities and entities in general is the subjectivity of the latter. For computational domains there exists exactly one well-defined conception. However, in "soft sciences" like the humanities there is no agreed-upon interpretation of contents and thus no single asset class for entity descriptions. Not only does the conceptual modelling of entities evolve over time as new findings lead to a better understanding of a domain, interpretations furthermore coexist as personalised views on entities.

Besides personalisation, there is an additional reason for coexisting asset models. Typically, domains are defined by using assets from existing base domains, which allows for reuse and also leaves asset definition to the experts of the field. To be able to incorporate base domain models into (multidimensional) derived domain models, inter-model relationships need to be established.

For both these reasons—subjective views and reuse—there is a demand for *openness* and *dynamics*. We call a CCMS open if it allows users to define assets according to their current information needs. Assets may change with time or context of the user and can be adapted to personal views. Dynamics is the ability of a system to follow redefinitions of assets at runtime without interrupting the users' work. Construction and dynamic evolution thus cannot be achieved with a manual software development cycle. We therefore adopt a generative approach to CCMS construction.

Just as content needs to be paired with a concept, open and dynamic systems cannot be based on a data model alone. Data models are limited by technical constraints of the target system (a database in most cases). To avoid such technical aspects in the domain model, a conceptual model is required. We briefly introduce our *asset language* for specifying such a model.

3.3   The Asset Model and Asset Language

In this section we give a brief description of the asset language as far as it is required for this paper. More details on the language can be found in [20,23,22].

A *model* consists of asset class definitions for entity descriptions. We refer to the corresponding part of the language as the *asset definition language*. First of all, it (intensionally) describes the structure of assets.

As an example, consider the following asset class definition:

```
class RegentImage {
    content image : Image
    concept characteristic title   : String
            characteristic epoch   : Epoch
            relationship   regent  : Regent
            relationship   artist  : Artist
            constraint     epoch = artist.epoch
}
```

In the content compartment a list of handles for multimedia content objects is given. Possible handle types are determined by a base language which is embedded in the asset language. Currently, we use Java as such a base language.

The concept compartment consists of a set of conceptual attributes and expressions. Characteristic attributes are ones that are inherent in an entity. In the above example, every RegentImage has a title and an epoch in which it was created. Just as for the content handles, possible values of characteristics are determined by the base language. Relationships are established between assets which describe autonomous entities. Here, each RegentImage has references to the depicted Regent and to the Artist who created that image. Constraints are imposed on assets of a class. In the above example it is required that the epoch in which a RegentImage has been created is the same as that of the associated artist.

While asset classes capture the structural aspects of assets, they can also be defined extensionally by naming a set of asset instances:

$$\textbf{class } \text{DeathOfTheRegent } \textbf{definedby } a_1, \ldots, a_n$$

Asset definitions are organised in models under the keyword model. As an example for the incorporation of base models (see the previous section) consider the sample models shown in fig. 1. One base model called Regents defines asset classes for descriptions of regents like kings or emperors. Another base model, Artists, likewise defines various classes of artists. Using these two domains as base domains, a new third domain on political iconography can be defined. It incorporates class definitions from the base models.

As can be seen in the example regent and artist information is reused in the political iconography. From the iconography point of view regent and artist information are objective so that one concrete model each is selected and used. Users from the field of political iconography build on these (objective) research findings in their (subjective) entity descriptions.

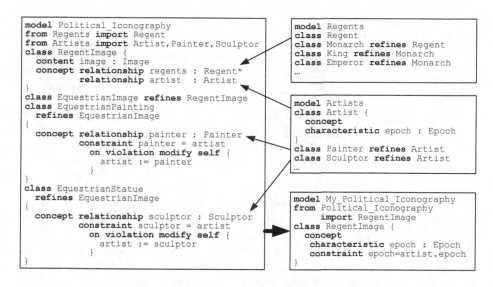

```
model Political_Iconography
from Regents import Regent
from Artists import Artist,Painter,Sculptor
class RegentImage {
   content image : Image
   concept relationship regents : Regent*
           relationship artist  : Artist
}
class EquestrianImage refines RegentImage
class EquestrianPainting
   refines EquestrianImage
{
   concept relationship painter : Painter
           constraint painter = artist
              on violation modify self {
                 artist := painter
              }
}
class EquestrianStatue
   refines EquestrianImage
{
   concept relationship sculptor : Sculptor
           constraint sculptor = artist
              on violation modify self {
                 artist := sculptor
              }
}
```

```
model Regents
class Regent
class Monarch refines Regent
class King refines Monarch
class Emperor refines Monarch
...
```

```
model Artists
class Artist {
   concept
      characteristic epoch : Epoch
}
class Painter refines Artist
class Sculptor refines Artist
...
```

```
model My_Political_Iconography
from Political_Iconography
     import RegentImage
class RegentImage {
   concept
      characteristic epoch : Epoch
      constraint epoch=artist.epoch
}
```

Fig. 1. Example of a model composed from base models

Subjectivity is possible because the openness property of the asset language allows the redefinition of assets. As an example, a user can change RegentImage by the definition shown in the model My_Political_Iconography in fig. 1. In the example a user added an additional characteristic attribute epoch plus a constraint. All content handles and conceptual definitions which are not named remain unchanged in the redefined class.

3.4   Conceptual Content Management System Implementation

Openness and dynamics as required for entity descriptions are not covered by contemporary information systems (ISs). Since ISs are usually based on database technology they share its typical constraints, the most crucial being that databases rely on one static schema.

Our approach to open and dynamic CCMSs is based on our asset definition language (see previous section). From models given in the asset definition language—by end-users—with little regard to implementation constraints open dynamic systems are generated by a technology that resembles model-driven architecture approaches [12]. It consists of a *model compiler* and a *modularised architecture* for CCMSs.

A system consists of a set of *components* reflecting one model each. These are broken down into *modules*. The model compiler creates modules, which are the basis of a domain-specific software architecture suitable for dynamic system generation [28]. The functionality of a component is defined by a component *configuration*.

Substitutability of modules is achieved by a separation of concerns. For our current purposes we identified five kinds of modules (see fig. 2):

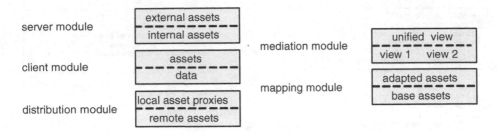

Fig. 2. Modules interface with each other in a layered architecture

- The description data of an asset (content, characteristics, and relationships) is stored in third party systems, databases in most cases. Mapping asset models to schemata of such systems is done by *client modules*.
- By use of *distribution modules* components can reside at different physical locations and communicate by exchanging data, e.g., XML documents generated from the asset definitions (comparable to the approach of [24]).
- Components are accessed via *server modules* using standard protocols.
- A central building block of the architecture of most CCMS applications is the mediator architecture [29]. In our approach it is implemented by modules of two kinds. One are *mediation modules* which delegate requests to other modules based on the request (operation and assets involved).
- The other kind of modules for the mediator architecture are *mapping modules*. By encapsulating mappings in such modules, rather than integrating this functionality into other modules, mappings can be added dynamically [11].

According to the two ways of combining asset models—model interrelation and personalisation—openness and dynamics in CCMSs happen along two dimensions: (1) the *organisation* and (2) the *application structure* [22]. Along the organisation structure users can define their own views (by personalising content and schema). Along the application structure, entity descriptions are shared and reused across domains.

In our approach the architecture of the generated systems allows changes along the organisation structure by its ability to enable dynamic system evolution through open redefinition of assets and dynamic invocation of the model compiler [23].

The association of models is realised by component configurations. Following the example from the previous section fig. 3 shows a configuration which combines two domains—regent and artists descriptions—into the new domain of political iconography. The component is accessed via mediation module m_{med1}. It distributes requests according to the type of the assets on which operations are invoked. If assets from one of the base domains *Regents* or *Artists* are affected, requests are delegated to the mediation module m_{med2}. This mediation module similarly delegates requests further to one of the components holding theses models. These components are accessed via distribution modules $m_{distrib1}$

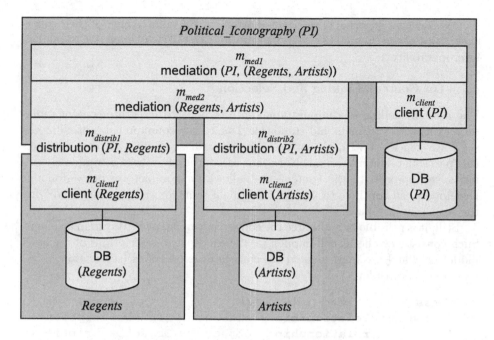

Fig. 3. Sample configuration of a system for a derived model

and $m_{distrib2}$. In the example of fig. 3 the components consist of client modules $m_{client1}$ and $m_{client2}$ and the respective base system only. Requests to the derived model *Political_Iconography* are forwarded by m_{med1} to the client module m_{client} which manages the users' assets from the political iconography.

As can be seen in fig. 3 the components for *Regents* and *Artists* are integrated into the overall CCMS without modification. This way the cooperating components remain unaffected, thus preserving their autonomy.

4   Asset Modelling and Software Engineering

The engineering processes of non-trivial software lead to a vast number of interrelated, but not explicitly connected, artefacts (e.g., requirements texts, various diagrams, code, tests, executables). In software development methodologies that are common practice today, most of the relations between artefacts of different type are not explicitly modelled. Instead, they are captured in the general knowledge of the developers or by "obvious" choice of naming. Both approaches lead to difficulties: The general knowledge of developers tends to diminish over time and obvious naming is usually only obvious to the one who chose it [13]. Thus, tool support for explicit modelling of such inter-dependencies is highly desirable. In fact, these interrelations are right at the heart of software engineering, as the transitions between development phases happen along them [9].

We therefore propose to model software artefacts by a domain independent conceptual content model, which is based on the asset technology discussed in section 3. This supports (1) retrieval of artefacts, (2) enforcement of their coherence, (3) a common and concise representation, and (4) exchange due to built-in interoperability.

4.1   On Content Linking and Selection

The asset modelling of computational entities aims to integrate content representations across formats and standards. Due to the common conceptual model a CCMS can work with all entities alike, regardless of the tool that supports this particular content format. Note that assets therefore take a completely unintrusive approach to the content that allows for complete owner autonomy. Developers can continue to use the traditional tools for creating and modifying the respective artefacts.

Still, it is possible to guarantee the consistency of changes to system artefacts. Such consistency checks can happen on the conceptual descriptions of the asset model level and are implemented via constraint expressions (see section 3). As an example, consider:

```
class SoftwareModel {
    concept relationship    classes : ClassDescription*
            relationship    objects : ObjectDescription*
            relationship    sequences : Sequence*
            constraint      sequences.objActs.msgs.name
                            <= classes.operations.name
                            and ...; matching signatures

        ...
}
class Sequence {
    concept relationship    objActs : ObjectActivation*

}
class ObjectActivation {
    concept relationship    obj : ObjectDescription
            relationship    msgs : Message*
}
  :
```

The constraint on `SoftwareModel` checks whether all messages used in sequence diagrams are available as operations in class diagrams. Of course, such constraints can also model inter-phase relationships, e.g., that every class in the conceptual model also needs to exist in the implementational one.

Violation of constraints can be reported for the system model as a whole, resulting in an integrated issue-list for the complete system. Some types of changes done by developers can result in violations of constraints (e.g., the renaming of a class in the transition from conceptual to implementational class diagram). This will show up in the issue list and can be clarified by the developer. The clarification serves a double purpose: It resolves what seemed to be a violation,

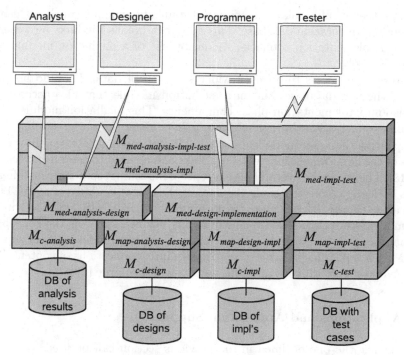

Fig. 4. A CCMS configuration for a software engineering scenario

but it also creates a link between two entities whose connection the system could not have detected automatically.

Fig. 4 shows a configuration for the management of SE entities with interrelationships. It is structurally similar to that of fig. 3. In the example there is a database for every phase of a typical SE process. According to the architecture of CCMSs there is a client module for each database. In conventional tool settings users in each phase work with exactly one of the databases at a time. In the example of fig. 4 this is the case for the analysts who store their results in the DB of analysis results.

For later stages the shown configuration supports the linking of contents as explained above. E.g., designers store their artefacts into the design database. To additionally relate their results to those of the analysis phase they do not work directly with the module $M_{c-design}$ which exclusively accesses the design database. Instead, they work with a mediation module through which they access both the analysis and the design databases.

The intermediate mapping module $m_{map-analysis-design}$ extends design assets such that relations to analysis assets are added. This way, designers can establish links between artefacts from analysis and design phases. These links can later (see section 4.2) be exploited to support a variety of functions.

Mediation modules do not only bridge the gap between analysis and design. They can also mediate between the other phases (see fig. 4). Programmers work on capturing the results of the design phase in actual code. In traditional environments, they would look at the design documents and then work exclusively with the implementation database. This approach breaks the links between design and implementation artefacts. Again, by use of a mediation module, this problem is resolved.

Testers need access to an even wider selection of data. They do not only work on the test database, but on a mediation module that also accesses the analysis and implementation phase components. This mediation module allows for seamless navigation through all the artefacts along the preserved links.

Obviously, the asset model supports linking of content between the various phases of the development process. Such links can be used to establish traceability [8,15]. Thanks to the overarching conceptual modelling, content from different phases is clearly connected along the lines of the corresponding concepts. These links can explicitly be modelled (as in approaches like "GRIDS" [30]) in the asset model (see section 3), but mostly this is not necessary, as the conceptual information persists across phase boundaries. With this model-inherent support of CCMSs it is possible to achieve concise semantic connections of content. This was previously very difficult and thus usually not attempted [9].

4.2   Applications and Application Support

A CCMS like the one outlined in the previous section can be used to support all aspects of the software development workflow. In this section, we will briefly introduce some interesting use cases.

Navigation through conceptual linking of artefacts. Through mediation modules that integrate various client modules, users are enabled to navigate along any path, even if it spans across multiple phases. This is beneficial for anybody taking part in software development to find artefacts that are related. A prominent example are implementers, who can now easily access the documentation for the code at hand. The same mechanisms allows them to reach back into design or even analysis to retrieve documents which concern the software entity at hand. This way it is much easier to understand what the entity does and why it is there. Especially the backwards links ("why do we need this class?") are not obvious in traditional software development. A CCMS is able to give a detailed account of the requirements and design decisions that lead to the existence of the entity in the implementation phase.

Custom perspectives for different roles. By means of personalised models different user roles can be provided with customised views on the development artefacts, e.g., to work on UML class diagrams with or without attributes shown. This way, users have to deal only with data which is relevant to their task.

Cross-phase constraints. Maintaining consistency between the artefacts of several development phases is a major problem in software development. Through the conceptual links that are also used for navigation, one is able to write constraints which span phase boundaries. An example of this was given in the previous section, but further use cases are not difficult to imagine: Tracking of changes from design to implementation (and the other way around), ensuring test coverage of analysis requirements, or monitoring the degree of completion of the implementation with respect to design documents.

Transparent distribution. Modern development happens in teams. This calls for remote cooperation of all the members of a team. In particular, they need to share a common information basis to ensure that the created artefacts are consistent with each other. Moreover, all the functionality outlined above needs to be available across several systems in a concurrent and transparent way. CCMSs support this by means of distribution modules (see fig. 2). In combination with the personalisation abilities, distribution in CCMSs goes beyond of what is traditionally used in software development. Through personalisation, users cannot only work on a common data base in a distributed fashion, but are also permitted to deviate from the community for some time and then remerge their artefacts. This can e.g. be used for branching source code.

5   Summary and Task Outlook

In this paper we present our asset-oriented information model as a conceptual content model gained by generalising the notion of functional abstraction predominant in the computational domain. Its safe and efficient use for the management of computational content is one of the fundamentals of state-of-the-art software development tools.

The presented generalisation step towards domain-independent conceptual content modelling makes CCMSs sound candidates for supporting the entire SE process ranging from application domain entities via artefacts for software design and architecture down to computational entities for system implementation and execution, thereby improving the coherence of SE processes.

Future work will address the extension of asset-based models for SE processes. This will include the development of models for the various development steps and their associated activities. Essentially, we address two goals: First, process portals can be built that collect examples of "best-practice" processes or parts thereof [25] which sometimes are more easily judged than abstract descriptions [17]. Second, making use of openness and dynamics allows the individualisation of software development processes to better suit a project's pragmatics [6].

Extending conceptual support beyond the traditional phases of software development into runtime will make information about the development of the system available during system execution. All sorts of services including debuggers and other inspection services will benefit from such extended information that allows to trace entities back to, e.g., the analysis phase.

Obviously, integration of CCMSs with traditional software development environments is essential in practical use. We expect that due to the modular architecture of CCMSs we will be able to create bridges to specific tools and representations (such as XMI based ones) which partially automate the conceptual modelling task of the developers. Also, with MDA [12] receiving much research interest lately, we will investigate how (semi-) automatic transitions between various development phases can benefit from the use of conceptual modelling.

References

1. Aho, A. V., Sethi, R., Ullman, J. D.: Compilers: Principles, Techniques, and Tools. Addison-Wesley (1986)
2. Brodie, M. L., Mylopoulos, J., Schmidt, J. W.: editors. On Conceptual Modelling: Perspectives from Artificial Intelligence, Databases, and Programming Languages. Topics in Information Systems. Springer-Verlag (1984)
3. de Alfaro, L., Henzinger, T. A.: Interface Theories for Component-based Design. In Proceedings of the First International Workshop on Embedded Software, volume 2211 of LNCS, Springer-Verlag (2001) 148–165
4. Egyed, A., Medvidovic, N.: A Formal Approach to Heterogeneous Software Modeling. In Proceedings of the Third International Conference on Fundamental Approaches to Software Engineering, volume 1783 of LNCS (2000) 178–192
5. Ehrig, H., Mahr, B., Cornelius, F., Groe-Rohde, M., Zeitz, P.: Mathematisch-strukturelle Grundlagen der Informatik. Springer-Verlag, 2nd edition (2001)
6. Fowler, M.: UML Distilled. Addison-Wesley, 3rd edition (2003)
7. Gawecki, A., Wienberg, A.: Report on the Tycoon-2 Programming Language. Version 1.0 (Draft). Technical report, Higher-Order GmbH, Hamburg, and Software Technology and Systems Institute, Hamburg University of Science and Technology (1998)
8. Gotel, O. C. Z., Finkelstein, A. C. W.: An Analysis of the Requirements Traceability Problem. In First International Conference on Requirements Engineering (ICRE), IEEE Computer Society Press (1994) 94–101
9. Duane Hybertson, D.: Strengthening the Modeling Foundation of the MDA. In Workshop in Software Model Engineering (2002)
10. Matthes, F.: Higher-Order Persistent Polymorphic Programming in Tycoon. In Fully Integrated Data Environments, ESPRIT Basic Research Series, Springer-Verlag (2000) 13–59
11. Mezini, M., Seiter, L., Lieberherr, K.: Component integration with pluggable composite adapters. In Software Architectures and Component Technology. Kluwer (2000)
12. Miller, J., Mukerji, J.: MDA Guide Version 1.0.1. Technical Report omg/2003-06-01, OMG (2003)
13. Musen. M. A.: Ontology-Oriented Design and Programming. In Knowledge Engineering and Agent Technology. IOS Press (2000)
14. Pratt, T. W., Zelkowitz, M. V.: Programming Languages: Design and Implementation. Prentice-Hall, 3rd edition (1996)
15. Ramesh, B., Jarke, M.: Toward Reference Models of Requirements Traceability. Software Engineering (2001) 27(1):58–93
16. Revesz, G.: Lambda-Calculus: Combinators, and Functional Programming. Number 4 in Cambridge Tracts in Theoretical Computer Science. Cambridge University Press (1988)

17. Rose, T., Fünffinger, M., Knublauch, H., Rupprecht, C.: Prozessorientiertes Wissensmanagement. Künstliche Intelligenz (2002) 16(1):19–24
18. Schmidt, J. W.: Some High Level Language Constructs for Data of Type Relation. ACM Transactions on Database Systems, 2(3) (1977)
19. Schmidt, J. W., Matthes, F.: The Rationale behind DBPL. In 3rd Symposium on Mathematical Fundamentals of Database and Knowledge Base Systems, volume 495 of LNCS. Springer-Verlag (1991)
20. Schmidt, J. W., Sehring, H. W.: Conceptual Content Modeling and Management: The Rationale of an Asset Language. In Perspectives of System Informatics, volume 2890 of LNCS, Springer (2003) 469–493
21. Schmidt, J. W., Sehring, H. W., Skusa, M., Wienberg, A.: Subject-Oriented Work: Lessons Learned from an Interdisciplinary Content Management Project. In Advances in Databases and Information Systems, volume 2151 of LNCS, Springer-Verlag (2001) 3–26
22. Sehring, H. W.: Konzeptorientiertes Content Management: Modell, Systemarchitektur und Prototypen. PhD thesis, Hamburg University of Science and Technology (TUHH) (2004)
23. Sehring, H. W., Schmidt, J. W.: Beyond Databases: An Asset Language for Conceptual Content Management. In Proceedings of the 8th East European Conference on Advances in Databases and Information Systems, volume 3255 of LNCS, Springer-Verlag (2004) 99–112
24. Shegalov, G., Gillmann, M., Weikum, G.: XML-enabled work-flow management for e-services across heterogeneous platforms. VLDB Journal (2001) 10(1):91–103
25. Simone, C., Divitini, M.: Ariadne: Supporting Coordination through a Flexible Use of the Knowledge on Work Processes. Journal of Universal Computer Science (1997) 3(8):865–898
26. Sommerville, I.: Software Engineering. Addison-Wesley (2000)
27. van der Straeten, R.: Semantic Links and Co-Evolution in Object-Oriented Software Development. In Proc. 17th IEEE International Conference on Automated Software Engineering, IEEE Computer Society (2002) 317
28. White, S., Lemus, C.: Architecture Reuse Through a Domain Specific Language Generator. In Proceedings of the Eighth Workshop on Institutionalizing Software Reuse (1997)
29. Wiederhold, G.: Mediators in the Architecture of Future Information Systems. IEEE Computer (1992) 25:38–49
30. Zamperoni, A.: GRIDS – graph-based, integrated development of software: integrating different perspectives of software engineering. In Proceedings of the 18th International Conference on Software Engineering, IEEE Computer (1996) 48–59

Using Step-Wise Refinement to Build a Flexible Lightweight Storage Manager

Thomas Leich, Sven Apel, and Gunter Saake

Department of Computer Science,
Otto-von-Guericke-University Magdeburg
{leich, apel, saake}@iti.cs.uni-magdeburg.de

Abstract. In recent years the deployment of embedded systems has increased dramatically, e.g. in the domains of sensor networks or ubiquitous computing. At the same time the amount of data that have to be managed by embedded systems is growing rapidly. For this reason an adequate data management support is urgently needed. Current database technologies are not able to cope with the requirements specific to embedded environments. Especially the extreme resource constraints and the diversity of hardware plattforms and operating systems are challenging. To overcome this tension we argue that embedded database functionality has to be tailored to the application scenario as well as to the target platform. This reduces the resource consumption and customizes the data management to the characteristices of the plattform and the application scenarion. We show that component techniques and feature-oriented programming help to face the mentioned limitations without focusing on special-purpose software. We present the design and the implementation of a database storage manager family. We discuss how feature-oriented domain analysis and feature-oriented programming help to do this task. Our evaluation criteria are the number of features and the flexibility to combine these features in different valid variants.

1 Introduction and Motivation

The domain of embedded systems is growing rapidly [15]. Approximately 98 % of all computer devices are deployed as embedded systems [34]. It is expected that pervasive and ubiquitous computing will push this trend in future [36]. Due to the low cost of embedded hardware, software-development on embedded systems is a hard challenge. The limitations on hardware, e.g. CPU-power, memory capacities or battery constraints make high demands on software-development. The result of these limitations is that applications developed as special-purpose software are tailored to a specific application scenario. Modern software-engineering methods, known from other domains are rarely used. We argue that component techniques, *Feature-Oriented Programming (FOP)* [8], and *Mixin Layers* [31] can help to reduce the devoplement cost and the time-to-market. Moreover, this software-engineering methods help to face the ressource restrictions without focusing on special-purpose software. Several promising studies [5,1,4,12]

J. Eder et al. (Eds.): ADBIS 2005, LNCS 3631, pp. 324–337, 2005.

show that FOP and mixin layers are appropriate to implement such layered, step-wise refined architectures. A further problem is the absence of standard infrastructure, e.g., database services. This makes developing embedded system applications more complicated. Due to the enormous number of variants of hardware and operating systems, software developers are swamped with finding the right vendor of infrastructure services. Since a few years the idea of product-lines is discussed in this context. Product-lines are supposed to maximize the reuse of existing components as well as to increase extensibility and customizability. This paper focuses on product-line technology for embedded data management infrastructure services.

In this contribution we present our first results towards a flexible, lightweight storage manager for embedded systems. The key idea is to implement the storage manager as a highly configurable program family [29][1]. Different family members (a.k.a configurations) satisfy the needs of different application scenarios: e.g. several embedded sensors require different data management functionality than data collectors or a mobile measurement unit in form of a PDA [37]. Furthermore, the high degree of configurability as well as the well thought design of the family allow to develop a highly portable storage manager. To implement a highly configurable program family we utilize feature-oriented domain analysis [22], feature-oriented programming [3] and mixin layers [31]. It is not obvious how the combination of these methods, integrated into the domain engineering process [16], leads to configurable, reusable and extensible data management software.

The article is structured as follows: Section 2 introduces a sensor network scenario and points to problems regarding embedded storage management functionality. Section 3 reviews the relevant software engineering methods used here. The subsequent sections present our storage manager architecture. In Section 5 we discuss our implementation results and review related work. Finally, we conclude in Section 6.

2 An Application Scenario

This section sketches an application scenario for embedded data management. Thereupon, we point out challenges of embedded data management.

2.1 A Sensor-Network Application Scenario

Due to the advances in wireless sensor-network technologies previous research focused on in-network aggregation and query processing. Most existing sensor applications rely on a centralized system for collecting data. Centralized data collection and analysis should provide cheap sensor nodes and minimal resource consumption. However, there are still a lot of problems: Sensor-networks are

---

[1] Although there is a subtle difference between program and product families (see [16]) we use these terms synonymously.

often intended for long-term deployment. Therefore, they underlay extreme resource constraints. One consequence of limited resources is that they are highly
communication constrained and therefore data buffering on the sensor node is
required. Another problem is that pre-aggregation and centralized systems lack
flexibility because data are extracted in a predefined way. However, an pre-
aggregation of raw data on nodes is possible only if the features of interest are
known a priori. This is not often the case in practice. Thereby an lightweight and
efficient buffering and access on raw data is essential for an ad hoc aggregation
on sensor nodes.

The following example scenario is borrowed in parts from [37,19]. We focus
on sensor-networks used in scientific applications, e.g. micro-climate and habi-
tat monitoring. Low-end sensor nodes are detecting environmental parameters,
e.g. temperature or light intensity. These modern sensors do not only respond
to physical signals to produce data, they also embed computing capabilities for
independent activity. Data collectors are special nodes to gather data from affili-
ated sensors to provide data for in- and out-network analyses. The different node
types are ordered in a hierarchical way and have widely varying requirements
on storage management services. For our scenario we point out two different
categories of heterogeneous devices:

- The first category are simple *sensor nodes* that only need a data structure
  to store data. Because of the hardware restrictions, all data are stored in the
  main memory. The size of a data record is known. The data structure needs
  only efficient insert, update, and lookup operations. Usually, sensor data are
  measurements. Therefore simple integrity checks of data are needed.
- The second category are *data collectors* that collect and aggregate data of
  different simple sensor nodes. To store data persistently the collector-node
  uses a secondary storage device (an additional flash chip). To optimize the
  processing of data a caching manager is required. Also complex integrity
  checks are needed.

2.2 Problems Occurring

In the scenario introduced certain problems occur: Common database implementations cannot provide the full range of the required functions by attending the
strong resource limitations. The monolithic system structure prevents the reuse
of logical device-independent functionality. These general-purpose systems are
not scalable[2] enough to satisfy the resource restrictions. The features of database services are not tailorable in such a fine-grained sense. The main reason
is well known as crosscutting concerns. Special-purpose data management services dealing with strong resource restrictions are not flexible enough to provide
services to all kinds of sensor-node types presented in the scenario. Application
developers have to choose the embedded database fitting best to their application, hardware and software requirements. This is a difficult, time consuming

---

[2] In the sense of scale their memory footprint.

and costly process, with lots of compromises. An adequate solution could be the concept of program-family architecture that can be tailored and optimized to the application scenario. Our goal are summarized as follows:

- systematic and detailed analysis of the domain of embedded data management
- customizability, reusability and extensibility through fine-grained features
- lightweight and portable implementation
- seperating crosscutting concern

3   Software Engineering Background

This section introduces the software engineering methods that we have used to analyze the domain of embedded storage management as well as to design and implement a program family of storage management. Following this idea we have used for the domain analysis feature-oriented domain analysis (FODA) [22]. Thereupon, we have designed a program family based on step-wise refinements and feature-oriented programming (FOP) [31]. Mixin layers are used as implementation technique.

3.1   Feature-Oriented Domain Analysis

With the domain analysis feature modeling is an appropriate software engineering method [22]. The goal of FODA is to analyze the considered target application scenarios and to derive the required and optional features. Since the focus of FODA is on a domain of applications the resulting features are chosen with regard to a whole family of systems. The results of feature modeling are feature models that describe the features, their relations, constraints, and dependencies [16]. These models express variation points and commonalities of the target-programs in an abstract and implementation independent way. Features are organized in a hierarchical way (see Fig. 1). Features are *mandatory*

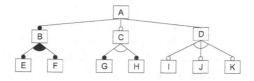

Fig. 1. Example feature tree

or *optional* stated by filled *(e.g. feature B)* and empty circles *(e.g. feature C,D)*. Moreover, they can be related in two ways: *alternative (e.g. feature G,H)*, connected by an empty arc and *or (e.g. feature E,F)*, connected by a filled arc. Feature models are one appropriate basis for designing and implementing program families [16].

3.2   Program Families and Step-Wise Refinements

Parnas [29] introduced program families first. The idea is to build software incrementally, using minimal building blocks and starting from a minimal base. This procedure is also known as *step-wise refinement* [31]. Exchanging, adding and removing such building blocks, also called *layers*, yields reusability, extensibility, and customizability. Batory et al. have mapped this concept to the object-oriented world [5,31]. They have observed that a new *software feature* often extends or modifies numerous existing classes. Based on this observation, they perceive features as *collaborations of class/object fragments*, also referred to as *roles*. Figure 2 shows a stack of collaborations. Classes are arranged vertically

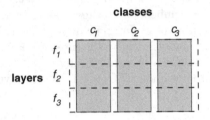

Fig. 2. Stack of collaborations

($c_1 - c_3$). Collaborations are arranged horizontally and span several classes ($f_1 - f_3$). Several features of a software system result in a stack of collaborations. In our context, examples of features are supported data types or caching strategies. Collaborations with the same interfaces are easily exchangeable. They are an instance of large-scale components [5]. In the sense of *Feature-Oriented Programming (FOP)* [31], a collaboration of objects implements a feature and is part of a layered stack.[3]

3.3   Mixin Layers

Mixin layers are one appropriate implementation technique to implement features in form of collaborations [31]. A mixin layer is a static component encapsulating fragments of several different classes (mixins) so that all fragments are composed consistently. Mixin layers are an approved implementation technique for component-based layered designs. Advantages are the high degree of modularity and the easy composition [31]. *AHEAD (Algebraic Hierarchical Equations for Application Design)* is an architectural model for FOP and a basis for large-scale compositional programming [7]. The *AHEAD Tool Suite (ATS)*[4], including the *Jak* language, implements AHEAD for Java.

---

[3] We use the terms feature and layer as synonym for collaboration.

[4] http://www.cs.utexas.edu/users/schwartz/Hello.html

3.4   Seperating Crosscuting Concerns

Pioneer work on software modularity was made by Dijkstra [17] and Parnas [29]. They have proposed the principle of *separation of concerns*. The idea is to separate each concern of a software system in a separate modular unit. They argue that this lead to maintainable, comprehensible software, which can be easily reused, customized and extended. Since a few years *Aspect-Oriented Programming (AOP)* and FOP are discussed as solutions of this problem. AOP was introduced by Kiczales et al. [23]. The aim of AOP is to separate crosscutting concerns. Common object-oriented methods fail in this context [23,16]. The idea behind AOP is to implement so called orthogonal features as *Aspects*. This prevents the known phenomena of code tangling and scattering. The core features are implemented as components, as with common design and implementation methods. Using join point specifications (*pointcuts*), an aspect weaver brings aspects and components together.

There are several discussions of pros and contras on separating crosscutting concerns using on AOP and FOP [25,24]. In this paper we are concentrating on heterogeneous crosscutting concerns. Heterogeneous crosscuts are distributed over several join points but apply varying code. That means different pieces of code are added to lots of different places. Homogeneous crosscutting concerns are distributed over several join points, but apply the same code fragments, e.g. locking or logging. Therefore the same piece of code is added to lots of different places. Current AOP languages focus on homogeneous concerns whereas FOP languages deal with heterogeneous concerns.

4   Storage Manager Design and Implementation

This section presents the domain analysis, design and implementation of the storage manager. Due to the limitations of space, we only focus on essential characteristics that are related to the presented scenario (see Section 2).

4.1   FODA

Figure 3 shows a subset of the feature model as result of FODA that describes the variability of our storage manager family.

The grey boxes symbolize features that have not displayed sub-features. This is because of the space limitations. The storage manager is separated in four mandatory features: (1) *Data Type (DT)* that represents the supported data types, (2) a *Buffer Manager (BM)* for storage data in primary or secondary memory, and managing the free space, (3) a *Storage Organisation (SO)* for structuring and accessing data and (4) *Records (Rec)* which represents the data in our database. Optional features are the *Integrity Checks (IC)* and supported *File Types (FT)*.

The overall feature-model of our small storage manager family has 93 features. We have not investigated in special data types, transaction management,

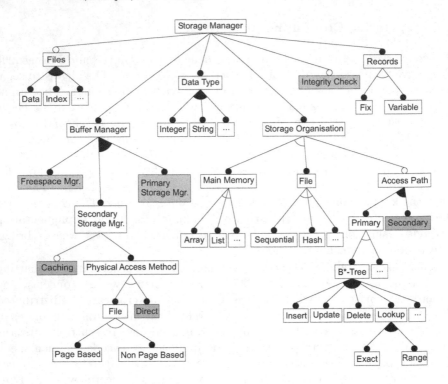

Fig. 3. Feature model of the storage manager family

recovery or specialized data structures for highly restricted application scenarios like smartcards [10]. An more extended analysis would produce hundreds of additional features for a storage management system.

Table 1 depicts variable parameters, e.g. number of supported data types (first two colums). The third column depicts the values for our experimental evalutation, e.g. for calculation of the permitted variants of the storage manager we assumed four different data types. Calculating the theoretical number of variants (cf. Table 1), we have determined 8.164.800 possible configurations (using a GenVoca grammar [6]).

$$\#SM = \underbrace{(2^f - 1)}_{FT} * \underbrace{(15)}_{BM} * \underbrace{(2^n - 1)}_{DT} * \underbrace{((m + s) * (6 * a * (2^o - 1)))}_{SO} * \underbrace{(2)}_{IC} * \underbrace{(2)}_{Rec}$$

The high amount of amount of feature combinations reforces the diversity of the database domain. The abstract description of variants and commonalities can be exploited to build a highly configurable database program family. The most combination differ only in a few details, e.g., the number of supported data types. However, we argue that only this fine-grained design can lead to optimally tailored database services.

Table 1. Adjustable parameters

parameter	description	# for caluculation
d	data types	4
f	file type	2
m	main memory organisation	2
s	data file structures	2
a	access structure	2
o	B^* Tree	6

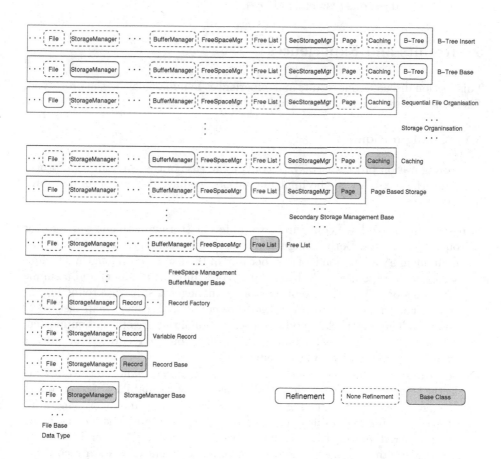

Fig. 4. Subset of implementes mixin layer

4.2   Design and Implementation

In order to evaluate our approach, we have implemented the storage manager, using the AHEAD Tool Suite which supports FOP for Java. It is also feasible to use the C++ template mechanism, nested classes and parameter-based inheritance [1,31,2]. Because of missing tool support and several problem regarding C++, we decided to utilize Java and AHEAD to prove our concept.

Figure 4 depicts a subset only. Mainly, the layers concerning the B^*-Tree access structure are depicted in bottom up order. Starting from the basic layers, which implement records, page storages and caching, the layer stack is refined to the B^*-Tree structure and several operations (Fig. 4 depicts the insert-operation only). The layer stack crosscuts about 26 classes and a couple of help-classes. In average, we have refined 3 classes per layer. To implement for instance the *Page Based Storage*, we had to refine three classes (*File, FreeSpaceMgr, SecStorageMgr*) and added one new class (*Page*).

5   Results and Experiences

This section discusses our results and experiences in implementing the prototype. Therefore, we use the scenario introduced in Section 2.

5.1   Configuration

The configuration process is easy.To convey the ease of the configuration procedure and the flexibility of the implementation, we have derived several storage managers:

Sensor Node. We have configured two different storage manager versions for our sensor nodes. Both configurations use main memory management. The main memory allocation is static, because of the fixed record length. The first sensor node type uses only basic data types (integer, number) and a simple array to store data. The resulting storage manager is step-wise refined by 11 layers. For the second category, we have configured a hash-map instead of an array. Thus the update and lookup functionalities are efficient supported. Furthermore, we have added an integrity check on the records. This storage manager is created by 16 layer refinement.

Data Collector. Due the application scenario the functionality of the data collector is more complex (cf. Sec. 2). Because of the availability of a secondary storage device, we have configured a secondary storage manager using a file oriented storing and an internal page based organisation. The file is sequentially ordered and for the access path we have used a B^*-Tree. To improve the performance we have chosen a cache management. The data record has variable length. Due to the task of the data collector we integrated a special integrity check on records. The total number of layers is 38 layers.

The correct syntactical composition of layers for a particular configuration is determined by equation files. The semantic correctness is ensured by DRC. We figured out that approximately 60 % of all possible configuration were excluded using DRC. We omit a detailed discussion because that is out of scope of this paper.

5.2   Discussions and Comparison to Related Approches

Incremental software development is an adequate process of building programs from simple ones by successively adding programmatic details. We have used these development methods to build tailored storage manager support for resource-restricted devices. Our implementation has shown that decomposition of storage manager into fine-grained components is possible. FODA, FOP and mixin layers are adequate software engineering methods to achieve highly scalable and lightweight software.

Direct comparisons e.g. performance analysis, code metrics, to other database solutions, e.g. COMET DBMS [26], Berkeley DB [28], are not meaningful at the current state of the work for several reasons:

- The set of implemented features of our storage manager is different to other approaches.
- We have not implemented any error-handling or logging functions, so that an objective performance analysis would be adulterated. We are going to implement this functions in future work.
- Our approach is implemented in Java. To the best of authors known, there is no other approach focussing on such a fine-grained tailorability of components by using Java implementing database functionalities.

For these several reasons we are comparing our approach to other solutions only on the concept level. First we compare our approach to Berkeley DB as known system in this area: Berkeley DB [28] is a common embedded database system, which is implemented in C and Java. The Berkeley DB consists of the following sub-systems: access methods, memory pool, transactions and locking. Hence, Berkeley DB is configurable on the sub-system level. However the components are coarser structured, as in our presented approach. An exchange of, e.g., the access methods, is complex due to a high degree of dependency of the sub-systems. This prevents an easy exchanging and extending of the database system. This fact is also confirmed by Tesanovic et. al [33]. They investigated on homogeneous crosscutting concerns in the Berkeley DB. With separating and implementing failure detection and synchronisation through aspects a code reduction up to 57 % was showed. This fact proves that crosscutting concern in Berkeley DB complicates tailorability and extensibility. Moreover Tesanovic et. al showed that there is a trade-off between the tailorability and maintainability of the system when aspects are used.

For the second comparison we choose COMET DBMS [26,32]. COMET DBMS is a component-oriented DBMS for embedded real-time systems. The research focuses on applying aspect-oriented and component-based software development to real-time system development. COMET is decomposed into seven basic components. These are: user interface component, transaction scheduler component, locking component, indexing component recovery and logging component, memory handling component, and transaction manager component. Furthermore the system is decomposed in three types of aspect: run-time, composition, and application aspect. One of the application aspects is the concurrency control aspect. This aspect crosscuts four basic components, namely the user interface component, transaction scheduler component, locking component, and transaction manager component. A clean separation of this aspect helps reconfiguring COMET to support locking or non-locking transaction execution. The COMET-project has shown that especially in real-time scenarios a lot of code is distributed as homogeneous crosscutting concern over several implementation units. Our approach has shown that in very fine-grained decomposed storage management systems heterogeneous concerns are challenging problems. Remaining on the discussion in [25,24] both types of concerns are common in today's system. Consequently, our objective in future work is to enhance our prototype with AOP features to deal with homogeneous crosscutting concern as well as with heterogeneous crosscutting concerns.

Finally, we have a closer look to more generalized results of our work. Choosing feature components in large scale database management software from a program family the system complexity can be reduced. This helps to reduce the maintenance overhead and new feature like automatic tuning can be easy evaluated and included in less complex software [14].

5.3   Related Work

Extensibility, customizability and flexibility on database systems are a research area that has been actively studied. An overview and classifications on extensibility can be find in [18,20]. Prototype systems like GENESIS [9], STARBURST [30], KIDS [21], EXODUS [13], etc, are commonly known in this research area. The XXL-library [11]is another prominent approaches to achieve extensibility and customizability based on using object-oriented design patterns. A more specific overview on embedded systems and real-time data management can found in Tesanovic et. al [32]. Olson points out in how to find the right database systems for embedded system environments [27]. Typical special-purpose database management solutions for embedded systems are e.g. GnatDB [35] for digital right management or PICO DBMS [10] for data management support on smartcards.

6   Conclusion and Further Research

Feature-oriented software methods and step-wise refinements advance the design and implementation of database functionality for embedded systems. In this article we have proposed a combination of FODA, FOP and mixin layers as feasible software engineering methods to implement a storage manager as a program family. A subset of basic features of a storage manager has been analysed and implemented, to show a high degree of flexibility and tailorability of our approach. Therefore we have presented an application adopted scenario from sensor networks, which shows different requirements on storage management in this area. Through an easy configuration process we derived three different variants form our storage manager product family tailored to the different application scenario.

As future work, we want to investigate and integrate more features. Our tokens of interests are special purpose algorithms resource restrict devices, transaction management, real-time feature and query processor. Furthermore, we want to investigate the performance and the memory footprint and how to encourage the configuration process for data management through deriving information from application scenario automatically. Furthermore we want to investigate our new language FEATUREC++ an extension to C++ that supports FOP [2]. Moreover FEATUREC++ improve the problem of crosscutting modularity by combining traditional FOP concepts with concepts of AOP.

References

1. Apel, S., Böhm, K.: Towards the Development of Ubiquitous Middleware Product Lines. In Cecilia Mascolo and Thomas Gschwind, editors, Software Engineering and Middleware Fourth International Workshop, SEM 2004, Linz, Austria, volume 3437 of Lecture Notes in Computer Science. Springer-Verlag, Berlin (2005) to appear.
2. Apel, S., Leich, T., Rosenmüller, M., Saake, G.: FeatureC++: Feature-Oriented and Aspect-Oriented Programming in C++. Technical Report Preprint Nr. 3, Department of Computer Science, Otto-von-Guericke University, Magdeburg, Germany (2005)
3. Batory, D.: Feature-Oriented Programming and the AHEAD Tool Suite. In Proceedings of the 26th International Conference on Software Engineering, IEEE Computer Society (2004) 702–703
4. Batory, D., Coglianese, L., Goodwin, M., Shaver, S.: Creating Reference Architectures: An Example from Avionics. In Symposium on Software Reusability (SSR), Seattle Washington (1995)
5. Batory, D., O'Malley, S.: The Design and Implementation of Hierarchical Software Systems with Reusable Components. ACM Transactions on Software Engineering and Methodology, 1(4) (1992)
6. Batory, D., O'Malley, S.: The Design and Implementation of Hierarchical Software Systems with reusable Components. ACM Transactions on Software Engineering and Methodology (1992) 1(4):355–398
7. Batory, D., Sarvela, J. N., Rauschmayer, A.: Scaling Step-Wise Refinement. In Proc. of the 25th Int. Conf. on Software Engineering (2003)
8. Batory, D., Sarvela, J. N., Rauschmayer, A.: Scaling Step-Wise Refinement. IEEE Transactions on Software Engineering, 30(6) (2004)
9. Batory, D. S., Barnett, J. R., Garza, J. F., Smith, K. P., Tsukuda, K., Twichell, B. C., Wise, T. E.: GENESIS: an Extensible Database Management System. In Readings in object-oriented database systems. Morgan Kaufmann Publishers Inc. (1990) 500–518
10. Bobineau, C., Bouganim, L., Pucheral, P., Valduriez,P.: PicoDMBS: Scaling Down Database Techniques for the Smartcard. In VLDB 2000, Proceedings of 26th International 2000, Cairo, Egypt, Los Altos, CA 94022, USA. Morgan Kaufmann Publishers. (2000) 11–20
11. Cammert, M., Heinz, C., Krämer, J., Schneider, M., Seeger, B.: "a status report on xxl - a software infrastructure for efficient query processing". IEEE Data Eng. Bull. (2003) 26(2):12–18
12. Cardone, R. et al.: Using Mixins to Build Flexible Widgets. In Proceedings of the 1st International Conference on Aspect-Oriented Software Development (2002)

13. Carey, M. J., DeWitt, D. J., Frank, D., Graefe, G., Richardson, J. E., Shekita, E. J., Muralikrishna, M.: The architecture of the EXODUS extensible DBMS. In K. R. Dittrich, U. Dayal, and A. P. Buchmann, editors, On Object-Oriented Database Systems, Topics in Information Systems. Springer, (1991)
14. Chaudhuri, S., Weikum, G.: Rethinking database system architecture: Towards a self-tuning RISC-style database system. In The VLDB Journal (2000) 1–10
15. Business Communications Company. Future of Embedded Systems Technology (2000) BCC Press release on market study RG-229.
16. Czarnecki, K., Eisenecker, U.: Generative Programming: Methods, Tools, and Applications. Addison-Wesley (2000)
17. Dijkstra, E. W.: A Discipline of Programming. Prentice Hall (1976)
18. Dittrich, K., Geppert, A.: Component Database Systems: Introduction, Foundations, and Overview. In K. R. Dittrich and A. Geppert, editors, Component Database Systems. dpunkt.verlag, San Francisco u.a. (2001) 1–28
19. Ganesan, D., Greenstein, B., Perelyubskiy, D., Estrin, D., Heidemann,J.: An Evaluation of Multi-resolution Storage for Sensor Networks. In Proceedings of the ACM SenSys Conference, Los Angeles, California, USA (2003) 89–102
20. Geppert, A.: Methodical Construction of Database Management Systems. GI Datenbank Rundbrief (1994) 14:62
21. Geppert, A., Scherrer, S., Dittrich, K.: KIDS: Construction of Database Management Systems based on Reuse. ifi-97.01, Department of Computer Science, University of Zurich (1997)
22. Kang, K. et al.: Feature-Oriented Domain Analysis (FODA) Feasibility Study. Technical report, cmu/sei-90-tr-21, Software Engineering Institute, Carnegie Mellon University, Pittsburgh, Pennsylvania (1990)
23. Kiczales, G. et al.: Aspect-Oriented Programming. In Proceedings of the European Conference on Object-Oriented Programming (ECOOP'97) (1997)
24. Lopez-Herrejon, R. E., Batory, D., Cook, W.: Evaluating support for features in advanced modularization technologies. extended report. Technical Report CS-TR-05-16, The University of Texas at Austin, Department of Computer Sciences (2005)
25. Mezini, M., Ostermann, K.: Variability Management with Feature-Oriented Programming and Aspects. In SIGSOFT '04/FSE-12: Proceedings of the 12th ACM SIGSOFT International Symposium on Foundations of Software Engineering (2004)
26. Nyström, D., Tešanović, A., Nolin, M., Norström, C., Hansson, J.: COMET: A Component-Based Real-Time Database for Automotive Systems. In Proceedings of the Workshop on Software Engineering for Automotive Systems at 26th International Conference on Software engineering (ICSE'04), Edinburgh, Scotland. IEEE Computer Society Press (2004)
27. Olson, M. A.: Selecting and Implementing an Embedded Database System. IEEE Computer (2000) 33(9):27–34
28. Olson, M. A., Bostic, K., Seltzer, M. I.: Berkeley DB. In USENIX Annual Technical Conference, FREENIX Track. USENIX (1999) 183–191
29. Parnas, D. L.: Designing Software for Ease of Extension and Contraction. IEEE Transactions On Software Engineering, SE-5(2) (1979)
30. Schwarz, P. M., Chang, W., Freytag, J., Lohman, G. M., McPherson, J., Mohan, C., Pirahesh, H.: Extensibility in the starburst database system. In Klaus R. Dittrich and Umeshwar Dayal, editors, 1986 International Workshop on Object-Oriented Database Systems, September 23-26, 1986, Asilomar Conference Center, Pacific Grove, California, USA, Proceedings. IEEE Computer Society (1986) 85–92

31. Smaragdakis, Y., Batory, D.: Mixin Layers: An Object-Oriented Implementation Technique for Refinements and Collaboration-Based Designs. ACM Transactions on Software Engineering Methodology (TOSEM), 11(2) (2002)
32. Tesanovic, A., Nystrom, D., Hansson, J., Norstrom, C.: Embedded Databases for Embedded Real-Time Systems: A Component-Based Approach. Technical report, Linkoping University, Mlardalen University (2002)
33. Tešanović, A., Sheng, K., Hansson, J.: Application-Tailored Database Systems: a Case of Aspects in an Embedded Database. In Proceedings of the 8th International Database Engineering and Applications Symposium (IDEAS'04), Coimbra, Portugal, Computer Society Press (2004) IEEE
34. Turley, J.: The Two Percent Solution. Embedded Systems Programming (2002) http://www.embedded.com/story/OEG20021217S0039.
35. Vingralek, R.: GnatDb: A Small-Footprint, Secure Database System. In VLDB (2002) 884–893
36. Weiser, M.: Hot Topics: Ubiquitous Computing. IEEE Computer, 26(10) (1993)
37. Woo, A., Madden, S., Govindan, R.: Networking support for Query Processing in Sensor Networks. Commun. ACM (2004) 47(6):47–52

BiChord: An Improved Approach for Lookup Routing in Chord

Junjie Jiang[1], Ruoyu Pan[2], Changyong Liang[2], and Weinong Wang[3]

[1] Department of Computer Science and Engineering,
Shanghai Jiaotong University, Shanghai 200030, P.R. China
jiang-jj@cs.sjtu.edu.cn
[2] Institute of Network and System,
Hefei University of Technology, Hefei 230009, P.R. China
pry@moe.edu.cn, cyliang@163.com
[3] Network Center,
Shanghai Jiaotong University, Shanghai 200030, P.R. China
wnwang@sjtu.edu.cn

Abstract. Efficient resource lookup is essential for peer to peer networks and DHT (Distributed Hash Table) provides an ideal solution for resource lookup in distributed networks. Chord is a representative peer to peer lookup service based on DHT. The topology of Chord is modeled as a directed graph. There is a unidirectional link from a node to its every routing table entry node.

In this paper, we propose to model the topology of Chord as a bidirectional graph. A reverse link is added for each original unidirectional link and such a pair of symmetrical links is maintained by a single heart-beat message. Then each node should maintain a finger table and a reverse finger table at very little additional cost. However, such reverse fingers may help to improve the lookup efficiency greatly. Theoretical analyses and experimental results both approve such improvements.

1 Introduction

Peer to peer computing has become a popular distributed computing paradigm. Many peer to peer systems, e.g. Napster [1] and Gnutella [2], have gained popularity quickly. Efficient resource lookup is considered essential for such systems.

By now, most of the deployed peer to peer systems are unstructured. Napster is based on a central directory while Gnutella and KaZaA [3] are decentralized and unstructured. All these popular unstructured peer to peer systems suffer from unscalability. Napster incurs the risk of a single point of failure and a performance bottleneck, because it completely depends on a single directory server. Gnutella uses a flooding approach with a maximum search depth to lookup and location resource. This approach can neither be scalable nor guarantee the perfectibility of a lookup. Some desired resources existing in the network may not be found. KaZaA takes advantage of super peers to improve its scalability but it still bears the deficiencies of unstructured peer to peer networks.

Fortunately, a new kind of peer to peer networks – that so called structured peer to peer networks such as CAN [4] and Chord [5], was proposed. Structured peer to peer

J. Eder et al. (Eds.): ADBIS 2005, LNCS 3631, pp. 338–348, 2005.
© Springer-Verlag Berlin Heidelberg 2005

networks are based on DHT (Distributed Hash Table) and DHT provides an ideal solution for efficient resource lookup in a distributed environment.

Chord is a representative peer to peer lookup service based on DHT. The topology of Chord is modeled as a directed graph. Each node maintains a finger table as its routing table. There is a unidirectional link from a node to its every finger node. Due to the dynamics of peer to peer networks, a heart-beat mechanism is required to perceive such churn, and such heart-beat messages are considered to be the dominating maintenance cost in Chord.

In this paper, we propose to model the topology of Chord as a bidirectional graph. For each original unidirectional link, a reverse link is added and such a pair of symmetrical links is maintained by a single heart-beat message. So each node needs to maintain a finger table and a reverse finger table at very little additional cost. However, such reverse fingers may help to improve the lookup efficiency greatly.

The rest of this paper is organized as follows. First of all, we show a brief overview of Chord in Section 2. Then in Section 3, we propose our bidirectional link model – BiChord and the BiChord lookup algorithm. We give some performance analyses of BiChord in Section 4 and provide the results from simulation experiments in Section 5. Finally, we survey the related work in Section 6 and conclude this paper in Section 7.

2 Chord Overview

In this section, we give a brief overview of Chord including its topology and lookup algorithm, which will help us understand the matter of BiChord better. To see more detailed description of Chord, please refer to the Chord paper [5].

2.1 Chord Overlay Network

In Chord, both data objects and nodes are assigned an m bits identifier by using a consistent hashing such as SHA-1. A node's identifier is obtained by hashing the node's IP address and service port number (or the user's private key) while a data object's identifier is produced by hashing itself or its name. We will use the term "node id" to refer to the identifier of a node and similarly the term "key" to refer to the identifier of a data object. The node id of node x is denoted by id(x). Sometimes, a node maybe denoted by its node id. Readers can distinguish such cases in context. Consequently, Chord defines a name space as a sequence of m bits and arranges such a name space on a scaled virtual ring modulo 2^m, which is called the Chord ring.

All the identifiers including node ids and keys are ordered along the Chord ring. Key k is assigned to the first node whose node id is equal to or follows k clockwise along the Chord ring and the node is called the successor node of k, denoted by successor(k). Also the successor node of a node x is the first node clockwise from id(x), denoted by successor(x).

In Chord, each node maintains a routing table, called the finger table and each routing table entry is called a finger of the node. The ith finger of node x, denoted by x.finger(i) contains the identity of the first node, s, that succeeds x by at least 2^{i-1} along the Chord ring clockwise, namely id(s) = id(successor(id(x) + 2^{i-1})) , $1 \le i \le m$. The finger table of each node may contain at most m fingers and in fact, the size of finger table is $\log_2 N$ with high probability, where N is the network size, i.e. the number of nodes in the network.

Figure 1 shows an example of a Chord ring with $m = 3$. There are four nodes in the network: 0, 1, 3, and 6. Also, there are four data objects, whose keys are 1, 2, 6, and 7 respectively. According to the descriptions above, the four data objects are assigned to their keys' successor nodes, i.e. nodes 1, 3, 6 and 0 respectively. In other words, the four data objects are located at nodes 1, 3, 6 and 0 respectively.

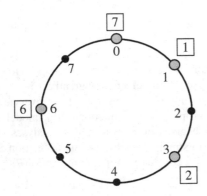

finger table of node 0

i	node id of the ith finger
1	1
2	3
3	6

Fig. 1. An example of Chord ring consisting of four nodes 0, 1, 3 and 6. Four data objects with keys 1, 2, 6, and 7 being located at the four nodes respectively. The numbers circled by a square denote the keys of data objects. The finger table of node 0 is shown at the right.

Figure 1 also shows the finger table of node 0. Based on the definition of finger table, the finger table of node 0 may contain at most 3 entries. The node id of the ith finger of node 0, id(0.finger(i)) = id(successor($0 + 2^{i-1}$)), $1 \leq i \leq 3$. Therefore, the node ids of these fingers are 1, 3, and 6.

2.2 Lookup in Chord

As a representative peer-to-peer lookup protocol, Chord just provides one operation that is lookup the node storing a given key's value, i.e. the physical location of the data object whose identifier equals to the given key.

The algorithm used for lookup through Chord is based on binary search. As stated above, each node in Chord maintains a finger table consisting of at most m fingers. To lookup a given key k, a node will check its finger table and forward a query message to the one that is closest to but doesn't overshoot k clockwise. Then the finger will do such in a same manner. After several bouts, the query message will ultimately arrive at the node immediately preceding key k and thereby the lookup is resolved. According to the construction of finger table, each forward will traverse 1/2 length of the remaining path at least. So the search space is reduced by half at least during each forward and it's very similar to bisearch.

It's easy to deduce that Chord can resolve a lookup within at most $\lceil \log_2 N \rceil$ hops, where N is the number of nodes in the network. Obviously, in Chord, all the lookup forward operations go clockwise along the Chord ring.

3 BiChord: Topology Model and Lookup Algorithm

As we have mentioned above, all the lookup routings in Chord go clockwise along the Chord ring. We take it as the start of our work. In this section, we propose a bidirectional link model that models the topology of Chord as a bidirectional graph. This bidirectional link model will improve the lookup efficiency greatly without too many changes to the simplicity of Chord. We also present the BiChord lookup algorithm.

3.1 Bidirectional Link Model

Two reasons inspire us to propose the bidirectional link model for Chord. The first is that the heart-beat message between each pair of adjacent nodes can be used by the two nodes to perceive the arrival or departure of each other. Such a single message can be utilized to maintain not only the original directional link but also its reverse link. The second is that in Chord, all the lookup go clockwise along the Chord ring and we think it's inefficient, because to lookup the keys being located near but preceding the node, the lookup has to traverse almost the whole Chord ring.

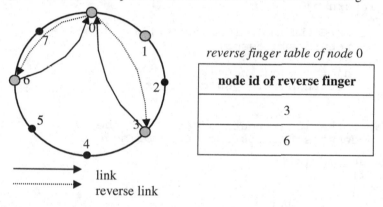

reverse finger table of node 0

node id of reverse finger
3
6

⟶ link

⋯⋯▶ reverse link

Fig. 2. An example of BiChord. Node 0 is the 3rd finger of node 3 and the 1st and 2nd finger of node 6.The reverse finger table of node 0 is shown at the right.

The bidirectional link model is rather simple. In the model, a node needs to maintain a so-called reverse finger table in addition to the finger table. If there is a link in Chord, we will add a reverse link that links the same two nodes but at the reverse direction. For example, if node A is a finger of node B in Chord, i.e. there is a link from B to A, a reverse link from A to B will be added into the topology based on the bidirectional link model. Then, B becomes a reverse finger of A. There are no changes to the responsibility of data objects in Chord. All the data objects are still located at the successor nodes of their keys.

Figure 2 shows an example of BiChord. This example is the BiChord version of the Chord example in Figure 1. In Chord, node 0 is the 3rd finger of node 3 and the 1st and 2nd finger of node 6. So node 3 and node 6 become the reverse finger of node 0 and are included into the reverse finger table of node 0. The original directional links between node 0 and node 3, node 6 are replaced by bidirectional links.

3.2 BiChord Lookup Algorithm

We take the finger table and the reverse finger table as a whole and call it the routing table. In the routing table, all the entries are ordered. To lookup a given key k, a node will check its routing table instead of only its finger table to find a certain table entry, namely one of its fingers or reverse fingers, whose identifier is closest to the key k among all these entries. Then the lookup message is forwarded to the node referred by this entry. Finally, this lookup message will arrive at the node closest to the key k among all the nodes in the network. Since we have not changed the responsibility of data objects, this node must be the predecessor or successor node of the key k. If the node is the successor node of k, the lookup is resolved. Or else, this node must be the predecessor node of k, the lookup is resolved too.

```
// ask node n to find successor of k
n.find_successor(k){
    if (k ∈ (id(predecessor), id(n)])
        return n;
    else
        if (k ∈ (id(n), id(successor)])
            return successor;
        else{
            n' = closest_node(k);
            return n'.find_successor(k);
        }
}
// search the local routing table for the closest node
to k, R denotes the routing table of node n
n.closest_node(k){
    m = 1;
    x = R(1);
    for i = 1 to ‖R‖
        if (|R(i)-k| < |x -k|){
            x = R(i);
            m = i;
        }
    return R(m);
}
```

Fig. 3. The pseudocode of BiChord lookup algorithm

The pseudocode of BiChord lookup algorithm is presented in Figure 3. Remote calls and variable references are both preceded by the identifier of remote node, while local variable references and procedure calls both omit the identifier of local node. The mechanisms to deal with the joins and stabilization remain unchanged, which is still same as that in Chord.

4 Performance Analysis

In this section, we will give some performance analysis on BiChord. The two main performance metrics we discuss are routing table size and lookup path length. We will give the precise proof on the routing table size and some intuitive analyses on the lookup path length in BiChord.

Theorem 1. *Each node maintains a finger table with at most m entries and with high probability, the size of finger table is O(logN), where m is the length of identifier and N is the number of nodes in the network.*

Proof.
Since there are no changes between the construction of finger table in BiChord and in Chord, the number of entries in the finger table of each node is also unchanged. So the finger table size in BiChord is same as that in Chord. It follows that with high probability, the finger table size in Chord is $O(logN)$ and is m at most. [5]   •

Theorem 2. *With high probability, each node maintains a reverse finger table with $O(log^2N)$ entries, and the expected reverse finger table size is O(logN), where N is the number of nodes in the network.*

Proof.
The expected distance between two successive nodes is $2^m/N$ on the Chord ring, and with high probability, the distance is $L = O((2^m/N) \times logN))$.

Consider a node n. With high probability, there are L continuous keys between node n and its predecessor node p, i.e. with high probability, $|id(n) - id(p)| = L$.

If node n is a finger of node x, we will have $id(n) = id(successor(id(x) + 2^{i-1}))$, $1 \leq i \leq m$. That is to say, $id(x) + 2^{i-1}$ is in the range between $id(n)$ and $id(p)$. So $id(x)$ is in the range between $id(n) - 2^{i-1}$ and $id(p) - 2^{i-1}$. It's clear that for a particular i, $id(x)$ locates in this range with probability $|(id(n) - 2^{i-1}) - (id(p) - 2^{i-1})|/2^m$, that is, node n is a finger of node x with probability $|id(n) - id(p)|/2^m$. As stated above, with high probability, $|id(n) - id(p)| = L = O((2^m/N) \times logN)$. Thus node n is a finger of node x with probability $O(logN/N)$ for any a node x and a particular i. And with high probability, for this particular i, there are $O(logN)$ nodes that finger node n because there are N nodes totally.

Since with high probability, a node has just $O(logN)$ fingers (i.e. all the values of i correspond to $O(logN)$ fingers), there are $O(log^2N)$ unique nodes that finger node n with high probability and so node n maintains a reverse finger table with $O(log^2N)$ entries, with high probability.

As shown in Theorem 1, every node maintains a finger table with $O(logN)$ entries, with high probability. So the sum of the finger table size is $O(N \times logN)$ and on average, each node is a finger of $O(logN)$ nodes. Then the expected reverse finger table size is $O(logN)$.   •

In Chord, all the lookup routings go clockwise along the Chord ring. However in BiChord, the lookup routings don't go only in one way any longer. In BiChord, the lookup routings may go clockwise or counter-clockwise alternately because at each step, the BiChord lookup algorithm tries to find the closest routing table entry to the desired key instead of the finger closest to but not overshooting the key. So if the closest routing table entry overshoots the desired key clockwise, the routing must turn back during remaining steps. Although the routing direction is not determinate, at each step, the current lookup forward node is closer to the destination node than the previous one.

The lookup efficiency is improved clearly. In Chord, each node maintains information about a small number of other nodes and knows more about the nodes closely following it along Chord ring than the nodes farther away. However in BiChord, each node maintains not only such information but also the information about more nodes (reverse fingers nodes). A node knows many about the nodes near it at both sides instead of only the clockwise side. Intuitively, the fingers and reverse fingers of each node partition the Chord ring finer and by these fingers and reverse fingers, a node will locate the region of a desired key more accurately at each step. Thus the nodes will resolve a lookup within fewer steps.

5   Experimental Evaluation

In this section, we evaluate the performance of BiChord by simulation. The simulator is implemented in Java and each node is modeled as an object instance of the Node class. The simulator uses the BiChord lookup algorithm shown in figure 3 and the remote calls are replaced by the local message passing between Java objects. For the comparison purpose, we also implement Chord lookup algorithm. We do implement the successor list in neither BiChord nor Chord lookup algorithm because the successor list is just to guarantee the correctness of routing during the churn process.

5.1   Routing Table Size

The routing table size is an important performance metric of BiChord. Although the reverse finger table brings very little additional maintenance cost, we still investigate the reverse finger table size to evaluate BiChord thoroughly. The finger table size is examined during the experiment too. From Theorem 1 and Theorem 2, with high probability, the finger table and reverse finger table sizes are $O(logN)$ and $O(log^2N)$ respectively, and the expected finger table and reverse finger table sizes are both $O(logN)$, where N is the total number of nodes in the network.

To understand the routing table size in practice, we simulated a network with $N = 2^k$ nodes. We varied k from 3 to 14 and conducted an individual experiment for each value of k. We measured the finger table and reverse finger table sizes of each node during every experiment.

Figure 4(a) plots the average sizes of finger table and routing table as a function of k. As expected, they both increase logarithmically as the number of nodes. Figure 4(b) plots the PDF (probability density function) of the finger table and reverse finger table sizes for a network with 2^{12} nodes ($k = 12$).

Figure 4(a) confirms that in BiChord, the average finger table size is $O(logN)$ and the average routing table size is $O(logN)$ too. Figure 4(b) shows that the distribution of reverse finger table size is much more uniform than that of finger table. The finger

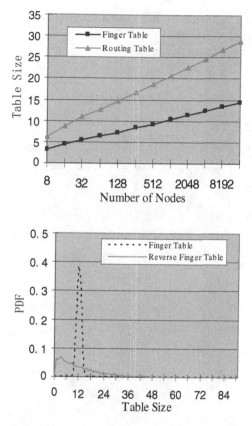

Fig. 4. (a) The average finger table and routing table sizes of BiChord as a function of network size. (b) The PDF of the finger table and reverse finger table sizes in the case of a 2^{12} nodes network.

table size of most peer nodes are around *log N* while the reverse finger table size of most peer nodes is smaller.

5.2 Lookup Path Length

The routing performance of BiChord depends on the lookup path length mostly. We also simulated a network with $N = 2^k$ nodes and 100×2^k data objects here. We varied k from 3 to 14 and conducted a separate experiment for each value of k. During every experiment, each node picked up a random set of keys to lookup using Chord and BiChord lookup algorithm respectively, and we measured each lookup path length of the two algorithms.

Figure 5(a) plots the average lookup path length of the two lookup algorithms as a function of k. Figure 5(b) plots the PDF of the lookup path length of the two algorithms for a network with 2^{12} nodes ($k = 12$).

Figure 5(a) indicates that BiChord has a great improvement over Chord in average lookup path length. Figure 5(b) shows more expressly that the average lookup path length in BiChord is shorter than that in Chord.

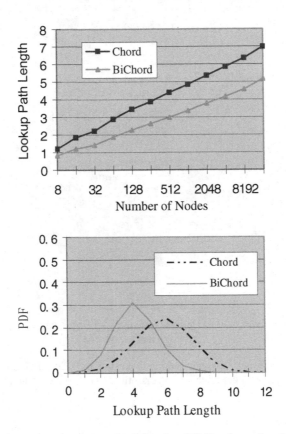

Fig. 5. (a) The average lookup path length of Chord and BiChord as a function of network size. (b) The PDF of the lookup path length of Chord and BiChord in the case of a 2^{12} nodes network.

6 Related Work

By now, Chord has brought up many novel distributed application systems. We also have implemented an experimental system for distributed text information retrieval based on Chord lookup service [6]. However, there is still some space to improve for the lookup efficiency in Chord.

There are two main ways to improve the lookup efficiency in Chord. One way is to optimize the logical topology of Chord such as the denser finger technique [7]. The other is to utilize the underlying network topology information such as geographic layout and proximity neighbor selection (PNS) techniques [8].

The denser finger technique places fingers of node x at points id(successor(id(x) + $(1 + 1/d)^{i-1}$)) on the Chord ring, $1 \leq i \leq m$ and d is a tunable integer parameter. The number of fingers kept by each node is now d times of that in original Chord and the maximum lookup path length is reduced to $1/(1 + log(1 + d))$ of the original. However, the average lookup path length is $logN / ((1 + d) log(1 + d) - d log(d))$. As declared, when d is larger, the improvement is less. In our another work, we present ChordPlus lookup algorithm [9] which generalizes Chord lookup algorithm to M-ary lookup. It also gets some improvements in lookup path length. There is some similarity between ChordPlus and the denser finger technique but the approaches are rather different in nature.

However, all the work remains to route lookup only in one way (clockwise) as in Chord. S-Chord [10] proposes to using symmetry to improve lookup efficiency in Chord. That is, each node maintains fingers at its both side and these fingers of node x are placed at points id(successor(id(x) + 4^{i-1})) and id(predecessor(id(x) − 4^{i-1})), $1 \leq i \leq m$. S-Chord shows the improvements on routing performance by experiments. BiChord is quite different from the idea of S-Chord. In S-Chord, each link is still unidirectional like in Chord, but in BiChord, we add a reverse link to the topology graph for each original link at very little additional maintenance cost and achieve remarkable improvements on routing performance too.

Exploiting the underlying network topology information has been considered for use in Chord too [11] and there some work is going on in this way.

7 Conclusion

Chord provides an efficient peer to peer lookup service based on DHT. The simplicity, provable correctness, and provable performance make it an attractive substrate for distributed applications. However there still remains some space to improve for its lookup efficiency.

In this paper, we propose BiChord, an improved approach for lookup routing in Chord. BiChord models the topology of Chord as a bidirectional graph and replaces every original unidirectional link in Chord with a bidirectional link. In nature, it utilizes the existing finger table in Chord and the heart-beat mechanism to construct a reverse finger table. Such a reverse finger table can help to improve lookup performance in Chord greatly. The theoretical analyses and experiment results both confirm such remarkable improvements. Another byproduct is that the fault-tolerance is enhanced due to more routing table entries and the relaxed routing selection policy.

References

1. Napster. http://www.napster.com
2. The Gnutella protocol specification v4.0. http://dss.clip2.com/GnutellaProtocol04.pdf
3. KaZaA website: http://www.kazaa.com
4. Ratnasamy, S., Francis, P., Handley, M. et al.: A scalable content-addressable network. In Proceedings of ACM SIGCOMM 2001, San Diego, CA (2001) 161-172
5. Stoica, I., Morris, R., Liben-Nowell, D. et al.: Chord: a scalable peer-to-peer lookup protocol for Internet applications. IEEE/ACM Transactions on Networking, Vol. 11, No. 1 (2003) 11-32

6. Junjie, J., Wang, W.: Text-Based P2P Content Search Using a Hierarchical Architecture. In Proceedings of the 7th International Conference of Asian Digital Libraries, Shanghai, China, LNCS 3334 (2004) 429-439
7. Li, Z., Feng, Z.: Understanding Chord Performance and Topology-aware Overlay Construction for Chord. http://www.cs.berkley.edu/~zl/doc/chord_perf.pdf, Project Report, (2003)
8. Ratnasamy, S., Shenker, S. and Stoica, I.: 2002. Routing Algorithms for DHTs: Some Open Questions. In Proceedings of the 1st International Workshop on Peer-to-Peer Systems, Cambridge, MA, USA, LNCS 2429 (2003) 45-52
9. Haihuan, B., Junjie, J., Wang, W.: ChordPlus: A Scalable, Decentralized Object Location and Routing Algorithm. Journal of System Engineering and Electronics, to appear.
10. Mesaros, V., Carton, B., Van Roy, P.: S-Chord: Using Symmetry to Improve Lookup Efficiency in Chord. In Proceedings of the International Conference on Parallel and Distributed Processing Techniques and Applications PDPTA'03, Las Vegas, Nevada, USA, Jun. (2003)
11. Dabek, F., Kaashoek, M. F., Karger, D., Morris, R.: Wide-area Cooperative Storage with CFS. In Proceedings of the 18th ACM Symposium on Operating Systems Principles, Chateau Lake Louise, Banff, Canada, Oct. (2001)

On Business Rules Automation: The BR-Centric IS Development Framework

Irma Valatkaite and Olegas Vasilecas

Information Systems Scientific Laboratory, Vilnius Gediminas Technical University,
Sauletekio al. 11, Vilnius, Lithuania
{irma, olegas}@isl.vtu.lt

Abstract. The business rules (BR) approach in information systems (IS) engineering responds to the need of business practitioners to maintain their ISs efficiently in the volatile business environment. The important requirement is to reduce effects to adapt IS to the changes in business environment. This problem can be solved by the explicit use of enterprise knowledge in the form of BR stored outside of the application logic. A number of BR-based systems, methods, frameworks, and languages were proposed, but only few address automatic BR implementation. In this paper we present the framework which outlines the main components for BR-based IS development using BR automation. In our approach we differentiate three abstraction layers where the understanding, representation, and use of BR differ accordingly. We give the definitions of the components, outline their role in the framework, and present the results of a short case study as an example of the framework instantiation.

1 Introduction

In the research of the business information systems (IS) development the business rules (BR) approach has achieved a lot of attention and already has a steady niche with a strong motivation behind [4, 5, 10, 24, 12]. Knowledge management initiatives drive enterprises to reveal their business knowledge and manage it as explicit asset. For knowledge management purposes business rules are used by business practitioners as the way to structure enterprise knowledge, i.e., to represent policies, procedures and constraints regarding how the enterprise conducts its business. Thus giving business rules the proper attention at enterprise management level enables enterprise to manage itself by making visible the individual policies that the organization puts in place as a guide to accomplish its goals. By manipulating the business rules the organization enables to fine-tune itself to the ever changing business environment thus becoming faster and more responsive than its competitors.

On the other hand, business information should support the ultimate goal of enterprises to quickly respond to environment changes. The business rules approach to IS development is intended to solve this task and enable IS developers to shorten the development cycle from business requirements to the actual implementation and also give the possibility to business users to maintain their business rules set by themselves thus achieving the intended speed of responsiveness and adaptiveness. Since business users are owners of the business rules it is a rather straightforward solution [12, 16]. The benefits of explicitly dealing with business rules may be stated as follows:

J. Eder et al. (Eds.): ADBIS 2005, LNCS 3631, pp. 349–364, 2005.

1. From the enterprise management perspective: the explicit business rules model, the elicitation and modelling activities reveal the implicit rules of running the business and serve as the means to first check and then ensure consistency and uniformity of those rules. The elicitation activity may have an additional positive "side-effect": uncovering of business rules is a learning activity and may be used as the auditing process to ensure that every single business process is in line with the enterprise strategic objectives. For example, if the enterprise strives to be customer-centric organization, it is important to ensure the smooth processing of all types of customer requests through the different departments. However, in large enterprises the prioritisation of customer requests may be done based on different criteria (depending on the localised targets of the departments).
2. From business rules enforcement perspective: explicit, consistent and uniform business rules model ensures that operational systems do enforce the right rules in the right way and conforms with the operating principles of the enterprise. Moreover, not only IS supporting operational level business processes may be built based on a single business rules model, but also the analytical level business IS (enterprise management systems, performance management systems, etc.) aligned with the same business rules model guarantee that the right measures are applied through all enterprise levels.
3. From business IS development perspective: the business rules are inherent concept of business itself adopted by IS engineering. Thus business rules elicitation and modelling serves as the bridge between business practitioners and IS engineers as the commonly understood language. If the selected business rules modelling language is understood by both parties and no transformations of the model is performed along the way, such modelling activity also secures that the right business rules are captured in a consistent way.

The research on business rules approach and the resulting technologies (business rules tools as well) may also be characterised by their intended purpose [13]:

1. Enterprise management: to provide an environment where business rules are captured, documented, secured, distributed to the relevant parties within both the business and technology organizations, and modified as the business evolves.
2. Enforcement: to integrate business rules into business application's architecture, but to hold business rules separately from the processing code.
3. Excavation or mining: mine through existing IS or enterprise documentation to uncover business rules held within application code or textual documents with the purpose to transform business rules uncovered from code into something that is meaningful to business people.

The three purposes (or characteristics) of technologies and tools are separate research topics, however, as technologies and tools evolve they are intermingled and tools emerge that serve for two purposes simultaneously. Most often technologies and tools are offered that are suitable for the first two tasks: enterprise management and enforcement. This is because these two require the same basic component – the business rules repository which serves as the central location of storing business rules data and metadata. The business rules mining is a different activity: (1) enterprise management and business rules enforcement are the activities that support daily business, while mining is a rather one-time activity results of which should be used as the input for the management and enforcement processes; (2) mining requires completely different algorithms and implementation architectures than management and / or enforcement technology. Thus it is not reasonable to combine business rules mining with the other two. However, some tools successfully combine all three (e.g., Infrex [11]; the survey of tools is given below in Section 2).

In this paper we present the framework for business rules approach to business IS development centred on business rules enforcement and enterprise management activities, not covering the mining or elicitation processes. We provide definitions for the components using three abstraction layers – that of business system, information system, and program system – where the understanding, representation, and use of business rules and associated framework components differ accordingly. The main goal of the framework is to give the necessary components and their interrelations for BR-based IS development with automatic business rules generation component.

The rest of the paper is organized as follows. The overview of the related work is given in Section 2. The basic idea of the framework and the description of the components are covered in Section 3, while the instantiation of the ideas are provided in Section 4. The conclusions are drawn and the further research directions are given in Section 5.

2 Related Work on Business Rules Approach

The business rules approach has drawn a lot of attention already and a number of architectures, technologies, frameworks have been proposed and a number of tools have been developed (both for research and commercial purposes).

The proposed BR-centric approaches are applicable for explicit work with business rules at various phases of IS development cycle. However, there are just few results reported on business rules automation. By business rules automation we assume the automatic generation of executable business rules specification from the declarative business rules statements or business rules model in some modelling language or interchange format.

2.1 Business Rule Concept

A number of definitions for business rule were developed. Business rules definition may be analysed from two perspectives: business perspective and IS development perspective [4, 14]. From business perspective ('Zachman [19] row-2') business rule is a statement that defines or constrains some aspect of the business; it is intended to assert business structure, or to control or influence the behaviour of the business. From IS perspective ('Zachman row-3') business rule is a statement which constrains certain business aspect, defines business structure, and controls business processes that are supported by enterprise information systems. In IS business rules may be implemented as facts registration (as data) and constraints applied during registration process. Von Halle in [23] summarizes the business rule definition problem as follows: "depending on whom you ask, business rules may encompass some or all relationship verbs, mathematical calculations, inference rules, step-by-step instructions, database constraints, business goals and policies, and business definitions".

In our research we use the definition given above providing the concept in business context – business rule defines the way of operating enterprise business (policies, guidelines, behaviours, etc.). However, we require that enterprise business rules model comprised only atomic business rules. Atomic business rules are such that cannot be broken down or decomposed further into more detailed business rules because, if reduced any further, there would be loss of important information about the business. This limitation comes from the IS implementation perspective and is reasonable because not-implementable business rules model can guarantee neither consistency, nor unambiguity.

The various taxonomies of business rules discussed in details in [15, 22] show the lack of standards in business rules community on types, classes and categories of business rules. However, the surveys show that the taxonomies of business rules presented by different authors depend on the intended purpose (for example, enterprise management or implementation of business rules in IS, or implementation of business rules in rules engines).

2.2 BR-Centric Frameworks

According to the survey of BR-centric frameworks, architectures and technologies given in [25, 15, 2], the proposed ideas are rather diverse depending on perspective or intended purpose and can be summarised as follows:

- From implementation perspective the proposed business rules approaches can be classified into three broad types: rules implemented as application logic components, rules implemented using active databases technologies, and rules implemented in rules engines (enforcement, inference, etc).
- From architectural focus: different authors stress different IS development life cycle phases – from elicitation to maintenance; accordingly their proposed frameworks vary. Some concentrate on business objects definitions and modelling, others go for automatic implementation frameworks and technologies.
- From modelling perspective: a lot of attention is paid to the modelling issues of business rules. Some proposed modelling techniques, for example, by Ross [17], are both modelling language and modelling method in one. Another approaches stem from adapting popular modelling languages, such as UML and OCL, to business rules modelling activity. However, none of the proposed languages or methods are accepted as technology standard yet.

2.3 Business Rules Tools Available

There is a number of different business rule management and enforcement tools available today. The common component of the majority of tools is the business rules repository which is later used for different tasks. However, as it was mentioned above, they employ different, sometimes very specific modelling languages. As for the functionality that the tools offer – it is centred on the following tasks:

- Manage rules – components for rules input and modification (rule editors);
- Store rules – rules repository;
- Enforce rules – rules engines or similar mechanisms.

The rules enforcement components offer the reference (transparent for business users) from declarative business rules statements stored in business rules repository to the actual enforcement mechanism thus achieving the required automatic dependency of the business rules implementation on declarative business rules statements.

Blaze Advisor [9] system offers the complete process for designing, running, and maintaining e-business applications. Blaze Advisor consists of the following 5 components:

- Builder – a rule creating tool targeted for developers;
- Innovator – a rule management and maintenance tool targeted for business users;
- Rule Engine – a scalable processing engine that determines and executes the control flow of rules, works together with the Rule Server;
- Rule Server – a dedicated rule server which supports rule execution, session management, scheduling, and dynamic load balancing.

Blaze Advisor uses its unique Structured Rule Language for input of business rules; decision trees and decision tables can be employed as well.

Infrex [11] is another type of tool – while Blaze Advisor is a totally stand alone application, Infrex can be embedded into applications written in C/C++/Java/C#. Infrex uses classes and variables of the application with the support for high level operators for rules specification. Rule Translator component generates C/C++/Java/C# code which is compiled and linked with the application to create an executable. The executable has the rules to be called at run-time, through the engine. Thus the adaptivity feature is achieved by the ability of the tool automatically create executable code from the rules specification. However, the language for rules specification is not suitable for business users because it directly operates with classes and variables which are not exactly the business terms.

QuickRules [26] is a business rules management system which allows inserting and editing business rules using the specific QuickRules Rules Mark-up Language. Rules are stored in XML format and may be executed by Business Rules Engine component.

ILOG rules are of ECA (Event, Condition, Action) type and consist of three parts: header, condition and action specifications [1]. The rules can be defined using BAL (Business Action Language), IF-THEN-ELSE rule format and TRL (Technical Rule Language).

The above mentioned tools have their own business rules engines therefore it is obligatory for enterprises to buy the respective product suit in order to be able to use their offerings. The opposite solution would be to use a wide spread technology (e.g., of active database management systems [1]) for rules repository and as an enforcement engine.

The Dulcian company (an Oracle consulting firm that specializes in data warehousing, systems development and products that support the Oracle environment) is working in this direction offering BRIM – Business Rules Information Manager [8] which offers the rules editing, designing and implementation functionality. The rules editing is done over two steps – analysis rules are entered using weakly structured *RuleSpeak* language (proposed by Business Rules Solutions [5]) and implementation rules are specified using UML [3] class and activity diagrams. The mapping between analysis and implementation rules may be done by business users manually associating rules with classes, states and diagrams. The automatic code generation component creates text files that either creates triggers on tables or alters the existing triggers on tables. The technology is completely Oracle-centred.

The survey of the tools given above is by no means complete but it highlights the trends within the field of interest. The lack of standards is obvious – for business rules modelling languages, repositories format, architectures. It is not possible to exchange business rules among different products or present to the business users more or less standard rules language. However, the promising step in business rules repository is the usage of XML as the business rules storage format which would enable the business rules sharing and exchange.

3   The BR-Centric IS Development Framework

In this paper we propose the generic BR-centric IS development framework which enables business rules automation. As the generic approach it does not require the specific technology to be used, however, in the instantiated version we use active database technology (namely, triggers) as the target business rules enforcement technology (as described in details in Section 4).

The BR-centric IS development framework (presented in Fig. 1) has several intended purposes:

- to describe the set of information objects and related modelling activities in the process of BR-based IS development;
- to give the information objects flow through different abstraction layers coming from the most abstract – business systems layer to the implementation layer;
- to give the information objects models flow through the same sequence of layers;
- to provide the possibility of tracing the flow of objects from business system down to the implementation layer and backwards in order to ensure the consistency between the concepts, especially traceability is required upon making any modifications in any abstraction layer – the corresponding modifications must be traced back to the modification origin.

3.1   Layers Description

During the process of the IS development and later in subsequent IS life cycle phases the information objects from different abstraction layers must be dealt with. The IS development cycle always starts from the elicitation or high level business analysis phase when the business system objects are analyzed. Business system abstraction layer represents the real objects – this is the business system itself which can be defined as the closed world with the input and output channels to and from its environment. The business objects under concern are those which must be mapped to information system layer objects in order to simulate the natural information processing with the mappings in information system objects.

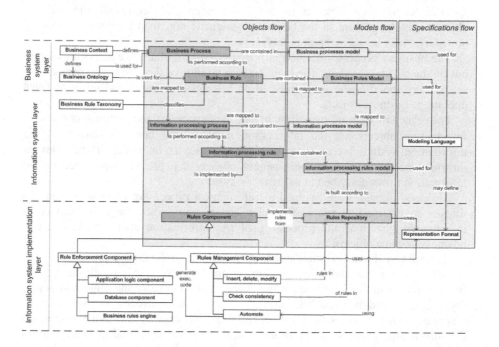

Fig. 1. The BR-centric IS development framework

Information system abstraction layer represents the information flows among the business objects. It deals with informational mappings of the business objects from business system layer. Therefore it may be called the informational mapping of the real business system. The type of objects in information system layer is information processing objects. These objects are also models of the business objects because they represent business objects only for their intended purpose. The information objects models are later used in the third abstraction layer – information system implementation layer where information objects are mapped to digital objects and information flows among the objects are implemented using the specific technology and architecture.

3.2 Objects and Models Flow

In Figure 1 the flow of the objects and corresponding models are shown through the different abstraction layers. The objects are:

- Business objects – the business environment objects, such as the physical order placed for the goods, etc. The purpose of having the business objects in the defined business context is to draw the boundaries of the business system in scope. The business objects definitions must be contained in the relevant business ontology. The business context defines the type of the business ontology to use. However, the business ontology also shapes the business context in the sense of being the reference of the uniformity and completeness of the business context (if the specific business ontology defines a set of concepts, the corresponding real life objects must be present in the business system; if not, then the business system boundaries may be set inappropriately).

The business processes defined in business context shape the activities carried out by the business system. The logic and constraints of the business processes are set by corresponding business rules. Both business processes and business rules operate on business objects.

The related models are two: those of business processes and of business rules.

- Information objects are the information maps of the business objects in the information system layer. Their intended purpose is to represent the relevant informational properties of the business objects that are of importance to the information flows described in information system.

Business processes are mapped to information processing processes, business rules – to information processing rules accordingly, since the only activity in information system is the processing of the information about the real life – business systems objects.

Accordingly the information processes models and information processing rules models are being created at information system layer. Here it is worth mentioning the differences in the definitions of the concepts used to name the same abstraction layer objects and models. The term "business rule" currently is used in very disparate ways – to name the business rules in real business environment, to name the information processing rule in information systems layer and even sometimes to name the implementation layer objects corresponding to business rules. In this paper we propose to distinguish among the mappings of the business systems layer concepts and their mappings in subsequent layers. Thus we say that business rules exist only in business system environment and they are mapped to information processing rules in information system environment. That is, we do not have "business" as such in information system layer – we have only mappings of the business information processing and flow.

However, despite the differences in the concepts, the same modelling language can be employed at different layers. For example, UML can be used for modelling both business objects and information objects.

- In the third layer which can be regarded as the physical layer – information system implementation as software components layer – the information objects are mapped to digital objects and implemented as various software components. In our framework we present BR-centric components, such as rules repository (information processing rules are mapped to implemented rules) and rules implementation (management and enforcement) components. In this layer we avoid using the term "business" – either for processes, or for rules. The implementation layer bears only the implementation of the information objects, information processing processes and rules which can be also considered as information layer map to executable specification.

4 Instantiation of the Framework

We have applied the framework using business system example. Since the framework is too generic for the direct application, we have instantiated it using the specific components instead of generic ones (where necessary):

1. The business context used: Production Ordering System;
2. The business ontology was not used for this phase of the instantiation, however, specific business domains ontologies should be investigated as sources of standardised set of business objects (entities) for modelling purposes;
3. Conceptual graphs were used for modelling both business system and information system layers objects;
4. Rules repository was created in active database management system;
5. Rules automatic generation component was implemented for the rules enforcement in active database as triggers;
6. The business processes modelling activity was omitted for the first application of the framework, however, the business processes modelling is a compulsory activity for traceability purposes. By traceability we mean the tracking of changes from business system layer down to the implementation layer.

The diagram of the instantiated framework is given in Figure 2.

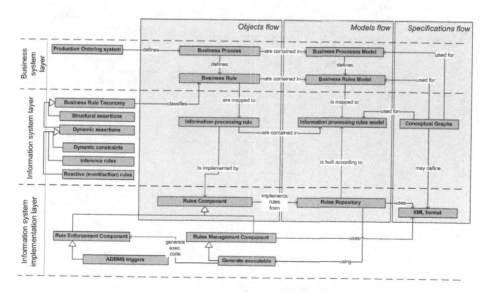

Fig. 2. The instantiated BR-centric IS development framework

In this paper we elaborate ideas presented in [22, 21]; and we are focused on the generic framework; therefore the detailed motivation of the choices for the instantiation is out of scope of this paper.

4.1 Automatic Implementation: Trigger Generation Component

In Figure 3 the flow of execution of the trigger generation component is presented: the business rules model serves as the input for creating the repository which again serves as the input for active database triggers generation.

In the current research as shown in Figure 3 we focus on the business rules model represented in conceptual graphs [20] CGIF notation (Conceptual Graphs Interchange Format, please refer to [6] for the draft standard of conceptual graphs and its notations including CGIF). However, the architecture is not limited in that sense and the extensions are possible (shown in Figure 3 on the left):

- Usage of another modeling language for business rules conceptual model;
- Usage of another underlying active database management system (because of syntactic differences of trigger definition in different active database management systems).

The XML based business rules representation thus is the central element which allows adding flexible extensions and serves as the business rules repository.

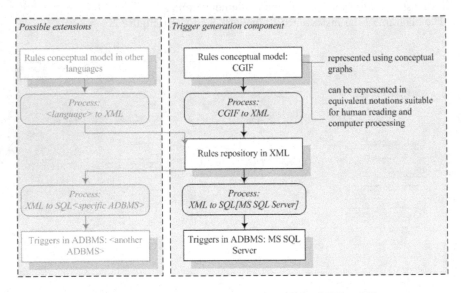

Fig. 3. The trigger generation component: from CGIF to SQL

The component consists of the two processes:

1. Process CGIF2XML. The scope of the process is a transformation of business rules representation from conceptual graphs model in CGIF format to the intermediate business rules representation in XML. The latter can be used as the basis for the business rules repository. In current implementation the input format is limited to CGIF; the output format adheres to the rules representation using XML structure.
2. Process XML2SQL. The scope of the second process is a transformation of rules contained in intermediate format of XML based structure to the actual

implementation representation – namely, active databases triggers. In the current implementation the Microsoft SQL Server active database management system trigger definition syntax is used.

4.2 Example of the Business Rule and the Resulting Trigger

To illustrate the flow of execution we present the example of the business rule, its intermediate representation in XML, and the resulting MS SQL Server trigger:

1. Business rule in natural language: *If manufacturing order is completed and it is not an internal order (the identification number is greater than 17 which marks the limit of the internal orders), its finishing date is set to today.*
2. In conceptual graphs visual notation: The diagram in Figure 4 represents the business rule using the standard conceptual graphs nodes – concepts (drawn as rectangles), conceptual relations (as ovals), actors (as diamonds) and links (as arrows connecting concepts with actors or conceptual relations).

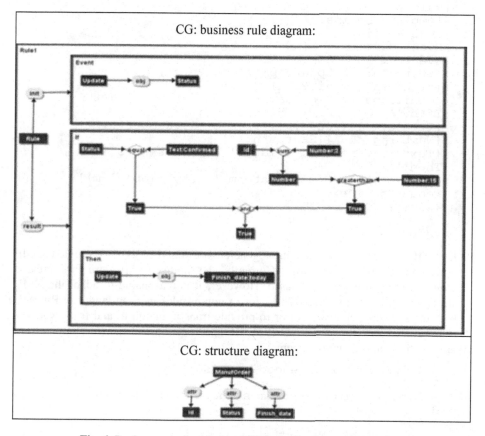

Fig. 4. Business rule modeled in CGIF using business rule template

The diagram is created using the conceptual graphs editor CharGer v3.0b [7]. The current version offers functionality to draw conceptual graphs diagrams, get the respective representation of the diagrams in CGIF and near natural English language, export diagrams to various picture formats, etc. In our research we rely on CharGer for generating CGIF representation of the diagrams.

While modeling the business rule we employ the following rule template:

```
Type Rule(*x) is T(?x) -
    <-(INIT)<-[Event:*y]
    ->(RESULT)->[If:*z[Then:*w]]
```

We have proposed the template to model business rules in [21] with the goal to standardize the business rule representation in order to make the automatic generation of the triggers possible.

3. In CGIF: the below presented CGIF representation of the business rule is generated by CharGer tool. Comments are added manually in order to increase the readability of the representation (comments begin by double slash '//').

```
//Rule name:
 [Rule1:''
//Template begins:
 [Rule*a:'']
//Event part:
 [Event*n:''
  [Status*o:''][Update*p:''](obj?p?o)]
  (result?a?b)(init?a?n)]
//Conditional action part:
 [If*b:''
  [True*c:''][True*d:''][True*e:''][Number*f:'']
  [Number*g:'15'][Status*h:'']
  [Text*i:'Confirmed'][Id*j:''][Number*k:'2']
 [Then:''
  [Update*l:''][Finish_date*m:'today'](obj?l?m)]
  <equal?h?i|?e>
  <sum?j?k|?f>
  <greaterthan?g?f|?d>
  <and?d?e|?c>]
```

4. In XML: the XML representation generated using the above presented CGIF representation is given below. Currently the unique XML structure created specifically for this project is used. However, it is reasonable to adapt the XML structure to the emerging standards, for example, rules markup language RuleML by Rule Markup Initiative [18] or to provide transformation to and from RuleML (the Initiative develops a modular RuleML specification and transformations from and to other rule standards/systems).

```
<?xml version="1.0" encoding="iso-8859-1"?>
<CGIF>
//Entity definition (from structural part of the
model):
<Tables>
        <Table Name="ManufOrder">
        <Column Name="Status"/>
```

```
                <Column Name="Id"/>
                <Column Name="Finish_date"/>
            </Table>
    </Tables>


    //Rule name:
    <Rule Name="Rule1">
    //Event part:
    <Event Column="Status" MainTable="ManufOrder"
    Operation="Update">
            <Condition>
                <Actor Name="jkf" Type="sum">
                <In1 Name="" Type="Id" Value=""/>
                <In2 Name="" Type="Number" Value="2"/>
                <Out Name="" Type="Number" Value=""/>
                </Actor>
                <Actor Name="hie" Type="equal">
                <In1 Name="" Type="Status" Value=""/>
                <In2 Name="" Type="Text"
                 Value="Confirmed"/>
                <Out Name="" Type="True" Value=""/>
                </Actor>
                <Actor Name="gfd" Type="greaterthan">
                <In1 Name="" Type="Number" Value="15"/>
                <In2 Name="jkf" Type="Number" Value=""/>
                <Out Name="" Type="True" Value=""/>
                </Actor>
                <Actor Name="dec" Type="and">
                <In1 Name="gfd" Type="True" Value=""/>
                <In2 Name="hie" Type="True" Value=""/>
                <Out Name="" Type="True" Value=""/>
                </Actor>
            </Condition>
    </Event>
    //Conditional action part:
    <Action>
            <Block Column="Finish_date" Operation="Update"
            Value="today"/>
    </Action>
    </Rule>
    </CGIF>
```

5. Resulting trigger: The resulting trigger implementing the business rule is shown below. The trigger is generated using MS SQL Server trigger definition syntax.

```
CREATE trigger Rule1 ON ManufOrder
FOR UPDATE
AS
IF UPDATE(status)
BEGIN
  if((SELECT status FROM INSERTED)='Confirmed' and
(SELECT id FROM INSERTED)+2>15 )
    BEGIN
      UPDATE ManufOrder
```

```
        SET Finish_date=getdate()
        WHERE id=(SELECT id FROM INSERTED)
  END
END
```

5 Conclusions and Future Research

In the research of the business information systems development the business rules approach has achieved a lot of attention and already has a steady niche with a strong motivation behind. The completed survey of current technologies and tools shows that despite the work already done towards technology standards there is still a way to go – the commercial products use their unique modelling languages for business rules, most of their rules processing and enforcement engines are stand alone, even the embedded ones use their unique rules representation format, the proposed business rules approaches are rather diverse depending on perspective or intended purpose.

We have presented a generic BR-based IS development framework which can be instantiated based on available techniques, methods or languages. We have carried out the experiment of framework application substituting the generic framework components with specific ones – such as selecting the ADBMS technology for rules repository implementation, conceptual graphs for business rules and information processing rules modelling, etc.

The other motivation for this paper and the framework itself was to show the diverse concepts depending on the abstraction level and the flow and mapping scheme of the objects from layer to layer. We have differentiated three layers – that of business system, information system and information system implementation – and have shown how the business objects map to information objects and to executable specifications.

The proposed BR-centric IS development framework enables business rules automation activity as the integral part of the development cycle; the traceability issues, although supported by the framework, were not elaborated in this paper and remain one of the important future research directions.

The next step in our research should be further refinement of the objects mapping and transformations in different abstractions layers and the full case study employing the proposed concepts and ideas.

References

1. ACT-NET Consortium. The Active Database Management Systems Manifesto: A Rulebase of ADBMS Features. ACM Sigmod Record, Vol. 25(30), 1996, pp. 40-49.
2. Bajec, M., Rupnik, R., Krisper, M. Using Business Rules Technologies To Bridge The Gap Between Business And Business Applications. In Proceedings of the IFIP 16th World Computer Congress 2000, Information Technology for Business Management (G Rechnu, Ed), Beijing, China, 2000, pp. 77-85.

3. Booch, G., Rumbaugh, J., Jacobson, I. The Unified Modelling Language User Guide. Addison-Wesley, 2000.
4. Business Rules Group. Defining Business Rules ~ What Are They Really? (formerly known as the "GUIDE Business Rules Project Final Report," November 1995), Business Rules Group, (3rd Ed.), 2000. (Also URL: http:// www.businessrulesgroup.org)
5. Business Rules Solutions homepage. http://www.brsolutions.com.
6. Conceptual Graphs Standard. Document type: International standard (Draft), Document stage: (20) Preparation, reference number of working document: ISO/JTC1/SC 32/WG2 N 000. http://www.jfsowa.com/cg/cgstand.htm, 2001.
7. Delugach, H. CharGer Manual. *http://www.cs.uah.edu/~delugach/CharGer/*, 2003.
8. Dorsey, P. Business Rules Analysis in the Real World. Electronic Proceedings of Oracle Development Tools User Group ODTUG 2003, http:// www.odtug.com/ 2003_papers.htm, 2003.
9. FairIsaac   BlazeAdvisor: How   it   works?   http://www.fairisaac.com/NR /rdonlyres/C3817720-3C36-4B43-9F65-3300B0B9AA29/0/advisor_how.pdf, 2003.
10. Gottesdiener, E. Business RULES Show Power, Promise, Application Development Trends, Volume 4, Number 31, 1997, http:// www.ebgconsulting.com/ publications. html#business_rules.
11. Infrex. Product overview. http://www.tcs.com/0_products/infrex/index.htm, 2002.
12. Morgan, T. Business Rules and Information Systems: Aligning IT with Business Goals, Addison-Wesley, 2002.
13. Moriarty, T. Business-Rule Stuff or Marketing Fluff? Intelligent Enterprise, Volume 3 - Number 3. http:// www.intelligententerprise.com/ 000209/ metaprise.jhtml, February 9, 2000.
14. Object Management Group. Business Rules in Models: Request for Information. URL: http://cgi.omg.org/cgi-bin/doc?ad/2002-9-13, 2002.
15. Rosca, D., Greenspan, S., Wild, C.: Enterprise Modelling and Decision-Support for Automating the Business Rules Lifecycle, Automated Software Engineering, v.9, n. 4, p. 361, 2002.
16. Ross, R.G. Principles of the Business Rule Approach. Addison-Wesley, 2003.
17. Ross, R.G., The Business Rule Book: Classifying, Defining and Modelling Rules, Database Research Group, Boston, MA, 2nd edition, 1997.
18. Rule Markup Initiave official homepage. *http://www.ruleml.org,*
19. Sowa, F., Zachman, J.A. Extending and Formalising the Framework for Information Systems Architecture. IBM Systems Journal, 31:3. IBM Publication G321-5488, 1992.
20. Sowa, J.F. Knowledge Representation: Logical, Philosophical, and Computational Foundations. Brooks/Cole, Pasific Grove et al., 2000.
21. Valatkaite, I., Vasilecas, O. A Conceptual Graphs Approach for Business Rules Modelling. In L. Kalinichenko, R. Manthey, B. Thalheim, U. Wloka (Eds.). Proc. of Seventh East-European Conference on Advance in Databases and Information Systems (ADBIS), September 3-6, 2003, Dresden, Germany. LNCS 2798, Springer-Verlag, 2003, pp. 178-189.
22. Valatkaite, I., Vasilecas, O. On Business Rules Approach to the Information Systems Development. In: H. Linger et al (Eds.). Proc. of Twelfth International Conference on Information Systems Development. Constructing the Infrastructure for the Knowledge Economy. Kluwer Academic/Plenum Publishers, 2004, p. 199–208.
23. Von Halle, B. Back to Business Rule Basics, Database Programming and Design, 1994, pp. 15–18.

24. Von Halle, B. Business Rules Applied: Building Better Systems Using the Business Rules Approach. John Wiley & Sons, 2002.
25. Wan Kadir, W.M.N., Loucopoulos P. Relating Evolving Business Rules to Software Design. Journal of Systems Architecture 50, 2004, pp. 367-382.
26. Yasu Technologies. QuickRules Discovery Guide. http://www.yasutech.com/ products/ quickrules/datasheet.pdf, 2003.

CFP Taxonomy of the Approaches
for Dynamic Web Content Acceleration

Stavros Papastavrou[1], George Samaras[1], Paraskevas Evripidou[1],
and Panos K. Chrysanthis[2]

[1] University of Cyprus, Department of Computer Science,
P.O.Box.20537, CY-1678 Nicosia, Cyprus
{stavrosp, cssamara, skevos}@ucy.ac.cy
[2] University of Pittsburgh, Department of Computer Science,
Pittsburgh, PA 15260, USA
panos@cs.pitt.edu

Abstract. Approximately a decade since it was first introduced, dynamic Web content technology has been gaining in popularity over static means for content dissemination. Its rising demand for computational and network resources has driven researchers into developing a plethora of approaches toward efficient content generation and delivery. Motivated by the lack of a comprehensive study on this research area, we introduce a novel research-charting, semi-formal framework called the CFP Framework, on which we survey and compare past and present approaches for dynamic Web content acceleration. Our framework not only serves as a reference map for researchers toward understanding the evolution of research on this particular area, but also reveals research trends toward developing the next generation of dynamic Web content middlewares.

1   Introduction

The Internet and the Web have become commonplace and their growth is unprecedented. This led to a proliferation of technologies to improve its usefulness and user satisfaction. Dynamic Web content (DWC) technologies facilitate (a) the adaptation of content served to a particular group of people (i.e., people that live within a certain time zone or Internet domain region), and (b) the personalization of content to meet an individual's expectations and needs (i.e., Web banking or e-commerce). According to [13], the above two categories of DWC comprise the 20% of Internet traffic each. DWC enables a new order of Web applications including online financial-related services, news sites, portals and e-learning brokerage platforms.

DWC technology involves a variety of cooperating components that are largely defined as content middleware systems. Arranged in an n-tier architecture, as seen in Figure 1, they cooperate with the goal of delivering content on demand to Web users. A Proxy server intercepts client requests to Web servers and delivers cached content, if certain criteria hold. Otherwise, the request is forwarded to

J. Eder et al. (Eds.): ADBIS 2005, LNCS 3631, pp. 365–378, 2005.

the Web server that invokes the appropriate application server, which generates the content by querying local and/or remote databases.

A dynamic Web page (DWP) consists of static and dynamic content junks called *fragments*, typically arranged in a *template file* interleaved with static HTML code. Dynamic fragments reside in templates in the form of script code blocks that must be processed by the application server. This processing, as illustrated in Figure 1, may require the execution of a significant number of script lines for performing tasks such as database queries, image processing, complex input Form generation, or even information retrieval and manipulation from remote hosts. For instance, the template file of the PC customization dynamic Web page of the www.higrade.com online computer retailer contains approximately 2000 lines of script code, having more than 20 database queries, distributed across 6 dynamic fragments.

Since the generation and delivery of dynamic Web content requires increased computational and network resources, especially during peak hours, various bottlenecks occur. The study in [5] identifies the bottlenecks on three typical dynamic content Web applications. A significant number of research approaches for accelerating DWC are proposed in the literature. As a result, state-of-the-art content middleware technology is found today in many commercial products that incorporate many of the proposed approaches, proving in this way the importance and applicability of this particular research area.

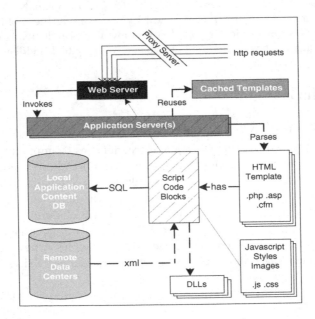

Fig. 1. The n-tier architecture and the process of generating dynamic Web Content

Motivated by the lack of a comprehensive study on this research area, we introduce the CFP Framework, a novel semiformal framework that facilitates the classification of existing research approaches based on their underlying methodologies and principles. We then attempt a complete literature review and conceptual comparison of the surveyed approaches on the CFP Framework. The purpose of the framework is not to reveal the 'best' approach, but to be a handy tool for researches toward understanding the evolution of research around DWC acceleration. The framework also reveals research trends that can guide researches into defining the next generation of dynamic Web content middlewares.

The next section introduces the CFP Framework and explains the reasoning behind its metrics. Section 3 surveys research on dynamic Web content acceleration and classifies the approaches. In Section 4, we gather and compare the surveyed approaches on the CFP Framework. We recap in Section 5.

2   The CFP Framework

Since a quantitative comparison (i.e., a performance comparison) between the approaches that we survey in the next section is rather unfeasible due to realistic and complexity constrains, we focused instead on establishing a theoretical, comparative semi-formal framework. We consider the fact that the majority of the surveyed approaches employ and combine to some extend three common characteristics or practices. Those are Caching, Fragmentation and Polymorphism and comprise the three principles of the CFP Framework.

The principle of Caching suggests a multi-tier reuse of content on network sites such as proxies, Web servers, application servers, or even at the client browser. The principle of Fragmentation suggests the breaking of a dynamic Web page down to computationally, but not necessarily semantically, distinct parts. This principle enables (a) finer-grained Caching and (b) concurrency in DWC generation. The notion of Polymorphism allows for a dynamic Web page to be assembled in more than one way without the need to regenerate any content. More specifically, the layout of the DWC fragments is decided dynamically according to, for example, the client's preferences. Polymorphism, in this way, enables another dimension of content dynamism by allowing the templates to be dynamic themselves. In the CFP acronym, Caching precedes the other two principles as the earlier to appear, and Polymorphism is the most recent.

The intuition behind the use of the CFP Framework is that the three principles of the framework can be viewed as orthogonal dimensions along which different research approaches can be classified. Thus, the framework can be represented as a cube as shown in Figure 2.

We make use of the CFP Framework by plotting a particular approach on the cube, given its corresponding values for each principle. For that purpose, we define value to be the *extend of employment* of a particular principle. Since the three principles are rather qualitative and subjective than quantitative, this evaluation requires assumptions and approximations in order to define the appropriate metric for each principle. For readability, Figure 2 illustrates the basic metrics only for the principles of Caching and Fragmentation.

The metric for the principle of Caching is the proximity of cached documents. Therefore, we state that an approach that supports Caching of dynamic

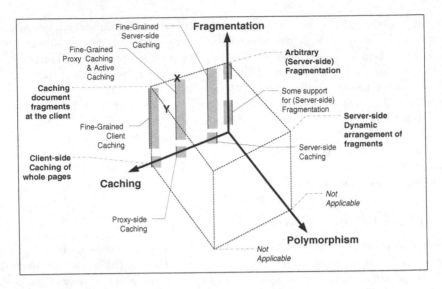

Fig. 2. The CFP Framework and its Approximate Metrics

content closer to Web users is evaluated higher from others that cache content closer to the Web server. Moreover, we state that an approach is fully employing Fragmentation if it supports for an arbitrary number of fragments in a dynamic Web page and of any computational type and size. Finally, an approach fully employs Polymorphism if it provides support for an arbitrary number of alternative arrangements for a dynamic Web page. Since we realize the notion of Polymorphism in combination with Fragmentation, we assert that it cannot be employed as a stand-alone principle or in combination only with Caching. Therefore, it appears as 'not applicable' at the corresponding edges of the CFP framework.

For example, the approach 'X' plotted on the framework in Figure 2 refers to an approach that (a) supports proxy-side Caching of DWC, and (b) fully supports Fragmentation. In another example, approach 'Y' caches arbitrary DWC fragments at the client-side and provides some basic support for different arrangements of the fragments.

3   Taxonomy of Approaches

In this Section, we survey the proposed approaches for accelerating the generation and delivery of dynamic Web content. We present the taxonomies in a more natural and reader-friendly way, rather than applying a strict technical order. Due to the lack of space, we exclude early, assorted and hardware techniques not directly related to the CFP framework.

3.1   Server-Side Fragmentation

The first class of approaches that we survey relate to the principle of Fragmentation. An early form of Fragmentation is encountered in Server-Side Includes

(SSI) [2]. According to SSI, some simple dynamic parts of a page can be isolated and regenerated every time the page is requested such as a counter, the time at the server, and date last modified. [8] suggests a more general form a Fragmentation that allows the dissection of a dynamic page into distinct parts (fragments) that are assembled according to a template file. A fresh version of a fragment is generated every time its underlying data objects are modified, using database triggers. With its fresh fragments in place, a dynamic page can be either immediately delivered or cached (as discussed next). More recently, [21] proposes a technique for accelerating template parsing and execution by processing the dynamic fragments of the template in a concurrent fashion. This approach, however, achieves increased server throughput and lower client response times when the system is not fully loaded. It is worth mentioning that the identification of the fragments takes place at run time (during parsing) and requires no a-priori compilation or special handling of the template.

3.2   Server-Side Caching

Content Caching boosts dynamic content generation by eliminating redundant server load. There are many interesting approaches for server-side Caching that vary mostly on the granularity and level of Caching. In [16] and [14], the Caching of dynamic documents at the granularity of a page is proposed for early content middlewares such as CGI, FastCGI, ISAPI and NSAPI. Extending their work in [14], the authors in [24] propose a Dynamic Content Caching Protocol (DCCP) that can be implemented as an extension to HTTP. This protocol allows for content middlewares, such CGI and Java Servlets, to specify full or partial equivalence amongst different URIs (HTTP GET requests). The equivalence information is inserted by the content middleware into the HTTP response header of a dynamically generated page, and stored at the Caching module along with the cached page. For example, the URI http://www.server.com/LADriveTo.php ?DestCity=newyork instructs the content middleware to generate a page with driving directions from Los Angeles to New York. Prior to transmitting the result page, the middleware inserts the "cache-control:equivalent_result=Dest=queens" attribute in the HTTP response header. The Caching module will cache the page, transmit it to the client, and store the cache-control directive for future use. A subsequent client request for the same URL, but for a different DestinationCity value, will be evaluated by the cache module for a possible mach with the value of "queens" or "newyork". If a much is found, then the cached page is transmitted to the client.

3.3   Fine-Grained Server-Side Caching

To achieve greater reuse of cached content, across both time and multiple users, Caching at finer granularities is proposed. The authors in [28] suggest the Caching of static HTML fragments, XML fragments and database query results. This approach, however, applies to Web applications that follow a strict declarative definition and follow a certain implementation. In addition, Caching cannot be applied to arbitrary parts of a DWP. A more general, flexible, and easier-to-use method for fragment Caching is introduced later on in [10] and studied more thoroughly in [9]. According to this method, Caching can be applied to an arbitrary fragment of a template by first wrapping it around with the appropriate tags (explicit tagging). XCache [3], is a commercial product that installs as a plug-in on popular dynamic content middlewares, and supports fragment Caching of any type using explicit tagging. Also, the Cold Fusion content middleware provides tags for explicitly defining the fragment to be cached.

3.4   Caching at the Proxy Server

Proxy Caching is the most popular approach for faster delivery of reusable static content such as static HTML pages and media files [26]. A Proxy degrades bandwidth consumption by eliminating unnecessary traffic between clients and servers, given that it is strategically located[1] between them. Proxy servers are found in many network points along the client/server path, with most popular those that reside on an enterprise's network boundaries. It has been identified that the usual hit ratio for proxy caches is around 40% [27], while another 40% of the traffic is redundant when proxies are employed [25].

A popular approach for Web sites to meet the growing demand on DWC delivery is to lease cache space on a service-based network of interconnected proxy servers called Content Distribution Networks (CDN). A typical CDN employs a set of proxy servers strategically arranged by geographical, or network location. Client requests for content are routed to the closest proxy server of the CDN network. The list of popular CDNs includes brand names such as Akamai, Yahoo, Intel and Nortel. It is noteworthy that for a Web site to be registered and served by a CDN network, an off-line procedure of tagging the source code (HTML script files) of the Web site is required. A thorough survey on the procedures, practices and performance of CDNs can be found in [17].

Despite the location of cached content, Server and Proxy Caching find their major implementation difference on how data consistency between the cached content and the underlying database objects is enforced. For the former, cache consistency is easier to be enforced since the Caching module is local to the content middleware (as seen in [8]). For the latter case, efficient cache invalidation techniques are required as discussed later on.

With the evolution of dynamic content middlewares, proxy caches had to adapt by providing support for dynamic documents. Early research conducted in [24], proposes the Caching of dynamic content at the granularity of a page by using the Dynamic Content Caching Protocol as previously discussed. The Caching protocol is applicable for both server-side and proxy-based Caching, and works by allowing the manipulating of HTTP header information and URL query string parameters (GET variables).

Another interesting approach for Caching dynamic pages is found in [19]. Analogous to the Caching protocol approach discussed earlier, this one suggests

---

[1] *Closer* in terms of network latency, topology or geographic location.

that the proxy server be allowed to examine the HTTP POST variables that are submitted as part of a client HTTP request for a URI . In brief, the proxy server attempts to reuse cached SQL query results by looking up on a predefined mapping called Query Template Info. This mapping establishes a relation between (a) the HTML form fields that are submitted with a URI request, and (b) the SQL query that uses those form fields as query parameters such as WHERE and ORDER BY clauses. Two strong points of this work is that (a) the proxy extracts and reuses portions of cached query results, if necessary, to satisfy future requests, and (b) it compliments a cached query result on demand by negotiating with the content middleware. Since the HTTP post variables are generated from HTML form fields, this approach is called *form-based*. The manipulation of cached content at the proxy server lies under the more general notion of Active Caching as we discussed later on in 3.10.

Both the *form-based* and the *protocol-based* approaches discussed above do not address the important issue of cache consistency. The authors in [6] propose an invalidation technique for cached dynamic pages, which uses a (triple) mapping between (a) the database content, (b) the SQL queries and (c) the dynamical Web pages. This mapping explicitly identifies the database objects that affect a set of queries which in turn are involved in generating a set of DWPs. According to this technique, a cached page is invalidated once a database object that relates to an SQL query which, in turn, is involved in generating that page is updated. Extending their work in [6], the authors in [18] illustrate how this triple-mapping invalidation approach is applied in a real world scenario when all four the database server, the content middleware, the Web server and the proxy cache are entirely independent Vendor products. Additionally, a technique for cached content freshness based on parameters such as user request, database content update rate and network latency is proposed.

3.5 Fine-Grained Proxy Caching

Caching at the granularity of a fragment is consequently proposed for proxy caches. According to fine-grained proxy Caching, the template file is cached at the proxy server whereas its dynamic fragments are either reused from the proxy cache or fetched fresh from the Web server. Edge Side Includes (ESI) was introduced as a standard for Caching page templates along with their fragments on proxy servers [1]. According to ESI, the dynamic fragments of a page are explicitly marked using tag-based macro-commands inside the page's template file. An ESI-compliant proxy server must provide support for parsing the cached template file and executing macros that dictate whether a fragment should also be retrieved from cache, or pulled from the original server. ESI macros have access to a client's HTTP request attributes (cookies, URL string, browser used) in order to choose between fragment alternatives. An example of that would be the identification of the client's browser version or vendor in order to pick the appropriate fragment that meets the browser capabilities. Endorses of the ESI technology are leading CDN brands such as Akamai, database vendors such as Oracle, and content management leader Vignette.

3.6   Client-Side (Fine-Grained) Caching

Surprisingly, the notion of assembling a dynamic page away from the original content middleware was firstly introduced in [12] not for proxy caches, but for client browsers. The proposed technique, called HPP (HTML pre-processing), requires from the client browsers the extra functionality of Caching and processing (parsing) a template file, containing blocks of macro-commands, prior to rendering a dynamic page. Each macro-command block generates from scratch a page fragment by manipulating local variables and strings. This idea can be overview as the client-side equivalent to Server-Side Includes discussed earlier.

Extending their work in [12], the authors in [23] propose the Client-Side Includes (CSI) by merging HPP and ESI. In order to provide support for CSI in the Internet Explorer Web browser, the authors propose a generic downloadable wrapper (plug-in) that uses JavaScript and ActiveX. The wrapper pulls and caches at the client side the template and fragments that are associated with a requested DWP, assembles them together according to the ESI directives in the template, and finally renders the page. According to the authors, CSI is suitable for 'addressing the last mile' along the client-server network path suitable for low-bandwidth dial-up users, even in the absence of an edge server (i.e., a CDN).

3.7   Polymorphism: A Second Dimension of Content Dynamism

Caching at the fragment level requires the existence of a page layout/template that dictates a strict arrangement for cached DWC fragments. If we loose up this restriction, by allowing for more than one template per dynamic page, we achieve Polymorphism (in Greek: the ability for something to show different phases-morphs) in DWC Caching. It is, therefore, left to the content middleware to pick the right template, according to the user's preferences (e.g., the Yahoo! Web site). A recent study in [11] proposes the use of multiple templates for a specific dynamic page along with proxy-cached page fragments. Following a client's request for a dynamic page (e.g., www.server.com/page1.php?id=2), the proxy server always routes the request to the origin content server and causes the execution of the original script (for example homepage.php). This routing is necessary for determining the desired template for page1.php at run time. The selected template is then pushed to the proxy server where it is parsed for identifying which fragments are reused from cache and which ones are requested fresh from the server. After all the fragments are inserted into the template, the complete assembled page is transmitted to the client. The performance analysis conducted in [11] demonstrated solid bandwidth reductions when applying fragment Caching, however, performance analysis for other critical metrics, such as scalability and responsiveness, remains to be seen. We believe that both the necessary routing of each request to the origin content server and the invocation of the original script can heart client response time and server scalability respectively. Nevertheless, the techniques introduced in this approach are an excellent starting point for further research. Polymorphism is also supported by the ESI technology in an indirect manner. Instead of choosing from a pool of templates, basic ESI branching commands may reorganize the layout inside a template according to client credentials (HTTP request header information).

3.8   Support for Inter-dependent Fragments

Caching of dynamic content at the fragment level, as employed today by proxy servers, assumes that individual page fragments have independent Caching characteristics. This assumption has simplified the design and deployment of proxy caches based on either the Edge Side Includes or other proposals. There exist, however, Web applications for which two or more fragments of the same dynamic page are dependent to each other. An example is an online retailer's Web page that includes among others (a) a fragment containing script code for evaluating and regenerating an HTML form used for product customization, and (b) a fragment with script code for calculating and rendering the shopping cart's total charge (including the value of the product being customized by the previous fragment). Upon client submission, the second fragment cannot execute to calculate the total charge unless the previous fragment has evaluated the HTML form input. In this case, the two fragments must execute in a sequential (serial) manner to ensure consistency between the total charge and the customized product's value.

The notion of fragment dependency in dynamic content generation has been studied first in [8] and later on in [21]. In brief, the former study suggests the construction of a separate Object Dependency Graph (ODG) where the objects in this case are the fragments ids (generated fragments are stored as separate files). Furthermore, a dynamic page is defined by a template file with references to fragment files using include statements. In addition, database triggers are installed to ensure that upon database content update, the affected fragments (and their dependent ones) are regenerated in the right order. Client requests for a particular page are fulfilled by inserting into the appropriate template the already generated fragment files. Although the whole procedure requires a quite complex setup, this approach is suitable for publishing heavily requested portals and news sites with frequently updated content and less client interaction. The latter study, suggests a simpler and more general approach for identifying dependencies between page fragments. Instead of using an external fragment dependency graph in conjunction with database triggers, the fragment dependencies are defined at the beginning of each template file. For example, the tag <dependency source_fragment=3 target_fragment=5> informs the content middleware that the third fragment to be encountered during parsing must be executed before the fifth fragment. This inline and immediate definition of fragment dependencies ensures consistency between dependent fragments, since this approach attempts to execute all the fragments of a template in a concurrent fashion (see Section 3.1). As opposed to the former approach, this one is suitable for more interactive Web applications i.e., an online retailer shop.

3.9   Caching with Delta Encoding

Delta encoding is a popular technique for efficiently compressing a file relatively to another one called the 'base' file [15]. This is achieved by computing and storing the difference between the file being compressed and the base file.

Streaming media compression, displaying differences between files (the UNIX diff command) and backing-up data are common applications of delta encoding. Under the assumption that consecutive client requests for a specific URI would generate a sequence of moderately different dynamic pages, Delta encoding can be exploited as an alternative for Caching dynamic content. [22] proposes the Caching of a base file for each group (also called Class) of correlated documents i.e., pages that share a common layout. With the base file cached, the next client request would force the content middleware to compute the Delta between the new dynamic page that the client would normally receive and the base file. The computed Delta is then transmitted from the content middleware to the side where the base file is cached for computation of the new dynamic page. Eventually, the result is transmitted to the client. An interesting feature of this 'class-based delta-encoding' approach, is that the base file can be cached either at the server-side, proxy-side, or even at the client browser itself as long as the required infrastructure exists. In the latter case, Delta encoding benefits could low-bandwidth users. [22] demonstrated solid bandwidth savings and reduced client perceived latency, however, those performance gains reduce the average system throughput to 75% due to increase the CPU overhead of computing the deltas. Nevertheless, we consider Delta encoding for Caching DWC as an exciting open topic of research.

3.10   Active Caching

The notion of Active Caching refers to the ability possessed by a Caching middleware to manipulate cached content instead of requesting fresh content from the server. The approach found in [7] piggybacks a Java object into a dynamically generated document, which is then cached at the proxy. The proxy provides a Java runtime environment in which that object executes in order to modify the dynamic parts of the cached document according to a client's preferences. Examples of document modifications include advertising banner rotation, logging user requests, Server Side Includes execution and even Delta compression. Besides these general types of modification, the Java object can personalize cached documents by retrieving personal information from the Application Database at the server side. Data chunks of personal information are kept by the object for future reuse. Building up on this approach, a more general form of DWC Caching with Active Caching is suggested in [20]. This one is very similar to the 'form-based' approach discussed earlier in the sense that the Java object manipulates HTTP post variables (the Form input) for filling the dynamic parts of the cached document. In general, those two Active Caching approaches differ from other approaches that support Caching and Fragmentation since the dynamic parts (or fragments) are not decoupled (stored separately) from the cached document (or template).

Active Caching of this form can be viewed as a means of content middleware migration. Original executable code and data, both parts of the content middleware, can be packed along with a mobile object (called Mobile Agent) that dispatches to a destination where it can better serve the client (i.e., a proxy server). This ambitious approach aims at alleviating the processing bottleneck from the content middleware, while reducing unnecessary network traffic by employing Caching and proxy-side computation.

Since the notion of Active Caching is supported by mobile code or function calls that accompanies relevant data, then an alternative or indirect form of Active Caching can be achieved by employing Active XML (AXML) [4]. Documents written according to AXML contain data in XML and calls/references to Web Services that fill-in on demand the missing (or dynamic) parts of the documents. In extend, AXML documents can be cached and materialized prior to transmission to Web users.

4   Conceptual Comparison of the Approaches

4.1   General Remarks

In this Section, we plot the surveyed approaches and technologies on the CFP Framework cube (Figure 3). This allows for a high-level comparison of the approaches, as well as for identifying research trends. In addition to the three dimensions/principles of Caching, Fragmentation and Polymorphism, we show how recent an approach is by using a gray scale background. At the heart of the framework, with null values for each principle, we place CGI as the primary dynamic content middleware. An immediate observation from Figure 3 is that the trend in research is toward refining and extending the employment of the three principles while attempting to combine them. In other words, dynamic content tends to be cached closer to the client, at finer granularities, and under different arrangements. This is crucial for modern Web applications that require content personalization and support for low-bandwidth (mobile) users.

4.2   Detailed Comparison and Discussion

As we observe on the CFP Framework, the majority of early research in accelerating DWC has focused on Caching whole pages (or slight variations of it). Page-level Caching does not meet the fine-grained Caching requirements of modern Web applications. However, within this group of page-level Caching approaches the most recent one that employs Delta Encoding appears very promising in-terms of performance, especially for low bandwidth users such as mobile users. Therefore, we recommend an implementation that supports Fragmentation that would encapsulate the Caching characteristics of modern Web applications.

Active Caching, as introduced in [7] and explored more in [20], combines the advantages of proxy-side Caching while providing some support for Fragmentation. Both approaches do not employ full Fragmentation since the fragments are not decoupled from the template (are not stored separately), and therefore cannot be cached and reused. For the same reasons, we assert that Server Side Includes (SSI), as discussed in Subsection 3.6, provides the same level of Fragmentation. On the other hand, the references to XML services that the Active

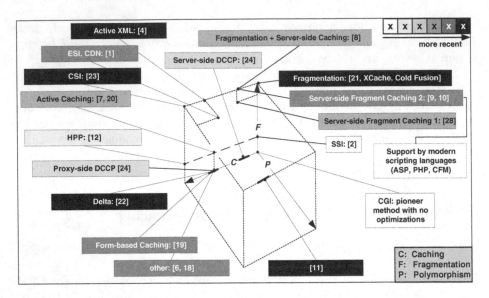

Fig. 3. The CFP Framework with the plotted proposed approaches and technologies. The numbers relate to the reference numbers in the bibliography

XML approach embeds within a template can be reused by other templates allowing in this way for arbitrary Fragmentation.

The early publishing system proposed in [8] supports arbitrary Fragmentation of DWC, however, it provides server-side Caching only at the granularity of page. The recent approach found in [21] supports arbitrary Fragmentation, inner-fragment dependency, and immediate execution of fragments with no Caching. The former approach is more suitable for less interactive Web applications such as portals and news sites since the generation of content is data-driven (i.e., triggered by database changes). The later approach better suits interactive Web applications, such as e-commerce, where fragment generation is user-driven.

The approach proposed in [28] provides server-side Caching but does not employ full Fragmentation. This is because even though the fragments are decoupled from the template, the approach allows for only specific forms of content (such as XML and queries) to be isolated and cached. The more recent approach found in [10] and [9] works around this problem by providing support for Caching of any type of content, at any granularity, on the server. To the same extend, scripting languages such as PHP, Cold Fusion, ASP and XCache provide programming-level support for arbitrary server-side Caching. Edge Side Includes extends [10] and [9] by moving arbitrary fragment Caching from servers to proxies. Finally, [11] compliments ESI (with Polymorphism) by supporting dynamic arrangements of the cached fragments at the proxy. The original Client Side Includes approach, as proposed in [12], employs full Caching, and it targets low-bandwidth clients. However, for the same reasons discussed in Active Caching and Server Side Includes, the approach does not provide full Fragmentation since it does not allow for arbitrary fragment Caching. The more recent and improved version of Client Side Includes, as proposed in [23], supports full Fragmentation by allowing arbitrary content fragments to be cached at the client browser.

5   Conclusion

In this paper, we surveyed and classified the research approaches and technologies for accelerated dynamic Web content generation and delivery. In order to perform a structured conceptual comparison of the approaches, we introduced the CFP Framework. We believe that our work can be used by researches not only as a study for understanding dynamic Web content technology, but also as point of reference toward developing the next generation of dynamic Web content middlewares.

References

1. The edge-side includes initiative. http://www.esi.org.
2. Server-side includes. http://hoohoo.ncsa.uiuc.edu/docs/tutorials/includes.html.
3. Xcache: The cache management solution. http://www.xcache.com.
4. Abiteboul, S., Benjelloun, O., Manolescu, I., Milo, T., Weber, R.: Active xml: Peer-to-peer data and web services integration. In VLDB (2002)
5. Amza, C., Cecchet, E., Chanda, A., Cox, A., Elnikety, S., Gil, R., Marguerite, J., Rajamani, K., Zwaenepoel, W.: Specification and implementation of dynamic web site benchmarks. In IEEE 5th Annual Workshop on Workload Characterization (2002)
6. Candan, K. S., Li, W. S., Luo, Q., Hsiung, W. P., Agrawal, D.: Enabling dynamic content caching for database-driven web sites. In SIGMOD Conference (2001)
7. Cao, P., Zhang, J., Beach, K.: Active cache: caching dynamic contents on the web. In Distributed Systems Engineering 6(1) (1999) 43–50
8. Challenger, J., Iyengar, A., Witting, K., Ferstat, C., Reed, P.: A publishing system for efficiently creating dynamic web content. In INFOCOM (2) (2000) 844–853
9. Datta, A., Dutta, K., Ramamritham, K., Thomas, H. M., VanderMeer, D. E.: Dynamic content acceleration: A caching solution to enable scalable dynamic web page generation. In SIGMOD Conference (2001)
10. Datta, A., Dutta, K., Thomas, H. M., VanderMeer, D. E., Ramamritham, K., Fishman, D.: A comparative study of alternative middle tier caching solutions to support dynamic web content acceleration. In The VLDB Journal (2001) 667–670
11. Datta, A., Dutta, K., Thomas, H. M., VanderMeer, D. E., Suresha, K. Ramamritham, K.: Proxy-based acceleration of dynamically generated content on the world wide web: An approach and implementation. In SIGMOD Conference (2002) 97–108
12. Douglis, F., Haro, A., Rabinovich, M.: HPP: HTML macro-preprocessing to support dynamic document caching. In USENIX Symposium on Internet Technologies and Systems (1997)
13. Feldmann, A., Caceres, R., Douglis, F., Glass, G., Rabinovich, M.: Performance of web proxy caching in heterogeneous bandwidth environments. In INFOCOM (1) (1999) 107–116

14. Holmedahl, V., Smith, B., Yang, T.: Cooperative caching of dynamic content on a distributed web server. In IEEE International Symposium on High Performance Distributed Computing (1998) 243

15. Hunt, J. J., Vo, K. P., Tichy, W. F.: Delta algorithms an empirical analysis. ACM Transactions on Software Engineering and Methodology (1998) 7(2):192–214

16. Iyengar, A., Challenger, J.: Improving web server performance by caching dynamic data. In USENIX Symposium on Internet Technologies and Systems (1997)

17. Krishnamurthy, B., Wills, C. E., Zhang, Y.: On the use and performance of content distribution networks. In Internet Measurement Workshop (2001) 169–182

18. Li, W. S., Candan, K. S., Hsiung, W. P., Po, O., Agrawal, D.: Engineering high performance database-driven e-commerce web sites through dynamic content caching. In EC-Web (2001) 250–259

19. Luo, Q., Naughton, J. F.: Form-based proxy caching for database-backed web sites. In The VLDB Journal (2001) 191–200

20. Luo, Q., Naughton, J. F., Krishnamurthy, R., Cao, P., Li, Y.: Active query caching for database Web servers. (2000) 92–104

21. Papastavrou, S., Samaras, G., Evripidou, P., Chrysanthis, P. K.: Fine-grained parallelism in dynamic web content generation: The parse dispatch and approach. In CoopIS/DOA/ODBASE (2003) 573–588

22. Psounis, K.: Class-based delta-encoding: A scalable scheme for caching dynamic web content. In ICDCS Workshops (2002) 799–805

23. Rabinovich, M., Xiao, Z., Douglis, F., Kalmanek, C. R.: Moving edge-side includes to the real edge - the clients. In USENIX Symposium on Internet Technologies and Systems (2003)

24. Smith, B., Acharya, A., Yang, T., Zhu, H.: Exploiting result equivalence in caching dynamic web content. In USENIX Symposium on Internet Technologies and Systems (1999)

25. Spring, N. T., Wetherall, D.: A protocol-independent technique for eliminating redundant network traffic. In Proceedings of ACM SIGCOMM (2000)

26. Wang, J.: A survey of Web caching schemes for the Internet. ACM Computer Communication Review (1999) 25(9):36–46

27. Wolman, A., Voelker, G. M., Sharma, N., Cardwell, N., Karlin, A. R., Levy, H. M.: On the scale and performance of cooperative web proxy caching. In Symposium on Operating Systems Principles (1999) 16–31

28. Yagoub, K., Florescu, D., Issarny, V., Valduriez, P.: Caching strategies for data-intensive web sites. In The VLDB Journal (2000) 188–199

Long-Term Temporal Data Representation of Personal Health Data

Tore Mallaug[1,2] and Kjell Bratbergsengen[2]

[1] Faculty of Informatics and e-Learning,
Sør-Trøndelag University College,
NO-7004 Trondheim, Norway
torem@aitel.hist.no
[2] Department of Computer and Information Science,
Norwegian University of Science and Technology,
NO-7491 Trondheim, Norway
{torem, kjellb}@idi.ntnu.no

Abstract. The demand for timely, accurate personal health data is continuously growing. The increasing volume of generated health data from different sources creates new needs for a national, or international, future intergraded personal electronic health record (EHR). The database plays an important role in such a future health system. All kinds of personal health data must be stored and represented for a very long-term access. For this purpose we are working on a temporal object model in order to represent different versions of health data content, schemas and ontologies. Mappings between versions of these concepts are used for a temporal search in the stored data. In this paper we are introducing the use and purpose of the temporal model related to the examples of data and schema updates. A contribution of this work is to solve the EHR-case by using solutions from temporal databases, schema versioning and ontologies.

1 Introduction and Research Objectives

1.1 Introduction to the Personal Health Data Case

In a modern health care system the need for data exchange of personal health data is increasing [1,2,3]. There are numerous reasons for this new demand. In a modern society citizens move and travel more frequently, and then they need to have their personal health data available where they stay or live at the moment. In Norway, citizens have a legal right for a free choice of a hospital, and a right for inspection of all their personal health data stored by different health care providers (today this is difficult to achieve since the data are stored in different local databases all over the country). A personal integrated EHR [4] makes it easier for citizens to collect, manage and control their own personal health data. These trends ask for national database solutions, and in a longer perspective, international solutions. From a database point of view, a future solution of a common integrated database is an alternative to message passing between heterogeneous information systems. This scenario can include database benefits, such as better data quality, better data availability, storage optimi-

J. Eder et al. (Eds.): ADBIS 2005, LNCS 3631, pp. 379–391, 2005.

zation, back up and logging administration, and common access control. We are going from a message passing system to a data sharing system.

Our research objectives can be summarized into two sub parts:

- To evaluate the future database solutions for a common integrated EHR – Electronic Health Record [4].
- To explore the long-term temporal data representation of lifelong personal health data and mappings of different versions of these data in a time space.

The second part can be used in an implementation of the first part. The EHR is a wider, extended definition of the Computer-based Patient Record (CPR) (e.g. [1,5]) that includes all kinds of personal health data and is not only limited to, for example, treatment at a single hospital.

Our contribution is to look how future EHR can be stored and how the data can be represented from a database point of view. We also focus on a long-term access of historical health data, since personal EHR must be accessible at least for the whole person's life (100+ years). Both the storage technology and the data representation will continuously change during such a long time period. This approach is different from traditional work on CPR since we do not constrain ourselves to commercial systems of today, by the situation of organizational problems in the health care sector or by legal limitations. Thus, we hope to offer applicable future solutions.

1.2   Dynamic Temporal Data Representations

Our goal is not to suggest one particular language for generating, or representing all possible elements of personal health data, since such a choice limits future ability, e.g. for representing expressions. As far as we know, no single mapping method can handle all possible mappings between heterogeneous data representations, and no ontological language is optimal for representing all kinds of semantic knowledge (and there is no common standard for representing ontologies today). However, the languages of today, like the XML-technology, can be used to demonstrate data representation that can work.

1.3   An Example of Data Updates and Update Causes

Changes, or updates, in the data content are *caused* by different reasons over time. A simple example of data content and schema changes over time is the updates of a citizen's postal code. We can use the postal code example to illustrate different reasons for updates. A citizen's postal code is updated because of one of the following causes:

Case 1: The citizen moved (geographically) to a new postal address, from postal code 7873 to 7870 on the date of 20.01.1999, and back again 01.06.2002 (illustrated in Fig. 1, case 1). This is an ordinary data update only concerning a particular entity in the database, and is not caused by any structural or semantically changes.

Case 2: The postal code 7873 (from now simply denoted code 7873) is not in use by the postal service for a given time period, so citizens having code 7873 are given the (neighbor) code 7870 from 01.10.2000 to 01.10.2000, when the code 7873 is reopened (Fig. 1, case 2). This is a temporal change which is not causing any schema change.

Case 3: Say, in the year 2008, the code 7873 is replaced with a new code, 37873, because of structural changes in the postal code system. This is a change causing structural schema versioning (Fig. 1, case 3). Note that dates into the future used in this example are only for the purpose of illustration. This is not a system for looking into the future, so the changes in the postal system is just hypothetical for showing possible schema changes.

Case 4: The code 37973 is replaced on 01.10.2010, and split into two possible new codes, 7800 GR and 7700 SN (Fig. 1, case 4). This is a semantical, or ontological change in the usage of the postal system. The update is causes a semantical schema versioning.

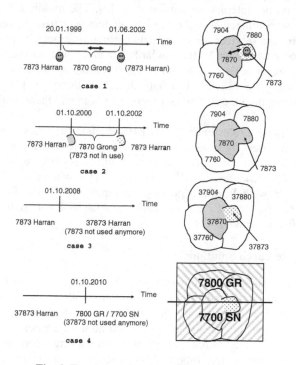

Fig. 1. Examples of updates in a postal code

Only the case 1 above is totally distinct from the other cases. The distinction between cases 2 - 4 are not clear, e.g. all can be related to (temporal) changes in the geographically borders of post blocks (a post block shows the geographically area where a postal code is used on a map - Fig. 1 shows simple examples of maps), and all these cases can be ontological if they are caused by the changes in the postal system. By store, or represent, such causes of changes over time, interpreting historical data in the temporal space is possible.

In the following, section 2 shortly mentions how our research relates to other work on EHR, and common database research. Section 3 describes how our temporal object model can be used, including the postal code example. Section 4 shortly introduces some usage of mapping objects, ontology objects and mapping rules in our model. Section 5 applies our model to usage the EHR-case.

2 Related Works and Present Realities

2.1 Electronic Health Record Realities

The fully integrated database solution for personal health data has not yet been developed. It is a lack of interoperable EHR systems (e.g. [6]). Studies on an integrated EHR [3,7,8,9] so far suggest message exchange solutions through a middle layer in health data networks or Internet. A future personal "virtual health record" activated by linking records on the Internet is mentioned by [2]. The middle layer in such health networks offer standardized solutions to set up message passing between different healthcare actors, and services for secure data communication. There are both national and international projects on XML standards for electronic message exchange (e.g. [10]) in health care. It is also a common suggestion that health networks can be used for data integration, for example to establish data warehouses [7]. However, these studies do not focus on a long-term data representation, and there is no database solution presented.

Data security issues are essential in the EHR context [8]. These include the identification of the end users by using a smart card or by biometrical solutions. We have chosen not to focus on the security, since data security is being rapidly developed and the situation will be different in, 10-15 years from now, when the EHR can start to be a reality. However, we believe it is possible to implement support for security mechanisms in our framework and database solution, such as a role-based access control (RBAC) authorisation model [11].

2.2 Database Research Solutions

Temporal database solutions have been discussed for many years [12,13,14,15]. Their use of temporal attributes and different time stamps along the time axes are quite useful in our model. An EHR is a temporal database, which is used for storing both system generated time stamps (like transaction time telling when the data was stored in the database, and time stamps generated by measuring instruments) and diverse user defined time stamps (like timestamps associated to a laboratory test result, including for example, the time/date the sample was collected, and the time/date the result was authorised by the clinical pathologist [7]).

Schema versioning [16] is supported if the database system allows the access to all versions of data, both data which are represented by the present schema version, and data represented by older schema versions. In our model we use schema versioning, but we also add the possibility to store new data through old schemas in the temporal space, which is not a requirement for schema versioning in general. *Mappings* between data representations, like methods for schema matching [17], are often related to the creation of common (global) integrated schemas, like used by mediators (e.g. [18]). Some of these mapping solutions are not "total" in the sense that they only map subparts of the original data content in different local schemas.

Schema transformation can be useful in our model, since some transformation techniques are generic across data models, for example [19]. Such generic methods can be one solution in defining mapping rules between schema versions in our model; however, research is needed to see if it is applicable in our case.

In the same way as our temporal framework supports versions of schemas, versions of related ontologies can be considered. There are studies on *Ontologies versioning* (e.g. [20]), and also in using ontologies to solve semantic heterogeneity (e.g. [21]). However, how ontologies can be used in our case requires further investigation.

3 Temporal Data and Data Versioning

3.1 The Total System Architecture

We are working on a long-term temporal data representation of the health data. Below we describe some of the design ideas for a framework, or a model for the data representation. The model works on a middle layer in a 3-tier client/server information system architecture (Fig. 2), containing the database, the middle layer and local applications. We call the middle layer the Data Representation Layer - DRL. The DRL offers common services, or tools to heterogeneous client applications, such as a mapping generator tool, request validation and request (query) execution (called request execution tool later in this paper), logging and access control. A local application is implemented to read and write data through a view to the DRL. This view is called 'XML View' in the Fig. 2 and simply 'VIEW' in the Fig. 3 and Fig. 5 later.

The underlying database must be a read-only / log-only database (e.g. [22]), where all updates is stored as new object versions. No deletion of stored data is allowed.

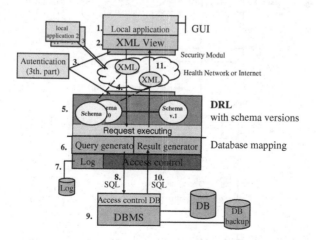

Fig. 2. The total information system architecture

3.2 Temporal Object Data Model

The goal of the data model is to represent data content and its metadata as objects in a temporal environment for a long-term use. In this paper we use three different object types from the data model: *Data object* is an object (instance) containing data content. Data content can be like elements in XML or part of a relational table. *Schema object* is an object containing a given schema version. The schema itself can be represented by a DDL (Data Definition Language) as standard (none-system related) SQL CREATE TABLE, or by other well-known syntaxes, for example a DTD or a XML Schema. Any syntax used here is assumed to be a well-known standard readable in the future. Any data content in a data object must be represented according to a schema in a schema object. Since both the data content and the corresponding schema is stored in the database, the data content is semi-structural (self-describing) in the sense that the schema is not implemented in the database, only represented in the DRL. The last object type is, what we choose to call, *mapping object*, which is an object representing data, or meta-data about a given mapping between two objects. Mappings can be present both for (instances of) data objects and schema objects. In Fig. 3 objects in the DRL are drawn as circles, 'Data v.0' is a data object, 'Schema v.0' is a schema objects, while 'map1' denotes a mapping object. The data content in 'Data v.0' is represented according to the schema in 'Schema v.0'. 'map1' is representing the mapping rules and metadata about the mapping between 'Data v.0' and 'Data v.1'.

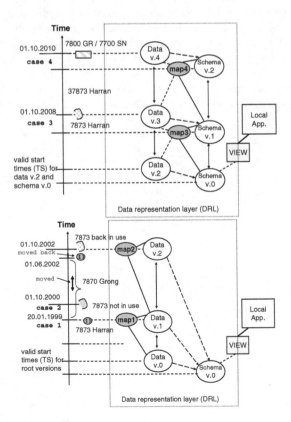

Fig. 3. Temporal object data model with example data-, schema- and mapping objects

All stored objects must be related to a set of time stamps (e.g. [13]). This set includes a fixed time stamp which stores the *transaction start time* (TS) when the new object instance was inserted into the database. A given object version is identified by its TS time stamp and a universal unique object identifier (OID). The model is bi-temporal [12], since we store both valid-time and transaction-time. Valid time can be used, for instance, to store / update historical data today. The model also supports user defined time stamps [14].

If following a linear time axis, as in Fig. 3, a time stamp can be seen as an accurate time line on this axis. The reader may then look at "the world" as it was expressed at that given historical date. The basic philosophy is that any object must be seen and interpreted according to its time stamps. This approach represents nearly unlimited ways for local client applications to query and view data versions both forward and backward in time.

3.3 Data and Schema Versioning

We can make a distinction between value mapping and schema mapping. A single *value mapping* is between two values, or more precisely two instances of a value of elements from two data object versions. A single *schema mapping* is between two elements in two schema object versions. Both types of mapping can be used in generating results of historical search in the database. Some mappings between data objects are value mappings only, without any schema changes involved, while others include schema mappings as well.

We can use the postal code examples to illustrate differences in mappings. In case 2 (Fig. 1), by using the combination of the cause of the change and the value mapping, a historical change in the usage of postal blocks can be found by searching postal code updates for the citizens' of Harran. By checking the causes of the change, we do not look at the citizens who have moved from 7873 Harran (case 1). In case 3 or 4, historical change in postal blocks, can be found by looking at schema versioning.

The causes of the changes in the four cases can be represented as functions at a logical level (the numbers refer to the cases):

```
1: Cause(EntityUpdate) = True;
2: Cause(TemporalChange) = True;
3: Cause(StructSchemaChange) = True;
4: Cause(StructSchemaChange, SemSchemaChange) = True;
```

These causes must be linked to the data objects involved. The mappings can be represented as follows:

```
1: no mappings
2: ValueMap(V0,V1) =
     ValueMap('7873','7870');
3: ValueMap(V0,V1) =
     ValueMap('7873','37873');
3: SchemaMap(S0.postcode,S1.postcode)
     =DomainScaleMap(char(4),char(5));
4: ValueMap(V0,V1) =   ValueMap
```

```
((ValueMap('37873','7800 GR')) or
(ValueMap('37873','7700 SN')));
4: SchemaMap(S0.postcode,S1.postcode)= DomainSemMap
(char(4), Concatenate(char(4), char(2)));
```

`ValueMap` represents a value mapping and `SchemaMap` represents a schema mapping, and `V0` and `V1` represent the values (the instances) in two temporal data objects. The schema mapping in the case 3 is a domain scale difference - the number of digits arises from 4 to 5. The schema mapping in the case 4 is a domain semantic difference, while the postal code in schema S1 is represented by two (sub) elements, one number code plus one code of two letters.

All these functions can be represented and stored in a relational database, for example, as shown in the Fig. 4. The `M_OID` attribute, in the tables of Fig. 4, is the OIDs of the mapping objects. We use an additional integer attribute, called `no`, as part of the primary key, since a mapping object can obtain several sub-causes and sub-mappings related to one (total) mapping.

CauseUpdate

M_OID*	no	cause_type*
1	1	EntityUpdate
2	1	TempChange
3	1	StructSchema
4	1	StructSchema
4	2	SemSchema

ValueMap

M_OID*	no	Vmap_type*	Vs	Vt
2	1	1:1	7873	7870
3	1	1:1	7873	37873
4	1	1:1	7873	7800 GR
4	2	1:1	7873	'7700 SN

SchemaMap

M_OID*	no	Smap_type*	Es_name	Et_name	Es_type	Et_type
3	1	1:1	postcode	postcode	char(4)	char(5)
4	1	1:1	postcode	postcode	char(4)	(char(4), char(2))

MappingObject

M_OID	VS	VE	TS	TE
1	20.01.1999	now	20.01.1999	UC
2	01.10.2002	now	01.10.2002	UC
3	01.10.2008	now	01.10.2008	UC
4	01.10.2010	now	01.10.2010	UC

Fig. 4. Tables for storing updates and related metadata

The table `MappingObject` is containing the temporal data about the mappings. The temporal attributes in the table is inspired by [23]. Our temporal data model is bi-temporal since it allowed both transaction-time and valid-time dimensions [12]. It is a principle that any object has a temporal dimension. Note that the usage of dates as time units in the example is just for illustration purpose. In an EHR the granularity of the time and time intervals varies from milliseconds in monitoring, for example vital functions, to years in preventive medicine [7]. This means a need for a flexible time stamp representation in the implemented temporal model, for representing time-varying from large time span to fine granularity.

4   Using Mapping Objects for Temporal Reads

4.1   Applications Usage of the Data Representations

Temporal data reads can be done both backward and forward in the temporal space, by using time stamps on the time axes (as in Fig. 3). Such time stamps can be called *read times*. There are two possible read time types; *horizontal reads*, which reads the data versions that were present at a given time stamp, or date, on the time axes. The other read time type is *vertical reads*, which is search in time, reading several versions of one or many data objects in-between two read time stamps. Vertical reads are also needed if an application needs to read the most current (most up-dated) version of data object content. Then the request execution tool in the DRL needs to read "forward" in time if the application 'VIEW' is older than the most current version (as in Fig. 5), or "backward" in time if the 'VIEW' is newer than the most current version. Fig. 5 shows one example for each read type, using the postal code example as a case.

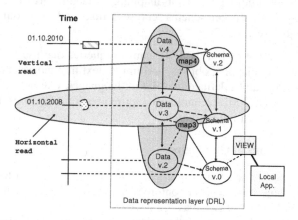

Fig. 5. Horizontal and vertical reads (searches) in the temporal space

4.2   Usage of Mapping Objects

Mapping objects are used to store mapping rules and possible metadata concerning the mapping. In Fig. 5, the mapping object 'map3' between Schema v.0 and v.1 can also be used to represent the mapping between Data v.2 and v.3, since data updates on the data content here are forced by the schema versioning (Fig. 1, case 3).

4.3 Mapping Rules

Mapping objects have to contain mapping rules for any schema (versioning) mapping. A mapping rule handles a particular (sub-)mapping between two elements in one direction. A mapping rule can be implemented as a function, which always returns the same answer for involved elements. A formal representation of a mapping rule can be stored in a functional programming syntax or XML. The rule must then be implemented in Java, as an example. A hierarchy of different types (classes) of mapping rules can be implemented related to the different reasons of data updates.

A *total mapping* for one object version is a set of (implemented) mapping rules in both directions, so that there is a mapping solution for all elements in the object to one or many newer objects versions (many if the version is split into several newer objects). Such total mappings are required for some of the health data in an EHR, since we, for instance, can not tolerate that any data in the case of emergency is missing due to none-complete mappings.

A system user can use a semi-automatical *mapping generator tool* maintained by the DRL for implementing a set of mapping rules for a total mapping. Some sub-mappings can be found automatically by the tool, but many have to be discovered and accepted by a system user.

For a *schema mapping*, between two schemas S0 and S1, the process of generating sub-mappings has to consider the following 3 circumstances:

1. If S0 and S1 defined by the same schema standard or not, and if the two standards using (build on) the same data model or not.
2. If a sub-mapping cardinality is a 1:1, 1:N, M:N or view-to-view mapping.
3. The (semantic) type of a sub-mapping, related to structural and/or semantic conflicts between schema representations. All such conflicts can be ontological (e.g. [24,25]).

The request executing tool in the DRL can run queries that use the mapping rules and the (meta-)data in mapping objects, and in the next turn generate results for local applications. Queries can be defined in different languages, like SQL (relational query languages), or XQuery (XML-technology). Optimalization of queries against the data representations is left for future research.

4.4 Linking Mappings to Ontologies

In the same way as for schemas, ontologies can be represented in the DRL as own objects, *ontology objects*. Changes in ontologies and their usage can also be one cause of changes in data content or schemas.

A schema object can have a relationship to one or many ontology objects if the schema elements are linked to the standardized (medical) concepts of ontologies. A data object can be also related to ontologies for included metadata about the elements / attributes if such metadata is present. Even mapping objects can be related to ontology objects if we have ontologies for describing mappings, or describing semantical heterogeneity between data versions [21].

In the same manner as we are mapping between different schema versions and schema standards, we can also map between different ontologies, or different versions of an ontology. If each of two different schema versions are linked to two different ontologies (the schemas are build on two slightly different understandings of reality, where these understandings can be related to the temporal time where a schema was created), a mapping between these two ontologies can help in interpreting replies to the local applications. An own mapping ontology can also include concepts for representing ontology heterogeneity. Mapping rules can be linked to ontologies including known medical domain ontologies (e.g. GALEN, UMLS, ON9, all shortly described in [26]) for understanding differences in the data representation in the two object versions. This shows some of the flexibilities of our framework for defining different object types for data and metadata.

5   Usage in the EHR-Case

Below we discuss shortly how our temporal framework is suitable for the personal electronic health record (EHR) case.

Grimson [7] mentions six major research issues for a future EHR. Among these she notes the need to improve data quality, temporal support, and preserving access to the record over time. We believe our solution matches these needs. In a longer run our solution also gives a possibility for storage of generations of population's EHR for (post-research) historical searches.

In term of a national database solution for storing an integrated EHR for each citizen, our idea is to have one common national database for the purpose. By using our framework, we however set very few constrains on how the database system is realized on the database layer, as long as it is possible to map data between the database layer and the DRL. Our solution relies on a flexible and scalable database solution, which can evolve over time.

The DRL and the database do not require any common standardization of health data representation. If local applications use medical standards or protocols, such standards can be represented as own schema objects and/or ontology objects in the DRL. Our temporal approach gives a good support for evolving medical standards / protocols. On the other hand, the DRL lets local applications store their data according to local schema specifications. In such cases it is up to systems on the application level. For example, a data warehouse can locally decide how to read, or to interpret, the stored data.

For the integration of common data that is typically used by many local applications we can choose a "light" solution, where parts of the EHR are stored only once in the database (though in different temporal versions). Such common health data can be a personal profile including demographical data about the citizen, the owner, of the EHR. Or a common set of data elements used for emergency, like data about the blood type, allergies and chronic diseases. A person's genome data (e.g. used by post-genetic research on genes together with data about disease, treatment and environment) is one more example of data that only needs to be stored in one common place in the database. However, our solution can not guarantee any normalized database, as long as we allow local applications to store everything in the database, without any restrictions.

6 Conclusion and Future Work

From a database point of view, the major problem for realization of our temporal data object framework in a future EHR is the handling of all kinds of mappings between versions of data content, schemas and possible ontologies. This paper presents general ideas about how mappings can be used in our model, and different types of mappings that have to be handled by mapping rules. However, more work has to be done by classifying different mapping problems and possible solutions on such. Examples on how to implement mappings in a conventional programming language, for example Java, can be implemented. For the DRL we can implement a test tool that uses mappings both forward and backward in the temporal space when generating replies on queries from client programs.

For the health care community, we must argue how a good database and related data representation solution can influence the reality of a future EHR system, including the data security aspect and the overall system functionality.

This paper provides some headlines of an ongoing work on using database techniques in the realization of a future integrated Electronic Health Record. The background and inspiration to look at a long-term temporal data representation of an EHR are presented. Linked to this is an examination of a possible temporal realization and a mapping between data content and schema versions in a temporal space. A temporal data object model is shortly described.

References

1. Dick, R.S, Steen, E.B, Detmer, D.E (Eds.).: The Computer-Based Patient Record - An Essential Technology for Health Care, Revised ed., Institute Of Medicine, National Academy Press (1997)
2. Fagan, L.M, Shortliffe, E.H.: The Future of Computer Applications in Health Care, Chapter 20 in Medical Informatics - Computer Applications In Health Care and Biomedicine, Springer-Verlag (2001)
3. Office of Health and the Information Highway Health Canada. Canada Health Infoway: "Paths to Better Health", Final Report of the Advisory Council on Health Infrastructure, February (1999) http://www.hs-sc.gc.ca
4. Waegemann, C.P.: The five levels of electronic health records, in M.D. Computing, Vol.13 No.3 (1996)
5. van Bemmel, J.H., Musen, M.A. (ed.): Handbook of Medical Informatics, Springer (1997)
6. Berner et al.: Will the Wave Finally Break? A Brief View of the Adoption of Electronic Medical Records in the United States, Journal of the American Medical Informatics Association, Volume 12, Number 1 (2005)
7. Grimson, J.: Delivering the electronic healthcare record for the 21st century, in International Journal of Medical Informatics 64 (2001).
8. Tsiknakis, Katehakis, Orphanoudakis: A health information infrastructure enabling secure access to the life-long multimedia electronic health record, CARS 2004 / International Congress Series 1268 Elsevier (2004)
9. Katehakis, Sfakianakis, Tsiknakis, Orphanoudakis: An Infrastructure for Integrated Electronic Health Record Services: The Role of XML (Extensible Markup Language), The Journal of Medical Internet Research, Volume 3 (2001) http://www.jmir.org

10. http://www.centc251.org
11. Ferraiolo, D. F. et al.: Proposed NIST standard for role-based access control, ACM Transactions on Information and System Security 4 (2001)
12. Jensen et al.: A consensus glossery of temporal database concepts, SIGMOD record, 23(1) (1994)
13. Snodgrass, R.: Temporal Databases, in Theories and Methods of Spatio-Temporal Reasoning in Geographic Space, Springer-Verlag, LNCS 639 (1992)
14. Clifford, Dyreson, Isakowitz, Jensen, Snodgrass: On the Semantics of "now" in Databases. ACM Transactions on Database Systems, Vol. 22, No.2 (1997)
15. Snodgrass, R.: The Temporal Query Language TQuel. ACM Transactions on Database Systems, Vol.12, No.2 (1987)
16. Roddick, J.F.: A survey of schema versioning issues for database systems. Information and Software Technology, Vol. 37, No. 7 (1995)
17. Rahm, E., Bernstein, P.A.: A survey of approaches to automatic schema matching. The VLDB Journal 10 (2001)
18. Kalinichenko, L.A.: Integration of Heterogeneous Semistructured Data Models in the Canonical one http://citeseer.nj.nec.com/kalinichenko99integration.html
19. Prakash, N., Srivastava, S.: Engineering Schema Transformation Methods, EMSISE (2003)
20. Noy, N. F., Musen, M. A.: Ontology Versioning as an Element of an Ontology-Evolution Framework. IEEE Intelligent Systems (2003)
21. Hakimpour, F., Geppert, A.: Ontologies: an Approach to Resolve Semantic Heterogeneity in Databases http://www.ifi.unizh.ch/dbtg/Projects/MIGI/ publication/ontoreport.pdf
22. Nørvåg, K.: VAGABOND The Design and Analysis of a Temporal Object Database Management System, Dr. ing. thesis, Norwegian University of Science and Technology, ISBN 82-7984-097-4
23. Wei, H-C, Elmasri, R.: Study and Comparison of Schema Versioning and Data Conversion Techniques for Bi-temporal Databases, Sixth International Workshop on Temporal Representation and Reasoning, Orlando, Florida (1999)
24. Sheth, A., Larson, J.: So far (schematically) yet so near (semantically). Interoperable Database Systems, DS-5 (1993)
25. Vestenicky, V.: Schema Integration as View Cooperation. Charles University, Prague (2003)
26. Gomez-Perez, A., Fernandez-Lopez, M., Corcho, O.: Ontological Engineering, Springer (2004)

Author Index

Lecture Notes in Computer Science

For information about Vols. 1–3578

please contact your bookseller or Springer